M000113265

BOSTON BOHEMIA

1881–1900

RALPH ADAMS CRAM:
LIFE AND ARCHITECTURE

Douglass Shand-Tucci

BOSTON BOHEMIA
1881–1900

RALPH ADAMS CRAM:
LIFE AND ARCHITECTURE

University of Massachusetts Press

Amherst

Copyright © 1995 by Paul Douglass Shand-Tucci

All rights reserved. No part of this book may be reproduced in any form or by any electronic or mechanical means (including photocopying, recording, or information storage and retrieval) without permission in writing from the author and publisher.

The lines from "A Walk by the Charles" are reprinted from *Collected Early Poems: 1950–1970* by Adrienne Rich, by permission of the author and W. W. Norton & Company, Inc. Copyright © 1993 by Adrienne Rich. Copyright © 1967, 1963, 1962, 1961, 1960, 1959, 1958, 1957, 1956, 1955, 1954, 1953, 1952, 1951 by Adrienne Rich. Copyright © 1984, 1975, 1971, 1969, 1966 by W. W. Norton & Company, Inc.

Printed in the United States of America
LC 94–11328
ISBN 0–87023–920–1 (cloth); ISBN 1–55849–061–2 (pbk.)
Designed by Dennis Anderson
Set in Sabon by Keystone Typesetting, Inc.

Includes bibliographical references and index.
Contents: v. 1. Boston bohemia, 1881–1900
ISBN 0–87023–920–1 (alk. paper); ISBN 1–55849–061–2 (pbk.: alk. paper)
1. Cram, Ralph Adams, 1863–1942. 2. Architects—United States—Biography.
3. Gothic revival (Architecture)—United States. 4. Avant-garde (Aesthetics)—
Massachusetts—Boston—History—19th century. 5. Avant-garde (Aesthetics)—
Massachusetts—Boston—History—20th century. I. Cram, Ralph Adams,
1863–1942. II. Title.
NA737.C7S44 1994
720'.92 — dc20
[B] 94–11328
CIP

Frontispiece: Portrait of Ralph Adams Cram by
Fred Holland Day, ca. 1895

This book is published with the support and cooperation of the University of Massachusetts Boston and is also supported by a grant from the National Endowment for the Humanities, an independent federal agency.

FOR F. W. ATHERTON

CONTENTS

Church of the Advent, Boston, Lady Chapel, from a painting
by Robert Douglas Hunter

PREFACE AND ACKNOWLEDGMENTS

Young oarsmen, who in timeless gesture seem
Continuous, united with the tide,
Leave off your bending to the oar, and glide
Past innocence, beyond these aging bricks
To where the Charles flows in to join the Styx.

— Adrienne Rich
"A Walk by the Charles"

"All scholarship," Jackson Lears has written, "is — or ought to be — a kind of intellectual autobiography." The obligations that truth implies (and not the debts acknowledged in the source notes) is what I wish to focus on at the beginning of this book. This involves telling tales religious, architectural, and psychological, often as reflected in a New England glass.

Consider Leslie Lang, a wise old priest and worldly, who when I was a young man rather entranced me in his last years. Sophisticated as only an old hand in the milieu of the Episcopal church in New York City could be, but not, I believe, in any sense, corrupt, Leslie (over much food and more drink, always in the Edwardian Room of the Plaza) used to regale me so well that even when I met and fell under the spell of Sir John Betjeman himself I never felt (as so many have) that Anglo-Catholic wit had invariably to be British. Leslie, I'm sure, had been there when Tallulah Bankhead told Tennessee Williams that they were the only two consistently high Episcopalians. Years later Leslie and I tried to be two others.

I remember another of his stories, also about Miss Bankhead, as he always called her, who for Leslie was a kind of lightning rod used rather as I have observed another clerical friend, Peter Gomes, uses Mae West — to disarm the listener about to be told a surprising or an unwelcome or even a threatening truth. It seems Grieg Taber, the rector of St. Mary the Virgin in New York, then as now the leading Anglo-Catholic parish in America, told Leslie that one Christmas Eve as he kept his vigil in the confessional before midnight Mass, he overheard Bankhead, perhaps his most notorious but not least devout parishioner, say quite clearly as she passed a large crucifix nearby, "Smile, darling, it's your birthday."

The point of that sort of thing, of course, is to tread relentlessly on the seeming romance (or is it sentimentality?) of all those images of Christ as true knight, best friend, tremendous lover, while still keeping the sense of a knowing intimacy with Jesus that these images express—in this book, as elsewhere—whether in Francis Thompson's word picture of the Hound of Heaven invoked in Chapter 2 or Ralph Adams Cram's Ashmont rood Christus explicated in Chapter 11. When these and other such images arise here, the reader should remember this story of Tallulah Bankhead (and that it happened on Christmas Eve, an important time for Cram).

Am I talking about camp? To some extent. Certainly one need not accept without qualification the view of Wayne Dynes that camp serves "to deconstruct the cult of seriousness and 'values' that sought to fill the gap produced by the fading of religion" in order to understand that camp's reversal of values is not only very modern (even very Nietzschean) but also very characteristically Anglo-Catholic. Grieg Taber and Leslie Lang, two very fine clergymen of the old school, found not irreverence but a useful truth in Bankhead's intimate salutation to Christ on his natal day. They knew it was one New Yorker's way of joining in "Yea, Lord, we greet thee, born this happy morning!"

Leslie had not known (though as I recall he had briefly met) Ralph Adams Cram. Another of the group of older priest friends I want to remember here knew Cram quite well: Alfred Pedersen, sometime Father Superior of the Society of St. John the Evangelist in the United States. While he never quite replaced Donald Davis, the senior curate at All Saints', Ashmont, in my youth and my first priest mentor, in my affections, Pedersen in the long run mattered much more because I knew him best when I was at Harvard (close by Cowley's monastery). Moreover, Pedersen thought well of my pose of agnosticism while in college (it was, he felt, only healthy), and he knew better than to try to persuade me back into the church. What he did was to engage me in a strenuous dialogue so as to expand my horizons beyond Cram's architecture to the wider religious and human aspects of his life and work. And when I resisted, he held simply that if this "effort of the imagination," as I remember him putting it with a glint in his eye, was too much for me, I'd just have to write about someone else.

In the same Harvard Square restaurants, when I was doing graduate work at the Episcopal Divinity School in Cambridge, Sewall Emerson, rector of Ashmont at another period, preached more or less the same sermon to me quite regularly, though he set it, as it were, to different music, being a very different sort of man from Pedersen. As his name suggests, a descendant of both Samuel Sewall, the New England Puritan jurist, and Ralph Waldo Emerson, Sewall would meet me after his daily hour on the river (he had rowed for Yale and was not about to give it up just because he was well into old age). Perhaps because he was a Bohemian who was also both an athlete and an intellectual, it may in truth be said he taught me how to row against even the stiffest currents, in a world in which we shared conflicts not easily resolved but with which both Sewall and I needed to cope. One could cope most successfully, Sewall thought, and convinced me as well, by opening up as one grew older rather than, as so many do, narrowing in and even closing down. Emerson was always there to remind me that there was a long and honorable *liberal* tradition in Anglo-Catholicism.

Quite a different sort of man was Peter Blynn of Boston's Church of the Advent, who was as flamboyant and shifty as the Italian opera he and my mother both loved. I could not help but admire, however, the way he seemed to minister to so many the church would otherwise have missed, and because of this I studied him all the more carefully in the differing roles I played in his life; whether swinging the censor for him as an acolyte at the Advent, or, scotch in hand, attending one of his famous parties (Blynn lived in a penthouse apartment across the street from the church, with a spectacular view of the Charles River). I never did figure him out. Years later an older and more perceptive mutual friend volunteered the opinion that Blynn was a bad man who was a good priest, and I saw this was the truth of the thing at once. Like Leslie's stories, the point is a characteristically Anglo-Catholic one, though a citizen of Rome might grasp it appreciatively, applying to Blynn Edmund White's observation about Genet, that like the prodigal son, the sinner is closer to God.

Then there was John Purnell, Sewall Emerson's successor twice removed at All Saints', Ashmont. John I cherished. One day I had been having a running argument with him about sexuality and the Oxford Fathers while, of all things, helping him to shop for his groceries; at the end of which, as I recall, I got huffily into the front seat of his car, and he shouted exasperatedly down his station wagon to me as he stowed away the last of the groceries: "If you can't see the connection between all-male choirs and the Oxford Movement you'd better look for another subject." "John Cardinal Ashmont" his friends often called him, for he was a big man in more than only a physical way. But there was just no cant in him at all. Others through the years—I think particularly of Peter Liberman at All Saints, James Deutsch at Harvard, B. Hughes Morris of the Advent, and Tom Cure of Cowley—have influenced my search for Ralph Adams Cram's elusive "center"; all built on my abiding memories of Pedersen, Emerson, Purnell, and Lang.

My architectural tales are less complicated than my religious ones. My mentors in architecture have not had to contend with quite such heavy weather as my priest friends.

Professor John Coolidge, late of Harvard's Fogg Art Museum, when I needed a paper topic one day in a course of his and mentioned I had been a chorister at All Saints' as a boy and thought it had some architectural significance, nudged me in the first place toward what would become in a sense a life's work. I learned much from his perhaps abrasive but certainly "hands-on" way of rubbing students and buildings against each other in one field trip after another. But Coolidge, though he cared passionately for good architecture in any style and in that influenced me greatly, seemed to me too much of a modernist. When I followed his advice and plunged into the history of Ashmont's design, he was not very sympathetic to my enthusiasms. And when I talked the local newspaper into publishing a series of articles drawn from my course project (my first published work), I fear my professor was more embarrassed than anything by what were, to be sure, undergraduate effusions of little merit. But oaks need acorns, after all. It was Walter Muir Whitehill who would reward me with a lunch at the Club of Odd Volumes, a free reader's card to the Boston Athenaeum, and — such was his prestige as *the* Boston historian of his generation — more or less license to kill on any topic in New England studies.

I well remember the building that occasioned my meeting of minds with Walter, who agreed with me (he was the first; I was quite surrounded by modernists at Harvard) that revivalist architecture, whether neo-Gothic, neoclassic, or whatever, like any other style from baroque to "modern," could spark creativity sufficient to yield admirable buildings. Lowell House, one of Harvard's original residential colleges, of which Walter had for a time been Senior Tutor, was, we agreed (daringly; this was the early 1970s), a masterwork. The implications for my increasing interest in Cram were obvious.

They were also underlined for me at once by a friend of Whitehill's who became my other mentor of those days, Kenneth Conant. Whitehill himself had known Ralph Adams Cram for years, never ceasing to marvel that when as a youngster he had written Cram for encouragement in some matter architectural, the great man had invited him into his office and devoted the better part of an obviously busy morning to young Walter's edification. But Conant, by the time I met him justly renowned for his seminal work in the reconstruction of the medieval abbey of Cluny, had been distinctly a protégé of Cram's and, indeed, years later, a colleague in the Medieval Academy of America. Conant got me much closer to Cram, and he was a great help in my efforts to detail Cram's aesthetic, for Conant was an unusual combination of scholar and architect, rather like my old friend, the architect (and, in fact, graduate of Lowell House), William Buckingham, whose scholarly neo-Georgian buildings of recent years at Roxbury Latin School in Boston may yet again breathe new life into that much-abused mode.

The architect, as distinct from the architectural historian (the gullible public notwithstanding, they are not the same thing), does have a role to play in training the scholar of art and architecture and culture generally. Indeed, I think while at work on this book I learned more about architecture in a practical way from overseeing the restoration of the Boston Public Library with Daniel J. Coolidge (ably seconded on the historical side by my colleague Professor Leland Roth) than from any study or research of my own. And this despite the fact that Daniel, though a superb restoration architect, was also a strict modernist. Dan's grandfather Charles Allerton Coolidge was the designer, as it happens, of Lowell House, and when Harvard on its 350th anniversary published my study of all the residential colleges, written originally for *Harvard Magazine*, Dan would have none of my view that they were truly distinguished architecture. As for Cram, it was not until Coolidge saw the nave of St. John the Divine in New York that he granted I might be on to something.

Daniel also disapproved of my older priest friends and was dismayed by my determination not only to write a study of Cram's design but to do so within the context of a very open biography. At our weekly lunches Daniel often played Emerson to my Whitman (and often enough actually in sight of the locale of that famous dialogue on Boston Common), Dan always arguing forcefully for discretion, I stubbornly determined the truth would set us free. He often would resign with the altogether typical pronouncement that he never *had* liked Wagner, thank you. Nor was it any good waxing theoretical in self-defense. When, for example, I put to him the view of some critics that architectural facades and interiors not in stylistic agreement might properly be called transvestite, even though he deplored such a discordance, he would not countenance the characterization. One such building (the Fogg Art Museum) had been designed, after all, by his grandfather.

Meanwhile, however, I learned in a thousand small instances how an architect thinks, works, rethinks, occasionally triumphs, and sometimes just covers up, and how architecture reflects all this. From Dan, from all my architectural mentors, I learned a great deal and not least from Professor Coolidge and others putting me in touch through the years with several outstanding contemporaries: William Morgan, a fellow neo-Goth for whom I gave my first lecture on Cram, appropriately enough in the Art Lecture Series at Princeton; Ann Miner Daniel, whose doctoral dissertation on Cram's early work I somewhat aided in 1978 and from which in this book I have greatly profited; and two Boston figures, Margaret Henderson Floyd and Robert Bell Rettig. (Margaret, an old friend now, was one of the readers for this manuscript, and her criticism was invaluable in my attempt to write both intellectual and architectural history here, never forgetting, however, that the biographical form had to encompass both.) After I took my undergraduate degree in history in 1972, and despite my determination to do only scholarship and not to teach and thus to forgo the doctorate, all these contemporaries generously welcomed me as a colleague into the guild of architectural history.

That was not a foregone conclusion nor an easy task, as it turned out, for I arrived in that realm having already formed independent and unconventional habits of mind, the result of the perhaps unruly but certainly stimulating influence of a small circle of family and friends of my boyhood and youth, to whom, as this biography has developed, my debt has seemed only to grow larger.

At the greatest remove this includes the inspiration I have always derived from the work of my two grandfathers, so striking a contrast of religion on the one hand and art on the other have these two men always seemed to me, in whom alone their genes meet. Lucien Groves (who as a graduate student at the Boston University School of Theology in 1904–1905 lived on Beacon Hill only a block or two from Cram's bachelor quarters but was the reverse of Bohemian and so most unlikely to have known Ralph) was a learned and idealistic minister from an old Ohio "log cabin" family of Revolutionary War antecedents. Peter Tucci, on the other hand, was an 1890s immigrant to this country from Italy, a superb furniture designer and maker and sometime architectural carver who had, in fact, started out in this country as an artist for Irving and Casson, Cram's carvers. Equally important in a different way were my grandmothers, who are in some measure the reason I have been so alert in this book to the power in Cram's life of the lost cause, be it Jacobitism, the culture of the American South, or Anglo-Catholicism.

My grandmother Tucci was a Waldensian, a member of an ancient Italian Protestant sect that predated the Reformation by at least five or six centuries, and I early observed how at odds she and my grandfather, by then parishioners of the First Congregational Church in Cambridge, were with Italian-American culture. My grandmother Shand Groves, moreover, was the proud and originally disadvantaged descendant of pioneer British settlers in the eastern townships of Quebec along the Richelieu River, the heartland of the American loyalists who fled Boston and elsewhere during the American Revolution for Canada only to be overwhelmed first by French Canadian and then, in this century, by American culture. The loyalist cause, particularly, than which there is no lost cause stronger on earth, molded my boyhood, for the dominant influences of those days were my mother and my maternal grandmother, Geraldine and Margaret Shand Groves.

It was the former who was the originator of the psychological tales that must keep company here with the religious and architectural ones already told. When still a senior at Simmons College, my mother met a Harvard undergraduate, John Tucci, who before they were married went on to Tufts Medical School, my mother meanwhile taking her bachelor's degree in medical administration. As she began, so she continued; aside from music, medicine was really the center of everything in my mother's life and by the time I was a boy, she, not content with having run the practice of my father (chief of anesthesiology at the Massachusetts Eye and Ear Infirmary), continued in this vein after they were divorced, performing a similar service for two Back Bay psychiatrists.

The first of these, Merrill Moore, caught my adolescent attention because he was also a poet, who had, in fact, for many years treated Robert Lowell. For the second, David Landau, my mother ran what I have been told was one of the first private electroconvulsive therapy (ECT) clinics in New England. She did so, as I recall, with some misgivings, for she was an ardent Jungian, and electroshock therapy (as it was then called) was a controversial mode of treatment (though not so much so as when Ralph Adams Cram authorized its use for his wife's treatment in 1942). Still, my mother felt she had helped many people and thought ECT promised something for the future.

I myself, coming from such a background, was regularly in therapy as a youngster (indeed, my Back Bay "progressive" school, the Kingsley School, encouraged students to have a "shrink"), and I was just as likely to encounter the same doctor whose office I'd been in that afternoon at my own dining-room table that night. When I add that the clinic my mother ran was in the historic old Pierce House on Beacon Street, which Landau was then restoring with my mother's help (my first experience of historic preservation) and that at the same time I was a chorister at All Saints', Ashmont (Cram's first church), it will be seen that religion, architecture, and the study of the mind (even my own) have never in my life been far from one another.

My mother, furthermore, enriched this rather challenging brew in a remarkable way by the family members she took care to surround me with as a youth, men intended to do duty, as it were, for my father, by my teens remarried and moved away. Two uncles, particularly, compassed seemingly limitless possibilities.

The first, James Shand, was to some of our relatives an embarrassment; a Checker cab driver, he was not well educated. But I knew well the family tales of how Jimmy, a strikingly handsome youth who remained a bachelor until his fifties, had departed Boston precipitously (in the wake of a reputedly misfired love affair), for the West, where he became a cowboy. He was founder of the pioneer prairie settlement of Shandleigh, Alberta, in 1908 (his letters to my grandmother Shand back in Boston are now in the Provincial Archives), but drought and depression drove Jimmy back to Boston in the thirties. Thus when I came along in the next decade, he was able (a cowboy being an instant hero to any youngster then) to serve the vital function of exposing me closely to someone who was by some standards a failure, but who was also a man of such grace and courage that failure, in that sense, meant little. Jimmy was that very rare thing, a gentleman.

The other uncle was an honorary one (he was actually, I believe, a cousin on my mother's side), and the contrast between Jimmy Shand and Harrison Hale Schaff could not have been greater. Jimmy was full of stories of life out West on the frontier; Schaff, who came to live with us in our old family home on Jones Hill in Dorchester when I was a boy, had been a Boston publisher at the turn of the century, and his tales were more often of London and Paris. He became my first and ever after chief mentor in a life blessed with many such.

Editorial director, in his prime, of a Beacon Street publishing house, the John W. Luce Company, founded in 1907, it was Schaff who in the early years of this century had introduced the Irish playwrights of the Abbey Theatre to America and who had, in a list conspicuously avant-garde for its era, also published H. L. Mencken's first book, as well as another by the same author that was the first book in English on Friedrich Nietzsche. And I think I may claim to be another, if much less renowned, discovery of Schaff's, for his opinion (which my mother found it hard to ignore) that I had it in me to be a scholar and a writer sustained us all in difficult days and still does me today when the ideas or the words just won't come.

More than anything else at the time, however, it was the immediately broadening vistas that opened up for me as a consequence of Schaff's role in my life; most important in the context of this book, he first opened the door of the fin-de-siècle for me, whether in Europe or in America. Through Schaff, to cite the most startling example, I came to know Prince Felix Youssoupoff, the murderer of Rasputin, whose correspondence with me (in my mid-teens, no less) is now part of the Romanov Collection at the Beinecke Library at Yale. Schaff was also an avowed atheist and early on urged the same upon me. Furthermore, he came complete with a mistress, introduced to us frankly enough, but only occasionally; he maintained her at an in-town apartment that to visit as a teenager I thought beat reading a novel by Arthur Schnitzler any day. Moreover, as Schaff was also conspicuously unmarried, the impression became clear as I got older that he was the complete Bohemian; an impression later strengthened when I came to know his friend Lucien Price, also unmarried, the distinguished author and editor (of *The Dialogues of Alfred North Whitehead*) who kindly took an interest in me as a youth.

By then I was away at school at Ashbury College in Ottawa, enrolled, so to speak, in a graduate course in Anglophilia from which (happily) I have never recovered. Ashbury was not called the "Eton of Canada" in those days only because it, too, produced outstanding civic leaders — and my experience of prep school life confirmed these youthful impressions absorbed from Schaff and Price. So did the aftermath of that prep school experience, back in Boston, where in the 1960s I found myself drawn to the company of a friend very active in the city's first homophile group, Joseph McGrath, then a student at Boston University who lived in the extraordinary Beacon Hill house (it had been, it was said, a stop on the underground railway) of the group's founder, Prescott Townsend.

Townsend, a Boston Brahmin and Harvard alumnus of high ideals and eccentric habit (so like an eighteenth-century English aristocrat he seemed to me then), was at that time as interesting for the summer colony he reigned over in Provincetown (to which I was *not* asked) as for his forthright defense at State House hearings and such (where I *was* welcomed) of the interests of homophiles, as gays were then sometimes called. Like Schaff, Townsend was already elderly when I first met him, and he figures in this book because, according to Lucius Beebe in his *Boston and the Boston Legend*, Townsend cut a considerable figure (raccoon coat and all) among the 1920s Beacon Hill Bohemians who succeeded the first wave of the youthful Cram and his friends. Thus, even aside from Schaff's friend Price (whose Beacon Hill rooms of the 1960s were in their way as Bohemian as Townsend's old town house), I may claim a significant link back to the edge of the world of this study, Cram's own Bohemia of the 1880s and 1890s. (As Volume One was going to press, I learned of another and rather more startling link when the estimable Claire Dewart, librarian of Boston's Trinity Church, told me that T. Henry Randall, the partner of Ralph Adams Cram's European travels of 1887–1888, about whom — since Randall had no descendants — I had not discovered much, was her granduncle, and that another of Randall's relations had been Father Daniel Randall Magruder. That priest, among all my older priest friends perhaps the most robust of my admirers when I was a young man, had, indeed, once told me he knew Ralph Adams Cram. But I saw no significance then to the fact or to Magruder's middle name. I do now.)

To return to Prescott Townsend, Schaff was dead by the time I met him, but I am sure my old mentor would have approved of Townsend's circle; of my decision to follow in my father's footsteps and go to Harvard, however, Schaff, a Williams College man in an era when such loyalties mattered a lot, would not have approved at all. But it was at Harvard and in its wake, in no small measure thanks to George Ursul of Emerson College (which I attended briefly and ingloriously in the misguided belief that I was destined to be an actor), that I found not only the key mentoring relationships with my older priest friends and with the professors and architect friends already recalled here but also my chief mentor in succession to Schaff and, in the last analysis, my role model ever since, Elliott Perkins.

The head tutor of Harvard's history department as well as the Master of Lowell House, Perkins in the first place taught me how to do history: how to search out the evidence, follow it, bravely if necessary, how to weigh and interpret and edit it, and, having judged its true significance, deploy it accordingly. But with Perkins, professional training played into what used to be called manners and mores. He was, for example, not above teaching a young man how to make a better snowball—and how to throw it better, too—as well as how to pay the bill graciously and manfully when you inevitably broke something. Indeed, Perkins taught me after years of failure how properly to tie a bow tie when, amid some roughhousing at a party, mine had got undone and I'd had to admit I was still depending upon the opposite sex to do it for me. Perkins would have none of it (and pretied bow ties were *not* his style), and he shamed me into learning how to tie my tie in about ten very embarrassing public seconds.

Am I drifting? Not really, for I've thought of Perk often while writing this book. His teaching, for example, came at once to mind when Paul Wright, my editor, sent me an article on a conference at Harvard on biography that dealt with "outing" historical figures; a conference that Paul attended (no doubt in self-defense) and where every other speaker seemed to allude to Janet Malcolm's piece in *The New Yorker* on the biographer today as increasingly a thief, exploiting the defenseless dead and robbing them of their privacy. In this article Professor Diane Wood Middlebrook of Stanford made a point I knew at once Perkins would have made had this issue arisen in his lifetime: the responsibility of the historian is to tell the truth as he or she sees it; that (as Perkins would have put it) is the whole ball game. Amen.

When another speaker went on in support of this view to assert that the dead have no wishes, it gave me pause, but I thought immediately of a talk on this subject I'd had one night with a gay friend who is a schoolteacher. He pointed out that, notwithstanding the fact that statistics show that most child sexual abuse is committed by heterosexuals (and, indeed, by the child's father), the fact that he taught children might mean he would have to go through life without ever being open about his sexual orientation, even though that meant that some of those he loved most (including his parents) would never fully know him. That, not so much the loss of his dignity as a person, was what seemed most to bother him; for notwithstanding whether the repression and the subterfuge weakened or strengthened him creatively—an issue I take up in this book—he knew how any such lie must twist and corrupt any human relationship. At least, he said, he would like to think that after his death someone might care enough for his memory to tell the truth about him. And here again I recognized again what would have been the view of Perkins, who would always have wanted the historian fearlessly to set any record straight that needed it.

The same conviction, in a different way, was the foundation of my relationship with the man who more than anyone else guided me in the post-Perkins era through the transition from Harvard to Boston and from student to historian, Francis Moloney, a Harvard man himself, in those days the senior assistant director of the Boston Public Library. Like me an admirer of Samuel Eliot Morison (whom I would reverently greet every week in the north aisle of the Church of the Advent, now that I was again going to church), Frank Moloney shared my view that Boston and New England studies had been in the doldrums since Van Wyck Brooks and badly needed shaking up after the manner of Morison, whose work had for some time, however, not been concerned, so to speak, with his back yard. Frank insisted all my disparate interests really *did* come together — in New England studies, a field in which Moloney could have made an even greater contribution under his own name had he spent less time helping others like me. Of course, that was, in part, Frank's job. But recall Jung's observation that exercising free will is doing cheerfully and well what we have to do anyway, what so many do meanly and poorly.

Alas, Frank's untimely death ended many of our plans. But the one that was, after all, fully realized was the Boston Gothicists Archive, the cornerstone of which was Ralph Adams Cram's office archives and private papers, which I had discovered in the course of the further research on Cram that Walter Whitehill had encouraged me to undertake after graduation. Frank found the interest and funds to support my foraging and ultimately to make possible the first retrospective exhibition of Cram's work, which I organized; it opened in 1975 in Boston at the library and the following year at St. John the Divine in New York. Moreover, Frank worked earnestly to help me rouse John Doran (the last survivor of Cram's office with any knowledge of that era) to the importance of the preservation of those drawings and also helped to incite Cram's by then only living child, Mary Carrington Cram Nicholas, to undertake a search for her father's private papers, in both cases with the idea of giving them to the library.

She it is above all who is to be praised and thanked here. Others of the Cram family, most notably Ralph Adams Cram II, have helped me greatly through the years. But Mary Nicholas was in the position to help most, not only because as the senior living Cram it was she whose decision about Cram's papers would be definitive, but also because she had been an astute observer of her parents and wrote down, on her own and then later at my behest, an enormous number of her recollections. Moreover, I early established the fact that she had been, not surprisingly, in Ralph Adams Cram's own wake, a good friend of Alfred Pedersen, the Cowley Father, dead by then, whose views on the need for me to address Cram not only as an architect but as a human being Mrs. Nicholas reiterated frequently, despairing as she did of ever convincing me. Thus she held back very little from me.

It was understood, of course, that when finished with Cram's papers, which she entrusted to me for my scholarly use, I would shepherd them into what today has become (since John Rivers's generous addition to them of Bertram Good-hue's sketches) the Cram and Goodhue Collection. Together with the other allied collections Frank and I secured for the library (the Wilbur Burnham, Charles Connick, John Evans, and Maginnis and Walsh archives), the material Mrs. Nicholas brought together is now the centerpiece of what is arguably the most important collection in the world on the art and architecture of the American Gothic Revival. Without Frank Moloney's perseverance and Mary Cram Nicholas's generosity, nothing — including this study — would have been possible.

Nor would it have been but for my aforementioned editor, Paul Wright, whom I have known since he and I worked together years ago in the Boston Public Library Learning Library program, of which Paul was the director and I a teaching assistant (to Professor Gerald Bernstein of Brandeis University). Although it was important to me when Maud Wilcox, then Editor in Chief of the Harvard University Press, told me that at the University of Massachusetts Press I would be in the care of her son, Bruce Wilcox, Director of the Press, who has been unfailingly helpful to me, it was most important that Paul would be the editor with whom I would work most closely. Paul is a historian who, like Frank Moloney, would be better known if he wrote more and edited less. But as an author of his I can scarcely complain. He has believed in my work and shared my interest in the little-known progressive and modernist tendencies of fin-de-siècle Boston for many years. And he has kept the idea of this book alive and performed what seem to the uninitiated miracles to ensure it would see print. His intellectual interest, moreover, and his editorial judgment (as well as the occasional gentle remonstrance about "the Shand-Tucci rhetoric") have been invaluable.

So has the zeal of my copy editor, Betsy Pitha. I first met Betsy, formerly the head of the Trade Copyediting Department at Little, Brown and Company, when she copyedited *Built in Boston* fifteen years ago, and since then I have never willingly written anything her eagle eye has not scanned and, if not always approved, at least allowed. Her labors over this manuscript have been prolonged, dedicated, and — only an author knows — absolutely vital. One cannot work day in and day out year after year with everyone. With Betsy, now long since a good friend, it is always a pleasure.

All these tales, all this catalogue of mentors and friends and editors, would have been for naught, however, but for F. W. Atherton. Fred originally sought me out (while studying Cram's work for a course project) when he was a senior in Harvard College, where, though he was in Adams House and I in Eliot House, he had heard something of the Architecture Table I had founded when Master Alan Heimert asked me to join Eliot's Senior Common Room. Fred and I actually met at All Saints', Ashmont, and thereafter became neighbors in Peabody Square in the shadow of All Saints' in 1991 — the hundredth anniversary year, as it turned out, of Cram's and Goodhue's own first meeting and of the design of the first church to bear their names. All Saints' was then between rectors and providentially presided over by a good friend of both Fred's and mine, E. Richard Rothmund, the parish's senior warden, whose help is also happily acknowledged here.

At that time, as a result of a prolonged bout of illness, this project had been all but abandoned, and it was Fred's friendship that revived both author and manuscript. It is because of that and because since then this aspiring architect has proved (on one expedition after another to explore this or that Cram building) so brilliant an interlocutor, that I gratefully dedicate *Ralph Adams Cram: Life and Architecture* to that keenest of critics and now best of friends, Fred Atherton. There was something here to be done which no one else could do.

PDS-T

Eliot House, Harvard University, February 1980 —
Boston Athenaeum, December 1994

BOSTON BOHEMIA

1881–1900

RALPH ADAMS CRAM:
LIFE AND ARCHITECTURE

1

PINCKNEY STREET

I went full of curiosity and the faint, unrecognized apprehension that here,
at last, I should find that low door in the wall, which others, I knew, had found
before me, which opened on an enclosed and enchanted garden, which was
somewhere, not overlooked by any window, in the heart of that grey city.

— Evelyn Waugh, *Brideshead Revisited*

New occasions teach new duties,
Time makes ancient good uncouth;
They must upward still and onward
Who would keep abreast of truth.

— James Russell Lowell, "The Present Crisis," 1845
(*The Hymnal*, 1940, No. 519)

1. Pinckney Street, Beacon Hill, a turn-of-the-century photograph. Cram lived in the lodging house visible to the far left, 99 Pinckney.

PINCKNEY Street, precipitate and Dickensian, cuts steeply down through the blocks of old brick houses and narrow courts that crowd the southwestern slope of Boston's Beacon Hill, where every street, in Ralph Waldo Emerson's words, "leads downward to the sea."[1] In my imagination of Ralph Adams Cram, this biography begins here: of a brisk New England morning a hundred and more years ago, in the quick descent of young Cram down Pinckney (*1*), from his bachelor rooms, to Charles Street, thence to Brimmer Street, and after a left turn and a shortish walk, to the Church of the Advent and the mellifluous Anglican murmur of early morning Mass.[2]

A century later, Cram's own imagination is nowhere more easily caught or more keenly felt than in the shadowy and beautifully timeworn interior of this Victorian Gothic church, where so much of his work is admired today, and in the surrounding streetscapes of old Beacon Hill, environs then as now that could not be more picturesque. If the steep prospect down Pinckney toward Brimmer Street (and the Charles River beyond) is worthy of Prague, the view up Pinckney Street Cram would have had on his return from Mass is just as reminiscent of London, for diagonally opposite Cram's rooming house, Pinckney opens unexpectedly into the amplitude of Louisburg Square, its brick townhouse blocks facing a tree-shaded center park and statuary.

Picturesque architecturally, Cram's Beacon Hill was also diverse socially. How much so is clear in the writings of the poet Robert Lowell, who, only a generation after Cram's, lived one block beyond Pinckney on Revere Street, on the much less elegant north slope. There, though their house was scarcely fifty yards from Louisburg Square, Lowell's mother once announced irritably that they were "barely perched on the outer rim of the hub of decency."[3] By this measure Cram's own perch on Pinckney Mrs. Lowell doubtless would have thought barely on the inner rim. Pinckney has always been rather a Bohemian street, mediating as it does between the socially ambiguous north slope and the much grander quarter of Louisburg Square and Mount Vernon Street—and, beyond that, Beacon Street itself, "street of the sifted few," as Oliver Wendell Holmes has somewhere called it.

Cram's address reflected not only youthful poverty of means but the ambivalences of his own background, for he was the son of a somewhat eccentric and controversial Unitarian minister, William Augustine Cram (*2*), of the New

Hampshire town of Hampton Falls. Scion of a seventeenth-century settler and sufficiently a Transcendentalist that Ralph Adams Cram, born on December 16, 1863, was given his first name in honor of Ralph Waldo Emerson, William Cram was nonetheless very much his own man. An ardent abolitionist, he was a pacifist and even a war resister who refused to serve in the Union Army in the Civil War and was scrupulous and, indeed, fierce enough to have rebuked a brother for buying him a substitute, though it saved him from prison. Forced, moreover, by a youthful promise to his parents that should never have been redeemed (to return home and take over the farm if the elder Crams felt unable to carry on), William Augustine Cram had, in order to do so, abandoned a successful pastorate in Westford, Massachusetts, much to the chagrin of his bitterly disappointed wife.[4] Reverend Cram thus endowed his son Ralph with rather a mixed heritage — a venerable family tradition, much learning, high principles, a stern independence, but also an overall sense of wasted gifts and stubborn if genteel poverty.[5]

Ralph himself, having been born just after the start of the Civil War, would not perhaps have felt too much the immediate psychological trauma of his father's actions, but their effect as he grew up was such that the younger Cram, always in later years very reticent about personal matters, admitted eventually that he had early felt his father to be a failure and that only after the death of Cram Senior (in 1909) did he come to terms with some of his Oedipal problems and begin to see a certain stoic heroism in the life of William Augustine Cram.[6]

As a boy Ralph was not perhaps conspicuously unhappy at Exeter High School, even though his father was an alumnus of Phillips Exeter Academy, one of New England's elite boarding schools.[7] But once in Boston, as a young man, Ralph would certainly have been made to feel the difference. This was all the more so as college was out of the question, a lack about which he would always be sensitive. It was in lieu of college that Ralph came to Boston in 1881 from rural New Hampshire in the first place, to take up an architectural apprenticeship at the age of seventeen.

FORETHOUGHT AND RECOLLECTION

The elder Cram, after all, was not without influence. And he was well known in New England Unitarian circles. What to do for his son rather than university was taken up in no less august a quarter than that of William Robert Ware, the head of the Massachusetts Institute of Technology School of Architecture, "a certain knack for drawing," as Ralph put it later, having suggested to William Cram an architectural career for his son. Ware, in turn, recommended Ralph as a draftsman to the new and rather fashionable architectural firm of Rotch and

2. The Reverend William Augustine Cram, Ralph Adams Cram's father, from the portrait that once hung in the younger Cram's study.

Tilden. (Years later, Ralph found out what really happened and told Larry Winship that "my father said he would give the architect $6.00 a week and that the architect could pay it [to] me without letting me know that it was he, not the architect, who was paying me.")[8]

Although in the long run an inspiration on his father's part, in the short run architecture did not entirely suit Ralph; at least not the kind of architecture practiced by Rotch and Tilden, where Ralph would doggedly plug away for the full five years of his apprenticeship, until 1886, but where (despite no little kindness from Arthur Rotch himself) Cram felt trapped in what he later privately called a "rotten office."[9] Not surprisingly, he was by only his second year of apprenticeship already submitting designs and sketches on his own to professional journals. The few of these sketches of 1882 that have come to light—designs for cottages published in *The Builder and Woodworker* (his first ever published designs)[10]—document that at eighteen Cram had a good eye for plan and volume and void and a nice ability to distribute wall and window (3). They were also evidence of the initiative and drive he would always demonstrate. However, nothing came of these early efforts.

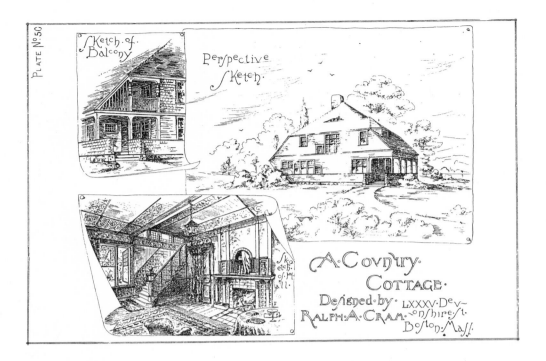

Sketch of Balcony

Perspective Sketch

Sketch of Hall

A · Covntry · Cottage · Designed by · Ralph · A · Cram · LXXXV · Devonshire st · Boston · Mass

3a, b. "Design for a small cottage, Ralph A. Cram, des. et del...," perspective and plans. One of a series of studies of 1882 by Cram in his second year of apprenticeship, these studies are his first known published works, at the age of eighteen.

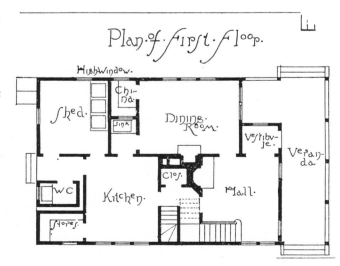

Plan · of · first · floor ·

Highwindow.

Shed

China

Sink

Dining Room

Vestibule

Veranda

WC

Kitchen

Clos.

Hall

Stores

4. Four years after his first published designs and sketches of 1882, Cram had become so skilled as to produce this superb perspective of Rotch and Tilden's design for the Church of the Holy Spirit, Mattapan, Massachusetts. The sketch is signed "Ralph A. Cram, del."

That Ralph Cram was not easy to get on with, thus frustrated, seems clear. He recalled in his memoirs that he had at Rotch and Tilden at least "one inveterate enemy," with whom he had "many militant encounters, some of them developing into actual knock-down brawls, to the great glee of the other members of the staff." The partners' designs scarcely pleased Ralph more. One case in particular, "a certain church design . . . [that] offended me mightily," he remembered years later, and he "began trying alternative schemes" for the Church of the Holy Spirit in the Boston suburb of Mattapan, which was the church he probably meant.[11] The final Rotch design carried out (4) shows, however, whatever Cram thought of the design, how competent a renderer he had become at Rotch and Tilden.

In 1884 opportunity seemed at hand. That year Ralph entered the first Rotch

9

Traveling Fellowship competition, established by Arthur Rotch; with every hope of winning, Ralph instead had to withdraw because he inadvertently saw the problem on his boss's desk. Then, the year following (and this must be accounted Ralph Adams Cram's debut as an architect, in 1885, at the age of twenty-one), what seemed to be his first success proved illusory; for while a design of his (now lost) won through to the next-to-last round of Boston's Suffolk County Courthouse competition, and he was awarded a five-hundred-dollar prize, it was only to be told that there would be no final round, the job having been arbitrarily awarded to the city architect. Boston politics! "So matters went," he called to mind years later, "for the full five years of my professional tutelage, with no appreciable results, either one way or the other, except a steady magnifying of my critical attitude towards the sort of work in which I was permitted to engage . . . though what I did like, apart from the Richardsonian evangel, I did not know."[12]

What did finally propel Ralph Adams Cram forward, however, was exactly his admiration for Henry Hobson Richardson. One of the reasons Ralph was able to move to Beacon Hill and to Pinckney Street at all (he had at first, in 1881, settled on Dwight Street in the declining South End),[13] from the periphery to the center of Boston's artistic and intellectual life, was that by the mid-1880s he had become, amazingly enough for a man of his years, the art critic of the city's most distinguished newspaper, the *Boston Evening Transcript*.

It all began in October 1884, a few months after the Rotch Fellowship fiasco, with a passionate letter by "C. A. Ralph" (as Ralph Adams Cram would always style himself as a critic) to the editor of the *Transcript*. In this missive young Ralph professed himself outraged by a plan to build an apartment house in front of Trinity Church, in what is now Copley Square.[14] So far as is known his first published writing, this letter declared not only Cram's ardent belief in art ("the measure of a people's worth is the record of the art that they can show") and his dislike for Victorian taste ("barren of art, as we now are, we must needs admit the truth"), but also the fact that while the young architectural apprentice, in Ann Miner Daniel's words, condemned in this letter "the money-seeking, selfish, fashion-conscious society he saw around him," he showed himself to be not just an idealistic scold but a practical problem-solver. All his life, Daniel continues, in a discussion of this incident in her invaluable doctoral dissertation on Cram's early work, "Cram, the dreamer . . . was always a pragmatist, and for every proposal . . . there was a practical plan."[15]

Indeed, Ralph's letter set in motion events that led ultimately to the city's buying the land in front of Richardson's famous church to make the present Copley Square. But the nature of his success pointed as well to a problematic aspect of Cram's personality, for the letter did not make him universally popu-

5. Cram's design for Copley Square, 1885–1893. Although this rendering, the only one known for the design, cannot date from any earlier than 1893, when the square's architectural background that Cram used was published in *American Architect*, the design is certainly a solo work of Cram's, for it is signed by him alone. Thus its origins perhaps may lie in the 1880s. It was Cram's agitation in 1883–84, when the larger part of Copley Square was purchased and named, that focused efforts under way since 1882 to create the now famous public square.

lar, embarrassing as it did not a few of his professional betters. (Where, one respondent to the *Transcript* wanted to know, were the famous architects, like Richardson, who seemed content to leave it to a young apprentice to defend their proud landmarks in aid of creating what would become the city's foremost square? [5])[16] For the first but not for the last time Ralph Adams Cram's enthusiasm and intensity would be both strength and weakness and arouse as much resentment as admiration. Meanwhile, one result of all this (and one or two other "letters") was that E. H. Clement, the *Transcript*'s editor (and Cram's Pinckney Street neighbor) offered his precocious young correspondent the post of art critic—along with a salary of eighteen cents per inch of text. Ralph accepted. By 1886 he had graduated from Rotch and Tilden and the following year was listed in the Boston street directory not as an architecture student but as a "reporter."

It is not likely that his family rejoiced in this development. Being so close as New Hampshire (to which Ralph often returned for weekends), they must have

6. Cram as a young man (back row, far right), pipe in mouth, in what is probably a Blake family group in New Hampshire. None of the other figures can be identified, though the bearded patriarch is surely Squire Blake of Kensington.

remained a formidable influence—not only the Crams but also the family of Ralph Adams Cram's mother, Sarah Elizabeth Blake Cram. More prosperous than the Crams, and thus better able to keep up the traditions of the New England country gentry, the Blakes (6), one gathers, distinctly caught hold of Ralph's imagination and played a large role in shaping his ambitions.

His maternal grandfather, Ira Blake, who will come up again when we take up our discussion of the sense of "past" that Ralph Adams Cram brought to his architecture, was an especially important figure. Master of a fine old country house, "the last of the squires," as Cram called him, had been a political power in the New Hampshire legislature and a great Federalist—which by family tradition accounts for Ralph Adams Cram's middle name, chosen by Squire Blake in honor of John Adams.[17] Also influential was the squire's son, and it was this uncle of Ralph's who, doubtless at the whole family's behest, as Ralph was poised on the cusp between architecture and journalism, wrote to him in 1885, admonishing the young man to hold a steady course:

Having been a boy once myself with perhaps as many ambitious schemes in my head as you . . . [I know well] *that all is not gold that glitters* . . . don't kick out of the traces . . . it is better to grow up solid; that is, mature slowly . . . in this battle of life . . . each and all of us should so live that the world will be the better for the fact we have played.[18]

It was a letter Cram took seriously enough to keep for a lifetime. But if the intent was to dissuade him from deserting architecture, it failed — at least at the time.

OSCAR WILDE IN BOSTON

Ralph Adams Cram's decision to abandon the "narrow environment" (the words are his)[19] of the architectural drafting room for the more cosmopolitan world of the *Transcript* newsroom seems in retrospect natural enough if one considers his youthful tastes. At about the age of eighteen, Cram later remembered, "when personal consciousness seemed to become operative," these tastes were three: Gilbert and Sullivan's operetta *Patience;* the paintings of the Pre-Raphaelite brotherhood; and the music dramas of Richard Wagner.[20] Avant-garde influences indeed, in the early 1880s.

The first, a satire of the aesthetic movement and its chief votary, Oscar Wilde (7), who would become the preeminent playwright writing in English of Cram's era, may be said to be the logical soundtrack for my imagining of Cram's fin-de-siècle passage down Pinckney Street to early morning Mass; in particular, I imagine much humming of "an attachment à la Plato for a bashful young potato. . . ." Not that young Ralph, who though slight was sturdy enough, was himself at all "a greenery-yallery Grosvenor Gallery foot-in-the-grave young man." Gilbert and Sullivan were all the rage in Boston during Ralph's first years in town. He probably first saw *Patience* in 1882 — and Wilde himself, too (of this there is no documentation, though one of Ralph's friends secured the great man's autograph), for the leader of the British aesthetes was in Boston twice that year, promoting Richard D'Oyly Carte's American tour with a series of lectures and staying at the Hotel Vendome in the Back Bay.

Wilde's time in Boston was highly controversial. Witness Richard Ellmann's description of how Colonel Thomas Wentworth Higginson, editor of the *Youth's Companion,*

a highly respected bore, [with] much to answer for in literary terms, since he had judged unworthy of publication [Emily Dickinson's] poems, . . . berated Wilde for writing prurient poems . . . [and] was especially agitated because . . . Julia Ward Howe, whom he all but named, had entertained this pornographic poet. . . .

Higginson was made to taste the grapes of Mrs. Howe's wrath . . . [in] the Boston

7. Oscar Wilde, dressed much as at Julia Ward Howe's soirée during his Boston visit. Alice Cary Williams recalled in *Through the Turnstile*: "The two large [Beacon Street] drawing rooms were . . . a brilliant scene. . . . Beneath the twinkling chandeliers ladies in brocaded gowns . . . milled about . . . their diamond tiaras and necklaces glinting. . . . I saw coming down the stairs . . . a pair of patent leather shoes with silver buckles, then black stockings and above them green velvet knee breeches [and] a matching green doublet, a ruffle running down its length, and . . . a pale white hand which held a lily."

Evening Transcript [where in a letter she denied] the colonel's right to decide who should be received socially. . . . "To cut off even an offensive member of society from its best influences and most humanizing resources is scarcely Christian in any sense," [she wrote, and] she received Wilde's thanks for her "noble and beautiful" letter. Higginson was silenced, but [in London] the *Pall Mall Gazette* . . . ironically endorsed Mrs. Howe's courage in trying to improve Wilde.[21]

Behind all the brouhaha there was, however, a serious purpose to Wilde's visit, and Ellmann discusses it with close reference to Boston. Observing that anti-Philistinism was fundamental to the values of the aesthetic movement, Ellmann writes:

> The United States had a subculture which was dissatisfied with money and power . . . [but] this [subculture] had no single and famed exponent. Neither the shirt-sleeved Whitman, nor the bearded Longfellow, nor the tense Emerson could remotely be thought of as Gilbert's model [for the aesthetes in *Patience*].

Actually, Wilde was fond of quoting Emerson's witticism that "I am always insincere as knowing that there are other moods," which suggests that Emerson was not entirely beside the aesthetic point. In any event, the purpose of Wilde's tour was to rectify this lack of focus in aestheticism in the New World: it was hoped that Wilde, Ellmann writes, "might gather the [aesthetic] strands together [and] give them the force of a program [in America]."[22]

Though it would be a while before the seeds sown in 1882 by Wilde flowered sufficiently to attract a wide national attention (as well as, back in London, Wilde's own notice), it has been too long overlooked that in Boston Wilde succeeded in setting in motion cultural developments (obscured in our collective consciousness because of his later downfall) that made the New England capital the center of aestheticism in America, thereby, admittedly, somewhat confusing the city's image. As Mary Blanchard has pointed out in her study "Near *The Coast of Bohemia*":

> To many Americans, Boston was a city that symbolized older standards that stood in opposition to the commercialism and modernity of a cosmopolitan New York. But it was also the seat of the new "gospel," aestheticism, a gospel that attacked those very standards.

And this gospel was early identified with Boston by the national media. Blanchard cites, for example,

> two stories in *Peterson's Magazine* in [1882 and 1884, in which] Boston's aesthetic circles were . . . portrayed as subversive and decadent. . . . One narrative, "The Utterly Utter Boston Browns," ended with the triumph of sensible country values. . . . [Another] catalogued the conversion of the youthful Cousin Tilly into a languid aesthete, seduced by the Boston summer boarders who . . . "belonged ter them estheticks."[23]

15

That Oscar Wilde and Ralph Adams Cram made their debuts in Boston within a year of each other in 1881–1882 certainly boded ill in the end for any "sensible country values" that Cram might have brought with him to the Puritan capital, it being if anything an understatement to call merely "subversive" the Wildean aestheticism Cram and his friends would soon become the effective leaders of in Boston. For the aesthetic movement, shaped chiefly by Walter Pater, buttressed strongly by Algernon Swinburne, and then developed vividly enough by Wilde that its image is still potent more than a century later, had to do not only with "art for art's sake" (art transcending both faith and morality as these are generally understood); it also had two clear subtexts.

First, clearly put by Richard Ellmann in his reading of John Addington Symonds's *Studies of the Greek Poets* of 1873, was the "Greek" theme, Symonds having in that work "confirmed the all-importance of the word 'aesthetic' . . . [and,] agreeing with Pater, conspicuously related it to the Greeks . . . [whose] morality [he held] was aesthetic and not theocratic . . . [because] the Greeks were essentially a nation of artists." Second, and following naturally upon the Greek theme, was the gay subtext. Again, it is clearly put by Ellmann, who notes that in the context of Wilde and Walter Pater "aesthete" was "almost a euphemism for homosexual."[24]

Both subtexts, Greek and gay (not unrelated), will be more important in the long run here than the aesthetic movement itself, whose pedigree we must not, however, for that reason lose sight of: for it was the *Pre-Raphaelite* who was reconstituted (at Oxford in the late 1870s; in America in the early 1880s) into what in Ralph Adams Cram's youth was increasingly called the *aesthete*, and the aesthete, in turn, who in the 1890s would be reconstituted into the *decadent*.

THE ROSSETTI-WAGNER REVELATION

Not all aesthetes regarded their Pre-Raphaelite background equally fondly. ("If you get sea-sick," said James Whistler to Wilde on the eve of the latter's departure for America, "throw up Burne-Jones.")[25] But the new art critic of the *Transcript* was, in fact, devoted to the work of the Pre-Raphaelites, the second of the three influences Cram judged formative in his youth. Of course, between the first and the second influences were many links: Wilde's Boston lecture of January 31, 1882, in connection with the opening of *Patience,* had been precisely on the subject of the Pre-Raphaelites. Nearly three years later, in November 1884, it was this same cause that Ralph Adams Cram took up in his first columns for the *Transcript.*

It was an appropriately *haute Bohème* topic to have chosen; there was then a Pre-Raphaelite exhibition at Boston's Museum of Fine Arts. And the series of articles also disclose that in this, his literary debut, "C. A. Ralph" showed himself as able a writer as he had a designer and draftsman two years previously in *The Brickbuilder and Woodworker* in 1882. Still, the prose was purple enough:

> When from Byzantium, laden with the newfound Oriental power of color, Art returned to Italy, it was not the crude, half-classical work of the earlier centuries, but as Christian symbolism, filled with the Eastern glory of color, changed by the strong Oriental rigidity and conventionality of form. Ravenna, Rome and Milan gave good record of this first consciousness of color as it came to the Italians of the north. But not for many centuries did it meet with its full and complete development. At first, as a subordinate means of expressing thought, it slowly grew more and more glorious and powerful, until at last, the work of Cimabue forgotten, Giotto, Fra Angelico and Botticelli — masters of thought — superseded beyond the mighty moderation of Titian, the subtle comprehension of Giorgione, color, utter sensuous color, achieved the climax of its supremacy.[26]

As the name implies, the Pre-Raphaelites sought their inspiration in the masters of the fifteenth century, and they are therefore part and parcel of the Gothic Revival. They were also vaguely socialist (the ideal twenty-first-century society of William Morris's *News from Nowhere* of 1890 had a very Pre-Raphaelite appearance). Nor was socialism their only modern signal, so to speak; even the Pre-Raphaelites' explicitly religious work, writes H. W. Janson, "radiates an aura of repressed eroticism."[27] Pre-Raphaelitism thus introduces here (in the wake of both the Greek and the gay subtexts of the first overall aesthetic influence) the general theme of the relationship of the aesthetic and the erotic on which this book will turn, a relationship dominant in the third and last of the formative influences of his youth Cram identified — Richard Wagner's music dramas.

As with Gilbert and Sullivan, Boston was in the forefront of the Wagnerian movement in the 1880s. Anton Seidl, "Wagner's personal emissary [in America]," as Joseph Horowitz called this important protégé of the composer, having conducted the American premieres in New York of *Tristan und Isolde*, *Siegfried*, and *Götterdämmerung* in 1886–1889, also in 1889 conducted the first performance of Wagner's Ring cycle to be given in its entirety, in Boston.[28] While Horowitz has contended that "in the United States the cult of Wagner did not, as in Europe, herald an iconoclastic modernism," his conclusion is rooted in an assumption that I will confront in this book: that "there were no American decadents or Symbolists poised to discover avant-garde aspects of Wagnerianism, . . . [which] was found not to challenge but to reinforce the [American] intellectual mainstream."[29]

In Boston, however, the dominating musical figure of the nineteenth century, John Sullivan Dwight, until his death in 1893, "resisted mightily," in John Swan's words, "the onslaught of 'modern' music, which . . . most particularly meant Wagner," while one of the leading critics of the era, Philip Hale, in a series of columns of 1889–1891, protested bitterly how Boston "divided into two unreasonable factions who quarreled over the name 'Wagner.' "[30] That composer's work was, in fact, of Cram's three formative tastes the most radical.

A half century later Cram would write: "It really is not too much to say that [in Boston in the early 1880s] with the 'Ring' operas, heaven opened for me. Then and there I became a besotted Wagnerite." He remained so for the rest of his life, cheerfully calling Wagner his "idol."[31] Perhaps only the name of Walt Whitman in Cram's catalogue of heroes in his autobiography would have been thought so much of a red flag, when, as many today hate rock music, so then many hated Wagner and for the same reasons. In what Nietzsche called Wagner's "narcotic art,"[32] sexuality is no subtext. It is central. Furthermore, note how the Wagner cult seems to Carl Schorske to have constituted then a sort of "theatrical psychotherapy," and how Jackson Lears can write of Cram's favorite opera: "*Parsifal*['s] . . . characters, . . . mired in psychological paralysis, are freed through exposure to Parsifal's pre-oedipal innocence and medieval ideas of heroism."[33]

It must all have been very heady for young Ralph. After all, it was not only T. S. Eliot (just a decade later) but everyone in Boston in this era who, when "evening quickens faintly in the street,"[34] had in hand or mind the *Boston Evening Transcript*, which is to say, in matters artistic in the mid-1880s, Ralph Adams Cram.

PARNASSUS AND THE BEAU MONDE

Never shy, Ralph was quick to find his way socially, discovering a home-away-from-home at 55 Mount Vernon Street, the Nichols residence, just above Louisburg Square. What first brought him there is not known, but Cram's elder daughter, Mary, remembered years later that this was "the first home to which RAC went familiarly and often in Boston as a very young man."[35] The more willingly, one assumes, for the elegance of this house, designed by Charles Bulfinch and superbly furnished (with such things as Chippendale chairs once owned by John Hancock, Venetian paintings, and Colonial portraits); for the refinement of the household, headed by Dr. and Mrs. Arthur Nichols (she was Augustus Saint-Gaudens's sister-in-law); and, not least, one imagines, for the charms of the three daughters of the house, Rose, Margaret, and Marion, whose company Ralph could hardly not have sought. Certainly, his papers of this period are filled with invitations to dinner parties and musical evenings at the Nichols home, while notes from Marion, thanking Ralph for lending her a play to read, or from Rose, grateful for his giving her Rossetti's *House of Life*, testify

BROOKLINE BOOKSMITH
Independent Store For Independent Minds
279 Harvard Street
Brookline, MA 02146
(617) 566-6660
www.brooklinebooksmith.com

74614 Reg 1 5:29 pm 02/23/98

```
S BOSTON BOHEMIA 18   1 @ 19.95    19.95
SUBTOTAL                           19.95
SALES TAX - 5%                      1.00
TOTAL                              20.95
VISA PAYMENT                       20.95
```

CHECK OUT OUR 10% DISCOUNTS!

HUNDREDS OF NEW HARDCOVERS 20% OFF!!

BARGAIN BOOKS AT UP TO 80% OFF!!!

BROOKLINE BOOKSMITH
Independent Store for Independent Minds
279 Harvard Street
Brookline, MA 02446
(617) 566-6660
www.brooklinebooksmith.com

Store Reg 1 61520 em 02/26/08 08

BOSTON ADMIRR IN 1 @ 18.95   18.95
SUBTOTAL   18.95
MIDDLE TAX 5%   .95
TOTAL
VISA PAYMENT   19.90

THANK YOU FOR YOUR PURCHASE!

HUNDREDS OF NEW HARDCOVERS 30% OFF!

BARGAIN BOOKS AT UP TO 80% OFF!

to a warmly familiar, almost daily relationship.[36] Rose Nichols, who would become America's first woman landscape architect, remained a lifelong friend and became in later years a valued colleague of Cram's.[37]

Rose Nichols was by no means Cram's only such friend. In his youth Cram showed a noticeable affinity for the company of women intellectuals. As we know from a portion (later cut) of an early typescript of his autobiography, though it was because of his *Transcript* writing that he made his debut in the great world, it was chiefly sustained in the 1880s through what he called in his manuscript "that notable circle of women who at the time preserved (and sometimes added to) the old and priceless quality of historical Boston."[38]

It is interesting that Cram should give pride of place to such a group as the most influential in his new life as a critic in Boston, and a Harvard professor he would later come to know has pretty well explained for us why it should not take us aback. Wrote George Santayana: "The American will inhabits the skyscraper; the American intellect inhabits the colonial mansion. The one is the sphere of the American man, the other, at least predominantly, of the American woman. The one is all aggressive enterprise; the other is all genteel tradition."[39] Ralph, to be sure, would exhibit a good deal of aggressive will in his life; but always in the service of heart and intellect — not the first time we shall observe Cram demonstrating a doubling in his personality of what we call, perhaps for lack of better terms, the masculine and the feminine.

First and foremost Cram mentions in his manuscript Annie Adams Fields (widow of James T. Fields, the celebrated publisher) and the writer Sarah Orne Jewett, of whom Boston historian and author Mark A. De Wolfe Howe wrote:

> The charms of the classical and continuing New England tradition were singularly united [in these two ladies]. . . . The hospitalities of 148 Charles Street [only two blocks from Pinckney led] . . . into stimulating and educative contacts with much that still survived from the authentic Boston which Mrs. Fields's dear friend and one-time neighbor, Dr. [Oliver Wendell] Holmes, had made known to the world over his Breakfast-Table.[40]

In being made welcome into this circle, Cram was also, in Sarah Sherman's words, exposed to a

> network of professional women whose lives centered not on their families and domestic duties but on their cultural, public contributions. . . . Some of the most important included Sarah Whitman, an artist who worked in stained glass and was a founder of Radcliffe College; Sally Norton, a cellist; Louise Imogen Guiney, a poet and essayist; Alice Brown, a short story writer; Celia Thaxter, a poet and story writer, and Louise Chandler Moulton, a poet.[41]

Here Cram was no stranger, either, for one of these figures was already known to him; Alice Brown hailed from Hampton Falls, Cram's birthplace, and

19

probably knew him from their childhood. Brown had, in her words, "picked up [her] petticoats and scudded off to Boston into the very odd precincts of the mind where books are written," arriving in town in 1880, a year ahead of Cram[42] (who briefly lodged with her in Boston). Her literary success was marked. Brown's work appeared in the *Atlantic*, *Harper's*, and *Scribner's*, while her skills as a writer were such that in his *Advance of the American Short Story* E. J. O'Brien judged Brown, with one exception, "the best living writer of New England short stories of her time."[43]

Cram would also have had much in common with Jewett, who grew up in a Maine family home not that far from his in New Hampshire. Moreover, she was known as a willing and skillful mentor, and that she advised Cram in his early Boston days is all the more likely because one of his problems has to have been one she herself had faced not many years previously: "when I was very young," she wrote to a friend, "and went from my quiet country home into busy city houses, I used to suffer very much from a sense of unrelatedness to my surroundings."[44]

That young Ralph stood in need of such advice is hardly in doubt. The dangers he faced were a commonplace of big-city life then, sketched darkly enough by William Dean Howells in his novel *A Modern Instance* of 1882. Published just a year after Cram's arrival in Boston, Howells's book depicts how a young man from rural New England could throw himself into Boston's cosmopolitan ways "so completely that he loses his moral bearings, becoming an unprincipled journalist, a drinker, and a philanderer."[45] Debauchery or retreat was always a likely option for young men like Ralph Adams Cram seeking to make their way in this period.

But Jewett would probably not have found even these dangers beyond her, for her circle was a very sophisticated one. How much so is clear in the remarks of Helen Howe (Mark A. De Wolfe Howe's daughter) in her *Gentle Americans*:

> There were, in my parents' circle of friends in Boston, several households consisting of two ladies. . . . Such an alliance I was brought up to hear called a "Boston marriage." Such a "marriage" existed between Mrs. Fields and Sarah Orne Jewett. Father wrote of it as a "union — there is no truer word for it." What Henry James, whose *The Bostonians* was published in 1888, found to "catch at" in the friendship between the Charles Street ladies we can only guess. . . . He writes of them both with such affection, nostalgia and downright chivalry that we are left confronting merely shadows.[46]

In fact, by 1881 Jewett had fallen very much in love with Fields. Though not an exclusive relationship, it was certainly for both the primary one, Annie Fields being, in Sherman's words, both Sarah Jewett's "lover and literary advisor."[47]

Fresh from a rural parsonage and only in his early twenties in the mid-1880s,

Cram, doubtless impressed by so cultured a milieu, must also have been rather taken aback. For all of Boston's much maligned provincialism, these women and their friends presided over a circle that was as advanced in its own stately way as that of Wilde and the new aesthetes of Cram's generation, and hardly any less challenging, either, of society in general in its pervasive feminism. Still, the Fields-Jewett circle was as highly respected and admired as any in the Puritan capital. Of course, it was doubtless for Ralph *too* stately. But here too, even at the city's heady heights of social and artistic intercourse, Boston did not disappoint. Enter Isabella Stewart Gardner.

Ralph Adams Cram came to know "Mrs. Jack," as everyone called that witty, stylish, irascible, and brilliant lady, also through his *Transcript* work. And the world of Isabella Gardner was only marginally stately: it verged, even in her married years, on being decidedly risqué in a way that must also have been a very new experience for Cram. For example, in the same year, 1888, that Henry James's *The Bostonians* came out, with its "shadows" of Fields and Jewett, Cram surely was among the art lovers who descended mightily upon the first solo exhibition anywhere of the work of John Singer Sargent, held at the St. Botolph Club that year. There he would have seen the celebrated portrait of Gardner,[48] notorious not only for the "revealingly tight, curvaceous black dress" in which Sargent depicted his friend and patron, but also for the witticism occasioned by the picture's rather daring décolletage that punned nicely on the name of the White Mountain resort that was the same as one of Gardner's reputed admirers, the novelist F. Marion Crawford; Sargent, it was said, had painted Gardner "all the way down to Crawford's Notch." (Her husband, for once provoked, withdrew the portrait, which was never again shown publicly in his lifetime.)[49]

Moving in the fashionable world, Cram, though not, perhaps, charming, had increasingly the reputation of being both earnest and brilliant, as well as precocious. With his sandy hair, firm chin, and boyish good looks, he was, one suspects, rather in demand, and more than one luminary of the beau monde seems to have taken him up: Maud Howe Elliott, for instance; a belle if ever there was one in Boston high society then, whose romance titillated and inspired all her friends, for it was a classic one, involving a ten-year courtship by a poor but talented artist — John Elliott — of a woman of great beauty.[50]

The result was not only a stellar marriage but a circle equally so. (Her husband did one of the first murals in McKim, Mead and White's new Boston Public Library, the other building, along with Trinity Church opposite it, that Cram most respected at this time.) And Maud Elliott was not only beautiful. Like Cram, she wrote for the *Transcript*. She was also an ardent suffragist; indeed, distinctly a modernist. Consider these entries from her diary of this era:

January 15th [1890]: Lecture from Professor Royce on Kant. . . . To a "Recollection of Tristan and Isolde," Mr. Preston giving the music on the piano, Ralph Adams Cram reading a description of the opera. . . .
January 17th: To dine . . . we met Dr. Holmes. . . .
January 18th: . . . To Mrs. Fairchild's. . . . John [Singer] Sargent was there. . . .
January 20th: With Mama to see . . . the "Merchant of Venice."
January 21: . . . To a Russian dinner given by Count Zuboff at the Tremont House. Very amusing. All sorts of queer fishes and queer dishes.[51]

What a catalogue! Could there be a better illustration of how diverse and au courant was just this one of the sets Cram moved in as a young man?

Boston, however, was still Boston. Just as lectures by philosophy professors kept company in Maud Elliott's diary along with Russian nobility (she was, after all, the daughter of Julia Ward Howe, for a biography of whom she would one day win a Pulitzer Prize), so, too, Isabella Stewart Gardner's mentor was the storied Harvard scholar Charles Eliot Norton (8). Wrote Van Wyck Brooks:

At Shady Hill [Norton's Cambridge home] still dwelt the tutelary sage or saint of [so many] Harvard prepossessions. . . . Twice I was taken . . . to Sunday "Dante evenings" in the golden brown study in which Henry James felt he had received his "first consecration to letters." . . . There in the presence of "Dante Meeting Beatrice," the picture that Rossetti had painted for Norton, half a dozen young men, interested, curious or devout, listened with copies of the *Paradise* open in their hands. . . . Norton read aloud, like a learned, elegant and venerable priest. . . . One felt there was something sacramental even in the sherry and the caraway cakes that a maidservant placed in our hands.[52]

It was, perhaps, through Isabella Gardner that Cram gained the entrée to Shady Hill, and, though still in his twenties, he was able to forge a close relationship with Harvard's first professor of fine arts, then in his eighties. Certainly that is documented by the unannounced calls and informal tête-à-têtes referred to in one of the few letters between them to have survived in Cram's papers:

My dear Sir,
I am very sorry to have missed the pleasure of seeing you yesterday when you were good enough to call on me.
Will you do me the favor to dine with me on Wednesday next, quite unceremoniously without other guests; — at seven o'clock? Should this be impossible, will you be so good as to come out on some Monday, Wednesday or Friday morning to see me, or on almost any evening you choose. In the afternoon I am apt to be out, for I use them for exercise or for rest.
I am,

Very truly Yours,
C. E. Norton[53]

Norton by the time Cram knew him was a legend. Famous for his lecture openings (for "The Idea of a Gentleman," Norton led off with: "None of you,

8. Charles Eliot Norton. This sketch by Edward Revere Little first appeared in *Harvard Celebrities* in 1901.

probably, has ever seen a gentleman"), he had a style that was much parodied. In fact, Norton himself is said to have enjoyed one parody in particular, in which he was made to open yet another lecture by saying: "I propose this afternoon to make a few remarks on the hor-ri-ble vul-gar-ity of EVERYTHING."[54] But Norton, whom John Ruskin called his "second friend . . . and first real tutor," also possessed, in Ferris Greenslet's words, a "magnetic sympathy with generous ideals, whether in life or in art" and an "urbanity, dignity and high seriousness" that did not interfere with an "exquisitely light social touch [and] wistful humor."[55] These are singular gifts that would surely have much appealed to young Cram. Furthermore, Norton's was a complex and rich persona, "constructed at once to communicate and to conceal"; he was as intriguing as he was charming.[56]

So, doubtless, in his way was Ralph Adams Cram, who was himself beginning to attract his own circle, which, though it would not take definite enough form to be noticed until the 1890s, when it will become a chief focus of this book, was coalescing already in the mid- and late 1880s. Its heart and center would ever be the neighborhood of Pinckney Street, that Bohemian quarter of Beacon Hill reaching out at its top into Joy Street and at its bottom spreading along Charles Street and leaking into lower Chestnut Street and its vicinity. Ah, Pinckney Street.

Queer Fishes and Queer Dishes

Maud Elliott's delicious phrase from her diary catches well the character then of Pinckney Street; "that *Rive Gauche*," as Cram called it, "of student life in Boston where all must, happily, sojourn for a time."[57]

It was interesting that Cram ventured a Parisian allusion; Pinckney is at first glance more comparable with the picturesque red-brick environs of London's Bohemian quarter, particularly Chelsea, where such as Whistler, Rossetti, Swinburne, and Wilde lived. But perhaps Cram was thinking of the fact that even before his time Pinckney Street already had a flavor of not only the literary and the artistic but also—and in much broader spheres—the radical.[58]

A leading Transcendentalist and abolitionist, James Freeman Clarke, lived at 58 Pinckney; a few doors away, 62 was a station on the underground railroad; while 66 Pinckney, in A. McVoy McIntyre's words, "offered hospitality to the disillusioned of the Brook Farm commune when that notable pre-Marxian experiment collapsed."[59] At 86 Pinckney in Cram's time lived J. L. Smith, the first black citizen of Boston to serve on the city's Common Council. Indeed, the area attracted many African Americans. On nearby Charles Street lived the widow of Judge Ruffin, the first black in Massachusetts to achieve this rank, whose salon drew W. E. B. Du Bois in 1888–1892, when he was at Harvard, where he would be the first African American to earn a Ph.D. (At Harvard Du Bois was a favored student of Cram's friend of those days, Barrett Wendell, who was the first to teach English composition as an independent subject, critically considered.)[60]

Pinckney Street's more literary associations were equally wide-ranging. Early and mid-nineteenth-century habitués included both Nathaniel Hawthorne and his admirer Herman Melville, who dedicated *Moby-Dick* to Hawthorne. Henry Thoreau lived for a time at 4 Pinckney; Louisa May Alcott's father, Bronson Alcott, an "apostle of progressive education" in his time, had rooms at 20 Pinckney, while across the street, 15 was the site of the pioneering American kindergarten of Henry James's *The Bostonians*, started, in fact, by that ardent feminist Elizabeth Peabody. Nearby, at 3 Joy Street, the progressive journal *Poet*

Lore, founded in 1889 by two other feminists, Helen Clarke and Charlotte Potter, was headquartered for many years; poets Bliss Carman and Richard Hovey, even Walt Whitman, and, years later, Cram himself, all appeared in its pages. And at the bottom of Pinckney, at the corner of Charles Street, Richard Badger's Gorham Press, an early twentieth-century avant-garde publisher (of Cram as well), was to be found.

Since Cram's day the literary and radical tradition has persisted. One thinks of Lucius Beebe's characterization in *Boston and the Boston Legend* of the "mode of life in Joy and Pinckney Streets" in the 1920s and 1930s as "sudden, raucous and boozy," centering on the Barn Theatre on Joy Street. A repertory group, it was surrounded by an artistic and literary colony, led by Elliot Paul, the novelist (later associated in Paris with Gertrude Stein and the poet-publisher Harry Crosby), and included Boston's post-World War II homophile activist Prescott Townsend and Catherine Huntington, the cofounder with Eugene O'Neill of the Provincetown Playhouse, who lived for years at 66 Pinckney. In our own time Anne Sexton, the poet, also spent no little time on this street in the late 1950s with her lover, George Starbuck, in what another poet and Beacon Hill neighbor, Sylvia Plath, called Starbuck's "monastic and miserly room on Pinckney."[61] Of all this Peter Davison has lately written most sagely in *The Fading Smile*.

In Cram's era, Pinckney was decidedly in its artistic and literary heyday, rejoicing in all kinds. For example, Thomas Bailey Aldrich of 84 Pinckney was notable for ensuring that Oscar Wilde's associations with Boston would not be entirely pleasant. Outraged by the aesthete Englishman, Aldrich, who was regularly visited by the great and famous (both Charles Dickens and Mark Twain were seen at 84 Pinckney), let it be known while Wilde was in town that he was not at home to *anyone*.[62] (In 1896 the Bohemians of Pinckney Street took their revenge: that year Stone and Kimball — a press, as we will see, that originated in the Pinckney Street milieu — published an impertinent, unsigned rhyme about Aldrich, who for many more reasons than his treatment of Wilde they did not favor. It ran in part: "What though, like a ladies' waist, / All his lines are overlaced? / What though, from a shallow brain, / Smooth inanities he strain? / In his emptiness content, / He achieves his ten percent. . . .")[63]

On the other hand, there was the publisher James Osgood, who bought 71 Pinckney from the profits of Dickens's American tour and added considerable luster to the street's avant-garde reputation by being an early and avid supporter of that other figure of the day even more controversial than Wilde, Walt Whitman, whose *Leaves of Grass* Osgood published in 1881 (Cram's first year in the New England capital), despite the shocking, homoerotic quality of that work. As well as Pinckney's associations with Hawthorne and Melville, the Aldrich-

Wilde fracas and the fact that Whitman's publisher lived on Pinckney point up the fact that this steep and romantic street's Bohemian tradition has also had the effect of endowing its history with somewhat of a gay subtext as well.

Indeed, 5, the first house erected on the street, ca. 1786, according to records, was built by two unrelated men, a "pair [of] presumably bachelor friends," variously described as a hairdresser and a horse breaker or, hardly less vividly, "a mulatto barber and a black coachman"![64] Moreover, one is also conscious of this subtext at the corner of Pinckney and Joy streets, the very heart of Bohemia, whose laureate in later years was T. S. Eliot. Having in mind the view of scholars like Robert Martin, who sees in "The Love Song of J. Alfred Prufrock" an expression of "the destruction of homosexual love,"[65] one may glimpse from that corner the Eliotean windows of Joy Street and Mount Vernon Place, behind which tradition has it women came and went talking — appropriately enough — of Michelangelo.

Closer to our own time, one thinks of the brilliant Harvard scholar who in the 1930s virtually created the full-fledged academic field of American literature (and was also Sarah Orne Jewett's first biographer), F. O. Matthiessen; he lived at 87 Pinckney with his lifelong friend and partner, the painter Russell Cheney.[66] At 51 Pinckney lived Lucien Price, the distinguished literary figure, friend of Samuel Eliot Morison, and author of *The Dialogues of Alfred North Whitehead*, who was for years the chief editorial writer of the *Boston Globe*. Here, too, at 6, lived for a time the gay novelist and essayist John Cheever.[67]

Even Pinckney's architecture has always been characteristically hidden and queer; George Weston has pointed out that of Beacon Hill's "many dark and mysterious tunnels" (the result of overbuilding) quite the "most interesting [are] to be found on Pinckney Street."[68] In fact, the lodging house in the 1890s that Cram resided in longest on Pinckney, 67, is located exactly across the street from the "hidden house of Beacon Hill," as 74½ Pinckney is often called because the house is completely hidden by later buildings and can be reached only by a long tunnel from the street that leads to a brick courtyard guarded by an iron gate, a fact it would be straining credibility to suggest was *not* Cram's source for a house created by him that we will remark on in Chapter 4. (Also close by Cram's lodging house, furthermore, was 40 Pinckney, the mysterious abode during Cram's day of Leonora Piper, a medium known not only to Cram — who attended her seances — but also to William James and Arthur Conan Doyle, both of whom aided and abetted Piper's international reputation.)

Cram's own circle, forming in the 1880s in these precincts in and around Pinckney, already endowed with so much history, was made up for the most part of Pinckney's younger element, the still struggling but thought to be promising writers, musicians, poets, sculptors, journalists, and artists of all kinds who often, as a matter of fact, chose Cram's rooms to forgather in and with whom he enjoyed relationships both ebullient and intense; in no small measure, he always insisted, because of the gregarious personality of his longtime roommate (whom he had known since childhood), Guy Prescott, a music student, who was, as Cram lovingly characterized him, "my first and lasting boy friend."[69] With Prescott Cram settled, after a year at 19 West Cedar, into 99 Pinckney in 1889, moving in 1892 to 17 Pinckney, near the top of the hill, and then in 1895 to 67, closer to Louisburg Square, where he remained until removing in 1900 to 112 Pinckney, the more elegant Brimmer Chambers, at the bottom of the hill.[70]

Probably it was Prescott who introduced Cram to a fellow musician, the composer Frederic Field Bullard, who was characteristic of the type of artist to be found in Cram's emerging circle, and to whom Cram forthwith became not only friend but librettist, particularly adept at the art songs that, along with church anthems, were the chief claim to fame of young Bullard. (In his *History of American Music*, Louis Elson went so far as to assert after Bullard's early death that "it is not too much to say that he was the most promising of American composers. Here, if at all, was an American Bizet.")[71]

This growing Bohemian circle of the mid-1880s brings to the fore the whole question of Boston's authorized version of the concept of Bohemia, of which in *One Boy's Boston* Samuel Eliot Morison revealed a little, telling of two "musical bachelors," Henry Goodrich and Francis H. B. Byrne, who lived, close to the Morisons on the corner of Mount Vernon and Brimmer,

> at 5 Otis Place [just a little more than a block from Pinckney], and William F. Apthorp, an eminent music critic [of the *Transcript*, and a friend of Cram's] and his beautiful wife Octavie, at No. 14.... They had late supper parties for most of the visiting divas, actors and actresses, and always included my parents, imparting a touch of Bohemia to their social life. I remember standing on the Otis Place sidewalk late one night to see the fascinating Sarah Bernhardt alight from a cab to attend an Apthorp party given in her honor.[72]

A more contemporary and less anecdotal characterization of Boston's Bohemia on and around Pinckney Street by Anna Farquhar, a contemporary novelist, is quoted in Frances Weston Carruth's *Fictional Rambles in and about Boston* (1902):

> "The majority of the old homes in Pinckney Street are converted into lodging-houses. ... There are to be found ... musicians; newspaper people; painters; incipient authors and a few full-fledged; impecunious youths with high spirits and one 'dress suit' among several; ... Here is the freedom of the Latin Quarter, with but a small amount of its license. ... In truth, this Boston Bohemia stands for good spirits and innocent

27

unconventionality, and is several times more virtuous than Boston society, no matter how pretentiously and flamboyantly the little country tries to disprove its virtue."

[Carruth comments:] This is the atmosphere of . . . *Margaret Warrener*, [by] . . . Miss Alice Brown. . . . And in Pinckney Street, we are sure, was the cosy third floor sitting-room of that splendid woman and sculptor, Helen Grayson ([of] Arlo Bates's *The Pagans*).[73]

Both Brown and Bates, like many of these fin-de-siècle Boston Bohemians such as Bullard, are footnotes a hundred years later and not, like Cram, chapter headings, but the work of a number of Cram's circle has survived well enough to figure, for example, in Jackson Lears's study of turn-of-the-century American culture, *No Place of Grace*.

Among those of Cram's Pinckney Street neighbors who at one time or another in the 1880s and 1890s became his intimates were not only Brown (at 11 Pinckney) and Bullard (at 22), but also the poet Louise Imogen Guiney, who lived at 16 and later at 42, and who in Cram's orbit was closest to her fellow poets Richard Hovey and Bliss Carman, the painter Thomas Meteyard, and an undergraduate named Bernard Berenson; the architect Henry Vaughan, who lived at 80 Pinckney; E. W. Clement, Cram's *Transcript* editor, at 85; the designer Daniel Berkeley Updike, who lived (in rooms designed by Ogden Codman, no less), at Pinckney Street's best address, the Brimmer Chambers; and the publisher-photographer Fred Holland Day, whose Boston studio and pied-à-terre was at 9 Pinckney, next to Brown's, and who may have brought the designer Bruce Rogers and the sculptor William Partridge into Cram's circle, as well as editors Herbert Copeland and Herbert Small and the poet Philip Savage, Harvard classmates all and frequent lodgers at Day's.

Interestingly, the name Updike would later give to his famous press, Merrymount ("an allusion to [the] hedonist and licentious establishment near Boston, attacked and destroyed by seventeenth-century puritans"),[74] was also the name Alice Brown gave to Pinckney Street itself in her novel *Margaret Warrener*. As she saw it,

Merrymount Street drops down to the river, across which the twilight flushes and deepens. . . . Traveled persons who come upon the street for the first time are apt to note its likeness to a foreign one. . . . The mellow red houses on either side project irregularly. [To one side the street opens into] elm-shaded . . . grassy . . . Quincy [i.e., Louisburg] Square. . . . The sisterhood [in real life the Anglican nuns of St. Margaret] occupies a great house . . . the bell from their hidden chapel in the garden measures rapid hours. . . . [To the other side] Benedict Square [i.e., Anderson Street] stretches into a tawdry quarter of old clothes shops and crazy tenements. [On Merrymount Street itself] the queer old houses were painfully converted into flats . . . prices remaining mercifully low. . . . Painters, musicians, writers drifted into the street because there they could get queer corners cheaply.[75]

La vie Bohème! The flavor is even better caught in a poem found in Cram's papers that (at a time when even Bohemians, as quickly as they could afford it, were deserting the declining South End for the friendlier precincts of Beacon Hill) gives a good account of the wit of these free spirits. The verses are written on a card to which is affixed a yellowed advertisement clipped from a newspaper:

WANTED — Sunny, airy, quiet, comfortable, unfurnished, inexpensive, independent room by non-smoking, tidy, middle-aged, unmarried poet. No. 126 West Concord St. Answering kindly mention price, with some other particulars.

The poem itself is signed [?].A.C., and one is entitled to conclude that the hard to read first initial is R.

> Oh, non-smoking, tidy poet, middle-aged and unmarried,
> Seeking something inexpensive, and an independent room!
> Something sunny, airy, quiet, comfortable and unfurnished,
> With the price most kindly mentioned, would that I could glad your gloom.
> Is West Concord Street untuneful? Is 126 prosaic?
> Does the road that's elevated jar your tidy little soul?
> Tell me in non-smoking verses in a middle-aged sonnet,
> In some inexpensive quatrain — why you seek another goal.

An even more lively souvenir is Cram's surviving correspondence with one Hendrie, his tailor — who clearly did not always give satisfaction. Ralph was having none of it:

I shall take the suit to Plante tomorrow, and if he can make the corrections in time (which I doubt) . . . I will accept the suit and charge the cost of the correction to you. But if the work cannot be done in time I will not accept the suit and shall return it to you. As it is I am of a mind to return it now. The coat collar is too low, the sleeves are too tight and too short. The trousers measure 21 inches around the knees, the style I believe of 1886.[76]

That Cram in his Pinckney Street days was distinctly a dandy, by the way, is hardly in doubt. Family reminiscences record that one weekend he was foolish enough to wear his prized peacock-blue suit and purple tie home; his mother *almost* forbade him the house.[77] He also sported pince-nez and owned a scarlet-lined evening cloak. And his dandyism is not unimportant. Long before Cram's era, Charles Baudelaire had attached great significance to "Le Dandy" (the title of his influential essay of 1863), and as the studies of Ellen Moers have shown, "the art of the pose . . . the mask . . . called upon to confound the bourgeois" had by the 1890s become a chief theme of aestheticism.[78] So much so that Karl Beckson concludes that "the image of the dandy, particularly as depicted in Wilde's social comedies . . . embodied the Decadent sensibility in its most subversive form."[79]

Leaves from a Diary

As he made his wary, brilliant way through fin-de-siècle Boston, Ralph Adams Cram seems often to have turned to his small pocket diary, and to explore it is probably as close as we can get now to his most intimate thoughts of those days.[80]

That he was, for all his passion for music and painting, an architect born and bred, is nowhere more evident than in this diary of the early and mid-eighties. For among the many certitudes one can excuse Cram for in his early twenties (he doubtless would have agreed with Wilde that only the mediocre develop!) is an observation that was to be the foundation of every church he designed; architects working in Gothic, he scribbled, too often

> not only copy the deficiencies as well as the beauties [of Gothic], but they make modern necessities conform to Gothic forms. It does not seem as though such servile copying is true art. . . . It is merely "chinese copying" [a means of reproducing drawings mechanically].

Above all, this diary documents how keen Cram was to get to Europe. And his stubborn, earnest, idealistic, hero-worshipping quest of truth and beauty and romance is, in fact, given most telling point by the lovingly worked out tour itineraries that take up so much of this diary, together with such exotic and marvelous things as a list Cram compiled on one page of the rulers of Byzantium, evidence of what Europe meant to a young American of Cram's sort in those days. As Allan Bloom has pointed out, a youth

> whose sexual longings consciously or unconsciously inform his studies has a very different set of experiences from one in whom such motives are not active. A trip to Florence or to Athens is one thing for a young man who hopes to meet his Beatrice on the Ponte Santa Trinita or his Socrates in the Agora, and quite another for one who goes without such aching need. The latter is only a tourist, the former is looking for completion.[81]

In this vein there are also long lists of books in Cram's diary, including textbooks in virtually all the standard academic fields, his reading lists for Europe, so to speak. Just as the lists disclose his wide-ranging interests, so do his sketches (in both his diary and his sketchbooks) show his impatience and restlessness. Cram's sketches suggest also that he was drawn invariably to the forceful, to the picturesque to be sure, but as achieved more by mass than by detail, as in the very carefully composed Shingle Style geometrics of the country house reproduced here (9). Still, the overwhelming feeling is that he frequently lost a good idea as his sketching ability failed to keep up with his more agile mind. It would be some time, and hardly ever on paper, before Cram's episodic fantasies evolved into sustained imagination.

Frurcklyn Cottage Elberon.

9. A page from one of Cram's sketchbooks, ca. 1885, kept while he was still an apprentice at Rotch and Tilden. Although his detail is very Queen Anne in feeling, the elevation study at the top of the page, "Frurcklyn Cottage," is decidedly more Shingle Style, foretelling Cram's first realized design of 1889, the Ide House (see 27).

More important than book lists or sketches are some glimpses of Cram's inner life that suggest that he was, indeed, "looking for completion." In his diary, in fact, self-regard is evolving into self-knowledge. Devastatingly honest, his self-analysis suggests that in his early twenties he was angry, arrogant, fanatical, moody, reclusive, and ascetic—or, alternatively, idealistic, disciplined, tough, frank, worldly, studious, tenacious, passionate, loyal, and dedicated. Dividing his paragraphs (and his life) into three periods, encompassing the years 1881–1886, between the ages of seventeen and twenty-three, Cram wrote as follows (the bracketed dashes indicate illegible material):

First Period
I am scornful, [—, —] given to swift, sudden anger, desperately advocating the principles of justice, truth, honor. I give up all bodily pleasure and indulge only in mental happiness. The discovery of the abuses of religion lead me to curse the whole system. Read Carlyle, Ruskin. I am full of despair at the hangers-on because I can do nothing to stop the rush of evil. I am moody, gloomy. I am always by myself, brooding over the evil of the world. I worship Art as the highest development of man, especially Pre-Raphaelitism [—]. I read much. Quite a wild letter to [—].

Second Period
Under the influence of [—] and my father I gradually commence to modify [—] I read Spencer, Darwin, Emerson. I take to Science and literature. I become studious [—] philosophical [—] I control my temper and advocate peace.

Third Period
I [—] beyond science. I grow interested in Buddhism. . . . I adopt many of the teachings of Buddhism and preach it to all I know. I become intensely religious and calm.

Increasingly the fashion among the Boston intelligentsia in this era, Buddhism will be alluded to again here. In this period, however, it yielded to Spiritualism, which, in Cram's case, took the form he called to mind years later of "Oriental occultism of the Madame Blavatsky type."[82]

Cram's youthful religious experience is easier caught hold of in all this than those sexual longings to the significance of which Bloom has alerted us; though there is a passage in the diary, evidently some sort of story-line, that may reflect these yearnings. A and B are letters he often uses to denote two persons, A usually implying himself:

A had no leisure for sleep that night, the mighty question that lay before him like the Sphynx [sic] offered no rest. . . . To reveal the truth of life to . . . B or to let him live on, in his pleasure, and discover what was possible to him of the falsity of things. The struggle was between the heart and the head. The question as to whether his friend would believe him or not [called for] little consideration, he had known B so long that no fear of his incomprehension came to his mind. The boy was but waiting to be awakened, he had shown unmistakable signs of great intellect, intensely quick understanding of a moral delicacy that . . . everything. Why then should he not be disenchanted? Few men would have hesitated, but to A came a sudden fear, the first that had ever entered his mind, that he could give him nothing in return.

Another source for these years is Cram's autobiography. Though it was written nearly fifty years later and heavily edited by him, Cram often signaled in it more perhaps than he knew, particularly in one rather revealing passage about his state of mind when he wrote his diary, by then doubtless long forgotten:

> I suppose that to everyone there comes a moment when a certain definite thing . . . acts as the precipitant on a fluid and amorphous personality, bringing some sort of order out of the chaos and dark night of immaturity, and in a way lifting self-consciousness out of the unconscious. With me, I know, it was music, — particularly that of Richard Wagner.[83]

The "chaos and dark night of immaturity," echoing Milton, whether consciously or not (just as "the unconscious" echoes Freud), is a vivid image, and probably a well-remembered one, of a young man in his late teens and early twenties, expected to negotiate successfully the difficult passage from late adolescence to young adulthood — on Pinckney Street.

OUT OF TIME

What friends Cram may have made at Rotch and Tilden he seems quickly to have shed, though he did once in later years refer to the effect on him of the "astoundingly amoral, yet very revealing and constructive influence and companionship of their head draughtsman," all trace of whom (one Bill Gilbert) has otherwise vanished from history.[84] Instead, his friends more and more after he took up his work at the *Transcript* were men like Fred Bullard, musicians, sculptors, and writers from the more general artistic world. Two particularly were to become close to Cram in the 1880s: William Ordway Partridge, a Bostonian who after graduating from Columbia College studied sculpture in both Rome and Paris (his work, though not well known today, is in the Metropolitan Museum);[85] and Bernard Berenson (*10*), the now much better known figure, then a Harvard undergraduate who lived in the seedier area adjoining the hill's north slope, for his Jewish immigrant family was quite poorly off.

Berenson always insisted that Boston and Harvard remained the *forma mentis* of his lifelong character.[86] Cram, too, in his old age recalled the importance to him of exchanging visits with his friend — often strolling over the hill to Berenson's rooms, where in his "diminutive library . . . I could forgather with him and discuss Art. . . . Of course we quarrelled delightedly" (over, among other things, Cram remembered, "which of us should succeed Charles Eliot Norton as Professor of Fine Arts at Harvard!").[87]

What would one not give to have been privy to those late-night talks! Yet so sympathetic were Cram and Berenson that, even after Berenson took up residence abroad, his and Cram's dialogue continued in written form — a medium we can therefore eavesdrop on these many years later. Herewith, from the papers of each (in the archives of Villa I Tatti and the Boston Public Library)[88] — the dates given only in the source notes — a Cram-Berenson sampler:

26 November: My very dear B.B. — I "shoot my arrow into the air," though if "it falls to earth, I know not where," I hope you may be there to pick it up. . . .
As ever, R. A. Cram[89]

10 January: My very dear B.B. — . . . Colour here is infinite in its variety and always exquisite. We do gain from it something of that "ecstasy" which you say is what is worth living for. . . . As for books I gain much satisfaction from "Baldy" Smith's ad-

10. Bernard Berenson, ca. 1885: "I still feel," he wrote more than half a century later in *Sunset and Twilight*, "that America is my only country, and Boston my only home [recalling his Beacon Hill 1880s youth, with] ample time for thought and conversation, delight in each other's personalities, and aspiration, in quiet awareness."

mirable book on Egyptian architecture, a new and very comprehensive study of Byzantium, another on Leonardo da Vinci. . . . If you have any treasure trove in the way of books let me know.

Always yours, RAC[90]

12 May: Dear B.B. . . . The fact that you say some of what you are doing would horrify me and another page would delight me is just the sort of thing I covet. . . . I need stimulus. . . and horrid things and delightful things in combination would do their work. . . . This [is] a fascinating place, both physically and socially. . . . You are quite right also in thinking that these blacks are, many of them, real aristocrats . . . so far as the women are concerned, strikingly beautiful; the men also . . .

Always and devotedly yours, RAC[91]

29 January: Dear B.B. . . . You may recall that I told you . . . that our particular era, which began about 1500 was bound to break down in ruins before the year 2000. Well, I was a true prophet, but I don't much like role of Cassandra. . . . You remember John B — said (per William Morris) . . . [that what was all important was] "the change beyond the change." My eyes are fixed on the "change beyond." . . . I'd give much to see you now, dear B.B., for I have for you a lasting affection. . . .

Faithfully yours, Ralph[92]

24 June: Dear Ralph, Yours of May 12 reached me a day or two ago and warmed my heart. I am happy to discover how completely we have reached the same conclusions although our paths have been at times so far apart. . . . I wish I could read Ortega y Gasset's "Toward a Philosophy of History." The only sure way of getting a book over is to send it as first class mail. Can I ask you to go to that expense. . . . I have always subscribed to Speculum. . . .

Write often. I shall answer. It is a real happiness to know that after at least 56 years of acquaintance we can both understand each other better than ever.

Yrs. affectionately, B.B.[93]

We have, indeed, jumped ahead here over half a century. But so constant were their mutual interests that we have surely heard more than one echo here of those late-night Boston talks of the 1880s.

Berenson's influence waned in a more immediate sense, of course, however enduring their affections and interests, when he decided to seek his future abroad. Cram's closest friends were instead found among those who remained in Boston. Among these, as he opined more than once, it was Louise Imogen Guiney (11) who exercised in the late 1880s and early 1890s "the most vital and creative personal influence" over him.[94]

POET OF LOST CAUSES

Guiney's and Cram's friendship began in 1887 with a characteristically charming letter, addressed to his *Transcript* pen name:

35

11. Louise Imogen Guiney. "She was that rarest combination: pure of heart, brilliant in mind," Henry Fairbanks has written, and added of "the lost lady of American letters" that " 'women's lib' owes her much, ecumenism even more," and that he had almost called her biography that of "the first modern nun."

Dear C. A. Ralph,
I have asked Mr. Hurd of the *Transcript* to forward you this note.... I want to say, first, what I once, indeed, asked Mr. Berenson to say to you for me, how sorry I was ... to miss seeing you on that showery Saturday ... for I have of old, a most hearty liking for that pen-name of yours and an earnest delight in everything written above it. I, too, am a good Bostonian, and on general principles love you for all you are! Now, can you not try my latch once more? ... I have a great deal to say to you.[95]

A published poet — in *Harper's*, the *Atlantic*, and *Scribner's* as well as in book form by Houghton Mifflin — Guiney was a devout Roman Catholic, though of liberal cast, not the easiest role in Boston in that period (she once admitted, for example, that while Sunday High Mass at the Church of the Advent, with all its pomp and music, was where she "should heartily enjoy being" from time to time, she couldn't "afford to scandalize the public" by being seen there).[96]

On the other hand, Guiney in more subtle ways was indeed a bridge builder:

36

"Bostonians resented the Irish," wrote Van Wyck Brooks, but "the case already had its compensations — the conquerors were bearing gifts for the joy of the conquered. . . . [One] was the lovely spirit of Louise Imogen Guiney."[97] Guiney's bridges spanned more than ethnic polarities. Wrote Stephen Parrish: "Irish by temperament and an ardent Catholic, Miss Guiney . . . [also] linked the genteel tradition [the death of which Brooks traces in *New England: Indian Summer*] to the rising aesthetic tradition of the 1890s."[98] Today she is considered a minor poet, though an important link between Emily Dickinson and Edna St. Vincent Millay, no small place to hold in literary history; even Van Wyck Brooks admitted that Guiney's poems had "a fragile beauty" and that "the prose of her later essays was precise and distinguished."[99]

It was not only her literary gifts, however, but also her character and personality that attracted Cram and so many other people to Guiney. Contrasts abounded, some of which explained why she was so good a bridge builder. For instance, her background. Her father had come to America from Ireland with very little means. Yet he worked his way up through college and the law, serving heroically in the Civil War, rising to brigadier general, and became the first well-known Irish Catholic to enter state politics as a Republican. And though his early death, when she was only sixteen, left Louise increasingly poor (she was forced to abandon her schooling after her father's death and eke out a living doing hack work or library jobs), she was a consistently cheerful person who did not burden others with her problems but bore them gallantly. Another contrast was that despite being an ardent Roman Catholic, she had so open and questing a mind as to be, for example, an advocate of women's rights. Nothing if not sophisticated, she was also an admirer of Aubrey Beardsley.[100]

A tall and lithe young woman given to such outdoor pursuits as hiking, she was as well an ornament in any drawing room; for all her formidable intellect she was pretty, with beautiful dark gray eyes. So much so that Alice Brown wrote of "her girl's grace, her mystic smile."[101] Guiney was warm and affectionate, even flirtatious, and altogether a buoyant free spirit with an irrepressible sense of humor that constantly delighted Brown.

Neither ever married and they were such close, lifelong friends that it is hard to believe they did not enjoy a lesbian relationship. Through the years everyone has bent over backward to avoid the word: Estelle Jussim refers to Guiney's "physically unthreatening young men"; Jackson Lears to her "physically masculine identity."[102] And so on. What is meant seems clear (see *15*).

Guiney's work, furthermore, dovetailed with all this: her heroes, it was said, always were "idealistic, pugnacious and died young." Guiney, wrote her biographer, did not have a "death wish," but a passion like Antigone's to risk her fortunes so long as any dead brother lay dishonored in the dust. . . . So she became the laureate of the lost. . . . Her best lyrics rank among the finest spiritual expressions in American literature.[103]

The kind of intense friendship she inspired is perhaps best caught by recounting the strange tale of the days when financial necessity forced her to accept the position of postmistress of suburban Auburndale. Here she fell victim to what appears to have been an anti-Catholic plot of sorts from which Cram and his friends had to rescue her. Cram recollected that:

> The revenue of the Postmistress was gauged by the business done . . . through the sale of stamps and so forth. . . . Suddenly the business began to decline rather alarmingly. Certain Sherlock Holmes procedures . . . revealed just what was happening: Auburndale was at that time a favourite retreat of retired Protestant missionaries; the Postmistress was a Catholic. The situation was intolerable to the evangelical mind; therefore the Papist incumbent must be driven out by the simple expedient of transferring the trade to other neighbouring post offices — which was done.
>
> Concerted action on the part of Lou Guiney's friends produced notable results. We all bought postage stamps . . . in such quantities that the Auburndale post office advanced in the matter of business done, and with such leaps and bounds that finally an emissary from the Post Office Department was sent out to ascertain what it all meant.[104]

Guiney, in fact, perceived immediately Cram's true character: "After thinking over some thirty-two available friends of mine," she wrote in connection with this fracas, ". . . I pick you out, for various reasons, as my knight. . . . Please forgive me for calling you up, good Lohengrin."[105] As to why she chose Cram she was more explicit, in another connection, in a letter to the wife of Herbert Clarke, the British critic. Noting that Cram was en route for a visit, she warned Clarke to beware because Cram and he

> will fight at sight, and "fierce fragments of no more a man" will bestrew [the Clarke residence]. R.A.C. . . . is extremely clever as an architect, a writer, and a mad agitator for "dead issues." But I am distinctly NOT introducing him to Herbert as I did Bliss Carman; for there would be blood on the moon in eight minutes after their conjugation. I have a "lunatic angel," as someone called Shelley.[106]

Guiney did, however, as we have seen, introduce Cram to several of her more Bohemian companions, including those three "vagabonds" Richard Hovey, Bliss Carman, and Tom Meteyard, so called because of their having collaborated on the then celebrated series of Vagabondia books.

Hovey, a Dartmouth graduate and convert to Anglicanism who had once studied for the priesthood, first surfaced in Boston in 1887, writing poetry then thought so stirring that Alan MacDonald has called Hovey "one of America's very greatest occasional poets."[107] (Hovey was, in fact, an early influence on

Robert Frost.) Very good-looking (in London, Hovey's wife recalled that at a party Oscar Wilde "raced after Richard all evening"),[108] the most raffish of aesthetes, Hovey sported a dark Whitmanesque beard. Witness *Town Topics*, for example, in 1896, which noticed him while reporting on the passing parade up Boston's fashionable Tremont Street:

> Mr. Richard Hovey . . . formerly looked like Dante, but now prefers to look like M. Alphonse Daudet. Wears a robe of blue and green serge, buttoned with miniatures of Mr. Maurice Maeterlinck — please pronounce Mah-ter-lingk. Wears a Spanish hat and feather; also rubbers for the purpose of stemming the tides of song without getting his feet wet. Is preceded by a gigantic Nubian slave in green livery, who continually observes, "My God! My God! My God!"[109]

Hovey, who was involved for many years with an older woman with whom he had a child before their marriage in 1894, was also a lifelong and intimate friend of Bliss Carman, who for the most part roomed with Tom Meteyard just across the Common from Beacon Hill in a bachelor flat at the Hotel Thorndike on Boylston Street. Carman, a Canadian, came to Harvard for postgraduate study in 1886 at the age of twenty-five, where he soon felt particularly the influence of Santayana. Another poet, Carman was often published in the *Atlantic Monthly*, for which he served as an editor for several years. A special favorite of Guiney's, he was also particularly close to Cram (he signed at least one letter to Ralph in this period "love, Bliss" and often tried to place Cram's literary work).[110] Tall, blond, handsome, and rather flamboyant, Carman was the chief link between the Harvard and Boston Bohemian "gangs," as Cram called them.[111] Meteyard, his roommate, the descendant of a distinguished New England family, was a designer and painter who had studied with Monet at Giverny and exhibited at the Paris Salon. He is best known today for his book design.[112]

Guiney having been, the reader will recall, a part of the Fields-Jewett circle, Cram may originally have been steered toward her by Alice Brown. Toward Fred Holland Day he was directed by Guiney herself. And while Guiney came to love Cram deeply if unromantically,[113] she appears to have harbored both kinds of love for Day, despite her relationship with Alice Brown. Whether that was true, it was all very complex, for Day's life, better perhaps than any of the Pinckney Street circle, illustrates very well Peter Gay's observation that in terms of sexuality the late Victorian era of Cram's youth was an "increasingly opaque, anxiety-provoking" period of problematic loves.[114]

STOLEN DREAMS

It is hardly possible to imagine a greater contrast than that between Louise Imogen Guiney and Fred Holland Day, Boston publisher, photographer, and collector (12). And the fact that after Guiney introduced Day to Cram she and Day emerge as Cram's closest comrades in the leadership of the Pinckney Street group is only slightly less startling than that Day and Guiney evidently came close to marrying each other in the first place.[115] Information is scant, for Alice Brown burned Day's letters to Guiney as indiscreet,[116] but the consequent darkness delineates all the better the sexual ambiguities of Pinckney Street in Cram's youth.

"She loved dogs, the outdoors, a fresh wind, and the smell of heather," wrote Parrish; "he thrived on stale air and incense."[117] (Cram, God bless him, loved it all!) Yet it is probably wrong to stress too much Guiney's and Day's divergences. As Day's biographer has pointed out: "She may have been playing at love with Fred as much as he was acting out his needs with her."[118] But what else is one's best friend for? Which is what Fred and Louise soon became. They traveled together, talked endlessly, honed and polished each other; she introduced him into Boston society, read manuscripts for him, procured him photographic models, and even posed for him; he published her books, often paid her bills, sought her advice, and was her eternal escort. They loved each other. They could not satisfy each other's sexual needs; others may have, but these were not, perhaps, the paramount needs for either. They did not marry. Instead, they cultivated what is sometimes called a "romantic friendship," by no means an unhappy resolution of affairs for two complicated people, whom circumstances had denied perhaps one prize, but who were not, despite that, willing to give up their feelings of love and loyalty for each other; or, indeed, the emotional support and intellectual stimulation each was uniquely able to give the other. Opportunists, really; they bore each other's burdens, alternately inciting and comforting as needed, in a wonderful exchange (knowing, as Charles Williams put it, one can never bear one's own burdens, only someone else's), and while they persevered in this relationship, their years were extraordinarily productive.

What is probable in Guiney's case is scarcely arguable in Day's.[119] And his homosexuality is evidenced above all in his photography, which also indicates his interests may have included the age-old sexual rituals of trust, sometimes called the exchange of imaginations, that it would be crude in this case to call sadomasochistic.

Day both looked and lived the part that he played. Slight, good-looking, graceful, with piercing blue eyes, he indulged in both a Van Dyke beard and pince-nez. In evening clothes, he typically preferred to the conventional white waistcoat a richly embroidered one; always poised in hand was one of his favorite black Russian cigarettes, fitted into his long holder. He also liked opium, though his drugs of choice, like Proust's, may have been veronal and trional. Wrote Estelle Jussim, his biographer:

40

12. Fred Holland Day, from a photograph by Alvin Langdon Coburn. Cram's close friend and neighbor, like Guiney, Day was not only the herald of the decadent movement in America, as both Wilde's and Beardsley's American publisher, but became, in his biographer's words, "one of the most famous photographers in the Western World."

F. Holland Day epitomizes the elegant, uninhibited artist of the decadent nineties . . . working in his Turkish robes and Chinese silk shirts, planning the secret panels in his Norwood library, bantering with Bernard Berenson or Yeats; dining with Lord Alfred Douglas and Oscar Wilde; . . . knocking about Algerian streets on a wild spree with Alvin Langdon Coburn; or lighting the thirteen candles of cabalistic ritual in his incense-fragrant studio on Beacon Hill.[120]

Oscar Wilde's American publisher, as Fred became, was also called the "Pied Piper of the South End," because, dressed invariably in his dashing cape and a broad-brimmed hat, he so often carried off the young men he "discovered" in the South End slums to country outings or to cultural events — or to his Pinckney Street studio to pose for his camera.[121]

Exactly what was going on is hard to say. Cross-class sex ("trade," as it is sometimes called, deriving from the feelings of so many upper-class Anglo-Saxons that sex cannot be without inhibition within one's own class and is more spontaneous outside it), may have excited Day; certainly it did Wilde, who

41

13. Day's portrait of Kahlil Gibran, his best-known protégé.

called it "feasting with panthers."[122] Yet appearances, as always, are hard to argue from, especially in the pre-Freudian era. More than once, for example, it was Louise Guiney, Day's intimate friend and both knowing and devout, who sent him models male and female.

The truth seems to have been that Fred Day's sexuality was unusually refined and idealistic for all that it may have been fierce enough. He was devoted to the concept of the "Platonic lover," a type of same-sex relationship that raises the stakes considerably, as it were, beyond the level of the kind of romantic friendship he had with Guiney; an idea Day seems to have absorbed from Balzac, who, as Fred understood it, in Jussim's words, "placed supreme value on attachments between men . . . heroic, devoted friendship, purified by *total chastity* [emphasis added]." Jussim suggests this is why "Day never documented his homosexual activities in terms of physical relationships."[123]

Day never attempted, however, to hide his "protégés." Often he brought them to concerts and such. ("Let's see who [Day's] got [with him] *this* week," a friend recalled someone saying at Symphony; "last week he had a Chinaman.")[124] And, whether he slept with them or not, he took a real interest in his discoveries. One of Day's models, for example, whom he plucked from utter poverty in the South End and started on his way to ultimately international repute was the Syrian mystic and author Kahlil Gibran, whose work Gibran's biographers admit owed a great deal to the influence of Day (*13*). Day introduced Gibran to the work of Maurice Maeterlinck and William Blake, from whom, both textually and visually, derives so much of Gibran's famous book, *The Prophet*. (That work, of course, still sells in the 1990s in the millions of copies, and such was Day's influence on Gibran as Guiney knew it, she may be forgiven for writing angrily to Day about *The Prophet*: "Why isn't this book dedicated to you?")[125]

Boston generally tolerated Day's outrageousness, one suspects, because he was a true Bohemian who stood up for what he believed in, which is to say certain aesthetic tastes or values. Fred's, wrote Guiney, was "the lofty taste of the true Emersonian, not of a sybaritic dilettante."[126] In Jussim's words, much of Day's work emanated from his passion for "the Keatsian romanticism that pervaded not only Pre-Raphaelite ideology but the aestheticism of Oscar Wilde."[127]

It is fundamental to understand, however, that Day was not an altruist. Gibran's biographers, though agreeing that Day may have been truly "concerned for the fate of [the] underprivileged," nonetheless point out that (as his own colorful appearance suggested) Day was an artist "honestly attracted to the exotic and unusual drama to be found on the bazaar-like streets" of the South End slum he found Gibran in, streets the average middle-class person would have avoided then or now, gay or not.[128] Day's photographs were the first of their kind, for instance, to ennoble the African American — in this case his black chauffeur and valet, Alfred Tanneyhill.[129]

Day's photographs of young men *were* erotic, masterfully so. But Day was no misogynist: his portraits of women were sympathetic and powerful. And his nudes only underline the point. It was, to be sure, quite a shocker the night of November 16, 1898, when Cram and Guiney and doubtless most of the rest of Bohemia trooped up to 9 Pinckney Street to see Day exhibit the first photographic frontal nudity seen in Boston (perhaps most shocking of all was the fact that the exhibit featured a very well-built and genitally well-endowed young man in a crucifixion study [*14*]).[130] But as one critic pointed out of such work by Day, one could not but notice his amazingly

> refined treatment of the nude. There is not the slightest suggestion of nakedness in any of his numerous studies in which undraped figures occur, and yet no photographer has ever given the varying values and multitudinous gradation of fleshtones with such appreciation, sympathy, and truth.[131]

43

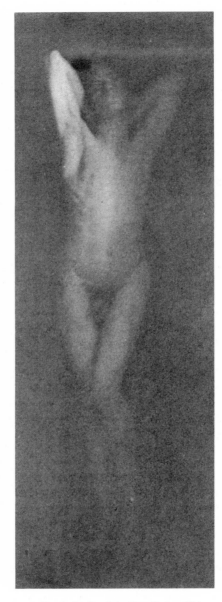

14. Day's *Study of the Crucifixion*. This
highly homoerotic work introduced
photographic frontal nudity to Boston in
1898.

Day suffered all his life not only from severe migraine but also — probably because of his drug use — from what Guiney in connection with another use of drugs aptly referred to as "the penalties intertwined with stolen dreams."[132] He had difficulty in both writing and speaking — his syntax was tortuous. Thus it was perhaps that photography appealed so, and he was undoubtedly a master of the pictorialist aesthetic, whose other luminaries included Edward Steichen and Gertrude Käsebier. An attempt to lift the revolutionary new medium of photography to the level of expressive art, pictorialism, though its triumphs were many and its influence on the history of photography great (through techniques such as soft-focus lenses and hand manipulation of prints), is not as widely known today because it was rejected in the 1920s. It was too "arty" and "moody" in appearance and often too "genteel" and elitist in subject matter (rather like the Boston School of painting) for the second wave of modernist artist-photographers like Edward Weston and Paul Strand, who preferred more crisply rendered prints of more apparently gritty subject matter. But Day's work, though certainly "arty" enough, was hardly ever "genteel" and often quite the reverse in its exploration of racial and sexual subjects (15). Long after his death, in fact, Day was a notable influence on that equally controversial photographer of our own time, Robert Mapplethorpe.[133]

Psychologically intense, mysterious and dreamlike in their probing into the mind of the subject, Day's photographs were sufficiently admired that by 1900 he was one of the most famous photographers in the world. Although perhaps more historically important as a publisher, whose mission, as we will see later, was to confront America with the title deeds of the aesthetic movement, Day in his photography discloses best how true on Pinckney Street — as for the avant-garde generally in the 1880s — was another significant assertion about this era by Peter Gay: that it was increasingly a *scientific truism* that "sexuality is the most potent ingredient in the human makeup."[134]

A DEEPLY CLOSETED LIFE

The last of the three Pinckney Street figures whose influence over Cram in his early and mid-twenties was pivotal, the Anglo-American architect Henry Vaughan was very different from the challenging and flamboyant Day, though hardly less fascinating (16).

By the mid-1880s Vaughan, who had come to America to design St. Margaret's Convent Chapel of 1882 on Pinckney Street (17), was fast becoming the leading church architect in New England, his design of St. Paul's School Chapel in Concord, New Hampshire, begun in 1886, having attracted wide and favor-

15. Louise Guiney by Day, a rare, if not unique, photograph, not previously published, of Boston's leading Catholic poet in drag. It was recently found by Patricia Berman. Guiney's masculinity, for all her feminine attributes, has often been commented upon.

able attention. A path-finding work, the chapel pointed inevitably to Vaughan's virtually unique credentials among architects working in America, for he had been chief draftsman to G. F. Bodley, then the preeminent English Gothicist, with whom Vaughan would ultimately design the National Cathedral in Washington, D.C.

Withal, Vaughan was as much a puzzle as a success. As a fellow architect put it, "Mr. Vaughan's life has been almost a mystery. . . . [He has been] a man who exerted a surprising influence in an almost totally unseen manner."[135] Even Vaughan's practice was, so to speak, shadowed by the fact that when he was not designing religious buildings for the Episcopal church he was designing all sorts of other buildings for Edward Searles, who was probably the person who (during an 1881 trip to England) first attracted Vaughan to America. And Searles, in the words of Vaughan's biographer, William Morgan, was "an even more shadowy figure than Vaughan."[136]

This is hardly the place to speculate on Vaughan's own relationships, but Searles (a New York decorator who in early middle age married a client's widow in her sixties, who then died four years later, leaving Searles in 1891 something in the vicinity of twenty-one million dollars) was a man of bizarre habits, not least of which was that he would spend whole fortunes on remote abodes for himself that involved moving roads and buildings he felt were too close. Perhaps his most astonishing commission to Vaughan was for Stanton Harcourt

16. Henry Vaughan, ca. 1900. "His life was apparently lonesome in the extreme," wrote George Barton. "From his rooms to his office, from his office to Marston's restaurant, and back again, was practically his entire life."

17. St. Margaret's Convent Chapel, Pinckney Street, as originally conceived by Vaughan in 1882.

in Windham, New Hampshire, an immense, forbidding pile that one is hardly surprised to discover was the model many years later, in the mid-twentieth century, for the dark castle of *Peyton Place*, Grace Metalious's exposé of the secret lives and passions of a small New England town.

Thus it was that while with his right hand Vaughan was creating the splendid architectural patrimony of New England Episcopalianism, which is to say that of America's most prestigious private schools (not only St. Paul's but also Groton) and of the devout parochial and monastic world of Anglo-Catholicism, with his left hand, as it were, Vaughan was just as diligently creating such dark medieval stage sets as Stanton Harcourt for an outré recluse who, as Morgan points out, may have been "shadowy" but was "as important a patron of Vaughan as the Episcopal Church."[137] Admittedly, it is an ancient human failing to believe ill of something sooner than good. But we know what Vaughan's churches were for; we do not know, and may do well to be wary of, the intent behind Searles's commissions.

One of the reasons Vaughan is, so to speak, a mystery within a mystery is that

48

he seems to have had almost no friends. Other, that is, than birds and mice. Perhaps the most personal and moving penetration of the life of this solitary architect that Morgan achieves is in this oddly beautiful but rather haunting anecdote:

> Vaughan always returned to the office [on the other side of Beacon Hill from his rooms] at night, although he never allowed his employees to do so. This was because Vaughan did not want his draftsmen to disturb the mice that came to feed on the crumbs of a roll that he brought back from his supper. The sparrows in Pemberton Square came to Vaughan's windows to be fed.[138]

Why does one want P. D. James to get to the bottom of this? Perhaps because no less than Charles Slattery, the bishop of Massachusetts (the respectable client), allowed himself with some amazement to say of Vaughan — who was, after all, the leading church architect of the ruling class in New England — "Few men have ever seen Henry Vaughan!"[139] Well; as it turns out, I believe one of those few to have been — and quite often — Ralph Adams Cram, the evidence for which is in part, at least, the extreme narrowness of Pinckney Street, out the front windows of any house on which one can hardly look without looking quite closely *into* the front windows of the house opposite. And if one stands on the doorstep of Cram's boardinghouse at 99 Pinckney, looking across the street, one inevitably is looking into the windows of 80 Pinckney, where Henry Vaughan lived until 1916, never, for some four critical years, much more than a stone's throw away from Cram.

Vaughan appears in Cram's memoirs as key to Cram's life story but in the vaguest possible way. Though Vaughan is the only person Cram calls "mentor" in his autobiography, where he even reproduces a portrait of the older man, and though it is clear Vaughan enormously influenced Cram's aesthetic and religious views, nowhere does Cram mention in his extensive reminiscences about Pinckney Street that Vaughan was once his closest neighbor. Unlike the case with Berenson, no letters survive with which to try to reconstruct Vaughan's and Cram's relationship, but Cram must have found the retiring Vaughan an intriguing counterweight to the rest of the Pinckney Street circle; all the more so when he came to practice architecture on his own.

A recluse Vaughan certainly was; but not, one may be sure, a dullard. On the contrary, for a recluse to achieve such eminence in his field would argue, like Vaughan's bold, piercing gaze (so evident in his portraits), for the reverse. And the shrinking away from all known human contact, the reclusiveness to the point of comment and, indeed, mystery, on the part of a public figure of such apparent magnetism, is suggestive not of dullness but of wariness. Vaughan was a "confirmed bachelor," in the phrase then common, and distinctly a High

Church aesthete, living, however reclusively, in Bohemia. Other evidence too suggests that, no less than in the cases of Guiney and Day, here again homosexuality is the explanation. (Significantly, in Renaissance Florence Leonardo was also called "withdrawn" and "mysterious." It is a classic defense mechanism of the anxious and deeply closeted.)

A scholar who has dealt with "mentoring" in the context of the closeted, Eve Kosofsky Sedgwick, in her *Epistemology of the Closet*, touches upon one of the most idealized and moving depictions of such relationships, that of Allan Bloom in his *Closing of the American Mind*. At the same time she gives us access to another view of the nature of Bohemia perhaps more penetrating than either of the two rehearsed here so far. For Bloom, writes Sedgwick:

> the history of Western thought is importantly . . . motivated by a . . . history of male-male pedagogic or pederastic relations . . . [a] narrative that goes from the *Phaedrus* to *Death in Venice*. . . . Bloom blames the sexual liberation movements of the [nineteen] sixties — all of them, but of course in this philosophic context the gay movement must take most of the blame — for dissipating the reservoirs of cathectic energy that are supposed to be . . . invested in cultural projects. Instead, as Plato's "diversity of erotic expression" has been frittered away on mere sex . . . "the lion roaring behind the door of the closet" has turned out "to be a little, domesticated cat." In Bloom's sad view, "sexual passion is no longer dangerous in us"; the "various liberations wasted that marvelous energy and tension, leaving the students' souls exhausted and flaccid."
>
> So Bloom is unapologetically protective of . . . a past in which "there was a respectable place for marginality, bohemia. But it had to justify its unorthodox practices by its intellectual and artistic achievement."[140]

The gloss Sedgwick puts on Bloom's views may help us to understand the likely nature of such a relationship as that of Cram and Vaughan. Surely Cram took careful note of the discretion necessary on the part of an architect identified with the Episcopal church and especially its schools — circles where Fred Holland Day, for instance, would not have been welcome and Henry Vaughan was — when, that is (as Bishop Slattery's remark indicates), they saw him!

ENGLAND AND NEW ENGLAND

Though undoubtedly the closest and for some time the most influential English friend of Cram's, Vaughan was really only the tip of the Anglophile iceberg, for nearly everything in this early period that shaped Cram was filtered through a pervasive Anglo-American cultural mist, the effect of which can also be seen in the lives of both Day and Guiney. The former would become best known for the English writers he would introduce into America; the latter so pined for Britannia that she spent the last two decades of her life there.

How English Boston was then is clear in Martin Green's report that "[Henry] Adams said that he was English to the last fibre of his thought."[141] So, really, was most of ruling-class Boston; equally so Ralph Adams Cram. And Cram's Anglo-American cultural milieu is especially worth exploring here because within a consideration of it we can try (by appealing back and forth from values and circumstances known and documented in one case but not another) to pencil in some of the gaps in our knowledge of Cram's late adolescence and young adulthood, venturing some ideas that can then be tested by our overall accumulating evidence.

Consider, by way of a case study, the youth of C. R. Ashbee, the celebrated British Arts and Crafts designer whom Cram later came to know personally and to admire sufficiently that he published Ashbee's work in America with no little enthusiasm. Ashbee is an apt comparison here because he came out of the same niche of the Anglo-American milieu as did Vaughan, but in Ashbee's case in Cram's own generation. (Both Ashbee and Cram were born in 1863.) In fact, Vaughan graduated from Bodley's office (to come to Boston — and to Pinckney Street) just five years before Ashbee entered the same office in 1886, after his years at Cambridge, for his own training by Bodley. And in the mid-1880s the cultural reverberations of Ashbee's life as an undergraduate at Cambridge were as significantly comparable to Cram's as were those of his life as an architectural apprentice in the late 1880s to Vaughan's.[142]

Cram, of course, never earned a degree. But he was a high school graduate, which meant more then, as would his soon to be undertaken European travel. (Only ten percent of Americans finished high school in Cram's day; and far fewer went to Europe than went to college.) Nor should Pinckney Street's resources be scanted either, whether one speaks of "students" or "faculty," resident or nonresident — or even the "reading list," which was, of course, the same on either side of the Atlantic. William Morris read Ruskin's *Stones of Venice* at Oxford as an undergraduate in the early 1850s; similarly, Cram read Ruskin *and* Morris as an adult in the early 1880s, as did Ashbee. As for classmates, not only were many of Cram's friends (Berenson, Updike, Bullard, and Partridge, for example) enrolled in, or recent graduates of, Ivy League colleges, but recall Cram's virtual tutorials (certainly tête-à-têtes) with Charles Eliot Norton. Just as Ruskin's invitations to Oscar Wilde at Oxford were important, so the fact that Ruskin's friend and mentor was so available to Cram illustrates that though Cram's Beacon Hill Bohemia was hardly Ashbee's Cambridge, it offered a comparable caliber of learning experience even before one entered on the "postgraduate" course with a Bodley (in Ashbee's case) or a Vaughan (in Cram's).

Thus it is not surprising to discover that Cram and Ashbee in fact accumulated not only many of the same tastes (Wagner, for instance) but also pretty nearly the same "isms," the same first principles, that would serve as their youthful starting points. Indeed, Cram's and Ashbee's journals were strikingly similar. Ashbee's biographer, Alan Crawford, has written:

> Ashbee's Journals allow us to eavesdrop on [his small group of Cambridge undergraduate friends], though generally all one can catch is certain recurring names and phrases — Plato, the soul, socialism . . . Emerson, Carlyle, transcendentalism, and others spoken more faintly, Schopenhauer, Swedenborg, even Madame Blavatsky. . . . [William] Morris added to what Ruskin had written.[143]

Ashbee's mention of Swedenborg and Blavatsky brings up again an interest of Cram's that will surface frequently here — Spiritualism and the occult.[144] Platonism and Ruskinianism — and Transcendentalism, which is American, of course, in origin — will also arise again and again in this study. Another American influence on Ashbee was evident — Walt Whitman — who also appeared in Cram's list of the heroes of his youth in his memoirs.[145] And that great American poet points up other continuities between Ashbee and Cram.

Whitman's name arose in Ashbee's life because of another "ism" he had in common with Cram — a rather literary but keenly felt socialism. In Ashbee's case it was introduced to him at Cambridge by Edward Carpenter, the influential British socialist thinker and friend of William Morris and George Bernard Shaw, whose views found expression at his farm community at Millthorpe, which, though it resonated with overtones of Concord and Emerson, was overwhelmingly Whitmanesque, for Carpenter, as Ashbee's biographer explains,

> believed, in a way that is characteristic of the Romantic phase of socialism in the 1880s, that . . . homosexuality could become a positive spiritual and social force, breaking down the barriers of class and convention, and binding men together in comradeship . . . that current of affection which he had recognized with a leap of joy when he first read the poems of Walt Whitman.[146]

Carpenter was an Anglican priest who after Cambridge was the curate of Frederick Denison Maurice, a founder of the Christian Socialism movement that Cram, as we will see, was to enroll under in Boston when he became a convert to Anglicanism in the late 1880s. For Carpenter as for Whitman, it is essential to note, homosexuality was seen as involving more than genital behavior and as a real force for social change.

Advanced Boston reciprocated Carpenter's interests. There was a branch of the Walt Whitman Fellowship International, which Jonathan Katz calls "the American counterpart to the [English] Carpenter circles," though it is not known, despite Cram's admiration of Whitman, whether he was a member, and Carpenter also sat for a portrait by Fred Day. Moreover, as late as 1902, Goodspeed's in Boston published the American edition of Carpenter's *Ioläus: An*

Anthology of Friendship, so forceful an effort to legitimize homosexual love that it earned the nickname among bookmen of "The Bugger's Bible." According to Warren Johansson, "the homosexual content [of *Ioläus*] was scarcely veiled," though in later (and post-Freudian) years the publisher somewhat disclaimed the project.[147]

Thus does another aspect of youthful experience surface. And, as was the case with Cram on Pinckney Street, its key expression for Ashbee was the way he pursued throughout the 1880s ardent friendships of great intensity that, in his biographer's words, "seem to be shot through with [homosexual] affections." That Ashbee had in his reading of Plato "a sense of these affinities" Crawford presumes. So may we of Cram, whose Platonic leanings are the subject of Chapter 4. But Crawford admits, as we must of Cram, that because of the great silence about this subject in this period all that one can really hazard is the general truism that "recognition" (in the form usually of a constant quarrel with oneself) "comes in stages."[148] Similarly, the sense of the probable costs involved.

That this was not a new issue, especially for an artist, emerged in 1896, when the publication of the town records from the Florentine archives disclosed that Leonardo da Vinci had been accused of homosexuality in 1476, a fact subsequently suppressed.[149] Closer to home, Cram probably knew of the rumors of same-sex inclinations that arose in connection with two mid-century Boston artists, Washington Allston and Anne Whitney. (Guiney, who dedicated one of her books to her close friend Whitney, chose with Day a bust by Whitney for the English memorial to Keats that Guiney and Day arranged.)[150] Cram also probably knew about the celebrated British painter Simeon Solomon, the leader of the aesthetic movement before Wilde. "After [Solomon's] trial and conviction for a minor homosexual offense in 1873, many of his friends," Emmanuel Cooper notes, "turned against him even though they were perfectly well aware of his sexual activities before his arrest."[151]

Above all, there was the example in Cram's own time and place of John Singer Sargent, about whom persistent rumors continue to circulate today that no biographer (as was until recently also true of Henry James) has effectively dealt with. Cooper writes:

> Sargent was cautious. . . . He declined to become a regular contributor to *The Yellow Book* for fear of being associated too closely with Aubrey Beardsley. . . . Sargent offered little information about his sexual preferences. He is generally described as being "emotionally inhibited." . . . He enjoyed close friendships [with, among others, Nicola D'Inverno, his valet of twenty-five years] . . . but much of the "evidence" for Sargent's sexual interest lies in his drawing and watercolors. . . . Sargent accepted a mural commission for the new Boston Public Library. He executed many preparatory drawings of the male figure, either naked or partially clothed. Angelo Colarossi,

the model, . . . sat for some of these drawings. Sargent later collated a selection of these studies into a sketchbook which is now in the Fogg Art Museum. . . . They give a glimpse of his response to masculine physicality. . . . [One such], viewed frontally, is given a particularly bold treatment and carries a self-conscious sense of masculinity.[152]

To Peter Gay's conclusions, already quoted here, that in Cram's youth it was becoming a scientific truism that sexuality was the most potent ingredient of the human makeup, and one that was increasingly opaque and anxiety-provoking, we might well add that among the reasons for that anxiety was the emerging sense in this period of homosexuality as an integral, if not an all-defining, aspect of self. It was an anxiety the evidence suggests Ralph Adams Cram shared.

RIVE GAUCHE, GROUP PORTRAIT

Pinckney Street in the 1880s is a very faded sepia picture now, more than a hundred years later, and perhaps the best way to conclude this introduction is to imagine it as a group portrait. Wrote Stephen Parrish: "The [Pinckney Street] circle was dominated by the versatile Cram. . . . But at Cram's elbow in all these enthusiasms stood Day."[153] To Cram's other side we must imagine Guiney, and in the background Vaughan. In between are the secondary figures: Carman, Savage, Hovey, Meteyard, Berenson, Brown, Partridge, Small, Rogers, Bullard, Updike . . .

Can we speed the sepia up, get it moving, add sound and color? If *Patience* wears thin as a soundtrack, there is always Bizet. Even Wagner! There is Cram again, striding up Pinckney — it is evening now and he is surely heading for the theater district. Undoubtedly he is in his black evening cloak lined in scarlet, which he would have worn over his dress suit in that more formal age. Walking stick and pince-nez are in evidence;[154] and it was his recollection as a old man that when he was young there were "few[er] pleasanter memories than that of waiting in the queue [at the old Boston Theatre on Washington Street] for the gallery doors to be opened and rushing dizzily up the circular stairs to the dollar seats."[155] *There's* a moving picture.

Then there were the evenings of dining and drinking with his friends in haunts Cram lovingly described in later years: "the old 'Bell in Hand' in Pi Alley. . . . One whiff of its unique atmosphere transported one back into the eighteenth century." There was also "Billy Park's, where you could revel in chump-chops and the justly celebrated musty ale . . . [and] Frank Locke's Brass House,"[156] all located in the then rather raffish area adjoining Newspaper Row. Above all, there was Marliave's, then as still today hard by the historic old Province steps, with its ancient ironwork and worn granite stoop (thought to be all that remains of the garden of Province House, the eighteenth-century residence of the royal governors). It was at Marliave's during this era that the Fox, one of Harvard's nineteenth-century men's clubs, was founded; there, too, John Boyle O'Reilly wrote: "And I'd rather live in Bohemia / Than in any other land."[157] Cram's description is best of all: "Marliave's of the theoretical French table d'hôte and the veritable 'red ink' as a beverage, with the incomparable Francise to serve us."[158]

But there was, of course, traditionally, another side to the artists' experience of *la vie Bohème*, about which Cram some years thereafter was frank: "I developed a certain repugnance to commenting *in extenso* on exhibits of pictures I considered bad, even when the proprietors of the galleries implicated were generous advertisers." The result was predictable:

> After hurling Quixotic defiance at the ever courteous and reasonable editor, I descended the long stairs [from the *Transcript*'s office] to Washington Street literally without a job. I had forsaken architecture; journalism had cast me out. . . . Still, one must live. . . . For a year or two I eked out a precarious existence by doing various odd jobs: designing wallpapers for the friendly George K. Birge of Buffalo, writing and illustrating articles for the *Decorator and Furnisher*,—most awful things they were, wallpaper, furniture designs, and articles,—and helping kind ladies with other designs for such "decorating and furnishing" as they might need.[159]

Actually, in his *Arts and Crafts Movement in America*, Robert Judson Clark points out that the Birge Company was "one of the leading manufacturers of artistic wallpapers in the country," some of the work of which is rather admired a century later and is illustrated by Clark. Alas, Cram's designs for the firm no longer seem to be identifiable.[160]

At the same time, yet another disaster befell Cram. He, Partridge, Guiney, Berenson, Maud Elliott, and others had joined forces to establish a monthly review of the arts, the name of which was to have been *The XXth Century*, but which collapsed somewhere between the matters of its staffing and of its financing—and amid no little disagreement among the aesthetes themselves. (Berenson proposed Isabella Stewart Gardner as a sponsor *and* columnist, but there were apparently doubters. Bliss Carman wanted to be involved, but not with Maud Elliott. And so on.)[161] Cram found this latest debacle, coming so soon after his having quit the *Transcript*, dispiriting in the extreme. Depressed and lonely in the fall of 1887, he accepted "at forty-eight hours' notice a sudden offer of a friend to go to Europe with him and his new wife as tutor to the stepson he had acquired by this same marriage."[162] Cram's first Boston decade of the 1880s—brilliant though it had been—was sputtering to a very inconclusive finale.

That decade's most enduring legacy from Cram is probably the preservation of what became Copley Square. And it is interesting that Martin Green, in his *Mount Vernon Street Warrens,* fixed on this square as the most telling backdrop for aestheticism in Boston. Writing of its landmarks — Richardson's Trinity Church, John Sturgis's Museum of Fine Arts, and Charles McKim's Boston Public Library, with all of which Cram was on intimate terms — Green observed (somewhat exuberantly) that they evidenced how Boston was becoming "the world capital of the aesthetic movement"; though, he continued more perceptively, in Boston "the aesthetic was still fused with an old-fashioned idealism and had not yet come to terms with the new eroticism."[163]

Green did not touch at all on the Pinckney Street group. Having seen here already, however, how Cram and Guiney and Day were beginning exactly to fuse Boston's characteristic idealism with the new aesthetic of the 1880s, we can also anticipate that it would be Pinckney Street where that aesthetic *would* come to terms with the new eroticism.

Meanwhile, for Cram, there was Europe.

2

BLACK SPIRITS AND WHITE

The more closely one reads the autobiography, the more convinced one becomes that there is *something that is not there*, "something" that eludes the reader. . . . The process of creativity *is* . . . a ghost story. . . . The cardinal rule of the ghost story was that "the teller . . . should be well frightened in the telling" — frightened partly by the unearthly visitations, but also by the strange and disturbing sexual innuendoes of violent, possessive, homoerotic or incestuous passion that vibrate through these tales.

> — Judith Fryer, *Felicitous Space:*
> *The Imaginative Structures of Edith Wharton and Willa Cather*

We are what we pretend to be.

> — Kurt Vonnegut, Jr., *Mother Night*

18. St. Mark's Basilica in Venice, from a photograph in Cram's papers. "In those far-away days of the middle eighties," wrote Cram in his memoirs many years later, "Venice was pure beauty . . . to youth just escaped, for a moment, from nineteenth century America."

ONE DAY in 1887, in the nave of Notre Dame in Paris, Bernard Berenson, his biographer reports, "bumped into Ralph Adams Cram, the brilliant young art critic for the Boston *Transcript*. . . . [Cram's] companion was William Ordway Partridge, at twenty-six the oldest member of the two and already well launched on his career as a sculptor. . . . The two kept Berenson on the go for three days and nights."[1] Behold, the Pinckney Street Bohemia convened abroad and quite recovered from the demise of their projected art review.

It was not hyperbole to call young Cram brilliant. Despite his leaving the *Transcript* and the foundering of *The XXth Century*, his reputation was still influential; as Joseph Chamberlin pointed out in his history of Boston's most legendary newspaper, "the *Transcript*'s first impression with art criticism was made with the notices of art matters by Mr. Ralph Adams Cram, then a budding architect and the leader of a circle of young aesthetes, in the eighteen-eighties."[2]

THE DIVIDED SELF

Cram's 1887 trip to Europe was actually his second; the first, a year earlier, funded by his prize money from the courthouse competition, had been a long tour through England, France, and Italy, climaxing in Germany; for Ralph Adams Cram did not first go to Europe to see architecture. "It was primarily," he wrote later, "for the purpose of attending the Wagner Festival at Bayreuth." Nor was he disappointed. To hear singers "personally trained by Wagner himself," he recalled, "[was] enough to make or mar any youth . . . who had just begun to open his eyes on a world of wonder and enchantment."[3]

Of course, there *was* architecture, most impressive to Cram the contemporary Gothic work in England of John Sedding and George Bodley, characterized, Cram felt, by both "vitality" and "modernism,"[4] as well as the dreamlike splendors of Venice, with which Cram at once fell in love (*18*). And in the long run the architectural impressions would matter most. In 1886, though, it was *Parsifal* that excited Cram. Although he did not scant the Pre-Raphaelites in his letters from Europe to his *Transcript* readers (Rossetti, wrote Cram after a morning at the Grosvenor Gallery, "seems to enter of a sudden into the consciousness of all the magic and mystery of life, love and passion, the intense and beautiful ardor of the middle ages"), he wrote above all of his time at the

Festpielhaus: "I do not suppose it is possible for anyone who is not a follower of Wagner to understand how he is taken by those who love him. . . . They find here in Bayreuth something they have wanted all their lives."[5]

That first trip also foretold Cram's eventual religious conversion. As he remembered it,

> when I was wandering through North Italy, I had come to Assisi, and there, . . . before the tomb of Saint Francis, by some unaccountable impulse I had found myself on my knees and trying to say something in the way of prayers. I did not make out very well, for it was actually the first time in my life when anything of the sort had happened. With a mystical philosopher for a father and a mother of keen rationalistic convictions (albeit a poet), prayer, or indeed, anything approaching formal religious action, was out of the question, and I had been allowed to go my own way. The sudden impulse, there before the tomb of the Saint, was, I think, genuine, but for the time without lasting results, and it soon passed out of mind.[6]

The comments about his mother and father, the only significant mention of them in his autobiography, are revealing. Beyond the bare facts already rehearsed here of Cram's father's controversial career and meager means, his mother's resentment and disappointment, and the influence of Squire Blake — and aside from a few childhood impressions and such that perhaps presaged architecture, to be touched on when we discuss Cram's early design work — there has been little to tell of Cram's adolescence because little is recoverable. Unless, that is, it is held to be of interest that Ralph as a child had a pet mouse he stoutly defended in a household of several cats — Cram was always feisty — or that he was unusually keen on amateur theatricals. Both author and director in high school of a play entitled *Faust*, he also designed the sets and the costumes — a total control of things that would in later years not have surprised any of Cram's clients.[7]

Of the long-range influence of his upbringing, however, more can be said because Cram's daughter Mary Carrington Nicholas, an unusually insightful woman, left behind some fugitive notes on the subject for a projected biography of her father. In these notes the background of Cram's comments here about parental influences emerges, for his daughter makes plain that if Ralph's upbringing was cultured (much reading of the classics, philosophic discourse, even chamber music with neighbors) and also full of a real love of learning (the family's small collection of books was thriftily "recovered in stitched brown paper by careful women who prized the books above almost everything"), it was also quite rigid: "Boys and men never cry," read the notes; "self-control, control of emotions, self-discipline [were] the essential truths. . . . Falling short was never condoned or excused."[8]

This environment nurtured not only Ralph Adams Cram but also a brother and sister, William and Marion Cram, neither of whom, interestingly, is even once mentioned in Cram's autobiography. Still, it is clear that any *emotional* life, religious or otherwise, must necessarily have been very limited, engendering not a little repression. Indeed, it was a commonplace of Cram's friends in his later years, in explanation of some one or another of his enthusiasms, to note that he came, as Walter Muir Whitehill put it, "from an austere New Hampshire farm, and so became a ready convert to Anglo-Catholicism, Gothic architecture, Brahms, Wagner, Browning, beer drinking and all kinds of non-New England passions."[9]

How much he had changed in his early Boston years surely became clear in that first experience of Europe. But the trip's results were indecisive. Not so the second one. In 1886 Assisi was en passant, Bayreuth the climax. In 1887 the climax would occur in Rome and change Cram's life utterly.

THE PATH TO ROME

At the center of events throughout this second and critical trip of 1887 was that necessary catalyst for Ralph Adams Cram — a stimulating and charming young man. We have already met the first of these in Boston and seen how Guy Prescott particularly widened Cram's horizons. Now, in Europe in 1887, there is suddenly another — quite unannounced, for about neither the manner of their meeting nor the nature of their relationship is very much known. But T. Henry Randall (19) was certainly akin to the "Beatrice or Socrates" Allan Bloom spoke of; fifty-five years later Cram wrote:

> the great thing was that [in Rome] I made a new friend who was to play a vital part, though only too brief, in my life. This was one T. Henry Randall, a young architectural student from Maryland. . . . Representing the best social tradition of the Old South, he had a personality of singular charm and a passion for good architecture that did much to rebuild the fabric of my vision and set me on the way to architecture again. Also, though unconsciously, he helped me to find a definite religion for myself. . . . When I first met him in Rome I was of the ordinary type of bumptious and self-satisfied youth that, in his mental superiority, scorns all religions. . . . Randall was an . . . Episcopalian . . . vitalized by Catholic tendencies.
>
> [Later, Cram continued, comparing this second trip with his first the year before:] . . . then I was alone. . . . Now, with Randall in alliance, there were revelations at every step; and under the stimulus of old beauty, and the increasing knowledge of the old Catholic culture . . . the inner conviction was growing daily that after all it was architecture as a profession that had claimed me as its own.[10]

Randall himself is a fairly mysterious character. Little is known of him personally beyond the fact that he was in his youth a considerable athlete (captain of his college crew at St. John's College, Annapolis, where he also played football) and that his marriage in 1901, when he was thirty-nine, to New York socialite Elizabeth Bradhurst, was both shortlived and childless; they were together for only one year, according to the New York Social Register. When Randall died in 1905, there was no mention of Mrs. Randall among his survivors, even though she did outlive him. Somewhat more is known of him professionally. Unlike Cram, he had outstanding architectural credentials (Johns Hopkins, MIT School of Architecture, and apprenticeships to both H. H. Richardson and McKim, Mead and White). But Randall never made his mark, designing little and dying young. In his memoirs Cram said little; only that "inexplicably, unhappiness pursued him after a few years, and he died before he could work out all the real artistic possibilities that were in him."[11]

About the overall relationship Cram was equally mysterious. Having thanked Randall profusely for being the means to no less than his religious conversion and also his final decision to take up architecture as his profession, Cram felt nonetheless bound to add: "I am grateful to his memory for more things than this";[12] surely an admission of intense feeling of an intimate nature. Yet Cram asserted as well: "I do not remember how I first met him,"[13] by no means the only time, as we will see, that he fell back on such an evasion (what else can it have been?), even in the case of some of his closest friends. He was perhaps franker about how he and Randall in turn met two others in that surly Roman fall of 1887, when

> it rained all the time, was bitterly cold; the pension on the Pincio was dreary . . . and, incidentally, I was, I suppose, the most ineffectual tutor at large. . . .
>
> By New Year's, conditions had just about become intolerable, but a way out was revealed. Randall and I had been [sketching] in the older churches, when in one of those churches we picked up two young naval officers. . . . We became rather friends, and later one of them said to us: "You fellows seem to be sharks on mosaics, why don't you go to Sicily? . . . Besides, the weather is fine and warm there. . . ."
>
> Incontinently, I severed relations with my patron and his family [and Randall and I took the boat for] Palermo. For three months we revelled in a new world of inspiring art. Daily we drew and sketched in the churches of Palermo or up at Monreale, going by tram to the latter shrine, sketching inordinately, eating our luncheons by the fountain in the corner of the cloister, then going back at night to our quarters.[14]

It was the romantic dash for freedom of which so many dream; and having chucked his job and taken off with his new friend, what follows seems indeed to have been a memorable peregrination. We know this, I believe, because of a book written by Cram some eight years later — *Black Spirits and White* — which even today, though it is a rare book, is by no means a forgotten one.

In fact, though Cram in his memoirs skated quickly past this very early book (dismissing it as a youthful indiscretion),[15] parts of this most bizarre and personal of all his works have since his death become his most widely read literary

19. T. Henry Randall. More than four decades later, remembering the effect on him of Rome in 1887, Cram wrote, "the great thing was that [there] I made a new friend."

work. A collection of horror stories, of all things, Cram's book is listed in the latest Oxford anthology of Victorian ghost stories in the "Select Conspectus of Ghost Stories, 1840–1910," where Cram is one of only twenty-five credited as being leading authors in that genre in the 1890–1910 period (including Rudyard Kipling, Henry James, H. G. Wells, and Conan Doyle).[16] Stories from Cram's book have also been reprinted several times since his death, notably in Edward Wagenknecht's *Fireside Book of Ghost Stories* and Richard Dalby's *Mammoth Book of Ghost Stories*, where Cram is cited as one of only six American writers to have developed the genre of the horrific tale in the wake of its progenitor, Edgar Allan Poe.[17]

Though it may seem improbable, these stories constitute pretty much a record of Cram's and Randall's European travels. For despite Cram's making no connection between trip and book in his autobiography (any more than he did between Vaughan and Pinckney Street; it is a pattern), *Black Spirits and White* takes the form of a series of adventures that befall the narrator in the course of a European trip with one Tom Rendel, an obvious animadversion to Thomas Henry Randall — the more so as Cram dedicated the book "to T.H.R." Under that dedication is printed this note: "*all* of [these stories] you know, and a part of them you were."[18] A surprising enough admission, for they all involve a fair element of dissipation (absinthe is duly drunk by our hero) and are not just occult in nature but often genuinely horrific, exceedingly violent, and full of homoerotic overtones. Also evident is a pervasive use of the technique scholars have identified as "mask and signal," a technique that reveals an inner conflict

20. Stone and Kimball's edition of Cram's *Black Spirits and White*, with its distinctive green cover design and carnation motif, the flower of Decadence that Wilde and others made into a symbol of homosexuality in Cram's youth. Stone and Kimball's imprint was notable also in a more strictly literary way: George Bernard Shaw's work was first published in America by the firm.

between what one wants to communicate — the signal — and what one needs to hide — the mask.[19]

There are two aspects of this. First, the visual aspect (20) is evident at once in the vivid green of the book's cloth cover and endpapers and in the repeated carnation motif that is the principal decoration of Cram's book. The significance of the matter of color is easy to overlook, but it is clear if one has read Oscar Wilde, who in his "Pen, Pencil and Poison" of 1889–1891 writes of that "curious love of green, which in individuals is always the sign of a subtle, artistic temperament, and in nations is said to denote a laxity, if not a decadence, of morals." And the significance of the flora, as it were, emerges also in the work of Wilde, as when, in *Salomé*, he writes of the Judaean princess's "little green flowers of perverse, forbidden desire" (for John the Baptist, never mind whether dead or alive). One flower in this respect is particularly significant, the green carnation, "the unnatural flower of Decadence," Karl Beckson calls it, which "Wilde wore publicly at the premieres of *Lady Windermere's Fan* (1892) and

The Importance of Being Earnest (1895) [Wilde's friends, including Aubrey Beardsley, were also seen to wear it] and that in Paris was worn as a symbol of homosexuality." That was a meaning which seems quickly to have migrated via Wilde to the English-speaking world; the satire written by Robert Hichens, himself gay, about Wilde and Lord Alfred Douglas, for example, was entitled *The Green Carnation*. As Beckson has observed, in "the prepsychoanalytic" world of the 1890s "symbols concealed as well as revealed the inner world of the symbol maker and symbol interpreter."[20]

To the visual aspect of mask and signal there is often allied a verbal or linguistic aspect; just in case anyone missed the visual carnations, Cram's book was published, for example, in Stone and Kimball's Carnation Series.[21] But the verbal aspect is harder to decode than the visual and will be taken up in Chapter 4. Meanwhile, consider this synopsis of one of Cram's stories in *Black Spirits and White*, "In Kropfsberg Keep":

> To the traveller from Innsbrück to Munich, up the lovely valley of the silver Inn, many castles appear, one after another, each on its beetling cliff or gentle hill — appear and disappear, melting into the dark fir trees that grow so thickly on every side. . . .
>
> But to us — Tom Rendel and myself — there are two castles only: . . . little Matzen, where eager hospitality forms the new life of a never-dead chivalry, and Kropfsberg, ruined, tottering, blasted by fire and smitten with grievous years — a dead thing, and haunted — full of strange legends, and eloquent of mystery and tragedy. . . .
>
> [While visiting at the first castle, the author and Rendel are told of the dark deeds of one Count Albert that have occurred at the other landmark and of how the consequent hauntings at Kropfsberg attracted the attention of a pair of modern-day travelers named Rupert and Otto. The story is thus told at one remove from Cram and his friend.]
>
> . . . Two young men who had studied painting . . . came down to Brixleg . . . partly to paint, and partly to amuse themselves — "ghost-hunting" as they said, for . . . they belonged to a certain set of people who believed nothing they had not seen themselves. . . . Their plan was to visit every place that was supposed to be haunted, and to meet every reputed ghost, and prove that it really was no ghost at all.
>
> [At Kropfsberg the two young men resolve to spend the night, and the tale really begins with the narrator falling into a fitful sleep.]
>
> It seemed to him that he woke almost immediately; the fire still burned, though low and fitfully on the hearth. Otto was sleeping . . .; with every passing moment the light died in the fireplace; he felt stiff with cold. . . . He shivered with a sudden and irresistible feeling of fear. . . .
>
> It had grown absolutely dark; a bat fluttered against the broken glass of the window. . . . He heard music; far, curious music . . . very faint, very vague, but unmistakable.
>
> Like a flash of lightning came a jagged line of fire down the blank wall opposite him, a line that remained, that grew wider, that let a pale cold light into the room, showing him now all its details . . . and in the very middle, black against the curious

brightness [there stood Count Albert, the] ghost, or devil . . . [who] beckoned to him. . . .

Without a word, Rupert rose and followed him, his pistol in hand. . . . Rupert found himself in a long, uneven corridor, the floor of which was warped and sagging, while the walls were covered on one side with big faded portraits of an inferior quality, like those in the corridor that connects the Pitti and Uffizzi in Florence. Before him moved the figure of Count Albert . . . the music grew stronger and stranger, a mad, evil, seductive dance that bewitched even while it disgusted [into the center of which the count leads Rupert, who is repelled by the] mad, seething whirl of sweeping figures. . . . Round and round the cursed room, a swaying, swirling maelstrom of death, while the air grew thick with miasma, [disgusts the young man, who is now addressed by Count Albert for the first time].

"We are ready for you now; dance!"

A prancing horror . . . leered at Rupert with eyeless skull. "Dance!"

Rupert stood frozen, motionless.

"Dance!"

His hard lips moved. "Not if the devil came from hell to make me."

Count Albert swept his vast two-handled sword into the foetid air while the tide of corruption . . . swept down on Rupert with gibbering grins.

The room, and the howling dead, and the black portent before him circled dizzily around, as with a last effort of departing consciousness he drew his pistol and fired full in the face of Count Albert.

Perfect silence, perfect darkness; not a breath, not a sound. . . . Rupert lay on his back, stunned, helpless, his pistol clenched in his frozen hand. . . Where was he? . . . Had he dreamed? Of course; but how ghastly a dream! With chattering teeth he called softly —

"Otto!"

There was no reply. . . . But why did Otto sleep so soundly; why did he not awake?

He stepped unsteadily across the room . . . and knelt by the mattress.

So they found him in the morning . . . kneeling beside the mattress where Otto lay, shot in the throat and quite dead.[22]

How striking that in Cram's tale the "seductive dance that bewitched even while it disgusted" (in which all Ralph's erotic yearnings can be read) and the triple demand that the narrator join it ("Dance!") are met by a bullet that finds its target, not in the ghostly provocateur but in the sleeping friend of the narrator, revealing, surely, no less than it conceals; and in a context not unknown in gay poetry of this period. One thinks of A. E. Housman's "Laws of God, the Laws of Men," where he writes of what today we would call homophobes, who would "make me dance as they desire."[23] Cram's story seems a literary rendering of what in the old textbooks used to be called homosexual panic.

Cram's murderous ending also calls to mind the distinction Freud made between *terror* (extreme and sudden fear in the face of a material threat) and *horror* (a fascinated dread in the presence of an immaterial cause in nightmares, phobias, or literature): "Terror can be dissipated by a round of buckshot. . . . Horror[s], on the other hand . . . [for example,] the frights of nightmares, cannot be dissipated by a round of buckshot; to flee them is to run into them at every turn"[24] — evidence, perhaps, of D. G. Hartwell's insight that what is essential to "the architecture of horror" is that it is "fiction that embodies psychological truth in metaphor," the purpose of which is to "release repressed or unarticulated psychological states." He believes, moreover, that this "project[ion of] the dark side of [authors'] sensibility — their most intimate, extravagant fears — in an uninhibited way" has, like the horror genre itself, "flourished most near the ends of centuries, during times of fearful social change."[25]

The reverberations now discernible are not only sexual but religious: "the Puritan sermon, with its hair-raising images . . . was the characteristic mode of horror literature in the United States before the invention of the short story," and the fact that so much horror literature has been written by ex-Christians "who have lost their firm faith in good but still have a discomforting belief in evil" ("all the best horror," it has been said, "is written by lapsed Catholics") only points up the ambiguities this story discloses about Cram. There is the sense in much of his work in this genre that no sensible explanation of the events he recounts is possible. It is, in Hartwell's words describing such a sense in the work of other authors, "the fiction of radical doubt," the sort that makes one realize that "Poe can profitably be considered as a contemporary of Kierkegaard." Some instinct in me wonders if this was true of Ralph Adams Cram, who also, after all, evolved through aesthetics to religion.[26]

What is most arresting is that by delving, through a reading of *Black Spirits and White*, into this virtually contemporaneous evocation by Cram of his 1887–88 trip to Europe, one gets an entirely different impression of it than from reading of the trip in his later memoirs, where there is more architecture, much more religion, less Randall, and no horror. Moreover, what *was* recorded in Cram's autobiography fifty years later, but not in the earlier book, takes on a different context — for it was in the midst of horrific, degenerate, and violent events, which, whether real or imagined, more than hint at a dark side to Cram's psyche, and which the evidence suggests are at least rooted in truth, that Ralph Adams Cram had perhaps the most intense and important experience of his life: his conversion to the Catholic religion.

"THIS TREMENDOUS LOVER"

It is interesting that Brigid Boardman, Francis Thompson's biographer, finds "an outstanding synthesis of the religious and psychological content" of Thompson's "Hound of Heaven" in the remarkable mural sequence based on

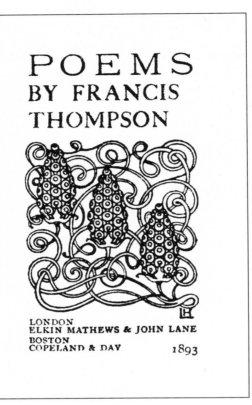

POEMS
BY FRANCIS
THOMPSON

LONDON
ELKIN MATHEWS & JOHN LANE
BOSTON
COPELAND & DAY   1893

21. Francis Thompson's poems (including "The Hound of Heaven") were first published in America by Copeland and Day.

that poem by the Boston painter (and later resident of Pinckney Street) R. Ives Gammell.[27] For it was Cram's own friends Day and Guiney who first published Thompson's poem in America (21),[28] and a hundred years later the Thompson Collection of his manuscripts and papers is to be found at Boston College. Clearly, Thompson, like Dante, must be accounted something of a Boston poet by adoption.[29]

"The Hound of Heaven" comes to mind because it is the most powerful contemporary image of the Catholic conversion experience as Cram and his friends knew it: uniquely worthy to keep company with those other images we have observed Cram evoking along the dramatic path taken by him and Randall to Rome and to midnight Mass there at San Luigi dei Francesi on Christmas Eve in 1887 (22). As Cram (in his quieter, autobiographical mode) later described it:

that night [the church] was blazing with hundreds of candles, crowded with worshippers and instinct with a certain atmosphere of devotion and of ardent waiting. For the half-hour after we arrived it was quite still except for the subdued rustle of

22. Christmas Midnight Mass at Boston's Church of the Advent, an early twentieth-century photograph of the splendid liturgy introduced there in the late nineteenth century. Often at the Advent in the 1890s, Cram must have recalled there his conversion at Midnight Mass in Rome.

men and women on their knees and the delicate click of rosaries. Then, in their white and gold vestments, [the priests] came silently to the high altar, attended by crucifers, thurifers and acolytes, and stood silently waiting. Suddenly came the bells striking the hour of midnight and with the last clang the great organs and the choir burst into a melodious thunder of sound; the incense rose in clouds, filling the church with a veil of pale smoke; and the Mass proceeded to its climax. . . . I did not understand all of this with my mind, but *I understood.*

On the way home, through the dark Roman streets, Randall remarked that he was going next morning to an early service of Holy Communion at the English Church. I told him somewhat to my own surprise, and to his, that I would go with him.[30]

What better company to keep in those dark Roman streets and the night watches following than Francis Thompson, who thus describes in his poem the Hound's pounce:

> I fled him, down the labyrinthine ways
>   Of my own mind; and in the mist of tears
> I hid from Him, and under running laughter.
>   Up vistaed hopes I sped;
>   And shot, precipitated
> Adown Titanic glooms of chasmed fears.
> . . . .
> I said to dawn, Be sudden; to eve: Be soon;
>   With thy young skiey blossoms heap me over
>   From this tremendous Lover!
> Float thy vague veil about me, lest He see![31]

Holbrook Jackson has observed that this poem is "a work which might well serve as a symbol of the spiritual unrest of the whole nineteenth century."[32] Its relevance to Ralph Adams Cram will arise again here.

Meanwhile, however, Thompson's mystic vision is in the post-Christian era not quite so apt.[33] As Ann Miner Daniel has pointed out, "the forces that produced [Cram] have certainly become unintelligible."[34] How then can we sort them out, if not through the image of Thompson's Hound?

More coolly, perhaps. Many Unitarians in the late nineteenth and early twentieth centuries, finding Christian ethics compelling but not self-validating and seeking the ethics' underlying sanctions, embraced Catholicism.[35] Cram was by no means alone in that it could be said of him that he had never, after all, been

anti-Christian or an atheist, it was only that he slipped away from the Unitarianism of . . . New England. (The best aspect [of which, he wrote elsewhere, was] not its allegedly comfortable nineteenth-century liberalism but rather "a kind of emotional reserve and intellectual integrity.") . . . Twentieth-century American Protestantism . . . had satisfied him neither intellectually nor emotionally. Yet the Christian patrimony he inherited from generations of upright New Englanders lay at the heart of his tradition; it could not be ignored; what he needed was *a grammar of assent* [emphasis added]. In the Church of England, with its grand liturgy, its ancient intellectual power, its splendid churches of every period, its virtual identity with English culture, he came to discover what he had found wanting . . . in the latter-day sectarianism of Beacon Hill. . . .

An Anglo-Catholic? . . . why . . . had [he] not proceeded all the way to Rome . . . [Because of] the Church of England's liturgy . . . [and its] splendid architectural monuments . . . [and the fact that] the Catholicism of Rome seemed an exotic thing, more Irish than Latin.[36]

These explanations I have imputed to Cram are quoted from Russell Kirk's explanation of the conversion (a generation after Cram's) of T. S. Eliot—another convert from New England Unitarianism to a Catholicism not Roman but Anglican. Though, like Cram, Eliot had, as we will see, other reasons than only liturgy and architecture and a certain anti-Irishness for preferring Canterbury to Rome, he was startlingly like Cram in this matter, even in detail: just as Cram had found himself on his knees at Assisi in the unknowing run-up, so to speak, to his conversion, so also Eliot, in a celebrated incident heralding *his* forthcoming conversion, inexplicably fell to his knees before the *Pietà* at St. Peter's in Rome.[37]

I make a point of quoting Russell Kirk for two reasons. First, that his explanations for Eliot's conversion can just as truly be advanced for Cram serves my purposes here in trying wherever possible to fit Cram not only into New England cultural history but into the wider context of the Anglicanism of his and the next generation, particularly with respect to figures of artistic hue such as Eliot and C. S. Lewis, W. H. Auden, Charles Williams, Evelyn Underhill, and Rose Macaulay. Second, Eliot's formative "modernist" poetry and criticism, though now somewhat in eclipse, have survived more creditably the critical onslaught of our own time than Cram's "traditionalist" architecture and writing. Invoking Eliot may the more easily open for us a door into the Anglo-Catholic world view Cram would make his own and then importantly shape himself in later years.

The modernist onslaught that has so disparaged Cram will be dealt with architecturally later. Its more general religious and cultural aspect (rooted in New England anti-Catholicism) arises now. It is never more evident than in the seminal work of Van Wyck Brooks, who complained in *New England: Indian Summer* of the enervating effect of "modish high-Anglicanism" on Boston's moral and intellectual life in the era of Cram's youth, when "young men who, in Channing's day, would have proselytized the West enjoyed a romantic destiny as high-church monks."[38] It was an odd remark, so obvious and crushing is the inevitable rejoinder: one wonders if Brooks cannot have known of men like

Charles Grafton, a Harvard graduate of old Boston family and one of the three founders of the Cowley Fathers, the first monastic order established within Anglicanism, who went from the rectorship of the Church of the Advent in Boston to become a pioneering bishop on the American frontier, ministering heroically on horseback over vast and dangerous distances, and thus exactly meeting Brooks's criteria both as to monkish fantasies *and* the proselytizing of the West. Grafton, in Andrew Mead's memorable phrase, "savored of sawdust on the one hand and incense on the other."[39] Today a High Churchman might be grateful for Brooks's attack; at least it speaks to how threatening Anglo-Catholicism was in Boston in the 1890s, an aspect of the subject that dealing with Cram's conversion so coolly obscures.

But if not coolly, what? Perhaps, after all, we need to deal with Cram's conversion imaginatively, but in more contemporaneous a way. Instead of Francis Thompson, let us have recourse to Rose Macaulay.

THE WINGS OF THE MORNING

It can be said only that it is likely that Cram knew of Rose Macaulay's travel books, for there is no record that he read them. But Macaulay read Cram's books; for her confessor was Father Hamilton Johnson of the Cowley Fathers (a close friend of Cram's and probably also his confessor), and in her published letters to Johnson the subject comes up of a book of Cram's she was reading. Macaulay forthwith delivered herself of a most penetrating observation: "I am *much* interested," she wrote in 1952, "in what you say of R. A. Cram. It confirms what one gathers from his book [which shows] unbalanced and child-like enthusiasm — even fanaticism — and idealism, combined with such good architectural knowledge. . . . It is a good and vivid book."[40] It would be fascinating if she had also read Cram's autobiography, from which comes the description just quoted of his conversion, because I believe Macaulay can help us to understand that conversion experience through her own best-known book — *The Towers of Trebizond*, a minor classic of the Anglo-American/Anglo-Catholic world view.

Laurie, the book's principal character, who is of indeterminate gender, is drawn strongly to what has been a lifelong Anglican religious heritage but as strongly away from it by a long-standing but problematic sexual relationship (we now know Macaulay's own life situation is reflected).[41] Throughout, the protagonist is repeatedly confronted not only by this relationship's consequences but by the analogous locale of the book, the old Byzantine capital of Trebizond, a minor Turkish port today, whose personality is redolent of the sort of lost causes we shall observe time and again Cram found so attractive and invigorating.

Macaulay describes the town in terms equally aesthetic and erotic; its spirit is still to be found in its ruined palaces and churches in the largely deserted hills above the harbor. There, she writes, they brood, "forlorn, lovely, ravished and apostate," each "still a lovely, haunting, corrupt and assassinating ghost," drawing Laurie repeatedly because "hidden in the town and its surroundings there was something I wanted . . . something exiled and defeated, but still alive, known long since and forgotten"[42]—a passage strikingly similar to that from *Brideshead Revisited*, also a conversion story, quoted at the head of Chapter 1.

Noting that "in the Middle Ages this famous but remote Byzantine city had been much addicted to magic and full of notorious wizards," and that even though the Turks "had driven it underground, . . . it still survived in corners among pseudo-Turkish Greeks who turned an honest lira by selling fair winds to fishing-boats . . . and making up love potions,"[43] Macaulay describes in a remarkable passage the result of her protagonist's twilight encounter with a sorcerer's potion; an encounter that yields an experience comparable to Cram's at midnight Mass in Rome but more accessible to us. For we are dealing, in the case of Cram's conversion, and according to his lights not with belief or conviction producing faith, but with grace, a gift freely received, acceptance of which by a person so predisposed documents Newman's teaching that "belief will follow action."[44] (Indeed, C. S. Lewis went so far as to describe the early stages of his own conversion under the title "Let's pretend.")[45]

Macaulay's recounting of Laurie's experience of grace is also very much in the key one suspects Cram himself might have used to describe his conversion experience (had he done so) in *Black Spirits and White*—though it is, of course, typical of Cram's mask-and-signal technique that he did not.

Wrote Macaulay:

The evening was very warm and still. . . . I was sitting in the banqueting hall . . . the four high walls were glorious with bright frescos of emperors and saints and Christ. . . . [The emperor was] sitting on his jewelled throne. Courtiers stood about . . . ecclesiastics with long Byzantine faces sat together, disputing with hieratic gestures about the aphthartocathartic heresy. . . . Marble pillars supported the starry roof; marble porticoes were seen dwindling in graceful perspective into the golden-fruited orchard and balsam-sweet woods. . . . Through open doors one saw other frescoed rooms, the chapel, the library, the audience hall, and beyond them a great range of towered walls swept down to the ravine. Through the windows I saw the circle of the Circassian mountains, indigo and brown and peach-pink in the sunset, and down the slopes a caravan of camels wound with their packs from the east. On the other side a fleet of cargo ships lay in the bay. On divans in the banqueting hall tall princesses reclined, and slaves knelt before them with palm-frond ferns. In one corner of the hall a young man sat playing chess with an ape, which brooded over its moves like a man, and chattered its teeth in anger when it lost a piece. . . .

73

The chatter died away to murmurs and became the voices of the sorcerer and his wife and the mutter of the long grass in the evening breeze.

The sorcerer asked me if I had had good dreaming, and I said I had.[46]

The climactic scene soon follows: a fierce attack of the sort Christians today especially (and no doubt rightly) are apt to make. Laurie is told in no uncertain terms that it will *not* do; that it is wrong that the church should be

"an opiate . . . a kind of euphoric drug. You dramatized it and yourself. . . . I know you read Clement of Alexandria: . . . 'We may not be taken up and transported to our journey's end, but must travel thither on foot, traversing the whole distance on the narrow way.' One mustn't lose sight of the hard core, which is, do this, do that, love your friends, and like your neighbours, be just, be extravagantly generous, be honest, be tolerant, have courage, have compassion, use your wits and your imagination, understand the world you live in and be on terms with it, don't dramatize and dream and escape."[47]

The point is, however, at this, the very outset of Cram's religious life, that it is likely that Cram, though sincere, *was* escaping, even if he was not dreaming. Certainly he was dramatizing, just as in *Black Spirits and White*. And of this early stage of belief, it may well be that we should say of Cram, if not Lewis's "let's pretend," then what Robert Crunden has said of Santayana, who, he thought (in this case all his life),

found in religion, broadly understood, perhaps the greatest work of the human imagination, something of far more value than anything generated by what is so casually assumed to be the "real" world. Just as he loved great poetry and great art, Santayana loved religion. . . . It was a great fairy tale of the conscience.[48]

Fairy tales and ghost stories, after all, are not dissimilar. Nor are they unworthy of profundity. I should like at this point to recall the observation Albert Camus made somewhere that "a man's work is nothing but a slow trek to rediscover, through the detours of art, those two or three great and simple images in whose presence his heart first opened." In what Cram called in his memoirs "the cold gloom and the mental depression of that Roman winter,"[49] Cram — in the Anglo-Catholic world view of things — had met not only Henry Randall but Jesus Christ.

However long the theme of "let's pretend" may have persisted for Cram (religion was to be for him the work of a lifetime), the fact is that in Cram's case belief *did* follow action, the reward, perhaps, for the brave; for action is always risky, though always necessary. And as in Cram's life, so in his art. Cram's conversion experience was, after all, *aesthetic* in the extreme. With great acuteness Jackson Lears has written:

Cram's aesthetic emphasis betrayed a new relation between art and morality. He departed from the conventional insistence that art must justify itself as uplift. In his
view, one did not proceed from absolute moral principles to an evaluation of art. Instead, one reversed the procedure: aesthetic judgments preceded and shaped moral
judgments. Beauty was an infallible gauge of moral worth.

Cram's developing outlook undergirded aestheticism, Ruskinian moralism, and
Platonic idealism with Anglo-Catholic theology. . . . He felt Anglo-Catholicism preserved the emotional legacy of the medieval church.[50]

That last aspect was, of course, the work again to no little extent of Henry
Vaughan, who was as important to Cram's experience of Europe as was Randall. Cram most clearly saw the glorious Catholic past (above all in Italy) with
the young Southern architect; but he had also seen the work in England of the
modern British Gothicists Vaughan had pointed him toward, and it was surely
the shock of the Catholic past that drove home to Cram the potential of the
Catholic future he was through architecture to make his own. Art and religion.
Old and new. Back in Boston, Cram wasted no time in beating a path to the door
of Vaughan's — and soon to be his — parish church.

Europe had been very much a breakthrough. As Freud so well observed, to
my mind pretty accurately with respect to Cram's situation on his return to
Boston:

> An artist is originally a man who turns away from reality because he cannot come
> to terms with the renunciation of instinctual satisfaction which it at first demands,
> and who allows his erotic and ambitious wishes full play in the life of phantasy. He
> finds the way back to reality, however, from this world of phantasy by making use
> of special gifts to mould his phantasies into truths of a new kind.[51]

CHRISTIAN SOCIALISM

In the Boston to which Cram returned in the summer of 1888, Edward Bellamy's just published and enormously influential national bestseller, *Looking
Backward: 2000–1887*, was all the rage. Perhaps the most celebrated of American utopian novels of the period, Bellamy's book (published by Ticknor) "contrasts the strangled souls of contemporary Boston," in Barbara Hobson's and
Paul Wright's words, "with the perfect Socialist state of Boston in the year
2000."[52] And Pinckney Street's Bohemians were naturally among the vanguard
of people enrolled in this cause.

Fred Day, for example, certainly had distinctly erotic reasons for haunting
the South End, but they did not exhaust the matter. *The Arena*, a Boston reform
journal of the period much concerned with slum life, was widely read, and
Robert A. Woods, the author of a book about Boston's poor, *The City Wilder-*

ness, that Hobson and Wright call "the first published scientific study of a poverty area in America,"[53] opened South End House in an effort to do something about it in 1895. Cram, having returned home fired with two causes—Anglicanism and architecture—found in the atmosphere of the time that he was being drawn out in more than one way: he was becoming not only Catholic but socialist. To be sure, his socialism was perhaps more Franciscan than Marxist; but it was also a reflection of concerns that were to be long-lasting; as we will see in Volume Two, by the 1930s Cram would be as well known to the American public as a social thinker—and disciple of Franklin Delano Roosevelt—as he was as an architect.

It is not clear whether Cram's socialist interests proceeded from his newfound Anglo-Catholicism (upon his return from Europe he had placed himself under instruction at the Cowley Fathers' Mission Church of St. John the Evangelist on Beacon Hill, where he came especially under the influence of Father Arthur Crawshay Hall), or whether he himself took the lead in this respect on Pinckney Street. Rather, William Ordway Partridge stood out in Cram's circle as seeking to bring together a group of men who were not only "artistic" but "progressive" (that is, socialist) and were "deeply stirred," in Edwin Mead's words, by the English Fabian Society essays and Bellamy's book; "all things," Mead continued, "considered dangerous by some of our proper [Boston] folk."[54]

A little group of Bellamy's disciples formed in Boston the Cold Cut Club, of which Partridge was probably a member (Cram may have been, too); Partridge's idea being, again in Mead's words, to establish "a center of a somewhat Bohemian character, where they could get together for simple good cheer, good dreaming and good talk."[55] That it was related to the Pinckney Street group is suggested not only by its Bohemian character but also by the fact that when the club was started it was called the XXth Century Club, surely not coincidentally the name as well of Cram's and Partridge's and Berenson's failed art review of 1887. (Eventually it resulted in the Boston City Club, "progressive" enough that in later years both Sidney Webb and Keir Hardie spoke there when visiting Boston.) Perhaps, also, Partridge's plans were seconded among Boston's aesthetes by Charles Eliot Norton, not for nothing so close to Ruskin; Norton ran a night school in his youth for the Cambridge poor and both planned and raised the money for worker housing in Boston.)[56]

In his memoirs Cram did link his socialist leanings to his conversion:

> Father Hall was preaching Anglo-Catholicism in [St. John's] on Bowdoin Street, and Father [William B.] Frisby at the Church of the Advent was doing the same.... Christian socialism came over from England and some of us even hired a vacant shop on Boylston Street and tried to start a "Church of the Carpenter" that was to follow the Catholic religion but combine with it a socialism that could but appeal to the working classes—which it conspicuously did not.[57]

The Church of the Carpenter Cram writes of here (which another early member recalled was not on but off Boylston Street, in an "Upper Chamber" on an alley called Boylston Place, then as now occupied by the Tavern Club), though it was an Episcopal church, was a decidedly unconventional one. The same could also be said of its founding rector, William Dwight Porter Bliss, who Bernard Markwell, in *The Anglican Left*, calls the "most famous Anglican social reformer in the history of the American [Episcopal] Church," and whose Church of the Carpenter "prefigured the more comprehensive ecumenical outlook of . . . the twentieth century." A graduate of Phillips Academy, Amherst College, and the Hartford Seminary, a disciple (as we saw in Chapter 1 Edward Carpenter had been) of the great Church of England Christian Socialist Frederick Denison Maurice, Bliss was a convert, subsequently ordained to the Episcopal priesthood, who organized in Boston in 1889 the first Christian Socialist Society in America, at the same time founding its journal, *The Dawn*. Bliss was its editor, as he also was of the *American Fabian*, and wrote as well a number of controversial books, including *The Communism of John Ruskin*. The Church of the Carpenter reflected these interests. It was, in fact, as much socialist as Episcopalian, and distinctly radical.[58]

Perhaps it is best understood through the work of Vida Dutton Scudder, like Cram one of Bliss's first disciples, unlike Cram a lifelong Marxist. A niece of sometime *Atlantic* editor Horace Scudder and also of E. P. Dutton, founder of the New York publishing house, Vida Scudder was one of a number of unmarried women in Boston marriages (another was Katharine Lee Bates, author of "America the Beautiful") who taught in this era at Wellesley College. A graduate of Smith College and possibly the first American woman to study at Oxford, Scudder was deeply moved by the powerful lectures she heard there given by Ruskin. It was his social thinking that Scudder helped to activate in the New World in the late 1880s and 1890s when (rather in the way that Norton and Cram were interested in workers' housing) she was a key figure in the founding of Denison House in Boston's South End, one of the earliest settlement houses in America.[59]

Scudder's involvement in the Church of the Carpenter reflected as equally formidable an interest in Anglicanism as in socialism, so much so that in *No Place for Grace* Lears compares her beliefs to Cram's own. Although Scudder, like Bliss, was more radical than Cram and attempted, in Lears's words, "to wed Catholicism with Marxism,"[60] she also, like Cram, formed more conventional Anglican associations with the Cowley Fathers and the Order of the Holy Cross (the first American religious order for men, established in 1884). The founder of Holy Cross, Father James O.S. Huntington, furthermore, was, Scudder recalled, "intimately connected" with her and Cram's Cowley mentor, Arthur Hall.[61]

These more conventional Anglican associations ought not to be misunderstood as necessarily less progressive; or the fact that Cram resigned in 1891 from the Church of the Carpenter after an unspecified disagreement with Bliss, who, if he was more radically socialist, was also much more Low Church than Cram. The Cowley Fathers themselves were involved with social issues. Of Father Hall's own ministry to Boston's emerging gay subculture we shall shortly have much to say. It was also Hall who urged the erection (and staffing by Cowley) of St. Augustine's Mission for Negroes on Beacon Hill, quite near Pinckney Street, where the first black priest in the Episcopal church in Boston was ordained in 1894.[62]

Jackson Lears, one of the few to notice this apparently less conservative aspect of Anglo-Catholicism, has written:

> The most successful Cowley Fathers were two Englishmen, Arthur C. A. Hall and Charles Neale Field. Hall . . . widened [the order's] concerns to include the back streets and slums near his Bowdoin Street church, where he organized reading rooms and liturgical festivals for the poor. . . . Sometimes naively paternalistic, Field [who founded a guild that backed labor unions and shorter work weeks] and Hall tried hard to wed traditional monastic asceticism and the nineteenth-century humanitarianism of the nascent social gospel.[63]

This was evident even to Oliver Wendell Holmes, who noted approvingly in the *Atlantic*, a journal hardly sympathetic to such as Cowley in the ordinary way, that St. John's, Bowdoin Street, was "a church with open doors, with seats for all classes and all colors alike." And it was the more effective and welcoming for its aesthetics; Holmes particularly noted the antiphonal singing: "their holy song floated from side to side . . . like a flight of birds that passes from one grove to another."[64] Probably it was this unusual alliance of a more moderate socialism with a higher, more aesthete churchmanship that drew Cram away from the Church of the Carpenter to an involvement with the Cowley Fathers that would become for him a lifelong commitment.

Catholicism, socialist or not, was one thing. Architecture was another altogether. Setting up in independent practice is a risky endeavor at any time, and the more so for someone like Cram, who, unlike Arthur Rotch, for instance, was not well off. But Cram did have a name, thanks to the *Transcript*, with which he could hope to attract a following. In 1889, at the age of twenty-five, he entered the Episcopal church in ceremonies at St. John's, Bowdoin Street.[65] In the same year he returned to the drafting board.

ARCHITECTURE RECLAIMED

Cram chose to launch himself professionally by entering yet another competition, this time for a gigantic block-long extension (eventually designed by

23. Cram's perspective of his design for the Massachusetts State House extension, 1888–89.
He won second prize.

Charles Brigham) to the venerable old Massachusetts State House. Again, though the design is bombastic to our eyes, Cram proved his worth (23). He won second prize[66]—the sum of thirteen hundred dollars, with which he not only paid off the accumulated debt of his lengthy stay in Europe but started his own architectural office: Cram and Wentworth, the first incarnation of a firm that would become world-famous. The name first appeared in April 1889 on the door of Room 60 of the Park Building at 2 Park Square in Boston, just across the Common from Beacon Hill.[67]

Room 60 was not impressive (it was only eight by twelve feet), nor were its furnishings (a drawing board, a high stool, a desk, and a chair), but it was inexpensive at only $29.17 a month. Its occupants, we know, were rather casual in their ways. Jack, Cram's devoted bull terrier, was much in evidence. And we know, too, that Ralph Adams Cram and his new partner, Charles Francis Wentworth, were if anything more trouble than the dog: "You keep the door of your office open into the hall constantly," their landlord complained to them, "which allows [your] tobacco smoke . . . to be driven through the building."[68] One knows what two young men would do with such a letter.

Especially Charles Wentworth (24). His partnership with Cram came about in a way that for once Cram detailed exactly. "I considered myself," Cram recounted, "as the designing factor in a putative architectural firm [in need of a] practical partner." But it says worlds for Cram and his circle that he had to admit, "Personally, I knew no one who would fill the bill."[69] The sort of people Cram had taken up with in his *Transcript* years would hardly do, and Cram was not likely to have sought what would have been a very frustrating junior partnership with Vaughan. Nor did he seem to have considered Randall, perhaps because his Southern friend was more drawn to New York, where Randall later opened his own office. What Cram needed was a *junior* partner; a *business* partner, moreover; and if possible a rich one; a tall order to fill for an aesthete art critic, and he learned of Wentworth only when he "was casually walking by the art store where [an acquaintance] was employed and consulted him on a sudden impulse."[70] He was told that Wentworth, a draftsman at Andrews and Jacques, might be just the man. And so it proved.

Cram came to think the world of Charles Wentworth, eventually naming his only son not Ralph Adams but Ralph Wentworth Cram. And after his first partner's death, he allowed quite frankly that without Wentworth he doubted

if I should ever have accomplished anything. Hard-headed,—even, so to speak, hard-boiled,—he was an unusual combination of sterling good sense, practical ability, keen judgment of men and things, and genuine enthusiasm for and appreciation of good architecture. He made no pretense to artistic ability, but he was a sound, fearless and reliable critic. If I started to go wild along any line he pulled me back; if I lost courage because of some casual adversity he pulled me together. . . . Withal, he had the most generous and charming personality, and a matchless sense of humor; he worked like a dog to build up the firm of Cram and Wentworth—and did it, by the sheer force of his own strong character and rigid integrity.[71]

The records of the firm now explored—including the partners' correspondence, for Wentworth traveled a good deal—more than bear out Cram's praise. That Wentworth was both critic and businessman is clear: "What do you mean by concrete and terra cotta?" he demanded of Cram, for example; "is it possible you have the nerve to use concrete walls with steel posts for roof trusses? That would be nervy. Write me all about it." Regarding another aspect, he wrote about Cram's plans:

Why is a window shown from kitchen into cloister and who in Hell is the Sacristan that he should have two rooms and how do you expect to move your foul air into the vent as shown on the plans? . . . Look out for this, Ralph. Make a false roof . . . and take out the foul air through the tower, you will be dead sure then. Barring the above, I think the whole thing fine and the widening of the aisles betrays ingenuity.[72]

24. Charles Wentworth. "I have never met, in forty-
five years," Cram recalled in his autobiography,
"another man who could have been so perfect a
balance-wheel for a certain congenital fantasy that
has often threatened to be my Nemesis."

Such a bristling impatience with Ralph's practical inadequacies, coupled
with so great an enthusiasm over his design creativity, speaks well of Cram's first
partner, documenting as it does exactly the strengths and weaknesses Ralph
Adams Cram would disclose all his life in the profession to which he had now,
on the eve of the nineties, finally committed himself.

3

THE PRAYER IS GRANITE

Architectural meaning . . . originates in the erotic impulse itself, in the need to quench our physical thirst . . . the effect of architecture is always beyond the purely visual, evoking the memory and expectation of erotic fulfillment. . . . Architectural meaning, like erotic knowledge, is primarily of the body. . . . Architecture is a verb rather than a noun. . . . The individual imagination of the architect with its capacity to construe history as it might have been and imagine a possible future remains the only true [meaning], one that must be implemented in the art of making.

— Alberto Pérez-Gómez, *Polyphilo, or the Dark Forest Revisited:*
An Erotic Epiphany of Architecture

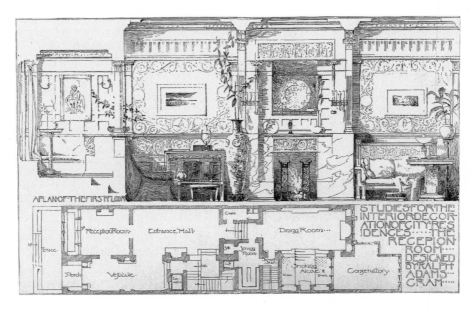

25a, b. Cram's sketches of his designs for his *Decorator and Furnisher* articles of 1885–1887
show his architectural tastes a few years prior to his founding of Cram and Wentworth. Most of
his sketches are very Richardsonian in feeling (*above*, a library), while a few attempt (in Cram's
words, explaining his reception room elevation, *below*) "to combine the vigor of the new
[Richardsonian] Romanesque with the purity and formalism and lineal beauty of the Greek."

AMONG Ralph Adams Cram's earliest memories was an almost Proustian sense of time past, an imaginative capability that even in adolescence was paralleled by his eye for the "art of making." In his earliest years as a practicing architect, somewhat at the mercy of contractors and craftsmen (especially as supervising construction was never Cram's forte), Cram's work can be disappointing; much more "temporary" wooden than stone tracery, for instance. Slowly, however, Cram accumulated the people (beginning with Wentworth) and the experience necessary, so that both his sense of the past and his eye for making had a practical effect.

About the former he wrote:

> As I look back over long years, it seems to me that almost my earliest recollection is of "The Old Place," as it was always called, and of . . . Ira Blake of Kensington. . . . My grandfather was in a sense the last of the squires.
>
> In this he represented more than a social episode, for the squirearchy of England, and of New England, was the last phase of that feudalism that came into existence as a social necessity after the fall of the Roman Empire of the West . . . and was the social basis of Medieval civilization for a thousand years.[1]

Having thus rooted his childhood memories virtually in time immemorial, Cram went on to write of the pastness of the house (the long East Room with "the solemn tall clock in one corner and in another the cupboard with its old china and pewter and its cut glass decanters") as both time past and time present, a continuum. After all, every Thanksgiving feast of his youth took place in that long room. And what Cram most remembered of the Old Place was the way the house was the "personification of its master"[2]—a most interesting observation, since, the house being so much older, one might have expected him to say the reverse.

As he grew up, it was noticed that Ralph also possessed an eye for the shape of things; his daughter remembered that it was said of him by Hampton Falls oldtimers that as a boy, though small of stature, Cram "had the reputation of being the best hay-stacker." Inevitably, perhaps, old hands were heard to say in the days of his fame (when, for instance, he was on the cover of *Time* magazine in 1928) that Ralph "built his cone-shaped stacks with as clear an eye as a boy as later he built church or cathedral."[3]

Cram also early demonstrated an interest in the basics of planning, as his own childhood memories attest. (Planning and arson, actually: one of his favorite pastimes being, in his own words, "the arranging of dried potato tops in streets and squares and alleys and then, with a good wind blowing, starting a fire in one place and playing the part of Nero.")[4] There were even childhood activities that combined mass and plan, described by Cram in his autobiography, where he remembered that he

> used to take the pictures of dwellings of various sorts out of *Harper's Weekly* and *Frank Leslie's*, . . . and then try to work out a plan to fit the perspectives. This I would do on the floor of the attic, working on the back of rolls of unused wallpaper. Also, I invented a game that absorbed me for long periods: I would cut out the pictures of all sorts of buildings . . . and then, with stiffeners of pasteboard and the utilization of many pins, arrange these in streets and squares on the broad shelves of an ancient cheese-safe. . . .
>
> In the year 1878 [at age fifteen] my father and mother gave me "House Building" by C. J. Richardson. . . . I shudder to think what might have been the result had the book chosen been Batty Langley, or Hobbs, or Wheeler. [Richardson's] was a different work indeed, for it contained many illustrations of old English manors and cottages and some not too bad modern houses and churches. . . .
>
> I fed on this book, made plans for the exteriors and exteriors for the plans . . . and all the while I was studying [Ruskin's] "The Stones of Venice" and "The Seven Lamps of Architecture" with avidity.[5]

In the pages of Cram's diary of the mid-1880s, which we have already consulted, he sustained this focus on domestic design, putting down the principles he was absorbing in his reading and apprenticeship: "on the exterior [of a house] there should be one principal feature or group which should govern the rest . . . [and] emphasize the more important part of the house. . . . [A house should] depend on the surrounding landscape; the color also."[6] And so on, in earnest enough colloquy that he did not neglect in the case of the dining room even the design of the china! Moreover, as be began to be published, he continued the discussion in print; chiefly in *The Decorator and Furnisher*, for which, in the years just after he left the *Transcript*, he wrote and illustrated in 1885–1887 an extended treatise on practical design in residential architecture that was not nearly so inadequate as he thought at the time.[7]

Focusing on the interior decoration of city houses, Cram laid down rules after the manner of Oscar Wilde in his lectures on "The House Beautiful," given in America in 1882 and surely known to Cram (whether or not he heard Wilde in Boston, he would certainly have read of them in the newspapers). Wilde's lectures offered very specific principles: for reasons of cleanliness, entrance halls should be tiled, not carpeted; in aid of intimacy, central chandeliers should be avoided in favor of side brackets; small windows were to be preferred as less likely to lead to glare; and so on.[8] And Cram was equally specific. Having decided to become a practicing architect, he by no means intended to give up his career as critic and polemicist. The sketches with which he illustrated his articles (*25a, b*) were skillful enough, and he was a good writer; he knew that he possessed the invaluable asset of being able to get the thing, as it were, coming and going: having on the printed page convinced people *what* to build, who better to build it? Time and again throughout his career he would create the need at his writing desk that he then met at his drafting board. It was fundamental to his success.

AMERICAN PLAIN SHAVIAN

Once he began practicing architecture, however, Cram proved less interested in the decoration of houses and more in their overall shapes and sinews, and in the larger questions that lay behind such concerns, both architectural and social, questions Cram's heroes also devoted themselves to; not only Ruskin and Morris but even Oscar Wilde, who, somewhat under the influence of Bernard Shaw, had allowed in his *Soul of Man under Socialism* that "aestheticism must deal with social and political ideas."[9] (Walter Crane was even more specific in the *Atlantic* in 1891, for which he wrote an article entitled "Why Socialism Appeals to Artists.")[10]

Cram took this line from the first, most conspicuously in 1895, when he published proposals in *The Brickbuilder* for workers' cottages. Arguing for the benefits of brick rather than frame construction, Cram urged not only architectural reform (brick was wisest because of sanitation and protection against fire and such), but societal reform, too; he opined: "Houses have more mental and spiritual effect on their tenants than we are willing to acknowledge."[11]

Cram and Wentworth's first realized work was, in fact, working-class housing. In Cram's words: "the first job I had on my own was making a two-family house out of a one-family house [a] saloon-keeper had in Somerville." Elsewhere, Cram refers to this historic project less picturesquely as "remodeling a tenement house in Brighton."[12] Regardless of which working-class suburb it was in, the job was for a wholesale liquor dealer by the name of Lee Hammond, who put into Cram's hands the first coin of the realm taken in by the firm, according to its earliest account books. But hardly any record and less knowledge of this work survive. And, as it turned out, a series of much grander commissions for country and seaside houses effectively launched Cram's career as an architect, the result of tireless opportuning of family and friends in the firm's behalf by Charles Wentworth's then fiancée, Marion Whittemore. Cram, who as he approached thirty still had no wife of his own to fulfill this traditional role, had chosen his partner well, no small asset in an architectural center like

Boston, from which many novice architects decamped as soon as possible because it was then as now very competitive. Just how much so is illustrated by the outcome of one of Cram's earliest, possibly the first, commissions to design and erect a fully new house—for the Buffalo businessman for whom he had designed wallpaper, George Birge.

At about the time Cram and Wentworth got going, another firm, Little and Brown, also set up in business, formed by one of Wentworth's ex-fellow draftsmen at Andrews and Jacques, Herbert Brown, and Arthur Little, who, with their mutual friend Ogden Codman, were christened—such was to be their influence—the "Colonial trinity." It was a formidable combination. Little, particularly, the designer in the 1880s of a series of brilliant Colonial Revival houses, could easily be called the real-life Seymour of William Dean Howells's *Rise of Silas Lapham* (the young architect who in 1884 talks the Laphams out of brownstone and black walnut for a Colonial-style house). And as it turned out, despite multitudes of sketches and plans prepared by Cram, the mansion finally erected in Buffalo was not Old English by Cram and Wentworth but Classical Revival by Little and Brown.[13]

Cram's second project—and first church design, of which more soon—also fell through, as did more or less half the jobs that Cram and Wentworth went after. But Marion Whittemore's friend James Ide, though he failed to deliver the church job, did commission for himself a country house in Williamstown, Massachusetts, almost certainly the first complete building built to Ralph Adams Cram's design (26, 27).[14] Happily, it survives today, though it has been hitherto attributed to Stanford White.[15] But that is quite a compliment to Cram, a designer then barely twenty-six years old.

Cram shows himself in the Ide House to be a disciple of R. Norman Shaw, the British master who had all but invented the Old English or Queen Anne style, and whose "freedom and vitality"—significant words—Cram praised in *Architectural Review* in 1891.[16] (Cram's affinity for Shaw is evidenced in his diary entry, previously quoted, about "copying" not being "true art." It is an almost exact parallel to a thought of Shaw's expressed in a private letter in 1882: "Look . . . and say if it is not *copied*. . . . Is it possible this can be great art? I think not.")[17] Thus Cram indulged himself in half-timbered gables, a wood-frame Gothic porch, several groups of banked small-paned casements, and rather a stylish third-floor dormer, where the wall plane has been thrust through the roof line after the medieval fashion taken up by Shaw (at Leyswood, for example). Yet for so large and ample a house, what strikes one is how relatively few are such features.

Cram's first documented work of architecture is, in fact, under scrutiny, as reflective of his New England roots as of his Anglophile tastes. A sparse, linear

26. The half-timbered gable of the garden front of the Ide House, Williamstown, Massachusetts, designed in 1889, as it appears today. It is rather Wrightian, although the overall character of the house is more Shavian. And Cram's Gothic porch (a precursor of a classical arcade and pavilion of some years later at Sweet Briar College in Virginia) is distinctly Lutyensesque.

elegance characterizes the Ide House; it seems, as it were, to ride serenely (like an ocean liner) the crest of its gently rising greensward amid the Berkshire hills—long, crisp, shingled, and rectangular, and made longer still by the covered porch that wraps around the house almost like the promenade deck of such a liner. And that basic long, rectangular mass and its so very American living and dining porch encircling it (such porches are distinctive to the modern period and the New World), far more than any medieval motifs, shape the house's character, which might best be called "American Plain Shavian." This is espe-

27. The gable end of the Ide House of 1889, the first fully realized and purpose-built design of Cram and Wentworth, photographed in 1992. The striking step-back geometry of Cram's massing and his starkly elegant wraparound porch, though very modern in feeling, enhance the seventeenth-century New England character of Cram's sparse design.

cially evident at each end, where one sees that, for all but the central bay of this four-bay house, it is virtually only one room deep. And the gables at each end (27) are the key to the house's basic genetic code. Not half-timbered like those on the entrance and garden fronts, the end gables are instead steep, flat, and plainly shingled — severely New England (*American*, Cram would have said). Suddenly it could be 1683 Topsfield, Massachusetts, and the Parson Joseph Capen House.

Actually, even the half-timbered gables on the long facades (26) are more American in feeling than English — and more forward- than backward-looking — because these features (like the overall long, low, horizontal feeling of the Ide House) are more Wrightian in feeling than Shavian; in which connection it is only fair to Cram to notice that Frank Lloyd Wright's claim that his Moore House of 1895 at Oak Park, Illinois, was "the first time . . . an English half-timbered house ever saw a porch" documents the fact that Wright knew nothing of Cram's Ide House of 1889.[18] Though it would be enthusiastic to a degree to claim for Cram's house the first such wedding of an English half-timbered house with an American porch, the design does illustrate Cram's originality.

In many ways the seventeenth-century New England feeling of the Ide House is even more pronounced at the Parker House on Brattle Street in Cambridge, probably Cram's second work.[19] (Plans existed by September 1889.) The Parker House is not at all as generously conceived as is the Ide House, of which in a sense the Cambridge house is but a fragment. But the rather sparse and thin feeling that comes through all the more strongly in this much smaller suburban villa also calls to mind American seventeenth-century Gothic, the Parker House being so much more than the Ide House the size and scale of houses like Parson Capen's.

The location of the Parker House — Brattle Street being, along with portions of Brookline, Boston's best address then outside of the Back Bay — indicates Cram was striking the right note in the right places in both town and country. So, too, did his third house, for the seashore is ever most important of all in New England. Equally, this house, also begun in 1889, underlines how vital a force Marion Whittemore Wentworth was in launching Cram's career, for this summer "cottage," called The Ledges, was built in York Harbor, Maine, for Marion's mother, Sarah Whittemore (28–31).[20]

We are fortunate to possess what is probably Cram's initial watercolor vision of the house, the ocean front of which, though it shows a shingled house encircled by another broad porch, is very different from the Ide House or its more pinched Brattle Street progeny. All hint of the Shavian manorial style has disappeared. And it would not be too much to say that Cram's design — Shingle Style if any style, but too simple really to speak of style (unless one just calls the house

28. The Ledges (the Whittemore House), York Harbor, Maine, is one of two country houses designed in 1889 that launched the firm of Cram and Wentworth. Its massive ocean-front foundations and overall severity of design are characteristic of the earliest independent work of Cram. So is his elegant watercolor rendering of 1898.

Gothic) — declares at once, this time on a principal facade (not a gable end), the not ungraceful but very severe aesthetic that was to be most characteristic of Ralph Adams Cram. There is not even the simplest half-timbering. In fact, there is hardly any detail at all. All there is, in a sense superbly emphasizing the house's situation on a promontory rising from the Maine coast, is the tremendous stone bastion supporting the veranda. Though the house was never built in this form, alas (for whatever reason, Cram built a much less pleasing ocean front), he more than redeemed that error by an entrance front that is neither Shavian nor Shingle Style, but instead a brilliant essay in the modernist Arts and Crafts mode (29).

Everywhere, there is interest: the syncopation of the ribbon windows; the opposing curves of the triple gable window and the adjoining tower; the way the two entrance doors are stepped and also the two first-floor windows above the lower doorway. Even the smallest things reward attention — the crisp and shapely brackets between the principal floors (30), for instance. Especially felic-

92

29. The entrance front of The Ledges (*above*) as it appears today, a remarkable design for only the second significant commission of an architect in his first year of practice.

30. *Right*: the Shavian oriels and the crisply profiled brackets of the entrance front of The Ledges (in 1992).

31. Cram's brilliant dormer and chimney composition on the south front of The Ledges (in 1992).

itous is the way one of the chimneys sustains on its flank a dormer that butts bluntly into it to create a lovely geometry of opposing planes (*31*).

Above all, there are the two elegant second-floor oriels (*29, 30*), surely inspired by Shaw's highly original and much-noticed elongated oriels at the Swan House in London, finished twelve years earlier.[21] But that should not mislead anyone into thinking less of Cram. Among English architects only Sir Edwin Lutyens and C. R. Ashbee used the motif with equal panache; especially the former, at Varengeville in 1898.[22] And Shaw's biographer is wrong to think that "after Swan House and Clock House these strange, thin windows . . . for all their originality . . . had to await Lutyens for their revival."[23] In fact, two American architects experimented strikingly with Shaw's elongated oriel motif as early as 1889: Arthur Little in his additions to 75 Beacon Street in the Back Bay[24] and Cram at the Whittemore House in York Harbor. That in the matter of style as well as of clients, Little and Cram were again quick on each other's heels is interesting in itself. But what is key is to notice that Cram, not widely thought to have been a very original designer on his own in his youth, was actually doing work somewhat in Lutyens's league in 1889 and comparable to Little's, an architect known for his precocity.

There are also at York Harbor, as at Williamstown, distinctly Wrightian accents (as they now seem to us), the closest reference in the case of the Whittemore House being to Wright's McArthur House of 1892 in Chicago, to the dormers of which the profile of The Ledges' ocean-front dormer is comparable. Of course, these Wrightian accents in Cram's work would have seemed more startling before the recent scholarship on the American Arts and Crafts movement that has cast Cram and Wright in the role of anchors of the Arts and Crafts continuum, Wright at the more radical end, Cram at the more conservative. Thus linked, the work of both discloses a certain unity. If we think of my characterization of The Ledges as basically Gothic, Richard Guy Wilson's comments on that word as understood then are pertinent:

> The use of the word "Gothic" for most of the Arts and Crafts designers did not mean a specific stylistic response.... Ralph Adams Cram once called Louis Sullivan "essentially the most Gothic of all," meaning not in style but in structural expression. In a similar vein, Frank Lloyd Wright argued for "a revival of the Gothic spirit."... Wright, Cram ...[and others were] expressing their antagonism for academic design.[25]

It was an antagonism evident all along the Arts and Crafts continuum from Cram to Wright — not least in those architects between them such as Sullivan, Greene & Greene of California, and Lutyens. Clearly, moreover, when Cram started in practice he was closer to the middle of that continuum. So, too, was Wright, with whom (all unknowingly, one assumes) Cram continued throughout the 1890s and 1900s to share many interests. For example, in the *Ladies' Home Journal* series of 1901, "A Country House of Moderate Cost," to which both Cram and Wright contributed designs, Cram's entry was a house whose reception rooms surrounded a large, paved terrace that he called "a kind of outdoor living room or dining room,"[26] evidence that Cram, too, sought to open out still further the American open plan to encompass even the outdoors.

Underlying affinities are also apparent in the fact that, when Wright's work became known to him, Cram, though not uncritical (he pronounced both Sullivan and Wright geniuses but thought Wright the "less responsible genius")[27] became an admirer of Wright. Whatever in later years Cram came to think of other modernists, Wright's own work won Cram's praise as early as 1916, when in a book of which he was a coauthor, *Low Cost Suburban Homes*, Cram remarked approvingly on the way "the low stretch of the Western plains has been symbolized in the parallel lines . . . characteristic of the work of Frank Lloyd Wright," and he allocated out of the eight illustrations in his "Promise of

American House Building" one to Wright's Boynton House in Rochester, New York, and another to a house by one of Wright's disciples. In a book otherwise filled with historicist designs, Cram's Wrightian illustrations of 1916 stand out as decidedly as do what seem to us now the Wrightian accents of Cram's own designs of the 1880s. So, too, does Cram's conclusion in 1916 (reaching back some three decades to exactly the era of his first house designs we are now discussing) that architects had in the intervening "thirty years redeemed the architectural art of the housebuilder from the pit it had digged for itself in the early and awful [Eighteen] Eighties."[28]

If in the late (and presumably better) 1880s Cram shared an interest in certain ideas with Wright because of their Arts and Crafts allegiances, so did they share a love for Japanese design. (It is fascinating to note in passing that the same Bostonians who nurtured Cram's passion for Japanese art and architecture should also have shaped Wright's, according to Kevin Nute, whose recent study of the influence on Wright of the "Boston orientalists," as Nute calls Sylvester Morse, Okakura Kakuzo, Arthur Dow, and Ernest Fenollosa, emphasizes particularly that J. L. Silsbee, the Chicago architect Wright apprenticed to in the 1880s before Louis Sullivan, was a cousin of Fenollosa, with whom Silsbee grew up north of Boston in Salem, and whom Silsbee may well have introduced to Wright when Fenollosa visited Chicago during his 1886–1887 lecture tour. Wright certainly admired both Fenollosa's and Okakura's writings, and though he was never quick to acknowledge the influence on him of any architect, it is hard to believe Wright was not familiar with Cram's writings on Japanese architecture, which were widely published [in *Architectural Review* in 1898, for example, and in *House and Garden* in 1902] and also widely influential—so much so that they were brought out as a book in 1905, the year of Wright's first trip to Japan, and, indeed, reviewed the next year in *The Dial* by Frederick W. Gookin, Wright's close friend and adviser on Japanese art.)[29] Cram, as we will see later, became an authority on Japanese art and architecture, and what seems to us now rather a Wrightian "modernism" kept company with a palpable Japanese timelessness in the fourth of Cram's early houses, the Gale House of 1890 (32–33).

Alas, our luck has run out with this splendid country house built (just across a meadow from Cram's first house) in Williamstown for Ide's brother-in-law, Edward Courtland Gale; Casa Loma, as it was called, has long since burned down—a great loss. But its importance is great, as Ann Miner Daniel has observed:

> One is struck by [its] almost modern appearance. . . . The veranda is one united piece. . . . The wall is strongly felt and punctuated by small, thin windows on the first level and by bands of windows above. . . . In execution all medieval picturesqueness has disappeared. Most importantly, the tower has [also] been changed into a recti-

linear block fitting into the corner between the entrance and the back wing of the house. The windows dominate this wall and have a Japanese quality in their simple, sleek setting in dark frames. The curve of the dormer roofs owes also to Oriental influence. . . . The medieval feeling of multiplicity of parts is there, yet it is not one of a variety of forms. Here are hard, sharp angles; repetitive linear forms progressing and receding from an inner core.[30]

The large grid window of the Gale House was an idea that would appear as well in another design of Cram's later in the same year for the Fellner House on Aspinwall Hill in Brookline, though not in the published design (34). This shows a full-fledged Shavian manor of most hard and mechanical mien, grand enough, but distinctly a dim contrast to the free style of the Gale House and its progenitors. However, Cram's initial idea in watercolor for this house (35), very different, has survived.[31] One cannot know about the plan—admittedly the published design shows Cram's gifts in this respect—but the exterior design of the initial Fellner watercolor is certainly much superior to the published design, even though it is wildly picturesque and in key almost "Wagnerian Revival." And among its chief features is the two-story grid formed by what appear to be banks of shapely casements.

Some such window configuration, of course, especially on a staircase, is not uncommon in neo-Tudor houses. But by flattening out the grid at Casa Loma and bringing it hard up directly under the eaves of its own surmounting hipped roof, and then at the Fellner House by developing it more robustly, Cram persuaded all this into a form recognizable as a motif Sir Edwin Lutyens was to employ masterfully at Deanery Garden, Sonning, Berkshire—though not for another decade, Deanery Garden being built in 1901. (Actually, Lutyens on a smaller scale evolved the same motif at Orchards, Munstead, Surrey, in 1896, but still this was five or six years after the Fellner House.)[32]

Alas, maddeningly, we cannot know which Fellner House was built. It has been torn down and no photographs have come to light of the house as built. Never mind. It is enough to observe that if Cram as a young man shared several interests with Frank Lloyd Wright, he shared at least as many with Edwin Lutyens and not a few with his fellow Bostonian Arthur Little. And those perhaps deeper affinities were such that I hold, for example, that Cram's superb small wooden entrance porch at the Ide House is as Lutyensesque as anything that master ever did.

THE UNEXPECTED MANNERIST

Although Cram's literary work in the eighties and nineties could be purple enough, his architectural work, as we have seen—when not of the grandiose

32. Casa Loma, the Gale House designed in 1890, in Williamstown, Massachusetts, the third of Cram and Wentworth's early country houses. It is the only one of Cram's early houses for which contemporary photographs taken for Cram survive. One such (*above*), ca. 1891, discloses the house's curiously modern and almost Japanese feeling.

type required of monumental public buildings — tended toward simple, bold massing articulated by a severe but elegant detail, rather "modern" in feeling. Because Cram in later years hardly ever initiated any of his firm's detail, limiting himself to criticism of the ornament he left to his designing partners to develop, it is startling to discover that these early houses document his ability to conceive good detail, and one is even more taken aback by its crisp, elegant nature.

Cram did attempt here and there to give a client some at least of the ornamental pomps the era expected; the result was generally the sort of elaborate free classic detail characteristic of Rotch and Tilden's work in the early and mid-1880s, when Cram was laboring away in that drafting room. But it is infrequently successful. Far more so are such things as the stairway at The Ledges. Cram's gifts as a planner are in the first place evident in the way he conceived of both the house's front *and* back staircases as part of one unified composition (*36*). The two staircases rise next to each other from the first floor in separate

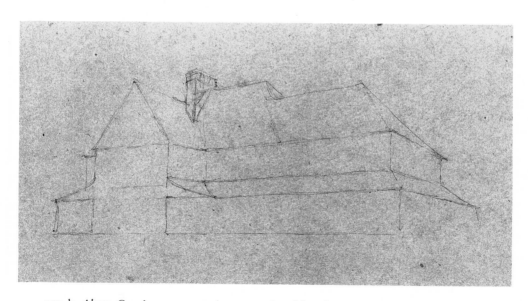

33a, b. *Above*: Cram's own presentation perspective of Casa Loma, 1890. *Below*: an example of the sort of basic sketch by which Cram thought through mass and scale, the first stage in his design process all his life. This sketch seems so much the genetic code of the perspective (*above*) that it is likely the first of Cram's sketches for Casa Loma.

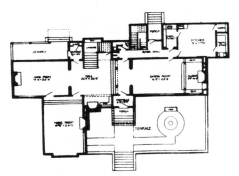

34–35. Two renderings by Cram of different schemes for Cram and Wentworth's Fellner House in Brookline, Massachusetts, designed in 1890. Most arresting is the scheme shown in the watercolor (*below*).

36. Cram's skill in thinking in three dimensions is evident in his design of 1889 for the principal staircase and parallel service staircase of the Whittemore House, seen as it appears today, somewhat restored.

halls that at the second-story level open generously into each other through a wide archway. A superb handling of spatial composition! In the second place, however, no little part is played in the overall effect by the balustrade, a striking example of the facility with minimal detail these solo house designs of Cram show. Reminiscent not only of Wright but of the work of C. F. A. Voysey and even of Otto Wagner, these balustrades could not be simpler or more delicate in their effect.

Cram's decorative gifts are particularly evident in three of his houses of 1890–1891: the Winslow House of 1890 on Beacon Street in Newton, so chaste in its detail and plain in its graces it could almost pass for a mid-1920s house; and the Merriam and Hamlin houses of 1891 on Winthrop Road in Brookline, each of considerable importance.[33]

Both Brookline houses show the exterior characteristics we have come to expect. Each is boldly massed, more or less Shingle Style, and beautifully articulated. But their interiors are of particular interest. In the Hamlin House, for example, in the dining room, the plainest possible corner cabinets, very early American in feeling (one thinks, of course, at once of the Old Place of Squire Blake), have delicately baroque scalloped edges to their shelving, while in the parlor the elongated Mannerist keystones of the overmantel could not be more justly proportioned (37). In the Merriam House next door the living-room mantelpiece is even more arresting. Here Cram is at his sparest — there are just plain, unfluted pilasters and simply profiled paneling, composed, moreover, so as to articulate yet another brilliantly conceived spatial configuration: above and below the mantel shelf (that is, the overmantel above and the brick facing around the firebox below), the front plane of the overall composition is dramatically sunk *into* the wall (38). The reverse of the usual chimney breast, here the entire design recesses rather than projects, a tour de force that may reflect in a diffident way Cram's admiration of Michelangelo's vestibule for the Laurentian Library in Florence, where that master treated his columns similarly, not projecting them from the wall, as was invariable, but recessing them. Cram had been to Florence by 1889, and even if it seems unlikely his idea had any such august pedigree as this, it is still interesting — bearing in mind our previous discussion of how both Cram and Wright used the word "Gothic" — that Erwin Panofsky, in his study of two Renaissance facades by Domenico Beccafumi, concluded that typically, in the sixteenth century, "Mannerism in architecture result[ed], to some extent, from the recrudescence of medieval tendencies within the framework of the 'Classic' style."[34] Certainly, in the nineteenth century Cram's mantel design, classical in style in a house that is itself medieval in style, is a kind of "Gothicist's classicism." It is also a modest masterpiece.

In the face of such striking detail, it is necessary to say that it was decidedly a

37. Cram's Mannerist tendencies are evident in this detail of the reception room overmantel of Cram and Wentworth's Hamlin House, Brookline, Massachusetts, designed in 1891.

mixed blessing for Cram that he landed as his first and forever after chiefly influential designing partner a decorative genius. There is no denying the seductive beauty of the firm's later ornament. Often compared with that of Louis Sullivan, it beguiled Cram as much as it does us today. But in a very real sense it also *corrupted* Cram, who, had he persevered on his own, might well have evolved a characteristic personal detail that, while it would not likely have been compared to Sullivan's, might have been to Wright's or Lutyens's.

Similarly, the various watercolor renderings by Cram reproduced here document that Ralph Adams Cram on his own was not only capable of good architectural detail but was as well a gifted renderer. Indeed, when James O'Gorman recently published some of these renderings, he was good enough to admire Cram's "impressionist's" handling and to wonder if it did not show the influence of the French-trained Arthur Rotch, suggesting that "Cram was a more accomplished artist than he has been credited" with being.[35] He was. Nor should it surprise us at this point. After all, Cram's quick, impressionist's technique in watercolor is an expression of the same characteristics we have seen in the crisp, sparse detail of Cram's solo houses. In both watercolor (as a renderer and painter) and architectural detail (as a designer), one sees Cram's restless (and distinctly modern) impatience with detail; all of which gave bite to the work by the young firm of Cram and Wentworth as seen at the Boston Architectural Club exhibition of Cram's renderings in 1890, work that cannot have left many unimpressed.[36]

38. Cram's masterful composition for the living-room mantel and overmantel of Cram and Wentworth's Merriam House, Brookline, Massachusetts, designed in 1891.

ARTISTIC APARTMENTS

Though offering much scope for a designer of Cram's proclivities, houses seem not to have sufficiently seized his imagination. Perhaps because of this and because his great passion was always for planning, Cram early on developed something of an allied specialty in what was in the 1880s and 1890s an innovative area of design where planning was of the essence — the apartment house. Here again, most of Cram's designs, such as the unidentified apartment block (or are they town houses?) Cram painted ca. 1891, were never built (39). But one such project that was carried through is of particular interest because it shows how Cram used his prominence in Boston's artistic world in aid of his newly established office.

The Grundmann Studios of 1891, located just behind the old Museum of Fine Arts in Copley Square, was intended as quarters for artists associated with the museum's school. Named after the school's first dean, it was a remodeling of a skating rink into exhibition halls and studios that became in its day, according to contemporary report, "the center of the artistic life of Boston."[37] Cram and Wentworth derived great prestige from the fact that the Grundmann was their design and that in Cram's two spacious, top-lit halls on the first floor (named Allston and Copley) Bostonians flocked to see such events as the first Arts and Crafts exhibition in the United States in 1897, the Sargent retrospective show of 1899, the 1905 Monet-Rodin exhibition, and even part of the historic Armory show of 1913.

Equally important, the thirty-four studios and residential suites upstairs were occupied by many of the city's leading artists, including William McGregor Paxton, one of the leaders of the Boston School. A great many younger artists, including three, Arthur Dow, Ethel Reed, and John Abbott, who were, as we will see, closely associated with Cram in local Bohemian circles, also lived at the Grundmann, Cram's design for which was judged at the time "a wonderful transformation [that] seems like a paradise to the artists." Each studio, raved the *Globe* in 1894, was "delightfully picturesque, with little, overhanging galleries which are reached by the tiniest flights of stairs . . . and there are the cunningest little windows divided into tiny panes."[38] Alas, no reliable illustrations of any of this survive, though when Boston's Museum of Fine Arts later moved to the Fenway and Cram's building was torn down, the Grundmann was replicated in the still extant Fenway Studios.

The same fate befell Cram's first purpose-built apartment house, The Gables in Brookline, even the memory of which over the years pretty much has vanished. Fortunately, however, Cram's design caught the eye of Louise Guiney in

39. Cram and Wentworth early developed a special interest in apartment house design, where Cram's gifts in planning were telling. Stuart Terrace Apartments, Beacon Street, Brookline, designed in 1891. The rendering is by Cram.

September 1891 ("the *Herald* cut of your Brookline apartment house," Guiney wrote Cram, "was a beauty"), and the *Boston Herald* report (since found) does indeed confirm The Gables to be another early Cram multi-unit design. Moreover, for the author of *Nine Sonnets Written at Oxford* to assure Cram, as Guiney did, that his latest work looked "as if it came out of Holywell Street, Oxford, circa 1480," whether that was an accurate reflection of Cram's sources, illustrates quite well the contemporary literary and cultural context of so much of Cram's early designs in the work of poets like Guiney.[39]

Architecturally, The Gables's significance emerges at once in the *Boston Herald* article, where it was trumpeted as a

> new idea in architecture: an artistic apartment house . . . giving the appearance of an old English country house. . . . In the designing of the exterior [the ground story was of rough cast plaster; the overhanging upper stories were half-timbered] the idea has been to remove all traces of its being an apartment house. . . . It has been studied from the early 17th century mansion of [the] southern English counties.[40]

L-shaped and set in ample lawns, this six-unit apartment block in the guise of a manor house was the beginning of a design concept that yielded within the decade Cram's nationally important prototype of the courtyard apartment house, Richmond Court (see 82).

Meanwhile, such was the success of the new firm that in 1891 the partners felt justified in hiring their first paid, full-time draftsman, Charles Alden (later a well-known Seattle architect), and in moving to the Exchange Building on State Street, the newest and quite the most prestigious building of Boston's intown financial and business district.[41] Later that year they hired a second draftsman, Frank Ferguson (eventually he would replace Wentworth as the practical and business partner, becoming the Ferguson of "Cram and Ferguson" after World War I).[42] Moreover, it was yet another mark of Cram's success in fusing his ongoing career as editor and critic with his newly taken up practice of architecture that in 1891 the designing partner of Cram and Wentworth was appointed, with C. Howard Walker, the first editor of *Architectural Review*, an almost immediately influential professional journal started in that year by Bates and Guild, publishers with whom Cram would continue to be associated to a greater or lesser extent for fully the next decade.

Institutional work, however, public or private, continued to elude Cram. This is curious, for he had won prizes in the previous five years in competitions for two of the largest institutional projects then under way in Boston, the Suffolk County Courthouse and the Massachusetts State House extension. It is true that in subsequent years Cram was inclined to depreciate the now lost courthouse design (it was, he wrote, "Richardsonian to the last degree, with towers and arcades and château roofs and vast arches with five-foot voussoirs, and all — I repeat *all* — the accepted elements in the master's style");[43] and the State House design *is* bombastic, but it was also entirely creditable in comparison with similar work of its type in the period.

It was certainly not for lack of trying that Cram and Wentworth built no such work; three designs for institutional projects not only document their efforts but disclose as well the new firm's stylistic range. That for the Seaside Club in Bridgeport, Connecticut, of 1889, is Colonial Revival (40). The second, an Odd Fellows temple in Cincinnati, Ohio, is an eclectic wonder. The third, for the Rockingham County Courthouse, Exeter, New Hampshire, includes two alternative designs, one classical and one medieval (41); thus documenting that Cram was never the hidebound Gothicist of later legend and was already in his first year of practice on his own not only designing in the Colonial style but also submitting more than one design in more than one style per job right off the bat. The medieval alternative for Exeter, which also dates from 1889, shows, too, that Cram continued faithful to Richardson and was not slow to appreciate his best and almost proto-modern work, for the Marshall Field Warehouse in Chicago, finished only two years before, was a chief inspiration for Cram's courthouse.[44]

40. Cram's sketch of one of the earliest Colonial Revival works of Cram and Wentworth: the proposed Seaside Club, Bridgeport, Connecticut, designed in 1889.

A Tower in Williamstown

One institution, of course, was of supreme interest to the new firm — the church. In fact, probably the very first designs issued by Cram and Wentworth — worked up by Cram, in all likelihood, in the fall of 1888 before he formed his partnership with Wentworth[45] — were for nothing less than the Cathedral of St. John the Divine in New York City.

Cram and Wentworth submitted two entries to this competition in early 1889, one Richardsonian Romanesque, the other Gothic (42; and see 51a); and while the former (a brazen enough echo of H. H. Richardson's design for Albany Cathedral) received little attention, Cram's Gothic submission did very well indeed for the first design by a brand-new firm making its first foray in another city and in a highly regarded national competition. According to Janet Adams Strong, six of nine board members voted for Cram and Wentworth's Gothic design on the first ballot, placing the firm in a fourth-place tie with only two other firms. Even in the second round Cram and Wentworth's entry survived, and it was one of the thirteen entries recommended by the board for evaluation by their professional architect advisers. Only at that point were Cram and Wentworth eliminated. How proud Cram must have been, in a field of some seventy entries, to have done so well and to see Cram and Wentworth's designs exhibited at the New York Architectural League in 1889 and at the Boston Architectural Club exhibition the following year.[46]

Still, it had obviously been a long shot, and, as we will see in Volume Two, the designs of Cram's maturity for this cathedral twenty years later embarrassed both these designs of 1889. As it turned out, the ecclesiastical building type that would in his earliest years stimulate Cram to creativity of the first order was not the cathedral but the village parish church, and Cram's genius was immediately aroused and evident in his striking designs of about six months later, in mid-1889, for St. John's Church, Williamstown, Massachusetts (the job James Ide did not land), which almost certainly may claim the distinction of being the first parish church design by Ralph Adams Cram (43).[47]

A primary document in the history of American architecture, this perspective shows a tower without spire, turret, buttress, or even parapet, only scant fenestration and virtually no decoration at all: crisp, severe, confident, it must

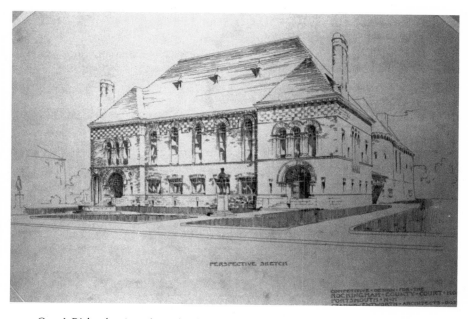

PERSPECTIVE SKETCH

COMPETITIVE DESIGN FOR THE
ROCKINGHAM COUNTY COURT HO
PORTSMOUTH NH
CRAM WENTWORTH ARCHITECTS BOS

41. Cram's Richardsonian scheme for the Rockingham County Courthouse, Portsmouth, New Hampshire, 1889, was much influenced by Richardson's Marshall Field Warehouse of 1885–1887 in Chicago.

have stunned more than one person. It seems the Marshall Field Warehouse of churches in an era when most warehouses were more picturesque in appearance. No church quite like this had ever really been seen before. Even so apparently similar a design as McKim, Mead and White's St. Paul's, Stockbridge, Massachusetts, of 1883–1885, is by comparison distinctly "Victorian" and picturesque in feeling. Cram's tower is actually more modern in appearance than either medieval *or* Victorian; and it is the first marker in his work of the design concept of the village or suburban "Cram-type" parish church, which was to become his most pervasive contribution to twentieth-century American culture.

Ann Miner Daniel's discussion of Cram's Williamstown project is worth quoting:

> Cram's first known church design has no specific English parish church as its model. Comparing it with English examples of similar size, such as the churches at Streatley, Sulgrave or Broy . . . the differences are pronounced. The tower is stark and simple.

42. Cram and Wentworth's Gothic scheme for the Cathedral of St. John the Divine in New York City, designed by Cram in 1889, was, like Cram's earlier competition entries, for the Suffolk County Courthouse and the Massachusetts State House extension, well received but finally unsuccessful.

43. The design concept of all Cram's half-century of church building in America was announced
boldly in his watercolor of 1889 of Cram and Wentworth's first church project, St. John's,
Williamstown, Massachusetts.

. . . The windows of the nave and aisles are more prominent features than in most
medieval examples because of their size and the repetition of the rectilinear shape.
The roof is interesting in the way that the various parts of the building are united by
it . . . [and shows] the influence of the Shingle Style. Cram has managed in this small
country church to combine a sense of strength and solidity with a light, open quality
by his contrast of wall and window areas.[48]

If Williamstown was the prototype of Cram's village or suburban parish
churches, the roots of the Cram-type city or town church are to be found in
another project (also published in *American Architect*), the Church of the Messiah of 1890 in Boston's Fenway section (44). As a city church, it was accordingly much more elaborate in design, but Cram's Messiah project has the same
clarity, if not the same strength of mass, as Williamstown, and shows as well
more than a little originality, especially in its tower, a worthy descendant of that
of Magdalen College, Oxford.[49] This job, too, Cram lost, to Rotch and Tilden.

Finally, around March 1890, probably through the good offices of R. Clipston Sturgis, Cram secured his first ecclesiastical commission. A young Boston

44. Cram's perspective and plan of the first city church of Cram and Wentworth's design, Boston's Church of the Messiah, designed in 1890. Its massing prefigures that of St. Thomas, Fifth Avenue, New York City.

architect and contemporary of Cram, of similar tastes but somewhat more advantageously placed professionally because he was the nephew and successor of the architect John Sturgis, Clipston Sturgis had many links to Vaughan through the Cowley Fathers and the Society of St. Margaret. He was quite supportive in the critical first few years of Cram and Wentworth's existence, writing to Cram in 1891, for example, of "the many fields of thought in which we shall be in harmony" and also agreeing to propose both Wentworth and Cram for membership in the Boston Society of Architects.[50] Overseeing the completion of the Church of the Advent after John Sturgis's death, Clipston seems to have parceled out many aspects of the work to other designers. Vaughan, for instance, was given the pulpit to design. And Cram was given the privilege of designing the credence (45) for the new high altar reredos donated by Isabella Stewart Gardner and designed by Sir Ernest George and Howard Peto.[51]

45. The first church commission actually carried through by Cram and Wentworth: the high altar credence of 1891 at Boston's Church of the Advent, visible to the right of the altar in this early twentieth-century photograph of High Mass.

Today, one is inclined to overlook this little job. Yet one can hardly help noticing, now that we have seen a good deal of his solo detail, that Ralph Adams Cram's first realized church design, if not conspicuously graceful, is nonetheless, like the detail of his houses, undeniably elegant in a very severe way. Moreover, this credence niche, though it plays a modest enough role at the Advent, would, when new, have been seen more as a creature of Gardner's huge new reredos, good company to be keeping for Cram and in so grand a place that it was not likely to be missed by Boston's small but elite Anglo-Catholic community. In fact, two prominent members of that community, who lived not far from the Church of the Advent, in 1891 brought to Ralph Adams Cram the complete commission to design and build a church he had so long and ardently sought.

That year Cram lost yet another church job—after still more labor over many plans—to Vaughan: St. Thomas, Dover, New Hampshire (see 48).[52] How it must have irked the younger man. Of course, he admired Vaughan, studied him, looked up to him, loved him for his quiet, grave, and deeply spiritual churches. But, after all, they were *English* churches, just as Vaughan was an *English* architect. And for all Cram's Anglophilia, his early work (as we have seen) was very much his own and, importantly, "American" (today, we would say "New England") in character; while Vaughan's "being in this country hardly affected or modified his work" at all, his biographer notes. Indeed, despite the fact that Vaughan had been a draftsman in the office of America's leading architect of this period, there was "almost no direct influence from Richardson."[53] Cram's first church would be very Richardsonian and very American.

OUR LADY OF ASHMONT

The Lady Chapel of All Saints', Ashmont, near Boston, is dedicated to Mary Lothrop Peabody in honor of Our Lady of Ashmont, as the celebrated figure of the Virgin by Johannes Kirchmayer over the altar is called. For it was Mary Peabody and her husband, Oliver,[54] the first of a long line of princely benefactors (extending eventually to the Browns of Providence and the Mellons of Pittsburgh), who commissioned All Saints', Cram's first church. It is a conversion story hardly less dramatic than Cram's.

"Rachel, weeping for her children, and would not be comforted, because they are not": that was the text of the sermon of All Saints' first rector on a stormy Holy Innocents Day in December 1879, when the Peabodys, on the way from their Milton estate to church in Boston, were stranded by a snow squall near the modest wooden mission chapel of All Saints'. The more eloquent for them because the rector had himself lost a daughter at an early age, his sermon deeply moved Oliver and Mary Peabody, who not long before had lost their only child. A small beginning, a type almost of a medieval miracle story, from it grew a commitment by the Peabodys that led to their conversion to Anglo-Catholicism in 1882 and culminated—for Oliver was a founder of Kidder, Peabody and Company, one of the leading investment banks of America—in the Peabodys' virtually building a new All Saints' Church and endowing it lavishly.

There was, in the first place, a family history of such things. Mary Peabody's father, Samuel Kirkland Lothrop, Boston's preeminent Unitarian divine, had in the early 1870s commissioned Richardson to design that architect's first important church, the Brattle Square Church in Boston's Back Bay. (When one notes in how many towns across America two of the leading churches are respectively Richardsonian Romanesque and Cram Gothic, it is fascinating that one man and his daughter should have played so key a role in launching both styles.) In the second place, the Peabodys themselves had much in common with Cram; not only had Colonel Peabody attended Phillips Exeter Academy, as had Cram's father, but both Oliver and Mary were, like Cram, children of Unitarian ministers who shared the Anglo-Catholic conversion experiences detailed here. That must have been decisive.

The logistics we can only guess. There was what could be called an architectural context. John Sturgis, the architect of the Advent, turns out to have been the designer of both the Peabodys' Commonwealth Avenue town house and their Milton Hill country house, and his nephew, Clipston, who as we have seen endowed Cram with his first ecclesiastical commission, at the Advent, was in the matter of All Saints' a logical adviser to the Peabodys.[55] So, too, was Henry Vaughan.

There was also a more strictly religious context. Anglo-Catholicism in Boston in the 1880s had not only a somewhat socialist but also a somewhat parallel medical aspect. The first superintendent of Boston's Children's Hospital (in 1869) was Deaconess Adeline Tyler, who was closely associated with the Church of the Advent in the effort "to make a Unitarian enterprise [as the hospital originally was] an Episcopal work and keep it out of Papal [i.e., Roman Catholic] clutches," a task taken over by the Anglo-Catholic sisters of St. Margaret in 1871, when the opportunity to staff the hospital brought them from England to Boston. And from 1883 on, Mary Peabody was a trustee of the hospital's convalescent home, while Oliver Peabody eventually became president of the hospital board.[56] Thus began an intimate relationship between the Peabodys and the Society of St. Margaret, with which Cram's friends Clipston Sturgis and Henry Vaughan were both so closely linked.

In fact, either Vaughan or Sturgis likely showed the Peabodys Cram's already published design (*48a*) for a village church. Certainly Cram's Ashmont

ALL SAINTS CHURCH
DORCHESTER MASS
Cram Wentworth & Goodhue
Architects State Street Boston

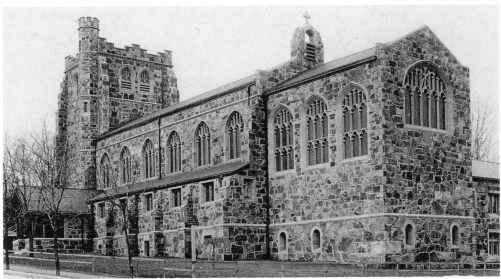

46a, b. The accepted preliminary design by Cram and Wentworth for All Saints', Ashmont, near Boston (*above*: from the southwest). Cram's perspective of 1891, with figures and lettering added later, includes the firm's new name of 1892, Cram, Wentworth and Goodhue, under which the All Saints' plans were published and the church itself erected in 1892–1894. *Below*: All Saints' as built.

design (*46a*), begun by the summer of 1891, proceeds in nearly every respect from that design. One can almost hear Cram's earnest proposal to the Peabodys; Gothic was not dead, only moribund; here was begun the high task of taking up again the thread of its development. The history of the Gothic Revival-according-to-Ralph ensued, and was repeated in Cram's essay accompanying the published plans of All Saints'. It is worth quoting from at length, as put in Cram's later *Church Building*:

> Everything stopped [after Wren], and for a century and a half religious architecture was nonexistent. What our ancestors did in America was only crude imitation. . . . The next phase was the first flush of the great Gothic Restoration. Unfortunately, however, this was with us only an episode, though the work done by its great advocates, Upjohn and Renwick, deserved better things. But as in England, so here. There the Pugins, with their sensitive appreciation of architecture as a living thing, had been succeeded by the masters of archaeology, Scott, Street and Pierson; and the Gothic Revival went backward. Here, Upjohn gave place to the practitioners of "Victorian Gothic." . . . The deplorable chaos that followed was lightened only by the . . . influence of Richardson, with his enormous vitality. . . . But his was an alien style, with no historic or ethnic propriety; its virtue was the virtue of its advocate alone; and with his death the fatal weakness of Romanesque became apparent. . . .
>
> In the meantime the steady and noble work of Bodley and Garner and Sedding had borne fruit in England. Victorian Gothic was suppressed, and continuity was restored with the original movement begun by [A. W.] Pugin . . . . Mr. Henry Vaughan came to America as the apostle of the new dispensation.[57]

And then there was Cram. And the Peabodys.

HAVE WE A RUSKIN AMONG US?

Notwithstanding this query, under which, according to Cram, one of his early effusions to the *Transcript* had been published, in his design of All Saints', Ashmont, Cram could not have more pointedly ignored that master. After all, in the preface to the second edition of *Seven Lamps of Architecture*, Ruskin had scorned Perpendicular and urged on neo-Goths the thirteenth-century Northern style.[58] All Saints', of course, is notably Perpendicular. Cram also rejected Ruskin's insistence that detail was key. All Saints' has almost none. Cram made a most persuasive case for this contrariness in the small booklet announcing All Saints'. There, having already ignored Ruskin, he also ignored Augustus Welby Pugin, whose assertion that "Christian architecture had gone its length" by the Reformation and that "it must necessarily have destroyed itself thereafter"[59] Cram was having nothing of. Instead, he argued that Gothic was

> neither a temporary phase not yet a sequence of episodes; it was a tendency, a progress, a development through various inevitable conditions to a certain point when,

not by reason of its consummation, not through its decay, but by a violent and sudden revolution [the Reformation], its wonderful career was terminated, half its possibilities undeveloped, half its glories unachieved.

Modern Gothicists, Cram concluded, should "go back to the sixteenth century, not to endeavor to build churches that shall pretend to have been built in that century," but, rather, in order that modern designers might then "work steadily and seriously towards something more consistent with our temper and the times in which we live." Hence, Perpendicular was the logical point of departure.[60]

Pugin, of course, was long dead and Ruskin far away. But Cram, charging ahead in his usual way, was certainly politic enough to seek out the opinion of Ruskin's closest American friend and mentor, and Charles Eliot Norton was clearly replying to such a query early in 1892, when he wrote to Cram that "the design [of All Saints'] seems to me well thought-out and pleasing." Norton wondered, however, if Cram could "justify for our modern needs so heavy a tower?"[61] A bit defensive, that; but the tower is at one and the same time the best thing about All Saints' and yet at first glance the least necessary.

What Norton meant by "heavy" is not entirely clear, but All Saints' as a whole is characterized by a sense of weight, deriving, I think, from its blue-gray granite walls, boldly laid up and seam-faced, the stones cut from quarry faces long exposed to weathering. Indeed, that most perceptive of critics, Montgomery Schuyler, thought All Saints' notable above all for "the skill with which the depth of wall is revealed."[62] That there is so little detail helps. There is, overwhelmingly, weight of mass. And consistency. Inside, where the nave piers, for instance, have no capitals at all, one is reminded of Cram's analysis of the Ypres Cloth Hall: "a simpler composition could hardly be imagined, or one more impressive in its grave restraint. . . . Its great quiet elements are left alone, not tortured into nervous complexity. . . . The great hall [is] broken only by columns and arches and roofed with a mass of oak timbering like an ancient and enormous ship, turned bottom up."[63]

Withal, this simplicity, that would so have disappointed Ruskin, is at Ashmont also part and parcel of an originality in design concept that would equally have startled Pugin. And it was characteristic of Cram that this originality by no means called attention to itself. The reverse of strident, it derives, as Robert Brown saw then, "not from any desire to be original, but simply to meet [then] . . . present conditions."[64] Thus the nave's unusual feeling, which is more basilican than Gothic, being both too wide for its length and too low for its width; the "present conditions" having been for Cram the modern American dependence on the fixed pew, every seat in which must needs command an unobstructed view of both altar and pulpit. As Cram would not give up arcades and their consequent spatial complexity and chiaroscuro (which a church needed, he thought, if it was to be a temple and not a meetinghouse), the very wide nave he needed to satisfy the agreed-upon seating capacity allowed only very narrow aisles, which it was inspiration for Cram to make not only narrow but low, compensating with an unusually high clerestory, which he endowed with the principal range of windows. It is a scheme that is at once traditional, in that it preserves the usual parish church proportions in elevation, and original, in that it reverses those proportions, the aisles being low and the clerestory unexpectedly high; the aisles are dark, the clerestory is brilliantly lit.

None of these elements was in itself new. But to have so logically and movingly expressed this plan in elevation was a tour de force. And it is, of course, the lofty clerestory that redeems the too-wide nave, making it instead a case of splendid amplitude; entirely apt for the church's massive severity of design, it is this amplitude that compels the breadth of the tower, the height of which is equally compelled by the clerestory. This was, truly (*pace* Pugin), to ascend to the realm of re-creation in the Gothic spirit — and all the answer Cram needed to make to Norton's query. The tower's heavy grandeur derives directly from the attempt to meet modern conditions in the Gothic spirit by Cram, who insisted, after the manner of his diary entry about copying, that All Saints' be "essentially a church of this century, built, not in England but in New England. . . . It is art, not archaeology, that drives us."[65]

All Saints's English roots, medieval and Victorian, are very evident. But so are its American sources, the chief being Richardson. Only a few have seen this; some vaguely, as in the case of Thomas Tallmadge, who asserted that "All Saints' was not entirely Gothic"; others more exactly: the leading Richardson scholar of our own time, James O'Gorman, has pronounced All Saints' quite definitely *Richardsonian* in feeling.[66] And in its disciplined picturesqueness and dark bulk and heft it does indeed owe much to Richardson. However, its austere simplicities and quiet but telling originality, its majesty of scale, and, above all, the authority with which the great tower leaves the ground and the stark grandeur of its tremendous volume — these it owes to Ralph Adams Cram, fired as he then was against his era's materialism and philistinism and the terrible effect of the consequent loss of faith *and* taste. Already for Cram art discloses religion; taste comes first; art being, after all, *im*pressive as well as *ex*pressive. Action precedes belief. Hence Cram's dictum of the 1890s, pronounced as he forged the rationale for his lifetime's work in the wake of Randall and Europe: "Art has been, is, and will be forever the greatest agency for spiritual impression that the church may claim. . . . Art and religion cannot be disassociated without mutual loss, for in its highest estate the former is but the perfect expression of the other."[67]

THE TWO MODES OF CRAM GOTHIC

All Saints', Ashmont, designed in 1891, and *Black Spirits and White* (whether one speaks of the experiences of the tales in 1887 or their publication in 1895) are no more than three or four years apart. Furthermore, Cram's horror stories, published the very year Freud published his first book, have perhaps survived the century of Freud with as much distinction, among the cognoscenti, as Cram's architecture has survived, among a different elite, the age of Le Corbusier and Frank Lloyd Wright.

The two sides of Cram's Gothic imagination seem to coalesce in a concrete way particularly in his "Notre Dame des Eaux." The opening paragraph is masterful:

> With the setting of the sun great clouds rose swiftly from the sea; the wind freshened, and the gaunt branches of the weather-worn trees in the churchyard lashed themselves beseechingly before the coming storm. The tide turned, and the waters at the foot of the rocks swept uneasily up the narrow beach and caught at the weary cliffs, their sobbing growing and deepening to a threatening, solemn roar. Whirls of dead leaves rose in the churchyard, and threw themselves against the blank windows. The winter and the night came down together.[68]

There is a sense here of Vaughan's lovely churches for Episcopalians and his dark castles for Searles finally also coalescing. For Cram, ever the artist more than the scholar, evokes the Gothic sensibility here very broadly and powerfully as it was then understood. From the scholarly point of view today the link between the overall feeling of the time for the Gothic with its architecture is best disclosed perhaps by Herbert Butterfield as quoted by Bruce Allsop:

> "the recovery and exposition of the Medieval world perhaps still remains as the greatest creative achievement of historical understanding. . . . [Gothic] ideas were capable of development towards a new aesthetic, whereas the classical manner . . . had completely failed to grow. . . . This is not to say the Gothic Revival was right and the Greek Revival wrong . . . it is to say that the Gothic Revival was linked with the rebirth of architectural history."[69]

All Saints' is the first masterwork of that rebirth in America, evidence so compelling that this "new aesthetic" would mature to good point in the New World that even so ardent an admirer of Louis Sullivan as the critic Claude Bragdon could compare Cram's churches with Sullivan's skyscrapers as equally vital. Cram, wrote Bragdon, could design Gothic churches "without dragging a train of absurd archaisms in their wake."[70]

Similarly, *Black Spirits and White* and Cram's other writings of the eighties and nineties would have rich issue in a long line of widely influential books and articles running into the hundreds that document Cram's vocation as an imaginative writer, critic, and thinker, a vocation hardly less serious than his calling as an architect, and only less important if not perceived *with* his architecture as parts of one and the same oeuvre of a man of many parts.

Cram's literary work, even his very well regarded horror tales, was, to be sure, somewhat overshadowed in later years by his other professional achievements, as, interestingly, was also the case with the author Cram as a writer in the horror genre has been most forcefully compared with, the Cambridge scholar (and sometime provost of Kings) Montague Rhodes James, whose work, in the view of one critic, Cram "anticipated in date and mood."[71] Yet Cram's literary writings inform all his work. For example, though all of Cram's horror tales are set in the Old World, none in the New, there is something profoundly New England about Cram's stories, something of Hawthorne and Poe, and this was noted by H. P. Lovecraft, the preeminent literary figure in this field in this century, in his comments on Cram's work in *The Supernatural in Literature.* There, in a wide-ranging discussion of the entire field in the last hundred years, Lovecraft singles Cram's stories out for exactly this regional quality: "Cram," Lovecraft writes, "achieves a memorably potent degree of vague regional horror through subtleties of atmosphere and description."[72] There is always about Cram's stories the underlying sense of Squire Blake's Old Place; and it is surely not beside the point that Cram's work is unarguably similar in this vein to that of his Pinckney Street neighbor and childhood friend in New Hampshire, Alice Brown.

Although in those few of her stories about the Pinckney Street Bohemia and "the difficulties of the artist surviving spiritually in urban culture centers like Boston . . . [Brown] lost her way," Kathryn Wheeler-Smith has written, her country characters—the spinsters and widows struggling in the "psychologically cruel wasteland" of late nineteenth-century "Tiverton," New Hampshire—are very well portrayed.[73] And no wonder they engender a sense of a shared milieu with Cram's stories. Brown's mythical Tiverton, the locale of many of her short stories and novels, has long since been identified by scholars as Brown's and Cram's childhood home of Hampton Falls, where, it must be remembered, Cram's gifted but thwarted father worked out a stony servitude to parents who had truncated his career, his wife all the while chafing at this while Cram Senior consoled himself with his Blake and his Emerson and his Swedenborg.[74] Though solaced by Ruskin and architectural pattern books, Ralph Adams Cram knew something of the sinister interior life of the New England small town that *Peyton Place* exposed three quarters of a century later.

Cram's attitude to the past is, in fact, exactly Brown's, whose characters, Wheeler-Smith observes, she always endowed with a sense that "when men and women only concern themselves with the present, or dream and strive selfishly for their futures, they dam the flow of life [and] . . . the past, present and future are disconnected into stagnant pools."[75] Brown's work is stout testimony to all these impressions of time past that Cram (and so many like him; T. S. Eliot comes to mind) felt so keenly.

Tiverton, and all that it represented, was surely also a key source as well of Cram's interest in Spiritualism and the occult. (One wonders if Cram harbored a "familiar" when Jack, the bull terrier, was succeeded by Damn-it, as Cram called his very black cat.) Boston was not only the New England Spiritualist center; rural Vermont — not very different from rural New Hampshire — played a vital part in the history of Theosophy, it having been in the wake of psychic "disturbances" in Vermont that Madame Blavatsky, the theosophical leader Cram was a follower of in the mid-1880s, journeyed to New England to undertake the study that led to her cofounding of the Theosophical Society. Although Cram never designed a Spiritualist temple — one wonders if he would have, if asked, and what form it would have taken — he did design the starkly beautiful Swedenborgian Church of the New Jerusalem (now the Church of the Open Word) in the Boston suburb of Newton in 1894, one of his firm's very first churches in a period when he was as yet not known for churches, and a commission that suggests Cram made his way in the 1880s and 1890s through more than Anglican circles in Boston (see *100*). (Nor did this connection dissipate over time: one of the major works at the peak of Cram's career was the so-called Swedenborgian Cathedral in Bryn Athyn, Pennsylvania. His Spiritualist interests also remained constant. During World War I, he collaborated with the legendary architect, psychic, and excavator of medieval Glastonbury Abbey, Frederick Bligh Bond, whose book *The Hill of Vision*, a Spiritualist triumph, Cram edited and prefaced.)[76]

If Cram's attitude to the past was so like Alice Brown's, so, too, his literary Gothic, for all its foreign settings, seems equally very American in feeling, just as, for all his admiration of the late nineteenth-century British Gothicists, his architectural Gothic shares the same "regional" (which is to say "American" in the sense that word then would have had, i.e., "*New* England") feeling. The stern granite walls of All Saints', Ashmont, may remind us of Edith Wharton, who also knew about New England villages and who likened Massachusetts's citizens to "*granite outcroppings*; but half-emerged from the soil," as she put it, so much was there so characteristically left unsaid.[77] One thinks, too, of Henry Adams at Mont-Saint-Michel, musing how, as between Normandy and New England, "the relation between the granite of one coast and that of the other may be fanciful, but the relation between the people who live on each is as hard and practical a fact as the granite itself." And his description of the Norman abbey could as well be of the Ashmont church: there is "the same directness, simplicity, absence of self-consciousness; the same intensity of purpose; even the same material; the prayer is granite."[78]

AN ASTONISHED AND NEEDY WORLD

The background of All Saints', its context, is easier to account for, however, than its effect, for after it American church building was never the same again. Perhaps Thomas Tallmadge came closest to describing that effect, pointing to how superlative Cram's design was and insisting that such an abrupt, unannounced excellence was "an essential quality for the work of [an architect like Cram] who aspires to be a prophet. There must be the element of surprise, and no time must be lost. . . . [Such a prophet-architect] must swim into the ken of an astonished and needy world."[79]

So Cram did at Ashmont. But we now know enough of the long decade of his work in the 1880s to realize that though the world was surprised by All Saints', it had been gestating in Cram's mind for some years and was really as much of a climax as a beginning. Starting with his cottage designs of 1882 and his early rebellious drawings for alternative schemes at Rotch and Tilden, continuing through the two big competitions of the mid-1880s, and then, above all, culminating in the results of the steady grind of his three Cram and Wentworth years, all on his own at the drafting board with only a business partner, laboring over houses and courthouses and churches, we have seen (alongside the overall artistic and critical growth of his *Transcript* work and the revelations of Randall and Europe) a development that has had already here its flashes of genius. Cram's early country houses and the church projects of 1889–1891, particularly that for Williamstown, clearly presaged All Saints'. When Ralph Adams Cram at Ashmont finally did "swim into the ken of an astonished and needy world" in 1891, he was, after all (so do biographies as lives proceed), nearly thirty years old.

There is another reason why All Saints', Ashmont, is more nearly climax than beginning: it was the last building that Cram designed entirely on his own. What followed All Saints' was a very different and quite new thing — for in the summer of 1891 Cram was not only joyously struggling with the designs of his first church, he was also corresponding with a young New Yorker who late that fall would move to Boston and become Cram's first and ever after incomparable designing partner.

In this connection I recall the observation of John Coolidge, considering the exterior of All Saints' with me one day in 1973. Its rugged granite walls, oxidized to rusty orange and deep gray, were, Professor Coolidge thought, the walls not so much of a mason as of a watercolorist; an observation I recalled three years later, when in his address at the opening of the Cram exhibition in New York, he insisted that above all he thought Ralph Adams Cram was *an artist*. This observation was accounted for, I suspect, by the fact that this distinguished scholar was feeling in New York the effect, as others have who have seen them for the first time, of Cram's watercolor perspectives, done when there was no one else to do Cram and Wentworth's presentation drawings in 1889–1891 — watercolors whose excellence startled viewers then as O'Gorman today.

Back in 1973 at Ashmont, neither I nor Professor Coolidge knew that the architect of those watercolorist walls was himself a fine watercolorist. All memory of Cram's skill in that medium had vanished, and for the same reason that Cram's solo designs had also receded and that the Ashmont church (too good for that) came to be seen, not as the final climax of Cram and Wentworth, but as the beginning[80] of Cram, Wentworth and Goodhue. The reason was Bertram Grosvenor Goodhue, with whom in 1892 Ralph Adams Cram began what was to become one of the most famous collaborations in the history of architecture.

4

THE DESIRE AND PURSUIT
OF THE WHOLE

Socrates [taught of male] homosexual love [that it] alone is capable of satisfying a man's highest and noblest aspirations [and that it] . . . has a range which extends from the crudest physical passion to a marriage of noble minds with no physical manifestation at all. . . . [The] ideal is sensuality entirely transcended. . . . Physical procreation is only one, and that the lowest, of the forms which Eros may take. Far nobler is spiritual procreation. . . . When a man's soul is pregnant with some creation or discovery he looks for a partner . . . with whom he may bring his spiritual offering to birth. Physical beauty will influence, but . . . [Platonic love] is a gradual progress comparable to the stages of an initiation. . . . The final vision is a religious rather than an intellectual experience. . . . Platonic love, in spite of the meaning commonly attributed to it, is a common search for truth and beauty by two persons of the same sex, inspired by personal affection.

— Walter Hamilton, Introduction, *Plato's Symposium*

Michael shrugged. . . . "We were too much like brothers. It felt incestuous [to have sex]."

The kid frowned. "That's too bad."

"I don't know. I think it freed us to love each other. . . . We just got closer and closer. . . ."

Wilfred's brow furrowed. "But . . . that's not really a lover."

"Oh, I know. And we made sure our boyfriends knew that too. We'd say: 'Jon's just a friend.' . . . If you've ever been the third party in a situation like that, you know that the difference doesn't mean diddlyshit. Those guys are *married* . . . and they're always the last to know."

"But *you* knew," said Wilfred.

Michael nodded, " . . . Yeah."

"Then . . . that's better than nothing."

Michael smiled. . . . "That's better than everything."

— Armistead Maupin, *Tales of the City*, "Babycakes"

47. Pictured in the 1890s in their office in Boston's Exchange Building, Cram is at his drafting board while Bertram Goodhue is chatting with a client. Also evident is one white Boston bull terrier (Cram's) by the name of Jack.

THE DESIRE and pursuit of the whole, declares Plato, is called love,[1] a pronouncement that may be as close to an acceptable definition of that storied state as has been ventured. I believe Ralph Adams Cram found that which he desired and pursued. That lust probably figured in the equation and soulmate may also have been bedmate added then, from a Platonic (and also, of course, from a Christian) point of view, a problematic element; but when one of the protagonists of *Brideshead* prayed, "Oh God, make me good, but not yet," he was quoting Saint Augustine himself.[2] Besides, with our changing conceptions of the share of the body in ideal love at the end of the twentieth century, we may now conclude that lust was a positive enough contribution. Still, the overarching categories are partners and brothers.

PARTNERS

It was in May 1891 that Ralph Cram and Charles Wentworth were first approached by Bertram Goodhue, then a draftsman in New York City at Renwick, Aspinwall and Russell, a venerable firm, the senior partner of which had been the architect of St. Patrick's Cathedral in that city. Only twenty-one, Goodhue had just won a competition for a cathedral in Dallas and was searching for an established firm that could offer him the experience and support necessary to carry forward such a major work.[3] Why he was drawn to Boston and to Cram and Wentworth is not known. At about this time his father died and his mother and several relatives relocated to the Boston area, but whether this was the cause or effect of Goodhue's advent in Boston seems to be no longer discoverable. Probably he admired the 1889–1891 church work by Cram published periodically in those years in *American Architect*, including the superb Williamstown church design that prefigured Ashmont.

In background and outlook both men (47) were somewhat alike. A *Mayflower* descendant, Goodhue had been raised in a genteel but none too well off Connecticut family that could not afford him access to architectural school or even college, and he was thus largely self-educated (and sensitive on the point).[4] With none of Cram's critical and literary credentials, it would perhaps have been difficult for Goodhue to set himself up in practice on his own. On the other hand, his abilities were such that he could offer Cram and Wentworth a much greater chance of their own practice's succeeding than was usual in highly competitive Boston. Money was a problem for both sides. As Cram admitted later, it was far easier to offer the New Yorker a partnership (and thus a share in nonexistent but hoped-for profits) than to pay him even a small salary.[5] Thus, though Goodhue himself later distinctly stated in writing that he "went to Boston and became head draughtsman for the firm of Cram and Wentworth [and] at the end of a year I was taken into partnership," it does appear that he worked only for a few months in 1891 in the capacity of draughtsman, very likely in the expectation that the firm would become, as it did in January 1892, Cram, Wentworth and Goodhue.[6]

Among Goodhue's first tasks was to take in hand the large watercolor perspective of the proposed design for All Saints', Ashmont (see 46a), which still hangs today in the cloister there. But as Cram's old draftsman, John Doran, noticed at once he saw it, in its Impressionistic flicker of Prussian blue, gray-green, and pale yellow this perspective is a representative example of *Cram's* artistry as a watercolorist; only the lettering and the figures in the foreground, intended to give scale, are so much more swiftly and deftly done as to be attributable to the hand of Goodhue.[7]

At the same time Goodhue executed a series of four pen-and-ink renderings of All Saints'. But whereas Ashmont's famous tower appears in Cram's watercolor in exactly the form, broad and massive, in which it was built, in Goodhue's renderings it is much more elegant. Even the fenestration is different. In fact, for all their exquisite technique, there is little sense in Goodhue's sketches of the realized design of All Saints', doubtless reflecting the fact that it is not likely he was much involved in the church's design. Moreover, details of the church as built support this view: the incised lines of the north door arch and the stone arches of the nave arcades are typical of Cram's plain detail and suggest the nave was built from Cram's drawings; the molded planes of the west door arch, on the other hand, not built until 1894, clearly reflect that they were detailed by Goodhue, whose lines die elegantly into the planes of the arch. Certainly Cram's plans for All Saints' were prepared before Goodhue's coming; in a letter of July 1891, Cram referred to a prior request by the parish for preliminary plans, which it is known the vestry was studying that month,[8] while Goodhue did not come to Boston and take up his association with Cram and Wentworth until November, by which time the parish authorities had already announced (in that month's parish newspaper) that the vestry "has accepted the preliminary plans for the new church drawn by Messrs. Cram and Wentworth"[9] — the firm name, interestingly, used in connections with All Saints' in the index of Cram's memoirs.

Most important, whereas the design of All Saints' clearly descends in all its key aspects from the parish church projects designed by Cram in his years with Wentworth (48), this is *not* true of the next church commission after Ashmont the new firm of Cram, Wentworth and Goodhue undertook. St. Paul's, Brockton (49), the plans for which, started in July 1892, well after Goodhue had taken up his duties, are startlingly different from anything Cram had ever put forward and more characteristic of Goodhue's later work.

This is particularly true of Brockton's west front, which centers on a deeply recessed archway with heavy buttresslike mullions, a motif also hardly ever used again in Cram's designs but one that was much favored in later years by Goodhue. Moreover, though clearly inspired by John Sedding's Holy Trinity, Sloane Street, London, this west front arch, in conjunction with the large square buttresses that rise at St. Paul's into turrets to either side of the arch, constitutes, as Ann Miner Daniel has pointed out, "a combination of [Gothic] form [that] is unique."[10] St. Paul's, though not so glorious a church as Ashmont, is more obviously unusual and arresting in design, thus declaring the nature of what would be Goodhue's characteristic contribution to the firm; for Cram always maintained that it was Goodhue's

> vivid imagination . . . that gave whatever came out of our office a quality of vitality that, to me at least, was very convincing.
>
> Little by little we began to learn something from each other; he came to see problems more in the large, as consistent and unified conceptions, where detail was *only* a detail; while I slowly sloughed off some of my archaeological predispositions and realized the inherent value in his originality and modernism.[11]

St. Paul's, Brockton, the first church for which the designs as accepted by the client bore both Cram's and Goodhue's names, was also very likely the first church design that was a result of a real collaboration between them.

To be sure, it may seem hard on Goodhue to deny him much of any share in All Saints', a masterful design, which St. Paul's is not. But St. Paul's is a fascinating beginning; the motif of the buttresslike mullions in the west front arch, for instance, first used there, would in future years be developed by Goodhue quite brilliantly in some of his best work, including the West Point Chapel. Nor does this suggest that in 1891 Goodhue was not, in his own way, as good a designer as the older and more experienced Cram. To see Goodhue's talents, one has only to look at the too often forgotten (because never built) Dallas cathedral design (50). Though the Dallas project, like All Saints', now became officially the work of Cram, Wentworth and Goodhue, the design was based on a competition entry of 1890 by Goodhue. He may have been influenced by Cram's church work of 1889 (published in 1890 in *American Architect*) but the award went to Goodhue

48a, b. Cram and Wentworth's design of 1890 for St. Thomas, Dover, New Hampshire, distinctly heralds Cram's design of the following year for All Saints', Ashmont (*below*), from the northwest.

49. St. Paul's Church, Brockton, outside Boston, the first church designed jointly by Cram and Goodhue; Goodhue's perspective of 1892 discloses at once the design's unusual vitality.

alone while he was still only a draftsman. Dallas, with all its elegance, was Goodhue's dowry to the new partnership just as surely as Ashmont, with its severity of mass and nobility of scale and proportion, was Cram's. Both promised much.

Meanwhile, differentiation had to yield to collaboration, no easy task, as one can see once Ashmont is pulled back from its traditional place as Cram and Goodhue's first church and seen instead as the climax of Cram's solo work and once St. Paul's, Brockton, is pushed forward as really Cram and Goodhue's first church. In fact, if the Ashmont and Dallas dowries show what each had to offer, and Brockton that their collaboration was not to be immediately easy, another comparison may disclose the nature of the challenge each man had to meet.

In 1889, so far as we know two years before they met, Goodhue as well as Cram entered the competition for the new Cathedral of St. John the Divine in New York. Neither won. But the differences between their designs (51) are nonetheless fascinating. As Richard Oliver, Goodhue's biographer, has pointed out, whereas Goodhue's rather fantastical offering was certainly "awkward," it was also "imaginative," both "impetuous and experimental." Cram's design, on

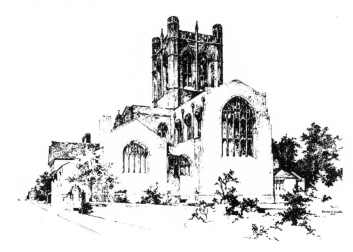

50. St. Matthew's Cathedral,
Dallas, Texas, published after
1892 under the new firm name of
Cram, Wentworth and Goodhue.

the other hand, Oliver rightly judged "calm . . . disciplined and ordered" though quite uninspiring.[12] Janet Adams Strong agrees, observing that Goodhue's design has an "ungainly exterior." She points out, however, that Goodhue was the youngest of the competitors (he was only twenty in 1889), and that, for all its faults, Goodhue's design was "free spirited" and even "daring," while Cram's designs, which she judges "disciplined [and] well organized," were also "cautious."[13] Each would have something to learn from the other, but Goodhue, being perhaps a quicker study, would learn more swiftly, and Cram, older, more dominant, and more experienced, would find it harder to assimilate the younger man's lessons.

Note the overwhelming Richardsonianism of Cram's Romanesque design as opposed to Goodhue's much more limited reference to that master. And note, too, that All Saints', Ashmont, in the view of the leading Richardson scholar of our day, James O'Gorman, is a "stylistically transitional work combining the seemingly irreconcilable characteristics of Richardsonian robustness and Gothic grace."[14] The fact that Ashmont is so Richardsonian—a thing to be expected of the young Cram, who hero-worshipped Richardson, but not of Goodhue—is critical to my contention here that the overall design of Ashmont (its detail, much of it added later, notwithstanding) is the climax of Cram and Wentworth, not the beginning of Cram, Wentworth and Goodhue.

Goodhue's originality was not the only or even the chief contribution he brought to the new firm. Rather, it was his gift for designing architectural detail. What a comparison Goodhue's Ashmont lectern (52) is with Cram's Advent credence (see 45)! In what is probably Goodhue's first important decorative work, this exquisite Gothic lectern is nevertheless very unmedieval (notice the

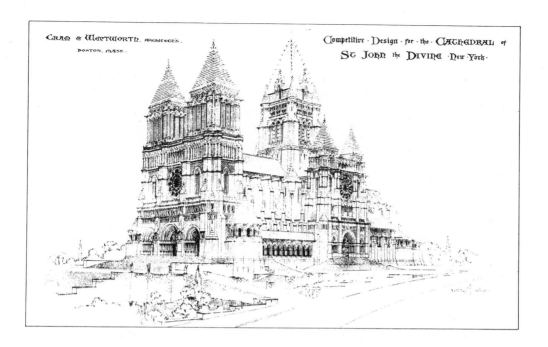

CRAM & WENTWORTH. ARCHITECTS.
BOSTON, MASS.

Competitive · Design · for · the · CATHEDRAL · of
St John the DIVINE · New York ·

Competitive · Design · for · the · CATHEDRAL · of
St John the DIVINE · New York ·

B · G · GOODHUE ARCHITECT.
· NEW YORK · N · Y ·

51a, b. Cram's Romanesque entry (like his Gothic entry; see 42) in the St. John the Divine competition of 1889–90 is in striking contrast to Goodhue's independent entry (*below*).

52. All Saints', Ashmont, lectern, 1894:
one of the first examples of Goodhue's gift
for architectural ornament.

scrolls at its base); there is no denial of the Renaissance, and the result is truly masterful.

More than impressed with Goodhue's gift for such detail, which he pronounced almost "elflike in its fantasy," Cram wrote the result was that

> From a professional point of view [Bertram] was my *alter ego* and I like to think that I was his. What ability I had stopped short at one very definite point. I could see any architectural problem in its mass, proportion, composition, and articulation, and visualize it in three dimensions even before I set pencil to paper. I had also the faculty of planning, and I generally blocked out all our designs at quarter-scale. There my ability ceased. I had neither the power nor the patience to work out any sort of decorative detail. At this point Bertram entered the equation. . . . Various books of the Pugins' treasured drawings might serve as a basis, but what in the end issued from his fertile imagination and deft fingers had suffered a sea-change into something rich and strange. In this alone he demonstrated very clearly that Gothic was not a dead style.[15]

As this extract shows, Cram was a writer as well as an architect, and here, too, Goodhue, in his originality of design and imaginative detail, brought a complementary gift, for to Cram's prose there was now added Goodhue's genius as an architectural renderer (*53a*), ultimately perhaps the best in the country. So much admired was his work that when in the 1890s Charles Maginnis, though he complained good-humoredly that *all* Cram, Wentworth and Goodhue's churches, as sketched by Goodhue, were always on magnificent street-corner sites, went on to praise the way Goodhue still invited challenge. Invariably, wrote Maginnis, Goodhue would illustrate

> one of the streets in sharp perspective, usually in the very eye of the vanishing point, and then follow it away into the landscape for a great distance, thus proposing to himself as fascinating a study in drawing as the illustrator could possibly meet with. It is a bold and difficult performance withal. Not many man would venture on it, and fewer still would we advise to try it. Mr. Goodhue can do it in a masterly way, still maintaining the breadth and scale of his drawing.[16]

Cram's writing and Goodhue's sketches were a persuasive combination. Consider Cram's writings of this period, the first in which he focused not on art in general but on architecture in particular. In 1891, in his article on Sedding in *Architectural Review*, he proclaimed Gothic "less a style than an impulse; the so-called Gothic styles of medievalism are complete and never to be revived; but the moving spirit which created them may come to life once more."[17] Then, in 1892, in "The Religious Aspect of Architecture" for the parish paper of the Church of the Advent (which may thus claim to have published Cram's first known article on church design), he argued that the Oxford Movement and the Gothic Revival were each part of the "same animating impulse,"[18] assertions that laid the theoretical groundwork of the last phase of the American Gothic Revival, a task Cram did well enough. When he rehearsed these arguments again in the 1892 booklet announcing All Saints', Ashmont, their force was far greater, however, because of Goodhue's sketches: not too exact a reflection of the actual design of All Saints', perhaps, they nonetheless lent tremendous new credibility to Cram's declaration that Gothic could still be a living style.

The new junior partner did bring some deficits. His biographer notes that as a young man Goodhue was argumentative and opinionated. "At his best," Oliver writes, "his outspokenness seemed a commitment to principles and ideals, and for this he was admired. At its worst, it made him appear arrogant, petulant and uncompromising, and suggested that his manner masked a darker and more problematic personality."[19] It is perhaps enough to say now that Goodhue in many respects was really quite like Cram, about whom Guiney once warned Day: "like most people wrapped up in causes, [Ralph] is hard on individuals, walking on one's corns while he gazeth upon the stars."[20]

Years later, long after Goodhue's death, Cram also recalled Goodhue's moods, but more forgivingly. Tactfully including Wentworth in his

DESIGN·FOR·THE·PRO
POSED·CHVRCH·OF
SAINT·IOHN·THE·EV·
ANGELIST·SAINT·PAVL·DIOCESE·OF·MINNE
SOTA··CRAM·WENTWORTH·&·GOODHVE·
ARCHITECTS·53·STATE·STREET·BOSTON

Interior·Looking·Eastward·

DESIGN·FOR·THE·PRO
POSED·CHVRCH·OF
SAINT·IOHN·THE·EV-
ANGELIST·SAINT·PAVL·DIOCESE·OF·MINNE
SOTA·CRAM·WENTWORTH·AND·GOODHVE
ARCHITECTS·33·STATE·STREET·BOSTON

Suggestion for
Colour·Decoration.
View looking toward
Morning·Chapel.

53a, b. Goodhue's genius for architectural rendering is evident in his interior perspective (*facing*) of 1892 of his and Cram's design of that year for St. John the Evangelist's, St. Paul, Minnesota — so much so that despite Cram's considerable skill as a watercolorist his own interior perspective of the same project (*above*) does not show to good advantage when compared with Goodhue's. This is a vivid example of the origins of Cram's increasing reliance through the years on the junior partner's presentation drawings.

reminiscences (though, as we shall see later, Wentworth was more likely to call to mind Goodhue's deficits), Cram remembered with evident pleasure how

> the charm of [Bertram's] personality . . . quite carried us off our feet. . . . Exuberantly enthusiastic, with an abounding and fantastic sense of humor, he flung gaiety and abandon widely around whenever he was in the temper to do so. On the other hand, he could be moody and dispirited on occasion, though this mood lasted only for brief moments, vanishing as quickly as it came.[21]

Cram's leniency discloses something of the nature of Cram and Goodhue's personal relationship. It was an intimate one. However, before they were anything else, Ralph and Bertram were brothers and comrades in Bohemia. Thus we must now enlarge our understanding of that country of the soul they shared.

BROTHERS AND COMRADES

So much of an oxymoron does Bohemia in Boston seem in the Victorian period, the reader will have observed I have edged into it here by very discreet stages; first claiming, in Chapter 1, the authority of no less than Samuel Eliot Morison that such a thing really existed in the Puritan capital; then quoting the quite benign contemporary description of it in Frances Carruth's book as proper Boston saw it; and only thereafter (in connection with Guiney, Day, and Vaughan) moving beyond "musical bachelors" and such to discuss Bohemia in general (wherever found) and its pedagogical and homosocial aspects as alluded to by Allan Bloom, whose comments pointed us toward Cram's European trip of discovery with Henry Randall. Now, as Bertram Goodhue succeeds to the central place in Cram's affections, it is timely to take more intimate testimony from that sure guide to the American fin-de-siècle, Gelett Burgess, who, as Cram noted in his autobiography, was a valued denizen of Boston's Bohemia[22] (though honorary; after attending MIT Burgess moved to San Francisco).

Burgess is all the more persuasive a witness because he took Bohemia's measure both coming and going: here is a part of his "The Bohemians of Boston," which does not leave out the expected allusion to the color green:

> The "Orchids" were as tough a crowd
> As Boston anywhere allowed;
> It was a club of wicked men —
> The oldest, twelve, the youngest, ten;
> They drank their soda colored green,
> They talked of "Art" and "Philistine,"
> They wore buff "wescoats" and their hair
> It used to make the waiters stare!
> They were so shockingly behaved
> And Boston thought them so depraved . . .[23]

Elsewhere, however, Burgess essayed a more serious discussion of the subject and one in which he pulled no punches,[24] writing that if the Bohemian ideal could lend its precepts "to some pretty vices . . . for in Bohemia one may find almost every sin except that of Hypocrisy," it also encouraged "generosity, love and charity; for it is not enough to be one's self in Bohemia, one must allow others to be themselves as well." Indeed, he asserted penetratingly, that there were "no roads in all Bohemia," only "signs in the wilderness." Here is his map:

> Within Bohemia are many lesser states. . . . On the shore of the Magic Sea of Dreams lies the country of Youth and Romance, . . . free from care or caution. . . . To the east-ward lie the pleasant groves of Arcady, the dreamland, home of love and poetry. . . . To the south, over the long procession of the hills lies Vagabondia, [for those who claim] . . . a wilder freedom . . . outlawed or voluntary exile from all restraint. . . .
>
> One other district lies hidden and remote, locked in the central fastness of Bohemia. Here is the Forest of Arden, whose greenwood holds a noble fellow-ship. . . . It is a little golden world apart, and though it is the most secret, it is the most accessible of refuges, so that there are never too many there, and never too few. Men go and come from this bright country, but once having been free of the wood, you are of the Brotherhood, and recognize your fellows by instinct, and know them, and they know you, for what you are. . . . Happy indeed is he who, in his journey of life . . . has found his way to the happy forest.

Why, one may well wonder, in describing so intensely urban a phenomenon as Bohemia, did Burgess have recourse to the imagery of Arcadia — the forest, the greenwood? But, of course, it is a *secret* country, is it not, hidden away, in the mind's eye, at the soul's center? And as the field of gay and lesbian studies has developed, its scholars have noted the propensity of homosexual writers from Whitman to Forster to see in that imagery of Arcadia "a place where . . . gay men could physically effect a pastoral escape route" (as Mark Lilly puts it in *Gay Men's Literature in the Twentieth Century* of the greenwoods role in Forster's *Maurice*). Less noted, perhaps, is that this propensity found important expres-sion in the Boston of Cram's youth and among his cohort — in such ideas as the nationally influential vagabonding movement Cram's friends Bliss Carman and Richard Hovey led (recall that on Burgess's map Vagabondia was the wilder refuge) and in the importance to Boston's Bohemia of such local retreats as Fred Holland Day's Little Good Harbor in Maine, the Meteyards' Testudo on the Scituate marshes, and William Sturgis Bigelow's island retreat on Tuckernuck near Nantucket.

Indeed, the art of Bohemia celebrated Arcadia significantly. Day shot many of his plein-air nudes in Maine, where he started something of a summer colony of pictorialist photographers, offering scholarships to poor but beautiful young men for summer residence that involved not only posing but a whole Whitmanic experience (including academic tutoring) after the ideal of Edward Carpenter,

Ashbee's homosexual mentor, whom Day knew. Often, too, Day posed his models by his outdoor statue of Pan, an image also evoked (in the poem "The Pipes of Pan") by Carman. In fact, Burgess's attempt to apprehend Bohemia through Arcadian images (popularized, in the case of Vagabondia, throughout America) speaks directly to what Byrne R. S. Fone has called, in the title of a landmark study, "This Other Eden: Arcadia and the Homosexual Imagination."[25]

The reader should recall how central to the socialism of Edward Carpenter was the idea of "comradeship . . . that current of affection which [Carpenter] had recognized . . . when he first read the poems of Walt Whitman." "Comradeship" is a word whose meaning in this context and in this era was very specific; it was, Karl Beckson has written, a "codeword among Uranians [homosexuals] for homosexual relationships."[26] Similarly, it is hard to miss the meaning of Burgess's "bright country . . . of the Brotherhood" where you "recognize your fellows by instinct and know them, and they know you, for what you are" had the same meaning. And if it sounds like Armistead Maupin's "28 Barbary Lane," where the richly varied sexual tapestry makes stereotypes both heterosexual and homosexual ridiculous, we may well recall that Gelett Burgess spent most of his life in San Francisco.

SOULMATES

Brothers in Bohemia, then, first of all; Ralph Cram and Bertram Goodhue were also, and I suspect from the first, soulmates and, after some fashion, lovers. Brilliant, nervous, a man of sharp edges but warm emotions, highly erratic, Bertram was graceful and boyish, blond, with bright blue eyes, and at times flirtatious; and he seems rather to have captivated Ralph, who, for all that he, too, was brilliant and strong-minded, was also idealistic, heartfelt, passionate (in Rose Nichols's words, "emotionally untrammeled"),[27] sensitive to a fault, and as a young man dashing enough to be worth captivating. Always a fit hundred and fifty pounds at five feet, seven inches, and with the strength to be expected of a farm boy, Cram was barrel-chested and strong-jawed, with sandy hair and steady, rather hard, eyes, and was vain enough to brag about his "well-turned limbs."[28] Nor was Goodhue all grace and nerves; he allowed once in defense of bullfighting that it was cruel, but also, he thought, "a gorgeous feast of bravery."[29] And he was socially very much hail-fellow-well-met; as one old friend remarked, at the time Cram met him, "Goodhue had a reputation for being able to drink more beer than anyone else."[30] Both men, of course, cultivated aesthetic convictions about which each was insistent.

Though he never failed to guard their privacy, Cram's published reminiscences of Goodhue, whom he outlived by nearly two decades, hardly obscure his affections. Some thirty years later, Cram described Goodhue when first he met him in these words:

> Blond, slender, debonair, with a "school-girl" complexion and a native grace of carriage, he presented a personality made up of joy of life, fantastic humor, whimsical fads and fancies blended with . . . an incomparable sense of beauty, an abounding friendliness. . . . With it all were a naiveté and boyishness that were lasting joys. . . . He certainly was a splendid sight, flaunting in medieval costume in the long-ago pageants in the old Art Museum or [Fred] Day's fantastic house in Norwood. The sense of romance possessed him. . . . And always with a laugh mixed in with supposedly serious matters . . . saving himself with the smile and the jeering word that spoke a redeeming common sense under the gay cloak of an untimely romance.

Cram also noted on the professional side Goodhue's "dominating ambition . . . and a capacity for hard work that nothing could daunt"; that was all: the personal aspect quite clearly outweighed any other. Consider Cram's two chief memories of Goodhue:

> Crouched over his board, working at such fever heat that his lips writhed in sympathy with the rush of his pencil or pen [he was ambidextrous]; a lock of hair flopped on his forehead, a cigarette burning holes in the edges of his board, and half the time he was singing or ambling on in fantastic humor; [or in the rooms of a club they belonged to] perched perhaps on the edge of a table, a broad hat slouched over his eye, a cigarette smouldering under his blond moustache, a Mexican "capa" flung over his shoulder while he strummed out improvised accompaniments on a battered old guitar.[31]

Like so much Cram wrote about Goodhue (although most of it was written after the acrimonious breakup of their partnership), one is always struck by the delicacy with which the survivor wrote of that "golden and engaging youth" (Ralph and Bertram were, respectively, twenty-seven and twenty-one when they first met).[32] Indeed, Cram would describe Goodhue as "the most stimulating and illuminating experience of a long and varied life."[33] The implication is hard to miss. Here was a case of the sort of memory of which Michel Foucault has observed: "There is not one but many silences."[34]

Yet the silences of each could be loud enough. Witness another of Cram's early books, *The Decadent*, published in 1893. With the overall importance of that book we will deal extensively in Chapter 9. Here the book's dedication and its frontispiece (54), which have their own specific significance, are our focus: Ralph dedicated the book to Bertram, who in turn executed the frontispiece, which in my view is surely a self-portrait of them both. It is a self-portrait, moreover, that returns Cram's compliment and constitutes a kind of reverse dedication; for in the frontispiece Ralph, not Bertram, is the focus, the idealized object. On the personal side as on the professional, the word is always Cram's, the picture Goodhue's.

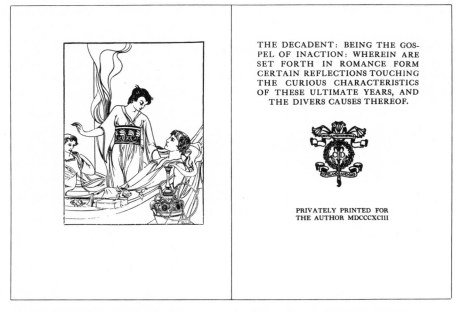

THE DECADENT: BEING THE GOS-
PEL OF INACTION: WHEREIN ARE
SET FORTH IN ROMANCE FORM
CERTAIN REFLECTIONS TOUCHING
THE CURIOUS CHARACTERISTICS
OF THESE ULTIMATE YEARS, AND
THE DIVERS CAUSES THEREOF.

PRIVATELY PRINTED FOR
THE AUTHOR MDCCCXCIII

54. Goodhue's frontispiece and title page for Cram's first book, *The Decadent*, published in 1893.

To recall our discussion of the visual aspect of the technique of mask and signal, particularly about things horticultural and green, in connection with Cram's *Black Spirits and White*, we should note that Goodhue's frontispiece for *The Decadent* (which was published in its most costly edition in "limp vellum with green silk ties") is not without significant horticultural adornment. The frontispiece brings to mind one of Beardsley's drawings for Wilde's *Salomé*, about which Karl Beckson concludes that a "single flower . . . suggests the green carnation."[35] Goodhue's Wildean, even Beardsleyesque, drawing includes just such a single flower, also suggesting the green carnation, the symbol of homosexuality in Paris and the preference of the chief character of Joris-Karl Huysmans's *À Rebours*, after which Cram's *Decadent* was modeled.

As was the case with *Black Spirits and White*, not only the visual but the literary technique of mask and signal is evident in *The Decadent*, and Goodhue's frontispiece, however more immediately arresting, is not really more telling than the form of Cram's dedication: TIBI . MEO . CARO . B.G.G.

In his *Christianity, Social Tolerance, and Homosexuality* John Boswell of Yale has observed that

from the scholar's point of view, any distinction between "friendship" and "love" must be extremely arbitrary. No scientific differentiation has ever been proposed. . . .

In Latin . . . "amicus" or "friend" and "amans," "lover," are derived from the same verb — "amo," "to love" — and are very largely interchangeable. . . . Exterior evidence of the erotic nature of relationships varies widely by culture and time.[36]

Thus Boswell, in his discussion of Alcuin and the court of Charlemagne, translates *caros* in one of Alcuin's love poems as "lover" because of its context — in that case the use of *amantem* in the very next line of the poem.[37] Similarly, I read into Cram's "MEO CARO" the same meaning, and in this case, too, because of its context — Goodhue's self-portrait of himself and Cram; "exterior evidence," after all, that is, visually, at least as "lover-like" as any reference of Alcuin's poem — or to take another and more contemporary (and architectural) example, the relationship between Louis Sullivan and Frank Lloyd Wright described by Brendan Gill in his recent biography of Wright, where he characterizes an argument of theirs as a "lover's quarrel."[38]

Of course, the word "lover," like "friend," though interchangeable, can mean different things. We have Helen Howe's word for it that in Edwardian Boston the word "lover" in conventional social usage among the upper classes had the meaning of: "I rather assumed that he was her 'lover,' in the sense that . . . he had asked her to marry him."[39] Similarly, even today and of specifically homosexual circles in the same period in Boston, one of Henry James's biographers, Fred Kaplan, has written of James as "an expressive and generous lover [of] Jocelyn Persse, perhaps because the drama was substantially in the words and in the heart," meaning, it should be noted, not that their relationship was without erotic desire (it wasn't; James, for example, wrote to Persse of the younger man's "enchanted physique"), but that James, Kaplan believes, "allowed himself the feelings and the language of transgression . . . but not more."[40] Of course, Victorian and Edwardian verbiage is often discounted. But this is risky; "actually the flowery words often expressed more, not less, than they meant," Peter Gay has noted of this era.[41]

"MEO CARO" thus is more likely to have meant, not less than it might have, but more, for the youthful Ralph Adams Cram; the accumulating evidence here from the beginning has been shading long since toward this rendezvous with Goodhue, marking Cram's finding of the other half, the forming of the Platonic whole, in what was to be the supreme relationship of his life and work.

"Homosexual," like "lover," is also a word of many meanings. Michel Foucault particularly has documented the evolution in Western thought that has led to our view today of homosexuality as a stable definition of identity related to personality structure, even quite aside from genital activity.[42] But, historically, that is to say that "the modern homosexual role is not the only homosexual role possible."[43] Thus one does well to note the definition of gay persons of John Boswell: "those whose erotic interest is predominantly directed toward their

143

own gender (i.e., regardless of how conscious they are of this as a distinguishing characteristic)."[44] I have adopted this definition here, despite the fact that (because American society so often equates gay with effeminate) to label the gay male whose behavior is gender appropriate as gay will seem misleading to many straights and also to the many (if not most) gay males whose behavior does not relate to the effeminate stereotype. But in a world of stereotypes, it is necessary, in order to tell the truth, to run the risk.

Another risk we must run is the sort of denial one has seen before in such cases. Because Cram became ultimately one of the leading figures of the conservative Catholic religious tradition in twentieth-century American history, his sexuality will pose for some the same sort of problem that arises, for example, in the case of an even more revered Anglican figure, C. S. Lewis, of whom many simply cannot bring themselves to accept that he willingly and knowingly married a divorced woman with a husband still living and, according to his own testimony, likely consummated his marriage. To enlarge somewhat upon a witticism of A. N. Wilson, in his excellent biography of Lewis, the result has been a stubborn enough cult determined to observe what I call the Feast of the Perpetual Virginity of C. S. Lewis,[45] against whatever odds to the contrary, as if the truth or value of religious belief could ever be dependent on any believer's adhering to it.

Those tempted to denial in the case of both Lewis and Cram are, of course, in John Moser's words, a part of that band of "sorry souls who seem always engaged in a perpetual novena to repeal the twentieth century."[46] Actually, their quarrel is in the case of Cram more with the late nineteenth century, when in Cram's formative years homosexuality as we now understand it began to take on its recognizably modern construction.

THE INVENTION OF HOMOSEXUALITY

The debate that must inform our study of those years is not difficult to compass, though it is profound enough in its implications. John Boswell puts what is called the "essentialist" position clearly enough in the subtitle of his seminal *Christianity, Social Tolerance, and Homosexuality: Gay People in Western Europe from the Beginning of the Christian Era to the Fourteenth Century.* Whether or not there really is sufficient continuity of such categories and identities between Saint Paul's time and our own is, on the other hand, thought doubtful by those influenced by Foucault, "constructionists" who argue that sexual categories and identities have varied so fundamentally over human history that they are newly constructed in each era to such an extent that the continuity asserted by Boswell is questionable.

144

This dialogue in gay and lesbian historiography obviously touches on "profound philosophical questions concerning the definition and constitution of the self."[47] And these questions arise here very pertinently, for scholars in all fields must, I believe, come finally to terms with the fact that, while genital activity would lose not a little of its value (as would also, to cite another example, auricular confession) if its privacy were to be violated during a person's lifetime, the larger universe of discourse of identity and personality structure of which genital tastes are one expression, what we have come to call in our era sexual orientation, is so central to human personhood that on the eve of the twenty-first century, a hundred years after Freud's and Jung's first work, it is equally central to the biographer. So much so that not to give the subject its due suggests less a concern with privacy than with shame.

My own view here is certainly "essentialist," that throughout human history there have been persons who identified themselves as primarily centered emotionally and erotically on their own gender, consciously or not, and there is in this respect sufficient continuity of identity from era to era to justify the non-anachronistic use of "homosexual" and, to use the less clinical sounding neologism I prefer, "gay." Equally, however, my view is "constructionist" in that it seems to me clear that such self-identification has varied so in the significance attached to it from period to period that one must be careful to differentiate between one era and another.

This last is key particularly in the wake of the gay liberation movement of our time, some aspects of which I believe to be related to the now almost total destruction of the formative and once male-only bastions of boarding school, college, club, and such, and even of certain walks of life (such as the arts, education, the armed forces, and the ministry), bastions that homosexual men once thought of as uniquely welcoming and open to their influence and even control. Nowadays, only sports (and the infantry!) remain. Moreover, while one can only celebrate the remarkable growth in gay and lesbian studies of recent years, to which this study is profoundly indebted, it is also key to guard against the manifold assumptions of superiority this movement often tends to with respect to the past. To accuse Oscar Wilde, for example, of dissembling about his sexuality is to read today's values back into a very different generation, especially as, like Charles I, Wilde showed his mettle late in the day; one does not have to admire Wilde, much less Lord Douglas, to see the truth in the observation Yeats associated himself with so publicly, that in not running away from his forthcoming imprisonment, as so many sophisticates urged, Wilde even to his detractors "made of infamy a new Thermopylae."[48] Similarly, while cherishing all the insights of Freudian and Jungian theory in the last hundred years, and of gay and lesbian studies and gender studies in the last decade, it is important to recall that our meanings now will in many cases not have been Cram's meanings then.

Ralph Adams Cram was nearly twenty-three years old in 1886, when that widely influential work, Richard von Krafft-Ebing's *Psychopathia Sexualis*, first appeared in advanced centers of learning like Boston. He was twenty-seven when the word "homosexual" first appeared (so far as is known) in English, in John Addington Symonds's *Problem in Modern Ethics*—in 1891, the year Cram and Goodhue first met. That was also the year Eve Kosofsky Sedgwick, in *The Epistemology of the Closet,* fixed on as "a good moment to look for a cross-section of inaugural discourses of modern homosexuality," citing *Billy Budd* and *The Picture of Dorian Gray* (the former written, the latter published, in that year) as the first two of the four works she cites as the "foundational texts of modern gay culture."[49] (The other two, issued in 1912, were Proust's *A la Recherche du temps perdu* and Thomas Mann's *Death in Venice*.) Ralph Adams Cram passed his young adult years in an era of which Peter Gay has written: "It is too much to say, but not by a great deal, that the 1870s and 1880s and 1890s invented homosexuality."[50]

That there are homosexual *persons* at all is in fact a relatively new (and still almost entirely Western) concept; so, in fact, is the concept Foucault asserts it begat, "their antitwins, heterosexual persons."[51] Goodhue and Cram and their friends, if pressed on the subject, would have spoken (as an Arab still would) not of homosexual *persons* but of homosexual *relationships*, agreeing, probably, with "the anthropological insight . . . that human sexuality is extremely plastic," that "all of us . . . have the capacity to be sexually attracted to members of the same sex . . . [and that there is] a huge variety of [sexual] patterns."[52] Our debate about nature versus nurture in the matter of the "origins" of homosexuality would not have seemed real to them. Today, recent research, such as the discovery that a pencil-sized bundle of nerve fibers linking the two hemispheres of the brain is larger in homosexual than in heterosexual men, and that gay persons may thus process not just sexual but all information differently from nongay persons, suggests that homosexuality can properly be called innate, that sexual orientation results from not only environmental but hormonal and also genetic factors. A hundred years ago this debate had hardly been joined. And neither Bertram Goodhue nor Ralph Cram would have thought of themselves as, in our sense of the term, homosexual persons.

On the other hand, like Copeland and Day, Carman and Hovey, and Brown and Guiney (to catalogue other names in Cram's circle often coupled), both Goodhue and Cram certainly appear to have understood well enough the homosexual *relationship*. Whatever one concludes about Cram's dedication of *The Decadent*, Goodhue's frontispiece to the book is *not* innocent, whether or not they were physical lovers. As to that, let us at this point consider the matter only to the extent of noting in the same period the case of Henry James, of whose request in a letter to a younger friend to treat him as "a brother and a lover," his biographer Leon Edel writes that he simply does not know "whether the use of the term 'lover' and the verbal passion of the letter was 'acted out.'. . . Most Victorians kept the doors of their bedrooms closed."[53] So did Ralph and Bertram.

That said, Charles Wentworth seems to have known enough to have raised the issue quite bluntly to Ralph Adams Cram.

THE HOUSE OF THE DOUBLE

Wentworth was a plain-spoken man, as we have seen, and not the sort likely to fail of friendship's supreme value, loyalty. Thus it was surely in a spirit of friendship that he wrote to Ralph in 1895 to warn him of the rather risqué company on Pinckney Street he and Goodhue were then keeping and of its effect on the firm's prospects. Admitting

> this is all very fatherly, isn't it? . . . [Wentworth, only two years older than Cram, goes on to say:] You are two innocents and besides you are both queer and queer things are looked at askance since Oscar's exposé. Poor Oscar, what horrid privations he will have to endure.[54]

It is important to note that the word "queer" was not then either an ugly slur or a somewhat surly if frank challenge, but rather one of a number of "code words" (we have already encountered several in Burgess's description of Bohemia) that I have deliberately conspired to use here without too much explanation so far, so as to rope the reader in to the experience, as it were. As Karl Miller has written in *Doubles: Studies in Literary History*, " 'odd,' 'queer,' 'dark,' 'fit,' 'nervous,' [were] the bricks which built the house of the double,"[55] meaning the words used in Cram's young adulthood (not all gays were aesthetes, after all) to describe and allude discreetly to the double life of homosexual behavior.

Two examples may be helpful here. One, cited by Miller, is taken from Henry James's "The Sense of the Past," begun in 1900, where of James's vocabulary (about a character named Ralph) Miller observes:

> So Ralph can be "gay" as well as "queer." These were favored adjectives of the fin-de-siècle and after, which in the fullness of time were to become in succession the names which the English-speaking homosexual community has used to identify itself. James's use presages this, just as his [story] may be accounted, like *Dorian Gray*, a form of early Camp.[56]

Second, that in the case of "queer" the identification had already become firm is Elaine Showalter's point in *Sexual Anarchy*, where she studies Robert Louis

Stevenson's vocabulary in *Dr. Jekyll and Mr. Hyde*, published in 1886. There not only does the butler at one point conclude there is "something queer" about Hyde, but Jekyll's abode, "Blackmail House," is actually located on "Queer Street," a connection underlined by another character's remark that "the more it sounds like Queer Street, the less I ask."[57]

Yet another aspect of the technique of reveal and conceal, or mask and signal, such code words are just as evident in some of Cram's work of the nineties. Consider, for example, this synopsis of his short story "252 Rue M. Le Prince":

When in May, 1886, I found myself at last in Paris, I naturally determined to throw myself on the charity of an old chum of mine, Eugène Marie d'Ardéche, who had forsaken Boston a year or more ago on receiving word of the death of an aunt who had left him . . . property. . . . [She was] a wicked and witch-like old person, with a penchant for black magic . . . [whose closest confidant was] a questionable old party known to infamy as the Sar Torrevieja, the "King of the Sorcerers," [a] malevolent old portent [of] gray and crafty face. . . .

[Having hunted up his friend] in three minutes we were sitting in the queer little garden of the Chien Bleu, drinking vermouth and absinthe, and talking it all over.

[d'Ardéche is not, he tells Cram, living in the house; the "King of the Sorcerers" having proceeded "to curse it elaborately and comprehensively," d'Ardéche cannot even rent it, not only because of "the queer goings on" in it in the past, but because since his aunt's death, even though the house has been perfectly empty] "a queer thing about the whole affair is . . . that everyone in the street swears that . . . the music and voices were heard again, just as when my revered aunt was in the flesh."

[The inevitable ensues: Cram joins d'Ardéche and "a couple of rake-hell fellows I know, Fargeau and Duchesne" in spending the night in the house, located in the Latin Quarter at 252 Rue M. Le Prince] running up the hill towards the Garden of the Luxembourg. It is full of queer houses and odd corners — or was in '86 — and certainly No. 252 was, when I found it, quite as queer as any. It was nothing but a doorway, a black arch of old stone. . . .

[They tour, by lantern-light, a series of fantastic rooms, of which perhaps the most arresting is] circular, thirty or so feet in diameter, covered by a hemispherical dome; walls and ceiling were dark blue, spotted with gold stars; and reaching from floor to floor across the dome stretched a colossal figure in red lacquer of a nude woman kneeling, her legs reaching out along the floor on either side, her head touching the lintel of the door through which we had entered, her arms forming its sides, with the forearms extended and stretching along the walls until they met the long feet. The most astounding, misshapen, absolutely terrifying thing, I think, I ever saw. From the navel hung a great white object, like the traditional roc's egg of the Arabian Nights. The floor was of red lacquer, and in it was inlaid a pentagram. . . . It is all just about as queer and *fin de siècle* as I can well imagine.

[They take up their vigil, each man in a separate room, each opening on to a corner corridor, and on to the mansion's interior court.]

It was very still without — still and hot. The great masses of rank wisteria leaves, with here and there a second blossoming of purple flowers, hung dead over the window in the sluggish air. . . .

148

Half a hundred times, nearly, I would doze for an instant, only to wake up and find my pipe gone out. . . . I felt numb, as though with cold. . . . I sank down in my window seat. How dark it was growing! I turned up the lantern. That pipe again, how obstinately it was going out! and my last match was gone. The lantern too, was *that* going out? I lifted my hand to turn it up again. It felt like lead, and fell beside me.

Then I awoke — absolutely. . . . I tried to rise, to cry out. My body was like lead, my tongue was paralyzed. . . . Darker and darker yet; little by little the pattern of the paper was swallowed up in the advancing night. . . . A thin, keen humming began in my head, like cicadas on a hillside in September. . . .

In the velvet blackness came two white eyes, milky, opalescent, small, faraway — awful eyes, like a dead dream. More beautiful than I can describe, the flakes of white flame moving from the perimeter inward, disappearing in the center, like a never-ending flow of opal water into a circular tunnel . . . the eyes of the unknown Horror swelled and expanded until they were close before me. . . . I felt a slow, cold, wet breath . . . against my face. . . .

Suddenly a wet, icy mouth, like that of a dead cuttle-fish, shapeless, jelly-like, fell over mine. The Horror began slowly to draw my life from me, but as enormous and shuddering folds of palpitating jelly swept sinuously around me, my will came back, my body awoke with the reaction of final fear, and I closed with the nameless death that enfolded me.

[The next day, when he awakes in a hospital, "a tall sister of mercy sat by my side." Cram is told of his friends' breaking in and finding him unconscious in a room streaming with a glutinous moisture, and of the fire, caused perhaps be his overturned lantern, that burned the old house to the ground. Perhaps the only explanation is offered by Cram in his introduction to the tale, when he writes that he believes in all sorts of curious things; "there are, in fact," he writes, "few things I can *not* believe."][58]

Edward Wagenknecht, when he republished this tale in 1947, after Cram's death, believed it would "reveal the great American architect Ralph Adams Cram to many of his admirers in a new and unfamiliar light."[59] More so, perhaps, than Wagenknecht knew. For to us today, in the post-Freudian era, Cram's tale, like 252 Rue M. Le Prince itself, is "just about as queer and *fin de siècle* as [one] can well imagine." Indeed, there is reason to believe that before the story was published Cram may have realized that the balance between what was hidden and what was revealed was awry from his point of view. More of the mask, less of the signal was surely the point to a suggestion of Cram's we know of because in a letter to Cram his editor, Harrison Rhodes, agrees to it: "As to rewriting 'No. 252 Rue M. le Prince,' putting it in the third person, if you think you can make it more effective that way, do so by all means."[60]

Cram's concern is understandable, for the level of self-disclosure is so high in this work that one is reminded of the assertion of H. P. Lovecraft that writers like Cram from other fields who "try their hands at [horror do so] . . . as if to discharge from their mind [themes] which would otherwise haunt them."[61] Lovecraft cites in this connection F. Marion Crawford's "The Upper Berth," the story, interestingly, that Edward Wagenknecht thought most similar in its nightmare struggle to Cram's. There is even a decidedly autobiographical aspect to Cram's tale, scholars having long since identified the motif of the "hidden" house as characteristic of work by men and women leading "double" lives. It is surely likely that 252 Rue M. le Prince derives from 74½ Pinckney Street, that "hidden house of Beacon Hill," across the street from which during the five years prior to the publication of the story Cram lodged.

If we must be alert to what colors like green and symbols like carnations and words like "queer" and motifs like tunnels mean, so also, however, we must not jump to conclusions. For example, the way Wentworth's letter brings up so prominently the name of Oscar Wilde, and in the year of his downfall ("Poor Oscar," writes Wentworth and not too subtly makes his point), is, when tested against other evidence, somewhat misleading.

In the first place, Wentworth's letter does not suggest that Goodhue and Cram were lovers, only that their sexuality made possible what I have concluded Cram's attitude toward Goodhue and his dedication and Goodhue's frontispiece suggest. Also, if one accepts my reading of the evidence of the dedication and frontispiece and reads Wentworth's letter in the light of my conclusion, Wentworth's immediately raising Wilde's name after his warning to Cram, taken in conjunction with the very Wildean frontispiece, suggests not only that Cram and Goodhue's relationship was Wildean, i.e., gay, but that their relational model was that of Wilde and Lord Alfred Douglas, who were, after all, *the* gay lovers of the era. But Wentworth also called Bertram and Ralph "innocents" as well as "queer," and neither he nor anyone else would (then or now) be likely to have called Wilde and Douglas innocents.

For Ralph's and Bertram's relational model I am persuaded we must look elsewhere. Granted the complexities of "the house of the double," any relational model proposed for Cram must be reconcilable with his values as we have come to know them here, especially with his newly embraced religion. One may well ask if there is such a model. It is a question we can hardly leave in abeyance while charging ahead into Cram and Goodhue's Bohemian lifestyle of the nineties. That must wait until we have cleared away the smoke screen of the last hundred years that obscures so much of Boston's cultural history. And before that, we must eavesdrop, as it were, on a vexing dialogue between Freudians and Jungians on the one hand and Christians on the other.

PREDISPOSITIONS

Persons whose interest in Cram is primarily religious need to be open to granting the Freudian-Jungian premise about the critical importance of our unconscious drives, while persons whose interest in Cram is mainly artistic need to accept the possibility that sexuality is related to creativity. Both themes will reoccur often here.

Freud's ideas, the culmination of the work of many others, did not come as a complete surprise (especially in Victorian Boston, where psychology flourished before Freud) to Christian moral theology, which has always recognized in what we should call today "neuroses" what moral theologians call "habitual impediments" to free choice and moral responsibility. Thus as our century has evolved, some things Freudian and some things Catholic have increasingly cohabited to the mutual benefit of each.[62] An excellent example, drawn from Cram's own religious universe of discourse, is Richard Ellmann's observation, so seemingly destructive of a key vector of Christian doctrine, that today's biographer typically "agrees with Freud that we must be skeptical of heroics . . . the existence of virtue itself [being] almost in question" — followed by Ellmann's citing of *Murder in the Cathedral*, where the last and most insidious temptation of Saint Thomas à Becket is, of course, that of *Christian martyrdom itself*.[63] Yet who would deny that the insight thus vouchsafed in this play by its devout Anglo-Catholic author, T. S. Eliot, deepens rather than compromises its religious content?

Freud's conclusion that we are virtually at the mercy of our psychological drives has, moreover, been somewhat modified by subsequent Freudian theory that takes into account developments in cultural anthropology, psychology, and linguistics, developments by figures like Jean Piaget and Noam Chomsky that seem to suggest human thinking is, if not as malleable as some have thought, neither as intrinsic. As Stuart Sutherland has written: "Though the mind is predisposed to act in certain ways . . . the neural circuits carry [our] predisposition[s] which may or may not be selected by experience . . . [and] all learning depends on the selection."[64]

Finally, it ought not to be necessary to point out, but is, that there is not only a Freudian but a Jungian school, whose founder, in Robert Hopcke's words, "eschewed a single-minded focus on sexuality as the basic element of the human personality or as the only key to understanding the psyche."[65] This is of special relevance to us because while Cram would not have identified himself as a Freudian, he did respect the work of William James, and in later years Cram became an ardent disciple of Henri Bergson, exhibiting an affinity for the Jungian mind-set, an affinity Jackson Lears has noticed,[66] and that is demonstrable artistically as well, I believe, in Cram's wholehearted love of Wagner. It is not only that the work of that great outlaw of Western music was concerned above all with the question of whether there is salvation for the sensuous artist and whether carnal and even violent love (as in *Tannhäuser*, for example) can co-exist with Christian love, but that the quality and finish, as it were, of Wagner's sound express our "collective unconscious," as Jung might have put it, so unerringly and beautifully—and, perhaps, alarmingly.

Having thus suggested to those whose interest in Cram is primarily religious that neither the Freudian nor the Jungian libido distorts or compromises Cram's accomplishment or scants his religious beliefs, it is equally necessary to insist to those chiefly interested in Cram artistically that they consider the effect of sexuality on creativity, all the more so in Cram's case because his sexuality, so long obscured, and thus the one thing missing, is now the one thing needful for a proportionate view of Cram; one hardly has to be a Freudian to see how distorting is sexual orientation *misunderstood*.

One of the few generalist scholars of stature who have studied historically the vexing question of the relationship, if any, between sexual orientation and artistic creativity is the Oxford historian A. L. Rowse, who cited an oft-mentioned example that sets up the classic standard:

> Michelangelo's love for [Tommasso] Cavalieri was the great passion of his life. This young artist [who was in his twenties and Michelangelo in his fifties when they first met] had everything that the artist worshipped—physical beauty, nobility of mind, a high intelligence, sensibility [i.e., what we would call today emotional maturity] and responsiveness. . . . Michelangelo's letters and poems express all the ardours and torments of his passionate temperament. . . . His mind became occupied by the beloved image. . . . This propensity has its disadvantages; but it has the compensation that it often predisposes to creation.[67]

It is a claim one has heard before. Unusually, however, Rowse went on to try to isolate "the predisposing conditions to creativeness, in [homosexuality's] psychological rewards." Though not neglecting what he called "the tensions that lead to achievement" (indeed, quoting Bacon that "whosoever hath anything fixed in his person that doth induce contempt hath also a perpetual spur"), Rowse concluded that "creative genius [had often] its source in the two elements [masculine and feminine] fertilizing each other in the same person," and that homosexuals thus enjoyed the benefits of what he called a "doubling [of] the potentialities of the personality" and a consequent "sharpening of perception."[68]

What is chiefly interesting about Rowse's analysis is that, like Karl Miller, he quite independently fixed on this idea of doubling, at once giving it a more positive aspect and relating it to the idea, broached first here in our discussion of the Whitmanic aspect of Ashbee's (and Cram's) Christian Socialism: that though homosexuality will always be erotic, its *eros* is not necessarily or chiefly genital, but is social and moral. And in this connection, Rowse essayed a most moving and significant comparison between the Western Greek tradition and the Japanese samurai tradition: that "though their reasons for it differ, the samurai and the [Western] homosexual *do not see manliness as instinctive, but, rather, as something to be gained by moral effort* [emphasis added]."[69] That aspiration is essentially Platonic. And that ideal pervades the specific relational model that I think was Cram's.

PLATONIC IDEALIST

Whatever Charles Wentworth meant when he called Cram personally an "innocent," I suspect Jackson Lears meant much the same thing when he described Cram intellectually as a Platonic idealist.[70] Thus the specific relational model with Goodhue that I suggest best dovetails with Cram's cultural, ethnic, religious, and artistic context and with his own character and temperament is the Platonic one. This is conjecture. But Cram, who agreed with T. S. Eliot about so much, would probably also have agreed (for himself) with Eliot's assertion that he was "more likely to be understood by someone other than himself, *as an optician knows his eyes*."[71] The historian, then, as optician.

Cram's surviving youthful musings and ruminations were likely, if they were not Anglophile or New England, to be more or less Greek. Witness this story-line of Cram's from his mid-1880s diary:

> The main character shall be a young Athenian, a soldier, yet with the first flickering of . . . artistic and religious feelings. . . . The hero shall be no particular [historical] person for I can better make [in that way] an ideal man who in the last book shall develop into a man of perfect justice, truth and wisdom. In the first book . . . his intense yearnings of truth shall be greatly hampered by his animal traits which he may gradually get rid of.[72]

Whatever the Greek classical experience really was, Cram's story-line can be seen in the era of his youth as central to an understanding of it, the development of manhood having always been central to what for simplicity's sake we call here the Platonic tradition.

At once devoted, heroic, and disciplined, integrating and celebrating equally both the life of the mind and of the body, the Platonic relationship, which is by definition homosexual and may exist only between males, arises out of shared values, admiring love, and ardent erotic desire rooted in a glorification of the grace and power of the male body and mind in perfect equipoise. Yet this is not to say that it was in any sense permissive or hedonist — quite the reverse; pleasure for pleasure's sake was held to be unworthy of a man. As David Greenberg has written:

> For Plato, the ideal life was to be spent seeking and discussing Beauty, Truth, and the Good. Although bodily perfection could inspire this pursuit, lust itself was evil because it leads to an undignified, slavish, animallike surrender to the passions. It

places temperance and reason in jeopardy, and fails to judge the worthiness of its object properly.[73]

Although Plato ultimately, Greenberg continued, "abandoned faith in the possibility that homosexual desire could be channeled into salutary forms" and fell back on the thesis that to avoid, as Plato put it, "the frenzied madness of love," only the minimal heterosexual love necessary between spouses for procreation of the race was tolerable, the ideals of his earliest thought never died. Though the various Greek schools of philosophy after Socrates

> all considered a life devoted primarily to physical pleasure to be noxious . . . yet none called for sexual abstinence for everyone and none thought that homosexuality should be suppressed. It was the quality of the relationship that was important, not the sex of the partner.[74]

Indeed, for all the glorification of the male body the Platonic tradition was founded upon, it *insisted* (in aid of a man's ascent of what has been called "the ladder of love" to yet higher and higher levels of philosophical beauty and truth) upon restraint and balance, encouraging understatement, admiring severity and balance, and exalting the achievement by a man, beginning in his earliest youth, of personal self-mastery, above all in the flesh; this self-mastery constituting one's highest duty to oneself (because predisposing the mind to its highest good) and the noblest good (because the noblest example) to others, including, first and foremost, one's beloved. One might almost say the moral effort that yields manliness is, to echo Rowse, the achievement of self-mastery.

This tradition was celebrated most splendidly, perhaps, in the heroic saga of Achilles and Patrocles, to whom homosexual thinkers such as John Addington Symonds were drawn because, as Symonds pointedly put it, "Achilles and Patrocles were *not* pederasts."[75] Harmodius and Aristogiton were another much-admired pair. Moreover, this tradition is enshrined in both the *Symposium* and the *Phaedrus*, Plato's lyrical exaltations of homosexual love, the first and surely the most noble of all considerations of the nature of love in Western history. Definitions are critical here. As Boswell puts it: "the origin of the concept of 'Platonic love' . . . was not Plato's belief that sex should be absent from gay affairs but his conviction that only love between persons of the same gender could transcend sex."[76]

It was, after all, Plato's conviction that a man's love for another man (love, not lust) cannot really *be* genitally expressed — worthily, that is — despite the deep desire to do so, a desire that lust constantly ministers to, whispering always in the friend's ear. No sexual acts, Plato believed, though they may easily and directly satisfy lust, are in the first place able to express Platonic love. Moderns often stumble unaware on this now unpopular insight. Note W. H. Auden's observation, even as a very sexually active college student, that love and lust were such very different things to him that the ideal was "deep devotion of one comrade for another" and "lechery in the back room as necessary."[77] A traditional British way of making this distinction is to speak of what was called in Rupert Brooke's day the "higher" sodomy or the "lower," referring in the first instance to a soulmate, in the second to a bedmate.[78]

The Platonic tradition also sees no incongruity between the covenants of homosexual love (Friendship, as it were, with a capital *F*) and heterosexual marriage; for however inferior as a love relationship marriage may have been in one sense in the Platonic scheme, it was hardly less important in a civic and social sense. Plato expected a man to do his duty to his community, his family, and his posterity. Everyone remembers Socrates and Alcibiades. Most forget that Socrates also had a wife and children.

So, too, did Oscar Wilde, and this is perhaps the place to alert the reader to the fact that in the period of Cram's youth, when the social pressures to marry were very strong, it must be assumed that many if not most homosexuals *did* marry and often had children, as did Cram and Goodhue and many of their friends. Thus marriage and even children are for that reason generally neutral evidence in assessing whether or not a person was homosexual, though that a person did *not* marry is for the same reason highly significant evidence for homosexuality. Similarly, I have not called Cram for this reason bisexual. Whereas today one might try to place a person on the so-called Kinsey scale, in Cram's youth the distorting effect of the pressure to marry would skew any judgment made from this distance and in the absence of detailed data. I have followed here Boswell's lead in assessing a person gay or nongay according to the perceived erotic center of his life. He gives the example of Alexander the Great, who slept with women but whose repute has always been homosexual.[79]

It is as difficult at the end of the twentieth century to understand Platonic love as it is to understand Cram's religious conversion, for even the tradition sketched here (admittedly an idealization that overlooked several to us problematic aspects of the ancient original) had its negative aspect, to which we are more likely to relate, as has Robert K. Martin in his study of another Platonist, Hart Crane. Observing that Crane and others of Plato's admirers seemed to him to have "inherited a tradition which held that homosexuality offered a higher, purer form of love, but that the price paid for that love must be a renunciation of physical passion," Martin describes this dilemma as "the 'trap' of Platonism."[80]

True enough. But one man's "trap" may be another's "triumph," especially if he has just converted to Anglo-Catholicism. Recall how suspect chasteness is today as a concept and note how very differently Cram and many of his contemporaries saw the matter. Think, instead, in our terms now, of skepticism, unlike chasteness still something of a virtue, and of Santayana's aphorism: "Skepticism is the chastity of the intellect, and it is shameful to surrender it too soon, or to the first comer; there is nobility in preserving [skepticism] coolly and proudly through a long youth, until at last, in the ripeness of instinct and discretion, it can be safely exchanged for fidelity and happiness."[81] Think of chastity as a skepticism of the body. Still, as with Cram's conversion to Catholicism, we need for our understanding's sake somehow to transpose the Platonic tradition of Cram's youth into what will seem to us more positive terms at the end of the twentieth century.

DOUBLE LOVE

In her study of Carl Jung and his distinguished follower James Hillman, Christine Downing observes:

> There are many different couplings, many different stories. The anima [the inner feminine capacity it is the primary psychological task of a man to establish a conscious relation with — DS-T] may appear in the imagery of a *woman's* unconscious; the animus [the inner male capacity] may be found working in men. [There is, perhaps, an] *inner homosexuality*, the possibility of a vital psychical relationship between a man's masculine ego and an inner masculine figure, [as well as] between a woman's female-identified ego and an inner feminine soul image.[82]

Downing goes on to describe what she calls "Double-love," writing with some eloquence that

> "Double-love is distinguished from Anima-love by uncanny feelings of unity, strength and reinforcement of personal identity." The Double is one's deeper support, a partner, helper, guide, a friend who is profoundly equal, deeply familiar, with whom "a mysterious, joyful sharing of feelings and needs, a dynamic intuitive understanding" is possible. The archetype contains the images of father, son, brother, lover . . . "but it is not necessarily a homosexual archetype. Rather, the Double embodies the *spirit* of love between those of the same sex." Thus Achilles and Patrocles exemplify the Double relationship, whether or not one views them as sexually involved.[83]

This modern concept of "double love" is in a certain sense comparable to Platonic love, in that while primacy is by no means yielded to genital experience (it is not even necessary), the share of the body in love is not on the other hand puritanically denied.

It is, of course, a very fine line we are trying to walk here, between what Peter Gay calls the "voluptuous rubbing [of the sensualists, at one extreme, and the ascetics,] for whom true love was a celestial emotion purged of sensual admixtures [at the other extreme],"[84] and when all is said and done, then as now that line is perhaps best negotiated with Plato's immemorial image before one (so apt because of Mary Renault's superb modern book *The Charioteer*); which is to say the tale of the Charioteer, the self, struggling to bring love and lust into proper balance on each side of a relationship. Plato declares:

> "[The beloved] comes to welcome his suitor and take a pleasure in his company; he comes to value this man 'in whom there dwells a god [Eros]' beyond all his other friends . . . [and] responds not just with *philia* but with Eros. . . . So when they lie, side by side, the wanton horse of the lover's soul would have a word with the charioteer. . . . The like steed in the soul of the beloved [also stirs] . . . he is minded not to refuse, to do his part in gratifying his lover's entreaties; yet [the wanton horse's] yoke-fellow in turn, being moved by reverence and needfulness, joins with the driver in resisting."

Downing's excellent commentary on this image, which incorporates more of Plato's text, draws out its meaning:

> If victory goes to the restraining elements, the pair's days on earth "will be blessed by happiness and concord" for they will have "won self-mastery and inward peace" . . . a life-long relationship in which each makes "*simultaneous* and *reciprocal* though *independent* progress. . . ." Socrates acknowledges the struggle is a persistent one: "Mayhap in a careless hour or when the wine is flowing, the wanton horses in their two souls will catch them off guard . . . and they continue therein, albeit but rarely. . . . Even such a pair (not only those who remain celibate) participate in the blessings of the love."[85]

Of course, one is entitled to assume such an outcome in the case of all such counsels of perfection, and if Cram (like C. S. Lewis) is not likely to have been any different from any of us, doubtless also he was capable of all the conventional ways of reconciling such incongruities. And those who find all this too much idealized need only note that it is by no means unlikely that it could be hazarded of Cram's circle in Boston's late nineteenth-century Bohemia what Maynard Solomon ventured about Schubert's circle in Vienna's early nineteenth-century Bohemia:

> That the young men of the Schubert circle loved each other seems amply clear. And, . . . it is reasonably probable that their primary sexual orientation was a homosexual one. By finding sexual release with anonymous partners, in Vienna's *Hallowett* [red-light district], they were apparently able to maintain idealized, passionate friendships with each other and to infuse those friendships with some stability.[86]

As we will see, Cram was also acquainted with such a red-light district, perhaps for the same reasons.

THE ARISTOTELIAN ALTERNATIVE

One final bit of underbrush needs clearing away: it is not always easy to distinguish between a homosexual relationship and a close nonerotic friendship,

Jeffrey Richards's point in his "Manly Love and Victorian Society," where he argues that there were *two* ancient Greek models: Plato's — clearly erotic and, indeed, genital and strongly oriented around older and younger men; and Aristotle's — found in his *Ethics*; and that this second, a nongenital relationship usually between equals, is, in fact, the supreme Greek same-sex model as well as the root of the Christian knightly tradition of the Middle Ages.[87]

The opposing view has perhaps been put most baldly by Stephen Coote, who, after describing the historical process by which same-sex love, so commonly accepted in the ancient world, was increasingly condemned in the Middle Ages by the church, ventured of the Renaissance and Enlightenment that "rather than wither as the love that dare not speak its name, gay emotion rechristened itself 'Friendship,'. . . receiv[ing] support from the classical concept of *amicitia*, and found its Renaissance prose-poet in Montaigne."[88] This point of view is echoed in much of the modern scholarly work of biographers of twentieth-century gay artists and poets. It builds on the homosexual experience of so many eras — one thinks no less in this connection of Whitman than of Plato — that, as Hart Crane's biographer Thomas Yingling put it, "homosexual satisfaction may reside in something *other* [emphasis added] than genital intercourse," a conclusion Yingling reached after a study of Crane's letters.[89]

Richards notes that Aristotelian friendship was limited to one relationship at a time between only two friends, a relationship even C. S. Lewis admitted in the case of knightly friendship was "lover-like."[90] Observe, moreover, that when Richards, citing as central to this tradition books like H. A. Vachell's *The Hill: A Romance of Friendship* (1905) and Ernest Raymond's *Tell England* (1922), asserts that their message was that "love between friends transcends sex,"[91] he is using almost the exact words of John Boswell quoted earlier to define Platonic homosexual love. There is a very real sense in which all these scholars are calling the same thing different things. And it seems to me that to make so much of a distinction and then to abolish it invites the suspicion of homophobia.

Consider Richards's assertion that though Alfred Lord Tennyson's friendship with Arthur Henry Hallam lasted only four years, those "four years probably [were] the equal in psychic importance to the other seventy-nine of [Tennyson's] life." Similarly, Robert Louis Stevenson's relationship with W. E. Henley was, Richards writes:

> a romantic friendship. . . . [Stevenson and Henley] were to part and quarrel and die unreconciled, but the power of the friendship . . . was never finally dissipated or broken, for between them was a strong, bitter, binding love.[92]

Surely each other's "significant other," were Tennyson and Hallam, Stevenson and Henley, Platonic homosexual friends or Aristotelian heterosexual friends?

Any answer will be controversial. And two extremes must be borne in mind. We must in the first place take seriously Edward Rothenstein's point in his beautifully entitled "Was Schubert Gay? If He Was, So What?" that we are only too likely to accept the premise that Schubert was gay because we sense that the only way to keep historical figures we admire alive and mattering in our era is to do so, "our cultural pantheon practically requir[ing] marginality and alienation as an entrance requirement." Thus we are not as suspicious as perhaps we ought to be of what may be, in fact, attempts to "create a contemporary [in this case gay] Schubert" — or Cram.[93]

Those alert to this danger, however, would do well to recall, historically, the enormous pressures to deny the effect and even the existence and certainly any positive aspect of same-sex love in the first place, pressures that do not by any means always derive from heterosexuals. Often they come from deeply closeted gay people, either those who suffer from the sort of self-loathing constant repression induces, or, conversely (in perhaps fewer situations), those who seem to rejoice in the almost Gnostic self-absorbed delight of an elite society hoarding a delicious and privileged secret. Both extremes — to seek out or to deny homosexuality — necessarily corrupt any answer to the question posed, about Tennyson or Stevenson or anyone else.

That there is such a thing as friendship — same sex *or* opposite sex — without any erotic component at all is obvious. But the most telling evidence is what type of relationship is *key* in a person's life, for there is the erotic investment the historian seeks to locate. And where the key human relationship, the strongest and most central in a person's life, is *not* an opposite-sex relationship but a *same*-sex one, a same-sex orientation is surely evidenced. If a man's "significant other" is not a woman but another man, that manly love is here called "homosexual"; quite aside from whether its erotic content is much or little, it is presumably the erotic content the person deems sufficient or, as it were, can muster: irrespective of whether it is acted out genitally, with the significant other (once, twice, or often), or with prostitutes (substituting for the image of the beloved), or alone (masturbation), or not at all. To conclude otherwise, I believe, is to fall into the mistake of people who, in Robert Martin's words, "assume that anyone is heterosexual until there is proof, not of homosexual feelings, but of homosexual acts."[94]

Accordingly, it is with both Plato and Aristotle in hand that I suggest we consider now how Ralph Adams Cram put it, writing only to himself in his diary between the ages of eighteen and twenty-three. Musing ostensibly about the fact that "sand dunes have a strange fascination for me. Why I hardly know," Cram is actually writing more about two people lying side by side, perhaps after some exercise and some kind of meal and surely "when the wine is flowing":

Then they both fell silent and in the hot shade of the dunes . . . the shadows almost purple . . . grass hardly moved in the heavy air; the crowded beach was hid from them by a lofty dune. . . . B broke the heavy silence, or rather intensified it, with a vague . . . line of half audible thoughts that were heard by his companion more by their echo in his own mind than from their own. . . . For hours they lay there in the shade, their bodies almost asleep, their minds alone dimly conscious and answering each other through the heat. The blue shadow of the dune grew long and longer and slowly reached out to the sea, which in turn crept slowly back up. . . . At last the two met, the soul of the dunes in the shadow of its substance.

The metaphorical treatment is hardly comparable to that of the *Phaedrus*, but it is nonetheless apt, for a period certainly interested in men on beaches: paintings such as Seurat's *Une Baignade* and Eakins's *The Swimming Hole* and poems like Gerard Manley Hopkins's "Epithalamion" come at once to mind; above all, Walt Whitman's "Song of Myself."[95]

And as for any dispute between varieties of friendship, consider C. S. Lewis's distinction between lovers — "face to face, absorbed in each other" — and friends — "side by side, absorbed in some common interest" ("seeing," as he puts it elsewhere, "the same truth").[96] One must imagine *both* of ideal Platonic love, the former inspiring the latter.

Finally, let us be clear that notwithstanding the weighty issues of religion and sexuality involved, self-mastery achieved, which is to say the absence of genital sex in a relationship, though in one sense less enjoyable, can in another sense be more so. Or thus at least one of Cram's most beautiful friends thought; in the first volume of his biography of Bernard Berenson, Ernest Samuels quotes that distinguished Bohemian as avowing: "after all, it is a *delightful* thing [emphasis added] to keep one's self in hand. I have enjoyed the effort not to possess, no less than the delight in possession. . . . Such suppressed desire immensely enriches life — and so it should."[97] It can also be highly erotic. As Patricia Otoole observed in *Five of Hearts* of Henry Adams's love affair with Lizzie Cameron, which seems not to have been a physical liaison, in this era "some *lovers* found it nobler [emphasis added] — and perhaps even erotic — not to act on their physical impulses."[98]

Of course, it was not so simple as that. But if such a thing seems strange to us today, it is because the richly variegated sexuality of the fin-de-siècle is still a closed book to many, particularly in the case of the developing gay subculture of that period, which in order to understand Cram's youthful role we must now explore more fully.

5

THE BELLS OF MY DESIRE

Alone beside the fives-court, pacing
Waiting for God knows what. O, stars above!
My clothes clung tight to me, my heart was racing:
Perhaps what I was waiting for was love!
And what is love? And wherefore is its shape
To do with legs and arms and waist and nape?
... Here, 'twixt the church tower and the chapel spire
Rang sad and deep the bells of my desire.

— John Betjemann, *Summoned by Bells*

I have been guileless long: angels and you
And beauty in my dreams together played ...
... What mystic love is this?
What ghostly mistress? What angelic friend?

— George Santayana, Sonnet 39

5. Cram's proclivities for things Greek arose not only in his writings. A sketch by him of 1887 of his design for a country house hall, in *The Decorator and Furnisher*, abounds in images both classical and sexual, in vases and statuary. Most arresting is the male figure Cram has labeled "Artemis," to the right of the staircase. Neither the boyish goddess of antiquity nor the Ephesian variant with her many breasts and penises could ever be confused with Cram's aesthete athlete. Note the "RAC" monogram in the lower left corner.

IN NEW England at the end of the nineteenth century, in the wake of the Romantic movement's rediscovery of things Greek, new meaning was being given to the Platonic ideal — the reason a young man like Cram might imagine himself in his diary to be an Athenian youth or endow an entrance hall of his design with more Greeks than most would willingly suffer (55). This new meaning derived from England, ever Boston's (and Cram's) "country of the mind," but was shaped as well by New England's own character.

The Boston marriage, that characteristic institution of the "Athens of America" (so like what Mark A. De Wolfe Howe called the "Boston religion," whatever that is, in that both fused incredibly high standards of personal devotion, loyalty, and rectitude to the most astonishing reserve), is a good example.[1] Nothing less than a full-blown female variation of the Platonic male relationship, it was as characteristically Anglo-Saxon as was its male Platonic original, the chaste male friendship of *Maurice*, for instance, about which E. M. Forster was so blunt; it was, he wrote, "precarious, idealistic, and peculiarly English: what Italian boy would ever have put up with it?"[2] Yet class has arisen here as well. The characteristic setting of the late nineteenth-century Platonic relational model was that upper-class Anglican institution, the English public school, such as Eton or Rugby, which in Cram's era New England was enthusiastically making its own in the "St. Grottlesex" schools founded in this period: St. Paul's, St. Mark's, Groton, and Middlesex.

"CHASTE, STRONG AND UPLIFTING"

Key to shaping the image of all these schools was Cram's Pinckney Street mentor. Henry Vaughan designed St. Paul's School Chapel and both the first and the second Groton School chapels, and the design of St. Mark's School is so Vaughan-like that William Morgan suggests its architect probably studied in Vaughan's office in the early 1880s.[3] St. Paul's School Chapel, particularly, a sensuously beautiful building and in 1886–1894 the first of its kind in America, seemed to Cram (who in later years would himself enlarge it), an "inspiration to young architects who were working toward a more sincere and expressive manner of buildings."[4] And, truly, it would have been hard to fault Vaughan's chapels. He was an Englishman, after all; St. Grottlesex got the real thing. And not least in

56. Henry Vaughan's St. Paul's School Chapel, Concord, New Hampshire, 1886, established the design concept followed thereafter in the St. Mark's School Chapel of 1889 in Southborough, Massachusetts. Such a seating plan, wrote Sir John Betjemann, was "an inducement to love, a corrective to lust."

the uncanny way these chapels brought not just the spiritual and the aesthetic, but also the erotic, into focus at the center of school life, as the late poet laureate Sir John Betjeman remembered so well in his autobiography, from which comes the first epigraph of this chapter, with its final lament: "Here, 'twixt the church tower and the chapel spire / Rang sad and deep the bells of my desire."[5] Why, one might ask, the chapel? Sir John is telling us where the action was; especially if the rows of seats, rather than facing the altar, were, instead, in the English choir style, raised up on tiers and facing each other, as Vaughan introduced at St. Paul's Chapel (56).

What the gymnasium was to the ancient classical expression of male ardor the English school chapel of this sort became to the modern Anglican expression, as generations of schoolboy memoirs testify. (In New England in 1891 St.

Mark's School followed Vaughan's example at St. Paul's, though in 1900 Groton opted for seats facing the altar.) Jonathan Gathorne-Hardy observed in *The Old School Tie* that only the fact that "the lavatories stood doorless" was a more important "architectural feature" of school life than the question of the choir stalls' placement. He writes of one school that the

> seats in chapel did not face each other, nor was the choir raised up; [because the headmaster] hoped to discourage the exchange of ravenous glances. Betjeman would not have agreed. Seats facing in chapel were all right: "An inducement to love; a corrective to lust."[6]

There it is again, the Platonic ideal — and now in Gothic guise. Ah, the beauties — architectural, musical, and male — of the Anglican school chapel in full bloom at Evensong.

What that august paragon of New England Episcopalianism in the mid-nineties, Bishop William Lawrence, made of all this one can only surmise. He was a distant figure. But when he was called upon to describe Vaughan's Groton and St. Paul's chapels, Lawrence's words seemed to catch not only the aesthetic aspect — seen through ethnicity, of course — but also the erotic and, as much as Betjemann's, the Platonic. Vaughan's chapels, Lawrence thought, "express[ed] . . . the Christian culture of the English speaking peoples"; they were "chaste, strong and uplifting."[7] The good bishop did not get it wrong at all.

He might just as well have been describing Cram and Goodhue's own Phillips Church, initially mooted in 1895, at Exeter, New Hampshire (*57*). The first of a long series of commissions at Exeter, nearly all for Phillips Exeter Academy, the Phillips Church, though it was erected directly across from the academy buildings, is Gothic, not Colonial — though Cram submitted schemes in both styles. So dominant was the British public-school image of Gothic chapels that even an old Colonial Congregational foundation like Exeter felt the need to remake its image the better to compete with St. Grottlesex. How chaste, strong (and perforce uplifting) was Cram's response at Exeter, one is reminded that on their exteriors at least (and in what was virtually Cram's home town), Cram's and not Goodhue's must often have been the decisive voice. Certainly there is at Exeter more than an echo of Cram and Wentworth's "constructional" detail, especially in the way the sandstone entrance ensemble is concentrated in a kind of recessed, built-in frontispiece formed by sheer-profiled granite pier buttresses, reminiscent of Cram's master recessed mantel and overmantel at the Merriam House of 1891 in Brookline.

The beautifully taut and elegantly severe Swedenborgian Church of 1893 in Newtonville (see *102*), Cram's best exterior between his first masterwork of the nineties at Ashmont and his later masterworks for Our Saviour's, Middle-

57. "Chaste, strong and uplifting": Cram and Goodhue's Phillips Church, Exeter, New Hampshire, designed in 1895–96.

borough, of 1897, and St. Stephen's, Cohasset, of 1899 (both of which are discussed later), is better composed than Exeter and better detailed. But Newtonville boasts nothing so harshly beautiful as Exeter's Spartan west front, so much crisper and harder even than Ashmont's tower. Ann Miner Daniel rightly stresses Exeter's "simple, geometric shapes, its only ornamentation being windows, doors, buttresses and other basic architectural features. . . . The tower . . . [is a] simple, almost stark mass."[8] Uplifting enough for one whose tastes are chaste and strong.

"Chaste," in the sense that Bishop Lawrence used the word, exactly points up the way in this milieu the Platonic ideal played into Cram's era. For at schools such as these — Anglican or nearly — throughout the British Empire (of which, culturally, New England has always been a part) "during the last quarter of the nineteenth century there developed," Jonathan Gathorne-Hardy has written, "a form of aesthetic, chaste homosexuality — a product of manliness crossed with the classical curriculum."[9] (All this proceeded from the revival of the Greek and Latin desideratum of a sound mind in a sound body; thus organized games in the seventeenth, eighteenth, and nineteenth centuries, in the wake of the Renaissance, assumed greater and greater importance in British public schools; this in turn is the background of the Anglo-American sports culture of the twentieth century.)

There were, to be sure, other currents; the homosexuals of Proust have little in common with their Whitmanic counterparts. Even in English public schools tastes differed. In *A Little Learning* Evelyn Waugh remembered that though as a boy he had been "quite pretty in a cherubic way," he attracted scant attention in his school, for the tastes for such things in his immediate vicinity "were more classical than rococo — 'Greeklove' as the phrase [was] . . . before the Wilde trial."[10] Which is to say manliness: youths (it was the milieu, after all, that produced Lawrence of Arabia) joining secret societies like the Order of Chaeronea, which took its name from the great battle won by Philip of Macedon, a battle famous for the valor of the "sacred band" of homosexual soldiers, while school heroes (Rupert Brooke is the classic case) seemed to be forever reading classical authors in the original Greek on their way to practice, for it was expected that they would throw javelins as well as they would compose sonnets — in each case in no small measure for the edification of the beloved.

That this tradition was well established in *New* England early on is documented by Peter Gay in *The Tender Passion*, where he quotes from the diaries of a Yale student in the early nineteenth century who "achieved self-mastery after tempestuous years," during which he exhibited a

> capacious gift for erotic investment. . . . [He] loved men and women indiscriminately without undue self-laceration, without visible private guilt or degrading public shame. His bisexual inclinations seemed innocent to [him] and apparently to others, because his bearing and behaviour, including his emotional attachments to others of his sex, did not affront current codes of conduct. He preserved the appearances; it never occurred to him, in fact, to do anything else.[11]

Why should it have? That was who he was, after all. "Bearing and behaviour" that did not affront codes of masculine behavior, indeed, that defined it, had been characteristic of homosexuality in the original culture from which the public school's model was derived. In John Boswell's words:

> Plato thought homosexuals naturally the most manly and an equation of homosexuality with effeminacy in men would hardly have occurred to people [like the ancient Greeks] whose history, art, popular literature and religious myths were all filled with the homosexual exploits of such archetypically masculine figures as Zeus, Hercules, Achilles, et al.[12]

Indeed, in such works as Michael Campbell's *Lord Dismiss Us* and Mary Renault's *The Last of the Wine* (assigned reading in at least one St. Grottlesex school as recently as the late 1980s) one can still hear the echo of all this quite clearly.

Such secondary school relations could be very enduring. The significant other is not always a lover; often an intellectual or artistic person's primary relationship is with a relative, best friend, or other mentor. Howard Sturgis,

Henry James's friend, had, in Fred Kaplan's words, "his closest relationship, other than with his parents, . . . with his Eton tutor, with whom he maintained a lifelong mutual devotion."

That New England prep-school culture was in general not very dissimilar to that of its English public school model can be documented again and again in this period. For example, there was Morton Fullerton (who probably knew Cram; certainly he was a close friend of Thomas Meteyard, one of Cram's inner Bohemian cohort), whose profile by Kaplan could well have been that of a better-off young Cram had his father been able to afford Exeter after all:

> A child of American puritan idealism and a Congregational minister, Fullerton grew up in [the then country town near Boston of] Waltham, with an adoring mother who loved him intensely with a sensual effusiveness that provided him with his ideal of feminine attractiveness. His father's New England limitations provided the counter-model for the males he most admired. At Phillips Academy and then Harvard . . . his interests were literary and [same-]sexual, including "two or three early love episodes." He briefly tried journalism in Boston, [then in London, ending up at the London] *Times* bureau in Paris, . . . a journalist . . . with a keen eye for people and a reputation for amorous adventure and sexual flexibility. . . . When he met [Henry] James in 1890 the attraction was immediate and mutual, quickly intimate.[13]

Fullerton graduated from Exeter and Harvard with the highest honors and more or less directly into Oscar Wilde's circle in London.

"OH, HARVARD — HARVARD"

There were many Fullertons; we saw the first of them in Gay's study of the early nineteenth-century Yale undergraduate. In America as in England college was, as we noticed in the case of Ashbee, a natural time for "coming out," at least in a limited way (from one of Gerard Manley Hopkins's undergraduate notebooks: "Looking at a chorister at Magdalen and evil thoughts");[14] and in Cram's circle college ideally meant Harvard.

That Harvard College has had its aesthetes through the years has never been in doubt. One thinks of the satirical jibe by Ezra Pound:

> This little American went to Oxford. He rented Oscar's late rooms. He talked about the nature of the Beautiful. He swam in the wake of Santayana. He had a great cut glass bowl full of lilies. He believed in Sin. His life was immaculate. He was the last convert to Catholicism.[15]

The nature and character of fin-de-siècle Harvard's aesthetes, however, have been generally obscured. Yet as early as 1882 it was a cohort of Harvard undergraduates, "dressed in the high aesthetic line," in Richard Ellmann's words, "with breeches, dinner jackets, Whistler locks of white hair, hats like Bunthorne's, each bearing, in a stained-glass attitude, a sunflower," their leader "limp and listless," who provoked Oscar Wilde at a lecture in Boston to a famous remonstrance. "I see about me certain signs of an aesthetic movement," he said, and then delivered himself (in a stage whisper) of a savage revenge: "Save me from my disciples." Nor did Wilde leave it at that. Having

> particularly liked [Harvard's] gymnasium [Wilde] urged [the college authorities] to combine athletics and aesthetics by placing a statue of a Greek athlete in that building. (In fact, he presented a plaster cast of the Hermes of Praxiteles to [Harvard] "by way of casting coals of fire on the Harvard students," as Robert Ross [Wilde's best friend] said. When Ross was in Cambridge in 1892, the cast was still there. It has since vanished.)[16]

By the nineties things had reached such a point that one author was bold enough to report in 1908 that among American colleges at the end of the nineteenth and the beginning of the twentieth centuries Harvard and Princeton stood out for their homosexual auras,[17] while George Santayana, Harvard's leading aesthete both as student and as professor, as well as one of its scholarly luminaries, could describe Harvard Yard as "distinctly Bohemian."[18] And the large intake of those days from the St. Grottlesex schools was no small part of the reason, if the tone of one of the most popular books published by Fred Day (designed by Bertram Goodhue) in the 1890s, Charles Flandrau's *Harvard Episodes*, is to be believed. This book, one chapter in which is about Santayana, caused a frisson because of such tales as that of the freshman who was translated from the "stained glass atmosphere of his imitation English 'fitting school'"; one of the beauties of Evensong there, he had been

> such a nice little boy at St. Timothy's — piping liquidly in an angelic "nighty" at Chapel — that when the inevitable rumors reached there, the rector and masters were deeply pained to learn that still another butterfly had burst [at Harvard] from the godly chrysalis. They assumed lank, Pre-Raphaelite expressions, and murmured, "Oh, Harvard — Harvard."[19]

Harvard Episodes is little read today. Yet, when asked what to read by friends seeking to take Harvard's pulse in the nineties, Santayana himself recommended Flandrau's book very highly.[20] And *Harvard Episodes* is full of the aesthetic life. An undergraduate's mother, visiting her son, is shown by his friends at tea a copy of Max Nordau's book *Degeneration*, and when they leave, she says, "They're queer young men," and asks her son, "Do you like them very much?" He replies indifferently, "Oh, yes," the blasé Wildean pose being pervasive in Flandrau's book. ("There was, I believe, some reason why I ought to go," observes one character, "and as it wasn't a very urgent one — I went.")[21] An aspect of the origins of Harvard indifference few are aware of, it accorded well with the attitude of Santayana, who always identified — it is a homosexual pattern — more with students than with fellow professors.[22] Typical of his influence was his helping to found the Laodicean Club at Harvard. It was a protest against Saint Paul, who denounced the church in Laodicea as neither hot nor cold. Santayana and his friends, naturally, thought that the only sane and balanced attitude worth taking up.[23]

It was through such clubs that Santayana presided over aesthete Harvard. One such, recalled by Van Wyck Brooks, was "the Stylus Club, [in] the straw-yellow wooden house [at] 41 Winthrop Street [still standing]. . . . Pierre La Rose, Santayana's friend . . . [was also] in the circle of the Stylus . . . [and] personified the Pre-Raphaelite aestheticism and dilettantish Catholicism that flourished at Harvard."[24]

Another recruit to Cram's circle, La Rose (née Peter Ross, according to Lincoln Kirstein!) was a graduate of Exeter, edited the *Harvard Monthly* and, after taking his degree in 1895, stayed at Harvard to teach in the English department. He was dubbed "the aesthete of Apley Court," and while he was not the last of what has become a long and distinguished line of such to reside in that Eliotean block of bachelor chambers, he may have been the most picturesque. Variously teacher, litterateur, book designer, interior decorator, and authority in heraldry, he achieved a national reputation in the last field, designing the arms of all the Yale colleges and Harvard houses, and fulfilling all Cram's heraldic architectural needs, including in the days of Cram's fame work at Princeton University and at St. John the Divine.[25]

When Cram first knew him, La Rose, while he would come to be well regarded in the overall Boston scene, was best known in Cambridge. There he is remembered even today for his restoration of the Faculty Room in University Hall and (with Cram and Goodhue; La Rose doing the heraldry, Goodhue and Cram the architecture) for his role in the remodeling of the house of the Signet Society (another artistic club; see 84), which Cram, Goodhue, and La Rose endowed with perhaps the most aesthete frontispiece of any facade in Greater Boston.[26] Doubtless it was also La Rose who got Goodhue to design the Signet's bookplate, as well as La Rose's own.[27]

The general impression La Rose gave was caught by Henry Ware Eliot, Jr., who conspired with two other undergraduates on a book of caricatures and verses, *Harvard Celebrities*, in which "Pierre" played a leading role. Wrote Eliot:

> Mon Dieu! What is it that it is!
> A-walking on the Square?
> We'll brush away the smoke — Voilà!
> Il est le bon Pierre!
> He has the figure — is it not?
> Petit et débonnaire!

At morn he punctures daily themes
With aphorisms neat,
At noon he "bubbles" with the sports
Upon Mount Auburn Street;
At eve he does the nobby stunt
With Mrs. Jack's elite.

See how the Radcliffe maidens turn
To rubber at his clothes;
He has a truly high-life way
Of turning out his toes.
The nifty Prince of Apley Court,
Our dainty, home-grown rose.[28]

Of all Cram's friends of this era, La Rose was the one, even more than Carman, whose manner was embarrassingly *not* gender appropriate, which the overall culture often does not understand is a problem for such men, even among other homosexuals. (Most gay males, not being effeminate, resent the widespread assumption by straights that gay men who are effeminate are thereby more "obviously" gay — as if masculine behavior was more characteristic of straight than of gay males.) Given how strictly gender-appropriate behavior was measured at Harvard, and how closely monitored, it says a good deal for La Rose that he won a place in Cambridge in the nineties. The same thing also could be said of his prep school and college roommate, Daniel Gregory Mason (later the composer), who remembered that "at Exeter most of the healthy young animals despised me as a 'mother's boy.' La Rose sought me out."

But Harvard, of whose Bohemian circles more will be said in Chapter 8, was apparently in the 1890s unselfconsciously a place of greater breadth than it is, for all its present-day lip service to "diversity," in the 1990s. Notwithstanding some current efforts to suppress all memory of the college's contribution to Boston's emerging gay and lesbian subculture of the late nineteenth and early twentieth centuries, the outstanding characteristic of such Bohemian circles then at Harvard was (aside from a high level of scholarly and artistic creativity) their diversity.

La Rose's and Mason's set, whose life centered on their rooms in Matthews Hall and could hardly have escaped notice as boldly Bohemian, included a wide range of types. There were some, like Charles Flandrau, who were equally as flamboyant as La Rose and Mason. It was Flandrau's "gay irresponsibility," wrote Mason years later, for which he especially prized him. There was also, however, the more robust and "vagabondian" William Vaughan Moody (he of "florid and careless dress," recalled Mason, "[with] a barbaric taste for magnificence in waistcoats and neckties"). Gaillard Lapsley, on the other hand, was a much more well behaved young man, one of Mrs. Gardner's cohort. Then there was the athlete Neddie Hill ("all forms of sport, so boring to me," wrote Mason, "filled [Hill] with enthusiasm"). Yet Mason and Hill, the extremities of the continuum, so to speak, each shared a passion for the Hasty Pudding theatricals, and each did one of the famous drag musicals of the 1890s, a fact that will not surprise any who have admired the Pudding's posters of the era, which do not undermine the assertion that college drag shows in this era were then seen as "homosexual influences."[29]

The late-night trolley cars and horse-drawn hacks that plied regularly across the river between Beacon Hill and Harvard Square carried more than one of this Harvard circle to Pinckney Street and vice versa, so akin were the tastes of each. Mason, for example, talking of the decor of his and La Rose's room ("there was a crucifix . . . more, I always felt, for artistic than religious reasons," a distinction Cram, of course, would not have allowed), might just as well have been Guy Prescott, Cram's roommate, had we Prescott's reminiscences. Mason also uncannily echoes Cram's memories of Goodhue when he wrote: "I can see [La Rose] at our upright, in red hair, . . . drooping his inseparable cigarette from a corner of his mouth." And Mason's descriptions of his evening with Moody not only are perhaps the most eloquent of New England Bohemian reminiscences but also recall haunts we have seen Cram loved, too. Mason wrote of

> hot rum toddy over my open coal fire, or walks in bleak sunsets across Harvard Bridge to Boston, to dine at Marliave's, where, as [another friend] said, "One played at being abroad" or to hear the Boston Symphony concert and discuss it afterwards over beer and Welsh rabbits. . . . There were in those days some new symphonies worth hearing. There was that feverishly exciting "Pathetique," . . . the fascinating "New World" of Dvorák. . . . As spring came on there were mint juleps in Boston, or boating at Riverside, . . . magical walks up Brattle Street, fragrant with lilacs, or to Fresh Pond, ghostly in mist and moonlight.[30]

That the coalescing gay community was so diverse in its types and personalities does not imply that the standard we first encountered here with Peter Gay's discussion of the early nineteenth-century Yale student had eased. When, for instance, Van Wyck Brooks allowed himself to deplore the "feline aestheticism that Santayana stood for,"[31] he was being, I suspect, not so much (as we would say today) homophobic as expressing his own identity with manly bearing and conduct. For example, in *Wallace Stevens: A Mythology of Self*, Milton Bates recalled that though Santayana's poetry readings in his Harvard rooms were popular occasions, when Santayana had his friend the poet Trumbull Stickney to read, the latter was evidently thought a little Mediterranean in his effusions (he had called a sunset "gorgeous"), and Santayana was informed that those men present had weighed the matter and had found Stickney "too literary and ladylike."[32] Therewith the glory of the New England prep school! Was that Achilles or Patrocles? And how sure is one that Santayana did not protest against a code of conduct and bearing he himself, after all, found erotically attractive? By definition gay men are invariably fascinated with what Brian Pronger calls "the arena of masculinity."[33]

At the collegiate level, however, Socrates and Alcibiades were more pertinent Platonic models than Achilles and Patrocles, because of the former figures' thirty-year disparity in age; Emmanuel Cooper, writing about the relationship between Tommaso Cavalieri and Michelangelo (already referred to here), put it best. Through such a relationship there

> echoes the Platonic ideal . . . an older, mature and successful man, teaching and loving a much younger man. It is doubtful their relationship was sexual. . . [The younger man] may not have returned Michelangelo's passion. . . . [Yet] Michelangelo's friendship with Cavalieri lasted for thirty-two years, until the artist died in his friend's arms in 1564.[34]

That the much older Socrates resisted Alcibiades' repeated attempts to seduce him is, of course, of the Platonic essence, and here again modern psychology can help us understand an oft-misunderstood subject. The judgment of Jung is pertinent:

> Homosexual relations between students and teachers may serve a valuable function: when such a friendship exists between an older man and a younger its educational significance is undeniable. . . . [It] can be of advantage to both sides and have lasting value. An indispensable condition for the value of such a relation is the steadfastness of the friendship and their loyalty to it.[35]

Just *how* Platonic the Harvard circle around Santayana was is unclear, but the weight of the evidence is that it was strongly so, at least in the case of perhaps Santayana's great love, Warwick Potter (the "W.P." of Santayana's sonnets). And it is significant that the senior intellectual figure in Cram's youthful era of what we would today call gay Boston chose to declare his Platonism so forthrightly as to say in one of his Harvard sonnets that being "wedded without bond or lust" meant to Santayana so much more intense a union. After all, the most moving modern witness we have to the power of the Platonic tradition is in *Maurice*, where E. M. Forster, who in the end argued for something else, nonetheless testified of his two principal characters, Maurice and Clive, that "it had been understood between them that their love, though including the body, should not gratify it," and that even when later looking back on that broken union (from a position of liberation not unlike ours as a society today) Maurice could still affirm that the Platonic code had yielded "the rule that brought the golden age, and [with Clive] would have sufficed till death."[36]

That code in Santayana's case also sustained not only his early poetry but his

173

58. "Harvard aesthetes," ca. 1888. Identifiable figures include, in the first row, Bernard Berenson (second from right); George Santayana (first on left); Fred Holland Day (center). Louise Guiney is probably on the far right, last row.

much more important early writings on aesthetics, including the first American treatise on the subject, *The Sense of Beauty*. Influenced as much by William James as by Plato, Santayana, John McCormick writes,

> applied certain findings of recent psychology to aesthetics, a novel and even startling procedure in 1896, particularly in his suggestion that sex and aesthetics are allied. . . . Berenson's sister, Sandra, remarked that "she thought Santayana's idea of beauty in his *The Sense of Beauty* was 'an overflow from the sexual passion.' " . . . Santayana's argument derived in part from Stendhal's *De l'amour*, but it also anticipated Freudian theory.[37]

That such pioneering work in charting the philosophical-religious axis of the aesthetic and the erotic was done at fin-de-siècle Harvard seems not unrelated to the emerging gay subculture of Boston's Bohemia, whether in the Yard or on Pinckney Street, the cross-fertilization between which is clear in a photograph (not heretofore published with the correct annotation) that shows Santayana keeping company not only with Berenson but also with Fred Day and Louise Guiney (58).

It was perhaps bad luck that Cram was not there that day. But his posterity would not be wrong to assume he was on other occasions. More than once we shall return to Harvard Yard.

DISTINCTIONS MADE AND UNMADE

The elite Anglophile circles of New England's educational establishment were discreetly supportive (indeed, to some extent, were an extension) of Boston's aesthetes. It remains to penetrate to the heart of the issue in Cram's case (Goodhue was cheerfully agnostic): Anglo-Catholicism, the emergence of which in the nineteenth century was in my view not by any means unrelated to the parallel emergence — already dealt with — of the modern construction of homosexuality. In both cases Boston would become a focal point.

A generation born after the publication of Evelyn Waugh's *Brideshead Revisited* will hardly need telling that Catholicism-and-homosexuality is an old tale, one that is at the heart of Waugh's book, perhaps the greatest Catholic novel of the twentieth century, and all the more fascinating because it argues for Roman Catholicism not on the basis of its most attractive aspects — its artistic glories, for instance — but on the basis of some of its harshest and least attractive teachings, chiefly touching on marriage and sex.

Historically, to be sure, Christ defended matrimony's integrity quite strictly. And it is possible to argue by extension, as does John Boswell, that among the ancient fathers

> Chrysostom [in *Epistolary and Romance*, homily 4, translated in app. 4] carefully notes that in derogating homosexual behavior among the pagans Saint Paul did not describe people who "had fallen in love and were drawn to each other by passion" but only those who "burned in their lust one toward another." . . . Enduring love between persons of the same gender, albeit erotic, may have seemed quite a different matter.

As this book was going to press, Boswell, an openly gay man and at the same time an active Roman Catholic, who had previously (in the work quoted above) argued that intolerance of gays did not develop until the twelfth century in Catholicism, has published what will surely turn out to be the magnum opus of Yale's A. Whitney Griswold Professor of History, *Same-Sex Unions*. This is a masterful study, even at first reading, in which he analyzes some eighty versions of Catholic ceremonies blessing same-sex unions from both East and West and from the eighth to the sixteenth centuries. Massively documented, it discloses how favorably the church in some eras viewed such unions so long as they were couched (as with opposite-sex unions) in a larger than only genital context, a context from our vantage point today that I can only call Whitmanic as much as Platonic.[38]

The similarity to formative Catholic thinking about heterosexual marriage is obvious. Saint Paul, for example, clearly felt that in opposite-sex unions, celibacy was the highest goal, while among the early church fathers Saint Jerome and Saint Augustine thought heterosexual sex between spouses sinful unless approached as a duty, reluctantly, and only with procreative intent. It followed, Thomas Aquinas taught, that any form of sex between husband and wife not open to procreative purposes was unnatural and sinful.

But the church's very ambivalence toward matrimony led, especially in the classically influenced Mediterranean cultures, to considerable toleration of male extramarital sexuality, which Reay Tannahill probably correctly sees as the root of what in our time has been called the "double standard": that is to say (in the Catholic tradition), "a certain leniency toward bachelors [as opposed to unmarried women] when they erred."[39] Bachelors, of course, do not always err in a heterosexual direction, any more than does the church always give the "right" lead. As Eve Kosofsky Sedgwick observes, Catholicism is

> famous for giving countless gay and proto-gay children the shock of the possibility of adults who don't marry, of men in dresses, of passionate theatre, of introspective investment. . . . And presiding over all are the images of Jesus . . . images of the unclothed or unclothable male body, often in extremis and/or in ecstasy.[40]

Even more disordered, seemingly, are the church's attempts to deal with all this and to "right" itself, historically. Whether it was the pope who ordered up loincloths for Michelangelo's Sistine Chapel *Last Judgment*, or those scandalized by the entirely nude and always well-endowed Christuses of Eric Gill, the famous English Catholic sculptor, or the prudes recently so offended by Leo Steinberg's brilliant exegesis of the relation of Christ's genitals to the doctrine of the Incarnation in Renaissance art, it is ever necessary to hold to the center and to fire back Gill's volley, which cannot be heard often enough: "The erotic and the spiritual are not opposites, nor separable."[41]

There is also a sense in which the center was Plato's before it was Paul's; Platonic and Pauline teaching, however antithetical to each other in other respects, are alike in this: they are both concerned with controlling lust, homosexual or heterosexual as the era and circumstances of each may be held to occasion. Indeed, all the celebrated biblical prohibitions about homosexuality are really about lust. The Catholic moral law (as opposed to zealous polemicism) has *always* held to the teaching that homosexual sexuality as such is not sinful and is morally neutral; it is only its genital expression (like all genital expression outside heterosexual marriage) that is problematic, as it was also to Plato.

It is possible to argue today, from the Catholic point of view, that in a stable, monogamous union proceeding from the sort of relationship Boswell cites Chrysostom as noting, one of the offices of love in such a homosexual union is to minister to one's partner's lusty needs. But in Cram's youth, lust — homosexual *or* heterosexual — was from neither the classical nor Christian point of view thought to be ennobling, though both traditions were sophisticated enough to accommodate failure. Plato, in *The Phaedrus*, allowed their wings to Platonic lovers who lapsed, an eventuality he seemed to think not unlikely; the Catholic equivalent is the old truism of the confessional (which eliminates any holier-than-thou aspect of all this) that the sins of the flesh are the least important and most easily forgiven.

The ideal of chasteness, Platonic before it was Christian (and in that sense homosexual before heterosexual), also descended, furthermore, to the Catholic Middle Ages, Cram's "period of the mind." We will discuss later the medieval knightly tradition. At this point it is enough to note the inexact but nonetheless striking fusion of what Cram's generation knew were originally Platonic homosexual ideals and Catholic moral thought, though only heterosexually understood then. Martin Bergman has written:

> The Middle Ages enlarged the vocabulary of [heterosexual] love by the creation of a new species of love — romantic love . . . [in which] unconsummated love was idealized. . . . Dante . . . is the poet of love deflected to higher aims. He therefore belongs to the tradition of romantic love, but at the same time his work is also a creative descendant of Plato's *Symposium*.[42]

The transference of the homosexual ideal of Plato to heterosexual love in Christian terms is quite fascinating. Similarly, such is the migration of ideas from culture to culture, the artistic expression of all this, the conviction that it was possible to develop Christian ideas through classical themes, is a constant of the Renaissance period that followed. Writes Emmanuel Cooper:

> For many [Catholics], admiration for the classical Greeks and their way of life implied an acceptance of homosexual relationships. . . . One of the most obvious situations in which homosexual sentiments could be expressed acceptably was in the male bath house. Michelangelo included such a scene in the background of the *Doni Tondo* [visible clearly behind the Holy Family] and Caravaggio set *The Martyrdom of Saint Matthew* in a bath house.[43]

We will have more to say of Boston bath houses in Chapter 6. Meanwhile, none of this can be said often enough at the end of the twentieth century, when the Christian Right, as well as hyperconservative Roman Catholics and Anglo-Catholics, have become mired in the defense of what is increasingly becoming a highly dysfunctional sexual ethic, and this despite the gallant efforts of intellectuals like Andrew Sullivan to keep the dialogue open between gays and the Roman Catholic church. It may or may not be true, as Paul Dinter has it, that from the Catholic point of view, "the fruit has already been eaten. . . . Most men and women are meant to seek holiness by enacting their sexuality, not by avoiding it."[44] But, insofar as the historical and biblical record is concerned, Peter Gomes, Plummer Professor of Christian Morals at Harvard, is surely correct in his judgment that, looked at without preconceptions, there are *no* references to homosexuality in Jesus' teaching, and no *anti*-homosexual teachings in Paul's work unless one accepts a very "tortured reading" of Paul's words. Observes Gomes: "To suggest that Sodom and Gomorrah is about homosexual sex is an analysis of about as much worth as suggesting that the story of Jonah and the whale is a treatise on fishing."[45]

INCENSE WREATHING TO THE LILY FLOWERS

Why Cram was drawn to the Anglican tradition, though he was converted in Italy at a Roman Catholic Mass, is a large subject, some aspects of which we have already addressed. Another was surely the Anglican mind-set toward homosexuality, long-standing and unusually liberal, as is evident in the teaching of Jeremy Taylor, the Caroline divine noted for his classic Anglican combination of High Church rigor and wide toleration. Of Taylor's work Vern Bullough has written:

> The most detailed of the Anglican writers on sexual matters, Jeremy Taylor (1613–1667), did not regard homosexual behavior as any worse than any other sexual sins. He insisted in all cases that such matters as motive, occasion and consequences of the act be considered; this [is], perhaps the first breakthrough in western [Christian] attitudes since St. Augustine.[46]

That this truly revolutionary attitude for its time made its way (though discreetly, of course, as with all things Anglican) not only over the centuries but across the ocean is illustrated vividly — in New England, moreover, and in this century — by a fascinating U.S. Navy investigation of homosexuality in 1919 at the Newport Naval Training Station in Rhode Island that nicely brings together both the educational and religious sides we have dealt with here. When the navy attempted to label an Episcopal priest attached to the station as a sexual pervert, the bishop of Newport protested that while the priest's obvious affection for young men was not in dispute, the church, in the words of George Chauncey, Jr.,

> offered a radically different interpretation of it. . . . The navy had defined [the] behavior as sexual and perverted; the ministers sought to reaffirm it was brotherly and Christian. . . . The Bishop . . . recalled that as [a] teacher at the Episcopal Theological School in Cambridge in 1908, he had asked [the priest] to help him develop a ministry to Harvard men, "because [he] seemed peculiarly fitted for it in temperament . . . and in general knowledge of how to approach young men and influence them for good." . . . The extent to which [the priest's] supporters were willing to interpret his intimacy with young men as brotherly rather than sexual is perhaps best illustrated by [their effort] to show how [his] inviting a decoy . . . to sleep with him was only another aspect of his ministering to the boy's needs.[47]

Anglo-Catholicism, Anglicanism's High Church wing, far more influential in Rhode Island than in Low Church Massachusetts, is the underlying factor here. Indeed, it has already surfaced here in our discussion of the St. Grottlesex school chapel as an image of the nascent gay subculture of the time in New England. For what is most striking in this connection (even in Low Church Massachusetts) is the critical role in the evolution of New England's splendid Anglican private schools that was played by Anglo-Catholics.

The founders of St. Paul's School (George Shattuck) and of St. Mark's School (Joseph Burnett) were both early leaders of the Church of the Advent in Boston, virtually the first Anglo-Catholic parish in America, and St. Paul's great headmaster, Henry Augustus Coit, is described by Robert Cheney Smith as "a staunch friend of the Cowley Fathers at a time when they had few friends at all in America."[48] Moreover, Coit saw to it that St. Paul's boys at Harvard knew how to find the Cowley Fathers' church, St. John's, Bowdoin Street, on Beacon Hill, where the great rood Calvary was given by St. Paul's old boys at Harvard (59), the corpus a memorial to Coit himself.[49] The whole design, homoerotic to a degree, was the work, of course, of Henry Vaughan. (It was at Bowdoin Street, by the way, that Cram collaborated with Pierre La Rose on the stained glass, among his earliest work there.)

The background of all this must be sought in Anglo-Catholicism as it developed in England; what is true of Cram's architecture is, naturally, true of his religion. Indeed, a telling link between the two is the church mentioned earlier here, Holy Trinity, Sloane Street, London (the work of Cram's hero Sedding), as having so much influenced the design of Cram and Goodhue's St. Paul's Church, Brockton, for Holy Trinity occasioned a justly famous poem by Sir John Betjeman that begins:

> *An Acolyte singeth*
> Light six tall tapers to the Flame of Art.
> Send incense wreathing to the lily flowers,
> And, with your cool hands white,
> Swing the warm censer round my bruised heart,
> Drop dove-grey eyes, your penitential showers
> On this pale acolyte.[50]

Lest any think this mid-twentieth-century effusion overdone, note how gentle a provocation of our own time it is, compared, for example, with one of Cram's time, "The Priest and the Acolyte," a late nineteenth-century example of Anglo-Catholic erotica, wherein a priest, caught in sexual embrace with his male acolyte, poisons the wine in the chalice before administering the Sacrament to them both — a *Liebestod*.[51] Although there is not in Catholicism, either Roman or Anglican, what Ihara Saikaku calls "the Buddhist priestly tradition of

59. Interior view of the Cowley Fathers' Beacon Hill mission, St. John's, Bowdoin Street, showing Henry Vaughan's rood screen, the gift of St. Paul's School "old boys" at Harvard.

homosexual love . . . between priests and acolytes to produce spiritual enlightenment," Peter Gay nonetheless notes that works like "The Priest and the Acolyte" generally proclaimed "the purity of [homosexual] loves, and their moral superiority." There was, Gay observes, "an exquisite snobbery about these productions, addressed as they were to an exclusive coterie, to a quietly superior, largely secret clan,"[52] into which clan we need to inquire much more closely.

ALL THE MORBID YOUNG MEN

Anglo-Catholicism in its earliest days was found by the Anglo-American establishment to be not just unpleasant but utterly contemptible; we are inclined to forget today that, in John Reed's words, "many of the practices championed by Anglo-Catholics were symbolic affronts to central values of Victorian middle-class culture," and that

> these countercultural themes in the Anglo-Catholic program help to account not only for its opposition, but for its support. It does not detract from Anglo-Catholicism's standing as a religious phenomenon to observe that its supporters were not moved solely by theological or spiritual considerations. . . . Support came disproportionately from groups that were culturally subordinate or in decline, groups whose members were threatened, oppressed, or simply bored by the values Anglo-Catholicism challenged.[53]

Consider the challenge to the traditional patriarchal family implied by the introduction into Anglicanism of such new customs, not sanctioned by centuries of use as in Roman Catholic countries, as auricular confession by a woman. Not only was another *man* — for only men could then be priests — interjecting himself authoritatively into the family so intimately as to subvert the father's or husband's primary role, but also, if the priest was attractive (confession being necessarily unchaperoned), opportunities for sin and scandal abounded. Similarly, women's religious orders affronted Victorian family values. "Sisterhood," Reed writes, "took women out of their homes. It gave them important and sometimes great responsibility . . . [demonstrating] that there were callings for women of the upper and middle classes other than those of wife, daughter and charitable spinster."[54] Nor was the nature of such challenges misunderstood. Edward Bouvier Pusey, one of the fathers of the Oxford Movement who Bernard Markwell in *The Anglican Left* characterized as "truly revolutionary on a psychological level" in his teaching, was himself enough of a feminist to observe: "I think that it is a wrong ambition of men to wish to have the direction of the work of women."[55]

Indeed, if Anglo-Catholicism seemed to appeal disproportionately to women who were distinctly independent of mind, those whom its detractors called "hysterical young women," the same detractors were quick to notice as well a good many "morbid young men."[56] (Why do we recognize what is meant at once? These are, of course, yet more Victorian code words.) Moreover, there *was* a dark side to all this.

Consider the story told by Geoffrey Faber in *Oxford Apostles: A Character Study of the Oxford Movement*, about a dream of W. G. Ward, a English Roman Catholic convert and controversialist:

> he found himself at a dinner party next to a veiled lady, who charmed him more and more as they talked. At last [Ward] exclaimed, "I have never felt such charm in any conversation since I used to talk with John Henry Newman, at Oxford." "I am John Henry Newman," the lady replied, and raising her veil showed the well-known face.[57]

Well might Peter Gay conclude that "classical Greece" was not the only "ideal" in which "the troubled" might find refuge at the end of the nineteenth century; another was the "intense Christianity" of the Oxford Movement.[58]

Whether one dwells on this aspect, or on the aspect previously noted of the "exquisite snobbery [of a] quietly superior, largely secret clan," on both the darker and lighter sides the fact is that Cram's Anglo-Catholicism is the *least* difficult to reconcile with homosexuality of all the elements of his character and convictions against which we have been testing my thesis here. Among the cognoscenti the Anglo-Catholic affinity for homosexuality has long been an open secret.

To say so in print is, admittedly, to break a long-standing taboo and will doubtless shock many, for the "apparent connection between Anglo-Catholicism and the male homosexual subculture in the English-speaking world," in David Hilliard's words, has hardly been explored at all by scholars, though in the British context there is Hilliard's path-finding, if undeservedly obscure, work, in which he does not hesitate to trace the connection back to the days of the Oxford Fathers themselves — not only to Newman (because of his intense relationship with Ambrose St. John, with whom at Newman's request he was buried) but also to Pusey and Keble, both of whom have been portrayed as sublimated homosexuals.[59] In the American context, however, the silence has been deafening. There are only such remarks as Martin Green's about Edward Perry Warren, a notable Boston aesthete and sometime parishioner of the Cowley Fathers, that this "figure in the aesthetic movement" had a career that "illustrates a philistine cliché of the times [in Boston], that Catholicism, aestheticism, paganism and homosexuality were interdependent."[60]

In England or America, however, the aesthetic explanation can carry us only so far, and it is to Hilliard's credit that he gets plausibly beyond it when he asserts that "at the heart of the correlation between Anglo-Catholicism and homosexuality was an affinity of outlook between a sexual minority and a minority religious movement" that allowed homosexuals to "express their sense of difference in an oblique and symbolic way [that was] a more socially acceptable type of rebellion."[61] Indeed, this may be the key to the enduring nature of the affinity between Anglo-Catholicism and the gay subculture. Certainly it was very evident as recently as my own experience in such Anglo-Catholic centers as London, Boston, New York, and Baltimore. And it was evident as well to Eve Kosofsky Sedgwick, who has traced this affinity back to yet another "minority"—the Caroline aristocracy of three hundred or more years ago. In her *Between Men* she contends that "high religion" has been since the seventeenth century one of a "cluster of associations about [the aristocratic homosexual] role (the King James version?)."[62]

The Caroline cavalier, a type of the medieval true knight—kind, loyal, tough, and idealistic, but also somewhat effeminate—is, like all things Caroline and Jacobite, precious to Anglo-Catholics, for many of Anglicanism's most cherished (and most High Church) title deeds derive from this period, not least the martyrdom of King Charles (the subject, by the way, of one of Cram and La Rose's Bowdoin Street windows). Cram, as we will see, was a besotted royalist, identifying strongly with the lost cause of that minority of old and fusing it, in the Jacobite Order of the White Rose (which Cram appears to have founded in America),[63] with the gay minority mind-set of his day, suggesting to me that the affinity Sedgwick finds between Caroline high churchmanship and the seventeenth-century English gay subculture was not dissimilar to the affinity Hilliard finds between Anglo-Catholicism, that later high churchmanship of the nineteenth century, and the gay subculture of that era, both of which not only emerged at the same time, but, as it turned out, were distinctly in aid of each other.

A crucial carrier of the earlier High Church tradition into the later Anglo-Catholic high churchmanship was Anglican monasticism, the American flowering of which occurred in Cram's youth, and which all his life fired him to do some of his best work. I think particularly of the dark, severely beautiful interior of his chapel for the Cowley Fathers near Harvard Square in Cambridge—in my judgment the undoubted masterwork of his last years—and also of the almost idyllic complex of tower, apse, and cloister high above the Hudson River that Cram designed for the first American Anglican monks, the Order of the Holy Cross, founded in the 1880s. I think too of a story from that order's superb history, an Anglo-Catholic anecdote worthy of keeping company with the Tallulah Bankhead stories with which this book opens. It seems that one of the brothers of the Holy Cross, secure enough in his vocation to hazard a witticism some would think inappropriate even today, used regularly—when returning to

West Park for the annual chapter meeting—to solemnly intone to a fellow monk, as they walked down the hill from the local railroad station to the monastery, verse eleven of chapter six of the Song of Solomon: the one about going "down into the garden of nuts to see the fruits of the valley."

STATES OF DESIRE

The Cowley Fathers, as the Society of St. John the Evangelist (the oldest Anglican monastic order, founded in England in the 1860s) was best known in Cram's day, were perhaps less likely to venture such drolleries, shadowed as they were then by a very unfriendly Boston and a scarcely more welcoming Harvard. Yet even the dustiest and driest of this band of intense young Anglo-Catholics (already touched on several times previously) must have taken notice of Ralph Adams Cram, whose passionate and intimate association with the society extended from 1889 to his death in 1942.

Sometimes called the Anglican Jesuits, this order has ministered through the years not only to the poor but to college students and intellectuals as well, serving these last with an unusual combination of worldly wise but strongly held religious convictions allied to intellectual rigor and artistic flair. Cowley's style is perhaps best briefly caught by parallel dashes of a little scandal and a little philosophy. As to the former: it is perhaps not startling to find in Isabella Stewart Gardner's library the work of Baron Corvo, the notorious homosexual outlaw of this era; and it is only somewhat more startling to discover it was the gift to her by one Father Powell of Cowley.[64]

As to the latter: consider the familiar Jesuit division of the spiritual life. Eric Gill's biographer, Robert Speaight, has described how it was put to Gill: there were

> two distinct compartments—one for ordinary folk who were to content themselves with discursive meditation to a set plan, the other for extraordinary folk who might be led to God by extraordinary ways about which the less said the better. . . . [When Gill inquired]. . . . whether the difference was fundamental, or whether it was no more than a difference of approach, [the monk] replied that the difference was indeed fundamental, and that it stemmed from the ancient Thomist and Molinist debate . . . the Thomist laying greater stress on God's action aiding and attracting the soul, the Molinist emphasizing human liberty and responsibility in the pursuit of holiness. . . . [One method] pushed to an extreme would lead to a sterile activism, the [other method] to an enervating quietism.[65]

My own studies and experience lead me to believe that while the Cowley Fathers have upheld the Catholic moral law as their communal ideal pretty strictly, in their counseling and direction of "extraordinary" converts (like

Cram), they have, historically, cultivated the individual's intellectual independence and moral freedom in guiding them through many and various "extraordinary ways." Hilliard catches a sense of this when he cites the Christian Socialist cause, in which we have seen Cram was active, as an example of the sort of thing Anglo-Catholic confessors (in the late nineteenth century conspicuously less rigid in the English-speaking world than their Roman brethren) encouraged among inquirers as a nonjudgmental and positive response to concerns about homosexuality.[66] Even today somewhat of a reflection of this attitude of mind is evident in the view Edmund White explores in *States of Desire* of how often the gay man does not so much reject "family," in the more limited meaning of the word normative until recently, as give himself through public service to the larger family of church or community.[67]

It is hard for us now to see how liberal this spiritual direction was a century ago. Today, even so orthodox a Roman Catholic prelate (and celibate) as Basil Cardinal Hume can frankly query in print if one can be "fully human in the celibate state" and admit that even if the answer be in the affirmative, there will always have to be pain, for "the celibate lacks something vital"[68]—a view that relates to conservative Catholic attitudes toward homosexuality because celibacy is the only approved Roman Catholic response. A century ago, aside from Newman, Cram and his cohort would have heard nothing from Rome except strident, judgmental anathemas and prohibitions.

It may have been meant disparagingly when one of Waugh's characters in *Brideshead* insisted all Anglo-Catholics were sodomites. Certainly, however, in the society of the beloved disciple, from its beginning, gay men have customarily found from their brothers understanding, acceptance, and good counsel.

THE GIFT OF SELF

The intellectual character of Anglo-Catholicism in the 1880s and 1890s, exemplified by the Society of St. John the Evangelist, may well astonish many now fully as much as its affinity for homosexuality. As David Hilliard has written:

> The intellectual and social ethos of the Anglo-Catholic wing of the Church of England was very different from that of English Roman Catholicism. Almost all its leaders, clerical and lay, shared a common upper-class background of public school and ancient university. Among its intellectuals the dominant theology from the 1880s until the 1930s was a liberal Catholicism which accepted the legitimacy of biblical criticism, used contemporary philosophical and scientific precepts in the study of theology, and asserted the central importance of the Incarnation . . . in its dogmatic system, . . . [which] also encouraged a slightly more accommodating attitude towards homosexuality than was commonly found elsewhere in the Christian church.[69]

185

60. Arthur Crawshay Hall, SSJE, whose liberal Anglo-Catholicism in fin-de-siècle Boston not only was an expression of his classical studies at Oxford but was in turn a conservative reflection of the movement Linda Dowling calls Oxford Hellenism, a movement that, as she shows in her *Hellenism and Homosexuality in Victorian Oxford*, laid important groundwork a century ago for the late twentieth-century thesis that homosexuality has a positive social identity.

Of course, it may be objected that I am relying too much here on the British and not the American experience. But remember that Boston's Cowley Fathers were overwhelmingly British. Consider, moreover, the teachings of the one American among Cowley's three founders, Father (later Bishop) Charles C. Grafton, sometime rector of the Church of the Advent in Boston.

A Bostonian born and bred (Boston Latin School, Phillips Andover, Harvard Law School) and from 1889 to 1912, when he was bishop of Fond du Lac, Wisconsin, the acknowledged leader of American Anglo-Catholicism, Grafton as a young man was a protégé of Wendell Phillips and a strong abolitionist, with liberal attitudes that he did not abandon after his conversion. Glenn Johnson, his biographer, has written that Grafton's views were widely divergent from the biblical literalism common in his day. "The Christian Church was in existence and in active operation before any of the gospels were written," . . . [Grafton] wrote in *Christian and Catholic*, one of his major books. Elsewhere he wrote: "The Church does not require us to believe in the Scriptures, but to believe in God, in Jesus Christ, in the Holy Ghost, in the Holy Catholic Church. . . . She [the Church] has separated some of her writings from other of her writings, which she calls her Holy Scriptures. She determines what writing are to be put in this class and by the power of the Holy Ghost dwelling in her she interprets them." With this outlook [Grafton] had no difficulty in accepting Darwin's explanation of the evolutionary development of life forms and in treating sections of the Bible as metaphoric expression [while] at the same time . . . [oppos[ing] particular explanations of the events of Christ's life . . . as no less than factual.[70]

Grafton's attitudes toward homosexuality are more difficult to discover. Surely, however, given his overall liberal views, it is significant that the author of the foreword to Grafton's autobiography took particular note of his ministry to those "whose temptations . . . proceed from tendencies to melancholy and morbid self-anaylsis,"[71] very nearly code words, as we have defined them here, and almost certainly meant to include gays. That Grafton, furthermore, was more characteristic than not of Anglo-Catholic liberalism (as opposed to Roman Catholic conservatism) in Boston in this era is evident, for example, in this stirring declaration by one of his fellow Cowley Fathers:

We are thankful to be free from many narrow definitions, from much mechanical exactness which prevails in the Roman system, from the dogged resistance to modern ideas which is bent on beating back the spirit of the age instead of trying to guide and Christianize it. We [Anglicans] rejoice to be able . . . to adapt ourselves to the needs and circumstances, political, social, and intellectual, of the country in which we find ourselves.[72]

These words go far to document assertions like Karl Beckson's that it was the overall liberal attitude and particularly the relatively positive view of homosexuality of Anglo-Catholics that drove (because it seemed to him so *threatening*) such as Gerard Manley Hopkins to Rome, where (however self-hating we might pronounce it today) converts like Hopkins hoped to find the necessary security in the cut-and-dried Roman condemnations.[73] (Recall that these were Anglo-Saxons concerned more with Roman Catholic theology than with Mediterranean mores.) And these words about the glories of Anglican adaptability were written by Arthur Crawshay Hall (60), who directed Cowley's ministry in Boston and who, as we noted briefly in Chapter 2, prepared Cram for reception into the Episcopal church.

An army officer's son, Hall grew up in Trollope's town-and-country-house England. A graduate in 1869 of Christ Church, Oxford, the college of Dr. Pusey (still there in Hall's day in the late 1860s, but in retirement) and of Pusey's friend and disciple, H. P. Liddon, who with Richard Benson was Hall's chief mentor, Hall was ordained priest in 1871, having already associated himself with the Cowley Fathers, who sent him to Boston in 1874. There he became the Provincial of the Cowley mission. A "tall and striking figure [with a] deep and powerful voice," Hall was known for "lucid thought and intensely practical counsel." Disciplined but outspoken, he was detached in judgment but strong in his convictions — though no one ever pretended that he did not suffer from a "quick temper and domineering will." (A colleague of his in the 1880s recalled that Hall "was a great *teacher*, and he had a following because he knew and others knew that he knew where he was going. I remember vividly an incident where an officious lady had provided for him a [kneeling] hassock which he loathed, and he kicked it several feet away across the room.")[74]

Hall was more pastor and teacher than original thinker, but his writings document that he kept abreast of knowledge in related fields. ("Our highest medical science," he wrote in 1896, "has established more and more clearly the traces of a correspondence . . . between thought and matter, between the faculties of mind and the structures of the brain").[75] Similarly, he cautioned that in the matter of "sensual indulgence" the attraction was often not chiefly appetite, but "the supposed assertion of manliness." Concluded Hall, on the eve of Freud and Jung, "Our temptations are wonderfully complex, and in the guidance and direction of the spiritual life . . . it is often of the first importance to recognize this."[76]

It was noticed early on (and these, of course, are more code words) that Hall had a natural way with young men; what a feast of Anglophilia Hall's sermons must have been in Vaughan's so very English chapel at St. Paul's School, and they were the more influential for the fact that Hall did not hesitate on occasion to shed his cassock and join the boys at their sport.[77] He was also popular at the college level, preaching in one year at Princeton, Williams, and Harvard. "A rather tall and slender youth," as a contemporary described him, "with an intellectual and profoundly spiritual face," Hall had, it was said, a "genius for friendship."[78] One of his most influential works was, in fact, entitled *Christian Friendship*, and a careful study of this and a number of his other writings of all kinds allows us to eavesdrop on Hall's instruction and counsel to Cram in his study at St. John's, Bowdoin Street (and to others from Pinckney Street; the Boston Public Library's copy of Hall's *Self-Discipline* was the gift of one of Cram's Bohemian neighbors, his friend Daniel Berkeley Updike).

"The essential evil of fleshly lusts," wrote Hall, ever a Platonist as well as a Catholic, ". . . consists in letting the body lord it over the spirit." To the use of every faculty was attached "a certain pleasure" that he did not disparage:

it is so with the mental powers. The orator experiences a pleasure in the sense of swaying the audience . . .; the man or woman of force in the conscious power of influence. But to use such gifts simply for the sake of the reflex gratification to one's self [aside, that is, from the cause the orator espouses] would indeed be base. . . . It is the same with the body. . . . The sin comes in when this pleasure . . . is sought after as an end to itself [i.e., sex without love].[79]

Note that Hall by no means depreciates the body. Indeed, far from denying the Platonic teaching of the body's leading the soul (in the sense that physical beauty, allied to nobility of mind, a high intelligence, and mature sensitivity, leads up the ladder of love to wisdom), Hall insists:

There is a more profound truth in the proverb "The eyes lead to love." Understood not merely of the bodily eyes, but of the eyes of the mind, it is indeed most true — true of all love, human and divine. Love is always based on appreciation. . . . True love . . . is based on the recognition of worth.[80]

And the Charioteer's struggle with the two sides of our nature is also discernable in Hall's teaching. Self-discipline for Hall is always the "sacrifice of the lower for the sake of the higher self . . . to redress the disproportion [between higher and lower] which, as a matter of experience, we find to exist." Yet Hall stresses in the same place Jesus' choosing among the apostles "three pairs of brothers, as if to teach us that He builds supernatural upon natural relationships, cement[ing] and hallow[ing] the lower by the higher."[81]

In *Christian Friendship*, Hall faces squarely the differences between the classical and Christian views of the matter:

Truly Friendship does not occupy in Christianity the exclusive position it possessed in the ancient world [because it] is no longer the only relation of love. . . . In the [ancient] world Friendship had to take the place which marriage and family life fill with us. . . . Friendship in Christianity is no longer all in all; it is but one ray of the moral sun.[82]

It has since been well argued, in fact, by John Boswell, that the "Greek" tradition *was* Christianized: "during the early Middle Ages the type of 'passionate friendship' familiar to the early church [from classical Greece] was common, and comprised the subject matter of much clerical writing, including almost all of the love poetry of the period," while "the loving relation of teacher and student in religious communities was very much a medieval ideal, despite its obvious parallel to Greek homosexuality." (Boswell cites, for example, Saint Anselm of Canterbury, who developed an ideal of monastic love that reflected its importance to his own life and work, for his theological treatises were very often inspired by such love.)[83]

But Hall's point was different. In contrasting classical pagan and Christian concepts of friendship and love, Hall was attempting to suggest, I believe, that moderns had lost their way somewhat. Hall did not disparage matrimony any more than he did friendship, but rather the attempt of the latter to mimic the former:

> May I give a word of warning concerning the folly, the danger of *excessive Friendship*, especially between two persons of the same sex. One has noted it again and again. . . . They live for a time entirely wrapped up one in another. And after a while there comes disappointment, jealousy, alienation. And the explanation . . . the friends were trying to be husband and wife to one another, and they were not sufficiently different; the very sameness of their sex prevented their being to one another that which they were trying to be.[84]

That the attraction of sames is not the attraction of opposites is an insight many gay commentators today find it worthwhile (more positively, perhaps) to study. The Charioteer's other shoe also drops, as it were, when Hall (who as we have seen emphasizes our two selves, higher and lower) counsels that a friend must when necessary "withstand a friend," noting that "if a friend is to be known in adversity, there is no adversity which so much needs his support as that of strong temptation," by which presumably he means to include sexual intercourse.[85]

Hall's context here is important, for his teaching about friendship love can only be fully understood if one takes careful note of his view that

> we are apt to think of Love as if it were a strong, passionate Desire. But in truth love is not desire. Love seeks union indeed with the object loved, but not by grasping at that object to make it one's own, but by self-surrender. *Love is the gift of self* to the object loved . . . the gift of ourselves to the friend we love . . . [for whom] we rejoice to spend and be spent . . . to place ourselves at the service of the one we love, to enable him, if it may be, to live a more perfect life by using any gift that we may have, while we feel that what is lacking in ourselves will be supplied in him, that we find ourselves truly perfected in and with that other.[86]

Thus does Hall echo Plato's teaching of the desire and pursuit of the whole, adding for good measure a truism of all ages that supports Platonic lovers: "as love is based on what is real and high it will be deep and lasting," wrote Hall, not ashamed to quote a very secular source: " 'a friendship,' said Madame Swetchère, 'will be young after the lapse of half a century; a passion is old at the end of three months.' "[87]

Finally, one finds in Hall's teaching exactly what Hilliard has led us to expect of an English Anglo-Catholic priest, wherever stationed. "What are [our] weaknesses, the dangers of our own characters," Hall asked, in aid of "remedy[ing] these faults . . . *in the light of those capacities for good* [emphasis added] which each one possesses." And elsewhere, but just as pointedly: "Remember, my

Brethren, it is not *every* cross which sanctifies a soul . . . [but the particular cross] He gives to each, to meet and remedy the special faults and needs of each."[88]

That is not to suggest, however, that Hall took a negative view of same-sex relationships. He had, in fact, as high a view of friendship as of theology.

THE GOSPEL OF FRIENDSHIP

For the most distinctive teaching of Cram's instructor and mentor in the Catholic faith, his text was always drawn from Saint John, wherein was to be found, Hall observed, Christ's "esoteric teaching, [his] more private, deeper, and more spiritual discourses delivered to his disciples, as distinct from the plainer teaching given to the multitude. . . . Have you ever noticed it?" Hall asked. Saint John's is "preeminently the Gospel of Friendship," recording as it does the admission of that saint "to the relation of peculiar intimacy with Our Lord, as 'the disciple whom Jesus loved,' who also leaned on his breast at supper, the bosom friend of Jesus." And then the good father ventured this commentary:

> it is all the more remarkable and noteworthy, and perfectly true to the genius of Christianity, that the Apostle [Saint John] who especially enforces the broadest universal charity, love to all men as men, and special love to all brethren in the Christian family, should be the one not so much to teach, but to illustrate *particular and personal friendship* [emphasis added].[89]

This is a more remarkable statement than it seems, for it cannot be too much stressed that in writing thus about "particular friendship" Hall was treading on dangerous ground, especially for a monk. Saint Benedict (as also Basil in the East) had urged (and for over a thousand years the church had insisted) that, in Boswell's words, "particular friendships of any sort — especially passionate ones — were a threat to monastic harmony and asceticism,"[90] a tradition continued into modern times, when as recently as the 1950s a "particular friendship" was grounds for expulsion from certain Catholic seminaries. The old maxim ever was: when two go together the devil makes a third.

Exceptional figures, such as Saint Aelred of Rievaulx, the medieval Cistercian abbot and friend to both Henry II of England and David I of Scotland, whose writings give same-sex love perhaps its most eloquent Christian expression, there certainly were. And in Boston in the late nineteenth century Hall was another such. Just as Aelred had gone so far as to call the relationship of Jesus and John a "marriage,"[91] so did Hall by implication, when to his New Testament citations from Saint John he added in support of monogamy Old Testament ballast (Proverbs 18:24: "The man that maketh many friends doeth it to his own destruction; but there is a friend that sticketh closer than a brother").[92]

Loyal Anglican that he was, he mustered as well a vivid supporting quotation from Jeremy Taylor, to the effect that particular friendships were truly "marriages of the soul."[93]

It was a phrase Hall could hardly have doubted would cause in the home of the Boston marriage a distinct frisson. But as Alexander Zabriskie has pointed out, "although a loyal defender of the faith, Hall had a keen mind and a passion for accurate scholarship, with a fearlessness which often led him along untried paths that frightened more timid souls."[94] Moreover, he appears to have had just such a "marriage of the soul" himself — with Charles Brent, a Canadian priest whom Hall met at one of his retreats in the same year, 1888, as he met Cram, of whom Brent was a contemporary.[95]

Brent, in his biographer's words, was "strongly and immediately attracted to Hall and began a lifelong friendship" that despite ecclesiastical disagreements or vast geographical distances "nothing broke or even seriously strained [for over forty years].... Hall was Brent's closest confidant."[96] And Brent's reminiscences of Hall's effect on his life are doubly interesting to us because Brent appears to have been a closer lifelong friend of Cram's than was Hall. Cram was, in fact, Brent's godson, Brent having stood sponsor for Cram at his baptism in St. John's, Bowdoin Street, in 1889. Forty years later Cram designed the splendid Celtic cross that serves as Brent's gravestone in Lausanne.

In later years the first missionary bishop of the Philippines, and after that bishop of Western New York, Brent, when Cram first knew him, was at Cowley to test his vocation to the religious life. Instead, Brent accepted the charge of St. Stephen's Church in Boston's South End, where he attracted a wide following, including "a number of social workers, pioneers in the great movement . . . [especially] Robert Woods [the settlement-house founder mentioned in Chapter 2], who became Brent's parishioner."[97] (Brent himself published in 1896 through the Diocese of Massachusetts *Early Christian Socialists*, a study of Frederick Denison Maurice and his coworkers.)

Though a genial man and a natural-born athlete (he excelled at cricket, polo, hockey, and tennis, even though he played left-handed), Brent — especially in his younger years — was quite as volatile as Cram, and between the two of them Hall can have had no easy time of it. Yet Brent's own influence on Cram would (because of Hall) have cut both ways. As Brent's biographer explains:

> Brent's inner life was turbulent. The outward composure [was] the result of strict self control. The constituents of Brent's being were discordant. . . . Limitless spiritual aspiration and a painfully acute conscience fought with physical appetites, pride [and] . . . a strong man's desire to have his own way and a hot temper. . . . He knew periods [according to his journals] of "abysmal depression . . . which just failed of becoming complete despair.". . . He also knew the heights of ecstasy. Most of the

time [he held] sternly to his duty . . . [disciplining and] captivating increasingly his imagination and emotions becoming the supreme value passionately sought by every factor of his manhood. . . . It was because Hall . . . fired him to espouse this idea [and] taught him the necessary discipline . . . that Brent felt under such profound obligation to him.[98]

Thus not only Hall's instruction and counsel and friendship to Cram but Brent's, too, must be factored in here, and perhaps because Brent's self-mastery was a harder victory won, Cram may have valued it more. Certainly Cram and Brent remained relevant to each other, longer, apparently, than Hall and Cram. Brent would in later years be called "the twentieth century's greatest champion of and crusader for church unity";[99] while Cram, when in the same century he achieved his own fame, has no greater claim on our attention than that he revolutionized the visual image of American Christianity, bringing *all* its various branches, from Romans to Swedenborgians, to worship in that marvelous ecumenical creation—the Cram church. The coalescence of Brent's and Cram's visions is striking. And it is rooted, surely, in the concept of Hall's "gospel of Friendship," that characteristically Anglo-Catholic concept (also Platonic, also Whitmanic), to which we shall return again and again in this study.

THE SUPREMACY OF CONSCIENCE

There *was* a Roman Catholic expression of this liberalism; of importance to Cram in the first place because of Guiney's constant influence, and also because though Brent's and Cram's ecumenism was years ahead, the seeds of it were sown with Guiney in the 1890s in and around Pinckney Street, whose liberal Roman Catholics were increasingly even more unwelcome in the Roman Archdiocese of Boston than High Church Anglicans were in the Episcopal Diocese of Massachusetts. Both the Roman modernists and the High Church Anglicans were aspects of Pinckney Street's incipient modernism.

Guiney and company's most immediate heresy was called "Americanism." An ideological position favoring a certain independence of Rome promoted by many American bishops (including Boston's late nineteenth-century Archbishop John Williams), this really quite moderate point of view by our lights today was condemned in 1898 by Pope Leo XIII in *Testem benevolentiae*, where he described it as the desire for "a church in America different from that which is in the rest of the world," a difference rooted, he concluded, in modernism, which Leo called "that fatal theory of the separation of church and state."[100]

As to these modernist Roman Catholics of Pinckney Street, they were the leading lights of a circle of Catholic writers, led by Guiney, whom Donna Merwick describes as

> supported by prominent [i.e., Protestant] Boston families. . . . They were friends of
> Bernard Berenson and Vida Scudder [note the scandal: respectively, a Jewish agnostic
> and an Anglican socialist] . . . [and they] were flippant and defiant, . . . consciously
> Catholic but tentative . . . always on the fringe of the congregation looking, as it
> were, at the snowfall rather than at the preacher. . . . Their lineage was from Holy
> Cross College in Worcester . . . [and] from Cambridge, through Catholic writers . . .;
> and it derived from Anglican Bostonians.[101]

It is thus not surprising that, as Merwick notes, "the foremost artistic thrust
of 'Americanism' at the end of the nineteenth century" came from Boston,
where the strivings of Guiney and company for "a glad Christianity that would
emerge out of the ambience of *aesthetics* [emphasis added] convinced Yankees
that a common liberal leadership of the divided city was possible and could be
effective"); nor that the work of these writers was particularly liberal in the
sexual realm:

> It is now commonly accepted that American Catholic writers . . . have been unable to
> make peace with the world of sex. . . . Nevertheless the circle of Catholic writers in
> Boston in the 1890s did have something of the range and humanity for which critics
> have searched vainly among Catholic writers until the appearance of Flannery
> O'Connor.[102]

Perhaps the most pointed example of the contemporary impact on Cram's
situation of all this was the controversy surrounding Bishop John J. Keane,
sometime rector of Catholic University and a popular lecturer in Boston, who
pronounced it an outrage to hold that "the Pope holds views contrary to our
[American] institutions, which we are bound to respect." On the contrary, insisted Keane: "The ultimate rule of every Catholic is his conscience."[103] Clearly,
there *were* Roman Catholics in Boston in agreement with Father Hall's teaching, and Romans Cram knew: when John Boyle O'Reilly warned that "paganism loves the beautiful more than it loves the truth," Guiney, devout Catholic
that she was, proudly fired back that in this respect she was glad to call herself
"bed-rock pagan," dismissing such warnings as O'Reilly's because as a Catholic
she had to "scrimmage" for the whole truth.[104]

That Catholic teaching about the absolute supremacy of the individual conscience should now arise here follows naturally, of course, from our discussion
of the link between homosexuality and Anglo-Catholicism in the context of
Cram's early life. Indeed, it was a Roman Catholic — albeit previously an Anglican; by no means unrelated to the ecumenical arena we have entered here — who
most convincingly addressed the whole subject: Cardinal Newman.

The teaching of Newman, who once observed that he would gladly propose a
toast to the Pope, but only after first proposing conscience, has lately been well
summarized in the homosexual context by Jurgen Liias, appropriately enough

today a priest on the staff of the Church of the Advent, where Father Hall first was stationed when Cowley sent him to Boston. Hall could have written every word Liias wrote:

> Christian moral thinking has always had the deepest reverence for the freedom of *individual* conscience; this itself was a deep honoring of the Holy Spirit in its immanent work within the believer. Such honoring did not, however, negate the *communal* [emphasis added] responsibility of moral law. [And he cites, with reference to the homosexual's struggle with that paradox, Cardinal Newman's teaching that] if your conscience tells you you may do this act but the church tells you you must not do it, you must obey the church. If, however, your conscience tells you you must do this act, then you must do it, though the church tells you you should not do it. Your conscience is mistaken, but you must obey it. And if you honestly do obey it, then it will eventually lead you on to the truth.[105]

A Decadent Footnote

Because for Cram art came first, religion second (as we have seen, in no small measure because his experience was that the first led to the second), a decadent footnote is now timely. In both culture and religion the Platonic ideal, far from frustrating Cram's agenda, as it were, reinforced it. But could the Platonic (and Catholic) view (which, though assuming failure and providing for reconciliation, still insists on the ideal of chasteness) be seen by Cram as reinforcing his artistic creativity? That *homosexuality* might do so was A. L. Rowse's point. But others have wondered especially whether the Greeks' "*attitude* [emphasis added] toward homosexuality had any relationship to the[ir] unusual creativity," in the words of Martin Bergman, who called this "an intriguing question."[106] Does the idea of self-mastery, which is to say chasteness itself, predispose to creativity? An issue that we know arose in Cram's circle (Fred Day ardently believed it did), it has of late been penetratingly dealt with by Camille Paglia in her remarkable book *Sexual Personae*.

She notes there that for the fin-de-siècle aesthete it was a case of aesthetics stopping where sex begins. Citing the affair of Oscar Wilde with Lord Douglas by way of example, Paglia observes:

> Wilde writes to Douglas of "the soul of the artist who found his ideal in you..." Therefore, Wilde's first encounter with Douglas after the release of *Dorian Gray* was a Platonic fulfillment, exactly like Shelley's with Emilia Viviani, stunning incarnation of the Hermaphrodite of his ... *Witch of Atlas*. But Shelley wrote a greater poem afterward, *Epipsychidion*, for there were *no sexual relations* between himself and [Emilia].... Wilde, forgetting the abstinence of Socrates with Alcibiades, made the fatal error of copulating with his representational ideal.... Douglas drew Wilde into Late Romantic infatuation and fascination, disordering his mature judgment and ending his career at the height of his fame.[107]

In this way Paglia takes note of the darker side of aestheticism, for as she points out, "aestheticism . . . assert[s] the primacy of beauty over all modes of experience" ("aesthetics," insisted Wilde, "are higher than ethics"), and because "the true aesthete is always a lover of narcissistic beauty," the aesthete can be endangered.[108] But though there is more than a whiff of this in Day's life, there seems little in that of Cram, who, I argue, most likely avoided Wilde's "fatal error" and held, at least in principle and intent, to the Platonic ideal. Indeed, it is critical to keep before us here in our discussion of Goodhue and Cram and, as well, of all their circle, Paglia's conclusion about the fin-de-siècle: "Decadence . . . is drenched in sex, but sex as thought rather than action."[109] The Platonic ideal is not only the model that best reconciles Cram's religion with his sexuality but also accords with the way in his era aesthetes and decadents were inclined to feel the creative process was sustained.

"THE IMAGED WORD"

That Cram's mind was nervously alert in this period to an inner struggle of his own seems clear from my reading of the third of the Gothic horror stories in *Black Spirits and White* we shall study here, "The White Villa":

> This was in the spring of '88. . . . We set off contentedly that white May morning . . . [thinking] in our innocence, that we should be alone. . . . We were *not*. . . . The inevitable English family with the three daughters, prominent of teeth, flowing of hair, aggressive of scarlet Murrays and Baedekers; the two blond and untidy Germans, . . . [a] terrible old man [who] had fastened himself upon a party of American schoolteachers travelling *en Cook*. . . . Our vision of two hours of dreaming solitude faded lamentably away.
>
> Yet how beautiful it was . . . three temples, one silver gray, one golden gray, and one flushed with intangible rose. And all around nothing but velvet meadows stretching from the dim mountains behind away to the sea. . . .
>
> The tide of tourists swept noisily [away to other temples] and Tom and I were left alone to drink in all the fine wine of dreams that was possible in the time left to us. We gave but little space to examining the temples the tourists had left, but in a few moments found ourselves lying in the grass to the east of Poseidon, looking dimly out towards the sea, heard now, but not seen, — a vague and pulsating murmur that blended with the humming of bees all about us.
>
> A small shepherd boy, with a wooly dog, made shy advances of friendship, and in a little while we had set him to gathering flowers for us: asphodels and bee-orchids, anemones, and the little thin green iris so fairylike and frail. . . . It was very still; suddenly I heard the words I had been waiting for, — the suggestion I had refrained from making myself, for I knew Thomas.
>
> "I say, old man, shall we let the 2.46 go to thunder?"
>
> I chuckled to myself. "But the Turners?" [Both were to have dined with the same that night in Naples and gone on afterward to the opera.]

"They be blowed, we can tell them we missed the train."

"That is exactly what we shall do," I said, pulling out my watch, "unless we start for the station right now."

But Tom drew an acanthus leaf across his face and showed no signs of moving; so I filled my pipe again, and we missed the train. . . .

[They end up putting up for the night in a vast and all but derelict old pile, where the huge and gloomy halls, lit only by fires, of course, and the surly old caretaker, bode little good.]

In a few minutes Tom was asleep . . .; but my constitution is more nervous. . . . Finally, I fell asleep, — for how long I do not know; but I woke with the feeling that someone had tried the handle of the door. . . . The latch rattled, and the door swung smoothly open. . . we did lock it, and now it was opening.

Then I heard a footstep . . . *in the room*, and with it the *frou-frou* of trailing skirts. . . .

The coverlid was turned back beside me, and in another moment the great bed sank a little as something slipped between the sheets. . . . With a cry that shivered between my chattering teeth, I hurled myself headlong from the bed on to the floor.

I must have lain for some time stunned. . . . When I finally came to myself it was cold . . . [and again] the door opened. . . . I stood trembling and listened . . . to heavy, stealthy steps creeping along on the other side of the bed. I clutched the coverlid, staring across in the dark.

There was a rush of air by my face, the sound of a blow, and simultaneously a shriek. . . . I sank crouching on the floor by the bed.

And then began the awful duel . . . of things that shrieked and raved . . . rushing swiftly down the great room until I felt the flash of swirling drapery on my hard lips.

. . . Came one long, gurgling moan close over my head, and then, crushing down upon me, the weight of a collapsing body; there was long hair over my face, and in my staring eyes . . . life went out, and I fell unfathomable miles into nothingness. . . .

[Later, in the village, the innkeeper tells them the story of *La Villa Bianca*.]

"Oh, Signori, certainly; and a story very strange and very terrible. . . . The Duca di San Damiano married a lady so fair, so most beautiful that she was called *La Luna di Pesto*; but she was of the people, more she was of the banditti. . . . Less than a year after they came to the villa the Duke grew jealous, —. . . it was in the spring — the Duke came silently down from Napoli, and . . . his carriage was set upon . . . the brigands were beaten off; but before him, wounded, lay the captain . . . and in his hand [he] saw *his own sword*. Then . . . he ran the brigand through, leaped in the carriage, and, entering the villa, crept to the chamber of *La Luna*, and killed her with the sword she had given to her lover . . . and as she died unshriven, so was she buried without the pale of the Church."[110]

Could Cram have identified himself any more explicitly or any more intimately with sexual transgression? The punishment is all but visited on Cram himself as he is crushed under the weight of the transgressor's collapsing body, her long hair clouding his staring eyes. Moreover, this hysteria, marking the night watches of the day of his and Randall's romantic idyll in the grass (and their missing of the train and general breaking of the rules) certainly implies some connection. Nor does Cram's ending of the story altogether reconcile the matter: the sexual transgressor with whom Cram seems to identify himself so completely is forthrightly assigned to the only proper place — "without the pale of the Church."

All things considered, despite the way his religion — and to some extent the elite New England establishment — sustained Cram as a young man, rescuing him from outright isolation and rejection, there is ample evidence in "The White Villa" that even Anglo-Catholics nurtured by Cowley had, after all, their own inner struggle between religion and sexuality, the intimate link between which at the deepest level of the psyche has been often commented upon.[111] It has perhaps for our purposes here been best put by John Crowley in his discussion of the conversion of the American travel writer Charles Stoddard. Crowley begins with a quotation of Stoddard's own:

> "I couldn't help it, you see; it [Catholicism] was born in me and was the only thing that appealed to my temperament. . . ." Catholicism, then, was as deeply "congenital" for Stoddard as his same-sexuality. Stoddard's coming out as a Catholic in his conversion narrative, A Troubled Heart (1885), was symbolically equivalent, as [his biographer] sees, to his revealing his sexual "temperament."[112]

Though Crowley goes on to say that "this equivalence remained inchoate for Stoddard because the idea of 'coming out' would not crystallize in sexual, rather than religious, discourse until the category of 'homosexual' had been fully established," his conclusion that a man's disclosure of his sexuality and/or religiosity may be "symbolically equivalent" (in whichever universe of discourse of "coming out" his epoch encourages him to) suggests to me (recalling Hilliard's point of how readily Anglo-Catholicism lent itself to homosexuals' "expressing their sense of difference in an oblique and symbolic way [that was] a more socially acceptable type of rebellion") that Anglo-Catholicism became for Cram the principal expression or carrier of his sexual orientation — and in a most characteristically Platonic way. Robert Martin has put the sharpest Christian point on it:

> As in the Platonic paradigm, [the artist's] love for a beautiful young man leads [the artist] to an apprehension of pure beauty. One cannot perceive Beauty directly, but may find it expressed in the perfect form of a young man; the form of that young man then leads to a truer, more eternal form. The final figure, "the imaged Word," expresses . . . [the artist's] . . . constant search for a balance between the claims of the body and the claims of the soul. Its source is in the mystery of the Incarnation, as expressed by St. John, that most Greek of Christians. The spiritual truth is conveyed through the physical form of the beautiful young man, Christ.[113]

These words come from a study of Hart Crane. Others might be quoted from Oscar Wilde; in his sonnet "Vita Nuova" he referred to Christ as "my Perfect

Friend," thus casting Christ, in Richard Ellmann's words, as lover.[114] So, too, George Santayana: Martin notes that the philosopher's sexual "guilt . . . expressed itself in an erotic vision of Christ: 'I sought on earth a garden of delight . . . / . . . And though his arms, outstretched upon the tree, / Were beautiful and pleaded my embrace, / My sins were loth to look upon his face.' "[115] All of a piece, surely, with Thompson's "Hound of Heaven"; hence my hazard that Cram's "tremendous Lover" of his Roman winter and spring of 1887–88 was only in the first place to be Henry Randall. Similarly with Bertram Goodhue. For "the form of that young man then leads to a truer, more eternal form." Father Hall would not have disagreed.

But if at this deeper psychic level Ralph Adams Cram in his youth was thus struggling manfully, he was gathering his experiences through the hurly-burly of contemporary society. And especially in view of how in this chapter we have found so readily at hand in that society a predisposition among the Anglo-Saxon elite for the Platonic ideal that was his and Goodhue's likely relational model, we need to make some of those experiences our own, especially as they relate to Boston's gay community of the period, the emergence of which has been so long hidden from us.

6

THE FIGURE IN THE CARPET

The bareness of Puritan plain style and the absence of inherited art works starved the American eye and aggravated the dangerous power of the visual when it arrived via Romanticism. Asceticism, fearing the eye, actually sharpens it. Hawthorne [in *The Scarlet Letter*] illustrates the sexual problematics of the visual when Hester is brought before the multitude: ". . . under the heavy weight of a thousand unrelenting eyes . . . concentrated at her bosom." . . .

Billy Budd belongs to the glamourous company of beautiful boys we have traced from the Athenian *Kritios Boy* to Donatello's *David*, Shakespeare's fair youth, and Wilde's Dorian Gray. . . .

The obscure late style [of Henry James] is itself a sexual projection, for whenever I labor under its enormous constraints, I think, "*Someone is there.*" ·

— Camille Paglia, *Sexual Personae*

A figure is nothing without a setting.

— Henry James, *The Bostonians*

61. Fifteenth-century ironwork secures the door of the Macknight Room off the Palace Road Cloister at Fenway Court, in Isabella Stewart Gardner's day her bachelor guest suite. Behind the antique grille is a smaller door through which to discern a caller's identity.

WHY DOES it no longer seem startling that Ralph Waldo Emerson, in Justin Kaplan's words, "had a crush on a fellow undergraduate at Harvard, Martin Gay, nicknamed 'Cool' by his classmates, and wrote ardent poetry about him as a fantasy laced with sexual symbolism"?[1] With our discussion in mind of both the continuity and the changefulness of sexual identity through the ages as we have begun to look more carefully at our highly edited past, the result has been that, in the case of New England's cultural history, our attention has been drawn not just to expected figures like Melville and Hawthorne. After all, in touching here on the life of the Yale undergraduate of the 1830s, we have already noted that even a highly genital homosexuality, so long as it was discreet, was acceptable in the early nineteenth century in New England. By the last third of the century, as the modern understanding of homosexuality began to develop, Boston played a key role in that process.

THE POET AS NAMER

Even before Cram's Pinckney Street neighbor James Osgood had published his edition of *Leaves of Grass* in 1881, that singular book had two decades earlier figured importantly in Boston's history. Although technically it was the third edition, *Leaves of Grass* was (as Whitman put it) "really published" for the first time in Boston in 1860, by the very brave house of Thayer and Eldridge ("We are young men," they pleaded with Whitman; "Try us"). In this edition the cluster of poems (called "Calamus") that marked Whitman's recognition of his homosexuality first saw the light of day.[2] No less than the Wilde trial of thirty-five years later, Whitman's 1860 debut was a seminal event. Nor was it done in a corner.

The scene is a famous one, though only in a very general way, the gay aspect having always been played down. It took place in 1860 on Boston Common. Whitman himself describes it:

Up and down this breadth by Beacon Street, between these same old elms, I walked for two hours of a bright sharp February midday . . . with Emerson, then in his prime, keen, physically and morally magnetic, armed at every point, and when he chose wielding the emotional just as well as the intellectual. . . . It was an argument-statement (like an army corps in order, artillery, cavalry, infantry) of all that could be

203

said against that part in the construction of *Leaves of Grass*. More precious than gold to me, that dissertation — it afforded me, ever after, this strange and paradoxical lesson; each point of Emerson's statement was unanswerable, no judge's charge ever more complete or convincing, I could never hear the points better put — and then I felt down in my soul the clear and unmistakable conviction to disobey all, and pursue my own way. "What have you to say then to such things?" said Emerson, pausing in conclusion. "Only that while I can't answer them at all, I feel more settled than ever to adhere to my own theory, and exemplify it," was my candid response. Whereupon we went and had a good dinner at the American House. And thence forward I never wavered or was touched with qualms (as I confess I had been two or three times before).[3]

The chief significance of this exchange is surely that emphasized by Robert K. Martin, who has observed of Whitman's overall attempt to name what we now call homosexual love (Whitman called it "adhesive" as opposed to "amative," borrowing terms from the language of phrenology) that while that love had hitherto "been recognized for thousands of years, . . . [and] implied in the language of the Bible" (he cites the description of David's love for Jonathan, "a love passing that of woman"), there was "no word for this love. . . . Whitman was indeed Emerson's 'poet as namer.' He gave that love," concluded Martin, "the first name it had of its own [adhesive], albeit a poor and borrowed one."[4]

Any who doubt the significance of this conversation on Boston Common between "New England's Plato" (which is to say America's), as Wilde called Emerson, and Whitman, the poet whose work (as much in England as in America) first celebrated as well as named homosexual love in the Western world in the modern era, should notice what Whitman later said about the event, words any author, this one included, might say: "If I had cut sex out, I must just as well have cut everything out . . . expurgation is apology . . . an admission that something or other was wrong."[5] Silence in his own behalf will always rob a man of his dignity, be he dead or alive.

As we saw briefly in our tour of Pinckney Street in Chapter 1, which the reader may recall began about 1786 with two bachelors setting up house together, the subject of homosexuality in Boston's history, though veiled for obvious reasons in some obscurity, is scarcely foreign to the Puritan capital. In fact, Boston is curiously identifiable with homosexuality. "Miss Furr and Miss Skeene," for instance, the playful piece by Gertrude Stein, written ca. 1908–1912, in which "gay" was possibly first used explicitly in its sense of homosexual, was originally published in Boston in 1922.[6] No wonder. Years earlier, when "Xavier Mayne" wrote *The Intersexes* in 1908, the first book by an American defending what was coming to be known as "homosexualism," he ranked ahead of Boston as one of the "homosexual capitals" of the United States only New York, the extent of whose homosexual life in the nineteenth century (among only the middle and working classes) is just now becoming clear in the path-breaking work of George Chauncey, whose *Gay New York* was published as this book was going to press.[7] After all, had not the Boston marriage been the most widely acknowledged same-sex relationship of the nineteenth century?

BOSTON MARRIAGES AND BOSTON BROTHERS

The city's preeminent Boston marriage, between Annie Fields and Sarah Orne Jewett, has already been discussed. So has that in Cram's circle of Alice Brown and Louise Guiney. Others of particular artistic importance included that of Edith Guerrier and Edith Braun, fellow students at the Museum School and friends of Charles Eliot Norton, which resulted, through the patronage of Mrs. James Storrow, in the now famous Paul Revere Pottery, and that of poet Amy Lowell and Ada Dwyer Russell. Nor is there any need to think such unions existed only between women. One of the reasons, in fact, that we dwelt so long on the teaching of Arthur Crawshay Hall is that his writings suggest that male same-sex relationships comparable to the Boston marriage also existed — relationships, it should be remembered, that Hall called, quoting Jeremy Taylor, "marriages of the soul."[8]

The proportion of such stable male unions to the presumably more promiscuous norm, or the extent to which stable same-sex friendships prevailed more among women than men, is a vexing subject about which there is more opinion to be found than fact. Of the widespread prevalence of homosexuality in Boston there seems little doubt. Admittedly, Dr. Magnus Hirschfeld in 1893 reported perceiving "almost nothing of homosexuality" in Boston.[9] But we have already seen that by 1908 *The Intersexes* told quite a different tale of Boston as a center of homosexuality. Moreover, Hirschfeld's report itself was challenged by others who pointed out that, on the contrary, "an awful lot was going on," and not least in the Turkish baths, Boston being so discreet and private a town and American homosexuals in general being so "astonishingly ignorant about their own true nature"; which as Antonio A. Giarraputo and William Percy have pointed out, "amounted to saying that while they were conscious of their physical desires, they had not yet been exposed to European concepts of homosexual identity."[10]

Therein, of course, lies one important reason that only scholars "on the lookout," as it were, and only recently, have seen the truth of the reports quoted by Katz that, whether one speaks of men or women, in union or living promiscuously, Boston in the 1900s had a significant homosexual population among all classes and in all sections, from the slums to the Back Bay.[11]

The habitat of the more promiscuous would, of course, likely have been the Turkish baths — not dissimilar, once imagines, from those celebrated by Michelangelo. And Boston's (and Harvard's) baths and pools will arise here soon, rather in the same way as have beaches and bathing in connection with Cram's diary. But the habitat most characteristic of the stable male relationship (admittedly much less domestic, very much more Bohemian, even risqué, than the Boston marriage — such things are sometimes said to be more likely of men than of women) was, in my view, at the upper-class level, Boston's clubland, especially the city's artistic and literary clubs that had their first flowering in the 1880s. There were three: the Tavern, the St. Botolph, and the Papyrus, the original character of which is easy to overlook and even to question today, when the two elite clubs that have survived are hardly Bohemian at all in comparison with the general culture, which in any event has become so liberated as virtually to have abolished the idea of Bohemia.

The geography of Bohemian Boston is a factor here. Although after the building in the 1900s of Symphony Hall and the New England Conservatory in a new section of the Back Bay, St. Botolph Street (the border between the Back Bay and the South End, and like Pinckney Street one mediating between quarters good and not so good) became very much a Bohemian enclave, complete with Turkish baths, in the 1880s and 1890s Boston's Bohemia was, as we have observed, strongly centered on Beacon Hill. It will be recalled from Chapter 1 that while Cram lived in the relatively genteel Bohemian area of residential Pinckney Street on Beacon Hill, he was as well a frequenter of the city's then roughest Bohemian quarter — the area of taverns and chophouses (for men only) between Province Street and Newspaper Row on upper Washington Street — and a habitué of the city's theaters and concert halls and their nearby cafés, which in the 1880s and 1890s centered in two enclaves at each end of Washington and Tremont streets.

The older enclave, still quite swell then but beginning to decline, centered on Scollay Square at the end of upper Washington Street, where, for instance, the fashionable Quincy House Café was open all night for after-theater revels. The newer area, at the lower end of Washington and nearby Tremont, which would become by the 1900s the city's principal theater district, was in Cram's youth just coalescing as another Bohemian quarter, distinct from Pinckney Street in being commercial and not residential, but also distinct from the rougher area of bars and taverns around Newspaper Row by being somewhat more stylish and aesthete. French and Italian restaurants, rather than chophouses, for example, tended to nest in this newer Bohemian enclave, particularly in the block bounded by Tremont, Boylston, Charles, and what is now Stuart Street, where the reader will recall Cram and Wentworth's first office was located in 1889. In this block were the legendary Vercelli's on Boylston Street, where the Tavern Club was begun in 1884, and also the buildings where the St. Botolph and the Tavern clubs first roosted when founded in the early 1880s. (Though the first of what we would call today gay bars was apparently the Pen and Pencil of the 1920s in Scollay Square — its name probably deriving from Wilde's "Pen, Pencil and Poison" — the area where during Prohibition such bars clustered was precisely that which Walter Muir Whitehill diplomatically called "The Neighborhood of the Tavern Club.")[12]

In no sense were the Bohemian artistic clubs when founded — the St. Botolph, the Tavern, or the Papyrus (the last the exception in making its earliest home in the older Bohemian enclave at the other end of Tremont Street in the Revere House, a hotel near Scollay Square) — in any sense clones of Boston's most prestigious male clubs, the much older and quite grand Somerset or the then only slightly less grand Algonquin, University, and Exchange clubs. In the case of the Tavern, which has studied its history sufficiently to be very clear on the subject, it is known that almost no members of the Somerset were among the Tavern's founders, the original membership of which was very young: in the 1880s and 1890s most Taverners were in their twenties.[13] A comparison of fees in the mid-1880s documents the fact that those of the St. Botolph, for example (fifty dollars initiation, thirty dollars annually), were half or less than those of the Somerset, the Union, and the Algonquin, all of which expected a hundred dollars upon initiation, and another hundred for annual dues. The Papyrus's initiation fee was only twenty-five dollars (ten for literary members); the annual dues, only five.[14]

Elaine Showalter of Yale has pointed out of the overall Anglo-American men's club concept that though "aggressively and urbanely heterosexual, even rakish, in their discourse," the membership of "fin-de-siècle Clubland existed on the fragile borderline that separated male bonding from homosexuality." Boston, to be sure, is not London. That in the British capital "the shadow of homosexuality . . . surrounded Clubland" does not mean that it did in the Puritan capital.[15] Still, Boston's artistic clubs especially, like the St. Grottlesex prep schools, all flowered in the late nineteenth century, on a universal Anglo-American-Colonial model; in the case of the club, the London gentlemen's club was an animating one in Anglophile Boston, and not least among homosexuals, who understood where, traditionally, they would be not only most welcome but, in some of the more Bohemian clubs, highly influential and perhaps even at times controlling. (Not surprisingly, in *The Intersexes* Mayne asserted that in 1908 "certain smart clubs [in Boston] are well known for their homosexual atmospheres.")[16]

The extent to which this was widely understood is hard to recapture. In his history of American Bohemianism, for example, Albert Parry wrote of the Papyrus Club:

> Boston's Bohemia was smuggled in by an adventurous Irishman . . . John Boyle
> O'Reilly . . . [first in his] commodious bachelor's den in Staniford Street and . . .
> [thereafter in] the Papyrus Club [founded in 1872]. . . . However, the dangerous
> word "Bohemia" was not passed too widely. . . . Certainly, when Thomas Bailey
> Aldrich and William Dean Howells were elected to the club they did not know of
> its scarlet lining. . . . O'Reilly waited till 1885 [significantly, after he had helped to
> found both the Botolph and the Tavern] to come out openly with his grand declaration of Bohemianism.[17]

The reminiscences of early Taverners, however, are very revealing, especially those of Francis Watson, who recorded that

> the members of the Tavern [only one hundred men in 1886] were thrown intimately
> together . . . tending to procure a quickly established comradeship. . . . The members
> were [also] for the most part young men. . . . Most of them had the tendency and
> many of them the habit of more or less Bohemian habits of living, and many of them
> had been students of art, of medicine, architecture or science . . . in Europe. . . . Most
> of them were either artistic of temperament or in close sympathy with those having
> this temperament.[18]

It ought not at this point to startle the reader to note a Tavern founder using words like "Bohemian," "artistic," and "comradeship" in connection with the club, words then widely understood, as we have seen, as euphemisms or code words for "homosexual." Usage may vary, of course. Yet whether the use is in a more positive or more negative sense (as then understood) is often the key to decoding a word's meaning. For example, another Tavern founder, Owen Wister, used the word "Bohemianism" in rather a telling way, surely, when in a club speech years later he assured his listeners that the Tavern "never *sank* into Bohemianism [emphasis added]" — which leaves little doubt that this now somewhat benign-sounding word once had about it more bite and challenge. Interestingly, Wister also appealed to his fellow twentieth-century Taverners to recall "the vanished world of 1884" by way of explaining the club's origins, in this century a more and more embarrassing burden, leading to such nervously defensive explanations as that "the Boston of 1884, and the little assemblage of young men who formed the Tavern Club, seem in retrospect of a naïveté almost Arcadian."[19] In the Tavern's post-Freudian club history all reference to Bohemianism is eschewed.

That Wister was correct in his reading of the club's original character could not be more aptly illustrated than by the well-worn tale of how a portrait of one Taverner by another came about. Its somewhat uneven quality (and the fact that the painter could never recall painting it!) gives credence to the tradition that it was the product of a very late night and early morning at the club, a tradition not contradicted in more sober moments by either the sitter, Dennis Bunker, or the painter, John Singer Sargent,[20] whose intimate relationship we know from other sources, such as Isabella Stewart Gardner, who, significantly, placed their portrait photographs side by side in the same display case at Fenway Court — even though, as Susan Sinclair, the Gardner's archivist, points out, there was no apparent reason to do so. Sargent and Bunker's relationship was probably not unlike that of another Tavern couple, Theodore Frelinghuysen Dwight and Thomas Russell Sullivan. About this second couple we know enough so that a discussion of their relationship will illuminate our exploration of Boston's clubland a century and more ago.

Town Topics

Sullivan, a well-known author and playwright who was highly influential in all three clubs (a founding member of each, he served as sometime president of the Papyrus, as secretary in the early 1880s of the St. Botolph, and on the very first elections committee of the Tavern),[21] was for years the intimate friend and confidant of Dwight, a librarian of considerable ability and charm whose interests ranged from rare books to baseball, and who, like Sullivan, moved in the highest circles in Boston intellectually, socially, and artistically.[22] Their friends included Henry Adams, Isabella Gardner, and the legendary Harvard figure George Pierce Baker, mentor of dramatists up to and including, in the next century, Eugene O'Neill. Indeed, no one was surprised when in 1892 Dwight, previously the Adams family librarian, was appointed to one of the city's preeminent positions as head of the Boston Public Library, just at the crucial point when the new building by McKim, Mead and White was nearing completion in Copley Square.

Dwight, Roger Austen writes of the library's head, was a man of very definite tastes:

> Dwight's private library was well stocked with pictures of naked young men [including] some Neapolitan photographs he had purchased from Pluschow, the notorious purveyor of erotica. . . .
> While touring Europe with Mrs. Gardner during the summer of 1892, Dwight purchased some additional material. . . . Dwight was also taking pictures of naked young men in Boston — and, if possible, going to bed with them. Sometimes his models were Irish, but more often they were Italians who had been procured for him by his barber. After he began earning five thousand dollars a year from the library [as director], he usually had one of these models living with him as his "valet."[23]

The library, it is important to note, was then so conservative in tone that when Hamlin Garland sought to borrow *Leaves of Grass*, he found that it was "double starred and lent only to serious students," a situation similar to what obtained at Harvard, where Whitman's book had been "removed from the open shelves of the college library and kept under lock and key with other tabooed books."[24]

Dwight's correspondence with Isabella Gardner is of considerable interest. Noting that what he writes "is of a nature quite too confidential to have been written with propriety,"[25] Dwight recounted to Gardner not only intimacies with Sullivan and Bunker, but also his and Sullivan's relations with Charles Loeffler, Timothée Adamowski, and Clayton Johns, all leading members of both the Tavern and the St. Botolph (Adamowski was one of five founders of the Tavern) and very well known musicians; especially Johns, a composer of romantic ballads. (Wrote a contemporary: "one has yet to hear of a summer hotel in this broad land that has not echoed to [Johns's song] 'I cannot help loving thee.'")[26]

Dwight's circle extended, moreover, as might be expected, to Cambridge. There his dinner companions included that fellow Taverner George Santayana, who himself introduced into the club as his guest in 1894 the second Earl Russell (one of the great loves of Santayana's life, Bertrand Russell's older brother), with whom by 1896 Santayana had forged a very un-Platonic relationship (described by his biographer as "an intense physical affair").[27] Dwight also knew very well a now lesser known but then quite important figure, William Woodworth. The head of Harvard's Museum of Comparative Zoology, Woodworth was also a friend of Louis Agassiz's, and the Woodworth home at 149 Brattle Street was famous not only for its exotic furnishings but also for its males-only Sunday socials, the cast of which included several junior members of the circle who have figured before here, such as Charles Flandrau, author of *Harvard Episodes*, and Pierre La Rose, who in addition to all his other activities had by then established himself as one of Brattle Street's favorite decorators, redoing, for example, H. H. Richardson's Stoughton House.[28]

In the summer this gay scene shifted to yet another lively locale: the estate of William Sturgis Bigelow, "where men," as John Crowley put it, "took their ease, often naked, in an untamed natural setting" on Tuckernuck, an island off Nantucket.[29] But for most of the year clubmen like Sullivan and Dwight and their friends called Beacon Hill home — Johns on Pinckney Street, Adamowski, Sullivan, and Dwight on Charles Street, often (in a pattern widespread in this period) rooming together in bachelor chambers where breakfast was produced by a resident servant and lunch and dinner were taken at the club. (McKim, Mead and White designed not only the public library but also Boston's most luxurious bachelor chambers, at the corner of Charles and Beacon streets.) Sullivan and Dwight, for example, each had a flat at 10 Charles Street, two blocks from Pinckney, near the intersection of Charles and Beacon streets, where they employed as concierge and factotum one Jacques Medus, late of the French army in Morocco (clearly unshockable), and his wife, Sarah,[30] who cleaned the flats while her husband valeted the young gentlemen and made their breakfasts and fetched their champagne at all hours, for much entertaining was done, especially when Mrs. Jack was in town. After a dinner one night, Sullivan and Dwight and a small party, including Gardner and the Paul Bourgets (he was a French novelist), all

> adjourned to 10 Charles Street. . . . Dwight opened his rooms [on the floor above], and we moved about between the two [floors], smoking, talking, and laughing. Then Bourget and I were left for a while alone. We talked of books. . . . They stayed late. . . . One more pleasant association for this small *salon*![31]

There were many such associations in the close-knit world of Boston's fin-de-siècle Bohemia, though there was, to be sure, not a little heartache, too. Wrote Dwight to Gardner in a very different vein from that of his friend downstairs:

> You would be amused could you know how in my secret thoughts of late I have been chiefly engaged in trying to penetrate my own disguise to find the real Dwight, for it is really ridiculous that I should all unconsciously have played a part so well as to deceive so many intelligent and respectable people. I dare not think of the time when they will discover their mistake.[32]

Eventually they did; within two years Dwight had resigned as head of Boston's library and departed for abroad — though nothing was ever said.[33] Boston being Boston, such notice as was taken in any pointed way that has survived of these young Bohemians was apt to be taken elsewhere.

Adamowski, for example, more in the public eye than Dwight or Sullivan, being not only first violinist of the symphony but also conductor of the Boston Pops (having been recruited by the symphony's conductor, fellow Taverner Wilhelm Gericke, whom he met at the Tavern; the aesthete network operated as well among musicians), was much noticed by that irreverent New York society rag, *Town Topics*. A merciless reporter of affairs Bostonian, in November 1896 it opined, surely with tongue very much in cheek, that Adamowski was "still holding his own as the blond Adonis among the violinists of the Boston Symphony, [and] . . . sails serenely on, the gay young bachelor, smiled on by all women, but conquered by none."[34] Not for the first (or the last) time here, the origins of our modern use of the word "gay" were never so obvious.

As with gossip then, so with history now: the documentation of this circle of gay Taverners (using the word in both senses) arises not from any Boston history or memoir but from my examination of the surviving correspondence of Isabella Gardner in the wake of Roger Austen's study of the papers of a Middle Western travel writer and professor of English at Notre Dame and Catholic

University, Charles Stoddard, whose biography by Austen, *Genteel Pagan*, documents homosexual circles all over America in the 1890s. Reticence, of course, has always been characteristic of the Boston tradition of historiography. That the New England capital was distinctly a part of Stoddard's "homosexual milieu" in the 1880s and 1890s is not suggested, for example, in Russell Sullivan's published (and very Boston) journals, any more than in Gardner's biography — *or* Cram's memoirs.[35] Sullivan's journals do muster Stoddard's Boston cast, not a few of whom appear also in the Gardner and Cram books. But in none of them is there more than the occasional hint of an important reason that all these people were drawn together in the first place.

Stoddard's papers disclose as well that though Dwight and his circle dominated for him, the gay Boston Stoddard knew in the 1890s was more extensive. Perhaps through Gardner, who knew Stoddard, he was also, Austen reports, introduced into what I have called here the Pinckney Street circle, where Stoddard

> met the Catholic poet Louise Imogen Guiney, who shared with him an interest in the trappings of medievalism and in the career of the young poet Bliss Carman. . . . Carman was *simpatico*. A tall, thin Canadian, whose unconventional appearance Stoddard found wonderfully picturesque, Carman wore his hair long and favored full flowing cravats, heavy tweeds, sandals and jewelry. . . . Carman apparently shared Stoddard's appreciation of good-looking young men.[36]

That, of course, was more than hinted at by Carman in poems such as "Verlaine" ("prowler of obscene streets that riot reels along") or "The Bather" (men are "so beautiful. / Their bodies are like the bows of the Indians. / They have the spring and the grace of bows of hickory").[37] But Carman was in Stoddard's case more explicit than that. Once alert to Stoddard's role in Boston (where he often visited Dwight, a close friend), no very diligent eye is needed to spot Pinckney Street's knowledge of his affairs in Carman's and Hovey's *Last Songs from Vagabondia*; there, in a little-known poem that is otherwise a charming poetic compliment to Auburndale's unusual postmistress, Louise Guiney, by her devoted Bliss Carman, the whole published by Fred Day, a telltale reference to Charles Stoddard has long waited to be recognized for what it says of all concerned:

> Now, there's a Romany in Auburndale,
> Wild as a faun and sound as cakes and ale,
> One of the tribe of Stevenson and Barrow,
> Who live today and let alone tomorrow.
> God keeps a few still living in the sun, —
> The man who wrote The Seven Seas, for one,
> And Island Stoddard, — just to prove the folly
> Of smug repose and pious melancholy.

So when I see her signal in the hedge,
(I mean her new book on the counter's edge),
"Ho, ho," say I, "that Guiney's broken loose again,
Cut a new quill and put her craft to use again."[38]

God keeps a few still living yet; that smug repose and pious melancholy may not prevail after all.

"Dear Boys"

Certainly neither repose nor melancholy prevailed for long at the Papyrus Club. This happy band of brothers, who regularly forgathered in that chophouse called Billy Park's we know from Chapter 1 Cram swore by for good fellowship, enjoyed a reputation caught best by Sullivan in a poetic effusion about the club's founder, which ended — and might as well have been entitled — "Dear boys!"[39]

The head boy (that is to say the founder, O'Reilly), described as a poet "who could and did relax with boyish *abandon*,"[40] though a cultured and refined man, was also physically highly aggressive, an ardent supporter, for example, of "the manly art," of which enthusiasm his biographer found it necessary to write just a tad defensively (even in the pre-Freudian early 1890s) that if O'Reilly was

> red-hot in his enthusiasm for the brawn and biceps of a famous pugilist, it is not . . . [as with] the dandies of old Rome who pinched the muscles of gladiators with slim, feminine fingers. In the society of the physically strong . . . Boyle O'Reilly is among his peers.[41]

Still, it is striking that a caricature of a seminude John L. Sullivan, muscular enough but very vain, not to say effete, appeared in this era in *Puck* magazine over the caption "Aesthetic Boston's New Hobby."[42]

Though O'Reilly's name, by the way, does not surface in Stoddard's biography, Stoddard's name did in the late nineteenth century in O'Reilly's.[43] And it was perhaps in part through O'Reilly that Stoddard sought out Cram's neighbor James Osgood, a Papyrus member, as his publisher, for Osgood did indeed publish Stoddard's homoerotic travel idylls as he had *Leaves of Grass*, apropos of which Sullivan allowed himself in his journal to recall that O'Reilly knew the poet (despite Whitman's notoriety, he *was* famous) and introduced him to the Papyrus Club. As Sullivan told the tale, one night after dinner O'Reilly took him to call upon Whitman, who was

> then passing a few days at a small hotel in Bulfinch Place [a street on Beacon Hill, now built over, that opened off Bowdoin Street, near St. John's, the Cowley church]. We found the old fellow correcting the proofs of his new edition of "Leaves of Grass," afterward published only to be suppressed [the Boston district attorney in 1881 put Osgood on notice about the book, which was withdrawn from sale]. One

or two other men came in, and as the room was small, we all adjourned to the Revere House and sat round the table in the Papyrus parlor [which was in the hotel], drinking, discoursing, and listening. . . . We talked of poetry and poets, of work generally, of the struggle for life, like that of ants in an anthill.[44]

Perhaps it was evenings like that which led a fellow Papyrus member, Mark A. De Wolf Howe, to complain that "the Papyrus club . . . took its Bohemianism a little too seriously."[45] (That was, no doubt, one of the reasons why the club did not survive. Nor did its founder for very long. Like so many treated in this book, he died in his mid-forties, reportedly of suicide.)[46] On the other hand, while Howe lamented the Papyrus's blatant Bohemianism, Santayana lamented the Tavern's increasing staidness. It was, Santayana later wrote, "the only club I ever belonged to in Boston; and [which] I frequented . . . until [it] became stuffy and tiresome." It is not difficult to catch his meaning.[47]

BACCHANTE AND NARCISSUS

All of this had its effect on Boston's art and architecture. For example, during Dwight's reign as head of the Boston Public Library, as the McKim building neared completion, not only did young men appear in the director's bed; they appeared, equally nude, this time in imperishable stone over the main front entrance, in the new library seal (62).[48] Wrote Russell Sullivan in 1892 to Gardner of Dwight's joy: "His library facade is now all done and very beautiful, the St. Gaudens' marble group [of the nude males supporting the library seal] over the door beyond compare."[49] These nudes were not beyond criticism, however, for they caused quite an uproar, as Walter Muir Whitehill recounted (though out of a context he did not suspect) with a perfectly straight face in the centennial history of the library:

The *Boston Evening Record* of 10 February 1894, under the headline "WIPE OUT THE BLOT" . . . told the sad tale of . . . "a pure-minded lad . . . [who] cried in anguish as he observed 'See that thing they have put up there, papa, isn't it horrible?' " . . . Because of the acute eyesight of this "bright, clean, Boston boy," the *Record* clamored: "*This indecency must not remain!*" . . . [But] . . . its crusade was too ridiculous to succeed even in Boston. Saint-Gaudens' seal remained, with its boys neither clothed nor castrated.[50]

Saint Gaudens's youths reflected an interest in the phallus this sculptor shared more than once with Stanford White. But, as finally designed by Kenyon Cox, the nudes of the seal are more like boys. In *Idols of Perversity* Bram Dijkstra pays particular heed to "how thin [was] the line separating idealist art and child pornography" in this era. He observes that in view of the fact that "to

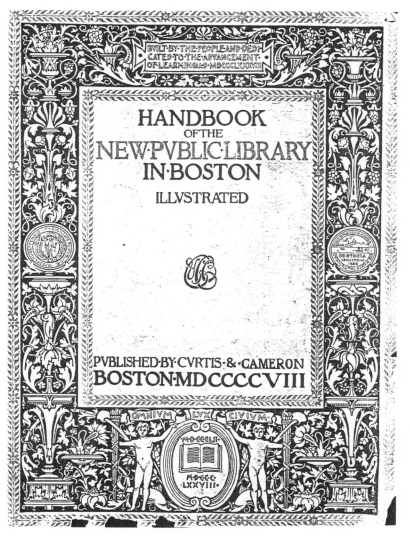

HANDBOOK
OF THE
NEW·PVBLIC·LIBRARY
IN·BOSTON
ILLVSTRATED

PVBLISHED·BY·CVRTIS·&·CAMERON
BOSTON·MDCCCCVIII

62. The Boston Public Library seal, carved over the central portal, appeared also at
the bottom of Goodhue's cover (*above*) for the library handbook. John Wheelwright,
the Boston gay poet and son of architect Edmund Wheelwright, later wrote scathingly
in his poem "Boston Public Library" of how the seal's detractors "were hardly
persuaded not to do the little boys/(who are not little girls) and who support/*Sigillum
Urbis Bostoniensis* a very great injury:/'Knock the balls off. Tut, tut!' "

the late nineteenth-century intellectual, one condition of being ceaselessly suggested its opposite," in such cases intellectuals typically "seeing purity [were] titillated — or disturbed — by thoughts of sin." Interestingly, moreover, though only Cox's work dealing with adult female nudes and bestiality is discussed by Dijkstra, his conclusion that much of the nude child art of the period "straddl[ed] the line between sentimentalism and obscenity"[51] echoes exactly Susan Thompson's estimate of Cox's work in *"The Art That Is Life."* There she notes that Cox, a New York artist best known today for his murals at the Library of Congress, produced work that seems now "an amusing combination of sentimentality and eroticism."[52] The library boys exactly. Moreover, much the same could be said of Fred Day's photographs of nude youths.

As it turned out, this fracas of 1892–1894 was distinctly a dress rehearsal for the cause célèbre of 1896, when Charles McKim's gift of a nude *Bacchante* (63) involved the library in yet another battle, Harvard's President Charles Eliot leading the charge against what was called (this time by the *Boston Post)* the "Naked Drunken Woman" in the courtyard![53] Sullivan stood up for the *Bacchante* as he had for the boys, but this time, he wrote, "the Philistines be upon us," and they prevailed.[54] That Sullivan and others of more tolerant tastes (or, alternatively, to the opposition, of private vices) who fought for all these nudities in Copley Square were not unaware of the significance of such contretemps for progressive causes of all sorts in Boston is clear from Sullivan's observation that "the depressing little incident [of the *Bacchante*] seems to drop us back a century or two toward the dark ages."[55] (How good it is to report that a casting of *Bacchante* has been returned permanently to the library to mark the building's centennial restoration.)[56]

The Tavern was, in fact, very much the center of the pro-*Bacchante* party, for Bohemians naturally took their art seriously in every medium, whether music or theater or sculpture — or painting, which now brings the St. Botolph Club to the forefront of this discussion because its art gallery was its chief claim to fame in the 1880s and 1890s.

In this club, too, Sullivan stands out, often in league with O'Reilly (especially before the Tavern's founding), with whom, as he had conspired to introduce Walt Whitman to the Papyrus, so also he arranged to introduce Oscar Wilde to the Botolph. O'Reilly invited Sullivan's aid to this end in a priceless letter, so evocative of Bohemian club life in Boston, of 1882:

> Dear Sullivan,
>   Tonight at about ten, I shall take Oscar Wilde to the St. Botolph. Please mention it to a few fellows so that we may have a welcoming smile for Narcissus.
>   Faithfully,
>   Boyle O'Reilly[57]

63. Frederick Macmonnies's *Bacchante and Child* in the Boston Public Library court. Seeking to explain why he found the statue "inappropriate" there, Robert Grant, though he admitted it was "spirited, graceful and airy," also pronounced it "somewhat decadent."

Although there is no firsthand documentary evidence — direct reminiscences and such — about the early days of the St. Botolph that there is about the Tavern, there is certainly contemporary literary evidence that the Botolph's character was such that Narcissus was not very likely to have been disappointed: a novel of 1884, *The Pagans*, by Arlo Bates, another Beacon Hill friend of Cram's.

The Pagans focused, according to Joseph Chamberlain in an 1898 article in *The Chap-Book*, on the St. Botolph Club, under the guise of the "St. Filipe Club." It was "a name which is so thin a mask that one wonders why it was put on at all," wrote Chamberlain, who went on to answer his own question when he reported how prone the club membership was to what he called "epigrammatic talk — consciously and very intentionally epigrammatic — and some philosophy of life which quite out-Verlaines Verlaine." *The Chap-Book*'s avantgarde readers, Chamberlain knew, would be quite familiar with the attitudes of that notorious French homosexual poet of the Decadence and would not misunderstand such snatches of club talk as one character's pronouncement that "Emerson lacked the loftiness of vice. He knew only half of life. He never had any conception of the passionate longing for vice per se; the thrill, the glow, which comes to some men at the splendid caress of Sin in its most horrible shape." This is just about as explicit as one got in 1898, and Bates, a member of both the Tavern and the Botolph, was in a position to know what was what very well indeed.[58]

Equally significant evidence of the early character of the Botolph, however, is the history of its art gallery. As Doris Birmingham has observed, that gallery in the 1880s and 1890s "showed some of the most advanced art available in the United States and therefore played a significant role in the development of American art." (The club's 1892 Monet exhibit, for example, was announced as the first one-man show of Monet in America and very nearly was, there having been only one previously, in New York.) Yet the gallery's avant-garde policy has never really been explained. Many founding members of the club were prominent enough, admittedly, to get what they wanted; even more, perhaps, than the Taverners, younger Botolphians took cover under august names recruited to lend weight to the club's invitations to the great and famous, and such people's tastes might be expected to be dominant in certain circumstances. But such tastes seem remarkable in the first place, and that the St. Botolph should "become," as William Gerdts has put it, " 'the major center for showing avant-garde art in [Boston],' is more surprising." This radical attitude, Birmingham notes, extended even to the club's exhibition "of the photographs of Fred Holland Day's protégé and relation, Alvin Langdon Coburn." She concludes, "Another unique aspect of the club's early activities . . . [was] its support of women artists."⁵⁹

Surely such avant-garde tastes are less startling, however, once one accepts that the evidently controlling Botolphians, in the eighties and nineties especially, were to a large extent Bohemian aesthetes. Similarly, of course, one would expect an increasingly older post-Freudian and more conventional (certainly less and less Bohemian) leadership to produce a decline in the cultural force of club and gallery, a decline (paralleling the one Santayana wrote of at the Tavern) that Birmingham does indeed detect: "the spirit of adventure that characterized the St. Botolph's first two decades began to diminish after 1900," she writes, going so far as to give as an example of the club's "succumb[ing] to a safe conservatism" in the new century the fact that it did not (though he was at the height of his fame then) exhibit any work of Fred Day himself.⁶⁰ Day had evidently become too outré even for a club of which he had been a charter member in 1887: the Club of Odd Volumes. Elected at its first meeting as a director and club librarian, Day was also asked to design the club's seal, as well as the printed constitution, actually his first book design. But a parting of the ways was not long in coming. As it turned out, wrote Day, its members were more apt to use a rubber name stamp than a bookplate.⁶¹ Aesthetes versus Philistines was probably the way Day and Santayana and Cram would have described the battle for all these clubs that perhaps they saw themselves gradually losing.

Meanwhile, however, Boston's aesthetes seized the day. For example, the St. Botolph Club Architectural Exhibition of 1890, in which Cram and Wentworth's first year's work was exhibited, along with that of twenty-three other firms,[62] shows how Cram's credentials as an art critic helped his young firm, for the club's gallery was a prestigious one, and its showing of Cram's designs extensive.

The Tavern, too, played a role in Cram's and Goodhue's affairs. Cram was elected to a by then much more staid Botolph Club only in 1932, when he was nearing seventy. But Goodhue, much more clubbable and with a special interest in dressing up ("flaunting," Cram called it), was elected a Taverner in his twenties in 1899.[63] Thereafter, moreover, and doubtless quickly enough, if only because of Russell Sullivan's equal propensity for costumery, Goodhue seems to have been drawn to Sullivan, whose writing style, by the way, Goodhue once compared to Cram's.[64] The subject of "Russell in his Cairo dress," such was its renown in Boston Bohemia, even arose in Dwight's correspondence with Isabella Gardner, and this is, no doubt, to what Sullivan referred when he noted in 1895 in his journal that at that year's Carnival Ball in Cram's Copley Hall he had first appeared in what he called "the outfit procured for me in Cairo six years ago, — caftan, robe, tarboosh, etc. . . . The scene was very gay and brilliant."[65] It was also probably what Goodhue was referring to in one of his sketchbooks, where under an exotic portrait indeed Goodhue wrote the line "Russell Sullivan as an Emir."[66]

Alas, there are no longer any emirs in Boston's clubland — though there are still a few aesthetes.

THE AESTHETIC MOVEMENT IN BOSTON

No Pinckney Street bell pull a century and more later is marked "Cram" or "Guiney" or "Day." Yet just a few doors up from Guiney's old rooming house and diagonally across the street from where Cram's rooms and Day's studio were, there is still the name "Warren" to be seen — in bronze, no less, now beautifully oxidized green, its raised letters very aesthetic in feeling, an escutcheon that may well have puzzled more than a few people through the years, for the Warrens, a well-known Boston family, lived on Mount Vernon Street on the other side of Louisburg Square from Pinckney. But perhaps it says something about New England that back doors there are always more significant than front doors, and it is typical of Beacon Hill that though the Warrens did live in one of the grandest mansions of Mount Vernon Street, 67, they also contrived (through a new red-brick Richardsonian block of bachelor chambers) an elegant and very private back door on to Pinckney Street.[67]

It was not the only time this happened: Mount Vernon Street did not disdain Bohemia. There was also 24 Pinckney Street, where about 1884 William R.

Emerson (designer of many a Shingle Style masterwork) remodeled an old carriage house of a Mount Vernon Street mansion into a house that most would agree today is Pinckney Street's most brilliant architecture, the only house in Boston's Beacon Hill Bohemia of the aesthetic era worthy of comparison with the houses in London's Chelsea Bohemia by C. R. Ashbee.[68] It is sometimes called the House of Odd Windows because none of its openings are the same size, and this sobriquet is more apt than most realize, "odd" being, as we have seen, another well-known code word for so many denizens of Pinckney, not least of whom was Edward Perry Warren.

Ned, as he was invariably called, was only three years older than Cram, a part of a parallel circle of Boston and Harvard Bohemians of the 1880s, not unknown to Cram's own circle on Pinckney Street, and one that seems to have constituted with Cram's set and the Dwight-Sullivan set the three leading of several not yet fully documented Bohemian circles of this period. Centered on separately domineering figures, such as Cram, how closely linked these sets were is not clear. Certainly all three shared associations with both Isabella Stewart Gardner and George Santayana, and at least two "overlapping" members in the circles forming in the late 1880s and 1890s around Cram and Warren can be identified: Daniel Berkeley Updike and Bernard Berenson, both friends of Cram and Warren. There are connections hinted at, as well, which we can only partially glimpse these many years later; for example, Warren's sister, Cornelia, was active (as was Cram) in Christian Socialist circles and contributed heavily to Denison House in the South End, where Fred Day and Kahlil Gibran met.

In a very real sense Boston's Edward Carpenter, Warren insisted on his sexuality in an exhibitionistic (and un-Bostonian) way for that era; even going so far as eventually to write, God help us, a three-volume work entitled *A Defence of Uranian* (i.e., homosexual) *Love*. He also spent most of his life in exile from Boston, if Lewes House, "a sumptuous retreat [for] bachelor scholars" in Sussex, as Walter Muir Whitehill called it,[69] which he shared with a dear friend and a number of companions from Oxford, where he studied after Harvard, can be described as "exile." Certainly it was far from fruitless: Martin Green in *The Mount Vernon Street Warrens* argues that if "the crucial imaginative experience for [Evelyn] Waugh and . . . John Betjeman and others . . . was Oxford in the 1920s [out of which came *Brideshead Revisited*]," it was Ned Warren in important ways who "was shaping that experience for them," so pervasive was Warren's influence on that generation of English aesthetes.[70] The brotherhood has ever been transatlantic.

"Exile" is also in another sense too harsh a word; even when it is only the back door that opens on to Pinckney Street, it is well to recall that things of this sort were never quite what they seemed in Boston's Bohemia, there being abundant evidence that Warren's problems were a good deal more complex than his sexual orientation and his community's reaction to it. Green notes that Warren's "most striking feature was his failure or refusal to be boyish — and later, manly. . . . As a boy he had bitter experiences as a sissy," which one can well believe of a lad known to smuggle pieces of his mother's china up to his bedroom so as to spend hours arranging them.[71]

Warren was effeminate by the standards of masculine conduct of his era. More to the point, however, he was himself deeply ashamed of his effeminacy, which ill accorded with his intellectual *or* erotic ideals, which were very Greek. (He realized a fact others doubtless cruelly underlined, that neither Achilles *nor* Patrocles would have cared much for him.) In fact, Warren yearned to be more manly and to attract the sort of public-school lover we discussed earlier who would, as he put it, "shout to him at football."[72] Still, it is notable that he was courageously unashamed of his sexuality, which he stood up for repeatedly.

The fact that Warren "in some sense hated his family" is, moreover, not to say that was because they rejected him; in fact, as Green points out, it is "not clear what his parents and siblings felt about his homosexuality — or what he felt they felt"; the reason for Warren's hatred of his family was that "he blamed the luxurious furnishings and art work [of his family home, decorated by his mother] for the effeminate sensuality [he felt] it developed in him"; even as a boy he had struggled unsuccessfully "to install men in the place of women [in his family house], Greek athletes instead of medieval Madonnas."[73]

Similarly, Warren had distinctly a love-hate relationship with Boston. As he was a very rich man, his exile was a case of *self*-exile. But one not exactly to his or Boston's loss; for in 1886 Warren began the process of endowing with one of the great classical sculpture collections of the world his native city's Museum of Fine Arts, of which his brother, Samuel D. Warren, was to become president of the board of trustees, and one of Ned's closest friends from Sussex, Matthew Prichard, the assistant director.

That Prichard could hold such a high post in a major Boston institution, despite the fact that his friend was so widely unacceptable, is significant. This is particularly the case because Ned Warren, though he was friendly with Robert Ross (Oscar Wilde's best friend and literary executor), was never conspicuously identified with the Wilde circle, membership in which after Wilde's trial in 1895 became naturally a thing few bragged about, while Prichard was so deeply involved in that group (and before his Boston appointment) that a collection of poems published in Paris *after* the Wilde trial by Lord Alfred Douglas included one poem dedicated *to* Prichard.[74] In fact, William Sturgis Bigelow, a trustee who disliked Prichard's influence at the museum and knew of the poem, tried to enlist Henry Cabot Lodge's help in seeking Henry James's aid in getting the goods on Prichard, so to speak; an unattractive episode, but one that shows Prichard's proclivities were not unknown.[75]

None of this mattered, however. The reason Prichard passed and Warren did not will be clear if one recalls Peter Gay's Yale undergraduate of the 1830s: it was masculine, which is to say, gender-appropriate behavior, that mattered, not a hetero- or homosexual temperament. David Hilliard notes of England at the end of the nineteenth century that society was "prepared to accept romantic friendship between men simply as friendship without sexual significance."[76] Similarly, in America, in Gay's words, just as "women sharing quiet establishments gathered only praise for their devoted friendship," so also, "as long as they preserved the appearances, bachelors were above suspicion."[77] And Matt Prichard was not only very masculine (only "bold manliness," not surprisingly, was cultivated at Lewes House) but handsome as well; his sexual temperament was much less important than that his "bearing and behaviour, including his emotional attachments to others of his sex, did not affront current codes of conduct."[78] The result, much resented by Warren, was that Prichard became increasingly influential in Boston and a key figure in the aesthete network we have been uncovering here; a network in which Ralph Adams Cram played no small part.

MRS. JACK

Just as it is relentlessly overlooked that Isabella Stewart Gardner's acquiring of art and building of Fenway Court was not a case of nouveau-riche ostentation but of tremendously original and creative museum design, so also her colorful lifestyle has been so repeatedly misunderstood that one really does wonder if it has not been deliberate. That her "temperament" was " 'artistic,' " as Morris Carter put it ("she had," Carter said, "the faculty of making artists feel that she understood them and their work. . . . [that] she was a friend who comprehended their aspirations as well as their achievements"),[79] is too often overlooked by those who stress her sharp tongue and restless neurasthenia. As a contemporary newspaper report opined, Gardner's purpose was to "break down social barriers and evidence her belief in society as a vehicle for the cultivation of art, music, and intellectuality and to create a social renaissance."[80] And Carter, who knew her well, testified that in Boston's high society of that era " 'the Brimmer set, which represent[ed] the old Puritan aristocracy' and 'the Apthorp set [the friends of Cram also mentioned previously here by Samuel Eliot Morison], which represent[ed] the new Bohemianism,' did meet in [the Gardner home] on a common ground."[81] But there was never any doubt which side Gardner identified with; she was herself as much of a Bohemian as a woman of her place in Boston society could be (*64a*).

64a, b. Two faces of Boston's Bohemia. *Above*: a Back Bay supper party presided over by Cram's most celebrated mentor, Mrs. Jack (pouring, to the right). *Below*: a summer call at the country house outside Boston of Cram's Beacon Hill friend and neighbor (on the left) Daniel Berkeley Updike. To the right is Ogden Codman. The other man is unidentified.

In her biography, *Mrs. Jack*, Louise Hall Tharp, though in common with so many others she suppressed much, did once lift the veil, albeit discreetly. Describing a part of Gardner's dear friend A. Piatt Andrew's home, Red Roof, in Gloucester, Tharp recounted that

> Andrew had an organ installed in the passage between the living room and a recently added study. Here, Isabella sat on the couch . . . to listen to his music. She was probably unaware of a hidden space above the books — too low to stand up in but equipped with mattress and covers where . . . guests could listen in still greater comfort. She had seen the Brittany bed in the living room, but that there was a small hole over it [opening out from an alcove amounting to a sort of built-in bunk bed accessible from another room] perhaps no one had told her. The sound of organ music [from an adjoining passage] could be heard the better through the hole — and was it just a coincidence that a person in the hidden alcove above could look down through it. Gossip had it that often [at the Red Roof] all the guests were men, their pastimes peculiar. Yet all the ladies on Eastern Point were fascinated by Piatt.

They were equally arrested by Piatt's best friend and neighbor, Henry Davis Sleeper, builder of Beauport, next door to Red Roof. That by now all but world renowned Arts and Crafts melange of architecture and decoration, which so influenced the thinking of Henry Francis Dupont, creator of Winterthur, has another and quite overlooked significance. Even more than in the case of the secret spaces of Red Roof, Beauport is a riddle whose explanation need no longer be avoided. Well might Nancy Curtis and Richard Nylander write in their *Beauport* that the house's "maze-like shape has always suggested secrets," and that "its crooked passages, doors leading into nowhere, secret staircases, dramatic surprises, and shadowy recesses is Sleeper's most revealing statement about himself." In the context of mask and signal and reveal and conceal, which has emerged so strikingly in this book, Curtis and Nylander's words take on new meaning, doubtless unintended by them, but apt enough nonetheless. Beauport, if not quite gay Gothic, is certainly an outstanding example in the history of Boston area architecture of "queer space," to use a term lately fashionable, reflecting the work of critics like Herbert Muschamp who are interested in the intersections of art and sexuality.

Eastern Point in Gloucester was doubtless the setting for only one of many such gay enclaves. (One thinks particularly, since Margaret Henderson Floyd's recent *Architecture after Richardson*, of the cohort at Little Harbor, Portsmouth, New Hampshire, where resided A. W. Longfellow, Edmund Wheelwright, and R. Clipston Sturgis — Boston architects with more than one link to Bohemia of whom one would like to know more.) But Eastern Point's gay character is sufficiently well documented that Isabella Gardner's intimate involvement there is telling, so much so that even Tharp's biography observes that at Piatt's "all the guests were men, their pastimes peculiar."[82]

This is, perhaps, the most explicit reference in print that points to the nature of Gardner's involvement in Boston's Bohemia. It was deep and knowing, but not reckless for all that it was blatant. And we now have Cram's word for it (from an unpublished section of the typescript of his autobiography) that Louise Guiney, the "sympathetic friend of everyone in the circle of young men I now could call my own, acted in some sort as a liaison officer between [Gardner and her generation and Cram's]"[83] — between Pinckney Street (and perhaps other aesthete Bohemian circles) and Gardner and her circle. If Guiney was mother to much of aesthete Boston (which is to say gay Boston), Isabella Stewart Gardner was distinctly godmother. It is a role we must not deny Mrs. Jack any longer.

It needs to be understood at once that Gardner was not in any sense an innocent. Her personal library at Fenway Court, for example, included books not only by Baron Corvo but also by Verlaine, Joris-Karl Huysmans, and Swinburne, of the last of whom Peter Gay reminds us that in that period Swinburne's "explicit images blurred the distinction between erotic literature and pornographic merchandise."[84] And Gardner's friends were in this respect scarcely less telling than her books. Even if one discounts the pervasive speculation that John Singer Sargent was homosexual, the gay mist that surrounded the chatelaine of Fenway Court is unmistakable.

Until now virtually unknown, the correspondence between Gardner and Theodore Dwight, which we have already quoted from, sheds much light in this area. For example, in one letter Dwight sighs: "I never cease thinking and talking of Angelo and Tito [the two gondolier boys at the palazzo in Venice where the Gardners stayed]"; in another he was even more daring, confiding to her that at lunch one day with the La Farges "the aesthetic John appeared. (Under breath — entre nous — I like Bancel very much — very much — the other — well, there is an infinite question involved). (Again — sotto voce — I like Mabel in the same way.)"[85] Nor were these letters in any sense unwelcome. Though we have necessarily only his side of the correspondence, there is no doubt (despite the fact that his name never arises in either Carter's or Tharp's book on Gardner) that she and Dwight were intimate friends. His signature appears in the Gardner guest book more than fifty times, and his letters (which open: "Dearest of friends") are very affectionate. Furthermore, it turns out that Gardner kept Dwight's photograph — and *only* his — on her writing desk in the Blue Room at Fenway Court.[86]

Nor was Dwight the only correspondent of Gardner's whose association indicates how au courant she was with things gay, for Dwight's friend Russell

Sullivan was her constant interlocutor, and, indeed, his letters make frequent reference to Dwight and more than once imply that Sullivan and Gardner somewhat competed for the good librarian's favors. Referring, doubtless, to the Neapolitan nudes Dwight had smuggled past customs (as he had also, with John La Farge's encouragement, a watercolor Gardner sought), Sullivan in a letter of 1892 to her reported: "The big boss librarian is having his photographs [of young men] framed, one by one. I go up[stairs at 10 Charles] for tea, and find him sighing before them, with clasped hands, wrapped in his brocades."[87]

Earlier the same year, when the Gardners were abroad and Dwight en route to join them, Sullivan, still in Boston and quite lonesome, held little back in another letter:

> I mourn for T.F.D. [Dwight] who has departed this house and sails for your shores in two days. . . . Sturgis Bigelow, M.D., has come in with hypnotic influence and carries me off to dine with him to-night, seductively, with the resident literati and tutti frutti. . . . I have ordered a new gown for the Nahant wedding when I mean to emerge from my cocoon for the only time this season. No visits, nothing — but just the ball and chain. You may laugh, but how could it well be otherwise, with those we care about in Europe. . . . Don't keep our librarian away too long.[88]

That Gardner responded to these missives in kind seems clear in Sullivan's riposte of March 1889: "you never so much as mentioned your adventure with the seven butlers! No matter. I heard it all from your Heart's Own, for our breach has been repaired, and we have kissed and made up. . . . But I am shocked at the 5 a.m. breakfast after the Hunt ball. Can such things be?"[89] That such things were, indeed, part and parcel of the set Gardner presided over seems no longer in doubt, or that it was not all fun and games. Wrote Sullivan to Gardner of Sargent's dear friend, whom we have already met:

> I am sorry to hear that [Dennis] Bunker means to give us up. Don't let him. And put a little more of the arlecchino [Harlequin] into him, if you can. It's the only role to play — except that of Colombina [the flirt] — and those who play it best (whether it hurts or not) get on best. . . . Give him a grip from me, and tell him to stay with us. But don't read him my moral philosophy, or he will swear strange oaths.[90]

Matt Prichard, not surprisingly, was one of the leading men of the Gardner set, and one of the joys of the Gardner Museum today is an etching of him by Henri Matisse, the gift of the artist to Prichard and his gift, in turn, to Gardner. It depicts very well the handsome, magnetic Prichard, who was Gardner's fervent second in the infamous "battle of the casts" that rid the Museum of Fine Arts of all but original works of art.[91] Indeed, the museum's history, like that of the Boston Public Library, was also much affected by the emerging gay subculture of the period in Boston, particularly through Prichard, he having vitally influenced the design of the museum's present building and through it American museum design generally. Insisting that "Joy, not knowledge," was "the aim of contemplating a [work of art]" and that a museum's task first and foremost was the establishment of taste, "Prichard and his friends," writes Martin Green, "gave elegant and lively voice to typical aesthetic ideas," ensuring, for example, that the new museum's architecture did not overpower its collections. Prichard was "one of the heroes of Whitehill's centenary history of the M.F.A., written so long after [Prichard's] death."

Prichard's battles in the 1900s at Boston's museum, over both "educational" casts and too much "architecture," remind me of the *Bacchante* controversy in the late 1890s at the Boston Public Library. Both times and places, not so many years apart, disclose very well the nature of the influence the developing gay subculture was exerting over both institutions.

There was, of course, in the *Bacchante* affair, a middle ground. Charles Eliot Norton, for example, who opposed the statue's installation, was hardly bothered by either nudity or wine. But he could not countenance such a statue as the centerpiece of what he saw as a solemn and serious repository of scholarly knowledge. How solemn educators can be the battle of the "educational" casts at the museum makes plain. And it seems to me that Prichard's battle cry — "Joy, not knowledge" — is equally the never quite understood argument for *Bacchante*.

The most persuasive defense of the propriety of Macmonnies's statue at the library, though so far as I know quite unnoticed by subsequent scholarship, was put forth by one of Boston's little magazines (so little it eventually published some of Cram's least known, perhaps best forgotten, and certainly quite minor effusions, including his lyrics for Fred Bullard's "secular cantata," *The Boat of Love*) — *Poet Lore*. Instead of railing against the philistines, making no distinction between Baptist preachers and scholarly solemnities of Charles Eliot Norton's sort, *Poet Lore* mounted a positive campaign of reasons why *Bacchante* was just what the library needed. Arguing for a distinction between "the books that are as oil," that is to say, "all learning of material facts and external utilities," and "the books that are as wine," defined by *Poet Lore* as "all the subtler breathings [of] religious ecstasies and philosophic exaltations of the . . . God-possessed consciousness [needed by] the soul of man," the magazine's editors skillfully invoked both Socrates and Shakespeare in aid of this view and concluded by triumphantly annexing to their cause no less than Emerson, against whom in Boston there is hardly yet any appeal:

> Let the *Bacchante* be looked upon with the vision of the seer of Concord. . . . Emerson's [poem] "Bacchus" enable[s] one to feel the peculiar appropriateness of the *Bacchante* [as] presiding genius of a building which treasures and imparts to all the express essence of man's experience and aspiration. So Emerson craves —

> ... That I intoxicated,
> And by the draught assimilated,
> May float at pleasure through
>   all natures.

It was the argument for joy, so to speak, as the highest knowledge Emerson spoke of; though it failed at the library, it triumphed thanks to Prichard at the museum. (And, a century later, thanks to Arthur Curley, it has triumphed, too, at the library, to which *Bacchante* has returned to preside.)[92]

Why is one reminded of another lambent light of Isabella Gardner's set, Morris Carter, whose aside to Gardner about Prichard in an undated (ca. 1890) letter is worth quoting:

> I had a little letter from Prichard today. He suggested that perhaps the day would sometime come when I would want to break out into the fresh air and pluck an apple from the forbidden tree. Doesn't he realize how many months ago, or years ago, that day came?[93]

Nor was it unlikely that it happened at Fenway Court, where Gardner lived on the fourth floor and Prichard, like Carter later, was one of the favored few invited to live in Mrs. Jack's ground-floor bachelor's guest suite.

"Our Fairy Queen"

To experience the feeling of Boston's fin-de-siècle Bohemia one must climb Pinckney Street, though it has now, so to speak, too many window boxes; ideally, too, one would visit the Tavern Club in Boston and a few landmarks of the nineties at Harvard, and Marliave's as well, though it is much changed. Above all, however, one should go to Fenway Court, Isabella Stewart Gardner's unique museum in Boston's Fenway.

The word "aesthetic" as we have used it here is nowhere better defined. One could argue easily that Fenway Court's whole design (its secret, really) is that it is in essence *Bohemian*: richly provocative in its striking and even mysterious juxtapositions of Raphaels and old brocades and Mercer tiles and ancient statuary and lovers' photographs, and, too, in its sincere love of old beauty and new knowledge, its cultivation of an unfailing melancholy, and its uncanny feeling for the modern mind's almost cinematic need for shifting focus and cross-cutting (as it were), as well as its instinctive sense of double vision. But then again, Mrs. Jack was no one's fool and had probably the lowest boring point in history.

Amid what inevitably will be larger thoughts such as these, the visitor will find it worthwhile to attend to some smaller trains of thought at the Gardner Museum, as it is now called. Soon, for example, we will visit the chapel at the end of the long gallery, which Cram knew so well. Just now it is the ground-floor guest suite that is of interest. He may also have known that well.

Imagine the approach to this suite by night through the darkened cloisters, then lit only by candlelight, that surround the intimate courtyard of flowering plants and ancient statuary, itself lit perhaps by moonlight slanting in through the great skylight four stories above. Looking into and up the court as one passes along, perhaps one might glimpse Gardner's great treasure rooms upstairs (again, lit only by candles); perhaps the sounds of music or muted talk might be heard if she happened to be entertaining that evening. Or, if she were not, one can imagine the silence of the palace as overwhelming, broken only by the sound of water sputtering in the courtyard fountain or, perhaps, by a returning late-night guest arriving at the private entrance on Palace Road. Making his way to the guest suite (today's Macknight Room), the guest would easily have found the suite's richly modeled black oak door with its small eye-level hinged panel, behind the iron grille of which its occupant could identify his caller (see *61*).

Occupancy of this suite (which then had a small kitchen and bath) was one of the prizes most coveted by Gardner's set, and aside from Gardner's nephew Amory Gardner, only Sargent, Prichard, Carter, Piatt Andrew, and the Japanese artist and museum curator Okakura Kakuzo (a friend of Gardner's and Cram's) are known to have been accorded this privilege, which was not, one suspects, unknown to several other people in Dwight's and Cram's circles. Something of the circumstances of residency there is disclosed, perhaps inadvertently, by Carter's response to Mrs. Jack's invitation to take up residence there: "If I make my dwelling place 'Fenway Court,'" wrote Carter, ". . . should you turn me out if I asked an entirely respectable gentleman to spend an evening with me?"[94]

I think not. Indeed, Mrs. Jack went so far with Carter in the end as to give him a piece of land she owned in Brookline and even to build on it the house (called in consequence by more than one wag "The House That Mrs. Jack Built"), where Carter lived for some years with his dear friend Stanley Lothrop, a Harvard architecture student who designed this structure that Carter in his memoirs frankly called "the house of our dreams."[95] Always there were guests and boarders, usually young men attached to the art museum — Ned Warren's menage in England can scarcely have been more interesting — and we have Carter's word for it that, forswearing her own table at her country house nearby in favor of the young men's company, "Mrs. Gardner . . . frequently came for dinner."[96] Well might Clayton Johns write to the ruler of Fenway Court: "Verily, you wield a wand, and you must have had many fairy godmothers. Thanks to them we have our Fairy Queen. Long may she live and reign."[97]

Wide as well as long was that reign and felt in many quarters. For example, one of the most ardently loved of Henry James's young men in his last and freer years, Gaillard Lapsley (whom we first discovered in Santayana's and La Rose's circle at Harvard), James met in London in 1897 through Gardner.[98] Nor did the Fairy Queen disdain the appropriate regal airs. The reason we know that Ralph Adams Cram was another of Gardner's young men is that she took an interest in Cram's picturesque Order of the White Rose (the aesthete Jacobite flummery of which will bring us back to Fenway Court in Chapter 8) and that, in Carter's words, "on Christmas Eve, when mass was celebrated in Mrs. Gardner's private chapel at Fenway Court, it sometimes seemed as if her costume had been influenced by her favorite portrait of Mary Stuart."[99]

If, as seems now clear, Isabella Stewart Gardner served as godmother to Boston's aesthetes, it must be said that the reasons for her involvement had not only to do with her artistic temperament. Nor was it either, as Carter put it, that she "remained tolerant of any moral or perhaps immoral code," even though it involved "ostentatiously flout[ing] Puritan tradition."[100] She had, in fact, reasons both deeply personal and tragic for her attitude, and they will lead us, via Harvard Yard (again) and Groton School, directly back to Pinckney Street and to Ralph Adams Cram.

"THOSE BRILLIANT BOYS"

Although much then as now has always been made of "the Isabella Club" (Paul Bourget's wife's term), or, in *Town Topics*' phrase, "Mrs. Jack Gardner's 'Little Brothers of the Rich,'" her biographer's characterization of this group as "Mrs. Gardner's bachelors destined never to marry" is (for all its witness to a deeper truth) misleading.[101] For even the most devoted of Gardner's "boys" did, in fact, marry, including Cram's friend of the 1880s, William Ordway Partridge, though in 1889 he had sent Gardner a poem entitled "The Beauty of Thine Eyes," only slightly less devoted than the sonnet sent her three years later by Santayana (an exception, assuredly: he did not marry), who told Mrs. Jack: "You have always been the bright spot in my Boston."[102] And except also for Clayton Johns (how typical his profile was of all of them: Harvard 1891, Tavern Club, Church of the Advent, Pinckney Street resident),[103] they mostly married well. Edwardians kept up appearances. Charles Loeffler married; so did Joseph Lindon Smith, Timothée Adamowski, and Dennis Bunker; even Russell Sullivan finally took a wife, as did Theodore Dwight, who in his Italian exile became a father, too.

For some it was a mistake. Dennis Bunker, whose sexual struggles Sullivan seems to be alluding to in the letter he wrote to Gardner quoted earlier, died within months of his marriage, an event that, it was said, produced a sexual panic from which only suicide seemed to offer him release.[104] And Bunker was by no means alone in finding it hard to keep a level course in such heady circles. Indeed, Bunker may very well have been taken up by Gardner somewhat in the wake of another tragedy that suggests Gardner's sensitivity to gay young men was not just a case of finding many uses for a cohort of brilliant and charming but sexually nonthreatening escorts, but was rooted in her experience with the three orphaned nephews of her husband, whom the Gardners raised. "Those brilliant boys," Henry James called them,[105] Joseph Peabody Gardner, William Amory Gardner, and Augustus Peabody Gardner: translated from Groton to Harvard, they could have been a chapter all to themselves in *Harvard Episodes*.

In *Artful Partners*, Colin Simpson, drawing upon an unpublished Berenson biography by Mary Berenson, his wife, remarks on the fact that of Charles Eliot Norton's four protégés in the mid-1880s Charles Loeser and Logan Pearsall Smith were already well-known homosexuals; George Santayana's homosexual inclinations were increasingly clear; and only about Bernard Berenson was there some mystery. Simpson notes, too, that all had the entrée to Isabella Stewart Gardner's home and that when

> proteges [such] as Bernard [Berenson] and such wits as Logan [Pearsall Smith were included] she [Gardner] was delighted. Their inclusion particularly delighted the eldest [of Mrs. Gardner's nephews and wards,] Joe. . . . Joe had been causing the Gardners some concern. He had bought himself a remote homestead at Hamilton to the north of Boston. . . . [Logan Pearsall Smith] said that Joe Gardner had bought the Hamilton homestead as a refuge from the censorious eyes of Boston, and his aunt's constant urgings to find a "suitable girl and settle down."
>
> Logan and his sister Mary had been frequent visitors, but it was Mary who had been the chaperone, for the object of Joe's attentions was Logan himself and it was Logan who had broken Joe Gardner's heart.
>
> Jack Gardner half suspected the truth and quickly included Joe on his annual European tour. The traditional solution for a broken heart did not work. On 16 October 1886 Joe Gardner committed suicide.[106]

Isabella Stewart Gardner's experience of homosexuality was neither social nor trivial.

Berenson, though of Norton's four protégés the only sexual enigma, whose relationship with Gardner would become critically important in the forming of her collection, was in this set, as in the Pinckney Street set (with Updike) and in Ned Warren's circle, a suspiciously perennial link. Certainly, there seems little doubt that Berenson was the link between Santayana and Cram, exact contemporaries (both born on 16 December 1863), who mention each other in their published works, but whose relationship is otherwise a mystery. Similarly, Berenson was a link between Mrs. Jack and Ned Warren (who most of the time did not get along); both of them for a time contributed to Berenson's support financially. Between Gardner and Warren, however, the link of chief interest to us here was William Amory Gardner, "W.A.G.," as he was affectionately called by one and all.

Of Amory Gardner Frank Ashburn has written words strikingly similar to those of Green about Ned Warren, for W.A.G., like his brother Joe, had an even more unusual environment to grow up in than Ned, the world of Mrs. Jack and her art: "It was said of [W.A.G.]," wrote Ashburn, "that he never had a boyhood with or like other boys."[107] Yet more code words, and they are not misleading. Amory, a tremendous classical scholar at Harvard and a man of striking character, left little doubt about his sexuality (or his closeness to his Harvard classmate Ned Warren) in his letters to Isabella Gardner from England, where he stayed with Warren in 1885. In one, full of admiration for Cardinal Newman, whom he saw preside at High Mass at almost ninety "in gorgeous scarlet," W.A.G. wrote:

> I have been spending a very jolly week here & expect to go over to Paris after about a week more. I have capital lodgings on "the High" quite near New College where Ned Warren is. We have had delightful walks & rides on horseback, besides numerous breakfasts, lunches & snugs (or high teas) which he or his friends have given for me. . . . It is just possible that Ned may go with me to Greece. . . . We should probably stay nearly three months.[108]

That was, of course, the trip to Greece that launched Warren's collecting and from which proceeded the legendary classical sculpture of Boston's museum. But Amory Gardner's contribution would lie elsewhere.

BACHELOR DONS

What college or school has not known well and much depended upon someone like this renowned figure, a type whose characteristics certainly included sexual ambiguity? In the annals of Boston and Harvard the most picturesque was probably "Copey" — Charles Townsend Copeland, Harvard's turn-of-the-century Boylston Professor of Rhetoric and Oratory.[109] The most famous, of course, of that era was Santayana himself. As might be expected, however, those free spirits under the influence of Isabella Stewart Gardner were especially interesting.

Consider, for example, another of her nephews, Archibald Cary Coolidge. Adams House, perhaps the most "Bohemian" of Harvard's present-day residential colleges, was the successor of Apthorp College, an attempt by Coolidge in the 1890s, while a professor at Harvard, to establish an Oxbridge-type residential complex in and around Randolph Hall, which he built in 1897 on Mount Auburn Street, a block from the Harvard Yard along Harvard's Gold Coast (a region of luxurious private dormitories and the setting, by the way, of more than one incident in *Harvard Episodes*). Coolidge himself resided there for over two decades, living with and mentoring carefully vetted undergraduates in his elegant lodgings in Randolph Hall, to which he attached over time not only a courtyard garden and squash courts but also an indoor swimming pool — an attraction not unrelated to Turkish baths and one that virtually constitutes in this context the collegiate homoerotic equivalent of that religious homoerotic architectural setting already considered here, the divided choir of an Anglo-American school chapel. (Coolidge also commissioned the famous artist Edward Penfield to adorn one of Randolph Hall's rooms with arresting murals celebrating Harvard athletes [65d]).[110]

I offer the comparison of choirs and pools because this is not the only instance of such a facility created by fin-de-siècle Bohemians in the Boston sphere of influence. Nor was Coolidge the only one of Isabella Gardner's nephews to carry to fruition such a fantasy to his own and his students' benefit. For Amory Gardner did almost exactly the same thing at Groton School, of which he was a cofounder and where he taught the Greek ideal in more ways than one all his life.[111]

More flamboyant than Coolidge (who had wrestled at Harvard as a freshman and then as later always eschewed aesthetes in favor of athletes), Gardner, though he too loved sports — he was a keen sailor and rode well — was distinctly an aesthete and in a place that stood in more need of that attitude. Groton's other founders, Endicott Peabody, the first rector, and Sherwood Billings, were both very unaesthetic Low Churchmen. Billings, for example, "looked askance at a copy of Michelangelo's *Pietà* on a colleague's classroom wall and strenuously opposed a reredos in the chapel."[112] Thus Amory Gardner's fantasy at Groton was more exotic than Coolidge's at Harvard. No "halls" for W.A.G. — he called his creation, attached to a large home he built for himself on the school grounds, the Pleasure Dome, presumably after Kubla Khan's, and the indoor swimming pool in this case kept company not only with squash courts but with a small theater and an attached maze.[113]

Lest anyone conclude the architectural setting sounds much more than the doubtless circumspect life lived in it or that this life was kept discreetly behind closed doors, consider the boy delegated to bring a distinguished minister visiting Groton to call upon Gardner after chapel and breakfast. Finding no one about on the first floor of Gardner's house, the boy called out and was summoned upstairs by W.A.G., who could be heard, as boy and minister ascended the staircase, saying excitedly to someone: "It makes not the slightest difference that you won the first rubber, my dear boy. . . . That is *la courtoisie de la maison*." The visitors having arrived at what turned out to be Gardner's

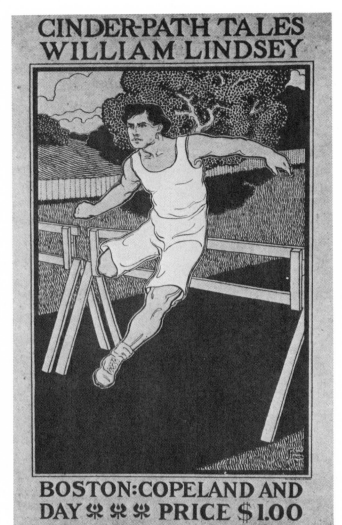

CINDER-PATH TALES
WILLIAM LINDSEY

BOSTON: COPELAND AND
DAY ✿ ✿ ✿ PRICE $1.00

65a, b, c, d. Boston's Bohemia celebrated both the "virile" and the "effete" homosexual modes; the former is evident in the work for Copeland and Day (*above, left*) of John Sloan, later a major twentieth-century modernist painter; the latter in F. S. Sturgis's sketch (*above, right*) of two members of one of Boston's elite men's clubs. Edward Penfield, famous for the stylish, asexual females of his brilliant 1890s *Harper's* covers, fused both modes in the aloof but sensuous male athletes of his homoerotic murals in Randolph Hall's Coolidge Room (*below, right*), Harvard's most evocative fin-de-siècle interior, part of Adams House, where the Westmorly tank, the indoor pool (*below, left*), was itself an elegant enough setting in the 1900s for Harvard men of all modes.

bedroom, it was at once clear that not only was W.A.G. stark naked before the fireplace (except for a pair of voluptuous bedroom slippers) but also so was the young man reclining on the sofa, to whom the remark had evidently been addressed. It is true that Gardner was eating his morning porridge and was flanked by a fully dressed butler (in morning coat, no less), holding more porridge as might be needed. But what dignity all could summon as the scene unfolded must have been utterly dissipated by W.A.G., who turned courteously to his new visitors and made the appropriate introductions, at the same time, according to Endicott Peabody's biographer, Frank Ashburn, "dropping an elaborate curtsey" *and* "without spilling the porridge."[114] Neither at Groton nor even at Harvard could any boy have such an experience today.

Amory Gardner's contributions at Groton were of a higher order than this. W.A.G. was the donor of the school's magnificent chapel of 1899, given in memory of Joseph Peabody Gardner — which surely explains why it is the only building at Groton School not by Peabody and Stearns. Indeed, I believe the chapel of Groton School to have been given by one gay man in memory of another, and designed by a third: Henry Vaughan. (Its stained glass, moreover, was likely the work of a fourth; certainly Charles Eamer Kempe was a confirmed bachelor all his life.) It was of a different kind than the book by Cram I will so characterize in Chapter 9, but Groton Chapel is gay Gothic nonetheless.

Amory Gardner had also given Groton's first and much smaller chapel of 1887, also the design of Vaughan, whose biographer speculates that "as donor Gardner no doubt exercised some say in the choice of the designer,"[115] and this would seem to indicate that Gardner knew the reclusive Vaughan over a span of many years. Does it surprise that one of the few things known about the private life of each man is that both Amory Gardner and Henry Vaughan were ardent Beacon Hill Anglo-Catholics, each devoted to the Cowley Fathers, Amory a parishioner of the Advent, Henry of St. John's, Bowdoin Street? One imagines many a Sunday lunch planning Groton Chapel.[116]

What a peregrination we have made through pre-Freudian Boston, beginning with Boston's club life and the new Boston Public Library; focusing on an aesthete circle centering on the benefactor of the Museum of Fine Arts, Ned Warren, a circle parallel to and interconnecting with Cram's Pinckney Street circle; from Warren's work we have followed a thread from him and Prichard at the Museum of Fine Arts and the Gardner Museum through several intersections presided over by Isabella Stewart Gardner in Boston and George Santayana at Harvard, and, via Berenson and the Cowley Fathers, have come finally to Amory Gardner at Groton School and at the Church of the Advent, where — behold, there is Henry Vaughan — and, at both places, like Vaughan, there is, too, Ralph Adams Cram. The reader will perhaps now better understand why the Advent published Cram's first writings on church art and gave him his first church commission, the credence of the high altar reredos donated by Isabella Stewart Gardner. And why it was Cram who designed the Groton coat of arms. And Father Hall, who in 1893 suggested its motto: *Cui servire est regnare* — Whose Service Is Perfect Freedom.

Trojan Horses

The fin-de-siècle Boston aesthete network we have been uncovering here was reflected not only in certain contemporary patterns of patronage but sometimes in the artistic work itself. The most spectacular example, cited forthrightly to his great credit many years ago by Walter Muir Whitehill in his *Museum of Fine Arts, Boston: A Centennial History* (although the museum does not itself widely advertise the fact), was Ned Warren's classical collection: "it was hate of Boston," asserted Warren, Whitehill reported, "that made me work for Boston. The [classical] collection was my plea against that in Boston which contradicted my [pagan] love."[117]

Nor must it be thought that contemporary society in Boston was oblivious to these things. We have seen how the Boston newspapers had a field day with the proposed nudities of the Boston Public Library. Similarly, they were provoked, to a certain extant, by Warren's classical art. As reported by Whitehill (the historian of both library and museum, who developed a deft technique in recounting these things with the straightest possible face and no little humor), "a lively controversy broke out in the Boston papers over the proposal to hold a YMCA reception at the Museum of Fine Arts, which [in 1901] was, in the view of some, obviously no place for a mixed social gathering because of the presence of nude male statues."[118] Indeed, even the museum's director was at one point so shocked by one of Warren's proposed additions to the collection, an archaic grave stele of about 500 B.C. of a beautifully muscled and well-endowed Greek athlete, that he rejected the figure. Though it was accepted later, it was not for half a century publicly exhibited.

Warren's effeminacy was also, as we have seen, a factor in this situation. It certainly did not go unnoticed in a city where not so much sexual orientation as gender-appropriate behavior was key, behavior by no means invariable, even with Cram. Though in appearance masculine enough apparently (even Teutonic), Cram was by universal report not only tart of tongue when displeased but overly enthusiastic when deeply engaged, "nervous" in his manner — rather like Santayana's poet friend describing the sunset — and likely to get carried away. In short, Cram was too passionate for Cold Roast Boston.

No wonder (though he did not complain, and in that showed his Yankee flint) that Cram revealed a very deep-seated love-hate relationship with Boston and New England, perhaps enhanced by family differences (did they really welcome his religious rebellion for all they accepted it?). Thus, when one considers in the light of Cram's sexuality a crack like Van Wyck Brooks's about Boston's youth degenerating from dreams of conquest in the Far West to Anglo-Catholic monkish fantasies, and puts remarks of that sort in the context of Hilliard's study of Anglo-Catholicism — when one does these things, the meaning of Cram's life and work takes on additional dimensions. There is distinctly a sense in which the life and work of Ned Warren (who shaped our whole sense of connoisseurship and has been called by those in the field one of the most important collectors of classical antiquities in American history) and the life and work of Ralph Adams Cram, who was to become America's greatest Gothic architect, were not dissimilar: Warren endowed Boston (and, indeed, the nation, such was his collection's importance) with Greek classical sculptures of beautiful pagan forms; Cram endowed Boston and its environs and, ultimately (so extensive was his practice), the nation itself with English Gothic churches of beautiful Catholic forms.

Though the aesthetic arena in which Cram acted out his relationship with Boston and New England was more religious than Warren's, more "Christian" than "pagan," as it were, one must recall Gay's and Hilliard's conclusions: aesthete Anglo-Catholicism, no less than classical Greece, typically attracted the sexually ambivalent during this period,[119] in no small measure because the religious minority position was a far better bastion from which to fight back than the sexual minority position — "fight back" being understood to mean contribute positively (after the manner of Father Hall's counsel) to one's culture. Thus Cram and Warren can be seen as doing something strikingly analogous both in motivation as well in effect. A remark of Robert Martin's, addressing an issue of the end of the *twentieth* century, seems uncannily apt: "To 'turn revolt into style' [in the words of the modern gay poet Thom Gunn] is, of course, to make art out of life; . . . an idea derived in large part from the aesthetic theory of Wilde."[120] Then as now!

It must be stressed that both Warren and Cram were entirely sincere in their aesthetic and philosophical convictions. Both also were unusually gifted and insightful in their appreciation of, respectively, classical and Gothic art — else, then or now, who would notice them? Nonetheless, each knew they forced on Boston what the powers that be mostly had not wanted and accepted only reluctantly; classical male sculpture in the art museum and Gothic Catholic churches on every other town green around Boston meant a very different Boston, a very different New England (a kind of artistic expression, if you will,

66. Goodhue's perspective of his and Cram's design of 1899 for the First Church of Cambridge, deliberately sabotaged, according to Cram's daughter, by Harvard's "anti-aesthete" president, Charles Eliot.

of the diversity derived from the effects of immigration). Boston had seen Greek nudes before, of course — in the Athenaeum Gallery, for example — and boasted already some good Episcopalian Gothic by Richard Upjohn, but Warren and Cram, in their respective fields (like Isabella Stewart Gardner in hers), challenged on a scale until then undreamt of. Cram's churches no less than Warren's sculpture were Trojan horses in Puritan New England.

How much so is clear in perhaps the most troublesome of Cram and Goodhue's church projects of the 1890s, their design for the prestigious First Church of Cambridge in Harvard Square, just opposite the main entrance to Harvard Yard (66). According to a note of many years later, written after Cram's death by his daughter Mary, the reason the firm's winning competition designs were never executed was that when Harvard President Charles Eliot "learned who it was whose unsigned plans had been unanimously chosen he nearly had a fit. He said RAC had 'peculiar ideas' and was 'very bad form.' . . . It was at the time a great blow. . . . They paid him for the plans, of course."[121]

A little on the bitter side, that; but ruling-class Boston was a tighter world then and Harvard was a far more important part. Even aside from the *Bacchante* protest, led by Eliot, there were many such stories. Cram's later partner, Alexander Hoyle, wrote years later about Cram's Second Church of Boston: "I remember how the old-fashioned people, especially old President Eliot of Harvard, were scandalized at the goings-on, especially at the altar candles used at the dedication service."[122] But that was *after* West Point, in the twentieth century, when the damage was more easily sustained.

Eliot's active distaste for what Cram stood for is also easily verified independently. For example, in 1896 Eliot wrote to Thomas Wentworth Higginson that "one of the most discouraging phenomena of the last twenty years has been the reaction *in the New England community* [emphasis added] toward ritualism [i.e., Anglo-Catholicism] and aestheticism."[123] Eliot utterly detested both. And that he was using aestheticism as a euphemism in the usual way is suggested by the fact that Eliot was also highly suspicious of George Santayana, whom he called "abnormal," another code word for homosexual.[124] A few Brahmins disagreed. Samuel Eliot Morison confessed once that he "revered Mr. Cram."[125] But Morison, unusually for a Boston Brahmin, was Anglo-Catholic and would not have shared Eliot's loathing for Cram.

Van Wyck Brooks did; he wrote:

> Mrs. Gardner was vulgar enough. In the game of self-glorification, in the game of sensation, she outglittered even the magnates of Nob Hill; and similarly Cram's Gothic churches gave the village meeting-house a dignity that even they had lost. There was something meretricious in all these manifestations, which were often sentimental and occasionally silly. Almost as much as Harry Lehr's Newport, they discredited religion, politics, art.[126]

Brooks, like Charles Eliot and Thomas Wentworth Higginson, bitterly lamented the passing of Puritan New England.

Thinking of Higginson, one senses that Cram must have appeared to many like him to be what Camille Paglia calls Emily Dickinson — "a Romantic terrorist."[127] Unlike Dickinson, however, Cram was not a land mine laid (all unsuspecting to such as Higginson) to explode in New England faces a generation or more later; Cram was exploding then, as it were, on every other town square. Cram and Goodhue's splendid St. Stephen's Church in Cohasset (67), outside Boston, designed in 1899, boldly modern in its square-headed fenestration and strikingly skewed in its profile, ravishingly picturesque for all its severity, quite

67. Exterior view by Paul Weber of Cram and Goodhue's St. Stephen's Church, Cohasset, outside Boston, designed in 1899. A modern Gothic masterwork.

overwhelms the old meeting house visible from its precincts across the town green. (Nor could Brooks be expected to appreciate St. Stephen's any more than Fenway Court. As a matter of fact, the way Goodhue stylishly elongated the carved oaken towers of St. Stephen's high altar reredos so that they reach up daringly, like exotic tendrils of detail, to engage the stained-glass window above the altar, thus integrating superbly reredos and glass in service to Cram's principle of liturgical art, distinctly foreshadows Goodhue's later masterpiece of reredos and glass, the high altar reredos at St. Thomas, Fifth Avenue, New York.) And if Paglia sees Dickinson's "metaphors [as] surprise renovations, polychrome statues and stained-glass windows added to a white New England church,"[128] then Cram was, so to speak, Dickinson's architect!

That Cram's churches were Trojan horses, agents for change on town commons everywhere, only enhances their spiritual power. Of course, "Trojan horses" is a very inexact term. And the seeming contradiction in all this points to a key underlying factor in Cram's life and work that is widely misunderstood:

Ralph Adams Cram was a traditionalist. His was a traditionalism, however, that, like Anglo-Catholicism then, was less conservative than what we would call today liberal.

This is easiest to discern in Cram's politics, for he was not a Republican. All his life he was an active, registered Democrat (in later years a supporter of Franklin Roosevelt), a very radical thing indeed to be in the Boston of that era. Similarly, in religious terms, he was a traditionalist of the sort of one of his great heroes, Cardinal Newman, who in the Catholic context was distinctly liberal in the best sense of that fine old word — in the sense that I have cited Pusey here as a feminist and will cite Keble as a proto-Freudian. And Newman's liberalism (which, after his conversion to Rome, importantly fueled forces there that ultimately flowered many years later in the Second Vatican Council) was distinctly and characteristically *Anglican* in just the way of David Hilliard's analysis, quoted in the last chapter, of how liberal Anglo-Catholicism in this period was as opposed to Roman Catholicism.[129]

This is the explanation, moreover, for Cram's attitude toward the use of Gothic by Protestant churches, a matter that has vexed many who find in Upjohn (who refused a Gothic design for a Unitarian church) their standard of "sincerity" and wonder why Cram was apparently so much less sincere — and, as we have seen here, right from the first; for example, in the 1890s for the Phillips Church at Exeter and for the First Church in Cambridge. Significantly, when Cram argued for the Gothic version in a letter of 1899, he saw an anti-Puritan affinity between his "liberal" Anglo-Catholicism and "liberal" Protestantism:

> While the Colonial style, so called, may have created propriety as the architectural style of Puritanism, it is not necessarily a logical expression of the liberal Christianity which successfully assailed the narrowness, the bigotry, of the Puritan regime.[130]

That "liberal Christianity," which he distinguished from Puritanism, was, of course, his father's. Like T. S. Eliot, Cram brought much of New England liberalism (via Unitarianism) to his Anglo-Catholicism, where it found good company in the Oxbridge liberalism of Newman and Father Hall.

However one reads the New England cultural map of the 1880s and 1890s, Boston's aesthetes were key in shaping progressive forces, both in Boston's major institutions and in the overall culture. And Cram's churches were a vital part of the change. Yet if we need to know this to understand Cram and his era, there arises at once a question. Given that twentieth-century Boston, for all that has been lost (*pace* Van Wyck Brooks), has on the other hand gained immeasurably and has built upon the work of Cram and his generation a vital new multiethnic American culture of which we are now proud heirs, why has that key part of those foundations, the dawning gay subculture of the period, been subsequently so obscured that its very existence seems now surprising to us?

LOST INNOCENCE, OR WHATEVER

Cross-dressing, evidently a habit of Russell Sullivan and Theodore Dwight, remains today a Tavern tradition at the now coed club's private theatricals. Once, perhaps, it was more homosexual fantasy; now it is more likely to be seen as heterosexual fetishism (and doubtless no less fun for that!). Thus have things changed between our own time and that of Cram's youth of the fin-de-siècle, an era that, if it began in Boston with the visit of Oscar Wilde in 1882, the impact of which on New England's cultural and intellectual history we are only now coming to comprehend, may be said to have closed in 1909 with the visit to New England of Sigmund Freud and Carl Jung. Occasioned by their being awarded honorary degrees by Clark University, this visit, though lately the subject of a good-sized book, also has not in the New England context been sufficiently explored.

Wilde and Freud and Jung seem, to be sure, strange bedfellows; and psycho-analysis, like aestheticism and the Decadence, at first glance very un-Bostonian. But just as we have traced here the beginnings of Boston's leadership in the development in America of the aesthete and decadent movements, so, too, Boston was to be in the next generation the leading edge of psychoanalysis in the United States. Like Wilde in 1882 at the start of the fin-de-siècle period, Freud and Jung in 1909 at that period's effective end, on the eve of World War I, actually found their most ardent American admirers in Boston.

Why this was so was answered in one sense by Freud himself, when he declared that "only Boston could be the starting point for the formation of a psycho-analytic group. . . . All important intellectual movements in America have originated in Boston."[131] A more detailed analysis was offered by Nathan Hale, and one that calls to mind here why Cram and his generation were so interested in the occult. Wrote Hale:

> Why did American psychotherapy . . . develop primarily in Boston? A lingering Uni-
> tarian and Transcendentalist tradition fostered among respectable Boston physicians
> a sympathy for hypnotism, suggestion, and psychic research, all major sources of the
> new psychopathology [of which the "Boston School" was the leader] in the critical
> decade of the 1890s. . . . The British founder [of the branch of the Society of Psychi-
> cal Research], F. W. H. Myers, probably brought Breuer and Freud's [first] work on
> hysteria to [William] James's attention.[132]

Freud's and Jung's visit even had a certain resonance in Boston's more aesthetic circles, largely because of Harvard. We have seen the influence of psychol-

ogy on Santayana's proto-Freudian work in aesthetics. And it was G. Stanley Hall, Clark University's then president, a close friend of Charles Eliot Norton's, who largely arranged Freud's and Jung's visitation to New England in the first place,[133] some of the circumstances surrounding which illustrate anecdotally the links in that period among occultism and psychotherapy and Freudianism and Boston's Bohemia. Hall, for example, and William James were at that time very much at odds over Leonora E. Piper, the famous Boston medium alluded to in Chapter 1 in whom Cram and Day also were interested. James had in 1884 instigated the American branch of the Society for Psychical Research, headquartered in Boston on Beacon Hill, just across from the Dwight-Sullivan menage, the secretary of which, Richard Hodgson (yet another Charles Street bachelor-scholar), had researched a study of Piper that James brought to the Jung-Freud lectures at Clark to give to Hall, who had himself just completed a much less favorable report on the lady. (Freud, it should be noted, was distinctly of Hall's opinion in such matters.)

Boston offered Freud not only admirers like James and Hall but also a key disciple, a Boston Brahmin and Harvard professor, James Jackson Putnam, who, according to Freud himself, was "not only the first American to interest himself in psycho-analysis" — probably a reference to an article of 1895 by Putnam in a Boston medical journal that showed even then familiarity with Freud's earliest work — "but soon became its most decided supporter and its most influential representative in America." The Clark lectures, moreover, are now seen to have been "a turning point," in Saul Rosenzweig's words, "in the life of Sigmund Freud and the history of psychoanalysis."[134]

Particularly important, according to Rosenzweig, was "the extensive coverage [of Freud's lectures] . . . in the prestigious *Boston Evening Transcript*."[135] But if this is evidence that, however staid that journal, it was alert enough to have played a key role in "introducing psychoanalysis to America," the tenor of its interviews with Freud did show a tendency to fight shy of Freud's controversial and vigorous attack on what Nathan Hale called the "civilized morality of the day" in America, an attack rooted, of course, in fin-de-siècle European thought of the sort reflected in the mores of Boston's Bohemia. Hale notes that although

> the American fin de siècle [which is to say, circles like that of Cram's on Pinckney Street] was but the palest reflection [of the European thought of the time] . . . there were signs of a crisis in sexual morality among small groups in America then. . . . Since the 1890s [a few] . . . intellectuals had been questioning some of the tenants of American morality, among them the founders of American psychology [including] G. Stanley Hall, [who] disliked what [he] called the "Puritan" suppression . . . repudiat[ing] in particular American prudery.[136]

President Eliot notwithstanding, we have seen how Cram was hurt by the Puritan party, and the need to destroy it, as we will see, was a chief theme Cram would develop in the nineties in his work; whether they knew it or not, Cram and Hall were on the same side, for Hall very much "disliked the 'Calvinist' New England rejection of joy and art," as Nathan Hale put it in words very similar to Cram's.[137]

Dr. Hall had very personal reasons for his attitude that Cram may not have had. One school Hall attended as a child was "rife with 'homosexuality, exhibitionism, fellatio, onanism.' "[138] And though there is no evidence that Dr. Hall's experiences were Cram's, they do speak overall to the era of Cram's youth in New England, widely held then to have a higher incidence of mental illness than any other section of the country. Alice Brown's and Cram's "Tiverton" comes to mind. So, too, do the published case studies of the turn-of-the-century Boston psychiatrist Eugene Emerson, which actually document at least one small instance of a nexus of those two significant visitations to New England — Oscar Wilde's in 1882 and Jung's and Freud's in 1909. For one of Dr. Emerson's patients asserted that his homosexual "affliction" was greatly exacerbated by his reading in the press of Wilde's affairs, surely a personal, anecdotal reflection of the larger, overall experience of an entire generation.[139] However, the truth of the matter is that however much Bohemia pioneered changing sexual mores, all that we have construed here so far of that Bohemia of Cram's formative years utterly collapsed in the wake of its "exposure" by Freud and his disciples, like Putnam. What Wilde had started Freud ended.

It is true in my view that the nature of Freudian love, if one may use that term, like Platonic love, has been greatly misunderstood. Martin Bergman, for example, sees Freud as reaching similar conclusions not only to those of Plato but also to those of Saint Paul. Bergman quotes T. Gould as asserting, in what I find a thrilling insight, that Freud was one of "the three men in the history of the western world [the others are Plato and Saint Paul, who have] created encompassing theories of love."[140] Bergman continues:

> Freud did not believe that sexual striving can be integrated into a matrix of an enduring human relationship. . . . Freud asserted his belief that "aim-inhibited" and "aim-deflected" strivings are the basis for sublimation and therefore more reliable for the building of an enduring relationship. . . . [Bergman goes on later that] Freud believed that ungratified wishes can be turned into motivation for psychic changes, whereas gratified wishes are conducive to inertia, [and, further] that the extent to which anyone is in love, as contrasted with the purely sexual desire, may be measured by the size of the share taken by the uninhibited instincts of affection.[141]

It is also true that Freudian, Platonic, and Pauline love have in common not only a high valuation of chasteness, but a similar attitude toward its effects. If

Freud did not quite endorse the views, for example, of Balzac, who, on achieving "unwanted" orgasm, is said to have exclaimed, "Well, there goes another book!"[142] Freud's own conclusions in this matter of creativity were still sympathetic, if mixed; a "young scholar," Freud wrote, may indeed through sexual self-denial "liberate energies for his studies"[143] (a fascinating use of the word "liberate"). And though he did think the harsher the denial the more likely was neurotic suffering ("an abstinent artist" Freud thought "barely possible"; more probably, he concluded, "his artistic achievement is powerfully stimulated by his sexual experience"),[144] he still insisted that, having in mind more overall societal affairs,

> it is precisely manifest homosexuals, and among them again precisely those that set themselves against an indulgence in sexual acts, who are distinguished by taking a particularly active share in the general interests of humanity — interests which have themselves sprung from a sublimation of erotic instincts.[145]

But this confluence of Freudian thought with Platonic and Pauline thought (which helps, I hope, our understanding as moderns of Cram's Platonic idealism) is more evident after a century of studying Freud, and was by no means what stood out in the early 1900s. Today, when the prevailing view among most progressives is that coming out is a matter of one's mental health, it is hard to realize that then Freudianism had the effect of marooning gay people in a morbid nightmare. Freud's view, that all people were to a greater or lesser extent bisexual, was hardly noticed; instead, in America, the emphasis was placed on homosexuality as a matter of arrested development. It was a conclusion that pleased nobody. But it changed everything. Particularly in Bohemia. Freud, though himself bitterly opposed to the moralism that was so striking a characteristic of his American disciples (the subject repeatedly flared up in his correspondence with Putnam), was unable to stop his views from being used to make homosexuality, already a sin and a crime, finally, too, a disease.[146]

Indeed, Freud changed the sexual landscape so utterly that not only was Bohemia annihilated and gay people stranded; by the 1920s another result was the distortion and discrediting of the whole Platonic tradition, making of it a kind of antique, idealistic footnote to an overall theory of homosexuality as morbid, perverted, and pathological.[147]

That is why we so easily forget that Pinckney Street was in the 1880s and 1890s, as Bloom suggested in our discussion of Henry Vaughan, both very Bohemian and very respectable. The same point has been made of London's Bohemia by Alan Crawford, who writes of fin-de-siècle Chelsea that it was "Bohemia with a dash of bourgeois reserve in it. There were easy morals and sometimes an electric air of homosexuality about the place; but there were also respectable, domesticated painters."[148] The lack then of Freudian labels meant, in fact, that in many ways 1890s Boston was *more* liberated, not *less*, than now. There was, if you will, a kind of innocence in Decadence, the effect of the loss of which, for example, can be traced in the legacy of the same-sex relationship of Annie Fields and Sarah Orne Jewett. Alas, the nurture and critical support Fields gave the younger Jewett, Jewett in turn (though she tried) could not really pass on to Willa Cather in quite the same direct and frank way: "Cather," wrote Johanna Russ, "was almost twenty-five years [Jewett's] junior and came of age in a different environment, [knowing] that what Jewett's generation would have seen as admirable, hers would consider abnormal."[149] Indeed, by the 1920s, it was decided that Fields's and Jewett's own correspondence could hardly be published uncensored. Without, that is, being misunderstood!

TRUTH AS MASQUERADE

Once recovered, our view of the gay subculture of Cram's youth in Boston must still be very skewed by how hypocritical it seems to us today. But that, of course, is itself a post-Freudian point of view, and though it is one we do well, perhaps, to cultivate for ourselves, it is never helpful (or fair) in trying to understand the past to read the values of one generation back into another.

Hypocrisy, of course, is an insistent theme in nineteenth-century cultural history, and Cram as a young man was enormously sensitive to it. In Peter Gay's catalogue of nineteenth-century moralists who "devoted themselves to the detection and denunciation of hypocrisy," all of Cram's chief heroes of the day appear—not only Morris and Ruskin but Pugin himself, who, complaining bitterly of "ornament and design *adapted to* instead of originated by, the edifices" themselves, bluntly "lampooned [the current Gothic fashion] by drawing an impossible Gothic building of his own, complete with ridiculous greenhouse, and commented that here 'all is mere mask, and the whole building an ill-conceived lie.' "[150]

The reader will recall that these views are reflected in Cram's youthful diary of his twenties, and one has to look no further than Cram's early houses and churches to see this concern in his persistent insistence on constructional honesty. Still, there was change then, too, of course (half-timbering, for example, was only for decorative effect by Norman Shaw's day; no other function for it was, as it were, functional). Even in so minor a project as a house, and one not in the medieval mode or entirely Cram's own (it was a remodeling, in the Colonial Revival style: the Huff House project of 1899 in Greensburg, Pennsylvania),[151] Cram was preaching stridently in private letters to clients that they must have *solid* brick walls, not a four-inch brick veneer on frame construction. The truth is: whatever the vices of Pinckney Street may have been, from its own point of view, as Gelett Burgess asserted was true generally of Bohemia, hypocrisy was not one of them.

That is not to say that it did not try to keep up appearances as good Victorians and Edwardians (and not only at English country-house weekends) always did. But it was James Fields, we now know, who suggested Sarah Orne Jewett be his wife's significant other after his death. "Victorian Americans," Carroll Smith-Rosenberg has noted, choosing her words with great care, "did not find their heterosexual and homosocial worlds incompatible. Here a husband himself recommended the woman who [in a Boston marriage] would replace him."[152] Similarly, there was Guiney, the mother of her sexually ambiguous "boys," as she called them, all of them, including both Cram and Goodhue. Such a devout lady; yet she admired the work of Beardsley, whom Paglia calls the "monastic pornographer."[153] Nor will it do, in lieu of hypocrisy, to call Pinckney Street, or even Guiney herself, naive. After all, she once wrote to Cram, who did somewhat resemble Beardsley: "the half-length portrait of Aubrey Beardsley in the current *Book Buyer* is a *little* like you. One thing only of his I wish you, one only, and that's his luck!"[154]

Perhaps the most striking illustration of how differently pre- and post-Freudian Boston dealt with such things is to be found in the life and work of Thomas Wentworth Higginson, the Boston critic and editor, who loathed Wilde and Whitman and was fairly clear as to why. Indeed, such was his "hatred" of the latter (the word is Justin Kaplan's)[155] that Higginson once said Whitman's chief mistake was not the writing of *Leaves of Grass* but that he did not burn it afterward! Yet consider how Higginson described *in print*, in a memorial biography, a friend of his youth:

> I never loved but one male friend with passion — and for him my love had no bounds. . . . I lived for him. . . . So handsome in his dark beauty . . . slender, keen-eyed, raven-haired, he arrested the eye and the heart like some fascinating girl.[156]

What would Freud have made of that?

The *nature* of the difference between the pre- and post-Freudian era is harder to illustrate, but is perhaps glimpsed in the respective Harvard careers of George Santayana and F. O. Matthiessen. Santayana, who affirmed that the only aspect of Harvard that "in any measure held my affections and with which I could almost have identified with, was that of the 'nineties' — or, rather, of 1890–95," which he described as "distinctly Bohemian,"[157] was open enough that President Eliot could, as we have seen, call him "abnormal."

Matthiessen, on the other hand, professor of English and Senior Tutor of Eliot House at Harvard in the early 1930s, faced quite a different situation. The

Greek tradition of manly love Santayana thrived on (a variation, after all, of "muscular Christianity") was fast blurring and (under the influence of what all too soon became Freudian stereotypes) breaking down into a new pattern of heterosexual muscle (athletes) and homosexual intellect (writers, artists, and such), a pattern already discernible here in the distinction between Archibald Cary Coolidge and William Amory Gardner, for example, and in the books of writers such as Robert Herrick, an author whose work is based on a rejection of Harvard aestheticism for football. (Herrick modeled one of his most uninspiring characters, Evard, in his *Gospel of Freedom* of 1898 after Berenson.)[158]

No one, it would seem, ever called Matthiessen abnormal. Indeed, Joseph H. Summers and U. T. Miller Summers, betraying very changed (and perhaps more cynical) standards of sophistication, wrote:

> for most of his students and younger colleagues Matthiessen's homosexuality was suggested, if at all, only by the fact that his circle was more predominantly heterosexual than was usual in Harvard literary groups of the time and that he was unusually hostile to homosexual colleagues who mixed their academic and sexual relations.[159]

Clearly, Matthiessen realized he was welcome at Harvard only as long as he adopted the proper pose of sharing the majority's distaste for such as he. Because of the era he lived in he could argue he needed to have a care not to allow his enemies a tool with which to discredit him. But he knew well that his dishonesty harmed no one more than himself, writing that "the falseness [of my position on this subject] seems to *sap my confidence* of power."[160] There, in the *post-*, not the pre-Freudian era, was the hypocrisy, and there, too, was the price of it.

Yet, what power was left was enough: Matthiessen's achievement is at least on a level with Santayana's. So much so that one can hardly help recalling A. L. Rowse's ideas about the value of tensions as spurs to achievement. And what was true of teacher and scholar would be doubly so, surely, of the artist. Consider Johanna Russ's catalogue, in her study of the work of Willa Cather, of the states of mind that necessarily intervene between our period and the pre-Freudian one of Cram's youth:

> The innocent rightness in feelings of love for and attraction to women which Jewett and her contemporaries enjoyed [in the Boston marriage] was not possible to Cather's generation; the social invention [not just via Freud, but in much other work, that of Havelock Ellis, for example] of the morbid, unhealthy, criminal lesbian had intervened. . . . The innocence, of course, had to go. If the next stage can be called guilty self-consciousness, and the stage after that self-conscious rebellion, no matter what aesthetic advantages they offer (and I believe they offer many not available to Cather, honesty being one of them) they do not have the same advantages of Cather's masquerade; they cannot possibly create the aesthetic completeness and richness of Cather's work.[161]

Honesty has already yielded gay artists and scholars and the culture at large great advantage. But will books like *Dorian Gray* and *Death in Venice* still be written? Certainly the figure in the carpet in fin-de-siècle Boston was challengingly intricate. Thus does one age speak to another.

7

DESIGNING PARTNERS,
ARTFUL CHURCHES

Art comes from the deep soul where a great force lives, and this force is sex and love and desire — desire for power, desire for possession, sexual desire, desire for beauty, desire for knowledge, desire for God — what makes us good or bad — and without this force there is no art, and no science either, and no — no man; without Eros man is a ghost.

— Iris Murdoch, *Acastos: Two Platonic Dialogues*

All that is builded here is built to bind
The gentle arch, the stone flower of desire
Into the sterner vision of the mind:
The structure of this passion is the spire.

— May Sarton, "Architectural Image"

68a, b. Ralph Adams Cram and Bertram Grosvenor Goodhue in their youth in the 1890s: photographs that show sides of each man not revealed in their more public portraiture. The photograph of Cram, as well, perhaps, as that of Goodhue, is by Day.

THE RICH texture of Boston's late nineteenth-century gay subculture, the context of Cram's first two decades of work in the 1880s and 1890s, having now been filled in, we must, as we turn our attention more closely to Cram's own work of the nineties, pick up threads long left hanging here while we focused on delineating Cram's sexuality and reconciling it with his developing cultural and religious values. We must now shift our focus back to his partnership with Goodhue.

In a sense, however, Cram had two partners during the nineties, if my conjectures are correct, one of whom may well be called his silent partner: Henry Vaughan first then, Bertram Goodhue thereafter.

HIS PERFECT READER AND LOVER

It is always easy to overlook Vaughan. Yet during the nineties Henry made his way up and down Pinckney Street twice daily past Ralph's door, en route to an office itself all but within sight of Cram's own, where Vaughan in his quiet way conducted the most prestigious architectural practice in New England of the Gothic and churchly variety — except on Sunday, when he and Cram were even more certain to see each other at High Mass at St. John's, Bowdoin Street, which both attended regularly from 1889 to Vaughan's death in 1917, a period of nearly twenty years. Since he was Cram's oldest friend and neighbor among his fellow architects and co-religionists in Boston and the only mentor Cram ever acknowledged, it would be most unwise to lose sight of Henry Vaughan.

We have already quoted Jung on the potentialities of a homosexual relationship between an older and a younger person. And Vaughan may very well have brought to his friendship with Cram the loving devotion and stimulating mentoring characteristic of the older person's role in such a relationship (all the more valuable because any sexual experience in such cases will naturally be uncompetitive). Cram would have brought all the characteristic gifts of youth — fresh intellect, physical charm and vitality, renewing ideals, and emotional openness. And to these gifts, which neither man could have hoped for from friends of his own age, each would have brought, too, his prodigious individuality. To be sure, such relationships fail. Among gay artists who have treated the subject of how tragic intergenerational relationships can be, one thinks of Ben-

253

jamin Britten's exploration of the romance of Elizabeth I and the Earl of Essex, *Gloriana*. Then, too, of Henry James's young men (to cite a homosexual instance), though Jocelyn Persse rose to the occasion (and inspired James's last novel, *The Golden Bowl*), others did not.[1] But one suspects better of Cram's and Vaughan's friendship.

Much of the value in such a friendship, of course, holds true whatever the sexuality of those involved. One thinks of Cézanne and Joachim Gasquet:

> When the two men first met . . . Cézanne was fifty-seven and Gasquet was twenty-three, ... [and in] the full bloom of a buoyant . . . highly energized youth. Ardor and enthusiasm flowed from him . . . and his blond beauty caused one of his contemporaries . . . to liken him to . . . Dionysus. . . . [It is] an archetypal situation that often occurs in the later years. . . . It is at this point that there may appear a youthful savior . . . who asks . . . to listen, to learn, to sympathize and to serve. With the arrival of this God-sent young man, renewal is at hand.[2]

Nor is the effect necessarily only to the benefit of the older man. In the case of Vaughan and Cram, one wonders if it was not the younger man who benefitted more, for the steadying by Vaughan of Cram in the 1890s probably explains the remarkable psychological stability Cram was to demonstrate when he plunged into the subculture of the Decadence with that most unsteadying of influences, Bertram Goodhue.

Such a relationship will usually have to be both personal and professional. One is reminded of Leonard Bernstein and the much older Aaron Copeland. Like many intergenerational relationships, it was not primarily genital apparently, though some "bonding" may have occurred. But it was intense and life-long. Though often it begins as a teacher-and-student one, the potential for learning and teaching will be present on either side. Indeed, the ideal will be an almost perfectly symmetrical exchange of inspiration in each other's work — an intimacy approaching the Platonic one that yields intellectual and artistic progeny referred to earlier by Walter Hamilton.[3]

An example of the younger man's being inspired by the older is found in F. O. Matthiessen's *American Renaissance*, the book that virtually created American literature as a field; it has been well described as the "ultimate expression of [Matthiessen's] love for Cheney [his partner and friend],"[4] who was twenty years older. (Vaughan was just about that much older than Cram.) An example of the older man's being inspired by the younger is perhaps the spare dignity of the Groton Chapel of 1899. I think it owes much to Vaughan's appreciation of Cram's thought, exemplified in churches we will discuss in this chapter at Brookline and Middleborough.

Cram and Vaughan, of course, did diverge in many ways. T. L. Steinberg, in his study "Poetry and the Perpendicular Style," is insightful when he concludes that what emerges as continuous in both media and is identifiable as characteristically English is a quality of individualism — self-contained parts that, whether in church or poem, are more additive in feeling than integral.[5] Such an individualism is very evident in Vaughan's work but hardly at all in Cram's, where the parts seems always more interdependent, even when, as is the case in all his 1890s Gothic work, he is working in a style more English than continental. Other differences will arise in a later chapter.

Yet both in Cram's inspiration by Vaughan and in his own considerable design initiatives, what Robert K. Martin has said of Hart Crane and Walt Whitman may also be said of Cram and Vaughan:

> Any reading of Whitman must take into account his need to be completed by the future. . . . As in any such relationship, imitation and homage are a double-edged compliment. Crane praises Whitman, yet suggests his own [Crane's] superiority, for only Crane can make Whitman whole [i.e., "complete" his work] by becoming his perfect reader and lover.[6]

Whether the younger man returns the older man's likely passion is not the point. A relationship that does not fully satisfy genital needs can still be primary if not exclusive if the people involved regard intellectual needs as primary and physical needs as secondary. As I have already pointed out, the significant other can be physical lover, teacher, mother, coach, or whatever. In that sense, Cram was certainly Vaughan's "perfect reader and lover"; all the more so as Cram's silent partner was in some important respects more sympathetic to him than his actual partner, since Goodhue did not share Cram's religious views as Vaughan, we know, did. And that was by no means the only aspect of Cram's partnership with Goodhue that was problematic.

PASSIONATE ACTS

"It sometimes seemed to me," wrote Cram years later, "that [Bertram and I] were less two individuals than two lobes of the same brain." Despite the fact that by Cram's own lights, his planning and massing were at least as important to their architecture as Goodhue's development and detailing, Cram added generously that for all they seemed one brain, "it was from Bertram Goodhue, however, that the inspiration seemed to flow."[7]

Of course, there will be those who will say that all Cram's judgments of Goodhue show how indulgent he was of his partner and friend. But we do not always like the work of a friend because we love him or her; sometimes we love in the first place *because* (among other things, to be sure) we love his or her work, for one may see there many a thing about a man or a woman well worth

255

the loving and otherwise undetectable. Cram's "two lobes of the same brain" is a drier, more cerebral attempt to get at what is put more warmly when speaking of the "one flesh" of the marriage bed; though having said that, we must be careful not to project back on another period our own era's obsession with genital sex as the supreme expression of love or even of physical intimacy; or indulge, either, the heterosexual suspicion that genital sex is all that homosexuality is about. Martin Duberman points out that the "sexual athletes [of today] have forgotten, or perhaps never knew, the pleasure and comfort to be had from nongenital physical closeness," so much so that "it's possible we're 'freer' than ever before sexually with members of our own gender — but more emotionally constricted."[8] As the biographer of several important Bostonians, including James Russell Lowell and Charles Francis Adams, Duberman commands particular attention in thus pointing to a sort of restrained and understated sexuality perhaps characteristic of New England, where the distinction between "sensual, without being sexual — that is, intensely emotional (and to some extent physical) but never genital" is hardly surprising to find.[9]

One thinks in this connection of Charles Ricketts and Charles Shannon, one of the few partnerships perhaps comparable to Cram and Goodhue's. These two British artists in the course of a lifelong professional and personal relationship (Ricketts was primarily a book designer, Shannon a painter) achieved so convincing a unity of expression that a friend wrote that "in their prime each was the other's complement."[10] Indeed, an exhibition of their work was subtitled "An Aesthetic Partnership," a title that comes particularly to mind here because they were known for having enjoyed drawing each other. After all, the most intimate sources we have as to Cram and Goodhue's personal relationship, aside from Cram's pronouncement, long after his marriage, that it was "the most stimulating and illuminating experience of a long and varied life" and Wentworth's that it arose between two men who were "queer," are Cram's word pictures of Goodhue and Goodhue's self-portrait of him and Cram in *The Decadent* frontispiece (very much, by the way, Nancy Finlay thinks, after the manner of Ricketts).[11] These pictures, surely, can be assumed to disclose something of Cram and Goodhue's mutualities without any necessity for complicated decoding; certainly not insofar as their sexual roles are portrayed by Goodhue. Without apparently tumbling to the identity of the two young men depicted, Estelle Jussim describes them as "one [man] bearded, the other limply Greek." And while in Cram's reminiscences *his* is always the more masculine role, in Goodhue's frontispiece Bertram is the bearded one!

We can, in fact, by dwelling exactly on smoking, go a little if not a great deal further in our speculation about Goodhue's and Cram's possible "gender" roles, at least as others (all of whom, after all, would have known each man for a dandy) might have then perceived the matter. For in their less exotic, more everyday guises, Ralph was hardly ever without his pipe or Bertram without his cigarette, and as Patricia Berman has observed in her riveting study of smoking in this era, not only were cigarettes a nexus for Bohemian social identities (in fact, without knowing of Cram's role in *The Mahogany Tree*, a Bostonian "little magazine" of the 1890s, Berman cites an editorial in that magazine as one of her references) but "the cigarette [having been from its first appearance at mid-century] widely understood to be an effete or feminized form of smoking," according to Berman, "the male smoker was feminized by his cigarette." Ralph's pipe would thus likely have signaled to contemporaries as clearly masculine a persona as Bertram's cigarette a distinctly feminine one.[12]

If reading (in the light of Cram's reminiscences) Goodhue's sketch of him and Cram in the way one might read, for example, an ancient Greek vase is the closest we can penetrate to their specific genital roles as conventionally understood, Goodhue and Cram's overall psychological relationship we can deduce more closely, for we have a quite personal and extended (if only one-sided) correspondence from two key periods of their lives in the 1890s and 1900s. (In using letters in this way, as I have Cram's youthful diary, his horror stories, and his autobiography, and, indeed, Goodhue's frontispiece to *The Decadent*, I am mindful of Peter Gay's point that "few diarists or autobiographers, no matter how sensitive or intelligent, really understand . . . how much they are really saying," and I am, of course, adopting his view, which I share, that "the methods and theories of Sigmund Freud . . . provide ways of digging beneath the surface of the written word . . . of enlarging the scope of an individual's report on himself.")[13]

The earliest letters, written to Goodhue by Cram while he was in Japan in 1899 (on affairs discussed in Chapter 10), document in the first place the design process of the 1890s as Cram remembered it.[14] In one letter he announces, "I have made an entirely new design . . ., based on the knowledge I have acquired since I came here. It is a good design and" — he adds, somewhat defensively (he is writing to probably the best renderer in America, after all) — "a pretty good drawing." Moreover, Cram begs off a plan Goodhue clearly expected: "the plan for Berkeley I simply could not do. On the steamer it was impossible and here I have devoted my [minutes?] to [another commission?]. Use your own discretion as to whether you go into it or not. I have full confidence in your judgement and Ferguson's." Support, though also seniority, is evident as well: "You did quite right in the Winchester matter [something otherwise anonymous] and the authorities can go to hell."

In the second place, more personally — and these letters are quite personal ("Let no one see this letter who is not discreet," Cram wrote across the top of one, then closed it with "Give my love to Ferguson, write every mail, and don't work too damn hard. Yours always, RAC") — Cram's letters also show how open and intimate he and Goodhue were. One missive, for example, details an experience of Cram's, which (as there cannot be too many descriptions of this sort by Bostonians from nineteenth-century Japan) I quote from at length:

> Would you could have seen me enacting another role three nights ago . . . [After returning with Arthur Knapp from a day out of town] we did *not* go directly home, but strolled . . . down the street gazing . . . into the doors of the great — well — [geisha] houses that line that avenue. . . .
>
> Well, we went in . . . and calmly surveyed the crescent of glittering girls perched in the cage to the right. They were all gorgeously in scarlet and gold and they had things in their hair and they giggled and stared at the awful sight of two foreign devils surveying "the ground where they must shortly lie." I chose Madame Butterfly, A.K. chose Madame Gold (O Cho San and Go Ken San).
>
> Thirteen old men and women wept on our shoulders and accompanied us to a five-mat room splendidly furnished with a hibachi. . . . There the thirteen old men and women told us the girls would cost one yen fifty (75¢) each and that the dinner would cost five yen. We acquiesced and while the repast was being prepared, A.T. and I toyed in a [delicate?] and Asiatic manner with O Cho San and Go Ken San, smoking many cigarettes the while, and drinking much sake.
>
> The room was seven feet high and 9x12, the walls were of rice paper screens and the only light came from a single candle in a holder three feet high and the glowing hibachi. The girls were as big as [dolls?] and . . . their skin like satin and they giggled consumedly at everything.
>
> *Mr. Cram lies.* [This and all that follows in this letter in italics are in another hand, presumably that of Arthur Knapp.] *We went to the M[ethodist] E[piscopal] church that night and afterwards drank lemonade with the parson's wife.*
>
> A.T.K. is too God damn drunk [Cram then inserts] to know *where* we went that night. . . . But to resume.
>
> *RAC heroically tries to preserve his reputation, but you know he lies. ATK.*
>
> All the same [Cram continues, presumably regaining the pen,] AT is drunk. Well: by and by we went upstairs. Butterfly and I hand in hand to a three-mat room with walls made of screens on the other side of which one could hear many sounds of movement. Butterfly was amiable, adequate and satisfactory in every way and it was with great sorrow that I led her downstairs and said farewell to the thirteen old gentlemen and ladies.

Midway in this perusal of Ralph's correspondence with Bertram, in aid of plumbing the sexual and psychological nature of their relationship, there arises again here, now quite dramatically, the issue of whether Cram should properly be called not homosexual but bisexual. As I pointed out previously (when I explicated my definition of "gay" from John Boswell, who cited Alexander the

Great as an example of a homosexual who slept with the opposite sex), being gay is hardly incompatible with heterosexual relationships, genital or not. One such of Cram's, with Ethel Reed, arises in Chapter 9, while love letters to a Southern lady reputedly exist. There was an American lady in Japan too! Does this mean Cram was bisexual?

"Bisexual" is a word that means, to my mind, at one and the same time everything and nothing. As much misunderstood as the term "Platonic love," it is certainly a universal truism, but one whose application to any one person is hardly clarifying. As Martin Bergman has written, echoing Freud, "bisexuality is a universal human endowment," and even though Freud thought it stronger in women, Bergman records that "every psychoanalyst discovers that even heterosexual men and women harbor the wish if not the drive to be both sexes." In a memorable phrase he asserts: "Paradise means having 'everything.' And everything stands for bisexuality."[15]

Admittedly, there is a bisexual midpoint on the Kinsey scale (3, midway between entirely heterosexual, 0, and entirely homosexual, 6) but the virtual impossibility of this category's existing in real life is well shown by David Greenberg, and the very nature of these categories in this context is effectively repudiated by Boswell.[16] To be sure, the point can be argued. In his *Homosexual Matrix* C. A. Tripp does defend the integrity of the word "bisexual" as applied to individuals like Julius Caesar, who was said to be every man's wife and every woman's husband, who are sexually attracted to both men and women, as Cram may have been. But even Tripp admits that it is a category hard to keep hold of, for nearly everyone one might so categorize is inevitably predominantly one thing even if significantly the other.[17]

Lord Byron, for instance, may not, according to the standards and definitions of one school of scholars, be properly called gay. But other scholars have found no difficulty in doing so. Byron is a leading figure in A. L. Rowse's *Homosexuals in History* (as also in more popular variants of this genre, like Thomas Cowan's *Gay Men and Women Who Have Enriched the World*), and his poetry is prominently featured in *The Penguin Book of Homosexual Verse*.[18] Boswell points out that one supposes "a homosexual person is one given to 'homosexual' acts. But in just how many such acts must one indulge before becoming 'homosexual' — one, two, ten, or four hundred? And what of the person who only dreams of committing the act but never realizes the ambition? Is he or she homosexual?"[19]

It is vital to my thesis here to recall the view we have seen advanced by so many that genital acts are not necessarily key to the stable personality type, as we would now call it, of a person of homosexual orientation. But neither are they incidental. And Boswell's emphasis on the act is well taken. But it gets us only so far and not much closer to answering the question under discussion. As the fashion for "queer het sex" (i.e., queers having heterosexual sex) of the early 1990s documents, genital activity is a murky and complex subject. Bergman, for example, in a book not primarily concerned with homosexuality, noting that successful heterosexual genital acts depend upon one's capacity to enjoy oneself as both subject and object at the same time, and that the latter is achieved through self-identification with one's partner of the opposite sex, argues that in homosexual sex "this state [of being an object] is accomplished by a denial of gender differences, through *fantasies* [emphasis added] of bisexuality." Similarly, he observes, masturbation has always been popular because it "lends itself to the feeling of being both sexes."[20]

The possibilities, of course, are endless. Shakespeare's sonnets are a case in point; they have been explained by a scholar who believes they are "the supreme love poetry in the world" as "a magnificent example of the split between homosexual love and heterosexual sex" in an era (before artificial insemination and gay parenting) when only heterosexual union could yield progeny.[21] Or consider prostitution, the subject that raises this whole issue here with Cram. All along, while I have insisted that both the Platonic and the Catholic ideals of self-mastery, in my reading of the matter, frankly provided for (if they did not encourage) genital acts and did not even necessarily condemn such acts if lust was seen as love's handmaiden, I have also suggested that Cram may have been like Schubert, sustaining his ideal relationships, what we have called elsewhere here the "higher sodomy" of soulmates, by recourse to the "lower sodomy" of bedmates, which will usually involve promiscuity and include prostitution. And, of course, the same forces that drove so many homosexuals to marriage in this era would have pushed them toward heterosexual prostitution. (How many gay men in the company of others — nothing very definite about Knapp, including his sexuality, is known — have called on such women and seen the matter through, while imagining quite a different partner indeed, later describing the affair to a fellow member of the brotherhood exactly as did Cram to Goodhue: "Would that you could have seen me enacting another role three nights ago.")

In marriage, of course, one reason was children, the rationale of that old and brutal saying of the British army in India: "a woman for business, a boy for pleasure." In such a situation as Cram found himself in, the need to dissemble and succeed can exist on so many levels — to one's friend, which is to say society, and to oneself, and in that in more than one way — that we can hardly go into it. Not the least reason, though, emerges in the comments of Gelett Burgess about Goodhue in a similar situation, which Burgess described in a letter to Cram: "I could have shown him the noblest work of God — the California girl . . . but he would have nothing but virtue, as he called it. . . . Such a picked collection as I could have given him, a different one to dinner each night in my rooms!" So

Burgess raved on. This was in 1901, when Goodhue pleaded his recent engagement; he married a year later. Still, Burgess protested to Cram: "You're mad — of course — I would hardly count you a friend if you weren't, but I can't yet see [what Goodhue was about] . . . God! That man . . . I had everything fixed."[22] It is not a reputation most men would want.

Whether Goodhue was more or less "bisexual" than Cram, and whatever his reasons for declining opportunities Cram accepted (which, evidently, Cram was known to do on more than one occasion; Burgess concluded his letter with the remark "I wish you had been there instead"), it is perhaps worthwhile to note that the gay icon of this era, Oscar Wilde, also was known to visit heterosexual brothels and to marry and to have had two sons by Constance Wilde. It is forever true that you don't have to be it to do it and you don't have to do it to be it.

THE MODERN MALADY OF LOVE

Cram did not spend all his time in Japan in amorous adventures, but they do tend to dominate his letters to Goodhue, and in that, as in so many other respects, they document the two men's intimacy. In another letter, for example, Cram wrote of yet other varieties of love:

> I am learning an enormous amount about Japanese architecture under the guidance of [Ernest] Fenollosa [one of the "Boston orientalists," of whom more in Chapter 9], who loves me like a brother and would cut off his hand to do something for me. As a return I have fallen hopelessly in love with a girl who is visiting him . . . Anne Dyer, who is beautiful, indulgent and a dead game sport. Last Sunday we all went down to Kamakura for the day and I don't hesitate to say it was the greatest spent of my life to date. No words can describe the glory of the old pre-Tokumgawa temples and their surroundings and as Anne was with me and there was a plentiful supply of sake, my cup of happiness was full.
>
> I needed it, for life here with the Knapps is simply HELL. Arthur is a surly, drunken, ill mannered, selfish chump. His Reverence [Cram's friend's father, a missionary] is a silly and fatuous old booby and Mrs. K is a doting, foolish, ill bred, superannuated baby — after which I feel better —. In spite of it all I like Arthur now and then. . . .
>
> For God's sake don't let anyone but Ferguson see this letter and burn it the moment it is read. . . . It is caddish in me to write as I do. Still, I am paying board, so why not? . . .
>
> Lord how I love Anne Dyer! What am I going to do about it? I can't afford to marry her. . . .

Poor Ralph, ever living at the peak of his emotions. Doubtless other figures than Ernest Fenollosa or Arthur Knapp or even Anne Dyer occasioned the next act, a "tradjedy" alluded to, without any further information than is quoted below, in yet another cri de coeur (the letter is dated 5 May):

The "tradjedy" is something awful. I may win through in the end: my damnable caution and procrastination brought it about. . . . Apparently, I am the only one who comes out it with credit. Really it has about killed me. I don't know whether to commit suicide or take the next steamer for home. I guess I should do the latter.

He did, of course, and this correspondence perforce ceased. But — to jump ahead a decade in aid of this topic — another and later correspondence also exists where we can again take up the theme of the nature and character of Bertram's and Ralph's friendship. This time it is Goodhue's letters from New York that have survived.

They are in striking contrast to Cram's letters from Japan, though it is only fair to note that Goodhue's later missives were written in the much-changed atmosphere of the 1900s, when each man had married and become the head of a separate office in separate cities. Still, Goodhue's letters clearly refer to deep-seated, long-standing patterns rooted in the 1890s and constant throughout Cram and Goodhue's relationship. In one letter, for example, Goodhue writes in respect of an issue he and Cram were rowing about regarding a church building committee:

> If by some miracle my arrangement seems to them to fulfil their requirements, and, even more miraculous, your rhetoric fails to shake this belief, I will not defy or check your exultation. . . . It is good of you to say that you wish to meet my feelings in the case of style just as far as you conscientiously can, but so far as I can make out even the metric system or Troy weights don't contain sufficiently microscopic units with which to mark the extent of your progress in this direction, for from the paragraph of your letter devoted to this laudable endeavour on your part, it is evident that almost the only thing left to us in common is a taste for Gothic, whatever that may be.[23]

Goodhue's bitter sarcasm here is quite revealing. In fact, Goodhue suffered from neurasthenia, a mild mental illness, and in seeking to understand Goodhue's and Cram's psychological relationship we have not just letters to read but also a presumed medical diagnosis of Goodhue to discuss.

It was an American physician, a graduate of Andover and Yale, the pioneering neurologist Dr. George Beard, later one of those New England admirers of Freud, who in the 1880s first isolated the syndrome of neurasthenia, causing an international furor,[24] which, like the new identification of homosexuality in this period, shows how modern were the spirits gathering to vex (or illuminate, according to one's point of view) Cram's life and, in the event, that of all of us in the twentieth century. A connection with matters sexual, moreover, was made almost immediately even in the general culture: Basil Ransom, for example, in Henry James's *The Bostonians* of 1888, certainly made the link in his tirades in that book. And the poet Arthur Symons did as well in 1897: "the modern malady of love," he wrote, "is nerves."[25]

It goes without saying that Goodhue's mental illness is shrouded in silence and never mentioned by Cram in his memoirs, any more than their sexuality was (or in later years Cram's wife's mental illness). Nevertheless, this malady of Goodhue's could hardly have been other than central to his and Cram's relationship. Indeed, Goodhue's biographer, Richard Oliver, is forthright about the matter, admitting that even before Goodhue and Cram met in 1891,

> the high-strung Goodhue was neurasthenic, a condition characterized by fatigue, anxiety, worry, and even localized body pains. As a result Goodhue experienced conflicts that caused him to oscillate between periods of elation and periods of depression, alternately magnanimous and mean, madcap and morose, sympathetic and supercilious, cautious and yet susceptible to his reckless will.

Oliver goes on, furthermore, to deal explicitly with Goodhue's behavior toward Cram over the period of their friendship; at one point, he writes, Goodhue became "distrustful, and even paranoid, about Cram's behavior. . . . Goodhue's behavior was petulant and even childish."[26] As Goodhue grew older, his condition did not improve.

That Cram (unintentionally) exacerbated Goodhue's illness is likely. We have, for instance, cited Cram's lavish praise in and out of print of Goodhue's gift for detail (and his skill as a renderer) as having more than a little of the element of faint praise about it. One can well imagine that Goodhue might be resentful of this tendency of Cram's to think of himself as the soloist, Goodhue the accompanist, however brilliant. Goodhue in the 1890s did not dispute that Cram was "the head" of the firm. But one suspects a long-standing complaint of Goodhue's in his assertion in one letter to his partner that it was a real question whether or not Cram was "marked by pre-natal influences toward domination."[27] Cram might have remarked (he didn't, so his biographer will) as did the composer Louis Holst about Martha Graham: that Goodhue like "every young artist need[ed] a wall to grow against, like a vine. I am that wall."[28]

From a different perspective, however, it is also worth noting, as John Tytell does in his *Passionate Lives*, a study of relationships among artistic and literary figures, that though romantics tend to be keen on the transforming power of love, mates of similar emotional intensity and ego do not over the long haul seem to match well.[29] Indeed, we should certainly assume, despite my sympathetic account here of Platonic love, that Peter Gay is right that "propagandists for the superiority of 'Greek' over other loves might say what they liked, but in real life homosexual affection proved . . . no more durable than its more conventional counterpart."[30] Having in mind our previous discussion about homosexuality's tending toward creativity, however, one can perhaps claim more for Goodhue and Cram's architectural partnership.

INTERNAL MADE EXTERNAL

In bringing to bear in this study Cram's life and work each on the other, we are seeking for a certain consistency. Neither the person nor the work must seem to deny (and ideally should confirm) the characteristics of the other. This is especially necessary in the case of Cram's church design because of my contention that Cram's churches, for all their spiritual power and artistic genius, are like Edward Warren's sculpture in also expressing in part a psychological revolt. This involves, however, accepting the proposition that if these churches have something to tell us about Cram, and Cram in turn has something to tell us about his churches, the churches themselves are not only expressive of Cram's conscious beliefs and convictions, religious and artistic, but also (no less than his books or his poems or whatever) expressive of his *un*conscious life.

It is still a controversial proposition. Long ago, in his *Varieties of Religious Experience*, William James worried about "the fashion," as he put it, ". . . of criticizing the religious emotions by showing a connection between them and the sexual life."[31] But criticism in that sense is hardly today the issue. Catholic scholars seldom any longer scruple to acknowledge the connection, or even, in Carl Capellman's words, that "religious enthusiasm and excessive sexual excitability often accompany one another."[32] Let us recall, too, the comment of Rose Macaulay, as shrewd as she was devout, that Cram seemed to her (beyond his superb gifts in art criticism) to disclose an "unbalanced and child-like enthusiasm — even fanaticism — and idealism." Morris Carter also used the word "fanaticism" in connection with Cram; so did Thomas Tallmadge of Goodhue.[33] Both men struck a number of people that way, including many admirers; perhaps that is why Goodhue and Cram shaped each other so strongly.

Where, then, is the difficulty? C. S. Lewis's biographer A. N. Wilson, writing of best friends, insists that "it was Lewis's friendship . . . which led Tolkien to write the works which made his name . . . just as it was Tolkien's friendship which *released* [emphasis added] in Lewis wells of creativity."[34] Philip Hodson, writing of Wagner, emphasized instead the lover in this role: "The sexual act released Wagner's artistic energies . . . [and] gave him ideas which he metamorphosed into music"; fulfilling his sexual needs proved for Wagner "conducive to the creative process . . . [and] his music retains the mood of its original sensual inspiration."[35]

Whether best friend or lover, surely, the only valid question to ask of sonata, poem, or building is that of its quality. This is true as well of what is called "displacement." Peter Gay has put it well; while displacement "cannot help inviting the charge of hypocrisy," because "it is unconscious . . . [it is] beyond the reach of moral strictures"; and that though "a dubious blessing, an attempt to escape from repressions which for many neurotics only tightens their grip," displacement does do well what defenses, after all, are meant to do: "reducing anxiety. . . . [and] permitting some satisfaction to clamorous drives" by directing them through socially acceptable paths.[36] Notwithstanding the jargon, Father Hall could hardly have put it better. Sex or not; release or displacement; what matter? So long as the sonata or poem or church is good of its kind: *laus Deo.*

Does it not all depend, in the final analysis, on how positively or negatively the matter is put in the first place? Consider Iris Murdoch's observation that the unconscious mind is "not just an abode of monsters, it's a reservoir of spiritual power."[37] Martin Bergman, furthermore, has pointed out that it was really from Plato, long before Freud, that we "discovered that the energy of love can be deflected to other channels than the sexual union" (whether through a modicum of genital contact or none at all), and that (appropriately enough as we take up again Cram's architectural Gothic) the Middle Ages, Cram's era of the mind, very much developed the concept of what we now call "romantic, that is, sexually unconsummated love."[38] It is an idea, by the way, that arises more than once in the music dramas of Richard Wagner that Cram so loved and also in Cram's own play, *Excalibur.*

"Deflected," however, like "displacement," has a certain negative connotation; certainly "unconsummated" does. Consider, instead, the way it was put by Havelock Ellis, who wrote of the "auto-erotic impulse [as frequently passing] its unexpended energy over to religious emotion, there to find the *expansion* hitherto denied it, the love of the human being becoming the love of the divine."[39] Put that way, it is virtually a mirroring of the Platonic concept of the ladder of love, and in such modern psychological garb that it sets forth all the better the proposition that religious truth and its artistic expression, and personal sincerity in the profession thereof, by no means necessarily stand in any uneasy relationship to our unconscious drives.

This is perhaps most clearly seen in our context here in the fact that the background of Freud's own thought in this area[40] was the nineteenth-century Romantic critical tradition, which associated artistic creativity with intense emotion, even pain, on the artist's part. And in that tradition there seems to have been a kind of suppression of the fact that there was no more striking a proto-Freudian than one of the fathers of the Oxford Movement, John Keble.

Keble, however unlikely it may seem to us today, was one of those critics of whom Ellen Spitz has written: "even before Freud's seminal work of the 1890s there were literary critics who understood that works of art may function not merely to express feelings but also to disguise and conceal them." A professor of poetry at Oxford as well as a priest, Keble, according to Spitz and M. H. Abrams, concluded many years before Freud that often "art," as Abrams explains Keble's thinking, "is an *indirect* expression of [in Keble's words] 'some overpowering emotion, or ruling taste, or feeling, the direct indulgence whereof is somehow *repressed*,'" and, as Spitz puts it, "not simply a direct, spontaneous expression of feeling but instead of an internal conflict between the artist's need to give utterance to his emotions and his [in Keble's words] 'instinctive delicacy which recoils from expressing them openly.'"[41]

That professional skills no more stand in any uncomfortable correlation with such unconscious motivations than do religious truth and personal sincerity is also important to concede. As in the case of the religious factor, so can the relationship of unconscious drives to the artistic factor be put very positively, as Bergman does in discussing the playwright Eugene O'Neill; he "had creative capacity that *opened* to him channels of sublimation not ordinarily available."[42] Then too, in discussing why the mid-twentieth-century school of the New Criticism allowed "nothing environmental or causal — not even its maker" to illuminate or explain a work of art, Cynthia Ozick has pointed out, using as example the life and work of T. S. Eliot, that "if Eliot hid his private terrors behind the hedge of his poetry . . . adoration, fame, and the Nobel Prize came to him neither in spite of nor because of what he left out; his craft lay in the *way* he left things out."[43]

So, too, with Cram. It is, surely, the *way* Cram made his work, the design itself, that is key to his repute as an artist; his motivation will, after all, bask in the reflected glory of design and execution, not compromise it.

Admittedly, there is a case to be made that Keble's truism is less true of architecture than of the other arts. In the case of architecture there is a level of client control and design development, more controlling, for example, than in the case of poetry. But does not M. H. Abrams's observation apply equally to architecture as to all the arts: "a work of art is essentially the internal made external"?[44] Granted, it seems easier to grasp the religious feelings of an artist and his or her studio assistants from a madonna and child than it is to sense the feelings of an architect and supporting draftsmen about God or the prayer life from a stone pinnacle. But I choose the comparison because a description in William Golding's *The Spire* is an excellent illustration of the fact that it is possible to see, even in so abstract a thing as a pinnacle (and therefore, presumably, so to design it), *exactly* a visual image of prayer. Wrote Golding:

> there against the sky, I saw the nearest pinnacle; and it was the exact image of my prayer in stone. There was the uprush, the ornamentation of side thoughts for others, then the rush of heart, rising, narrowing, piercing — and at the top, still carved in stone, the thing I had felt as a flame of fire.[45]

How one probes the internal workings of the mind of the maker, as Dorothy Sayers called it, especially in tandem with a partner, as between *ex*pression and *re*pression has never, admittedly, been an easy matter. Freud's pathography, whether seen (as he did) as the study of an artist through his work or as the study of the work through the artist, has never been judged entirely a success. And architectural history, which no less than intellectual history and biography this study must encompass, has not really ventured down this road. Literary criticism and musicology have, however, and I propose by appealing somewhat from one field to another (an allowable indulgence in a biography of a man proficient in both letters and music) to hazard this uncertain terrain in aid of the 1890s churches soon to be studied here.

CROSS-MEDIA

Consider Richard Taruskin's spirited defense of Peter Ilich Tchaikovsky, whose stature as a composer has been somewhat compromised by the extremes of reaction to him. On the one hand, there are critics who complain of the "hysterical" and "indulgent" character of the Sixth Symphony and of its "melancholy" and "passive" qualities as well, exactly the criticisms Taruskin suggests male heterosexual critics are apt to make of women composers and also of male homosexual composers. On the other hand, critics who argue from a frankly gay perspective equally alarm Taruskin when they analyze the *Pathétique*'s first movement as "a record of anal sex [between Tchaikovsky and Aloysha Sofrano]."[46] Yet that would be a perfect case study of what Keble meant when he wrote about the role of repression and expression in art. All the more so as Tchaikovsky himself seems to have agreed with the view that his art was not unrelated to his sexual life when, in correspondence with Nadezhda von Meck, he asserted that *"music alone"* could *"convey the all-embracing characteristics of the feeling of love."*[47]

This relationship of music (of the Romantic era especially) to love and erotic desire is important to us here because one of the ways we can fill in what, perhaps (to use Keble's term), Ralph Adams Cram's "delicacy" may have led him to repress, is to refer instead to music, about which Cram was more open about his feelings, and which, because of subsequent scholarship, we now can relate to his sexuality, allowing us a clearer view of what Gerard Manley Hopkins would have called Cram's "inscape." Cram's lifelong admiration of the greatest Romantic composer of his youth has already been discussed here sufficiently to allow us to do just that by setting Cram's devotion to Wagner in the context of what we now recognize about the overall meaning and effect of that composer's work, which was tinged with Eros even more than was Tchaikovsky's.

267

Cram was hardly unusual in being besotted by Wagner. Igor Stravinsky thought, for example, that T. S. Eliot found *Tristan*, which he first saw in Boston in 1909, to be "one of the most passionate experiences of his life."[48] No one would argue, either, with Philip Hodson's conclusion that Aubrey Beardsley "perceived the profound sexual tendency of Wagnerian art" and that what Hodson calls "the Yellow Book movement of the 1890s embraced Wagnerism with indecent enthusiasm."[49] Nor would many dispute the view of Eve Kosofsky Sedgwick that though Wagner himself was heterosexually active, he,

> like Nietzsche, crystallized a hypersaturated solution of what were and were about to become homosexual signifiers, set up under the notorious [homosexual] aegis of [King] Ludwig II [of Bavaria]; the Wagnerian operas represented a cultural lodestar for what Max Nordau . . . refers to as "the abnormals"; that tireless taxonomist Krafft-Ebing quotes a homosexual patient who "is an enthusiastic partisan of Richard Wagner, for whom I have remarked a predilection in most of us [sufferers from "contrary sexual feeling"]; I find that this music accords so very much with our nature."[50]

With that in mind, consider Peter Gay's analysis of "the overheated, heavily perfumed eroticism pervading Wagner's works" generally, and especially in the Bayreuth productions Cram himself attended, which created a kind of "Wagner cult" (Boston, led by Isabella Stewart Gardner, was always well represented at Bayreuth). Gay also focuses on *Tristan*, which he finds hardly less explicit in its impressions than others quoted here found Tschaikovsky's *Pathétique*, describing the effect of *Tristan*'s music as

> a long drawn out and reiterated representation of sexual congress . . . its luxuriant themes . . . rising, rising, and those final satiated moments. . . . It evokes the thrilling journey to what the French call the little death, which seals sexual intercourse happily completed.[51]

Nor does he neglect *Parsifal*—the other opera Cram so admired at Bayreuth—referring bluntly to its "erotic religiosity" and concluding that some there were even then prepared publicly "to recognize [in *Parsifal*] a sensual orgy when they saw one, and not too genteel to call it by its right name" (indeed, D. H. Lawrence called *Tannhäuser* "pornographic").[52]

Fundamental to understanding all this is Gay's conclusion that it was another case of mask and signal, that "such eroticism in the nineteenth century masqueraded in high pretensions; the more sensual the work, in fact, the more exalted the rhetoric. . . . Wagnerians, especially the most assiduous devotees, treated Wagner's music as revelation."[53] It was Cram's very word; the reader will recall his hymn to the Wagner-Rossetti revelation in Chapter 1 and his affirmation that "heaven opened for me."[54] Assuredly, Cram falls very much into Gay's category of an "assiduous devotee," suggesting the nature of some at least of the erotic urges Cram expressed in one art if not another. Yet is that likely? Architecture, after all, was Cram's first love.

That said, and no objection being raised to applying to architecture as to music, and to Cram as to Tchaikovsky, Taruskin's truism that "in responsible hands the fact of Tchaikovsky's homosexuality is potentially a viable critical tool,"[55] there remains, however, a considerable problem in applying to the architecture of the period the approach applied to its music.

Can architecture be passive? Indulgent? Hysterical? Melancholy? Some of the well-known architectural productions of Wagner's good King Ludwig might, indeed, properly be called "indulgent," even "hysterical." But when musicologist Susan McClary writes, for example, of finding the "homosexual character" of Franz Schubert's work in the "casual pleasures and encounters in the music," or when Maynard Solomon writes that "desire, of course, is fundamental to nineteenth-century music,"[56] it is hard to transpose those categories to architecture. Is desire fundamental also to nineteenth-century architecture? Are there such things as "casual pleasures and encounters" in buildings? And if there are (Cram's Gothic is full of unexpected vistas around unsuspected corners and such), can we really assign meanings to them of this sort quite so confidently or readily.

Cram himself was by no means adverse to appealing back and forth from music to architecture; writing in 1899, for example:

> How explain the difference in words, how differentiate the right from the wrong? When you hear *Tristan* one night and *Traviata* the next, you are enlightened and become convinced of the gulf that lies between good and evil; but this is not to be demonstrated in words. So with good and bad Gothic.[57]

Henry James once called a character the "keystone" of the family arch, thus "viewing an emotional state through an architectural metaphor."[58] Surely Cram, in likening good Gothic to *Tristan* and bad Gothic to *Traviata*, was viewing architecture through a musical metaphor, though metaphor is somewhat aside from the point here. So also is analogy, though in aid of making such categories more pliable, one can invoke it, as does Camille Paglia:

> House and body have been in analogy since the birth of architecture. . . . The tall, flat-chested Pre-Raphaelite New Woman . . . is a bony Mackintosh chair; tea and sympathy on a Scottish torture rack. Mannerist Art Nouveau['s] . . . whiplash, a sado-masochistic trope, stings the eye.[59]

But something about architecture resists all this.

More plausible, perhaps, are literary categories. Harold Beaver has stressed the fact — one has only to read Proust to agree — that homosexuals, historically, have tended for obvious reasons to be all but "beset by signs . . . hidden meanings, hidden systems . . . the reverse image."[60] And, indeed, in the New England of this era there is a perfect example of this (and a key instance of the way the Boston gay subculture would influence the national culture, in this case the twentieth-century rediscovery of "Americana") in that "riddle" of a house in Gloucester, Massachusetts, as Nancy Curtis and Richard C. Nylander have called Beauport, built by Cram's fellow aesthete and sometime collaborator, Henry Sleeper, the significance of the "maze-like shape" which we have already touched on.[61]

In Cram's own early work, meanwhile, there is surely more than an echo of this theme when Proust's Paris and Cram's Boston seem to coalesce in the Left Bank mansion of Cram's horror story "252 Rue M. de Prince," which the reader will recall was (aside from a single entranceway) invisible from the street exactly as is "the hidden house of Beacon Hill." But there are not, so far as I can see, the architectural equivalents in Cram's work of, for example, the drawers that will not open in Jasper Johns's paintings.

Certainly, the "reverse image" can be found in Cram's work, some of the charm of which, like that of Lutyens, derives from the way Cram occasionally reversed the expected—as, for example, in the masterful Winthrop Road mantelpiece (see 38), which is sunk into the wall rather than projecting outward after the usual manner of a chimneybreast. In Volume Two, examples of similar inversions in the detail of some of his later churches (at Calvary, Americus, Georgia) will be noted. On a larger scale, All Saints', Brookline, does actually reverse All Saints', Ashmont's proportions. Ashmont's wide nave and very narrow aisles, which are also very low, and high clerestory with the principal range of windows becomes in Brookline a narrow nave with wide aisles and a low clerestory with the principal windows in the aisles. But this is all very speculative.

A more promising category is wit, with which Cram's work abounds. Consider, for instance, the irony of the miters invariably carved into Cram's bishop's chairs, which he knew only too well would be occupied equally as invariably by Massachusetts bishops we now forget would not, in the 1890s, have been caught dead in a miter (69). (By way of more provocation, Cram also sometimes incorporated figures of better dressed [i.e., fully vested and mitered] bishops into the carvings around such bishop's chairs as well. Equally, the thurifers with their smoking censers in Cram's reredoses were at least ironic in churches where any appearance of such figures would have caused a near riot; against which joyless Puritanism, by the way, Cram himself was reported on one occasion to have mounted a more lively protest. According to John Nicholas Brown, at a Low Church consecration service of a Cram church at which the architect was present, Cram caused a minor uproar by secreting incense in the hot-air furnace.)[62]

69. Four characteristics of camp — irony, aestheticism (shaping irony), theatricality, and humor —
have been identified by David Bergman. *Above:* All Saints', Ashmont's, episcopal throne is
splendidly theatrical in its flamboyant carving, and aestheticism never shaped irony more truly
than on such thrones, espeically in the motif of the miter, which no Massachusetts Episcopal
bishop would then have worn on or off what *he* called his "bishop's chair." If camp's fourth
characteristic, humor (the blacker the better), seems missing, it is not so in Cram's Our Saviour's,
Middleborough, throne. There the carving of the gridiron on which Saint Laurence was martyred
is surely a High Church-aesthetic riposte to Massachusett's Low Church-Puritan "prelate" of those
days, Bishop William Lawrence.

Wit wears many guises, of course. It was in Cram's time not only evident in
his own work, but, most conspicuously in my view, in that of a contemporary
and rival in 1890s Boston, a leading figure of yet another aesthetic circle of
bachelor designers whom *Town Topics* was forever mincing about — Arthur
Little. Some of his seaside houses on Boston's North Shore of the 1880s and
1890s and his additions to historic Boston-area houses are stunningly witty.
And Little probably was gay.

Then, too, was not Michelangelo in this respect the master? And is not

271

Mannerism's modern progeny "camp"? Now, surely, we are very close, as Hilliard seems to intuit when he writes:

> To the extent that "camp" (in its meaning of "elegantly ostentatious" or "affected display") was a prominent attribute of the homosexual style as it developed in England from the 1890s onwards, it found ample room for expression in the worship and decoration of many Anglo-Catholic churches.[63]

"Homosexual style"! That such an explicit reference should surface in connection with the *decoration* of Anglo-Catholic churches seems, once the shock of the term wears off, hardly startling. Easy to see, and then name (the reader need only leaf through a book such as Peter Anson's *Fashions in Church Furnishings*); to explain homosexual style as Hilliard comes upon it is more difficult.

One way would be to seize on camp and follow that thread. David Bergman has observed that "camp plays with the categories of the classical and the grotesque" and, invoking some names we have heard before here, he cites

> a long line of gay photography that has played with the aesthetic tensions between the classic and the gothic. At the turn of the century, Frederick Rolfe, better known as Baron Corvo, Fred Holland Day, Wilhelm von Pluschow, . . . and perhaps most famous, Wilhelm von Gloeben, recorded beautiful young men in the nude or nearly so.[64]

Is homosexual style connected somehow with erotica? Or with extremes of "style" in the more conventional sense? Is homosexual style in Gothic terms more "Flamboyant" or more "Decorated" in feeling than "Norman" or "Perpendicular"? More curvilinear than rectangular? Was it more or less "homosexual" that Ned Warren's style was so severe? Was it, in the first place, insightful or provocative of Hilliard to identify "affected display," or Anglo-Catholicism, for that matter, with homosexual style? Bishop Lawrence characterized what I have perhaps no less provocatively called the "gay Gothic" of St. Grottlesex as "chaste, strong and uplifting." Is there (as Waugh tells us there is, with young men) *both* a rococo gay taste and a Greek taste? Are both affected? And if both are gay tastes, are both homosexual style?

Perhaps the full context of Waugh's remarks — about his boyhood relationships with J. F. Roxburgh, a famous headmaster, and Francis Crease, a friend of Ned Warren's — will be clarifying. Writes Waugh:

> J. F. did not approve of Mr. Crease. . . . he would not allow boys in his House to go to Mr. Crease's. Mr. Crease, as I have said, was effeminate in appearance and manner; J. F. was markedly virile, but it was he who was the homosexual. . . . Most good schoolmasters — and, I suppose, schoolmistresses also — are homosexual by inclination. . . . J. F.'s passions ran deep. I do not think he ever gave them physical release with any of his pupils, but as distinct from the general, romantic pleasure of association with the young . . . he certainly fell in love with individual boys. . . . [He was especially] ardently attached to a golden-haired Hyacinthus. He gave this boy a motor

cycle from which he was immediately thrown and much disfigured, but J. F.'s love remained constant until the friend's death in early middle age.[65]

Among homosexual men both masculine and feminine modes of behavior (what Waugh calls here "effeminate" and "virile") are, of course, historically discernable. In English history, for example, the evolution since Caroline and Jacobite times, mentioned before as tracked by Eve Sedgwick, is in her view the origin of at least the more reserved and refined version of the effeminate homosexual mode, while on the other hand she concludes it was the nineteenth-century middle-class tradition that yielded what she calls the virile homosexual mode, which she describes as "emphasiz[ing] the virile over the effeminate, the classical over the continental." It tends (though it is probably now the majority gay mode) to be overlooked because it stands out naturally much less from the accepted gender behavior of the overall populace.[66]

Sedgwick cites Lord Alfred Douglas as an example of the first, or effeminate, mode and Edward Carpenter as an example of the second, or virile, mode, noting that "the educated middle-class man looked to classical Sparta and Athens for models of virilizing male models in which the male homosocial institutions (education, political mentorship, brotherhood in arms) and the homosexual seemed to be fully continuous," and that such men "seem to have perceived the exclusion of women from their intimate lives as virilizing them, more than they perceived their choice of a male object as feminizing them." Especially significant for us (since Cram, after all, was not only middle class but artistic) is her conclusion from the published case studies of John Addington Symonds's and Havelock Ellis's *Sexual Inversion* that upper-class gay men disclosed "a far higher incidence of self-described femininity or effeminacy than the professionally or even the artistically employed men."[67]

The contrast—whether put as "the virile over the effeminate, the classical over the continental," or as "more classical than rococo"—must be central to any discussion of "homosexual style." And it is interesting that (as with Ned Warren's attempt to replace medieval madonnas with classical athletes in his mother's house) for both Sedgwick and Waugh artistic and/or architectural style is central to clarification of the meaning of "masculine" and "feminine." Today even more so than a century ago, these words of gender are slippery and controversial to deal with. Still, they are all we have; that and Freud's warning that the adjectives "masculine" and "feminine" really beg all the interesting questions.[68]

THE STRUCTURE OF THIS PASSION IS A TOWER

Readers of Louis Sullivan's writings are often startled by his deeply passionate response to H. H. Richardson's Marshall Field Warehouse in Chicago; "a real man, a manly man . . . an entire male," his biographer quotes him as asserting.[69] But listen to Ralph Adams Cram in connection with Trinity Church in Boston exclaim about Richardson: "Here was a real *man* at last." Nor did he leave it at that, exulting in Trinity's "masculine scale," always "bold, dominating, adventurous," and adding, leaving little doubt of the meaning he gave to masculinity, "there was neither grace nor sensibility [about Trinity] but there was power."[70]

Is it not fascinating that just as both Evelyn Waugh and Eve Sedgwick have recourse to artistic and/or architectural character (classical, rococo, and so on) to define and express in homosexual behavior the categories of masculine and feminine, so Sullivan and Cram quite reverse the thing and have recourse to those categories of masculine and feminine to express and define artistic or architectural character in a particular building? And this ought to be borne in mind by those suspicious of, as it were, sexing architecture, either in whole or in part; whether it is Sullivan or Cram in the case of Richardson or a present-day scholar in the case of Sullivan or Cram — Robert Twombly, for instance, who contends in his insightful biography of Sullivan that the architect's likely homosexuality is supported by evidence of two kinds: "some personal, some architectural." Sullivan's "sexuality informed and is visible in his work," Twombly insists, even though it was "so repressed [Sullivan] may not have known it himself."[71]

This is, of course, to claim more than does Hilliard with "homosexual style." That was interior decoration. Now we have presumably advanced to "architecture." But the question remains: can one see such things in architecture any more than in decoration? It may seem that Twombly sees in Sullivan's ornament, which he calls "almost ejaculatory,"[72] too much. Certainly this is reminiscent of the analysis of Tchaikovsky's *Pathétique* previously referred to. Yet Twombly is surely close to the heart of the matter when he writes that "bonding 'male' structural [underlying] forms to 'female' ornament [meant] that Sullivan [saw] the 'male' rationality of a building's shape [as] provid[ing] the occasion for 'female' embellishment."[73]

So did Cram. Note that all of his descriptions of his and Goodhue's collaboration reserved the masculine and leading role for himself (the building's shape and mass) and assigned the feminine role (its embellishment) to Goodhue, a design dynamic Sullivan encompassed in himself; it is a nice question whether it was with more or less stress than arose between Cram and Goodhue in their partnership.

One can, perhaps see this design dynamic best in four of the earliest of the firm's churches, built in 1892–1894, all in suburban Boston — St. Paul's, Brockton, already discussed in Chapter 3; the Church of the New Jerusalem (later called the Church of the Open Word), Newtonville; Christ Church, Hyde Park;

and All Saints', Brookline — and especially in the original 1890s designs for the towers of these churches, only one of which was built, but the sketches for all of which have survived.

The first of these churches, St. Paul's, Brockton (see *49*), was endowed with a tower design of 1892 whose basic contours are entirely appropriated from All Saints', Ashmont (see *46*). Cram's mass has been ornamented very superficially by Goodhue, who grafted two rather flamboyant and overscaled windows onto its highest stage and topped it all of with a not very plausible flèche; altogether a very awkward performance.[74]

The tower design of 1893 for the Church of the New Jerusalem in Newton-ville (see *102*) is much better. It is still Cram's Ashmont tower, calmer now, but Goodhue's hand is surer than at Brockton, more reserved but more telling. Even better is the tower design for the other village church of 1893, Christ Church, Hyde Park (*70a*), which spreads out behind a corner tower that while chiefly felicitous in its mass and in its balance of volume and void is also appropriately detailed. Cram has adjusted a bit to Goodhue here; his proportions are more elegant. Not, however, that it succeeds; as Ann Miner Daniel has pointed out: "taking its basic shape and arrangement of forms from several towers that Cram had designed, [the Hyde Park tower] loses its force in [Goodhue's] ornamentation of the top stage."[75] But this ornamentation is much less grafted on and arises more from the tower's overall and basic character; one sees the beginnings of the partners' ability to fuse the taste for mass and proportion of one with the taste for detail of the other, stage by stage, as the tower rises, to a kind of crown that at Hyde Park shows how much Cram's severe volumes and noble scale and proportions had to gain from Goodhue's delicacy of line and detail.

The tower of All Saints', Brookline (*70b*), the design of which was begun in 1894, shows this fusion growing into imperceptibility; Goodhue's detail, now molding itself to the mass from which it seems to emerge organically, does not compromise the underlying mass but shapes it. At Brockton, Goodhue grafted ornament onto Cram's tower; at Hyde Park and Newtonville he detailed Cram's towers ever more adroitly and justly; at Brookline he not only detailed the tower, he completed it, making All Saints' tower as much his as Cram's. Goodhue was a very fast learner.

In *Significant Others*, a study of artistic collaboration between personal as well as professional partners, Jasper Johns, for many years the presumed partner in every sense of Robert Rauschenberg, is quoted as analyzing their collaboration as a case of "if you do something, then I do something, then you do something";[76] really quite the most satisfying description of the creative and critical dialogue of many designing partners I have ever run across, not least

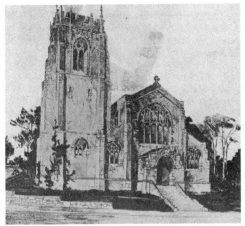

70a, b. Goodhue's perspective of his and Cram's tower designs for two churches in Boston's suburbs: Christ Church, Hyde Park, designed in 1893 (*right*); and All Saints', Brookline, Massachusetts, designed in 1895 (*below*). For their tower at St. Paul's, Brockton, see 49.

because it is so totally straightforward and for that very reason discloses the depths of the psyche such a collaboration reaches. Depths we can only catch at here, but which it is not to be denied are those of the "two lobes" of the same brain or the "one flesh" of the marriage bed. Nor should we (in Gill's words in his biography of Wright) "resist seeking to discern the sexual message implicit in [Cram's and Goodhue's any more than] Sullivan's architecture."[77] So long, that is, as we persevere in the balanced view outlined earlier in this chapter. James Jackson Putnam, who the reader will recall was Boston's leading Freudian of the period, "could perfectly easily accept a bell tower as a phallic symbol," Nathan Hale has written. But for Putnam, Hale added, "that did not exhaust the significance of the tower; it also had, properly, a real religious meaning on another level."[78]

It has, finally, an architectural meaning, and that its architectural meaning is continuous with its psychological and religious meanings is suggested in the response then of some critics; for instance (to jump ahead a bit in aid of the best example), to Cram and Goodhue's culminating work of the decade of the 1900s at West Point, which elicited this pertinent criticism of their work:

> One of the most fascinating things about Cram, Goodhue and Ferguson's work is always the termination of their vertical lines, which, starting *bulky and powerful* at the base, by wonderfully modulated degrees, become *slim and decorative* at their crowns. This treatment has never been exhibited to better success than in the side of the [West Point] headquarters building, where the buttresses, placed in a natural position to brace a high wall, are stepped back from their faces, and terminate in a crown of vertical members. This treatment, *which I believe to be of modern development entirely* and largely due to Cram, Goodhue and Ferguson, is the most excellent manner of decorating the coping wall that comes to mind, since it treats the top of the building as integral with the base [emphases added].[79]

Notice that even in the most formal terms this analysis unconsciously echoes our categories here when Cram's "bulky and powerful" (i.e., masculine) base becomes Goodhue's "slim and decorative" (i.e., feminine) crown.

Meanwhile, it must not be imagined that Cram and Goodhue in any sense, even at the earliest stage of their collaboration, in the 1890s, purchased their artistic unity at the cost of their individuality, as will be evident in a consideration of another of their mid-nineties church designs (alas, in this case, *none* of the church was built): that of St. Paul's, Rochester, New York (71).[80] This is one of the first instances (long before each partner headed a separate office) of Cram's unusual habit of submitting *two* designs to a client (which we saw in his solo work with Wentworth) becoming now, with the advent of Goodhue, a way of accommodating the independence of two very insistent designing partners. As Montgomery Schuyler pointed out, Cram and Goodhue adopted the habit of "submit[ting]

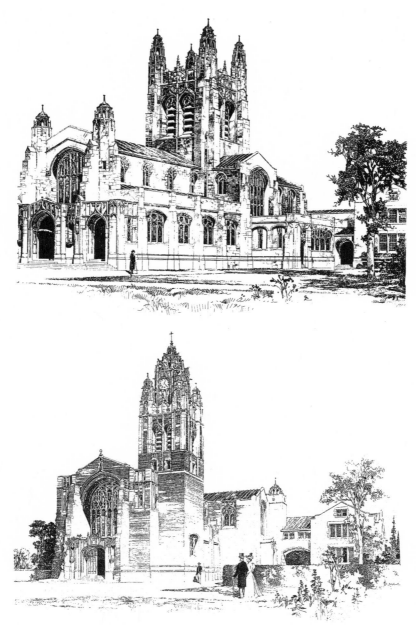

71a, b. Two schemes drawn by Goodhue for the competition to design St. Paul's, Rochester, New York, in 1896. In its breadth of mass and notably structural ornament, the first scheme (*above*) is very representative of Cram's tastes since his first solo church designs of 1889, while the second scheme (*below*) is, in its distinctive profile and unusual ornament, more akin to Goodhue's tastes. That Cram took the lead in the first scheme and Goodhue in the second is also suggested by the inclusion of only the second one in *Bertram Grosvenor Goodhue: Architect and Master of Many Arts*. Neither scheme was built.

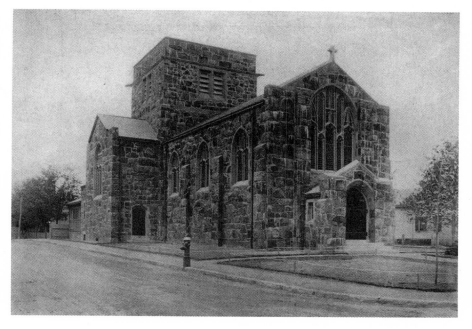

72. Exterior view of Cram and Goodhue's Church of Our Saviour, Middleborough, Massachusetts, Cram and Goodhue's masterful design of 1897.

to [the same] building committee [for the same job] differences of view they found irreconcilable between themselves," a proceeding Schuyler pronounced "probably unexampled, certainly uncommercial and as certainly artistic."[81]

Just as one can see in the fusion and unity of the four towers what needs and skills drew Cram and Goodhue together, so in the two Rochester submissions one can see the factors that boded the two partners' eventual divorce. To continue in the vein we have been pursuing here, a comparison with Sullivan and Wright is instructive. Brendan Gill's sense that Sullivan and Wright on at least one occasion had a "lover's quarrel" is as evident in Cram and Goodhue's opposing designs as it was in some of the letters we discussed earlier. It is hardly surprising. If "what Wright [who was not gay] and Sullivan [who probably was] felt for each other at the time of their first meeting amounted to an infatuation . . . [and] there were powerful sexual overtones in the relationship," how much more one could say of that of Goodhue and Cram?[82]

More than enough, as it turned out, for after only five years of partnership, Cram and Goodhue achieved the first and still not the least of their masterworks, the Church of Our Saviour in the Boston suburb of Middleborough (72).

279

Reminiscent in many respects of Ashmont, Middleborough's random-coursed, burnt-orange, and deep gray Quincy granite exterior is like the December ground in New Hampshire, hard as iron. Architecture does not get more manly than this, the feeling of which is overwhelmingly Richardsonian while not at all Romanesque. And this suggests to me that in trying to understand Middleborough's character we take a tack different from Twombly's, though in aid of the same purpose: one taken to very good point by Richard Mohr, a professor of philosophy at the University of Illinois.

Using *Chest*, a superb photograph of 1986 by Robert Mapplethorpe, Mohr discourses imaginatively and controversially on "the natural rectilinearity [as opposed to curvilinearity] of male chests and male bodies generally," seeing in this a key to understanding Sullivan's description of Richardson's Marshall Field Warehouse, which Mohr quotes as "four-square, . . . a *man* you can look at, . . . a real man, a moral force." Middleborough exactly. Nor is it beside the point (for Middleborough has a crisp, hard-edged, blunt square tower with no spire and no need of one) that, like Richardson's warehouse, in Mohr's words about it, Middleborough "achieves [its] distilled masculinity without appeal in any way to genital sexuality [which is to say] . . . the phallus."[83]

Our Saviour's is, however, by no means only strength and power. It is also, compared with Ashmont, sharper and cleaner; Goodhue's "line" is everywhere evident — not only his detail but now his "line." The masses are still Cram's but now the edges, one could almost say the geometry, are Goodhue's. Notice the molding and waterspouts of the central tower. Doubtless economy denied the partners the fiercely carved gargoyles they craved. But if the joy of Middleborough is in no small measure its severe, square tower of the crisp edges and sharp profile (still very reminiscent of St. John's, Williamstown), it must also be said that the four elegantly plain splayed waterspouts, almost Art Nouveau in feeling, are a truly lyrical outgrowth.

One of the reasons Our Saviour's is such a triumph is that Goodhue and Cram encountered at Middleborough that rare benefaction, a knowing and supportive client. Any architect's best work will arise in such a case. The deep religious unity of the Peabodys and Cram had not a little to do with the genius of All Saints', Ashmont. At All Saints', Brookline, it appears to have been a case of shared artistic tastes with the rector's formidable wife, Julia deWolf Addison. Educated at art schools in England and Italy and author of several art history books, she was a designer of ecclesiastical ornament, particularly of metalwork, mosaic, and illumination, and an incorporator with Cram of Boston's Society of Arts and Crafts. (Not surprisingly, All Saints' has two reredoses richly painted in the medieval style by Mrs. Addison.) At Middleborough both elements coalesced ideally. An Anglo-Catholic religious ideal and a like aesthetic vision were shared by Cram and the parish's rector, William Bayard Hale. Nor did it hurt that Hale was a handsome and winning young man, a bachelor aesthete who was also very much the confidant of Bishop Phillips Brooks. And thereby hangs another tale.

PHILLIPS BROOKS AND THE AESTHETES

C. F. Thwing long ago pointed out that John Henry Newman (far advanced today along the road toward canonization in the Roman Catholic Church) and Phillips Brooks (who already appears in the calendar of saints and heroes of the Episcopal church) were each "a liberal, one for the liberal branch of the [Roman] Catholic Church, and the other for a liberal Protestant [Episcopal] faith." But that is to be two very different kinds of liberal. "Newman is never a modernist," wrote Thwing; "Brooks is a modernist from the beginning."[84] Thus it was only to be expected that Cardinal Newman figured in Ralph Adams Cram's roster of youthful heroes — and that Phillips Brooks did not.[85]

These legendary Victorian prelates may be said to stand for the two great opposing forces in late nineteenth-century Anglo-American Christianity; each may also be said to point to the differing sensibilities emerging here in the matter of "homosexual style"; sensibilities that set off Ned Warren's athletes from the family madonnas, sensibilities that Evelyn Waugh expressed through his varieties of young men ("Greek" or "rococo") and that in more blatant architectural terms I have tried here to signify through, on the one hand, Hilliard's "affected display" of homosexual style in Anglo-Catholic churches, and, on the other, Bishop Lawrence's characterization of the work of New England's foremost Anglo-Catholic designer in the 1890s, Vaughan, as "chaste, strong and uplifting."

Building on nearly contemporaneous work (in 1895, for example, James Rigg, in his *Oxford High Anglicanism*, described Newman as "characteristically feminine,"), Thwing put the comparison thus: Newman, he wrote, possessed a "refined, gentle, said to be half-effeminate diffidence," while "Brooks was direct, forcible";[86] a perfect match, of course, for Brooks's architect at Trinity Church, H. H. Richardson. Note that if Cram was Newman's in the matter of religion he was just as decisively Richardson's in the matter of architecture.[87]

At least one High Churchman, however, did not find Brooks offputting. Arthur Hall, by 1891 the leading figure in the Cowley Fathers in Boston, doubtless startled Cram as much as everyone else when he took a most unexpected position in this respect. Robert Cheney Smith tells us:

One day en route to Nova Scotia Father Hall met Dr. Phillips Brooks. . . . It was the beginning of a warm friendship — and also of difficulties. . . . When [in 1891, Brooks was elected bishop of Massachusetts], Father Hall, . . . although he did not vote for Dr. Brooks, did affix his signature to the endorsement required. . . . Furthermore, from this date on Father Hall publicly and vigorously supported the cause of Phillips Brooks. [Anglo-]Catholic Christians, deeply distressed by Dr. Brooks's marked theological liberalism (some, indeed, thought Brooks an Arian), were scandalized! Soon letters began plying the Atlantic Ocean.[88]

Hall was summoned back to England in consequence of this furor in 1891 and relieved of his position by his distressed colleagues as head of the Cowley Fathers' American province. Thus Cram, within three years of his conversion, lost at one stroke the man under whose instruction he had become an Anglican as well as his chief sponsor in that undertaking, for Father Brent, though he stayed in Boston, left the community over it. The Sunday after Hall's departure there were at High Mass at St. John's, Bowdoin Street — assuming Vaughan and Cram were there — only six people!

Why Hall, the monastic Oxonian High Churchman, was so drawn to the Boston modernist Low Church bishop is best left to the future biographers of both men. Of course, Hall was equally a great friend of Isabella Stewart Gardner's, who always responded promptly to Hall's pleas for money for this or that cause and who is known also to have invited Hall to spend his summer vacations with her at her country estate. (A book of Hall's teachings is dedicated to her.)[89] Though he was Boston's foremost High Churchman, Hall did not avoid controversial relationships with those he grew to trust, no more in the case of Gardner than in that of Brooks — the former being, of course, more scandalous to the populace as a whole than the latter, who scandalized only Anglo-Catholics.

There were links between Gardner and Brooks through Groton School; Brooks, a most powerful influence on headmaster Endicott Peabody, was chairman of the board of trustees of the school of which William Amory Gardner had been a cofounder. And Father Hall, so important at St. Paul's School, was not unknown at Groton either; the reader will recall that it was Hall who suggested in a sermon of 1893 the motto Peabody adopted for Groton School — which Ralph Adams Cram, in turn, incorporated into the coat of arms he designed for Groton.[90]

Groton thus arises here yet again and not as might seem in any contrived or superficial way. An even closer scrutiny, for instance, discloses that before asking Amory Gardner's help in founding the school, Peabody had asked the same help of Joseph Gardner (whose affair with Logan Pearsall Smith led to Gardner's suicide), help that Joseph refused on the grounds of being too "nervous"[91] — exactly the same code word, the meaning of which has been explained, used of

Bishop Brooks himself, who was described by Edward Wagenknecht as being, though "in excellent health" generally, also of "highly nervous constitution." (Of course, as befitted the more masculine of our two prelates, no tales of the sort already floated here about Newman are extant about Brooks — who was evidently not given to appearing at Boston dinner parties in drag.) But Brooks nonetheless occasioned his share of gossip. Certainly, Wagenknecht found it necessary to observe of Brooks that his "attitude toward women and marriage [was] something of a puzzle. . . . [He was] very much a man's man [yet more code words] and some thought him indifferent to women. . . . There were even those who thought Brooks greatest as a preacher to men, especially to young men." Perhaps, Wagenknecht concluded, "too much of a mystery has been made of the matter."[92] Indeed!

It is controversial of me to conclude that perhaps the most forceful Christian preacher of his era in America was probably gay, but that conclusion proceeds naturally from our adherence here to the rule that the best and most fundamental documentation for sexual orientation, as we should now call it, is to be found in a person's demonstrable same-sex feelings (whether known to have been genitally expressed or not) as well as, in some measure, the extent to which similar feelings were thereby aroused in others who (again, whether genitally expressed or not) reciprocated them. Certainly the homoerotic aspects of his appeal are clear; Brooks excited men — so much so that one result was the Phillips Brooks House at Harvard.[93] And one such man was William Bayard Hale, Cram's client in Middleborough, the founding rector of Our Saviour's, whom Cram might have known already from the Christian Socialist Church of the Carpenter, for the journal of which Hale wrote, or from the Cambridge Episcopal Theological School, where Cram lectured on church architecture at about the time Hale was a student there.

Like Arthur Hall, Hale was another aesthete High Churchman oddly drawn to his charismatic Low Church bishop. Hale's relationship with Brooks emerges in an extraordinary peroration he preached in 1893 after Brooks's sudden death. Hale recounted how ardently he had watched Brooks's face

hundreds of times . . . when the eyes of great assemblies were upon it, and then when we two were alone. I have seen it in all sorts of lights and in the darkness, always so gentle, so kind, so sweet. . . . That handclasp of his, I can feel it now. . . . And then the close bond of . . . his bishopric. I suppose there can be no more intimate, no more sacred, relationship than that between two men, one of whom takes his life and brings it to the other and gives it to him in trust for God and humanity, and the other of whom accepts the trust. . . . When that other is Phillips Brooks, I think you cannot imagine the trust and love which the young man's heart pours out. . . . I cannot think that in all this sorrow there is a loss like mine.

283

Citing a most specific instance of that intimacy, the fact that Brooks's "first act as bishop of this diocese was to lay his hand on [Hale's] head" in ordination, the rector of Middleborough added the altogether remarkable observation that

> among us, who in these days have grown so sadly wise, who have ceased to be artists, and have become scientists pursuing a remorseless, morbid scrutiny into the dark corners of the human heart, and brooding over the presence of disorder — among us [Phillips Brooks] walked protesting against despair.[94]

Controversy is not far off here. Nor Freud's tread.

Hale was, in fact, evidently in a position to say these things. He had taken up the rectorship of Middleborough in 1892 at Brooks's earnest request. Though only twenty-three, Hale already held several degrees. And as it turned out, Hale's career in the Episcopal church survived the death of his beloved bishop by only eight years. Noted as a "contributor of radical magazine articles to *The Arena*," Hale went on to become an editor and foreign correspondent for the *New York Times*, of such stature that he was once accorded a personal interview with Kaiser Wilhelm II; while in the field of diplomacy he also became a trusted friend of and adviser to Woodrow Wilson, whose biographer Hale was, as well as the President's personal representative in Mexico. A Germanophile, Hale was (during the period of American neutrality in World War I) virtually the director of the German propaganda service in the United States.[95]

In the mid-nineties, however, when Cram first met Hale, all this could scarcely have been imagined. Nor Hale's marriages, either — the first, in 1899, lasted scarcely six months — nor his subsequent divorce and remarriage abroad, nor the fact that Hale would ultimately be defrocked and leave the priesthood. (There is something very reminiscent of Theodore Dwight and his brief reign at the Boston Public Library about William Bayard Hale.) The author of Hale's entry in the *Dictionary of American Biography* referred pointedly only to Hale's "engaging presence" and (in yet another bevy of code words) to the "handsome young rector's high-strung temperament."[96] Never mind. High-strung, nervous people like Hale and Cram and Goodhue appear to be well suited to build splendid churches. Only six years younger than Cram, Hale was exactly Goodhue's age. Of old American stock like both Goodhue and Cram, Hale was an officer of the Sons of the American Revolution and a deputy governor of the Society of Colonial Wars; also like Cram, he was of German ancestry and (as was in the 1890s quite the norm) very much as well the Anglophile; good-looking, unmarried at the time, of aesthetic tastes, a High Churchman, scholarly, interested in Gothic architecture — the ideal client for an architect like Cram, who complained in a letter to another churchman in the 1890s that "the majority of the clergy are half-hearted artistically [and tend to] . . . demand work that expresses their jejune predilections."[97] 'Twas ever thus. But one doubts that Cram made such complaints about Father Hale.

The result at Middleborough is a wonderful church. And strikingly High Church for so low a diocese. At a time when, beyond the Church of the Advent and St. John's on Beacon Hill, a Solemn High Mass was unheard of in the Episcopal Diocese of Massachusetts, it was surely this time more a case of war than of wit that virtually the entire cast of characters for such a liturgical extravaganza (as it must then have seemed) was arrayed atop the poppy heads of the choir stall ends at Middleborough. Exquisitely carved in oak, according to Goodhue's sketches, this assemblage includes a fully vested priest, deacon, and subdeacon, a crucifer, cantor, and organist, and even a thurifer with censor in hand, any one of which in the flesh, as has been noted (outside the two Beacon Hill churches, where alone the bishop tolerated such things), would have been a news report the next morning in the *Boston Transcript*. Worse yet, one of these carved figures is carrying a reliquary, the appearance of which in *any* Episcopal parish in Massachusetts in that era certainly would have caused official apoplexy.

Our Saviour's also boasts an unusual conjunction of the antique (for example, the clergy stalls have medieval "misereres" on the bottoms of the seats, which, when the seats are folded back, support clerical posteriors fatigued by standing too long) and the modern, apparent in the ten carved grotesques in modern garb among the canopy work of the high altar reredos. By local tradition these depict the faces of the designers and carvers of the reredos. Certainly they all differ in physiognomy, are quite naturalistic, and obviously portray contemporary persons, for such things as a slouch hat are visible on one, a goatee (Bertram's?) on another, and, just as clearly, on yet another, spectacles (Ralph's?). More serious, perhaps, are the carved devils lurking in odd corners of the reredos alongside the saints. Still, amid the war there *is* wit, appropriately pointed. The reader will recall our discussion under All Saints', Ashmont, in the caption of figure 69, of the four elements of camp and of the gridiron here above the throne that is assuredly a rebus for the name of the bishop who succeeded Phillips Brooks to the see of Massachusetts, William Lawrence, no friend to High Churchmen.

Anglophile touches also abound, from the roses and thistles of England and Scotland carved above the sedilia to the altar's stone mensa from Shakespeare's parish church in Stratford-on-Avon. The aesthetic sensibility is everywhere, especially in the superb panel in oil of an angel (by George Hallowell, of whom more later) on the choir's north wall; and a fine architectural sensibility, too: there are, for once, cathedral chairs that Cram only rarely convinced a client to prefer to pews (which, of course, by obscuring the junction of piers and pave-

73. Exterior view of the first of a princely series of commissions from the Brown family of Rhode Island: Cram and Goodhue's Emmanuel Church, Newport, designed in 1900.

ment, ruin any church interior so endowed). But Hale doubtless agreed with Cram that pews were a vulgar Americanism.

Being a good preacher, Hale would have had a special concern for sight lines and may thus very well have proposed (as he wrote) the church's unusual plan, from which Cram contrived Middleborough's quite original profile. There are no arcades (to obscure altar or pulpit) and in consequence no aisles; thus rather an unusual Gothic parish church elevation results: the nave walls are very high, the principal range of windows being not quite high enough to suggest a clerestory, yet too high to suggest aisle windows. And thereby Cram nicely solved the problem of how to design a Gothic church that dispensed with aisles, arcade, and clerestory — without losing the requisite mass and weight (and dignity) that was so sadly lacking in most Victorian churches, whose immense roofs plunged down past a parade of porthole-like dormers (attempting to serve as a clerestory) to crush the churches' low walls almost claustrophobically.

Indeed, Our Saviour's affords an excellent comparison with one such Victorian church, strikingly reminiscent of a Rotch and Tilden design that Cram worked on about a decade earlier, around 1886. Cram had loathed this design (the reader will recall the Church of the Holy Spirit in the Boston suburb of Mattapan) and called its twin "an example of vicious design."[98] In both, spreading out around a huge, overweight tower, the church's steep roofs drop precipitously down to squat side walls. At Middleborough, on the other hand, the tower is a crisp, sheer, flat cube of severe mien, plain of parapet and with hardly any detail at all, carried (the roofs are unobtrusively flat) on all sides by very high walls of great severity, articulated only by very shallow, planar pier buttresses, altogether very taut and compact. Thus the fundamental change in the appearance of the American church, first broached in Cram and Wentworth's St. John's, Williamstown, design and followed up so brilliantly in Cram's first church, All Saints', Ashmont, was at Middleborough carried forward to new distinction by these insistent young men, upon whose mid-nineties' design collaboration we are focusing here.

In aid of this focus, one more of Cram and Goodhue's New England parish churches of the 1892–1900 period needs to be considered at this point (though it is to jump forward a bit) — Emmanuel Church, Newport (73), which marks Cram's first contact with the historic Brown family of Rhode Island.

How Cram and Goodhue made this important connection — for the Brown family (as we will see in Volume Two) was to be the most princely of all Cram's patrons and John Nicholas Brown the younger a prodigious stimulator of Cram's genius — is not known. But probably it was through Daniel Berkeley Updike, whose Bohemian life in Cram and Goodhue's circle was apparently extended as well to Harold Brown, brother of John Nicholas Brown Sr. Such at least one is entitled to infer from the coded references of Updike's biographer, George Winship, who pointed out that Updike—distinctly effeminate—revealed a "sensitive unfitness for the vigorous comradeship of school-fellows on the playing fields" and that it had early been noticed that Updike and Brown "were much alike and not like other boys."[99] Updike certainly introduced Ogden Codman to Harold Brown and entertained both at his country house, and Codman's correspondence with Updike documents both that Updike was acquainted by 1896 with Harold's brother, John Nicholas Brown Sr., and that Cram was known in this milieu.[100] Indeed, it would have been very odd if Updike had *not* introduced both Cram and Goodhue. Updike shared with Harold Brown and Cram an ardent Anglo-Catholicism and with both Cram and Goodhue no less ardent an interest in its church art. In fact, in Cram's memoirs (though in his usual maddeningly vague way he says nothing of how they met) he recalled doing ecclesiastical work for John Nicholas Brown Sr., before his marriage.[101]

Moreover, the distinguished work of art one would expect of such a mutual acquaintance of Cram, Goodhue, Updike, and Harold Brown—the justly celebrated *Altar Book* (of which more later)—duly appeared in 1896. Of this, more in the next chapter. Meanwhile it was for John Nicholas Brown's widow, Natalie Bayard Dresser Brown, that Cram and Goodhue began to design Emmanuel Church, Newport, in 1900, the records of which so much illuminate their partnership.

THE MAN OF TASTE

Henry Adams (Cram's odd relationship with whom must await Volume Two), in his famous distinction between the Dynamo and the Virgin, between force and taste,[102] can hardly be understood to have meant anything other than masculine and feminine. Equally, Judith Fryer has pointed out in *Felicitous Space* that even "the distinction [Mario] Praz made between exterior and interior is a cultural distinction between male and female."[103] And if this distinction seems pertinent here to Cram and Goodhue, so did it seem to critics then.

"In the austere quality of his mind and the logical enterprise of his pencil," Cram's gifts were as like to Charles McKim's, wrote Charles Maginnis, an ardent admirer of Goodhue particularly, as was the "flamboyance" of Goodhue's skills to that of Stanford White.[104] Similarly, Thomas Tallmadge, who thought enough of Goodhue to wax eloquent about the way Goodhue's "fanatic devotion to beauty would make him brother soul to that seraphic traveler in the realms of gold [Keats]," called Goodhue, famous for his exquisite drawings, "the darling of the draughting-room," concluding that the firm's work "show[ed] the perfect unity of the austerity of Cram and the exuberance of Goodhue."[105]

For "force," "exterior," "austere," and "logical," read "masculine"; equally, for "taste," "interior," "flamboyance," and "exuberance," read "feminine." Whatever Goodhue's view, then or later, even his keenest admirers seem to have agreed with Cram's view: that it was Cram who dealt with "mass, proportion, composition, and articulation and . . . had also the faculty of planning, [and] . . . generally blocked out all our designs at quarter-scale," while Goodhue did the "decorative detail . . . to the completion of the work," and that later, when Goodhue had learned "to see problems more in the large, as consistent and unified conceptions, where detail was *only* a detail," he took "one project subject to [Cram's] advice and consent in plan and composition [and Cram] another, up to the point where [Goodhue] applied all the decorative detail, where also [Cram] advised and approved."[106] It was a very masculine-sounding Cram that led and then collaborated with a very feminine-sounding Goodhue. Nor was it an unusual division of labor in the sense that any inquiry will discover that typically in major firms up to the Depression there was always (sometimes heading a whole department) "the man of taste,"[107] i.e., the decorator, responsible for detail and particularly interiors. That Goodhue was in the 1890s Cram's "man of taste" is well documented in the surviving correspondence about Emmanuel Church.

Emmanuel itself is an excellent example of Cram's spare aesthetic, a fact Ann Miner Daniel fixes upon at once:

> As was Cram's characteristic tendency, ornamentation, when used at all, was carefully directed to specific parts of the building. . . . [An] example is seen in the thin pilasters which rise from the top of the tower buttress to the top of the tower parapet. . . . Rigorously controlled ornamentation that was used to strengthen the mass of the building was a characteristic of the strongest early designs.[108]

On the other hand, Emmanuel's chancel, with its woodwork by Irving and Casson, stained glass by Harry Goodhue, and superb wall paintings by Robert Wade (the only chancel where Cram and Goodhue, who had wanted such decoration at Ashmont, finally talked a client into going, as it were, the whole way), is very richly and imaginatively detailed in Goodhue's best manner. The extant correspondence tells the expected tale. Having been led from chancel carving that would cost about $650 to work expected to cost $4,000, the donor bridled (as who would not) when confronted with estimates that finally came in at nearly $8,000. A handwritten note from Cram made such amends as he could and explains for us a good deal:

> The whole trouble lies here—or largely here—that one man [i.e., Cram] gave you the approximate figure of $4000 while another man [i.e., Goodhue] made the designs. Mr. Goodhue is so thoroughly a genius in this particular direction that he is

neither "to bind nor to hold" when inspiration strikes him. When I talked with you I had something very simple, almost severe, in my mind, but I was utterly unable to instill this idea into him and the result was that his pencil ran away with him.[109]

Another contretemps arose soon enough, and this time it was Goodhue who made the explanations, writing to Natalie Brown to say that "after talking the matter over with Mr. Cram we decided that [such and such an] arrangement would be quite impossible," involving a stall so placed that "it would be very awkward for the rector to have to keep moving back and forth from his seat to his kneeling desk." Cram, it will be observed, is the planner, Goodhue the detailer. Admitted Goodhue: "at the time [I] talked with you, [I] didn't consider this very particularly."[110] One can almost hear the two partners arguing.

Notice that there is in this private correspondence, as in Cram's public explanations, the same masculine-feminine distinction behind the scenes that critics like Maginnis and Tallmadge, who if anything admired Goodhue more than Cram, saw in the work *itself*. Yet Goodhue was a decorator. So, for a while, was Cram. What else does one call a man who, as he himself put it, made his living "helping kind ladies with other designs for 'such decorating and furnishing' as they might need"?[111] But (Stanford White notwithstanding) do not fail to note the self-ridicule in Cram's choice of words, not unrelated to why several of the first decorators (including Ogden Codman) were repeatedly rejected by architects' professional societies. Indeed, one way of explaining the differing architectural sensibilities emerging here is to note that they reflect Sedgwick's categories of the virile and effeminate homosexual modes; Hilliard's discussion of the "affected display" of homosexual style arises in connection with *interior decoration* and by extension to the practitioners thereof; and Bishop Lawrence's "chaste, strong and uplifting" has more to do with the building as a whole, with structure as opposed to detail: that is, with the architect.

How deeply ingrained in us are these polarities can be seen in a contemporary example, Edmund White's *States of Desire: Travels in Gay America*, where White comments on two historical examples of "gay taste" of interest to us here, Decadence and camp, and describes the former in terms uncannily pertinent to our discussion: "Decadence, attracting such figures as Oscar Wilde . . . was a movement characterized by exquisitely rendered surfaces, a concentration on detail rather than overall structure."[112]

These could almost be Cram's words, about interior decoration generally and the "man of taste" particularly — and about Goodhue most particularly and most condescendingly, as when in his memoirs Cram extols Goodhue as a genius of ornament and detail in one chapter and in another, hymning the importance of mass and composition, assures his readers that "detail and ornament were a minor factor in architectural design." Mask and signal again.

Similarly, Cram in one place will sing Goodhue's praises for his stunning drawings, then write elsewhere that "ability to draw [does] not necessarily mean anything so far as the practice of architecture [is] concerned."[113] (He was defending himself, of course; but he was also defending his convictions.)

The origins of the mind-set evident here reach back to ancient times. It was Vitruvius, in the only architectural treatise of its kind to have come down to us from antiquity, who defined the severe and stately Doric order as masculine (exemplifying "the proportion, strength, and grace of a man's body,") and the elegantly detailed Corinthian as feminine, exemplifying "the slight figure of a girl." In his *Classical Language of Architecture* Sir John Summerson accepted the distinction, with only the footnote that "the Ionic in between [represented] something rather unsexed — an ageing scholar or a calm and gentle matron." Moreover, one knows what Summerson meant when he wrote in connection with post-Renaissance English work of the "toughness" of the Tuscan and of the "soldierly bearing" of the Doric. One even knows what Serlio meant when he counseled that the Ionic order should be used in churches dedicated to men of learning and matrons; the Corinthian in churches dedicated to virgins; and the Doric in those dedicated to the great extroverted and militant (of course, male) saints such as Saint Peter, for example, or Saint Paul.[114]

One knows, too, what Sullivan meant about Richardson, and what Cram meant, and not only about Richardson either; when Cram wrote, for example, in 1899, of "the masterful, manly, fearless Gothic of the middle ages,"[115] he might have been describing his own modern Gothic. Think of the Middleborough tower.

WHITE BUILDINGS ANSWER DAY

We have come very far indeed from the "affected display" of Hilliard's "homosexual style," having seen in the 1890s Cram and Goodhue churches, from Ashmont to Newport, another and very different "homosexual style," if style it be. It is one we have, I think, fairly associated with what Vitruvius called the Doric. Notice the Platonic resonance of the phrase "the proportion, strength and grace of a man's body" unmistakably akin to the definition I have fixed on here for "gay Gothic": "chaste, strong and uplifting." Equally so is Cram's own definition of Gothic itself: "masterful, manly, fearless."

To test Cram, moreover, against these 1890s churches of his and Goodhue's is to see clearly that both the man and his work are consistent, each with each other. The masculine and the feminine were in Cram himself, quite apart from the combination with Goodhue, delicately balanced. (Within Cram it was a dialogue, within Goodhue it was often a quarrel.) Cram's "Doric" taste was not just an expression of his more masculine sensibility as against Goodhue's (in the 1890s) more feminine sensibility. Cram's Doric taste, the reflection of a more ancient homosexual style, if you will, than that noticed by David Hilliard, marked the place on the continuum where the two sensibilities were cross-fertilized. Thus does Cram's work invariably disclose "that quality of emotionality which is the earmark of erotic involvement even though no overt sexual acts or even conscious sexual impulses are present."[116]

That emotionality could be strident. More often it was justly passionate; recall that Cram was "emotionally untrammeled," in Rose Nichols's words. So much so that one might say of Cram's overall work of the nineties in relation to its era what Robert Martin has said of Santayana's:

> to the soft dreaminess of the nineties he opposed a toughness of mind that was perhaps necessary, [Santayana having, after all, transformed his sexuality into] an aesthetic of restraint which is expressed as an attempt to provide a classic hardness of line and clarity of vision . . . [creating] . . . an art of simplicity and rigor.[117]

Cram's churches exactly — which, not surprisingly, Santayana admired. What Cram *was* (what he wasn't he took care to secure from Goodhue) is evident in what he built, which, in turn, expresses his values very well.

Today, when the effeminate homosexual type has for so long all but defined homosexuality in the overall heterosexual context, as opposed to the virile or manly type, this may surprise. But Cram's homosexual style reflected the Platonic tradition we have discussed here and was quite a different thing, its character reflecting the fact that anciently it centered on martial valor. As David Cohen has observed of classical Thebes:

> In a world where all male citizens were warriors . . . and where pederastic relations between older and younger men represented a culturally privileged form of homosexuality, . . . such relations in military affairs inevitably arose. . . . Spartans also practiced pederasty, [but] they idealized it, . . . transform[ing] it into a chaste, educational and inspirational experience that promoted martial valor. . . . The indomitable valor of Spartan armies was regarded with awe and fear in classical Greece. It was the Thebans, however, who crushed the Spartan army at the battle of Leuctra, apparently led by an elite force of 300 warriors constituted of pederastic pairs of youths and their lovers.[118]

To our modern ears Thebes' triumph is perhaps more easily accepted than would Sparta's have been, but (with the almost solitary exception of some of Mary Renault's work) the whole idea of a "culturally privileged form of homosexuality" associated with martial valor is so foreign to us today that it is hard to credit. There has been really only one influential contemporary reflection, in the controversial work of Camille Paglia, who insists not only that "male aggression and lust are the energizing factors in culture," but that it is "male homosexuals of every social class [who] have preserved the cult of the masculine, which will therefore never lose its aesthetic legitimacy." Though she discourses elsewhere on the English epicene and camp homosexual style, Paglia is describing in these remarks Ralph Adams Cram's style.[119]

This is certainly not to deny the importance of Cram's feminine side. Even Edward Carpenter, whom Sedgwick cites as an exemplar of the virile gay mode,[120] was clear (in an observation obviously pertinent to Cram) that it was, indeed, "the dual nature and swift and constant interaction between [the homosexual's] masculine and feminine elements . . . [that made] it easy or natural for [him] to become an artist." However, wrote Carpenter, "finding himself *different* from the great majority, sought after by some and despised by others, [the homosexual] was forced to think. His mind turned inward on himself would be forced to tackle the problems of his own nature, and afterwards the problem of the world and of outer nature. He would become one of the first thinkers, dreamers, discoverers."[121]

To me, thinking of David Bergman's view that "the creative process is directly related to specific psychic conditions . . . which propel the artist into the creative act,"[122] it does seem reasonable to assert that, no less than Tchaikovsky in music or Santayana in poetry or Warren in sculpture collecting, Cram in architecture spoke the language not only of religion and of art but of Eros. To think otherwise is to be content only with the surface of things. We have to do here in the deepest sense with what Susan Sontag has called the "erotics of art."[123] And with what Plato called the desire and pursuit of the whole.

What was it Keats opined about the imagination? It "may be compared," he mused, "to Adam's dream — he awoke and found it truth."[124] So, too, perhaps Hart Crane, whose words catch for me so much of the resonance of Ralph Adams Cram and Bertram Grosvenor Goodhue's partnership:

> Look steadily — how the wind feasts and spins
> The brain's disk shivered against lust. Then watch
> While darkness, like an ape's face, falls away
> And gradually white buildings answer day.[125]

8

WHITE ROSE, PURPLE ROSE

However forcefully a man develops and seems to leap from one contradiction to the next, close observation will reveal the *dovetailing*. . . . This is the task of the biographer: he must think about the life in question on the principle that nature never jumps.

— Friedrich Nietzsche, *Menschliches, Allzumenschliches*

If there's any subject in which you're content with the second rate, then it isn't your subject.

— Dorothy Sayers, *Gaudy Night*

74. The chapel at the end of the Long Gallery at the Isabella Stuart Gardner Museum in 1904.

"THEY LAID Jesse James in his grave and Dante Gabriel Rossetti died imme- diately. Then Charles Darwin was deplored and then, on April 27, 1886, Louisa May Alcott hurried to write in her journal: 'Mr. Emerson died at 9 p.m. sud- denly. Our best and greatest American gone.'"[1] So begins *The Mauve Decade*, that strange but rather brilliant record of the fin-de-siècle by Thomas Beer. Why *was* the Empress of Russia's celebrated "mauve boudoir" the same color as one of Ralph Adams Cram's favorite ties? All one can say is that Beer's juxtaposi- tions are no odder on a transatlantic cultural stage than are those of Boston's own Bohemia.

Not the least strange of these—and altogether characteristic of Pinckney Street—was that at its midpoint, halfway up the steep slope, where Louisburg Square opens out into the hill's more aristocratic quarter, there should have been at Bohemia's heart what else, for heaven's sake, but a convent, that of the Anglican Sisters of St. Margaret, its chapel the design of Pinckney Street's senior aesthete, Henry Vaughan. Among its significant sources of support was the cre- ation (by the nuns and their students in the St. Margaret's School of Embroidery) of textiles, mostly for the adornment of churches also designed by Vaughan and, increasingly, by Vaughan's chief disciple, Ralph Adams Cram, and his partner, Bertram Goodhue. Their architectural careers, recall, were given a critical leg up at Ashmont by the Peabodys, who had probably their first experience of Anglo- Catholicism at Boston's Children's Hospital, the staffing of which was the good work the nuns of St. Margaret had come from England to take up in the first place. Juxtapositions indeed.

Yet as the sisters doubtless saw it (perhaps because the order's founder, John Mason Neale, had been a distinguished authority on church art), art was scarcely less a good work than nursing, as their embroidery school acknowl- edged. Thus Vaughan's advent in the Puritan capital ought to be seen as the artistic side of an overall Anglo-Catholic thrust into New England, the educa- tional aspect of which is evident in the advent of the Cowley Fathers in Boston (where they would be close to Harvard in the same way Cowley in England was close to Oxford), and the medical and charitable aspects of which are discern- ible in the St. Margaret's sisters' response to the call from Children's Hospital. For all these Anglo-Catholics religion had important educational and charitable aspects; equally important was the artistic one. Art and religion, on both sides of the Atlantic, kept in these circles very close company.

Thus it is probably not incongruous that there was nothing at all amateur about the St. Margaret's School of Embroidery, which in 1897 became a founding member of Boston's Society of Arts and Crafts,[2] one of the cluster of societies and clubs through which in the 1890s Cram and Goodhue made their mark in the larger world.

ARTS AND CRAFTS

The founding members of this society, the result of the historic first Arts and Crafts exhibition ever held in America (in 1897; 75), included people drawn from a great many of the circles we have traced in and around and through Cram since his arrival in Boston in 1881, such as Annie Fields's and Sarah Orne Jewett's friend the stained-glass designer Sarah Whitman; Pinckney Street's Daniel Berkeley Updike; Sam Warren, Ned Warren's brother and the president of the trustees of the art museum; Joseph Lindon Smith, Theodore Dwight's and Isabella Gardner's dear friend; and, as the society's first president, the presiding elder of the era, Charles Eliot Norton. Indeed, perhaps the only circle conspicuously absent was that of Cram's old masters, Rotch and Tilden, and explaining the probable reason for this, while carrying our story forward into the purposes of the Society of Arts and Crafts, will enable us (now that we have sufficient threads in our hands) to tie up the important loose end of why Rotch and Cram seemed to do so little for each other and went, as we have seen, so completely their different ways.

Both partners of the firm of Rotch and Tilden were protégés of William Ware,[3] and having hired Cram at Ware's behest, they were admitting Cram into a milieu where he had arrived pretty well proposed. To be sure, Cram lacked Rotch's family wealth and social standing, but that had not hindered Rotch's partner (Tilden was also the son of a rural New Hampshire Unitarian minister). And although Arthur Rotch does not seem to have socialized with Cram, despite being only nine years older and very much the bachelor (a member of both the Papyrus and the Tavern,[4] he married late, at forty-two, and died childless), Cram nonetheless made it plain that there was no personal animosity.[5] It thus makes sense to consider whether or not there might have been some professional discord, which Cram somewhat hinted at when he noted in his later years his dislike of the too-Gallic quality of Rotch's work.[6]

Trained at the Ecole des Beaux-Arts, Rotch was, in fact, a leader of that small elite of Boston designers thus educated and a leading proponent in Boston of the French academic school of architectural education.[7] And it is not perhaps un-

75. Goodhue's principal decorative motif for the catalogue of the first exhibition in America of the Society of Arts and Crafts, 1897, in Boston.

duly Freudian to conjecture that Cram's later and well-known opposition to the Beaux-Arts type of graduate training was not unrelated to his contact with Rotch, whose rather Francophile Architectural Association, for example, Cram seems to have avoided. Yet when it was reconstituted as the more Anglophile Boston Architectural Club, Cram's footprints were suddenly everywhere. Certainly Cram and Wentworth early identified with the club,[8] exhibiting there in 1891. In fact, by the turn of the century, the club's Beacon Hill house had a great hall of which Margaret Henderson Floyd has speculated that Cram or Clipston Sturgis might well have been the designer.[9] When one notes that the hall was on the ground floor of a building the upper part of which was "rehabilitated into studios and offices," this becomes even likelier, for echoes certainly reverberate here from Cram and Wentworth's Grundmann Studios of 1891.

Note also the reappearance of Clipston Sturgis's name here. The man who helped Cram secure his first church job, the Advent credence, was one of the organizers of the new Boston Architectural Club, a great lover of *English* church art in general (in which he designed very well indeed), and also very much a High Churchman, closely associated with the Sisters of St. Margaret and, in fact, an authority on ecclesiastical needlework. Sturgis was also a founder of Boston's Society of Arts and Crafts. His English banner was as conspicuous as Rotch's Gallic one had been. And Cram would have had no difficulty picking sides. At the Arts and Crafts Society as at the Architectural Club, Cram would noticeably thrive in a milieu that (to tie up the loose end) had little sympathy with Francophile and Low Church figures like Rotch and (to carry our tale forward) much more with Anglophile High Churchmen like Sturgis.

The Arts and Crafts Society, moreover, the happy outcome of that 1897 Arts and Crafts exhibition (held in one of Cram's halls at the Grundmann), was so tremendous a success, writes Beverly Brandt, that it "initiated a movement which spread throughout the United States" and looked always to Boston's society — and charter members like Cram and Goodhue — for leadership.[10]

TRANSATLANTIC GIFTS

One senses again, in this domain of the Arts and Crafts as elsewhere, the influence on Cram of Vaughan, who in his years as Bodley's head draftsman, had absorbed wholeheartedly his master's Arts and Crafts philosophy of total, overall decorative harmony in architecture, a philosophy Cram shared. One also sees just as clearly a characteristic way in which Cram parted company from Vaughan. The older man insisted on importing, whenever possible, traditional Gothic Revival stained glass, by Clayton and Bell and Charles Eamer Kempe, whose American representative Vaughan was. However, as Peter Cormack has pointed out, "Kempe, Clayton, and Bell [and others] scarcely strayed beyond historicism [and] in the 1890s their supremacy was challenged by an emerging new approach, one which aimed for the spirit of medieval work and respected its traditions without copying its precise forms."[11]

Cram, not surprisingly, immediately allied himself with the newer British school, the American prospects of which were much encouraged by the Boston Society of Arts and Crafts' 1897 exhibition, which included the work of both William Morris and C. F. A. Voysey,[12] and by visits to Boston in the 1890s by both Walter Crane and C. R. Ashbee. Both were impressed: Ashbee noted later that in America "craftsmen actually work for and with the architect,"[13] while Crane praised Goodhue's graphic work particularly.

Both Ashbee and Crane met and came to know Cram and Goodhue personally, and it may have been through them that contact was made with two up-

and-coming artists of this new English school. The first was not a glassman. Henry Wilson, John Sedding's assistant and successor, was an architect and sculptor. The brilliant Wilson, who became a close friend of Cram's, was, according to Cormack, as completely the aesthete Bohemian in 1890s London as was Cram in 1890s Boston. He and Cram seem to have hit it off at once, and by 1910 they had joined forces at St. James, Roxbury,[14] outside Boston, where Wilson did for Cram a superb bronze font cover (*76a*). In later years, moreover, Cram would give Wilson his last and crowning commission, the great bronze doors for St. John the Divine in New York.

To return to the arena of stained glass, Cram also introduced into the United States the work of the artist whose glass perhaps most seriously challenged the older firms such as Kempe's — Christopher Whall.

Son of the rector of Thorning-cum-Gidding, Northamptonshire, Whall studied at the Royal Academy and abroad, beginning his career as a painter (exhibiting at the academy in 1895), and though he spent part of his life in Italy, he worked mostly in England, where Ruskin and the Pre-Raphaelites were key influences. A founding member of the original British-based Society of Arts and Crafts and also of the Art Workers Guild, he taught at the Royal College of Art and was the author of an influential book, *Stained Glass Work*, in which medium he became best known.[15] Such was Whall's standing, he was, along with Henry Wilson and W. R. Lethaby, one of "six men who belong to an advanced school" who submitted a brilliant if unconventional design in 1902 for the decoration of the apse of Liverpool Cathedral.[16]

Whall's was an advanced taste in more than one way. A friend of Ashbee's, for whose Chelsea town house Whall did the stained glass (Ashbee it was, surely, who introduced Cram and Whall to each other), Whall was a fierce individualist, very antagonistic to publicity, and like Vaughan a bit of a recluse though not for similar reasons.[17] Whereas Wilson may have been gay, Whall probably was not. Yet Whall seems to have had an affinity, unusual then, for working well with women, whom, as Emmanuel Cooper has pointed out in *The Sexual Perspective: Homosexuality and Art in the Last Hundred Years in the West*, the Arts and Crafts movement inevitably attracted, particularly if they were lesbian, because in such circles there was a freer acceptance of same-sex relations than elsewhere. And it was one such likely lesbian artist, the noted stained-glass designer Mary Lowndes, whom Whall helped to found the firm of Lowndes and Drury in the 1890s.[18] Whall's daughter, Veronica, also worked with her father, whose work when criticized, interestingly, was faulted only for "an occasional excess of feminine qualities."[19]

More often praised, and highly (Whall's Lady Chapel glass, for example, at Gloucester Cathedral, is a glorious achievement), Whall was admired in the first

76a, b. *Left*: probably Henry Wilson's earliest
work in America: his splendid bronze font cover
of 1910 for Cram at St. James's, Roxbury, near
Boston. *Below*: another famous Arts and Crafts
name figures in the Lady Chapel of All Saints',
Ashmont, 1912: the Cram office's pattern plan
for the Grueby tilework pavement.

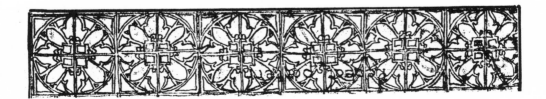

place for being "an 'artist' in stained glass [who] not only draws his own cartoons, but chooses all the glass and does much of the painting himself."[20] His was thus the Arts and Crafts ideal. Whall, wrote Cram, was the "greatest of all [English stained-glass workers]."[21]

Whall's design proclivities were such as to suit Cram exactly, weary as he was of commercial stained glass, for Whall disparaged nineteenth-century glassmen trying to do thirteenth- or fourteenth-century glass. Rather, he tried as he saw it to do nineteenth- and twentieth-century glass in the Gothic spirit. And Whall's glass, though recognizably Pre-Raphaelite, was highly original and modern in feeling; much more so, for example, than the Kempe glass always favored by Vaughan. In fact, Cram did not care at all for the work of Kempe, who relied on painted glass. Whall, on the other hand, pioneered in the use of slab and clear glass and tried to achieve his effects through a silvery white translucence. A "true believer" exactly of Cram's sort, Whall shared with Cram (as more "modern" designers like Louis Tiffany and John La Farge did not) the same philosophy of stained glass: that though it must be telling and, indeed, brilliant (hence the clear glass and direct action of the sun), it must also be a part of the overall organic art of the church, never assertive, always reticent, holding to the plane of the wall without perspective or modeling, its design not interrupting the wall but persuading it suddenly to brilliant but quite flat color. ("Efface yourself, my friend, sink yourself," wrote Whall in his *Stained Glass Work*; "illustrate the building . . . enrich it, complete it.")[22]

Whall did more than that for Cram at All Saints', Ashmont (77), and at Boston's Church of the Advent, the two churches for which Cram commissioned from Whall what Peter Cormack has called "the first major examples of English Arts and Crafts glass to be seen in America." Furthermore, Whall's and Cram's collaboration inspired a young American, Charles Connick, to take up the cause of a Gothic but modern and *American* glass just such as Cram needed.[23] Of Whall's Boston glass Connick said: "He has broken with some of the old traditions, but so gently that one hardly senses rebellion. His use of canopy designed from natural forms, instead of the more formal architectural canopies of the fourteenth and fifteenth centuries, is a distinct mark of his inventiveness," Connick concluded, while on the other hand it was also a sign of Whall's "adherence to architectural principles."[24] And forthwith, in his first representative windows for Cram at All Saints', Brookline,[25] Connick succeeded Whall (after Cram had helped him get to Europe to meet Whall and others) as Cram's favored glassman, laying the foundations for the American stained-glass renaissance Cram and he would lead all the way to St. John the Divine in New York in the 1920s and 1930s. Soon enough, Henry Vaughan too was using Connick glass.

77. Christopher Whall's design for his clerestory glass for Cram at All Saints', Ashmont:
The Risen Christ, 1906.

THE AMERICAN RESPONSE

Connick's success points to the solution Cram found for the resentment among American artists Cram's commissioning of English artists aroused: ever the practical dreamer, Cram made use of the Boston Arts and Crafts Society to encourage American work of high quality; that of William Grueby, for instance, whose marvelous Arts and Crafts work is so admired today, was used by Cram in the Lady Chapel of All Saints', Ashmont (76b). But Cram went further; in aid of ensuring the necessary economic incentives to yield, at prices clients could afford, the type of art he wanted, he made at least one deal with an artist that benefitted all concerned, though it is not clear that clients knew of the arrangement. A letter survives in which Connick, before he was in a position to start his own studio, accepted a position in another studio "with the understanding that, in addition to the salary, I am to receive one-half of all profits that may accrue from work placed in any [Cram and Goodhue building] or from work that is obtained through the influence of Mr. R. A. Cram."[26] Verily, a Gothic Revival kickback! And one for which we can all be very grateful. Later, moreover, Cram helped Connick financially to start his own studio.

Cram also struck gold in his and Goodhue's early patronage of Lee Lawrie, later a notable modernist sculptor, whom Cram commissioned to do work for the office in 1898, when Lawrie was only twenty. In Vaughan's wake Cram was also fortunate in his early association with the John Evans Company (and its chief sculptor, Domingo Mora) and the Irving and Casson Company, where he seized at once upon the work (which he would enormously influence) of the sculptor and carver Johannes Kirchmayer.[27]

Another mysterious and reclusive figure (Cram really was surrounded by them), Kirchmayer (78), trained as a woodcarver in Bavaria, had come to America at about the age of twenty in 1880 and had worked for a while for Herter Brothers in New York, where he was said to have been befriended by Stanford White. Kirchmayer came to Boston in 1884 to associate himself with Irving and Casson. (Robert Casson was Vaughan's closest friend, and young Kirchmayer's advent may have been through that still more mysterious figure, Edward Searles, Vaughan's leading client, who had been a decorator at Herter Brothers.) It was for Irving and Casson (and Vaughan) that Kirchmayer did the figure sculpture in 1894 for the high altar reredos of St. Paul's School Chapel in Concord, New Hampshire, work that had as striking an effect on Ralph Adams Cram as Whall's on Connick. In the course of the next twenty years Cram would lead Kirchmayer to the point where his sculpture would be exhibited in the rotunda of Boston's art museum and his work praised by a learned critic as

78. Cram soon extended his patronage from British artists like Wilson and Whall to Americans such as Lee Lawrie, Otto Heinigke, Charles Connick, and Johannes Kirchmayer, whose pew-end self-portrait of unknown date is illustrated here.

that of "one of the indubitably great artists of his era," comparable in his own medium with both Sargent and Prendergast.[28]

Cram's affinity with Kirchmayer, as also with Wilson and Whall (and, later, Connick), related to philosophy of design and to craftsmanship. Kirchmayer, for instance, used to say the secret of both was in the drawing, not in the carving, for while he did sometimes model in wax for metalwork, in the case of figures carved in wood he drew his figure directly on the balk of wood — the nude in charcoal, to get his proportions right and ensure that the figure not get lost in its vesture, and the drapery in crayon — and with no other guides then roughed out and carved the figure, thinking it through as he worked. Though, like Cram, Kirchmayer was partial to the carving machine for running ornament (because he thought it saved a carver's spirit from being deadened by hour upon hour of labor better used for figure work), he abhorred using the machine for anything else. Even when the figure was finished by hand, he pointed out, it would fail if it was first roughed out by the carving machine, for "when the carver receives the piece roughed out, he does not have to think; the shape is there."[29]

There was, in fact, in Kirchmayer's and Connick's work the same unusual combination of traditional form newly imagined as in Wilson's and Whall's. As Cram himself wrote, though Kirchmayer "was possessed by the whole Mediaeval tradition he was bent on working this out in vital contemporary forms, and if you didn't like it, it was just too bad."[30] And for all his figures' extreme individuality, they are also very reticent and architectural. Their modernness is of many kinds. The facial expressions of his figures are not more naturalistic but more personal, more American, he would have said. And in terms of overall concept and form? Asked about his inspiration for the rather elongated character of Our Lady of Ashmont, Kirchmayer spoke to one critic of "something of the skyscraper," an aspect of America this immigrant sculptor never forgot, for skyscrapers had made quite an impression on him as a young man in New York.[31] Like Goodhue's ornament, the achievements of all these artists Cram worked with so closely would lend strong credence to Cram's contention that Gothic was not dead, only moribund, and could again be given new life.

Toward a Liturgical Art

Cram himself, it should be noted, was much more than the facilitator of this embryonic circle of designers and artists that in the days of his fame I have called the Boston Gothicists. And while it would be an error to introduce at all fully here Cram's philosophy of liturgical art before completing our study of the philosophical axis of the aesthetic and the erotic out of which it arose, still, something must be said in order to take due note of what Cram's *creative*—not just theoretical—contribution was to all this. Thereby, moreover, our understanding of the firm's 1890s church work will be immeasurably strengthened.

The Lady Chapel of the Church of the Advent, which Cram and Goodhue designed in 1894, is the key work of the nineties in this respect, as seminal an interior as was All Saints', Ashmont, an exterior. Conceptually Cram's first authoritative, complete interior, the first masterwork fully to illustrate his principles of liturgical art, in this chapel altar, reredos, bishop's chair, clergy stalls, credence, and altar rails are integrated beautifully into one enveloping, unifying work of art, the distribution of the weights and accents and overall balance of which artistically are practically faultless. Granted, it is clumsily detailed; Goodhue had not yet hit his stride; but three years later, at Middleborough, he did, and, as we will soon see, not long thereafter at Ashmont he surpassed himself in that chancel's interior detailing.

Note that at the Advent, if the altar is central and elaborately set off, the adjoining stalls and credence are also given their attributes of ornament as of use; and just as a rich iconography by no means overwhelms the design's overall order and simplicity, so neither do any of the several necessities of the chancel assert themselves. Necessities and ornament in themselves are quite worth independent notice, but they are not at all additive; all work *together*, taking their cue in a supremely functional way from the corporate nature of worship as a part of one overall organic work of art, each part, like each person in the liturgy, praying, so to speak, a greater prayer than its own.

It was a concept Cram fleshed out in later years into a unity of the music, poetry, rhetoric, and gesture of the High Mass with the architectural setting of stained glass, embroidery, metalwork, sculpture, and painting as one all-encompassing work of art that was truly Wagnerian in its integration of the arts as the visible expression of the life of the Catholic church before her Lord. But that must wait for Volume Two.

A CONGERIES OF CRAFTS

Pinckney Street itself was a center of Arts and Crafts activity. In the 1890s and 1900s more than thirty members of the society lived there, ranging from little-known lace makers and embroiderers to such well-known artists as Joseph Lindon Smith, the sculptors Bashka and Bessie Paeff, and many of the society's leaders such as Cram, Vaughan, Day, and Updike.[32] Often, too, it was in neighborhood studios that Cram's commissions were carried out. For example, the trinity of superb gold- and silversmiths (George Hunt, George Gebelein, and James Wooley) Cram cited as his earliest such artist-collaborators in those media had their studios within a block or two of Pinckney Street on nearby Lime or lower Chestnut Street.[33] And so pervasive did the society's influence become that even Fenway Court itself was to be endowed with an Arts and Crafts component, a striking tile pavement by Henry Chapman Mercer (a onetime student of Charles Eliot Norton at Harvard), the color of which Cram (who often used Mercer tiles in his churches) so admired that he once asked to borrow one as an inspiration for another tile maker.[34]

The advent of Goodhue, as we have seen, was of particular significance with respect to all this, and the resulting cross-fertilization of the arts, given much emphasis by the Arts and Crafts Society, was legendary. A striking example is the way three members of the society, Cram, Goodhue, and Updike, joined forces to make a book, *A Description of the Pastoral Staff Belonging to the Diocese of Albany, New York*,[35] that celebrated the artistry of goldsmithing as well as architectural design, and, in another craft, that of bookmaking. Indeed, Goodhue, the designer of the book, was the principal designer of the work of art it celebrated. Not surprisingly, as James O'Gorman has pointed out, Goodhue's borders in this book, distinctly more architectural than just floral or figural, in

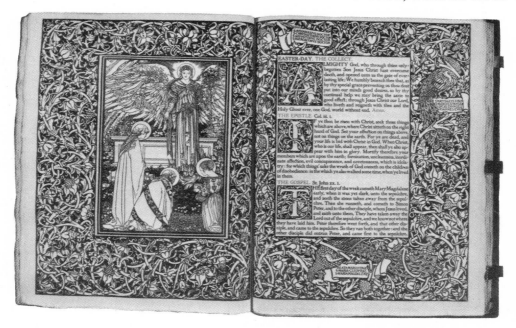

79. Born of Harold Brown's and D. B. Updike's affection for the church and for each other, the *Altar Book* of 1896, with illustrations by R. Anning Bell, also rejoiced in page borders, initials, and typeface by Bertram Goodhue.

the way they set up the text achieve a real confluence of book and architectural design.[36]

Far more significant, and of the greatest importance in the history of American bookmaking, was the *Altar Book* of 1896 *(79)*, the joint effort of the distinguished Rhode Island patron Harold Brown, his friend Daniel Berkeley Updike, and Bertram Goodhue, another founding member of the Society of Arts and Crafts, that heralded the society's founding the following year. To be sure, a distinguished British designer, R. Anning Bell, was called upon to collaborate with the Americans, Bell doing the illustrations, Goodhue the page borders and other decorations. But it is Goodhue's work that stands out; in *American Book Design and William Morris* Susan Otis Thompson makes the point about Goodhue's book decoration so often made here of his church detail; it was, she writes, "not only charming but rather original. Taking Kelmscott bookmaking as a point of departure, [Goodhue's book decoration] is a fresh creation."[37]

It was characteristic of their work that Cram and Goodhue (as well as Cram's fellow Anglo-Catholic Updike) were no less interested in the design of the altar missal or its stand, so important a part of the function of an altar, than in the altar itself; and how consistent Cram was in this respect is evidenced in the fact that three decades later Updike was busy making a magnificent one-of-its-kind memorial book for Cram for St. John the Divine.

The *Altar Book* itself remains unchallenged. An outstanding work of art that came out of the gay subculture of Boston in this period—comparable to that equally outstanding work of scholarship of the same time, Santayana's *Sense of Beauty*—the *Altar Book* is entirely comparable to Ashbee's *Prayer Book of Edward VII*, another landmark of its era. For many years no altar in America was worthy of it, and it is not too much to say that this missal, a masterpiece of the 1890s of the American Gothic Revival, is in the league of All Saints', Ashmont.[38]

THE PEWTER MUG

As likely as not, the masterpiece was conceived after too many beers at Billy Park's, where Cram and Goodhue were wont to forgather with Updike and others of their friends of the Pewter Mug. For although the Society of Arts and Crafts was the most public (and most respectable) place for many Boston Bohemians, artists, and craftsworkers, it was only one of a network of artistic groups Cram and Goodhue and their cohort belonged to in the nineties, of which the most diverse was probably the Association of the Pewter Mug. It was made up, in Cram's words, of

> all the younger males I [knew]. . . . Anyone was eligible provided he did, or tried to do, something constructive along any line, was companionable with his fellows, enjoyed a certain Elizabethan tang in the social proceedings and had a sound taste in malt liquors. Our headquarters were in the field, so to speak; we met at any time when the call went out, and anywhere that good entertainment was offered. The presence of any literary or artistic light from far afield was cause enough for calling a meeting.[39]

In comparison with the Society of Arts and Crafts, the Pewter Mug was boisterous enough, and in a distinctly masculine way. But though Boston's Bohemia had quite a good deal in common with Bohemias everywhere, of course, it was also its own thing, a point critical to understand because Stanford White's New York Bohemia was so close in terms of time and geography.[40] White's Bohemia was very different from Ralph Adams Cram's. New Yorkers looked more to Paris in this era, Bostonians to London, and White's Sewar Club had little in common with Cram's Pewter Mug, where neither pubescent girls nor boys ever emerged from anybody's birthday cake. Pinckney Street preferred medieval costume dinners, welcomed women, and encouraged intellectual discourse as much as picturesque behavior — and did not inquire too closely about whatever happened upstairs afterward.

The Pewter Mug, for example, as another member called to mind years later,

> prided itself on having only a single rule, an elaborately silly one that reveals the kittenish air of its festivities: a member was forbidden to buy a drink for either of the members seated beside him at the dinner table, though he might for anyone else — he could treat his immediate neighbors only by taking them out of the dining room into a bar.[41]

Kittenish *and* artistic; for a goodly number of Cram's earliest and most important artist-collaborators were members. None was more important than Goodhue's younger brother, Harry Eldredge Goodhue.

A student in the early nineties at the Boston Art Students Association, Harry thereafter apprenticed at the Horace Phipps stained-glass studio, where he remained until striking out on his own. Cram relied on Harry, a devout Roman Catholic and a dedicated member of the Boston Society of Arts and Crafts, when he could not afford Christopher Whall's work, for Harry, who, as Connick pointed out, experimented with curious color schemes, showed just the kind of originality Cram liked, and some of the best of the earliest glass Cram commissioned, characterized by masses of lambent, amber-colored canopy work over intensely colored figures, adorns Cram and Goodhue's parish churches of the nineties.

Bertram Goodhue, of course, probably proposed his brother to the Mug; Cram probably recruited George Hawley Hallowell. An apprentice at Rotch and Tilden just a few years after Cram's graduation from that office and then, after study at Harvard with Charles Eliot Norton, a student at the School of the Museum of Fine Arts in Boston, Hallowell trained under Edmund Tarbell and Frank Benson and then made a lengthy tour through Europe. A painter of landscape and genre scenes (several of which were bought by Isabella Stewart Gardner), Hallowell was also a book and poster designer (for the *Atlantic Monthly*, among others) and dabbled in stained glass, collaborating on works for Cram with Otto Heinigke, the New York glassman Cram also approved of.[42]

The other artist member of the Mug important to Cram was Updike. A much respected typographer at Houghton Mifflin and the Riverside Press in the early 1890s (it was noted, wrote William Dwiggins, how Updike "manipulates space [on the page of a book] with the discrimination of a Renaissance architect"),[43] Updike, after he founded his Merrymount Press in the early nineties, pioneered the notion of historical revivals of printing styles appropriate to a book's content, an idea that paralleled, of course, Cram's and others' architectural use of Revival styles.

And, indeed, architecture, in the sense of realized building rather than book designs of architectural character, now arises, for St. Andrew's Church, Detroit, of 1894 is a fine example of how Updike's work served Cram and Goodhue.[44] A compendium of the work of both men in this period (the idea of a central tower is derived from Goodhue's Dallas cathedral design; the west front is reminiscent of Christ Church, Hyde Park; the tower is of the Ashmont type; and so on), St. Andrew's was the first church actually erected to the firm's designs at any great distance from Boston and was so much admired that it would lead to a great deal of later work for Cram in the Detroit area. Not the least reason for its success, moreover, was a marvelous booklet, embodying not only Cram's prose and Goodhue's sketches, but also Updike's gifts as designer and printer (80). How it reflected back on Updike (Bohemians being ever on the alert to second one another's causes and help make their fortunes!) is clear in the observation by Updike's biographer, George Winship, that Updike's early work

> shows connections with various Episcopal churches in and about Boston, . . . and the way the designer's fame spread is shown by *An Appeal in behalf of the Memorial to Rev. S. S. Harris* [St. Andrew's was built as a memorial to Harris] issued in Detroit . . . and printed from Designs by D. B. Updike at 6 Beacon Street, on behalf of a memorial designed by Cram, Wentworth and Goodhue.[45]

Updike was, in fact, a central figure in Boston's Bohemia. Though eventually a businessman of resounding respectability, in the 1890s he was involved in nearly all of the Bohemian circles or clusters that we have linked with Cram: the primary Pinckney Street circle, the Mount Auburn-Brattle Street circle, the

80. Goodhue's perspective of his and Cram's St. Andrew's, Detroit, from Updike's booklet of 1894 about it.

Charles Street-Tavern Club group, the museum circle, the "Colonial Trinity" and their friends, the Copeland and Day group, and the Grundmann circle; each separate but interlocking. Copeland, too, figured in several Bohemian circles, as did Thomas Russell Sullivan. But only Isabella Stewart Gardner (and, for a while, Bernard Berenson) turns up as consistently as does Updike in *all* these interesting circles.

Except when they all did at some Bohemian frolic, such as the perennial artists' fêtes.

ARABIAN NIGHTS

At least once a year in the gay nineties, sometimes more often, Boston's Bohemians, like the artists of fin-de-siècle Paris, made rather a grand public splash at a gala fête, often involving a masquerade as well, and usually sponsored by the Boston Art Students Association, yet another of the societies with which Goodhue and Cram were involved.

Just how extravagantly Boston responded to such goings-on is clear in a *Town Topics* description of Isabella Stewart Gardner at one gala in 1896. Noting that lady's propensity for startling attire (including, on another occasion, "a halo-like arrangement on her head—gold wires tipped with diamonds that made her look like a cross between a Burne-Jones and an Aubrey Beardsley"), the writer reported that

> Mrs. Jack . . . outshone everybody . . . in a costume she had brought from Egypt, . . . tightly swathed round and round with layers of gauze, gold embroidered . . . her famous diamond and ruby necklace, with her ropes of diamonds, bound her throat. But it was upon her head that eyes were fastened with breathless admiration and awe. Everything was covered but her eyes. . . . [She was] swathed in soft mull as tight as a bandage; two big diamonds held strings of jewels with a pendant in the center, which hung just above her nose.[46]

We have no description of Cram at any of these balls, but in his study of Day and Guiney Stephen Parrish is almost certainly alluding to the aftermath of one such when he writes that Cram had

> mastered a dramatic presence that was beyond even Day's grasp. At a masquerade at the old Art Museum [where several such artists' balls were held] in the spring of 1893, to which Bohemia flocked . . . Cram made a tremendous hit as Henry VIII. . . . [Louise Guiney, not in attendance] caught sight of Cram in his costume [after the ball in the studio of a Back Bay photographer,] a sight that took her breath away.[47]

One ball particularly, held in 1894, a fête entitled Arabian Nights, is of interest to us, for the Art Students Association, a "club of young and mostly impecunious students," who had already succeeded in the "daring and perilous

81. Jack Abbott in costume at the 1894 Boston Students' Association Artists' Fête.

undertaking" of establishing the Grundmann Studios, placed in charge of the decorations of this fête Bertram Goodhue himself. Opined even that rather sedate bourgeois journal, *The Bostonian*: the city should "make much of such artistic fraternities among us, and take counsel of them, profiting by their vital enthusiasm for aestheticism."[48]

It was a point of view that for such a journal was being enthusiastic to a degree, even with the usual middle-class lag in mind. By 1894 most aesthetes were already decadents, though the continuum of the two words as euphemisms for the same thing is constant. Consider the way Richard Ellmann concludes, as I have of Warren's statues and Cram's churches, of Henry James's aesthetes: that at the end of his career James saw clearly that he had used the [aesthetic] movement as a stalking horse because it enabled him to represent people like himself. . . . In *The Golden Bowl* . . . [he] makes the fastidiousness of aestheticism and its insistence upon beauty central to life's concerns. . . . In other words, aesthetes, like homosexuals, may have their place in the scheme of creation.[49]

Certainly they did in Boston, which then took its fêtes and their artistry with a seriousness few would credit today, and where in 1894 they were hard at work on their Arabian extravaganza. The editors of *The Bostonian* in their report of the fête assured their readers it was "wholly the work of the youngest set in art in Boston" and that the tableaux, musical selections, play, and various dances and such, all had gone off perfectly amid a brilliant throng of young Bostonians in period Arabian costumes "in the court of the Caliph, Haroun Al Raschid," as Copley Hall of the Grundmann was transformed into for the delight of all concerned. Some humor seems to have marked the occasion — witness the "entrance of the [Boston] Society of Architects representing the Forty Thieves" — as well as untold magnificence of costumery. And when the evening ended, it was at four in the morning with a call to prayer! Nor was that all. Thereafter, the correspondent reported:

> The quaint little studios which were thrown open [upstairs] for the reception of guests and later became the scenes of private banquets were cosy and inviting. . . . The secret of it all was that the [Grundmann Studios] is the home of this delightful art colony.[50]

One of these studios would have been that of one of the fête's other inspirers, John C. Abbott, an artist who wrote the play, acted one of the parts, designed the program, and generally did whatever Goodhue didn't, including doubtless giving one of the cozier supper parties afterward, for Abbott was of all Goodhue's and Cram's Bohemian friends one of the most lively and imaginative. Abbott certainly appears to have been one of the stars of the evening as grand vizier and master of ceremonies, in which capacity he attracted more than a little attention as he led in the Caliph, "making room for him in the hall by waving a huge scarlet poppy"! Well might our correspondent describe him as "the gracious and vivacious Mr. John C. Abbott [81]."

In another year — 1898 — the theme was Gothic. And that indefatigable Bohemian Thomas Russell Sullivan, who never missed Bohemia's fêtes, took enthusiastic note of this one in his diary:

> Tonight, at Copley Hall, the medieval festival of the Art Students Association. The place was transformed into a huge tent set up in a primeval forest, hung with Gothic tapestries, shields and banners, and crowded with a gay company in costumes of the time. . . . The Tavern Club, *en masse*, represented the returned crusaders. . . . There were processions, dances, sports, and a Gothic play, "Rosemonde." . . . The whole fête, from first to last, was certainly a brilliant spectacle.[51]

315

WHITE ROSE IN BOSTON

Cram may have played a larger role in the Gothic fête, but Goodhue, it will have been observed, had rather taken the lead from him in the matter of the Arabian Nights affair, and at first glance this may seem to accord with what Cram wrote in his autobiography—that for the success of many of their activities in the 1890s "Goodhue was largely responsible, through that singular quality that drew all sorts of interesting and provocative people within the sphere of his dynamic personality."[52] But Cram was being generous; Parrish points out:

> As the youth movement of the eighties flowed into the youth movement of the nineties, Cram stood out more and more clearly as one of bohemia's dominant personalities. His "high wind of a mind" [as Guiney characterized it to Day in 1891] blew him into the center of every esthetic or cultural activity. . . . "A very Proteus is he in his different characteristics," wrote Goodhue a little ruefully [in 1896].[53]

The truth is that one seldom hears of either Goodhue or Cram apart from the other in the nineties; to be sure, Cram had a considerable name in Boston that counted for much in such things as the first Arts and Crafts exhibition—the hall it was held in, after all, was of Cram's design—but the cover of the Arts and Crafts show catalogue was, on the other hand, of Goodhue's design; the usual roles, of course. Increasingly, in the nineties, both were equally influential. Because, as Cram pointed out, "for the first few years of Goodhue's coöperation, the affairs of the [architectural] office went on after a fashion not any too glittering in their financial results . . . [and they thus] had time, individually, to immerse [them]selves in a lot of invaluable outside activities,"[54] there were manifold opportunities for either or both to throw themselves into. One of the most important for Cram (not, however, for Goodhue) was the Order of the White Rose.

It says a good deal about Ralph Adams Cram that he was a leader not only of the earnest and highly serious Society of Arts and Crafts, and of the hearty and somewhat boisterous band of the Pewter Mug, but as well of this much more rarefied circle of souls of the White Rose. Beer, champagne, absinthe, even afternoon tea—Cram cheerfully drank them all in whatever drag he thought appropriate. The Order of the White Rose, however, is a particularly good example of the integration of divergent elements in Cram's life, celebrating some of the most surprising and intimate connections of aesthete Boston in the 1890s.

Actually, however outré the White Rose strikes one as being, it is possible to find a good many roots of Cram's ardent Jacobitism in his family background, to which we are never really able to give the weight here one might like as opposed to his later Boston period, because so relatively little is recoverable of

Cram's childhood. But to his sense of the past mentioned earlier as deriving in no small measure from Squire Blake's country house in Kensington must be added the fact that the seventeenth-century New Hampshire land grant of the Crams was from Charles I, a fact weighted with meaning for someone of Cram's temperament. And though the Jacobitism of Cram and his friends in America in the 1890s was certainly more cultural than political and more than marginally Anglophile, to the extent that it *had* political content it could best be described as Hamiltonian, a view of things Cram also inherited from his strongly Federalist family.

Cram may well have been the first to introduce the cult of King Charles the Martyr, whose roots in Anglicanism are quite venerable, into America. In July 1892 he invited a small group to his Pinckney Street rooms to meet the Marquis of Ruvigny, compiler of *The Jacobite Peerage*. And even then it was necessary for Cram to write to Fred Day ("you may be very sure that there will be no scoffing")[55] to ensure that Day understood Cram's purpose was a serious one: to establish an American branch of the Jacobite League. Four years later, Cram and Day and others decided to incorporate it into a new American branch of the more successful Order of the White Rose, founded in Britain in 1886 and taking its name from the chief ornament of the badge of the House of Stuart. In this cause Cram would achieve a sort of Bohemian apotheosis (which even Guiney shook her head over) as North American Prior of the order.

From the beginning, these American Jacobites were identified with the Church of the Advent, especially during the rectorships of Fathers William Barroll Frisby and William H. Van Allen, who always celebrated White Rose Day, as the feast of King Charles the Martyr appointed in the old English Book of Common Prayer is often called. The striking statue of Archbishop Laud in Cram's Lady Chapel at the Advent was given from offerings collected at King Charles Day masses.[56] After Fenway Court was built, however, with a fully functioning chapel duly consecrated by the Advent's rector (see 74), chapter meetings were as apt to be in that more exotic locale, where, Morris Carter recalled, Isabella Stewart Gardner (costumed often, the reader will remember, somewhat after the manner of Mary, Queen of Scots) presided:

> In the picturesque fanaticism of the Order of the White Rose, she took an aesthetic interest [as well as in the] first and only issue of "The Royal Standard," . . . when "Ralph von Cram" was Prior of the Order in North America. . . . The death of Charles of England, king and martyr, was occasionally . . . commemorated at Fenway Court by a little supper for a few enthusiasts, and an intimate, romantic service in the chapel.[57]

What marvelous aesthete evenings those must have been. No doubt as part of such an evening Mrs. Jack brought out for her guests' edification the magnificent Book of Hours she owned that had, indeed, once belonged to Mary of Scotland. Religion, art, scholarship, collecting, family—what a rich web of interconnections.

Furthermore, the society had a wider than only religious meaning, Nancy Finlay, a scholar of book design, having noticed that "many of the Boston artists [of the book] and writers were interested in seventeenth-century England, and a number of them belonged to the Order of the White Rose," a subject that arose in the most avant-garde publications of the 1890s.[58] Indeed, there was also a more scholarly dimension to all this, for Louise Guiney especially (though inclined to impatience with some of Cram's more enthusiastic Jacobite proclamations) was well known for her writings on this period in English history. Furthermore, Fred Day's Caroline collection was a centerpiece of his library, one of the notable American private collections of books of the period.[59]

It was easy enough to make fun of the White Rose. And, again, it was Van Wyck Brooks who did so, with a fine bravado, in *New England: Indian Summer*:

> In their revolt from democracy and realism, their desire to expunge all remnants of the Puritan past, [these Bostonians] conceived a monarchist movement. . . . They organized a local branch of the Jacobite Society, the "Order of the White Rose," namely; and they offered expiation on the feast of St. Charles. . . . Ralph Adams Cram, the archaeological architect, who was bent upon reversing evolution, was the prior of the chapter.[60]

This polemic (any more than those quoted in previous chapters) is not, however, very penetrating. It reminds one of those many, to jump a generation and again compare T. S. Eliot with Cram, who could hardly believe after Eliot's conversion to Anglicanism that the author of *The Waste Land*, *the* "poetic modernist, could find it possible to take refuge in an antique orthodoxy," perhaps forgetting that Eliot and Cram were also alike in their love of lost causes. ("Eliot assumed that he was casting his lot with the vanquished," in the case of Anglicanism, writes Russell Kirk, for Eliot expected its disestablishment and disintegration.) Moreover, it comes as less of a surprise to us today, doubtless, than to Brooks in his day, to learn from Kirk that Eliot, too, had a "veneration of King Charles the Martyr," an important part of the background of "Little Gidding," one of Eliot's *Four Quartets*, arguably the most sublime religious poetry of the twentieth century.[61] *Pace*; good King Charles has inspired more than his share of modern art.

In other realms as well. The Advent's Lady Chapel is not the only example of what might be called the architecture of the White Rose. As discussed in Chapter 3, one of the earliest aspects of design other than churches in which Cram seems rather to have specialized was that of the apartment house, quite a new thing in American life in the 1890s; and in some way, Cram's mind, having already generated a Jacobethan English country-house type of apartment house in Brookline (The Gables, in 1891), seems to have made a further connection between massed flats and things Jacobite and triggered a very creative response. In 1891 the connection was sufficiently mature that Cram had insisted a client change the name of a projected apartment block Cram had been approached about designing to "Stuart Terrace."[62] Nothing came of that project. Seven years later, however, another such opportunity did not disappoint, and Cram persisted in the connection. The result was one of the most innovative and beautiful American apartment blocks of the period — Richmond Court (*82a, b*) in the Boston suburb of Brookline.[63] The name undoubtedly commemorates the court of King Charles I at Richmond; moreover, the apartment house is divided into "entries" or "halls" whose names are suggestive; Grafton Hall, for example, surely commemorates Father Grafton of the Advent.

The English Richmond, of course, was a great Tudor palace, as is the American Richmond Court. Important architecturally, because it is perhaps the first Tudor-style courtyard apartment house on the East Coast, thus resolving in a highly original manner many problems of overall size and light that had until then plagued the development of the apartment house, Richmond Court has been criticized by many, including Cram himself, for being (in its architect's words) "the first attempt to camouflage an apartment house through the counterfeit presentment of a great Tudor mansion."[64] Yet what *were* Charles I and his court doing at the original Richmond? That palace — even Versailles — was essentially an apartment house. Cram's royalist instincts did not mislead his architectural ones. Or perhaps it was the other way around. Nor was Richmond Court at all, despite Brooks's lament about Cram's not only royalist but archaeological propensities, at all antique-looking. Interestingly, a later and more commonplace neighbor (Hampton Court), another Tudor apartment house, has battlements; the earlier Richmond Court has none, just Cram's typical clean, sharp cornice line.

Notice the deep consistency emerging here. Think, in the first place, of Cram's earliest Shavian houses of 1889 and of W. Knight Sturges's point that "Shaw's Queen Anne [was] . . . an attempt to adapt freely elements borrowed from the vernacular architecture . . . of Stuart England . . . [and] to combine Queen Anne motifs with late Gothic effects of mass."[65] Recall as well how we linked not just Cram's favored styles but also his favored designers (Shaw, Sedding, and Bodley) to another of Cram's sources, seventeenth-century New England Folk Gothic. And, finally, bring to mind the fact that not only Cram's earliest architectural sources and his first works, both domestic and ecclesiastic, but also the historical link between his religion and his sexuality — Anglo-

82a, b. Richmond Court's crisp modern profile (no battlements here) aptly expresses the innovative design of this apartment house, designed in 1899 by Cram and Goodhue. It was one of the first of the open court type in the United States. *Above*: Goodhue's exterior perspective; *below*: Cram's plan.

Catholicism and homosexuality — date from Stuart England, from the Caroline and Jacobean eras. Is it any wonder (especially when one adds to this jigsaw the fragment of Cram's own ancestors' New England origins in that era) that Cram's first politics, the earliest expression of his youthful socialism, should be a form of Jacobite monarchism that fused American Federalism, socialism, and a forecast of the New Deal? I think not.

So rich and varied were the byways of the minds of Cram and his fellow Jacobites — essays by Guiney, collecting by Day, architecture by Cram — that it all somehow spilled over into wholly new and surely unexpected dimensions of creativity. First of all, Cram took to writing poetry — Jacobite poetry, of course. Even Louise Guiney was impressed, writing to Cram that one of his poems "is as worthy to rank with the best royalist lyrics of that time as Browning's." She followed up with page after page of serious criticism, culminating in her naming of the work, Cram's best poem by far:

> Consider every suggestion tentative, for I offer each with humility, wishing all the while . . . I were the author! I should be vainer than a peacock if I were. First of all, the title [evidently originally "The Cavaliers"]. The Cavaliers had none of these high spirits, this confidence and swagger, after the real fighting began; reverses followed too fast. I thought therefore a definite date could give color and force. . . . How would "Nottingham Hunt" do? . . . It was at Nottingham, you remember — of course you remember, since you were there! — that the white standard was first raised in 1642, and war proclaimed by the King. Most of my emendations are to cover up your wicked generosity in making many uses of one word: three "hounds," two "foxes," two "games," too much "hunting," too much "riding." The lines appear to gain by a freer vocabulary. . . . You never did a better, nor did anyone else.[66]

In the event it was in *The Century* — distinctly a coup for a nonpoet — that "Nottingham Hunt" was published in 1895.

Then, of all things, Cram's poem went on to achieve a wholly new lease on life as a song, set to music by the composer Fred Bullard, Cram's Pinckney Street neighbor. And its popularity was immense; Bullard's wife, in a letter to Cram years later, recalled "the concert, years ago, in Symphony Hall, when [Fred] gave a gorgeous rendition of your 'Nottingham Hunt,' the only encore allowed that evening."[67] Evidently, too, there was also a theatrical dimension to the influence of the Order of the White Rose, for in a letter of February 1894 Marion Nichols describes a scene somewhat reminiscent of Oscar Wilde's Boston lecture of twelve years previously, when she writes Cram from Italy: "I was glad to hear that at your request [Henry] Irving acted Charles I when he was in Boston. I hope that all the good Jacobites were there, as you planned, sitting together in the front rows of the theater."[68]

Many have smiled, and still do, over Cram's enthusiasm for the Order of the

White Rose, upon which one *does* wonder if even Baron Corvo could have improved. (It is perhaps not by the way that Fr. Rolfe was himself, in his biographer's words, known for his "devotion to the Royal Stuarts.")[69] But to design the Advent Lady Chapel, dine at Fenway Court, incite acting by such as Henry Irving and collecting by such as Day and essays by the likes of Guiney, win repeated attention for things Jacobite in a widely read journal such as *The Chap-Book*, essay a new kind of apartment house, be published in a national magazine, and have Symphony Hall at one's feet? We should all make such fools of ourselves as Ralph Adams Cram.

LITERARY LUNCHES

The earnest crusade of the Arts and Crafts Society, the frolics of aesthetes and artists, the hail-fellows-well-met Pewter Mug, and the more precious Order of the White Rose did not exhaust Cram. To these groups one must add rather a leftish literary lunch club in order to catch the full flavor and variety of his leadership role in Boston's Bohemia. Rather more intellectual in character than the others, this club met invariably in the Hotel Victoria diagonally across from the Public Library in Copley Square and was described by the legendary Houghton Mifflin editor Ferris Greenslet:

> An informal lunch club met every day around a table at the Victoria, in a basement so far below the level of the street [a restaurant is still there today] that one looking up could sometimes see even the scalloped tops of passing ladies' shoes. It was a gathering of literary lefties, Hunt and Chevalier from the [Boston Public] Library, Professor Weiner and once in a while Lanman from Harvard, Truman H. Bartlett, sculptor, Ralph Cram, Prior of the Order of the White Rose, Tom Meteyard, amateur of all the arts, the partners of the minor publishing houses of Small and Maynard, Curtis and Cameron, and Copeland and Day, who were convinced that they, not Little, Brown and Houghton Mifflin over on the hill, were carrying the torch of Boston letters.
>
> They were, too, up to a point. Sometimes Richard Hovey would come in, black-coated, black-hatted, black-bearded, a revenant from the boulevards of Paris, or Bliss Carman . . . to read some Anacreontic just finished, to inquire whether it were suitable for *Songs from Vagabondia*. I recall a particularly agreeable one, beginning "Who is this I cannot see / Tumbling over me?" and my regret when it was decided to be suitable but not possible.[70]

Though no figure from the *Atlantic Monthly* is mentioned, these authors and editors were as likely to be courting that medium as they were book publishers and editors, for it was one in which Pinckney Street residents played a conspicuous role, as designers (Hallowell) or editors (Carman) or writers (many, including Guiney and Cram). Jackson Lears explains:

> During the 1890s historical romances ... flooded American magazines ... romantic adventure pervaded the "quality magazine" — *Harper's Monthly*, *Scribner's*, the *Century*, the *Atlantic Monthly* — as well as the upstarts [such as *Munsey's* and *McClure's*, the background of which flood was] an assault on the "feminization" of American culture [and the] displacement of Gothic romanticism. ... Many activist critics [concluded it] was necessary to rediscover the Middle Ages, when "men sang [in] a manlier way."

In his ensuing analysis Lears enfolds no less than three of Pinckney Street's luminaries (not to him identifiable as such, of course; he is dealing with American writers in general) into his discussion:

> Martial lyrics like those of Louise Imogen Guiney and Richard Hovey filled magazines ... whether set in medieval England or the American West — the revival of historical romance embodied longings for psychic rejuvenation. To Bliss Carman, the popularity of Kipling, Stevenson, and other "masculine world wanderers" suggested ... [as he wrote in 1894] "we must have a revolt at any cost." ... [Carman's and Hovey's *Songs from Vagabondia* (1894)] ... mingled ... sword and buckler with ... the camaraderie of the open road.[71]

Immediately evident here is a predisposition toward the manly (no less than in Sullivan's and Cram's hymns to Richardson's architecture) that was also reflected in the boys' literature of the day as well, a corollary particularly significant because this was an aspect of things to which the ethos of Pinckney Street was closely linked. Editors (including Cram's own at the *Transcript*) lived on that street, too, and many an author by night was (by way of supporting the habit) an editor by day. Indeed, many of the missing links between these and others, on Beacon Hill and in Cambridge, are disclosed only at that often overlooked "daytime" level; Alice Brown, Herbert Copeland, and Charles Flandrau were all, for example, fellow editors at the *Youth's Companion*.[72]

Of course, nothing in Bohemia is ever quite what it seems; and this was true as well, scholars now hazard, of the authors Lears quotes Bliss Carman as so much admiring. Of an era when "the homosocial 'romance' of adventure and quest, descended from Arthurian epic" replaced the "heterosexual romance of courting," Elaine Showalter writes:

> Boys' fiction ... conveyed an illusion of eternal masculine youth. ... "Boy" was the euphemistic Victorian terminology for the male lover, as "lad" would be for [a later] generation. Masculine romance, its advocates believed, "tapped universal, deep-rooted, 'primitive' aspects. ..."; these included strong if unconscious homoerotic feelings. ... [In this literary genre, called the male quest romance by scholars, it was] usually Africa or ... a mysterious district of the East [that was the setting for sexual experience unobtainable in Europe, often involving] ... a blurring of sexual boundaries. In [his translation of] *Arabian Nights* (1885–86), for example, Sir Richard Burton delineated ... [what] he called the "Sotadic Zone" in which ... Burton claimed, "there is a blending of the masculine and feminine temperaments."[73]

The medieval and Arthurian overtones of this literary activity were paralleled to a varying degree in nearly all the artistic work of Pinckney Street, of course, where the literary Gothic Revival of Guiney and Hovey found an echo in the medievalist book design of Updike and Goodhue; men singing in a manlier way was not unreflective of Vaughan's and Cram's grave and austere church design. And it is surely also reflected — admittedly, to push the point — in yet another medium in the powerful and severe music of Pinckney Street's leading composer (with whom, we have Cram's word for it, he collaborated as beautifully and usefully as with Goodhue), Fred Bullard.

Not only did the same causes and themes and attitudes resonate in their naturally quite varied and individual ways among all these artists and in their several media, but they did it so contagiously and effervescently that Cram, as likely to be a poet one day, an architect the next, or a critic or an interior designer or a lyricist or whatever, so abounding were his gifts and enthusiasms, was scarcely less involved in the literary Gothic Revival than in the architectural one. In 1893, for instance, Cram's poem "Saint George of England" was published in *New England Magazine*, a year before his design of the interior of the Lady Chapel at the Church of the Advent, the setting for the statue of Saint George that was finally installed there under his direction years later. Cram refused to confine himself to any one medium. For him the *idea* was key; art, he would often say, was a *result* of an idea. It might — in his case, it usually did — move one first (action precedes belief), but it was always toward an idea of which it was the result, the expression. Cram preached Saint George, as it were, the True Knight, in words or wood or whatever as occasion presented itself. And this cross-media propensity was characteristic of Pinckney Street. Poet Bliss Carman, for example, wrote for *Craftsman* magazine, even as book designer Will Bradley was photographed at home in the Boston suburb of Concord comfortably ensconced in his Morris chair in a *Craftsman*-like house.[74]

Few, however, went at it with quite Cram's gusto. No less than seven of his poems were published in 1892–1895 in various American magazines, including the prestigious *Century*. Often somewhat mawkish to our ears today (as compared with his prose, which still moves us), to be properly evaluated they need to be considered in context; which is to say, for example, that Cram's "Saint George" needs to be read as a caption for, or, perhaps, as a gloss on, his statue of Saint George in the Advent Lady Chapel. Indeed, this kind of context is essential in respect to all of Cram's poetry, which falls almost invariably into the first of Showalter's categories, "the homosocial 'romance' of adventure and quest," and hardly at all in her other category, the "heterosexual romance of courting." A chorus from his "secular cantata," *The Boat of Love*, is characteristic:

"Swords were made for men to use; / Soldiers only crave / Now to win, if then to lose, / Now to love, if then to choose / Fame or shallow grave." Another chorus from the same work is a vivid example of Cram's word painting: "Silence: save a sound of grieving / While the looming moon of brass / Lifts above the ocean, heaving / Hungrily. As in a glass / Dusky shadows stagger by, / Waving wings along the sky, / Where the tangled winds are weaving / Webs of tempest as they pass." Cram was quite a success as a poet. In *The Chap-Book* Goodhue claimed that as of 1895 it was "in verse that [Cram's] best known and appreciated work has been done," catching in Cram's poetry echoes of Rossetti, Tennyson, and Swinburne.[75]

Moreover, though it seems improbable now, Cram appears in the nineties to have written as many plays as poems. ("Cram is taking a so-called rest," wrote Wentworth to Edward Gale in 1892; "He is working hard on a play and calls that rest!") It was a lifelong passion however. We have seen that even as a boy (recall *Faust*) Cram was keen on the theater, and all his life a propensity on his part for amateur theatricals was widely noticed—a propensity that also plays into the theme of mask and signal, reveal and conceal, so important in this study. For homosexuals, obviously, something akin to acting has long been second nature. In Cram's case it would appear that in no aspect of the theater was he lacking in talent. Thanks to the Harvard Theatre Collection's record we know that Cram's play *The Angelus* was given its premiere by New York's American Academy of Dramatic Arts before 1893 and also that Cram was asked to do the costume design. And in at least one instance Cram himself and Goodhue too did the acting, playing the leads in a production of 1900 in the Boston suburb of Brookline of Lope de Vega's *The Duenna Outwitted*.[76]

The best known of his plays, published in a sumptuous edition by the Gorham Press, was *Excalibur*, written about 1895. A full-scale Arthurian epic, it was apparently suggested by a prologue entitled "Excalibur" to *King Arthur*, a play with music by Sir Arthur Sullivan and scenery by Sir Edward Burne-Jones, which, according to a news clipping in one of Cram's scrapbooks, opened in London in January 1895.[77] Cram's play was also suggested by Richard Hovey's efforts in the spirit of Morris and Rossetti that were among the most popular Pinckney Street contributions to the general culture in the nineties. Cram himself recalled Wagnerian influences in an introduction he wrote for the play's publication seventeen years later and rashly pronounced it, when he was old enough to know better, the "best thing I ever wrote."[78] Written in blank verse, it is terribly earnest but very bombastic; though that is too easy. Taste no more than morals should not be so readily projected backward by one generation on to another. Santayana, for example, also in the 1890s inflicted *Lucifer*, a verse drama, on the world, and Santayana's biographer has well observed that that great philosopher was "*not* a dramatist."[79] Cram's biographer must take the same view of a certain great architect.[80]

Alas, in the nineties Cram never quite gathered his forces sufficiently to create an "Arthurian" architecture to match his literary work. Yet other hands ensured that Boston was endowed with a splendid Arthurian (even Wagnerian) decor: under the aegis of McKim, Mead and White, Edwin Austin Abbey's murals, *The Quest of the Holy Grail*, created just such a setting in the Abbey Room in the new Boston Public Library. Thomas Russell Sullivan remembered in his journal the architects' private viewing in April 1895, at which it is very likely Cram and Goodhue were present:

> There were two hundred guests. . . . It was a splendid affair of brilliant jewels and costumes. . . . An orchestra played on the landing of the marble staircase, up and down which the pretty women strolled in all their glory of satin, lace and diamonds. It happened to be a very warm night, and through the open windows of the court the fountain flashed and sparkled, throwing its tallest jet almost to the roof. The Abbey and Sargent pictures overwhelmed us all. . . . [The Holy Grail murals] are brilliant dramatic scenes, well composed, glowing with color. . . . After the reception some of us were invited to a supper at the Algonquin Club.[81]

Thus did the beau monde and Bohemia occasionally briefly commingle in Boston's brilliant nineties.

ALL MUST BE EXPRESSED

The donnish and leftish lunch club that launched our discussion of some of Cram's efforts in the literary Gothic Revival met in the shadow of the new public library Cram admired so, architecturally, and that it involved not a few of its librarians reflects that institution's importance to Boston's Bohemians. So many strands intertwine at the library, which is more associated with aesthete-decadent thinking than is at first apparent. The pallid spirits of the gallery murals by Puvis de Chavanne (whose work was much admired by Rosicrucian circles in Paris and also by both Verlaine and Mallarmé) inhabit a silvery sacred wood equally as mystic and ethereal as the darker Wagnerian glades of Edwin Austin Abbey's murals of the Knights of the Holy Grail nearby, and neither conception is far removed from the rainswept Celtic vistas of Yeats. As for Sargent's tremendous cycle of murals: their depths, hardly suspected by most, are decadent enough to arise repeatedly in the fascinating volume of Philippe Jullian, *Dreamers of Decadence*.

Boston's own also made their timely contribution. Maud Howe Elliott's husband, John, as noted previously, did a ceiling mural. The Venetian Lobby is the superb work of Isabella Gardner's friend and Cram's Pinckney Street neighbor, Joseph Lindon Smith. In Bates Hall is a bust of Whittier by another of Cram's friends, William Ordway Partridge. Even the library's first architectural guide was distinctly a production of Cram's set: the text was by Herbert Small, the cover design by Bertram Goodhue.

Other Bohemians had more practical associations with the library. Francis Watts Lee, who collaborated with Cram and Goodhue as the printer of *Knight Errant*, was for years the library printing department's chief. Philip Savage, whom Day was very much enamored of, supported himself for some years as the director's secretary. And poor Lou Guiney called the windowless and airless cataloging department her workaday home for too long (in aid of her always fragile finances). With her usual good humor she made the best of it, writing to Savage: "Perhaps we shall collide on the back stairs, at intervals, and swear in hexameters *viva felix*."[82] Besides, quite often Fred Day would be waiting for her by the main entrance at midday to waft her off to a smart lunch she certainly otherwise could not have afforded. Even more than Trinity Church, the library was Bohemian Boston's pride and joy. And this was especially true of Cram, who exulted over McKim's masterwork, calling it an example of "serene Classicism, reserved, scholarly, delicately conceived."[83]

The library was not stylistically, to be sure, Cram's chief passion, any more than was Trinity. But as we have seen in so many of Cram's early projects, though he was an ardent Goth, he by no means — not since his awed fascination with Randall and the glorious stylistic chaos of Sicily in 1888 — deprecated other styles in every varying circumstance. And poised as we now are here on his and Goodhue's first realized major non-Gothic (and in fact classical) institutional architecture (very much in the wake of the Boston Public Library), it is timely to explore at some length this key matter of Cram's attitude to style, so widely misunderstood, as that attitude can be documented in the 1890s, *before* the days of his fame.

Cram thoroughly discussed this matter, hardly less important to his overall work than his theory of a developing modern Gothic school, in a speech given in 1899 to the American Institute of Architects, in which he reviewed the whole subject before what was likely to be, after all, a highly critical audience.[84] Asked to deal with the influence of French architecture, he addressed as one of his themes the eclecticism of his own era, and he did so with wit and perspicacity, even having kind words for the tortured Queen Anne (some would have called it Gothic and/or Richardsonian Romanesque) of his Rotch and Tilden days:

> The Queen Anne craze served the part of the swallow of salt water in the case of seasickness — it prepared the system. [Richardsonian] Romanesque gave us some idea of what vigor and power and honesty meant. . . . Colonial suggested to us the

value of historical association — of ethnical continuity. And the Parisian Renaissance? I honestly think it will do more good than any of the others, [teaching] . . . a certain self-restraint, [ending] . . . our period of aesthetic anarchy.

Not only historical time but also historical place mattered also to Cram, who observed pointedly to his fellow architects:

The Parthenon would be grotesque in Paris, the Opera is admirable. Architecture is good if it expresses the time and the people and the spirit that made it possible; it is bad if it is an affectation. . . . The Paris Renaissance of the boulevards is better architecture than would be the Doric of Greece . . . or the Gothic of the Ile de France on the Rue de Rivoli, and yet, in the abstract, . . . the Greek and the Gothic are good, the Renaissance bad.

So, after all, it is worse than useless to dispute as to whether Parisian Renaissance is really a good style or a bad — for France. It is inevitable, it expresses the time, . . . therefore it is a thousand times more respectable than the archaeological Gothic of the thirteenth century pasted over the outside of English law-courts.

Central to Cram's view, however, was that what was good for a Paris boulevard was not good for a New England town; what was fine as an expression of the genius of one ethnic group was not necessarily fine for every ethnic group; and, above all, what was fine for apartment houses or shops was not fine for Anglican churches, for example. Continued Cram, still in a cosmopolitan vein: "If we are English by blood and sympathy, we are French by perversity, and all must be expressed. There is much in our society that can be better expressed through the French style than any other." And by way of example he had already in this speech, speaking as an advertised Gothicist, taken pains to point out that "Gothic would be an offense in a fire house or a Turkish bath." He had also noted that "skyscrapers demand an utterly new architectural expression" (an opportunity for which Cram waited another thirty years). It was religious, collegiate, and domestic design that concerned Cram, and especially for churches he argued for

the splendid Gothic that Bodley and Sedding and Austin and Paley and their . . . associates have restored to life and vigor. . . . As for our commercial work . . . it demands a new style and we are achieving it, but not by way of the Ecole; rather by obeying the dictates of our common sense. . . . All hopes of a single style are vain. What our civilization is, that must our art be also, and our civilization is as various as our population.

Multiculturism in 1899! Finally, Cram concluded with a scathing attack on a sometime hero — which shows that his mind was not nearly so closed or his views so static as many have thought. Arguing that architects must not allow themselves "to be led away by [any] tempest of fanaticism," Cram pleaded: "above all things, let us have — in architecture — no bigotry." And his warning

83. Exterior view of Cram and Goodhue's Sayles Public Library, Pawtucket, Rhode Island, 1898. The figure sculpture of this major example of the firm's classical tastes is by Lee Lawrie.

of 1899 could not have been more blunt a repudiation of his views a decade earlier:

> Ruskin was a bigot, and he made himself absurd by his frantic advocacy of certain forms of architecture; frankly, I think some of those who now must religiously uphold exactly what he with equal vigor denied are laying themselves open to the same condemnation.

No wonder, books and buildings having kept such close company for so long in Cram's life, and McKim's new Boston library having so won Cram's admiration, that in 1896 and 1898 respectively Cram and Goodhue began the design process for the Fall River Public Library in that city south of Boston and the Pawtucket Public Library in Rhode Island, both of which are, in very different ways, distinctly classical. (This is not to suggest that Cram thought Gothic unsuitable for libraries; only a few years later he designed the Nashua, New Hampshire, Public Library in Gothic, and it won high critical acclaim.)

The Pawtucket library (83) is perhaps of the most interest, for Goodhue was out of the country for much of the time during which it was designed, which no doubt accounts for its severe style and more than usually austere mien. Correspondence with the client documents the facts that for Cram then (this would change in later years when a Mediterranean cruise altered his perspective) Greek classical design did not, he thought, have the potential for development that Gothic (and to a certain extent Colonial) design had, and that he was

329

"anxious to make [the library] a perfectly correct and scholarly piece of Greek Ionic design." So correct, indeed, that on more than one occasion Cram felt forced to defend his work against his client, protesting in one case that a certain carved molding was "an integral part of the Greek Style and were it omitted the result would be simply ignorant and ungrammatical."[85] The result is a stunning building, rising splendidly above its indifferent surroundings, showing just the severe beauty one would expect of a romantic Goth who was also a Platonic idealist.

In the more Italianate Fall River library, as in the Pawtucket library, Cram and Goodhue demonstrated much more than competence in classical design, for McKim's glorious Boston library seems never to have been very far from their minds. At Fall River, particularly, they used McKim's brilliant modernistic Arts and Crafts flush-panel door designs — very reminiscent of what I have called here the "constructional" detail of Cram and Wentworth — and also a great deal of beautifully veined colored marble. They also planned an extensive cycle of mural paintings, after the manner of the Boston library. This plan was never carried to completion, but the Fall River mural scheme was succeeded by an even more grandiose sculptural scheme at the Pawtucket library, notable as having been the first extensive work for the office by Lee Lawrie,[86] who in 1918 would model the figure sculpture of the high altar reredos of St. Thomas, Fifth Avenue, the acknowledged masterwork of its type of Cram and Goodhue's maturity.

In the nineties, meanwhile, doubtless all concerned were grateful that between the Pewter Mugs and the artists' fêtes and the literary lunches there was at least some chance for more permanent glory in the odd church or library. But there was in the end always enough time for the important things: White Rose in Boston and . . .

PURPLE ROSE IN CAMBRIDGE

Cambridge (which, not unreasonably, thinks of itself as Boston's Left Bank) was then as now the New England capital's better half. Van Wyck Brooks, for instance, recalled that at fin-de-siècle Harvard there were two popular cults among his friends: "the cult of Dante, which Mrs. Gardner also embraced," presided over by Charles Eliot Norton, one knows; the other was "the semi-serious cult . . . [of the] Order of the White Rose . . . led by Ralph Adams Cram."[87] Cram, of course, was never in those days in any way connected with Harvard (President Eliot, as we have seen, could not stand him), but it was a very short trolley ride from one place to another across the river, which bears King Charles's name, after all.

In fact, Boston's Bohemians sought out in other Boston suburbs, far from Pinckney Street, more unlikely locales for their activities. Norwood and Gloucester come quickest to mind, of course. But Herbert Small and his wife gave literary soirées at their apartment in the Hotel Nightingale in Dorchester; there was even a distinctly Bohemian artistic and literary colony in the suburb of Scituate, to the south of Boston, clustering around Meeting House Lane and including Testudo, the Meteyard house. Here Meteyard, Carman, Hovey, and Goodhue joined forces for a time to produce the *Courrier Innocent*, a paper the first numbers of which had been produced at Giverny by the young American artists (including Meteyard and Hovey) who wintered there at the feet of Claude Monet. Text and decorations, wrote Nancy Finlay, "were painstakingly cut in wood by the contributors, and printed on tan tissue-like paper by D. Dawson-Watson, using a rolling pin and a piece of felt." Inevitably, Dawson-Watson followed up on all this with an article in *The Literary Review* entitled "The Rolling-Pin in Art."[88] Amen.

Cambridge, however, contained Bohemia's heaviest concentration (indeed, Goodhue actually lived there, on Buckingham Street) beyond Beacon Hill, particularly such haunts at Harvard as the Stylus Club and the Signet Society, remodeled, as we have noted, by Cram, Goodhue, and La Rose (*84*). At the Stylus, as Van Wyck Brooks recalled, everyone read Walter Pater's *Marius the Epicurean* (a defense of life as chiefly aesthetic appreciation), and the bookcases overflowed with Joris-Karl Huysmans and Oscar Wilde.[89] Even Swinburne; Martin Green observes that everywhere it was Swinburne who provided "the litanies of aesthetic/erotic rebellion" so vital to the fin-de-siècle.[90] Van Wyck Brooks remarks that, especially in Boston, Swinburne "charmed the latter-day New England mind [because he was so] 'capable of passion.' . . . [His] freedom and extravagance . . . cast a spell," Brooks felt, even over "Henry Adams [and] enchanted the souls of . . . other inhibited Yankees."[91] And, indeed, moved the habitués of the Stylus to their own excesses, albeit highly creative ones, such as commissioning no less than Bruce Rogers to "design the menu for [a Stylus member's] twenty-first birthday dinner" at the Somerset Club on Beacon Hill.[92] Rogers, a denizen of Pinckney Street and a member of the Pewter Mugs, was then employed at the Riverside Press in Cambridge, on the eve of a career in bookmaking that would be of national importance.

If aside from Beacon Hill the neighborhood of Harvard Square was the favored quarter of Bohemia, a "little magazine," such as the *Courrier Innocent*, was the favored cause of Bohemia everywhere, the occasion for various of its cohorts to group and regroup as needs and enthusiasms suggested. Thus Cram recalled the Santayana-La Rose circle in Cambridge as generating the first of Boston Bohemia's magazines of the era, one that took its name from William

84. Signet Society House, Cambridge, Massachusetts, as remodeled in 1902 by Cram, Goodhue, and Pierre La Rose, according to the last of whom it was intended to restore the house, not as it originally was but as it "originally ought to have been"! Thus the architectural solecism of the two orders (Doric and Ionic) of the porch was retained but elaborate decorative features were added, including the pedimented pavilion blazoned with the Signet arms — a signet ring circled by bees, surmounted by a forearm and hand holding a book inscribed *Veritas*, and beribboned with a motto from Plato's *Phaedo*: ΜΟΥΣΙΚΗΝ ΠΟΙΕΙ ΚΑΙ ΕΠΓΑΖΟΥ (Work and ply the Muses).

Makepeace Thackeray's poem "The Mahogany Tree" and in which both Cram's and Day's work appeared. This effort (which lasted only six months, starting in January and folding in July 1892) was dominated by Harvard undergraduates, although *The Mahogany Tree* originated, not at Harvard or even in Cambridge, as Cram's account in his memoirs suggests,[93] but in a downtown Boston bar. Its inception was, in Thayer Lincoln's words to Cram in a letter forty-some years later, at

> a serious, but not altogether sober party at the Bell-in-Hand . . . [in] Pi Alley. The idea originated, I think, with Herbert Small and Phil Winn. . . . Winn, as I remember, was unable to keep sober long enough to become a contributor and most of the editorial work fell upon Herbert Copeland as Editor-in-Chief. Phil Savage contributed each week a translation from *Horace*. Arthur Taylor Knapp wrote the musical criticism, Herbert Small many of the book reviews.[94]

Quite new and entirely American work also appeared in the *Tree*, recalled today chiefly as the journal that first published Willa Cather.[95]

"Little care we / Little we fear / Weather without / Sheltered about / the Mahogany Tree" appeared always on the cover. Inside, more seriously, but not wearyingly so, the *Tree*'s editors opined:

> We have tried, of course, to reform the world, — to induce mankind to turn now and then from the mad chase after the Almighty Dollar, and smoke cigarettes and read Oscar Wilde. We have taken sides against electric cars, bicycles, and Mr. Howells. We have played at Theosophy because we found it amusing. . . . We have sung the praises of cigarettes and coffee, not for themselves alone, but because they stand for a mood opposed to that prevailing one of our times which turns life into an express train.[96]

That mood, expressed by all the little magazines of the 1890s and 1900s, yielded also *The Cult of the Purple Rose*, written by Shirley E. Johnson and published in 1902. As might be expected, it is a curious book, part fact, part fantasy, wholly sardonic.

There *are* some clear links to reality. Bliss Carman is mentioned, and many of the works Fred Day published — including John Davidson's *Ballad of a Nun* (the cult's "criterion of excellence") and *The Yellow Book*, all of the numbers of which the members are said to own. In fact, in an allusion to *The Yellow Book*, *The Cult of the Purple Rose* has a yellow binding on which is emblazoned a vastly vulgar purple blossom.

The most intriguing of the links to the real Boston Bohemia is that *The Purple Rose*'s publisher, Richard C. Badger's Gorham Press, was also Cram's publisher of his play *Excalibur*. And as with *The Chap-Book*, the character of Cram's publishers and the company he was keeping (a part of our enlarging mosaic of evidence) are of no little interest to us.

In the case of *The Chap-Book*, it published during the 1890s and 1900s some of the most advanced of the European decadents. In the case of Gorham Press, between the turn of the century and the First World War, the character of this house is evident in the fact that Badger is known to have initiated talks on shared distribution of materials with the British Society for the Study of Sex Psychology, led by Edward Carpenter himself and backed by Havelock Ellis. And Badger did not exaggerate when he asserted that his publishing house was issuing "a number of advanced sex books which are meeting with a very remarkable reception in this country." Among the titles that surrounded Cram's (published in 1909) on Gorham's list in the same time frame were books both scholarly and artistic that featured homosexual themes, ranging from Sándor Ferenczi's *Contribution to Psychoanalysis* (1916) to Badger Clark's *Sun and Saddle Leather* of three years later.[97] And even in the nineties Gorham's character was such as to suggest close links to Harvard's Bohemia especially.

The Cult of the Purple Rose, with all its allusions to the Boston Bohemia of the nineties, rather more exotic than *Harvard Episodes*, is also almost certainly derived from the Santayana-La Rose circle at Harvard. It is a very roundabout series of tales of clever social climbers who give "purple teas" and nervous hothouse flowers who pass out at Theosophist rallies held on Boston Common under purple banners, tales the author writes are by no means representative of Harvard College; but though they are "the doing of a few extremists . . . many of the episodes here recorded actually occurred," which begins to sound similar to Cram's disclaimers in his dedication of *Black Spirits and White*.

It is a nice question, indeed, how much is fact and how much fable, given the cult's emphasis, above all things, on *incongruity*. Here, for example, is a description of the study of one of the cult's leading lights:

> Eddie DeLancy belonged to the most original set at Harvard, and his study . . . [reflected this]. . . . On the wall were pictures hung with incongruity, for beside a large photograph of St. John's Cathedral was a nude from the Salon; and there was a group of college editors hanging between a pen imitation of one of Mr. Aubrey Beardsley's drawings and a picture of Phillips Brooks.
>
> In a cozy nook, made by a fish net and some ribbons, was a small wood carving, and on the mantel stood a statuette of Apollo Belvedere, surrounded by queerly-shaped pipes, daily themes and glasses which alternately held beer and dust.[98]

One thinks at once of the odd juxtapositions from *The Mauve Decade* that opened this chapter. Yet the cult was in its own way consistent. It had, for instance, no officers—the host of every meeting became the leader—and no regular meetings; any member could call a meeting at any time by placing as a signal a pale purple light in one of his windows in Harvard Yard or along Mount Auburn Street. And its "little magazine" was intended to be "unique, original,

334

striking and impossible." Only *one* issue was to be published, rather like the small magazine Alice Brown and Louise Guiney are said to have published, with a masthead tagline that read "Ave morituri te salutamus."[99]

Nor were the nature and character of the cult hardly ever in doubt. In fact, the discussion that launched it (in Eddie DeLancy's study) turned upon the whole subject of Robert Hichen's *Green Carnation*, the book mentioned in Chapter 2, where the significance of the color green and the carnation to homosexuality in this era first arose here. Declaims one of the aesthete Harvardians in Johnson's book: "The Green Carnation — 'tis absinthe / in far more ways than one; / It makes me long for crème de menthe — / My last debauch is done." Another member of the Purple Rose agrees: "It [*The Green Carnation*] is verily the most modern of modern books; so modern, indeed, that its very modernity makes one regret one is modern." Even more pointedly, another member then chimes in: "It's so original to make the best of what one has, just as if it were one's ideal."[100]

If the point of the novel is the meaninglessness of modern life, that certainly explains the book's fairly ghastly ending. Not content with the suicide of the little magazine, *The Cult of the Purple Rose* climaxes in the suicide of one of the members, who leaves behind for the support of his lady fair a bulky manuscript he declares to be of great value but is found upon investigation to be "a great package of blank paper." Except the top page, that is, upon which is written: "A Poet Without a Soul: A Novel of Modern Life."

In real life, however, Cram and his Boston and Cambridge cohorts were about to achieve a triumph few literate New Englanders failed to notice. Like Guiney and Day, Cram was an enthusiastic contributor to *The Mahogany Tree*. But in Stephen Parrish's words, "Cram had never lost his vision of *The XXth Century*,"[101] the journal he and Berenson and Partridge and Guiney had sought to bring into being in the late 1880s.

Years later Rose Nichols used to say that, after Cram's marriage, what his wife, who did not approve of Cram's Bohemian friends, did not understand was that Ralph Adams Cram was "a man's man" — it was another euphemism of the day — "who enjoyed and needed [such] friendship . . . had always been a popular leader in a group of men, and after marriage [when] this was discouraged, he missed the association and inspiration very much."[102] What both meant to him is, in fact, best glimpsed in his project for *The XXth Century*. Cram would be a founder of many other magazines (one, *Commonweal*, survives still). None equaled *Knight Errant*, as it was finally called when the first issue appeared in 1892.

9

GAY GOTHIC, DECADENT GOSPEL

In Freud's theory, the mental forces opposed to the reality principle [operate] from the unconscious. . . . [These forces constitute] Phantasy (imagination) . . . a thought-process with its own laws. . . . The truths of imagination are first realized when fantasy itself takes form. . . . This occurs in *art*. . . .

Like imagination, which is its constitutive mental faculty, the realm of aesthetics . . . has retained its freedom from the reality principle at the price of being ineffective in the reality. Aesthetic values may function in life for cultural adornment or as private hobbies, but to *live* with these values is the privilege of geniuses or the mark of decadent Bohemians.

— Herbert Marcuse, *Eros and Civilization*

A·QVARTER·YEARLY
REVIEW·OF·THE·LIB-
ERAL·ARTS·CALLED
THE·KNIGHT·ERRANT·
BEING·A·MAGAZINE
OF·APPRECIATION

PRINTED·FOR·THE·PROPRIE-
TORS·AT·THE·ELZEVIR·PRESS
BOSTON··A·D·MDCCCXCII···

VOLVME·FIRST   NVMBER·ONE·

85. *Above*: Goodhue's cover design for *Knight Errant*, April 1892. *Knight Errant* was intended to be "an expression of the most advanced thought of its time," wrote its editors. It is not clear if, in addition to being *Knight Errant*'s editor (with Goodhue), Cram was still (with C. Howard Walker) editor of *Architectural Review*. If so, editorial cross-purposes surely vexed Cram when the older journal in June 1892 pronounced the newer one an "aesthetic anarchist" not much to its liking.

THE CHAP-BOOK, that avant-garde banner of the gay nineties, first issued by Herbert Stone and Ingalls Kimball in 1894 from an office on Brattle Street, when both were undergraduates in Harvard College (Bliss Carman was the editor), is perhaps today as celebrated as *The Yellow Book*. Most of the leading fin-de-siècle figures of two continents did work for *The Chap-Book*; Paul Verlaine, Aubrey Beardsley, Max Beerbohm, Anatole France, Charles Ricketts, Robert Louis Stevenson, Stephen Crane, and Stéphane Mallarmé all appeared in its pages, to the chagrin and bewilderment of the American establishment. So, too, did the work of native decadents and proto-Modernists like Will Bradley and John Sloane and, perhaps most prominently among Boston's Bohemians, Ralph Adams Cram, whose repute in this context largely reflected his having been the founder and editor of *The Chap-Book*'s illustrious forerunner, *Knight Errant*.

MEN AGAINST AN EPOCH

It lasted for only four issues (the last one almost a year late when it came out); it boasted only a fraction of the famous names who wrote for *The Chap-Book*; it never enjoyed a wide, national circulation. Yet Stephen Parrish is surely correct to name *Knight Errant* "the crowning artistic achievement of Bohemia."[1] And it must be said as well that Cram, for us today of interest as a great architect and not as the indifferent poet, playwright, and librettist we now judge him to have been (even as art critic and short-story writer he is hardly a major figure), still ranks fairly high as an editor, having discharged that office with Goodhue so brilliantly that *Knight Errant* has been called by one major critic hardly less important to the history of typography and bookmaking than the founding by William Morris of the Kelmscott Press.[2]

Cram ruled over the words, Goodhue over the decor, particularly the cover (85), which was his, while Herbert Copeland seconded Cram by reading manuscripts and Fred Day seconded Goodhue by serving as page designer. Francis Watts Lee (whom Cram would have known from the Christian Socialist Church of the Carpenter, where Lee was very active in the nineties) was what we would call today the production editor. The contents of the magazine were also impressive. Charles Eliot Norton besought America to elevate its tastes, taking his friend Ruskin's view that art was a civilization's best measure and test of value. From England Walter Crane weighed in enthusiastically; Day essayed an elaborate review of Oscar Wilde's *House of Pomegranates*; Berenson (writing from abroad) was brilliant on Correggio; Lee was ardent about the Kelmscott Press; Cram played the historian and Goodhue the critic; and two others — Ernest Fenollosa and Arthur Wesley Dow — held forth on the glories of Japanese art.[3] Well might both. Fenollosa, a Harvard graduate and the first curator in this field at the Museum of Fine Arts, would become as well a great benefactor of Boston when his collection came to the museum, while Dow, who "had a major influence upon art instruction in American schools" in his era, was an artist known for his wood-block prints, in which he "applied Japanese techniques to New England expression.")[4]

Knight Errant's design was, in Guiney's words, "as Medieval as possible";[5] more important, design was given equal weight with text. Cram and Goodhue as joint editors showed their true colors at once, announcing that their knight had been summoned "to ride for the succor of forlorn hopes and the restoration of forgotten ideals." ("Men against an epoch; is it not that after all?" they asserted.)[6] The contributors were brave and their work winning, not least Ralph's: "The doughty Cram," wrote Guiney, "swings his sword at the world generally."[7] Nor did Guiney herself disappoint. Her title poem is worth quoting in full:

> Spirits of old that bore me,
> And set me, meek of mind,
> Between great dreams before me
> And dreams as great behind,
> Knowing humanity my star
> As first abroad I ride,
> Shall help me wear, with every scar,
> Honour at eventide.
>
> Let claws of lightning clutch me,
> From summer's groaning cloud,
> Or ever malice touch me
> And glory make me proud.
> O give my faith, my youth, my sword,
> Choice of the heart's desire:
> A short life in the saddle, Lord!
> Not long life by the fire.
>
> Forethought and recollection
> Rivet mine armour gay!
> The passion of perfection
> Redeem my faulty way!

> The outer fray in the sun shall be
> The inner beneath the moon;
> And may Our Lady lend to me
> Sight of the Dragon soon![8]

The triumph was not only regional. It was national, indeed, transatlantic. Just as Ashbee praised (and joined) the Boston Society of Arts and Crafts, so also Walter Crane saluted *Knight Errant* enthusiastically in his *Artist's Reminiscences*.[9]

Scholars have agreed with Crane ever since. Nancy Finlay has pronounced it "the beginning of a new period of bookmaking in America." And with good reason, given *Knight Errant*'s progeny. Explained Finlay:

> Although the *Knight Errant* disappeared in 1893, after just four numbers, within the year two of its contributors, Fred Holland Day and Herbert Copeland, had founded Copeland and Day. . . . The formation of Stone and Kimball by Herbert Stone and Ingalls Kimball, two Harvard undergraduates who had fallen under the spell of the Visionists [of whom more shortly], followed quickly. Herbert Small, Laurens Maynard and Daniel Berkeley Updike were all in touch with the same group, so that in a sense, the firms of Copeland and Day, Stone and Kimball, Small, Maynard and Company and even Merrymount Press, all owe their existence to the same influence.[10]

It was an astonishing roster of presses. Of Copeland and Day, who became the chief thrust of the aesthetic-decadent movement in America, we shall have much to say shortly. Of Stone and Kimball (publishers of Cram's *Black Spirits and White*) it is sufficient to note that in 1894 they not only began issuing *The Chap-Book* but also published Santayana's first book and gave Will Bradley his first commission to design a book. Small, Maynard and Company would ultimately publish Cram's most famous book, *Church Building*; and Updike's Merrymount Press became in its day the most influential printer in America. If Ralph Adams Cram had never designed a church, he would be remembered for his role in the history of American bookmaking.

A House Divided

It cost Cram dearly, however, this creative ferment of the mid-nineties heralded by *Knight Errant*. For Cram's increasingly complex life after his thirtieth birthday in 1893 — a life that can be more or less reconstructed by a careful reading of his correspondence of this period, kept all his life, such was its importance to him — must have been discouraging and exhausting in equal measure. Nor was the heart of his life, architecture, by any means exempt. It was not just that the artistic success of Cram, Wentworth and Goodhue's early churches was not replicated on the financial side. Their troubles went much deeper.

341

Certainly there is in his mid-1890s letters to Ralph Adams Cram clear evidence that Charles Wentworth found Bertram Goodhue more than a little trying. Perhaps Wentworth resented the personal closeness of his original partner and the newcomer; it would have been only natural for him to feel in some ways excluded. But it would seem Goodhue worried Wentworth on several grounds, an impression certainly conveyed by a letter of January 1894, in which Wentworth writes:

> Dear Ralph
>   I enclose you a cheque for $200.00. This is the best I can do and you will have to make it go as far as possible. . . . The Boylston Bank would not advance us a note unless it had my wife's endorsement. . . . Jam the people that owe us; there is no reason why we should carry people who can afford to pay. . . . I have loaned you since the first of last August . . . nine hundred and fifty dollars and 500.00 of that I borrowed and am paying interest on. . . . Damn the arch, it is only a waste of time and money making drawings for it. . . . Love to all.
>
>   C.[11]

The "arch" was Goodhue's pet project of 1894–1895, the proposed Chickamauga, Georgia, Memorial Arch, a job brought to the office by Goodhue (but with very little chance, Wentworth opined to Cram, of ever being built). As a matter of fact, it was not erected (though there is a possibility the client-to-be played some role in the West Point competition years later, so perhaps it was not a complete loss in the long run), but the subject was clearly a delicate one in the mid-nineties. It comes up again in a letter of September 1895 that discloses just how close a thing the Cram firm's survival was that year. Enclosing yet another check, Wentworth admonished Cram:

> I will not caution you how carefully every cent must be spent. . . . Deposit this yourself and tell Mr. Church that on no account is the bank to accept any signature but yours or mine. . . . BG's year [a reference, apparently, to the term of Goodhue's partnership agreement, which has not survived] terminates the first week in November and I am firmly resolved that at that time the firm of CW&G will be dissolved. . . . If you prefer to open up the matter with BG, why do so, but whatever you do must be done soon. Don't make any statement of division of profits until I talk it over with you and *get all the information you can at once*. . . . I am still inclined to feel that if G. will take the arch and get out we should save a lot of trouble and recrimination. . . . Goodhue must not forget that I hold first lien on all profits. . . . If I'm not mistaken this will count him out of any share in future profits. He has had what there was to have for four years and must now get out. Let me hear from you as soon as may be.
>
>   C[12]

In the event Wentworth, increasingly ill, retired from practice himself in 1895, though not, apparently, from the partnership; his name remained on the letterhead until his premature death in California in 1897. But before his influence inevitably waned, he continued to argue fiercely against Goodhue. Indeed, Goodhue's actual work seems also to have distressed Wentworth; just a few months before the above letter he wrote Cram to record his reaction to the All Saints', Brookline, booklet Cram had sent on to him in North Carolina. Wentworth was not impressed, indeed justifiably so, given the quality of the sketches:

> The Brookline book came. . . . It certainly is elaborate, but the sketches [of ca. 1894–1895] in my opinion do not equal the Dorchester ones [of early 1892] by a long ways: the large interiors are rotten, quite the worst I think we have sent out for many moons. I hope you have — [?illegible] — in the sketch showing roof over widening of aisle on Dean St. side; for if we ever built a pitch running into a side wall we should lose our reputation as practical architects. I am surprised you should allow such a mistake to appear even in a sketch.[13]

To troubles with his partners there must also be added family difficulties as Cram's financial situation worsened and he was forced to appeal to his parents for help. In 1895 the firm's credit (never, one suspects, very good) seems to have come close to failing, and Cram, having approached his mother and father, received this gallant but pointed response:

> They will not accept your note at the bank, even with your mother's and my name for endorsement. We do not wish to go outside for help in the matter. Only one thing is left for us to do since we have concluded to try and help you this time. Your mother withdraws $200 from savings bank and sends you herein check. . . . We trust your business if it is a sound one will meet both notes on time and save further trouble, and the *Cram name*.[14]

Yet another plea of Ralph's, this time for only one hundred dollars, provoked a longer remonstrance. Headed: "Please sit down when you can read this quietly, for we have tried to put all our good will and help for you into it," it proceeds for several pages of very harsh advice indeed. For example:

> Your letter was not unexpected. . . . Our best judgment says, better for you as to business not to send the $100, but our feelings and sympathies say, perhaps a year hence we shall all look at life more kindly and hopefully if we give the $100, though quite sure it will only procrastinate, *not help* save your present business. To us there appears but one thing before you, insolvency. . . . We judge that Wentworth feels the same. You may think it strange, but we feel that it is the one thing to be desired. The longer you struggle on, the harder the change you must finally make. The grand turning point in your life appears to us close before you. If you can now *honestly* fail, then steadily put yourself to begin in a quiet, simple, strong way of real business, you can do a good deal of grand, helpful work for the world, and find real joy in the doing, *which we cannot think you have the past five years* [emphasis added]. . . . Don't keep borrowing, and miserably struggling on, sinking deeper. Close your business as to its present form as soon as you can, in a manly, honest way. Pay the most

343

86. Watercolor portrait (1894) of Ralph Adams Cram, by Thomas Buford Meteyard. This artist, who caught Oscar Wilde's eye in 1881, was the complete Bohemian, a part not only of Cram's Boston circle but of Wilde's in London as well.

you can on your debts, then try again in a strong, economic, business way. We all feel that you have talents for much good work. . . . We send the $100, not feeling in the least that it will help tide you over — we do it [to] express our love.[15]

There is just the slightest whiff here ("we judge that Wentworth feels the same" and "which we cannot think you [have done in] the past five years") that his parents, too, thought Cram had been somewhat led astray by Goodhue, and doubtless in more than one way. It would have been a characteristic parental reaction. That aside, however, no young man, least of all Cram, likes to be lectured that way. And of course, lectures such as this were always an excuse to bring up other points of dispute, never lacking between parents and their offspring. Ralph, in his early thirties by 1895, was not yet married, evidently protesting to such maternal queries as he had fielded previously that he could not afford it. Now his mother, in her part of the March 23 letter, did not miss the opportunity (what parent would?) of observing that her son was "at an age when a home and a wise and sympathetic wife would be [his] greatest happiness and help." Poor Ralph. It was not a very good time for him that way, either, for in the mid-1890s he became intensely involved with, of all unhappy souls, Ethel Reed.

"Menages-à-Trois"

A student of Goodhue's at the Cowles Art School, Ethel Reed lived in the Grundmann Studios nearby. So great a beauty that she posed for Day, who delighted in her statuesque profile and "great dark eyes the color of a violet gray spring twilight," Reed was an artist of such remarkable talent that, in Nancy Finlay's words, she "achieved an international reputation at the age of only twenty-three."[16]

Even now, the details of Reed's story are not very clear. It appears that in 1895 she met and became engaged to Philip Hale, a young Boston artist (the son of the noted author Edward Everett Hale). Then (having either jilted or been jilted, in the phrase of the day), Reed abruptly went abroad. Surfacing in England, Reed — perhaps the greatest gift of Boston's Bohemia to the Old World — succeeded Aubrey Beardsley as art editor of *The Yellow Book*, where she was seen by more than one critic to serve as a "neutralizing counterbalance [to] Beardsley's aggressive and confrontational homosexual style."[17] Scarcely had she joined *The Yellow Book*, however, than she "vanish[ed] into obscurity." Said Richard Le Gallienne, her mysterious disappearance "robbed the world of a great decorative artist."[18]

It would seem that Ralph Adams Cram was intimately involved in that mystery. A startling and until now unpublished correspondence (87) with Cram (ca.

345

87. A page of one of Ethel Reed's recently discovered letters to Cram, with a sketch in her own hand, presumably a self-portrait.

1896–1898) has come to light that clearly reflects directly on her last year in Boston.[19] Beginning "My own dear mad moth," Reed writes to Cram:

> Your letter which came to me Sunday was unexpected. I thank you for proving to me that I was right in believing you kind and good. And I am going to ask you not to think unkindly of one whom I advise you not to see here. I leave it to you to decide — for I have no reasons beyond that of mortally wounded pride to forbid you coming. Don't think that I am angry — that I even suffer from the aforesaid wounds now. I forgave everybody everything long ago. I am my own — self. But like you I find it difficult to forget sometimes. And frankly I am too tired, too thoroughly heart broken — or heart-healed? — whichever it is — to seek or even desire the forgiveness . . . that your kind heart would like to be able to give me. But come — look in my eyes, if you will. You will see there what you saw in the beginning — what you could always have seen with a clearer vision. Do you deny it? But there is nothing else, nor — will be. As you know perhaps, this is near Paris, and there are woods to walk in if you wish to come. But why do you wish to? And that's all —

Why, indeed? Though another letter hints at reason enough:

> I didn't write before because being prey to many maladies, I had not the heart to throw a shadow on your shining way. But since you entreat so splendidly, I obey. And in truth I write to thee with more ease than to any others. I wonder why? Perhaps because you are as mad as myself (or as sane) and I know that all will be swallowed with (a *jug*, wasn't it, *beneath the bough*? Fancy my forgetting my Bible — my Omar!!) But who is the Thee that is there now? Never mind. It is indeed possible that I shall be *She* when you go there on your two years madness. . . . Yes, I received your letter this morning — the breath of a cherry blossom against my lips! — and lo, I awoke to find it lying slim and yellow underneath my hand! That you should have met me in your wanderings. . . . Your words are intoxicating, and if I were alone in the world, nothing more than that [letter] would be necessary to lure me to your side — not even those — coloured pictures you draw between the lines . . .

The strong suggestion here of a deeply romantic love is echoed in other missives ("Only a line or two tonight — to say . . . that I love ya lots and lots dear. . . . I've been drinking Absinthe . . ."), and in one there is the distinct suggestion that Ralph (whose own letters do not seem to have survived) is not unresponsive when Ethel remarks, "And yet I almost [want?] to see you NOW that I may understand thoroughly the nature of the '*All*' that you speak of so despairingly."

On the same type of stationery and in all ways similar, which is to say evidently of the same period, are other letters, however, that seem to involve some kind of menage-à-trois with Goodhue. In one such letter to Ralph, Ethel calls Bertram a "dear horrid Child! — he never had answered my letter — but I shall always love him I'm afraid — yes — that's the secret of all my *vagaries*." But she goes on to say in a further démarche to Ralph:

> So Bertram [plans?] to ignore my "love letter" — Did the fool really think it *was* a love letter? Do you know I never realized before that he was trying to insult me. . . .

347

What a fool thing I am always! I have always clung to the affection I felt for him and believed that he was sweet and young and goodnatured enough to understand me. But really — he is too absurd. . . . Adieu, Bertram . . . for Bertram is dead.

So, it seems, was Ralph soon enough, if one is to believe perhaps the most strident of Reed's missives:

Dear Ralph,

I hope that I shall say only what I *mean* to say this time — and that you will try to understand a little better, or be a bit more lenient. You are so quick to misjudge me. And yet — I shall never believe that just what you say is true, — that is — that you love sincerely one whom you consider the incarnation of deceit — That cannot be — Either you do love me for what *I am* — through intuition — or you do not love me — but only a memory — made vivid by the name of this month.

And in either case you must see why I cannot see you. If you do love me the result would be that you would say, as of old, she is playing with me — I have heard that too often — You beg me to come to you — only to tell me later that it was a devilish thing to do. I know — and now I must and will protect myself. . . . And if you do not love me and are only dreaming as poets can and may — well then, Dream on — for Dreams are best.

As Jessica Todd Smith has pointed out in her Harvard senior thesis on Reed, it is not entirely clear that Ethel was heterosexual.[20] And Cram's role here — whether as lover, confidant, friend, or broker (as Goodhue's second, for example) — is also not at all clear. That Reed played some romantic role with Cram, however, who obviously cared deeply for her — even if it was "only dreaming as poets can and may" — would be apropos in the mid-nineties for Cram particularly. Pressures were, after all, beginning to mount on a man eager for success to do the expected thing. Surely Cram's mother wrote from that point of view when she responded to some lament of her son's that may well have referred to Ethel Reed:

As regards your own private unhappiness, I can only express my sympathy and sorrow that you should find only disappointment in such relations, though you would find it a severe trial to put aside the temptation to marry if your financial condition were the *only* obstacle. . . . But I doubt if you would find [a wise and sympathetic wife] in a person so much younger than yourself even if her affection were yours. [Reed was nine years younger than Cram.] I think you will see some day, that hard as it may be, it is better as it is, for both of you.[21]

The mystery of Ethel Reed remains unsolved. When she died and where are not known.

ANGLO-CATHOLIC UNDERWORLD

Whatever the nature of the menage-à-trois of Cram, Reed, and Goodhue, Cram, under the guise of "Brother Clement," was also conducting throughout 1895 another complicated and highly picturesque correspondence, this time with a young man—one "Brother Anselm," a priest stationed in Swanton, Vermont. And nothing is clearer than that "Brother Anselm" was devoted to "Brother Clement." (Cram's side of the exchange does not survive. On the other hand, he kept "Brother Anselm's" curious letters for nearly fifty years.)

Their joint purpose appears to have been to start a religious order. (In one letter Brother Anselm refers to the necessity of "training in the religious life before starting a new order"; in another place in the same letter to "our friars.")[22] And a considerable manuscript of Cram's has, in fact, survived from this period,[23] outlining the role of an American congregation of the Canons Regular of Saint Norbert, the twelfth-century archbishop of Magdeburg, who, after leading a very worldly life as a young noble at the court of Henry IV, founded the Order of the Canons Regular, known as Premonstratensians. (Saint Norbert, surely not accidentally, also figures, like Saint Charles the Martyr, in the heraldic stained-glass windows designed at Cram's behest for his own parish church, St. John's, Bowdoin Street, by Pierre La Rose.)

It should be stressed, however, that the tone of the letters suggests that Brother Anselm had Brother Clement on his mind quite as much as any order. Clearly aware Cram was a Bohemian (Anselm writes in one letter, "you had better come and retire with me for a while and forget the world and the decadents, et cetera"), the good brother was nothing if not insistent:

> I would give anything to see you for just a few hours that we might talk over the plans for the future monastery. So much has troubled me since our meeting in Danvers[?] and it is a matter about which I do not feel quite at liberty to *write* you.[24]

One understands what is meant soon enough as one letter succeeds another, each with its pleas to "come as soon as you can and stay as long a time as you can with me"; or, in another: "I cannot bear the thought of losing you again so soon after renewing our friendship."[25] That these torrential missives are signed "aff'ly" seems an understatement.

There do seem to have been other brothers, though none ever inspired Anselm as Cram did. ("I have just heard from Brother Theodore," reports Anselm, adding rather dryly, "who does not seem to be in a very religious frame of mind.")[26] And there were also mutual acquaintances: "Apropos of our conversation anent St. Agnes," Anselm writes another time, "Fr. Richards of the Messiah is a great friend of [Arthur] Hall and was there with a boy soloist at his choir jubilee."[27] Well, here we are back in the choir stalls! And here is certainly a familiar name: Arthur Hall, who as the former Provincial of the American Province of the Cowley Fathers was a natural enough adviser for anybody considering starting a religious order, entirely a typical project, by the way (though it may seem incredible to us today), of Cram's aesthete Anglo-Catholic circle. As David Hilliard has pointed out in his study of Anglo-Catholicism and homosexuality, in the 1880s and 1890s "the Anglo-Catholic underworld was producing a succession of short-lived, often clandestine, brotherhoods and guilds whose members delighted in religious ceremonial and in the picturesque neo-Gothic externals."[28] And certainly Cram throughout the 1890s seemed to be founding "orders," "guilds," "fellowships," and "brotherhoods" sufficient to populate a small town.

Of course, Hilliard is reporting chiefly about English affairs. But the Order of the White Rose, after all, just about the most exotic bloom of this nature the New World produced, was also a good example of the frequent colonial and American reflection of the activities Hilliard refers to. As late as the 1920s at Oxford, for example, Evelyn Waugh recalled that he "joined the White Rose . . . devoted to the Stuart Cause, [which met] at the Golden Cross. . . . Those who could sang Royalist songs."[29] The aesthete-Anglo-Catholic-gay network in Boston was never for long out of touch with its parent networks in London and Oxbridge. And hints of other such groups abound throughout Cram's correspondence of this period. In 1891, for example, Guiney wrote Cram:

> Fred Day was here yesterday, but dropped in suddenly, and so went "Sudden and swift, and like a passing wind" and you know whose line that is. With him was M. J. Savage's unSavage son [Philip, the poet], the nicest fellow, who is beginning to do some charming work in verse. And whom you may want to bag sometime for your guild. I will manage it somehow, sometime this summer, at your convenience, to knock all your heads together.[30]

"Guild"? Alas, nothing more is known of this. Though Guiney's exchanges with Cram during this period include mention of losing as well as gaining first one person and then another from all sorts of groups, like Brother Anselm Guiney had things to say she wished not to write: "Your question," she wrote Cram, "whether B.B.'s [Berenson's] 'defection' was conscientious maketh me for to smile. I fear it wasn't and will tell you why when next I see you."[31]

Brother Anselm, meanwhile (who was probably Father Frederick M. Garland, according to the records of Holy Trinity, Swanton, its then rector),[32] when he mentioned Hall to Cram was referring to his bishop, Hall having been in 1893 elected Vermont's diocesan as something of a consolation for his dismissal by his English superiors at the time of Bishop Phillips Brooks's election. And it should surprise no one that among the achievements of Hall's episcopate were a number of Cram-type stone Gothic churches: St. James's, Woodstock, of 1907; St. Peter's, Bennington, of 1909; and, in 1910, Holy Trinity, Swanton.[33] Indeed, this last may actually be Cram's design, for Anselm (that is to say, Father Garland) does in one of his letters to Cram refer to "the sketch you sent,"[34] which, moreover, the rector of Swanton insisted on paying for so it could be kept on hand for the future. But Cram's design, if used (it could have been the basis for the present building), was never credited to him.

Anselm in general did his best for his friend, remarking that he had met "with Bishop Hall and we had a very interesting talk on the [proposed] new church [for Swanton] and other things," and that at one point during one of Hall's visits to Swanton the bishop, leafing through Cram's Ashmont booklet, which Anselm probably had purposefully left about, had told him how "happy" it made him that Cram and Anselm were friends and that he, Hall, must try to get Cram some Vermont commissions.[35] In fact, he seems to have done nothing of the sort. Henry Vaughan found commissions in Vermont in Hall's episcopate;[36] so did R. Clipston Sturgis, whom in 1894 Hall himself commissioned to design Bishop's House, with its chapel and library, in Burlington, Vermont.[37] For Cram there was nothing.

Vaughan, a parishioner and friend of Hall's, was in 1894, to be sure, the leading High Church architect at this time, while Sturgis was, of course, a fine architect and also an intimate friend of Hall's; the exterior of Cram's first realized church at Ashmont, on the other hand, was just being finished in 1894. Still, as late as 1909, yet another Vermont church went to Vaughan; none went to Cram, however, until after Hall's death in 1930. Too striking a fact not to invite speculation, there is an explanation readily at hand that bears the right date, for the letter from Wentworth to Cram quoted in Chapter 4, in which Wentworth warned that his and Goodhue's being queer required them to be more cautious of the company they kept, dates from just these apparently rather chaotic years for Cram. Moreover, as we will discover soon in our further discussion of Cram's and Goodhue's Bohemian activities, both their reputations plummeted in the mid-1890s, for unlike Vaughan and Sturgis, they were in this period becoming alarmingly indiscreet. And Hall, for all his heterodoxy about "particular friends," was bound (especially in the wake of the Phillips Brooks fracas) to seek to avoid scandal, particularly now that he had become an American rural bishop and one of the few Anglo-Catholic prelates in the Episcopal church.

On the other hand, no more with Hall than with Charles Brent (whose ecumenism has been mentioned), one should not lose sight of the fact that in the long run not a little of the most significant architecture of Cram's later and most productive years derived from the associations Hall (in league with Vaughan and Clipston Sturgis) first opened to Cram. For, however awry things got for a bit, Brother Anselm's reports with respect to Bishop Hall have again briefly allowed us another fugitive glimpse of the aesthete network we have several times run into here. One of the clearest signals of its reappearance is the name of R. Clipston Sturgis.

An aesthete Anglo-Catholic who guarded his privacy and whose life has yet to be looked at closely (after the births of their children, he and his wife parted company, assigning the blame to a never-seen mistress in England), Sturgis, according to correspondence in the Cowley archives, was "a devoted friend of Fr. Brent's in [the 1890s] and for many years afterwards." And he also designed and superintended for Father Hall the erection of St. Augustine's in Boston for no charge.[38] Moreover, it seems now almost to follow, does it not, that the good father's urgent need for funds for construction was generously met by — Isabella Stewart Gardner.

Always, to be sure, the names are the same. Who was the donor, after all, of the Advent's high altar reredos? Indeed, of the painted altarpiece of Cram's later reredos at St. John's, Bowdoin Street? All that is recorded is that St. John's wonderful altarpiece is the work of Martin Mower, a Harvard-trained artist whose name arises in Bohemian circles during this era with some frequency. Certainly Gardner favored Mower so much that she bought his work for Fenway Court and allowed him to hold an exhibition there of his paintings, some of which were for sale.[39] And if one recalls the connections delineated in previous chapters, especially the links between Hall and Vaughan and Cram at St. John's and between Vaughan and Cram (at the behest of Clipston Sturgis) at the Church of the Advent — Gardner presiding at every intersection — it now appears that Arthur Hall was also a part of the aesthete network the contours of which we have been filling out as evidence accumulates. Young men in Cram's era "grew up" and settled down (usually marrying). But they did not forget the friends of their youth.

Note, too, that the links between the English and American networks multiply rapidly in any discussion of this sort. It is significant, for instance, that the English Gothicist Cram most admired, John Sedding, was a close friend of Sister Louisa Mary, the first Mother Superior of St. Margaret's Boston house and herself a close friend of Clipston Sturgis (who did much needlework and may have studied with her).[40] Note, too, that just as Bodley decorated the original oratory chapel of the Order of St. Margaret in East Grinstead, Sussex, and later designed Cowley's Oxford church, so did Vaughan design the Beacon Hill interiors of both his St. Margaret's Convent Chapel and the old Cowley church on Bowdoin Street.[41] Cram would inherit both orders as clients, as well as the first American monastic order, that of the Holy Cross.[42]

Similarly, as Vaughan designed the tomb in Wisconsin of Bishop Grafton, Cowley's first rector at the Church of the Advent, so did Cram, as we have seen, after the death of Bishop Brent (who himself is now in the calendar of saints and heroes of the Episcopal church) design the bishop's tomb in Lausanne. Indeed, the interlocking network was profoundly involved. To remain with Brent: he

was, for instance, Vida Scudder's pastor, and the cover design of his book of
1899, *With God in the World*, was the work of Bertram Goodhue. And to
extend the matter: the ceiling art at Bodley's Cowley monastery church outside
Oxford is by the same Bodley draftsman who did the ceiling art at St. Margaret's
Convent Chapel on Beacon Hill, *Brother* Maynard — for that architectural
draftsman later entered the Cowley Fathers and became a monk. So too did the
son of Cram's architect-hero, John Sedding.

If in the long run the architectural yield of this aesthete Anglo-Catholic
network far outweighed Father Hall's never delivering on his promise to
Brother Anselm about Cram, that certainly cannot be said in the short run
about 1895; that year the fact that there was no job forthcoming from Vermont
was the least of Cram's problems. Perhaps not surprisingly (given the litany of
Charles Wentworth's complaints), Cram and Goodhue's architecture of that
year was somewhat problematic, including their first Spanish baroque work.
Problematic but fascinating.

Cram, of course, would naturally be drawn to this flamboyant and exotic
style, so like the Sicilian baroque churches he and Randall had marveled at in
the late eighties, when Cram first realized that Gothic, though he loved it best,
hardly encompassed all beauty. And Goodhue, ever since his 1892 visit to Mexico (which yielded a small book, *Mexican Memories*), was equally responsive to
things Hispanic. The result: two designs in this mode near Boston, one a church
in Fall River (discussed in Chapter 10), and the other a Methodist church in
Newton Corner (*88*) that seems more than appropriately to mark Cram's *annus
miserabilis* of 1895, for he called it the worst he ever built.[43]

Actually, in its crisp, four-square, stepped-back massing and handsome dome
(it is an auditorium church built on a Greek cross plan), and the superb contrast
between its richly detailed churrigueresque ornament and sparse wall surfaces,
this church is quite striking, Mexican baroque in detail, rather modern in massing, and, oddly enough, rather English baroque in feeling, especially inside (in
the manner of Wren's part of Hampton Court). Still, it *is* a bit of Hollywood
ahead of its time, and one can understand Cram's chagrin.

SICUT LILIUM INTER SPINAS

One after another, these intermingled professional, familial, and romantic difficulties we are trying to reconstruct as bedeviling Cram's thirty-second year all
occurred in the wake of what must have loomed then for Cram as a disaster
hardly less cruel than the likely failure of his architectural office — the demise in
1894 of *Knight Errant*. That it was the January *1893* issue that brought the
magazine to an end (more than a year later) speaks clearly enough to the travails

88. Exterior perspective of Cram and Goodhue's Newton Corner Methodist Church, designed in 1895.

of those years for Cram, who had been chasing this dream of an arts journal of quality since 1887. How great was his triumph in establishing *Knight Errant* at all (as it seems to us now in the knowledge not only of its distinction but of the importance of its progeny) would hardly have occurred to Cram then; none of its offsprings, after all, was his. Whereas *Knight Errant* had involved both Cram and Goodhue as partners, only Goodhue evidently was asked to be a partner in Copeland and Day. Cram (who at about this time had rather conspicuously *not* remodeled Day's Norwood home into a medieval manse another architect was commissioned to create) was, perhaps, a part of yet another menage-à-trois. Goodhue apparently declined Day's offer. But he nonetheless was repeatedly besought to design and decorate Day's books, while Cram was only rather grudgingly accepted by Copeland and Day as an author.

Money, too, quite a lot of it, seems also to have been involved. Letters found in Cram's papers document, at one and the same time, both the intimacy he and Day enjoyed in the early nineties and the decided estrangement that seems to have ensued. Thus Cram writes in one letter:

My dear Day,
   The White Rose papers are, alas, at Norwood [Day's home]. . . . You can get them if you go over to the house. They are in the middle tray of my steamer trunk in *my*

354

bedroom [emphasis added]. Rummage as much as you like. . . . I can't send them to you for I do not go to Norwood tonight. . . . I am not quite sure that Copeland will be at the Procrastinatorium [a club all three belonged to] tonight, but he will be there tomorrow night.

Yours always,
Ralph Adams Cram[44]

But in the wake of *Knight Errant*'s demise, other correspondence indicates a distinct strain between the two Bohemians. Letters from *Knight Errant*'s printer to Cram actually threaten legal action for unpaid bills, noting that "[Mr. Day] says, substantially, that in pledging the credit of the four editors [apparently Cram, Goodhue, Day, and Lee], you [Cram, as principal editor] acted without [Mr. Day's] knowledge or consent."[45] However the matter was settled, the strains of the *haute Bohème* life were beginning to tell. Certainly Goodhue made so bold as to say in print in 1896 that Cram's prose was marked by

a Ruskinism so turgid and with such a barbaric wealth of adjective, as might cause even that much discussed master to lift his lids. . . . Whether he is critically discussing the pictures of the English pre-Raphaelites, or rhapsodizing over some opaline Italian landscape, it is always in the same luxuriant and Persian manner, which bespeaks strange modes of thought in one reared in such simple fashion.[46]

Actually, as we know, Cram wrote very well. But he could also get carried away. And fight back! That Ralph was capable of equally crushing rejoinders is clear in his criticism of Bertram's cover design for *Knight Errant*; it was, Ralph remembered carefully even four decades later, "most decorative, . . . admirable in all respects — barring the one item [the centerpiece of the whole design] of figure and animal drawing, the only field in which [Bertram] was not proficient, for this sort of thing he could never learn to do."[47] Of course, Cram was right. And so was Goodhue. One is reminded of two boys who fight each other to a draw and become best friends.

Doubtless the jockeying back and forth got on even the most artistic nerves from time to time (which may explain both Goodhue's and Cram's outbursts in print), and it cannot, from either man's point of view, have helped that Wentworth, in seeking to expel Goodhue from their partnership, was in effect seconding Day's efforts to lure him away. Add to this volatile situation, furthermore, the fact that whereas Cram, Wentworth and Goodhue was barely sputtering along financially, Copeland and Day, with Day's family money behind it, scored one triumph after another.

The success of Copeland and Day stemmed most of all from each partner's careful cultivation of very different contacts, aided always by Guiney's editorial judgment. First, Day's ties with John Lane at the Bodley Head ensured that he

89. Aubrey Beardsley's cover for the first issue of
The Yellow Book, April 1894, published in
America by Copeland and Day.

and Copeland became the American publishers of such authors as Oscar Wilde, Richard Le Gallienne, Francis Thompson, and William Butler Yeats, to say nothing of illustrators and designers like Aubrey Beardsley;[48] and of *The Yellow Book* itself (*89*) (in the pages of which even Baron Corvo's writings appeared), for few recall today that the American publisher of this controversial journal of the Decadence was a Boston one. (So great were the excitements involved that one incident, characteristic of all concerned — and of Boston's Bohemia generally — "strained [Day's] relationship with Goodhue almost to the breaking point." It seems that Goodhue "was so eager to see [the latest Beardsley sketches just arrived from London at Day's offices] that he stole a key to the publisher's offices to give himself and Daniel Berkeley Updike first crack at them." Estelle Jussim, who tells the story in Day's biography, points out that he had every right to be furious: "Updike, after all, was Day's competitor at the Merrymount Press.")[49]

Second, Copeland's Harvard contacts enabled the firm to publish (and also to return the favor by giving the British rights to Lane) a number of works by contemporary American and Canadian authors. These included Bliss Carman and Richard Hovey's *Songs from Vagabondia* and Charles Flandrau's *Harvard Episodes*, national bestsellers.

Carman and Hovey's work was, in fact, quite as popular in England as in America. Vagabondia, Henry Leffert has written, "took the country by storm and collegians went about chanting Hovey's poems as more than twenty-five years before Oxonians had chanted Swinburne's first series of *Poems and Ballads*"[50] — or, one must add, the way the generation after Vagabondia chanted

The Wasteland, in the manner of Anthony Blanche in *Brideshead Revisited*. Pinckney Street Bohemians never had a headier time than when virtually the whole country and not a few Britishers were quoting the poems of two of its luminaries. Copeland and Day's even greater achievement was to have first published *The Black Riders* by the radical realist Stephen Crane.

In design, too, the firm excelled. Goodhue's work was notable (*90*). And that of Will Bradley (a member of the Boston Society of Arts and Crafts) was exceptional. His cover for Copeland and Day's edition of Richard Le Gallienne's *Robert Louis Stevenson: An Elegy and Other Poems* (*91b*) explains at a glance why Bradley's genius is so universally acknowledged.[51] Ethel Reed, often inspired by Bradley, was hardly less good; her poster for the *Arabella and Araminta Stories* by Gertrude Smith can hardly be called anything but astonishing (*91a*). And to original poetry and distinguished design, moreover, Day added the expected dash of socialism—publishing a translation from the Yiddish of Morris Rosenfield's book *Songs from the Ghetto*. But it was the reputation of Copeland and Day as the aesthete publishers of America—who had made Boston the port of entry, so to speak, for the Decadence, as the aesthetic movement had become—that claimed then as now the most attention.

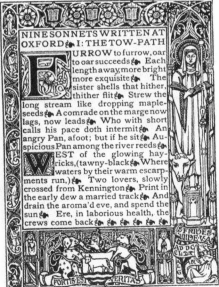

90. One of Goodhue's most splendid—and most architectural—book designs, for Louise Imogen Guiney's *Nine Sonnets Written at Oxford*, 1895.

357

ARABELLA AND
ARAMINTA STO-
RIES BY GERTRV-
DE SMITH WITH
XV PICTVRES BY
ETHEL REED

BOSTON COPE-
LAND AND DAY
PRICE $2.00 NET

91a, b. Two examples of Copeland and Day's outstanding book design: Ethel Reed's poster for the *Arabella and Araminta Stories* of 1895 (*facing*) and Will Bradley's cover for Richard Le Gallienne's *Robert Louis Stevenson* of the same year (*right*). Bradley's design includes one of Goodhue's printer's marks for Copeland and Day, lilies amidst thorns; hence *Sicut lilium inter spinas.*

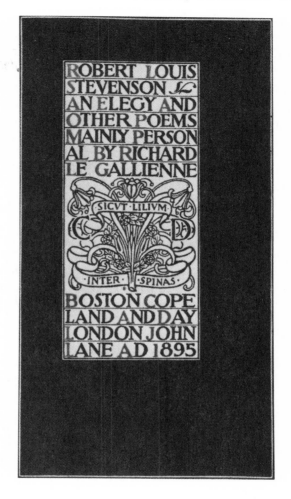

THE DECADENCE

In one sense it was hardly more than a change of words. What was true of the *aesthete* of the 1880s was equally true of the *decadent* of the nineties. Eve Kosofsky Sedgwick has observed that "Decadence is a notably shifty idea" and that "many of [the word's] uses can be simply explained by its being a euphemism for 'homosexual.' "[52] But the scene does both deepen and darken for aesthetes become decadents, the reason that in the epigraph to this chapter we have called upon Herbert Marcuse as our final witness as to the nature and purposes of Bohemia. For all the high frolic and sometime innocence of Boston's

359

Bohemians, their doughtier spirits — above all, Cram, Guiney, and Day — lived their values so intensely that at the end of the decade many had hardly survived the experience.

Let it be said, too, as we open this Pandora's box of the Decadence, that we are not entirely concerned with Americans earnestly catching the latest breeze from Paris or London. As H. P. Lovecraft pointed out in *Supernatural Horror in Literature*,

> [Edgar Allan Poe's] elevation of disease, perversity, and decay to the level of artistically expressible themes was likewise infinitely far-reaching in effect; for avidly seized, sponsored, and intensified by his eminent French admirer, Charles Pierre Baudelaire, it became the nucleus of the principal aesthetic movements in France, thus making Poe in a sense the father of the Decadents and the Symbolists.[53]

Just as we have seen that Boston's welcome to Spiritualism was not unrelated to its Emersonian heritage, and that, later, Boston's spearheading of Freudianism was equally not unrelated to Transcendentalism, so the aesthetic movement and now the Decadence (not a moral or artistic decline but rather a moral and artistic vision) had an American and even a New England genealogy (Poe was born in Boston) that not even Paris despised.

The Boston face of the Decadence has, however, been little studied, for New England historiography has hardly been comfortable with this phenomenon, which achieved its most exotic blooms, to be sure, in Vienna and London and Paris. There, amid much absinthe and more hashish, poets like Verlaine and writers like Huysmans, forever fascinated by the symptoms of degeneracy, both of whom Cram was brave enough to mention admiringly as great lights of his young adulthood (though without explanation) in his autobiography, joined forces with Stéphane Mallarmé and Arthur Rimbaud (who, it is not too much to say, believed in the progressive derangement of all the senses through any available stimulus) to claim proudly in the mid-1800s the epithet "decadent" thrown at them by shocked traditionalists.

Cram and all the Boston circle were most influenced by the British decadents, chiefly Wilde and Beardsley, the former a pervasive influence here from the start and the latter as we move through the nineties hardly less so, for the "much edgier" Beardsley, in Robert Taylor's words, whose "psychic anxiety lent him a harshness as kinky as any contemporary punk rocker's" ("*have* pools of blood ever been so decorative?" asked Michael Kimmelman),[54] was admired by Day, Guiney, Updike, and Goodhue especially. But whether in Paris or London or Vienna or Boston, the authors read were pretty much the same and also the underlying themes. The brilliant Viennese novelist Arthur Schnitzler (no doubt deliberately echoing Tolstoy) well explained the lure: "There are so many sicknesses," observes his hero somewhere in *Anatol*, "but only one state of health." Does this seem too far away from the Puritan capital? That is because we know fin-de-siècle Boston so little and its philosophical axis of the aesthetic and the erotic hardly at all. It was Louise Guiney, in a letter of in 1894 to Louise Chandler Moulton, who named the nineties "the sick little end of the century."[55]

DOING THE OSCAR

In her *Sexual Anarchy: Gender and Culture at the Fin-de-Siècle*, Elaine Showalter of Princeton, one of our most perceptive cultural historians and critics, details the revolution in sexual mores and behavior that marked the end of the nineteenth century; and it is quite fascinating that, Boston's contribution to the Decadence having been sufficiently obscured, the only figure from the Pinckney Street circle (though in her own right, of course; nothing is said of any circle) that surfaces in this superb study of both Europe and America is Alice Brown.

Deservedly. Brown, Pinckney Street's senior bluestocking, did not shrink from calling a spade a spade in the matter of Robert Louis Stevenson's *The Strange Case of Dr. Jekyll and Mr. Hyde*, published in 1886. Showalter (embroidering modernist nonsense, some will say) calls *Dr. Jekyll* a "gay Gothic" and "a fable of fin-de-siècle homosexual panic."[56] Brown (whether or not she was in whatever sense a modernist) was just a plain-spoken New Englander. But she really settled the matter a hundred years ago, putting it simply but no less clearly in 1895 in her *Study of Stevenson* (published by Copeland and Day): "Mr. Stevenson," she wrote, "is a boy who has no mind to play with girls."[57]

Pretty much the same thing could be said of the characters found in another book published by Copeland and Day, actually the first book the firm issued, aptly titled *The Decadent; or, The Gospel of Inaction*. It was published anonymously in late 1893, the author having thought better of exposing himself in the matter. But if Alice Brown did not learn the author's identity from her next-door neighbor, Fred Day, she probably learned it soon enough from the author himself, another neighbor and her old friend from Hampton Falls, Ralph Adams Cram.

It is, of course, provocative, as it was in the case of Vaughan's Groton Chapel and its issue, for me to appropriate Showalter's term and call Cram's book "gay Gothic." But *The Decadent* of 1893 (its dedication to Goodhue and frontispiece showing him and Cram have already been discussed here) and Cram's other early book, *Black Spirits and White* of two years later (already dealt with extensively because it records Cram's 1880s trip to Europe, even though it was not published until after *The Decadent*), are *both* gay Gothic. It is true that *The Decadent* abounds with sometimes heavy-handed preaching, but it would. In

361

Boston even the Decadence was apt to be fired by moral effort. And Cram, after all, was a minister's son.

Not that one could not read *The Decadent*, at least plausibly, in all innocence. Witness Marion Nichols's letter of thanks to Cram for her presentation copy:

> Your book arrived just as I was leaving Naples for Capri. . . . At times I almost felt that I was . . . talking once more with you.
>
> [I am] convinced more strongly than ever of the sad truth of the [decadent] Gospel of Inaction. But I cannot entirely agree with [you], so I am glad that you quoted for me those words of Oscar Wilde. . . . I think your Rhodian dreams [another of Cram's projected orders, planned to exist on the isle of Rhodes!] offer a more attractive ideal life than that pursued among Eastern luxuries.[58]

Is there a rebuke in this well-bred rejoinder? It is hard to tell. What is clear is that the kind of books likely to be found in a decadent's library, as Peter Gay put it of Walter Pater's *Studies in the History of the Renaissance*, was such as to "permit an innocent reading but invite a sexual interpretation"; so much so, indeed, in the case of Pater's book that it seems to Gay "a distinguished performance in the covert theatrics of homoerotic propaganda."[59] Certainly this was true of the two immediate models for Cram's *Decadent*, Huysmans's *À Rebours* and Wilde's *Picture of Dorian Gray*, the former based on the life of Proust's and Huysmans's notoriously homosexual patron, Robert de Montesquiou, and the latter, as Gay points out, though it was "a homosexual tale by suggestion only," nonetheless, with its "lush coloring, its theatrical male friendships, and its polemics against social repression, it . . . deceived no one."[60]

Neither is it very likely Cram's book did, the title alone of which is explicit enough. (Recall our discussion of Sedgwick's study of the word "decadent." Showalter also focuses exactly on this word: "Decadence," she writes, "was also a fin-de-siècle euphemism for homosexuality.")[61] Indeed, one cannot say too often here what Robert Martin has observed of *Dorian Gray*: "Gay literature has always, since the Greeks, been a literature of indirection . . . of more or less coded references. [Because of] gay liberation . . . it seems certain no one will again write a novel like *Dorian Gray*."[62] Or a romance like *The Decadent*, which is, I believe, a key marker in terms of New England cultural history of the coming into being in Europe and America then of what Showalter calls "a new community of knowledge, if not of life and feeling, amongst many men with homosexual leanings [what I have called here the emerging gay subculture of Boston's Bohemia—DS-T] . . . an identity around which a sub-culture [began] to form and to protest . . . [and ultimately] forge its own identity and culture. . . . The record of this culture emerges in the 'decadent' art and literature of the fin-de-siècle."[63]

In the case of Ralph Adams Cram we are, of course, studying a maker of both art and literature, and it is well to recall at this point another observation of Martin's that the so-called gay sensibility (so widely discussed in the 1980s), involving, in his words, "a sensitivity to the surfaces of things, a taste for order, and an ironic distance between the self and the world [had its] roots . . . in the 1890s, with the witness of the aesthetic tradition,"[64] all of which refers, of course, to our discussion in Chapter 7 of "homosexual style" in Anglo-Catholic church design. It might seem to be stretching things to call All Saints', Ashmont, decadent or to call *The Decadent*, as I have Cram's 1890s churches, "chaste, strong and uplifting." But the fact is inescapable that Cram's first church and his first book were conceived at virtually the same time by the same hand. Both were aspects of Cram's exploration of cultural and social and religious ideas, first discussed in *The Decadent* (as Robert Muccigrosso has pointed out), but still central to Cram's thought forty years later, when he enjoyed a large national readership in an America always eager to hear from him about much more than architecture.[65]

The plot of *The Decadent* is easily summarized.[66] Malcolm McGann, a political activist of ardent socialist convictions, has been invited to the country house of a friend and former disciple, Aurelian Blake. McGann arrives in a Boston full of fetid air, dirty streets, loud, money-grubbing citizens and ugly buildings — "in fact," wrote Cram sarcastically (of a city where he would one day be chairman of its Planning Board), "none of the adjuncts of a thriving, progressive town were absent." This urban scene is contrasted vividly with the idyllic country estate outside town to which he is driven for his weekend. But Vita Nuova, as the estate is named (an obvious reference to Boston's Dante cult), is by no means what McGann expects; nor is his host, who, though he has remained a socialist, has become also a monarchist — and distinctly a decadent. Forthwith, Aurelian tries to convince Malcolm that the life of Vita Nuova is the only possible one; that however necessary the revolution, now is not the time; that however well-intentioned socialist agitation, it is too dangerous. Once loosed, the revolution can never be controlled, still less its corollaries, and the result is likely to be a grosser materialism and a more deadening uniformity. Instead, Aurelian counsels, one should seek solace in one's pleasures, awaiting a better day.

To Malcolm's vehement assertion that he will not give up, Aurelian replies, in words Marius the Epicurean would not have disclaimed:

> Dear Malcolm . . . you have mistaken the light that is on the horizon; you have waked from sleep, but the flush of light that is in your eyes is not the dawn, . . . it is sunset. You taught me that we lived in another Renaissance; I know it to be another Decadence. . . . Here [at Vita Nuova] I have gathered all my treasures of art and letters; here may those I love find rest and refreshment when worn out with hopeless fighting. . . . Suffer me to dream in my cloister through evil days. . . .

All of Cram's lost causes come up in the course of the book (Arnold's "Dover Beach" is even quoted) — and most of his heroes, too (including Wagner, Turner, Burne-Jones, Pater, Rossetti, King Charles, Arnold, even Cardinal Newman). But heroes and causes alike are seen as household gods in a truly astonishing household, for the setting is extraordinary. Here is Cram's description of Vita Nuova's great hall:

> The room was vast and dim . . . a mysterious wilderness of rugs and divans, Indian chairs and hammocks, where silent figures lay darkly. . . . And everywhere a heavy atmosphere which lay on the chest like a strange yet desirable dream; the warm, sick odour of tobacco and opium, strong with the perfume of sandalwood, and of roses that drooped and fluttered in pieces in the hot air.

Ministering undismayed by these vapors are an obsequious little black boy in a red fez and a Beardsleyesque Japanese geisha, whose depiction by Goodhue in his frontispiece brings to mind Camille Paglia's remark about gender in Beardsley — "constantly in doubt. . . . As they used to say in television schedules, to be announced."[67] Nor are the details of this service reassuring: the boy at one point comes "out of the darkness," for example, "and at a gesture from Aurelian filled the great hookah of jade and amber with the tobacco mingled with honey and opium and cinnamon, placed a bright coal in the cup and gave the curling stem wound with gold thread to his master." Why has it taken so long, one suddenly wonders, for drugs to make their appearance? And not only drugs: "Aurelian's ardent eyes gazed on the man before him through the writhing smoke [of the opium] in the pallid dawn; his voice was like the voice of a velvet bell. . . . His eyes grew soft and he smiled gently. 'Malcolm,' he said, . . . laying an arm lightly over his broad shoulders . . ." And Malcolm, perhaps not comforted that "the 'divine Plato' " is now invoked by Aurelian, appears as he weakens to refer to other than the force of Aurelian's arguments: "The slow and musical voice, so delicately cadenced, had grown infinitely pleasing to his unfamiliar ears, strangely fascinating in its mellow charm." It would seem to be of more than philosophical discourse, moreover, when this scene is followed at once by Aurelian's saying to Malcolm: "Yet the night is at hand, and the darkness at last will cover our shame. It is better so." It is hardly any wonder that, somewhat ahead of this scene, Malcolm should have mused about Vita Nuova that "there was something awfully wrong."

Both these themes of drugs and sex converge most strongly, perhaps, when Cram conjures an exotic scene illuminated only by

> a fitful light on heavy tapestry curtains wrought with the story of the loves of Cupid and Psyche. Its two halves parted slowly, and a flush of red light fell through as, in the midst, appeared a dark figure with closed eyes, swaying softly as it leaned forward, and, while the curtains closed, fell with a long sweep gently towards the brazier —

not as men fall, but as a snake with its head lifted high might advance slidingly, and, as it came, droop lower and lower until it rested prone on the uncrushed flowers. So Enderby, heavy with the suave sleep of hashish, came among the smokers and drooped motionless in the midst of the cushions. The movement sent a tall glass quivering until it fell to one side, and the yellow wine sank slowly into the silky fur of a leopard skin.

At first glance it may seem curious that drugs generally appear to get the better of sex as Cram's leading theme in *The Decadent*, and, overall, socialism the better of both. But again it is necessary to caution the reader in the matter of the period's coded references; of one of *The Decadent*'s models, *Dorian Gray*, Sedgwick notes that not only in the case of opium, but generally, "drug addiction is both a camouflage and an expression for the dynamics of same-sex desire."[68] An example of this, of particular relevance to our study, is *The Last Puritan* by George Santayana.

Though published many years later, the earlier parts of Santayana's famous book were conceived and first written in the Boston Bohemia of the 1890s, and some passages relate to that era as much as does Cram's work here. In Santayana's book, for instance, after a nude swim and much conversation — both with homosexual overtones — between the chief protagonists (two young men on a family yacht), the conversation appears to veer off (but actually focuses in) when, talking of many "strange worlds — the sea and the Klondike and the British Navy and Anglo-Catholicism," the two men have this exchange:

> "Did you say," he asked with an effort, "that my father takes drugs?"
> "Of course he does," [Jim replied]. . . . *Dope* [Oliver said to himself] was the worst thing possible. *Dope* was the very denial of courage, . . . a betrayal of responsibility. *Dope* was a cowardly means of escape. . . . And yet [seeing his father in comatose slumber later, for the first time, Oliver felt] a new possible dimension of moral life. [It seemed, after all, that] in close association with that miserable *dope*, appeared this strange serenity, . . . this smiling and beautiful death in life. . . . Could it be that life, as the world understands it, was the veritable *dope*, the hideous, beastly, vicious intoxication [of] obedience to convention and custom and public opinion.[69]

Clearly, Santayana, in the wake of a scene with unmistakable homosexual overtones, is speaking here of more than drug taking.

That drugs are in this context that kind of camouflage underlines, moreover, how dense is the literary technique of mask and signal in Cram's work. Indeed, to decode the meanings just of the names of *The Decadent*'s characters is a challenge one could easily regret taking up. Consider "Aurelian Blake." The first name of Cram's principal protagonist seems to echo not only a certain underlying Yankee stoicism, but, because Pater's protagonist in *Marius the Epicurean* lived during the reign of Marcus Aurelius, that philosopher's view of life as well as Pater's own; while Aurelian Blake's second name is almost certainly an allusion of some sort to Cram's family: perhaps to his father (who much admired the poet William Blake, another mystic and rebel) or, more likely, to his maternal grandfather, Squire Blake, whose estate was where Cram as a youngster first experienced the aesthetic of place and past together.

Socialism also, of course — though this is not to impugn Cram's sincerity here any more than in his Anglo-Catholicism — is part of the coded references. Recall that Cram's socialism can reasonably be seen, as I have here, closely linked to his sexuality through "Christian Socialism" and Edward Carpenter, just as was Day's through his ministry in the South End, a reflection of Martin Green's point that "in Boston the aesthetic was still fused with an old-fashioned idealism and had not yet come to terms with the new eroticism."[70] And *The Decadent* signaled the fact that Boston *was* being led to confront that new eroticism — albeit controversially, for *The Decadent* did not go unnoticed.

A succes d'estime in one sense it certainly was. Cram must have been pleased at the standing it gave him that his first book (the ghost stories, recall, were not actually published until two years later, in 1895) should also be the first book published by the prestigious new firm of Copeland and Day, and it cannot but have delighted him to see his book featured in the new firm's catalogue, gallantly keeping company with so many of his betters: for amid books by Dante Gabriel Rossetti, Walter Crane, Francis Thompson, and Oscar Wilde, Cram's was the only one by an American. And, of course, historically, *The Decadent* has become an important book, always noted, often illustrated, in histories of American book publishing, its design much praised and, increasingly, its literary value as well. (Estelle Jussim calls it a "fascinating indiscretion"; Stephen Parrish even goes so far as to conclude that Cram's "weird philosophical 'romance' . . . deserves to be better known today.")[71] But the reaction when *The Decadent* was published was a great deal more problematic. Probably based on experiences in the summer of 1892, which, according to the *Boston Courier*, Goodhue and Cram spent keeping "bachelor's hall" with Day and company at Day's Norwood manse,[72] *The Decadent*, even within Cram's closest circle, stirred a largely negative reaction. Even Guiney, so enthusiastic about some of Cram's other writings, despised it, writing to Cram in 1894: "I don't believe I ever told you how 'The Decadent' stuck in my throat. I am glad I made up my mind about you before I read *that*."[73]

Even Day disliked *The Decadent*, and it must have somewhat unnerved Cram to be harassed in this respect not only by the virtuous Guiney but by Day too, of all people. But Day, who wrote to a friend in 1893 that Cram had "tried so very hard to 'do the Oscar' [in *The Decadent*] but had failed ignominiously,"[74] likely had the most personal of reasons to be alarmed, for whether or

92. The great hall of Fred Holland Day's country house in Norwood, near Boston, as it appears today.

not Cram had used that summer of 1892 he and Goodhue spent with Day at Norwood (taking photographs of each other indulging in opium on the lawn; see 94) as his chief source, more than one person gained the impression, reading the novel, that the "dim . . . mysterious wilderness of rugs and divans" of the hall in the book, to say nothing of the "warm, sick odour of tobacco and opium," was a fairly accurate description of the much talked-of goings-on rumored to take place at Day's Norwood estate (92). And Day, for all his flamboyance, was a very private man who had, one assumes, good reason to be.

In any event, Day was careful, in the letter of November 1893 announcing Copeland and Day's founding, to distance himself as much as he could from *The*

367

Decadent, writing that Cram "will probably not put his name to it, but no persuasion of Herbert's or mine has had the least effect to leave it in M.S. It will appear most 'queer' before Christmas," sighed Day. Most "queer" indeed.[75] For though Cram withheld his name from the title page, he was, as we have seen, more revealing on the dedication page (and Goodhue equally so in the frontispiece), and Copeland and Day made no attempt at all to dissemble in their advertising. Their catalogue, which appeared in December 1893, heralded Bertram Grosvenor Goodhue as the illustrator, thus at once decoding the "BGG" of the dedication page and, indeed, for any who knew either man, surely the frontispiece as well; while *Publishers' Weekly* (not very helpfully from the Boston point of view) trumpeted *The Decadent*, the firm's first book, as a "revolutionary essay."[76]

Not surprisingly, disapproval was even more pronounced beyond Cram's and Day's own circle. Indeed, so alarming was the public reaction that Copeland wrote to Day (who happened then to be in London) that he was "really afraid we have a bad reputation as I find some people take the *Decadent* wrong and everyone naturally takes [Wilde's] *Salomé* wrong."[77] (What company Cram kept! Both appeared on the firm's list.) Exactly what was the *right* way to take either, Copeland did not explain. But his alarm proved prescient, and his coupling of Wilde's and Cram's books illustrates how dangerous the situation would become for Cram by 1895; for what was, as we have seen, an awful year for Cram got much worse very quickly when the tremendous international scandal of Wilde's downfall burst shatteringly on aesthetes and decadents everywhere during the spring and early summer of that year.

Meanwhile, there was a little good news. The publication of *Black Spirits and White* also occurred in 1895 and attracted quite favorable attention in *The Chap-Book*, distinctly a national publication by then, having moved to Chicago. One of Cram's short stories from the book, "Notre Dame des Eaux," was published as the magazine's lead article in August, and in April of the following year *The Chap-Book*'s editors shamelessly puffed all Cram's literary work by way of a lengthy and enthusiastic article, "The Written Work of Ralph Adams Cram," written by the highly disinterested Bertram Goodhue. He was both loyal and tart enough to conclude with the remark that *Black Spirits and White*'s publication was "a high fulfillment of the hopes of its author's friends, and, besides this, shows a degree of [literary] power in him which was hardly suspected even by the most sanguine."[78] And then, in the following year, under his more respectable guise as art critic, Cram's "Painting, Sculpture and Architecture" was published in the *Atlantic*, his debut in that legendary periodical, and a milestone in any life.

Even amid these successes, however, there are surely echoes of the trial of

Wilde, who was convicted at the end of May 1895. The full-page portrait sketch of Cram that illustrates the *Chap-Book* article, probably by Goodhue, is not only a recognizable (and brilliant) abstraction of Day's portrait photograph of Cram (the frontispiece to this volume) but also a much less aesthete and more robust image of Cram than either Day's portrait or Goodhue's frontispiece for *The Decadent* of only two years before. Moreover, from that earlier book Goodhue goes to great lengths in his *Chap-Book* article to distance both himself and Cram, whose "love of beauty," he wrote, had proved in *The Decadent* "a dangerous taste." The result was "too opium-saturated to be altogether agreeable," huffed Goodhue, uncharacteristically, adding that Cram, too, had by 1895 concluded that *The Decadent* was "a mistake."[79]

One could hardly blame either man for so conspicuous a retreat, given the magnitude of the Wilde scandal, of which will shall have more to say. There was another reason (not unrelated to events taking place in London, but much more definitely germane to Cram's affairs in Boston) why both he and Goodhue should try to disassociate themselves from *The Decadent*. Too many had decided there was more to the book than just a reflection, however outré, of the bachelor lifestyle at Fred Day's Norwood manse. For its habitués went by a name of which many unsavory things were said in Boston. As Jussim points out: "In reading Cram's description of the supposedly fictitious library in which the action — or, rather, the inaction — takes place, one can only wonder how much of *The Decadent* was modeled after . . . the Visionists."[80]

That highly reclusive and vaguely notorious secret society must now claim our attention.

10

THE RIDDLE OF THE VISIONISTS

Grounded in the Acts of the Throne and the pacts of the themes, / it lived only by conceded recollection, / having no decision, no vote or admission, / but for the single note that any soul / took of its own election of the Way; the whole / shaped no frame nor titular claim to place.

The Table may end to-morrow; if it live / it shall have new names in a new report. / Short is Our time, though that time prove eternal. . . . / We declare the Company still / fixed in the will of all who serve the Company, / but the ends are on Us, peers and friends.

> — Charles Williams, from "The Founding of the Company"
> and "The Prayers of the Pope"

Most people are only a very little alive, and to awaken them to the spiritual is a very great responsibility; it is only when they are so awakened that they are capable of real Good, but that at the same time they become first capable of Evil.

> — T. S. Eliot, in his study of demonic influence

93. Province Court, though itself fairly wide by Boston standards, opened off Province Street, which was then barely six feet from curb to curb. In a city of many grimy alleys and byways, it was one of the grimiest in the 1890s when this photograph was taken of the locale where the Visionists forgathered on so many late nights and early mornings.

THE PROPHET of Fred Day's protégé Kahlil Gibran, and not the work of once-celebrated poets such as Hovey, Carman, and, most deservedly, Guiney, has become in some curious (and probably dubious) way the most widely known today of the literary effusions whose origins can be traced back to Ralph Adams Cram's Boston Bohemia. As early as 1917, in an article in the *Boston Herald* by F. W. Coburn, it was clear how quickly Gibran had come to the fore in Boston's then consolidating memory of the 1890s:

> This Syrian artist . . . [was an assistant] of F. Holland Day. . . . More than perhaps any of the then group of symbolists [as various aesthetes styled themselves, Gibran] has carried forward the sort of vague, mystical expression that was then the beau ideal of advanced Boston in the days when white roses were worn on the birthday of Charles the Martyr [by Cram and his fellow members of the Order of the White Rose, of course] and when wealthy ladies [i.e., Isabella Gardner] scrubbed church steps [at the Church of the Advent, according to legend]. . . . The phase passed. . . . Erstwhile wearers of the white rose now build imperishable cathedrals [i.e., Cram at St. John the Divine in New York]. . . . But Mr. Gibran . . . has run true to the quest of the inchoate. . . . Art conceived in a sublimated ether this of Gibran's surely is.[1]

And most enduring ether it proved; for all of the disdain of so many for "Kahlil Gibberish," *The Prophet* has become a sort of underground bible of the twentieth century. Cram (a disciple later of the French philosopher Henri Bergson) was not himself ever a conspicuous admirer of Gibran. Nor, interestingly, was Isabella Gardner. But *The Prophet*, whatever its shortcomings, does preserve a sense of the mystical vapors that pervaded Boston's Bohemia and found its focus in the Order of the Visionists.

RATS' PARADISE

In June 1894 Herbert Copeland wrote to his sometime classmates at Harvard, Herbert Stone and Ingalls Kimball:

> My dear fellows,
>   We all hope that you will be with us at Visionists. . . . We . . . have had lots of fun at the Hall of Isis and we hope to have more. You know the room — it's surely a pleasant place to loaf in and invite your soul, a pleasant place to meet or take a friend. . . . You know who we are — Abbott, Day, Baldwin, Cram, Goodhue, Small, Knapp, Lincoln and your humble His Most Superfluous Highness — At any rate

whether you are with us or not — be sure that we all want you and sincerely hope you will join us —

Your friend, Herbert Copeland

PS. The address at Province [Court] is not very safe. Should you write to me at 69 Cornhill I am surer of getting it.

H.C.[2]

Safe? Province Court? In that picturesque antique volume by Henry D. Blaney, *Old Boston*, the author, portraying late nineteenth-century Boston locales hardly less uncanny than the Paris Cram delineated in his first horror story, describes Province Court (*93*) under the heading "Rats' Paradise": "Passing along Province Court . . . half-way down, you find a doorway leading into darkness and gloom . . . you grope your way" along this old Revolutionary passage, "amid groaning of hidden machinery above, [in a large block of newly built offices] and the squeak of rats below."[3]

To have found the lair of Cram and his cohort of so many midnights in the nineties, you would, after a similar excursion, have had to go through another doorway that led up a tightly twisting mid-nineteenth-century staircase (described by Cram as "dusty and decrepit") to the top floor of 3 Province Court, an old brick tradesman's house of the 1840s that by the 1890s had deteriorated into cobblers' and locksmiths' dens. It was, Cram recalled, "disreputably decadent."[4] But what you would have found within the Visionists' inner sanctum is by no means as clear. The police, suspecting gambling, once raided the place but found little to complain of.

There were, to be sure, visiting actresses who accepted post-theater late-night invitations. And much alcohol and tobacco and, above all, according to Cram, talk. That was Thayer Lincoln's recollection of a characteristic Visionist evening that had centered on a poetry reading by Hovey:

> the discussion continued [in Province Court] until after two in the morning, when we all adjourned to an all-night restaurant somewhere in Dover Street [then Boston's least respectable quarter] and then went to early Mass at the Cathedral [of the Holy Cross]. . . . When Mass was over, Copeland and I discovered to our dismay that Hovey was sound asleep on his knees.[5]

That more than talk and good cheer went on, however, is suggested by other firsthand testimony found in Cram's papers: a letter to him of some years later from Herbert Copeland. In the context of congratulating Cram on the birth of Mary, his first child, in 1902, the letter suggests (taken in conjunction with "a pleasant place to meet or take a friend") a somewhat risqué aspect of the Visionists:

Isn't it extraordinary what family men "the gang" is getting to be. I suppose it's well to have at least one old bachelor in the crowd to carry out its traditions of sugar plums and telling the stories of Papa's youth. . . . How interesting . . . the Visionists will be to Mistress Mary when she's about 16 — may I be there to tell![6]

Certainly Charles Wentworth had been upset enough about something or other when in 1895 he wrote to Cram, warning him and Goodhue in the strongest possible terms:

I hope you boys have given up the Visionists; certain questionable characters belonging to the society are liable to give it an extreme black eye. Avoid Jack Abbott and don't be seen in public with him; he is rapidly getting a most questionable reputation; even I got rumors of it in the South, this is on the [qui vive?] and be careful, no word is said concerning what I have written.[7]

Abbott, he of the artists' ball, had by the 1890s moved to 11 Joy Street, diagonally across the street from Day's pied-à-terre at the head of Pinckney. Evidently by then quite intimate with Cram (from whom he borrowed, on the security of his gold watch, a substantial sum of money in 1893),[8] Abbott seems also to have been close to Goodhue and to an even older friend of Cram's, Henry Randall, then practicing architecture in New York. Such, at least, is the implication of a letter of 1895 to Cram from Randall, who after detailing plans for a forthcoming Boston visit ended it with "warmest regards to Goodhue and Abbott."[9] In the letter to Cram quoted above, moreover, Wentworth left little doubt as to the nature of at least one thing all these people had in common: though Cram (unlike Day) was not really all that devoted to Oscar Wilde, clearly he had felt the need to defend Wilde to Wentworth, who replied, quite unsympathetically:

Your friend Oscar Wilde is about to have his unnatural practices shown up very strongly to the world according to the London papers: it will be interesting reading to some. A propos of Wilde, no I won't say that, is Abbott still on the turf? Mrs. Washburn advertises him so well in the Sunday Herald that he ought to be doing a good trade. . . . Love to all.[10]

Whatever distinctions Wentworth was trying to make, what is very clear is the association made between Wilde's "unnatural practices" and Jack Abbott and the Visionists.

To the subtext of homosexuality must also be added that of drugs, as we saw in our discussion of *The Decadent* hardly incongruous. The environment, after all, was sufficiently friendly: not just the Wildean lily of Copeland and Day but also the poppy turns up often enough in Pinckney Street's works in everything from choir-stall "poppy heads" (in Cram and Goodhue's church at Middleborough, for example) to book designs such as Ethel Reed's (for Julia Ward Howe's *Is Society Polite?*). What such blossoms meant may, of course, be debated. However, not only does Nancy Finlay point out that "the poppy was an extremely popular flower with Boston's fin-de-siècle artists, who were well aware of the many meanings associated with it," but Jessica Todd Smith concludes, in connection with Ethel Reed's use of the poppy (and she must have been Goodhue's star student), that it was widely interpreted then as an "emblem of sexual uninhibition and signifier of transgression."[11] Jack Abbott, the reader will recall, was waving a huge poppy at the 1894 artists' fête when he led in the Grand Vizier. Rossetti was, in fact, believed to work under the influence of opium.

The issue of drugs, of course, like Cram's sexuality and, indeed, his conversion to Anglo-Catholicism, poses for us the usual problem that a century ago the issue was very differently framed from the way it is today. So much so that in her *Architecture after Richardson*, Margaret Henderson Floyd documents the existence at Vancroft (a grand West Virginia estate of 1899 designed by Alden and Harlow, sometime partners of Boston's A. W. Longfellow) of an architectural interior designed to be an "opium den," complete with the necessary divans and such and all the requisite brass accoutrements for the use of the drug — a room Floyd compares to a "Moorish hunting room" Longfellow designed at 37½ Beacon Street in Boston two years later.

Ethan Naderman, the chair of a Princeton working group on drug use, has written,

> in turn of the century America, opium, morphine, heroin, cocaine, and marijuana were subject to few restrictions. . . . Coca-Cola . . . [was] laced with cocaine. . . . The violence, death, disease, and crime that we today associate with drug use barely existed, and many medical authorities regarded opiate addiction as far less destructive than alcoholism. . . . Many opiate addicts, perhaps most, managed to lead relatively normal lives and keep their addictions secret. . . . The imposition of drug prohibition . . . occurred almost simultaneously with the advent of alcohol prohibition, [though] contemporary Americans tend to regard Prohibition [of alcohol] as a strange quirk in American history and drug prohibition as entirely natural and beneficial.[12]

That alcohol prohibition in the United States was ended after only fourteen years and other drugs are still prohibited nearly seventy-five years later did not reflect any consensus that alcohol was the least dangerous or the least associated with violence of these drugs. Rather, it reflects the fact that alcohol, of all of them, was and is the most popular. (Cram and Goodhue were, in fact, formidable drinkers, Ralph's liquors of choice having been wine, especially brandy, Bertram's beer.)[13]

The use of drugs in Cram's circle is hardly arguable. One of his Bohemian friends, Gelett Burgess, when forced to eschew his accustomed opium for some reason, not only had recourse instead to hashish but was so far from secretive about it as to write (anonymously, he said, because of his mother) an article on his experience, "Some Experiences with Haschisch," for MIT's *Technology Review*.[14] Of Fred Day's drug use we have already spoken.[15] And even if Cram and Goodhue themselves used no other substances than alcohol, certainly Cram not only was knowledgeable enough on the subject (*The Decadent* betrays this), but chose in that work to romanticize drug use. Furthermore, both he and Goodhue ostentatiously posed as taking drugs in photographs by Day (94). One calls to mind the assertion of Lord Alfred Douglas's father, with respect to Oscar Wilde, that "to pose as a thing is as bad as to be it."[16] In this respect, at least, one cannot argue with that unpleasant man. Nor is this drug subtext surprising. In her *Opium and the Romantic Imagination* Althea Hayter's observations about opium users' characteristics certainly relate to those of the Visionists, particularly "a delight in secret rites and hidden fellowships" and "curiosity about strange and novel mental experience."[17]

Just as in his memoirs Cram suppressed the gay subtext, however, so, too, did he mislead his readers in respect to the matter of drugs, insisting that tobacco and incense were the extent of Visionist dissipation.[18] (This is not to disparage the effects of incense, by the way; it was, as we have seen, distinctly a potent

94. Cram, Copeland, and Goodhue take their ease with gurgling nargilehs, ca. 1892, photographed probably by Day: "These young writers are keeping bachelors hall [in Norwood]," reported the *Boston Courier* in 1892.

377

THE RIDDLE OF THE VISIONISTS

weapon in the hands of Cram). Yet such suppression was obviously necessary in his memoirs in the post-Freudian mid-1930s, by which time Cram was, indeed, to use Copeland's phrase, very much a "family man" and in a very much more proper Boston. Doubtless for the same reason, in the list of his works that appeared in his books of those later years, *The Decadent* and *Black Spirits and White* were both discreetly omitted.[19]

The way Boston hearts (never in the first place very warm in this respect outside of Bohemia) had hardened to aestheticism by the time Cram wrote his memoirs is clear in the life of Harry Crosby, the outré Boston Brahmin poet-publisher who in the 1920s took off for Paris, adopted as his heroes Huysmans and Wilde, and determined to live the whole decadent creed (not excluding drugs and flagellation). Although Crosby also followed the more constructive Bohemian tradition of establishing his own publishing house—the Black Sun Press, which published at least one of Copeland and Day's old authors, Stephen Crane, and also a number of the new generation's heroes, including James Joyce, D. H. Lawrence, Ezra Pound, Archibald MacLeish, and Marcel Proust—of Crosby's life, "shining like a black pearl in a cup of dead-green absinthe," his biographer has quoted Morse Peckham's words about aestheticism-according-to-Boston, every one of which strikes home here:

> It excited [Crosby] to know [in the 1920s] that Bostonians despised the Decadents [of the 1890s] . . . [because they seemed characterized by] "relaxation of nerve, self-indulgence always hinting in the direction of sexual perversity, and often enough arriving there, remoteness, an unrealistic worship of art for its own sake, of a commitment to Aestheticism as a strategy for escape from a real world which these artists did not have the courage or manliness to face, an escape which often enough involved a return to the more sensate rituals and forms of religion, especially if they were anti-intellectual and mystic in the worst of the many senses of that word."[20]

By way of illustrating this widespread Boston view (President Eliot's, surely) of the 1890s, imagine an aesthete of that era, a bit of a dandy in his dress, who adored Gilbert and Sullivan and the Pre-Raphaelites; loved all beauty, Venice particularly, Wagner most of all; wrote odd books; lived a very Bohemian life; was artistic, a critic, writer, and poet, as well as a medievalist and scholar; and was besides an ardent Catholic and a besotted Jacobite, forever projecting some sort of monastic order or guild. It is the notorious Baron Corvo I have been describing[21]—but equally the young Ralph Adams Cram, whose thankfully much sounder character ought not to be allowed to obscure the similarities between them from Boston's point of view. Cram, on the other hand, would have been a fool not to have tried to obscure them by the 1930s. Instead, he wrote of the nineties: "In some way . . . word got abroad that [the Visionist rooms were] a queer sort of place; and in certain more conservative circles this did no good to our budding reputations — which was most unjust."22

Ah, Ralph; but what of the Procrastinatorium — so secret that what it *was* is unclear — and, above all, what of the Sacred Cat? Thayer Lincoln wrote to Cram about this at around the time Cram was preparing his autobiography for publication, and though Cram slid past the subject there (allowing only that there was "a gutter-cat called Pasht"), Lincoln didn't at all, writing his old friend about

> the cat — the Lady Pasht. . . . The legend was, you remember, that as two somewhat intoxicated Visionists were walking through Salt Lane on a warm, summer night the Boston Stone suddenly cracked open and the Lady Pasht jumped out. At least, this was the story told us by the two young men when they returned to Province Court.23

The reader need not worry that there now portends a discussion of the significance of the cat in homoerotic literature. But as a matter of fact, the literature of the day is relevant, for in Arlo Bates's novel *The Pagans*, that society, limited to seven "earnest and sometimes fiery young men" who were dedicated "anti-Philistines," rather "anti-Christian" and also "anti-women," is quite fixated on a cat of the same name; not the "gutter-cat" of Cram's dismissive memory, but a statue in the Ware Collection at Boston's Museum of Fine Arts of "Pasht, the cat-headed deity. . . . 'It is the patron saint of our Pagans,' the artist said . . . '[a fitting] figure-head of a society like the Pagans where we fight with words but may come to blows at any time.' He spoke gayly."24 Indeed! The date, mystifyingly, of this novel is 1884; either the Visionists were already in existence then (and have had more than one period of activity) or, if founded about a decade later, they adopted this custom of *The Pagans*, which is surely too exact to be coincidental. And too important for Cram to have forgotten. But Ralph, after all, was always agile in defense: a "gallant fellow, and I love him well," wrote Claude Bragdon, ". . . his mind is so active and eager that Frank Bacon once said of him: 'Conversing with Cram is like holding a squirrel in your lap.' "25 His autobiography is a little like that, too.

BLACK MAGIC OR WHITE

"They tell me I am a visionary in some ways, but I do not know that I am therefore a Visionist. May I seek light from Dies?"26 Thus did Francis Watts Lee inquire of Day (*dies* is Latin for day; it was a habit of the Visionists to take Latin nicknames) as to the advisability of his accepting an invitation (probably Day's) to join this obscure but storied group. In another letter of this period Cram extended the same sort of invitation to Carman we have seen Copeland issue to Stone and Kimball.[27] That those three—Cram, Day, and Copeland—accounted, with their candidates, for seven of the original nine members argues for the three having been the founders of the order. Carman, Meteyard, and Stone became Visionists. Of the others, Thayer Lincoln was a law student; Herman Baldwin, a classmate of Copeland's at Harvard, was a medical student; and Arthur Knapp was the son of a missionary to Japan. Still other names— Bullard's, Randall's, Hovey's—arise in connection with the Visionists from time to time. Two women, Guiney and Brown, were, if not members, certainly frequent guests.[28]

One would give a lot to read Day's answer to Lee as to whether he was truly a Visionist, for the Sacred Cat is by no means the only indication that this group was much more than a club like the Pewter Mugs. Even in his memoirs Cram admitted that only the Mug's "madder and more fantastic members" made it into the Visionists, and despite his making every effort to depict their Province Court headquarters as the most harmless thing in the world, Cram's description is bizarre enough and the code scarcely hard to break:

> On the walls, the painter-members had wrought strange and wonderful things: the Lady Isis in her Egyptian glory, symbolic devices of various sorts, mostly Oriental and esoteric. There were pictures, oddments of varied types, rugs. . . . In some indefinable way its place had a mildly profligate connotation, which misrepresented it utterly. . . . When from time to time a light shone in its windows at a late hour . . . the police force would make investigation, . . . [but there was present] no beverage more potent than beer; while the smoke, which was indeed dense, was innocent of any aroma other than that of pipes and cigarettes, or, on occasion, the lingering perfume of incense when Herbert Copeland officiated as Exarch and High Priest of Isis, clothed garishly in some plunder from Jack Abbott's trunks of theatrical costumes.[29]

Strange and wonderful things, indeed. And as Cram's description, as usual, conceals more—or tries to—than it reveals, it naturally raises more questions than answers. Black magic or white?

Perhaps, actually, none at all. In 1894, with the publication in *Harper's* of George du Maurier's *Trilby*, a tale of the Parisian Latin Quarter that was extraordinarily widely read, a wave of what can only be called middle-class "parlor Bohemianism" swept over America. And it included Boston, where by 1900 there actually was a magazine called the *Bohemian* that reflected this more broadly based and much diluted Bohemianism so well that it misled Albert Parry to the conclusion that "even the Nineties, the decade of the *Trilby* craze and Bohemian or pseudo-Bohemian circles in every large center of America, left no imprint on Boston."[30] As for the Visionists' Egyptian splendors, Theosophy was wildly popular in this era; Madame Blavatsky's world-famous *Isis Unveiled* of 1877 had issue in innumerable and quite harmless societies fixated on ancient Egyptian cult gods and goddesses.

Of the few scholars who (only slightly and reluctantly in every case) have hazarded on this terrain, Nancy Finlay, for instance, argues that the Visionists "played at being wicked" and that their ritual was no more than "youthful silliness." In aid of this view she points to Bertram Goodhue's depiction of the Visionists on the first page of *Saint Kavin: A Ballad* (see 96), where Carman, the author, is seen to droop in rather a puckish way, noting that "this unsuspected touch of humor in a lavish 'ecclesiastical' design is a reminder that these young men did not always take themselves altogether seriously, and is a fitting complement to the mocking tone of the poem itself."[31] Nor is other evidence lacking to support such a view. For example, it was Thayer Lincoln's recollection that the order's head, the Exarch, "was required to sit on the stove in setting forth all official edicts." In consequence, he continues, "no serious business of an important nature was transacted during the winter months."[32] Humor there certainly was—and a strong, masculine, roistering element as well, reflected in Bliss Carman's then-famous verses: "Midnights of revel / And noondays of song! / Is it so wrong? / Go to the Devil!"[33]

But there *was* a more serious side to Isis, who had in ancient times enjoyed a highly decadent following in late Imperial Rome, as in the 1890s in fin-de-siècle London; it was a nervous, sick little decade, after all, as well as a brilliantly creative one, just such an era for Isis. And Boston, it is often forgotten, was in one sense just such a place. In fact, *Isis Unveiled* has distinct New England roots. In the first place, the reader will recall that Helena Petrovna Blavatsky, the founder of modern Theosophy, and her disciple, Colonel Henry Steel Olcott, a Civil War officer and New York editor and lawyer, who cofounded the Theosophical Society in New York in 1875, actually met in New England while studying séances held the year before near Rutland, Vermont, at the farmhouse of the Eddy brothers, uneducated farmers who, according to Blavatsky's biographer, nonetheless boasted "a long history of mediumship in the family. (A grandmother four times removed was condemned as a witch during the Salem, Massachusetts, trials of 1692)." And in the second place, when Blavatsky, who in the 1870s lived and worked in Boston in the critical period just prior to the founding of the society (explaining why J. R. Bridge calls Boston then the "Mecca of Spiritualists"), decided to make what her biographer calls "her first public disclosure" of her formative teachings, it was in an article written for a Boston journal, *The Spiritual Scientist*. That was also the year she began the writing of *Isis Unveiled*, which the august *Boston Evening Transcript* certainly

THE RIDDLE OF THE VISIONISTS

took seriously, asserting in its review that it "demands the earnest attention of all thinkers."[34]

Nor does this exhaust Madame Blavatsky's Boston connection, for she wrote *The Voice of the Silence*, a notable theosophical work, while vacationing with an old Bostonian friend, Ida Chandler.[35] It was a book William James cared enough for to quote from in his celebrated *Varieties of Religious Experience*, hardly surprising, as Boston had always been interested in such things; Ralph Waldo Emerson was said to have gone about with a copy of the Bhagavad-Gita in his pocket.[36] And one of the grandest of the new Back Bay churches of the 1880s, for example, was the First Spiritualist Temple, later the Exeter Street Theatre.[37] Moreover, a local lodge of the Theosophical Society, still in existence today, was established by 1885.[38] Encouraged doubtless by his father, who, recall, was not only a Transcendentalist but an admirer of Swedenborg, Ralph Adams Cram, like many other Bostonians in this era, is known to have attended séances in the 1880s and 1890s in Boston; so, too, did Day.[39] The reader will also recall from our discussion of Freud the founding in Boston by William James of the American branch of the Society for Psychical Research. This is to force together disparate things, perhaps, but the occult and Spiritualism and such had a very serious and distinctly Bostonian aspect at this time that we ought not to forget.

Perhaps not surprisingly, therefore, there is another view of the nature and character of the Visionists, and if Nancy Finlay's conclusions illustrate the benign view, Estelle Jussim's advertise the darker one. Jussim pronounces the Visionists "an eccentric and sometimes notorious group of young poets and artists who combined worship of the occult and the supernatural with aestheticism, ritual and drugs." Factor into her use of "aestheticism" the gay subtext and this seems to me the more likely situation, especially as Jussim convincingly links the Visionists with the celebrated British Order of the Hermetic Students of the Golden Dawn, into contact with which Day was drawn when Guiney introduced him to William Butler Yeats at the Rhymers' Club in London in 1890, where Day also met Oscar Wilde (whose wife was an initiate of the Golden Dawn). Yeats, with whom Day shared an interest in black magic, may have confided to Day more than he should have. "It seems likely," Jussim goes as far as to say, that "Fred Holland Day joined [the Golden Dawn] but there is no sure evidence. . . . For obvious reasons, that is difficult to verify"—and that when Day returned to Boston his involvement with the Visionists was "inevitable."[40]

Other evidence that links the Visionists to the Golden Dawn includes, for example, the form of Cram's dedication to Goodhue of *The Decadent*, which reads in full:

TIBI . MEO . CARO . B . G . G .
CVIVS . LABORIBVS . PRETIVM . NON . PROPRIVM . EI . FIEBAT .
OPERA . TVA . EXARCHO . FRATRIBVSQVE .
EIVS . ORDINIS . QVAE . SVMNIA . SIBI . FINGIT .
DENIQVE . OMNIBVS . DELECTIS . PER ORBEM . TERRARVM .
HVNC . LIBRVM . GRATE . DICO .

[To you, my dear B.G.G., due to whose efforts a reward which was not his alone was being paid to that man who, thanks to your help, is the Exarch and to the brothers of that group which defines its own dreams and finally to all the select members over the entire world I dedicate this book with thanks.][41]

Although this statement would be opaque in any language and is open to many interpretations, the dedication of *The Decadent*, like the identity of the dedicatee, the book's authorship, and, indeed, the text itself, is no less decipherable in our context here than is *Black Spirits and White*. The reader will recall the initial analysis of Goodhue and Cram's relationship in Chapter 4. I concluded there that as well as being "partners" in design professionally and "soulmates" and "lovers" personally (perhaps "lovers" also in our sense of the term today, when society invalidates the word without regular genital involvement), Ralph and Bertram were also, and fundamentally, "brothers" or "comrades" in Bohemia, that is, fellow homosexuals. And that certainly seems to me the meaning of "brothers of that group which defines its own dreams."

But the phrase that follows, set off by "finally," and thus apparently referring to some other category, seems to me more specific in meaning: "to all the select members over the entire world" surely refers to an *organization*, one with "members," as that word is almost invariably used. Moreover, not only is the word "Exarchos" a direct link to the Visionists, but the clear meaning of that word from ancient classical times to the present (the term is still used in the Eastern church) is that of "viceroy" or "deputy," which, in conjunction with the phrase "over the entire world," suggests the Visionists saw themselves as a cell, temple, or branch of some kind of larger organization led elsewhere.

Nor does this evidence exhaust the matter. It should not be overlooked that the Isis-Urania Temple of 1888 in London was the senior founding temple of the Order of the Hermetic Students of the Golden Dawn and that S. McGregor Mathers, one of the Golden Dawn's founders, was celebrated for his "rite of Isis." Or that Pasht, the cat-god of *The Pagans*, was equally Egyptian. And both Isis and Pasht—and incense—most certainly figured in the Golden Dawn's secret rituals, now long since published (95).[42]

The notoriety of the Golden Dawn (which reflects on the Visionists in much the same way Wilde, Beardsley, and *The Yellow Book* did on Copeland and Day and *The Decadent*) derives from its association with such colorful figures as

383

95. Pasht, the cat-headed deity, as depicted in the once secret ritual of the Golden Dawn, now published.

Mathers (who married a sister of Henri Bergson, whose ardent admirer Cram would become in mid-life) and, above all, Aleister Crowley. Educated at Trinity College, Cambridge, Crowley was "one of the most brilliant magicians of modern times." But his unstable personality undermined and made destructive what seem to have been undoubted occult powers; besides which, he argued for violent sexual excess to the extreme limit compatible with survival so as to precipitate breakthroughs of consciousness. Although he enjoyed a wide influence in the United States, where he lived for some time (in New Hampshire, among other places), Crowley's scandalous lifestyle was such that the Golden Dawn's reputation suffered considerably.[43] (No such specific charges were ever made about the Visionists, but it is only fair to note that Cram *was* linked to sexual adventuring as a concept insofar as he and his father were associated with Swedenborgianism, for David Reynolds has pointed out that "Swedenborgianism['s] . . . doctrine of "permissions and 'conjugal love' opened the way for sexual adventure in a religious context.")[44]

But as there are two views of the Visionists, so there are at least two of the Golden Dawn, which also hardly sought attention; one member "described the Golden Dawn to [John Symonds] as 'a club, like any other club' "—rather as Cram described the Visionists. That aside, there were also more moderate elements that struggled in the nineties to purge the English order of its unsavory elements with such success that among those drawn into the Golden Dawn were persons who, like Cram, would become leaders of the High Church Anglican movement in the twentieth century. Kathleen Raine has gone so far as to assert that though the published rituals do not reflect the fact, having been edited, "there was at one time [in the Golden Dawn] a strongly Anglo-Catholic bias." She notes that a number of members of the Anglican Society of the Resurrection were initiates of the Golden Dawn, and both Charles Williams and Evelyn Underhill belonged to it.[45] As Christopher Armstrong wrote, in the Golden Dawn

384

the emphasis was undoubtedly on what to outsiders appears to have been the ac-
quisition of a certain "gnosis" or private experimental contact with ultimate realities
through the deliberate deployment of incantations and rituals . . . some genuinely ancient and associated with the historic rosicrucian movement, some . . . of very recent
concoction. [Some] took it all in a fairly light-hearted spirit. On the other hand, the
possibility of notable "happenings" cannot entirely have been precluded.[46]

In this connection one recalls again Cram's horror stories, the first of which
in *Black Spirits and White* was about black magic. But the *writing* of these
stories is in itself of significance; the fact that Cram wrote them, or at least
prepared them for publication, in 1894–95, when he was in the thick of his
Visionist involvement, may well be significant. Edward Wagenknecht noted
that Cram's "No. 252 Rue M. le Prince" (one of the characters in which, Sar
Torrevieja, whom Cram calls the "King of the Sorcerers," may well have been
modeled on the Abbé Constant, himself an inspirer of the Golden Dawn) was in
the same mold as Edward Bulwer-Lytton's "The House and the Brain," a story
H. P. Lovecraft was quick to see showed "hints of Rosicrucianism," another
link, perhaps, between the Visionists and the Golden Dawn.[47] Such stories seem
to have been an important aspect of the experience of the Golden Dawn for
Underhill, whose biographer has written that her own stories

> belong to a genre . . . of the supernatural short story. . . . It is to this taste or fashion
> that we owe the ghost stories of M. R. James [with whose work, the reader will re-
> call, Cram's was compared] or . . . A. Conan Doyle, H. G. Wells and others . . . [in-
> cluding] *The Turn of the Screw* by Henry James . . . reflect[ing] a widespread
> interest . . . in the phenomenon of diabolical possession for which Huysmans and,
> behind him, Edgar Allan Poe and others were ultimately responsible. But . . . the
> deepest impression on Evelyn's stories . . . falls to *The Picture of Dorian Gray* or the
> Emile Zola of *Thérèse Raquin*. . . . For most educated people of the era of Wilde and
> Evelyn Underhill art is the mirror of that in humankind which men themselves can-
> not express in other words in that age, still largely ignorant of the findings of the sys-
> tematic exploration of psychological depths.[48]

The Golden Dawn, which "during its height . . . possessed perhaps the greatest repository of Western magical and occult knowledge"[49] (*not* the so-called
low magic of sorcery and spells and such, but high or mystical magic, which
having survived its discrediting in the seventeenth- and eighteenth-century scientific revolution had been revived in the nineteenth century, the Golden Dawn
constituting the peak of this revival), was significant less for its rituals and more
for its studies. Thus two of Underhill's books, *Mysticism* and *Worship,* books
that remain today acknowledged Anglo-Catholic classics of scholarship in their
fields, owe much to the influence of the order. And while no specifically mystical
works came out of the Visionist brotherhood (*The Prophet* was a grandchild, as
we have seen, of Day at least, and probably of the group as a whole, but of a

quality several members would have found suspect), there was still a profoundly creative aspect of the Visionist idea. For example, Cram mentions that there were "bookcases [at Province Court] to hold the contributions of the members, as it was a basic law that whoever wrote a book must give a copy, while those who did not indulge in authorship must contribute a volume consonant with the spirit of the institution."[50] And the Visionists' more purely artistic achievement was, after all, formidable. Never mind individual works like *The Decadent* or the "Stein Song"; *Knight Errant* itself, indeed, even Copeland and Day *and* Cram and Goodhue were all in truth Visionist ventures.

THE DREAM TOWN OF SAINT KAVIN

Creative collaboration pervaded Cram's circle. George Hallowell, for example, designed the cover of Stone and Kimball's 1894 edition of Bliss Carman's *Low Tide at Grand Pré* and in more than one church designed stained glass and murals for Goodhue and Cram.[51] The book *Patrins* was written by Guiney, dedicated to Carman, published by Copeland and Day, and then, God help us, reviewed by Carman.[52] (Worse, perhaps: Santayana once felt able to assure his publisher that a review by Bliss Carman would be good.)[53] Meteyard designed all the volumes of Hovey and Carman's Vagabondia series (see *106*), including *Last Songs from Vagabondia*, a book that included a poem by Carman called "The Girl in the Poster" inspired by Ethel Reed, not only Goodhue's student but also a model for Day (who initiated the Vagabondia books).[54] And the Visionists seem to have been at the center of this pattern of collaboration; a key, perhaps, to our understanding of the brotherhood.

The Visionist accomplishment most immediately felt in the popular culture of America in this era is alluded to by Stephen Parrish:

> One of the [Visionists'] most famous and popular triumphs, the "Stein Song" seems to have come into being when Frederic Field Bullard put together a musical accompaniment to a lyric by Richard Hovey, with the boisterous cooperation of a band of singers gathered about a piano in one of the group's clubrooms.[55]

Cram, too (whose poem "Nottingham Hunt," the reader will recall, Bullard set to music successfully enough that it was heard in Symphony Hall), had his own memories of this song, recalling that "one of the first hearings . . . of the 'Stein Song' occurred in my bachelor quarters in Pinckney Street, when Stephen Townsend sang it gloriously to the admiration of a few fellows who had gathered there."[56] And one can certainly see why Bullard and Cram would have worked well together. Even Bullard's drinking songs, Louis Elson has written,

96. The Visionists are shown in the topmost panel of Goodhue's opening page of Bliss Carman's *Saint Kavin: A Ballad*, 1894. Note Harvard's Memorial Hall in the third niche from the bottom on the left.

"suggest[ed] wine rather than lemonade" and showed "virility and straightfor-wardness . . . [and even] Viking vigor."[57] Bullard's more serious work, mostly church anthems, would surely also have appealed to Cram, for Bullard appears often to have set to music, as it were, All Saints', Ashmont; or so, at least, Rupert Hughes suggests to me in his *Contemporary American Composers*, where he wrote of Bullard's work as disclosing "a fine ruggedness." Bullard, Hughes felt, characteristically always "found the right occasions for wild dissonances and dared to use them. The effect is one of terrific power."[58] All Saints', exactly.

Of more relevance to Goodhue was the work of Bliss Carman, whose *Saint*

Kavin: A Ballad Goodhue designed in 1894 (96). Distinctly Bertram's sort of saint ("This St. Kavin was a most / modern sort of saint, indeed; / His philosophy involved / No more theory than the wind; / With his own smile he absolved / Every sin he ever sinned"),[59] Saint Kavin, a sort of Visionist alter ego, perhaps, appeared many more times in print, usually presented in a rather mocking tone: "When Kavin comes back from the barber, / Although he no longer is young, / One cheek is as soft as his heart, / And the other as smooth as his tongue."[60] Soon enough, Kavin appeared in Goodhue's more visual realm, so to speak, for Bertram seems to have appropriated him. Perhaps one could commandeer or at least share in fellow members' alter egos. Certainly, Goodhue created out of Carman's work, if not an alter ego, a dream over and against his professional practice — and one that is clearly in its origins Visionist, when he cast Saint

97. Goodhue's 1896 perspective of St. Kavin's Church and the Kavinplatz in the imaginary town of Traumburg. Goodhue locates Traumburg, of course, in Bohemia!

Kavin's Church as the centerpiece of a brilliant series of pen and ink sketches (97) of 1896 entitled "Traumburg" ("Dream Town"), a place that existed, in the words of Goodhue's biographer, "on no map except that of [Goodhue's] imagination."[61] (Unless on Burgess's map of Bohemia!)

Previously, we have seen how Cram and Goodhue grew from a clear differentiation of their abilities as designers in their early churches to an increasing unity of design in the mid-1890s that was not achieved, however, at the expense of each other's individuality.[62] And in the specifically Visionist collaborations just discussed (Hovey's lyrics, Bullard's music; Bullard's music, Cram's poetry; Carman's poetry, Goodhue's design) there is evident just this sort of mutual sparking, rooted, it goes without saying, in very personal relationships. For example, it is surely not coincidental that about the time Goodhue appropriated Carman's alter ego, he and Carman (without Cram) undertook a walking tour together in 1896 through England and France.[63]

A long-standing Visionist relationship, comparable to Cram's and Goodhue's, was that of Hovey and Carman, who combined artistic partnership in their coauthored poetry books with personal partnership. Seeing them in tandem and from Carman's perspective, his biographer has written that Carman's

> particular friend was Hovey, and they reacted violently upon each other, to the advantage of both. They both had high opinions of each other's verses, [both] published in *Harvard Monthly* [a journal founded by Barrett Wendell and others in 1885, which published some of the earliest American studies of Verlaine].... They were earnest and young, both around twenty-five, and considered themselves quite unique; after all, poets were rare in America at that time. Together they turned away from things academic ... and became practicing poets instead.... They complemented each other both in looks and attitude. Hovey was dark and muscular, Carman was fair and lanky.... The aesthetic Carman, the pale youth, became a counterpart for Richard Hovey.[64]

How similar to Cram and Goodhue, to whom the phrase "reacted violently upon each other, to the advantage of both" is strikingly apt. The similarity is equally striking in more personal terms. Certainly Cram, like Hovey, can fairly be characterized as representative of what Eve Kosofsky Sedgwick calls the "virile" type.[65] Goodhue was not, apparently, as effeminate as Carman, who was conspicuously fond of his long, flowing blond hair, cultivated even at Harvard (where he spent so long attending to it that it became a sort of fetish) and in the early 1900s began to wear more and more outlandish turquoise jewelry. But fragments here and there (recall that Goodhue's girlish complexion was commented upon in one case)[66] do seem to indicate that in his youth, particularly, Goodhue may have been representative of the more "effete" type.

Psychologically, moreover, Carman—lacking initiative though not power, once he got going—and the more dominant and gregarious Hovey seem to have been counterparts in a way one can just catch a glimpse of in the affairs of Cram and Goodhue. Hovey and Carman also seem in their Vagabondia books to have hit on a joint philosophy ("love is often found outside wedlock," William Linneman writes, while on the other hand, "all things are possible in brotherhood. Comradeship is the greatest of all values; it lasts when wine, women and song have disappeared").[67] But they appear to have advanced it each in his own way—Carman more traditionally (Cram-like, as it were), in four-line stanzas, Hovey more boldly in more experimental (Goodhue-like) free verse, short lines, and varying rhyme combinations. Cross comparisons occur, too: Hovey as poet (like Bullard as composer) is comparable to Cram as architect. Though a dandified enough aesthete that he once compared himself to the character of Bunthorne in *Patience*, Hovey grew rather away from the Wildean aesthetic and more toward the Whitmanic as he matured. So much so that his biographer describes Hovey's last work ("poems which speak to men for men") in words reminiscent of those applied here to Phillips Brooks's sermons and as intended "to reanimate an effeminized poetry,"[68] words also reminiscent of Cram's analysis of the nature of the reform needed in church art.

To be sure, this can all be carried too far. It is only fair to note that Alan MacDonald contends that such was Hovey's disdain for Wilde that " 'the love that dare not speak its name,' which Wilde defended, was [for Hovey] the evil, inverted shadow of comradeship." Even in 1957, however, that was surely to take too strenuous a view of the matter in the face of Carman's homosexual reputation and MacDonald's own rather coded admission that "Carman . . . as blond and tall as Hovey was dark and solid . . . [formed with him] a friendship that was the richest and closest of [Hovey's] life."[69] But just as the professional and personal similarities between Carman and Hovey on the one hand and Cram and Goodhue on the other are striking, so are Carman's and Goodhue's affinities and Hovey's and Cram's.

In the case of Hovey and Cram, of course, it is the more striking because Hovey, like Cram, took up (in the wake of Bohemian heroes of the era such as Richard Wagner and William Morris) the medieval Arthurian epic and in a fashion similar to the way Cram took up medieval art and architecture. Of Hovey's *Launcelot and Guenevere*, for example, Linneman has written:

> The real culprit is the puritanical society with its material values and conforming pressures. . . . Hovey's contemporaries were not fooled into thinking he had written another Medieval romance. His characters were different from Tennyson's—they were modern. Guenevere was certainly the "new woman," and Arthur and Launcelot were also modern. They were alive with modern problems—especially the con-

flict between individual and social interests. Hovey . . . appears to be one of the first American writers to use a myth to present modern themes.[70]

Today, in the wake of *Ulysses* and *The Waste Land* and such, this is commonplace. But Hovey wrote before Yeats, Joyce, and Eliot, and he was "not escaping [despite his medieval theme] from modern life; he was dealing directly with it."[71] So, as we have seen, was Cram, whose churches I have called here Trojan horses.

This was true of the Visionists in general, a thing we too easily miss because a century later the connections between all the activities of Cram and his cohort seem obscure. But Wayne Dynes is correct to insist on the fact that

> disgust with the squalor and alienation brought by the coming of the industrial revolution went hand in hand with a demand for thoroughgoing reform of society, religion and art. This agitation called forth such diverse results as Christian socialism; the Oxford movement and Anglo-Catholicism; the Gothic Revival in architecture; Pre-Raphaelitism in painting and poetry; and the arts and crafts movement, . . . meld[ing] a nostalgic yearning for a supposed organic society of bygone days with utopian hopes for a new social and aesthetic order.[72]

Cram's and Goodhue's architectural design was as modern in comparison with Pugin's as Hovey's and Carman's poetry was in comparison with Tennyson's.

The finale of this Visionist creative pairing was the one crafted by Cram and Goodhue, a finale that yielded eventually a prodigious national success (promised, but not delivered quickly enough, by All Saints', Ashmont) — a series of articles written by Cram with some sketches by Goodhue (and numerous photographs) that began to appear in 1899 in *The Churchman*, a highly influential Episcopalian journal. Such was their reception that these articles were brought together and published in book form two years later, scoring at once an immense success.[73] Running to several editions well into the twentieth century, *Church Building* (98) was not Cram's first architectural book. In 1898 Bates and Guild brought out a huge book by Cram, *English Country Churches*. It was, however, a series of plates without text. *Church Building*, on the other hand, was mostly text and became a kind of bible of church design for its era, ultimately the most influential book in its field published in America and the foundation for Cram's forthcoming revolution of the visual image of American Christianity in the twentieth century.

Appropriately, it was dedicated to the firm's cofounder, Charles Wentworth, who died of tuberculosis in California in 1897 (thus necessitating the firm's change in name to Cram, Goodhue and Ferguson — the latter the draftsman whose advent was noted in Chapter 3). *Church Building* was also a collaboration with Goodhue, who, as in the case of *The Decadent*, did several illustrations as well as the elaborate cover design. Very different from *The Decadent*,

98. Among Goodhue's and Cram's most famous collaborations was Cram's seminal work of 1899, *Church Building*, published in book form in 1901. Goodhue designed this elaborate cover.

Cram and Goodhue's second collaboration was not only written by a Visionist and illustrated by another, it was published by a third, Herbert Small, whose press, Small, Maynard and Company, was, as we saw earlier, another of the progeny of *Knight Errant*.

VISIONIST ARCHITECTURE

Goodhue's imaginative use of Carman's work in the "Traumburg" project is also important as disclosing what is surely the last phase of the several we have explored here in the decade-long collaboration of Cram and Goodhue in the nineties, for in these drawings it is evident that Goodhue's maturity as a designer

THE CHELTENHAM FONT

¶ It is in characters not differing in any material item from these (the designer trusts) that this new font will be cut.

THE CHELTENHAM TYPE

Quaint enough will be this type lacking exactly what chiefly gives the Italic, its qualities of dash & zip; i.e. the kerns. J.

99. Designed by Goodhue (*above*: his original drawings) for his and Cram's fellow Visionist, Ingalls Kimball, the Cheltenham typeface, first used to present Cram and Goodhue's plans for West Point, was distinctly modern in concept, being probably the first typeface devised for setting both by hand and by the Linotype machine. According to Alex Lawson, in his *Anatomy of a Typeface*, Cheltenham went on to become "in all probability the most widely known type designed in the United States" — a Visionist artistic triumph that outlived even the "Stein Song"!

(he would turn thirty in 1899) was at hand and his need of Cram coming to an end. As Goodhue's biographer put it, however, these designs' very excellence, the "degree of order and restraint evident in [these drawings], as compared with Goodhue's 1889 scheme for the Cathedral of St. John the Divine, also suggests that he had profited from his association with Cram."[74]

But "Traumburg" is by no means the extent of what might be called Visionist architecture, which is to say architecture (like so much literature also discussed here) done *for* Visionists *by* one or more other Visionists, such as the Gothic mortuary chapel for Fred Day's family in Norwood (*100*) by Cram[75] or the several works by him and Goodhue in, of all unlikely Visionist locales, Fall River, Massachusetts.

That rather foreign-looking workers' port city of lofty stone church towers and hardly less towering factory chimneys, rising from the immense ranges of stone and brick mills that dominate this once-great textile center south of Boston, seems to have had a most mysterious affinity for the work of Cram and Goodhue in the nineties, and their most eclectic work at that, including an

100. Exterior view of the Day family chapel in Norwood, the work of Cram and Goodhue in 1902.

Italianate public library (already discussed), an Anglican Gothic parish church, a Roman Catholic church in Mexican baroque, and, as a finale, of all things, a full-fledged Japanese-style house that would have been the astonishment of many more cosmopolitan centers than Fall River, where we are certainly justified in thinking Cram had more than one good friend. In fact, there is a surviving letter to Cram (found among his papers), in which probably one Visionist refers to yet another, Arthur Knapp (or, perhaps, his father), with respect to certain possibilities in Fall River. The salient paragraph:

> My dear Cram,
>   What I am writing you is strictly personal and I would rather you would say nothing about it at present. The city of Fall River is going to build a Public Library to cost about $100,000. . . . I know all the trustees very well and you may be sure I will do all I can for you. Already, I have been at work. I will watch the affair carefully and let you know when to make a [?illegible]. Mr. Knapp will have some influence. . . .[76]

Here again, one suspects, is the aesthete network. It is evident as well in the commission for the Roman Catholic church in Fall River, SS. Peter and Paul (*101*)—stylistically a reflection of Cram's Sicilian adventures with Randall in

101. Interior view of Cram and Goodhue's striking baroque extravaganza, the Church of SS. Peter and Paul, Fall River, Massachusetts, designed in 1895.

1888 and Goodhue's fascination with Mexico (the reader will recall all this from our discussion of the Newton Corner Methodist Church, sister church, so to speak, of SS. Peter and Paul, built in the same year).

This Fall River Roman Catholic commission came to the office through Louise Guiney, who in an effort to bolster Cram's flagging architectural prospects had arranged for him to write an article on Roman Catholic church architecture for a widely read magazine of the period, *Catholic World*, and the nature of the job was well described by Cram in his letter of thanks to her thereafter (it is his only known work of the 1890s for a Roman Catholic parish, except, perhaps, for some interior fittings at the Gate of Heaven Church in South Boston):[77]

> It is for Father McCahill of Fall River. A little Irishman and a square man and a gentleman if ever there was one. It is going to be a good church too, all domes and vaults and great arches à la San Marco [illegible]. Father McCahill says it is going to revolutionize Roman Catholic architecture in America. Is not that fine?[78]

A curiously naive sort of letter! Guiney, in reply, gave Cram good advice: "Go slow and sly," she wrote, "and don't let the cost exceed the calculation [Goodhue again, no doubt] and I know you will be in furious demand."[79]

Cram, in his usual fashion, had not minced words in his *Catholic World* article.[80] The Catholic church, he wrote, was visually a town's "barest, commonest, red brick and granite structure," with an interior focused on a "high altar of bluish white marble, ready-made, looking, alas! like a glorified soda-fountain in its frantic elaboration." Though he thought Holy Cross, the Roman Catholic cathedral in Boston, had "outward dignity and reserve," he savaged its interior, with its "gas-pipe columns and very ugly windows," and asked: "apart from this is there one Catholic church in all of Boston which glorifies God by its material worth [or] . . . its charm? I do not know of one." To the argument of economy, moreover, he replied that "the best churches, architecturally, in America are precisely those that cost small sums of money." And he met equally head-on the difficulty of his not being Roman Catholic: "it is surely better to glorify the Almighty by the hands of unbelievers than to wrong him by the incompetence of those in the fold." Noting that "inside [the Catholic Church], indeed, is salvation," he went on: "Inside, also, is an apotheosis of the ugly and the annoying. That it should be so is, with no exaggeration, the greatest pity, the greatest blunder in the world." Nor did he neglect pointedly to remind his Roman friends of "the great success of the High Church [Anglican] movement . . . due [not least] to its restoration of sumptuous ritual and inspiring architecture."

The church that followed this blast, SS. Peter and Paul of 1895–1898, if it did not revolutionize American Roman Catholic architecture (that was to be left to

Charles Maginnis), certainly must have revolutionized more than one person's conception of Cram and Goodhue's church work. There was to be no chaste Perpendicular this time.

Yet as we have noted before here, no more now than then should one be surprised by Cram's stylistic eclecticism, even in church design, and even considering Cram's tastes quite aside from Goodhue's. Cram's hero, after all, John Sedding, though a famous English Gothicist and an ardent Arts and Crafts man, earned his reputation for boldness and originality in design not primarily for those virtues; nor even for the fact that, above all, he possessed "a sensibility nervously alive to proportion, mystery, splendor, color, sheen; in a word, the aesthetic sense"; but for his determination to enrich his vocabulary of church design with classical as much as with medieval modes. As Cram pointed out (and as things like Goodhue's Ashmont lectern evidence), Sedding

> realized that the [more strictly and narrowly Gothic Revival] method of his own master, [George] Street, was lacking in vitality . . . [and was] not artistic. . . . Sedding's work was simply this . . . to prolong Gothic to its logical conclusion. In other words, unite Gothic and Renaissance in a coherent whole.[81]

Notice also that it was in the late 1880s, when Sedding had been doing his first important classical church work, that Cram himself had been bowled over by the baroque churches of Sicily he and Randall had been exploring. By the time he started his firm in 1889, Cram's eclecticism, so soon demonstrated in his work, was to have been expected, whatever area he might specialize in.

One must, on the other hand, assign to Goodhue and Mexico much of the stylistic content of the church he and Cram built at Fall River, which surely must have been the astonishment of that city: two bell towers (reminiscent especially in their cupolas of those of the great seventeenth-century cathedral of Mexico City), each tower's upper stages a riot of rusticated columns, broken pediments, bulbous balusters, and nearly everything else imaginable, rose from a richly sculptured facade whose fantastical detail was very churrigueresque in feeling. And the interior, as completed by 1898, was even a greater astonishment: filled with fresco, stenciled color decoration, and much elaborate wood and plaster detail, the "reredos wall" at the east end, behind the high altar, was conceived as a baroque fantasia of every other motif ever imaginable — roundels, shells, garlands of fruits, cartouches, and draperies, with putti and angels poised precariously amidst such profusion of detail that the underlying cornice must somewhat have to be taken on faith. And all this in papier-mâché and plaster enriched with gold leaf! (It was, nevertheless, a highly disciplined and effective composition.)

What tremendous fun it all must have been — one imagines Cram, Goodhue,

397

and Guiney making Sunday excursions to see the work as it progressed. Years later, a priest on the staff there who had grown up in the parish recalled a marvelous story that quite captures this high-minded and earnest but very jolly attempt (and no less Visionist for that) to put American Roman Catholic architecture right; Cram, he and Goodhue having conceived of the interior color as "an integrated pattern . . . rich and subtle" (muted fawn tones were blended with red, blue, and many gold highlights), could not for the life of him decide what color to paint the sets of doors to either side of the high altar. "Cram was at breakfast," the story goes, "and suddenly said, 'We'll paint one [set] the color of coffee with milk, the other the color of coffee with cream.' "[82]

Alas, it is all gone now, destroyed by fire in 1973. And so all that remains of this sudden summer affair of Cram and Goodhue with fantastical baroque in 1895 is the much less successful Newton Corner Methodist Church of the same year. Still, it must be remembered that in the post-World War I period both Cram and Goodhue, each on his own then, would return to this baroque enthusiasm with great success.

Patronage (what such projects as the Day chapel and SS. Peter and Paul had chiefly in common) may not have been the only aspect of Cram and Goodhue's work of their early period that suggests the term Visionist architecture. Another aspect may just perhaps be glimpsed in their other Fall River church of the 1890s, St. Stephen's Episcopal Church.

ARCHITECTURE, MYSTICISM, AND MYTH

Toward the close of Cram and Goodhue's brilliant if erratic decade of the nineties, there is, in the church work of the firm particularly, a discernable growth in the partners' power of design. Cram himself later thought that in the late nineties they had done "too many churches and were getting hidebound."[83] Evidence that his own restless modernism, as he would have called it, was as critical if not as inventive as Goodhue's, Cram's judgment, however, does not seem to me at all reasonable. Just as the first major ecclesiastical designs of 1892–1894, in the wake of Ashmont (St. Paul's, Brockton; Christ Church, Hyde Park; the Open Word, Newtonville [102]; St. Andrew's, Detroit; All Saints', Brookline; and the Church of the Advent's Lady Chapel) constituted something of a unity (and one that for all its unevenness boded well for the future), so does another group of ecclesiastical designs, of 1897–1900, form a triumphant climax to Cram and Goodhue's decade together.

These five works are Our Saviour's, Middleborough; St. Stephen's, Fall River; St. Stephen's, Cohasset; Emmanuel, Newport, Rhode Island; and the interior of the chancel of All Saints', Ashmont. Having jumped back and forth

102. The Church of the New Jerusalem (now the Church of the Open Word), the Swedenborgian church in Newton, Massachusetts, designed by Cram and Goodhue in 1893, evidences the fact that in the nineties Cram moved in other than strictly Episcopalian circles.

in this volume, topicality and chronology often being incompatible masters for a biographer, among all the firm's 1890s churches (which, whatever subgroups they form, are all sufficiently of a piece to allow this), we have already discussed three of these churches: Our Saviour's, Middleborough, St. Stephen's, Cohasset, and Emmanuel, Newport; in the next chapter we will deal with the interior design of the chancel of All Saints', Ashmont. Now we must focus on the one of these last five powerful church designs of the late nineties not yet dealt with: St. Stephen's, Fall River, the only one of the five not completed, yet in many ways the most interesting of them all.

In this connection it should be borne in mind that although Cram always expressed himself both publicly and privately as chiefly a disciple in church design of John Sedding ("who most inspired me," Cram wrote years later to his son, "when I began work in ecclesiastical architecture"),[84] the more conservative Bodley, not Sedding, has often seemed to scholars more influential with

399

103. St. Stephen's Church, Fall River, Massachusetts, designed by Cram and Goodhue in 1897, rejoices in one of their most avant-garde west fronts.

respect to Cram's early work. Sedding died at the outset of Cram's career, in 1891, while Bodley lived through the 1890s, as did Cram's local mentor, Vaughan, who was, of course, a product of Bodley's office. But Vaughan's opposite number in Sedding's circle, the architect and sculptor Henry Wilson (not only Sedding's successor architect but a far more innovative designer than either Sedding or Vaughan), was also known personally to Cram. While I am sure Vaughan's influence on Cram both professionally and personally was considerable, I suspect that the same was true, albeit at a distance, of Wilson. And where Wilson is in the 1890s, there frequently is also William Lethaby, making for a formidable combination.

The most important British Arts and Crafts theorist of Cram's generation (only six years older than Cram), Lethaby was in turn much influenced by Philip Webb, William Morris's collaborator and the architect who took the lead in England in translating Arts and Crafts principles into architectural practice — a mission that in the area of architect-craftsman collaboration was preached perhaps most ardently by Sedding, who, like Wilson, was both architect and crafts-man in equal measure.[85] It is not clear whether Cram knew Lethaby personally, though it is likely, but it is certain that Goodhue did (and wrote about him in *Knight Errant*),[86] and Wilson was a close and lifelong friend of Cram's, commis-sioned by Cram to do several works for him. As usual, beyond his admission that he had met Wilson in England, we know nothing of the nature and circum-stances of Cram's friendship with Wilson, except, perhaps, that Guiney referred in her correspondence with Cram to "your adored Henry Wilson!"[87] That the friendship was close is also indicated by the fact that in an age when such usage was rare, Cram and Wilson corresponded on a first-name basis.

Wilson and Lethaby were themselves close friends, collaborators, for exam-ple (with Christopher Whall, whom, as we have seen, Cram also knew), on perhaps the most radical plan submitted for Liverpool Cathedral,[88] and it is known that Wilson was very much involved with Lethaby during the middle and late 1880s, when Lethaby was putting together his famous *Architecture, Mysticism and Myth*, published in 1891, a book about symbol and meaning in architectural shape and form. Whether it directly influenced Cram I do not know. But Lethaby's ideas certainly influenced Wilson's work (which Cram much admired), as I think St. Stephen's, Fall River (*103*), designed in the months just after Middleborough's plans were completed, discloses.

St. Stephen's was described in contemporary reports based on interviews with Cram as being in style

> developed Gothic, worked out in a truly original style. The front is thoroughly
> unique. . . . The mason work will be of the simplest kind. The plainness and severity
> is plainly noticeable, with the exception of the front porch. The aim of the architect
> was to give dignity and majesty to the building, and what little exterior decoration
> there is has been wonderfully effective by concentration in the porch.[89]

Even sharper and crisper than Middleborough, though perhaps less timeless, St. Stephen's west front, a stunning magisterial composition, has so obvious a past in St. Paul's, Brockton, and so much more of a future in Goodhue's work than in Cram's solo work, many may well conclude St. Stephen's is more the junior than the senior partner's work. But more likely it is one of both partners' most successful collaborations. Cram was deeply invested in it, writing in one of his books of how "lofty, massive and commanding" the design was, and how in its majesty "the amenities of Gothic are done away with, and stress is laid on its attributes of power and domination"—words very reminiscent of Cram's youthful Richardsonian hero worship and of his own as opposed to Goodhue's side of the architectural equation.[90] And though it is only fair to add that Goodhue was evolving rapidly (and in his own way) in the direction of what had originally been chiefly Cram's emphasis on mass and scale and volume and void, the west front of St. Stephen's is also very reminiscent of two contemporary British churches by Wilson, who was, it would seem, more Cram's friend and mentor as Lethaby was more Goodhue's. Certainly the finlike piers of the arch framing the west window recall Wilson's at St. Peter's, Ealing, London, of 1892; and the massive, fortresslike west front as a whole, so flat and square to each side of so deep a void, is surely a development from Wilson's pylonlike entrance front at St. Andrew's, Bournemouth, of 1895. In each case what Alistair Service has called Wilson's "splendour of scale" is very evident.[91] So, too, at St. Stephen's. (Alas, potentially Cram's and Goodhue's masterwork between Middleborough and Cohasset, this church survives today as only the rump of a design, gallant but forlorn.)

If Wilson's ideas seem more specifically pertinent to St. Stephen's, more generally it is Lethaby's ideas that carry a Visionist connotation, especially as laid out in his book, the basic thesis of which was that there were three "ultimate facts behind all architecture." Two were Vitruvian prescriptions, hardly controversial: man's own functional needs and the means and materials of construction. The third, however — "the connection between the world as a structure, and the building" — seems almost Jungian in feeling, relating as it does to what are virtually *architectural* archetypes.[92] And that idea is perhaps the closest one can now get to what one might call Visionist architecture in the largest sense, to what may have most stimulated Cram and his fellows, who, if they were not forgathering in the Hall of Isis or in Saint Kavin's Cell by the sea in Scituate[93] or in Day's mysterious and magnificent Norwood manse, were instead in Mexico or Japan or Persia, or wherever, following one dream or another.

Japan? Persia? Truly, we are not done with exotic architecture here. Goodhue, for example, not content with another trip to Mexico at the end of the nineties, rode more than four hundred miles on horseback from the Caspian Sea to the Persian Gulf at the turn of the century, as the guest of his lifelong friend and client James Gillespie, paying particular attention to the Persian gardens he would ever after always love. From Shiraz to Samarkand, Goodhue saw them all, often by daylight and then again by moonlight. And as always, there was architecture: El Fureidis, outside Santa Barbara, California, the splendid estate Goodhue and Cram designed upon his return, was set in Persian-style gardens scarcely less romantic or beguiling than the originals, as Goodhue painted them in one exquisite rendering after another.

It was all in the best Visionist tradition, whether with Goodhue in Persia or Mexico, or Cram in Japan. For the most improbable architecture conceived by Cram and Goodhue at the behest of a fellow Visionist was a case of far away and (as it turned out) never built, but nonetheless more important for all that in

104. Goodhue's perspective of his and Cram's designs for the Imperial Japanese Parliament Buildings, Tokyo, 1898. Their design was never carried out.

the long run than much Cram and Goodhue did build: their project for the Imperial Japanese Parliament Building in Tokyo (*104*).

BOSTON AND JAPAN

It is by now a legendary relationship, Boston and Japan, played out in the late nineteenth and early twentieth centuries on so many levels that it was not unusual that one of Cram's wealthier Visionist friends, Arthur Knapp, should exhibit an enthusiasm for Japanese architecture. Especially since Knapp's father, a Unitarian missionary in Japan, was as much a convert to Japanese culture as any of his disciples were to Knapp's New England religion. But only a pair of Boston Visionists could have worked up the scheme of 1898 best left, perhaps, to Cram himself to describe:

> The father of one of the original Pewter Mugs and Visionists, the Reverend Arthur May Knapp, was a sort of Unitarian emissary to Japan, and was then living there. [Knapp, it should be noted, wrote on Japan for no less than the *Atlantic.*] The Empire was at the point of building fine new Parliament Houses in Tokyo. We had earlier discussed the essential unrighteousness of the general principles of Westernizing this ancient land, with its unique and beautiful culture. . . . Why should we not work out a scheme . . . based on the indigenous architecture . . . but sufficiently adapted to modern conditions? . . . Mr. Knapp, who first put the idea into our heads, was sure

403

that through his [Japanese] affiliations he could get it before the Government, . . . particularly if I would bring the designs over in person. . . . We decided to take a chance. . . . I developed a set of plans, [Goodhue] produced one of his most brilliant and beautifully rendered perspectives, and I set forth, via San Francisco, for the long Pacific voyage.[94]

In Japan (the sojourn that produced the letters to Goodhue on Japanese geishas quoted earlier here in another context), Mr. Knapp's connections proved efficient. The forthcoming budget of the Marquis Ito, then the prime minister, provided for a substantial sum for fuller plans from the Cram office. Alas, Ito's government did not endure long enough to build. But that is not to say that nothing came of it all. Geishas aside, Cram fell seriously in love with Japan, a country whose temple architecture particularly he found supremely moving: "Black lacquer and gold and cinnabar, . . . massive ropes and tassels of blood-red silk; . . . great lotus plants sheeted with beaten gold; . . . deep tongued bells, sonorous drums; strange, unearthly chanting . . . pale incense."[95] For any Visionist and habitué chez Day the real thing, as it were, must have been over-whelming.

At least, in his artistic and historical musings during this peregrination, Cram was judicious, even understated, in his reports back, entranced, above all, through his friend Ernest Fenollosa[96] with the temple gardens. He wrote, soon after his return, of the Koshoji Temple that for him it was

> full of some kind of enchantment; once there one would never leave. We had heard each evening down at our inn at Uji . . . the velvety boom of some enormous bell, a sound that seemed to draw one irresistibly to rise up in the still night and search for its source under the great, pale moon. . . . We found the bell and much more. . . . [Japan] concentrates itself and becomes really quite irresistible, in the form of scented temple garden in some forgotten monastery where the odour of incense mingles with that of box, where the patterned sand retains the lines of a thousand years ago, where tonsured bonzes [monks] in yellow robes move silently through the shed petals of a pink cherry, and a thunderous bell gives tongue at the rising of the moon.[97]

Yet there was, too, a very contemporary aspect to this peregrination, quite aside from the hope of a job. Years later, Cram recalled:

> It was all mixed up with curious happenings of diametrically opposed nature, for this was the year [1898] of the Spanish[-American] war, and by sheer accident I happened to be in the Imperial Hotel in Yokohama at the moment when the U.S.S. *McCulloch* came in with the first word of the Battle of Manila Bay. Strange conjunction of the ancient East and the youthful West; of history in the past, of history in the making. The contrast in thought and action, once I was back in Boston, was no less, for from the temples of Kyoto and Uji, Nara and Nagoya, and the painting and sculpture and drama of twelve centuries, I returned to work out the designs for Rich-

mond Court in Brookline, which was the first attempt to camouflage an apartment house through the counterfeit presentment of a great Tudor mansion.[98]

As I observed earlier, this is an unfair judgment of Richmond Court, one that reflects the harsher views of Cram's later years in the 1930s, when he wrote his memoirs. There also, undoubtedly for the same reason, he omitted any discussion of another of his acts of counterfeiture, as he would have by then called it: the Japanese architecture of his design that *was* built in the 1890s, at Mr. Knapp's behest and well enough to have somewhat explained the subsequent Parliament House project—the Knapp House itself of 1894 (*105*), which, despite published reports to the contrary, still stands more or less complete today, the last of our trio of Fall River landmarks of the 1890s by Cram and Goodhue.

At first glance this house seems ordinary enough in a period when, such was the continuing fascination in New England for the Oriental, Fenollosa's wife, writing under the pseudonym of Sidney McCall, could describe in her novel *Truth Dexter* a fashionable Boston drawing room of the era:

A coil of burning incense wrote gray hieroglyphics upon the silence of the room. Above her hung a great carved ostrich egg, and, near it, a Venetian lamp of fretted ironwork. It was a strange, rich, luminous room, set about with oriental treasures in unexpected patches of pure color, like a brilliant unorganized mind, that draws into itself refulgent images.[99]

But at second glance, the Knapp House is not more decor than architecture. For example, though it is crowned by "a magnificent irimoya roof," as it has been called, "with deep, flaring eaves and a curvilinear Tokugana gable piercing the front slope,"[100] that substitution for the conventional Western roof is not so easily accomplished as one might think, given the need to provide for Western features such as attic dormers, stairwell skylights, and at least two working chimney stacks, all of which Cram had to contrive so that they should occur behind the main ridgepole (and thus be hidden at least from the front of the house). Cram, who in 1895 knew little of Japanese architecture and had not yet been to Japan, had, it is true, a client who knew much and had lived there. But that client also wanted Western amenities, as a contemporary newspaper report made plain:

Of course [the house] is not strictly Japanese; it was not intended that it should be. Mr. Knapp wanted first of all to build a house in which he and his family could live comfortably—a house which should be duly respectful to New England and 19th century ideas of propriety and convenience. Liking the Japanese style of architecture, he believed that it could be adapted perfectly well to warmth, convenience, and an improved system of plumbing; and also, that its combination of piquancy and simplicity was quite as well suited to a New England street as the colonial perversions and Queen Anne absurdities with which it is usually lined.[101]

105a, b. Exterior view (*above*), ca. 1896, of Cram and Goodhue's Knapp House, Fall River, Massachusetts, designed in 1894, showing in the foreground the tea house, designed between 1895 and 1898. Interior view (*below*), ca. 1898, of the Knapp tea house.

With a client like that such a idea was bound to be in so unforgiving an art as architecture an enormously challenging task. What *was* only decor — the actual palm tree trunk (with its original bark), for example, incorporated as a post into an alcove in the dining room — must have been the easiest part, and Cram's designs were, in fact, frankly if carefully worked up from Sylvester Morse's definitive *Japanese Homes and Their Surroundings*.[102] (Important aspects of the parlor, for example, are drawn from an illustration that appeared on page 139 of Morse's book.) But Morse, if he knew nothing of chimneys outside, knew nothing either of fireplaces and mantelpieces inside. Thus the Knapp House was, as Cram reported in *Architectural Record* in 1898, distinctly "an architectural experiment," and one of which in *The Japanese Influence in America* Clay Lancaster has much good to say:

> The interior of the Knapp house showed a synthesis of East and West . . . [combining] Occidental fireplaces and Oriental recesses filled with art. . . . Western stair flights, niche and hinged doors juxtaposed against Eastern railings, open panel carvings and unstained woods. [The main stair] ascended to a gallery lighted overhead through a translucent ceiling screen [of wood lattice and rice paper] upheld by a series of slender square posts connected by railings [in some places of bamboo] and pierced *ramina*. Although a bit cluttered the stair hall [is] a more agreeable fusion of components from two hemispheres than the adjoining rooms.[103]

Particularly difficult was the question of how to make any type of Western window — a necessity in New England — do duty as sliding shoji screens. Cram arranged some of the windows in sets of ribbons, contrived the blinds or shutters to slide rather than pivot on hinges, and, as a contemporary report noticed, some of

> the windows are so built as to be easily removed, like shoji, and the pleasant little conservatory, from which they look out, is so finished that the summer winds and rains may enter it without harm. . . . Thus, in a small way, Mr. Knapp will be able to taste that indoor outdoor way of living which is universal in Japan.[104]

Equally interesting was the way Cram introduced ceiling shoji under the stairwell skylights and contrived a protruding window seat (rather like a pagoda-oriel) over this stair hall, one of several interior windows that make the stairwell itself seem to participate more in the outdoors and also give cross ventilation on the bedroom floor, thus using Eastern decor to solve, as it were, what is, after all, a very practical Western problem on all bedroom floors everywhere.[105]

Indeed, in one respect the Knapp House seemed to its client an improvement on the Eastern abode. As he told an interviewer, the Japanese

> are great lovers of beautiful graining and choose their [exposed] beams and planks with a careful eye to a rich and various marking. . . . The Japanese themselves use a great deal of black cypress in the construction of their houses. . . . The American va-

riety [used in the Knapp house] is much superior in texture . . . and Mr. Knapp says that there is nothing in his house which a Japanese would so envy him as the luxurious grain of his woodwork. . . . The woodwork throughout the house has been left perfectly plain, as is the Japanese custom . . . merely smoothed, shellacked and rubbed down.[106]

Today one might not be so enthusiastic as to claim that the Knapp House is an improvement on its inspiration. But Clay Lancaster, in the work already cited, leaves little doubt of the historical importance in American cultural history of Cram's still too little known and quite charming response to his Visionist friend and client. Lancaster emphasizes Cram's role, along with those of Frank Lloyd Wright, Richard Neutra, and Raymond Hood, in advancing knowledge of Japanese design in America, and he notes that

regard for authentic Japanese architecture first manifested itself in America among a small selection of intellectuals. The foremost among them was Professor Edward Sylvester Morse . . . curator of Japanese ceramics at the Boston Museum of Fine Arts. A Japanese friend, Bunkio Matsuki, settled in Salem, and in the 1890s built a house there that was mostly Japanese in character. A larger contemporary house in Fall River, Massachusetts, was constructed for the Reverend Arthur May Knapp, . . . [who] succeeded in getting his architect, Ralph Adams Cram, over for four months [to Japan].[107]

The most significant part of the Knapp House was, in fact, designed by Cram after his trip to Japan, the one-story pavilion, or tea house, opening off the dining room and more intimately related than the rest of the house to the elaborate Japanese garden that surrounded it. Built in the authentic Japanese fashion — on posts, with no masonry foundations, and ornamented only with carved grilles of cryptomeria — the tea room's white pine and rice-paper sliding screens, protected by stouter exterior sliding doors of wood and glass, could dispense with this exterior protection and slide back to form a whole with the garden, though obviously during only a few months of the year. Yet Cram felt the effect in winter as fine as in summer, an effect he was able to describe without self-praise by assigning the larger share of the achievement to his client. Said Cram: "It would be impossible to imagine anything more quiet and delicate than the effect of this room, either in winter when the shoji [screens] are drawn and it is full of soft diffused light, or in summer when they are run back and two sides are open to the fresh air."[108] (Much changed today, this superb interior awaits restoration.)

Cram was similarly generous with credit for the mantelpieces of the main house, but nothing is clearer than that the Knapp House was Cram's preeminently, and not just so far as the client was concerned; for just as things Persian and Moorish were, in his biographer's view, Goodhue's particular passions and the chief sources for the firm's work in those veins (Japanese architecture is not even mentioned in the Goodhue biography), so Cram's biographer can affirm here that Japanese architecture and garden design, equally as obviously, were distinctly Cram's passion. And, of course, it very much accords with what we have seen here of their partnership that each man, in addition to their joint Gothic and Bohemian passions ("Traumburg," after all, is in Bohemia), should seek out and find his own individual romances of the far away and long ago and then bring the passions of each back to the other and exploit them to the architectural full.

For us here, concerned as we are more with Cram's side of things, his Japanese interests were especially significant as allowing him to keep alive his own "constructional detail" of the Cram and Wentworth period, so likely to be overwhelmed by Goodhue's decorative genius. For the firm's Japanese work was the one aspect of Cram's design partnership of 1890s with Goodhue where Cram was able to maintain and develop the kind of sparse, constructional, almost abstract detail that characterized his solo houses of 1889–1891.

Seen now in the context of the newly rediscovered Cram and Wentworth houses of five or six years earlier, the Knapp House interior is recognizable, for all its exotic overtones, as Cram's own. The balusters of the staircase, plain and square in plan but finely molded in the center; the simple, spare bracketing of the mantelpieces; their feeling for recession and projection — all these are so reminiscent of the Ide House in Williamstown and the Whittemore House in York Harbor that the affinities with Frank Lloyd Wright's work we noticed earlier in the Wrightian accents of both of Cram's early houses seem now in this setting much more inevitable.

Cram and Wright, after all, shared a very similar passion for Japanese art. And as *The Craftsman* magazine, reviewing Cram's writings on Japanese design, pointed out, in an article entitled "Japanese Architecture and Its Relation to the Coming American Style," those writings were "notable" for pointing to "the trend of modern thought and art, with its strong revulsion toward simplicity" and its "rejection of all false ornamentation and the meeting of all actual requirements in the simplest and most direct way."[109] Indeed, it was as this sort of modernist that Cram most prominently appeared in *The Craftsman*, that bible of the American Arts and Crafts movement, where many of the threads we have been following in this volume met. Wright's master, Louis Sullivan, wrote about architecture in the same issue (May 1906) in which Cram's Japanese work was reviewed, and in the summer of 1906 *The Craftsman* also published Bliss Carman and Edward Carpenter on Walt Whitman! All of which, as much as Cram's proclivities for Japanese architecture, was part and parcel of what the anonymous author of the Cram piece called the "gospel preached by *The Craftsman*."

If Cram's affinities with Wright are evident at the Knapp House, which in its day was widely admired and published in architectural journals and books (copiously illustrated, for example, in C. E. Hooper's *Country House* of 1904 and 1913),[110] so also does this house disclose shared ideas on Cram's part with the Greene brothers, those remarkable West Coast architects of the turn of the century, whose interest in Japanese architecture can be dated at the latest to "a volume on Japanese houses and gardens" first seen by one of the brothers about 1903.[111]

Probably this was yet another edition of Morse's book. But it could have been a book by Cram on the same subject published just about then. For the greatest significance of this Visionist architecture in the Japanese mode is that it would lead, a decade later, in the new century, to one of Cram's most famous books (*Japanese Architecture and the Allied Arts*) and to a series of Japanese interiors at the Museum of Fine Arts in Boston by Cram that played their part in the history of the greatest Japanese collection in the Western world and not incidently reflected the continued validity, even in the face of Goodhue's gorgeous detail, of Cram's own pre-Goodhue aesthetic from Cram and Wentworth days.

Cram had in the Japanese parliament design no more reformed or rejuvenated Japanese architecture than Goodhue and he had reformed or revived American Roman Catholic church architecture in the Church of SS. Peter and Paul. But in future years much came of what Cram rather embarrassedly called his "pseudo-Japanese house."[112]

THE XXTH CENTURY

When or if the Visionists were disbanded is not known. The last evidence of the order's activity is to be found in Bliss Carman's Harvard Phi Beta Kappa poem of 1914. Of interest because it shows the wide reach of this small group of never more than twenty or so young men — from such popular nationwide successes as the "Stein Song" to the elite solemnities of Harvard's commencement — the content of this poem (not in itself of any great literary value) also discloses how very personal, on even so public an occasion, were its references. Both Hovey and Meteyard are alluded to (see, respectively, a "poet . . . from Dartmouth" and "a painter's paradise . . . by the Scituate shore") and, by their actual names, so are Cram and Goodhue:

> One band of scholar gypsies I have known,
> Whose purpose all unworldly was to find
> An answer to the riddle of the Earth —
> A key that should unlock the book of life
> And secrets of its sorceries reveal . . .

106. "Three men in a decadent moon" — the cover design of *Songs from Vagabondia*, 1894. From left to right, Thomas Meteyard, Copeland and Day's designer, and Bliss Carman and Richard Hovey, the authors of the book.

> Our dark young poet who from Dartmouth came
> Was told the secret by his gypsy bride,
> Who had it from a master overseas,
> And he it was who first hinted to the band
> The magic of that universal lore . . .
> They stood intoxicated with delight before
> The poised unanxious splendor of the Greek;
> They mused upon the Gothic minsters gray . . .
> (Like a remembrance of the Middle Age
> They rose where Ralph or Bertram dreamed in stone);
> Entranced they trod a painter's paradise,
> Where color wasted by the Scituate shore
> Between the changing marshes and the sea . .
>
> Ah, softly, brothers! Have we not the key
> Whose first fine luminous use Plotinus gave,
> Teaching that ecstasy must lead the man?[113]

Much here enforces our long-standing surmise. In the first place something is made of magic. "A master overseas," for example, may well have meant one of the magicians of the Golden Dawn, or it could have referred to one of Madame Blavatsky's teachings, that all those who come together for occult purposes need to seek out one of the constantly reincarnating "masters" who sustain such things. There are also telling references to things Greek, evidence that

Jussim's instincts were right when she called the Visionists "fin-de-siècle neo-Platonists,"[114] and a specific reference to one neo-Platonist teacher in particular, Plotinus, a very apt mentor for the Visionists. Wrote Evelyn Underhill, "In the high place [Plotinus] gives to Beauty, which is to him one of the three final attributes of God, the strongly poetic character of his vision of Reality becomes evident. . . . His doctrine gives a religious sanction and a philosophic explanation to those special experiences and apprehensions of artists, poets."[115]

Furthermore, if subtexts both occult and Platonic are evident in what Carman said, so is the gay subtext in what he did *not* say. His overall theme, after all, is an old one here — Whitmanic comradeship; though by 1914, as much as the Decadence itself, in a quickly changing post-Wildean and more and more Freudian context, such a theme was increasingly suspect.

But if Carman's poem really was, as it turned out, a eulogy (1914 and all that) for a cause increasingly lost, surely it is at this point in our study beyond argument here that for Cram and his friends lost causes were always the best causes. Consider Stephen Parrish's analysis of the Decadence as served up in *The Mahogany Tree*. The decadent, its editors opined, had to live in luxury and idleness, his only solace absinthe, Wilde, Burne-Jones, and such; his only desire the woman of his dreams, whom, however, he would never find. Of course. And even if he should, and escaped with her to the tropical isle of his bliss, they would be in that ideal life, Cram and his fellows wrote (and here the key signature changes curiously),

> the new Adam and Eve, whose children would not go wrong at the first touch, because they would have no consciences and couldn't do wrong. The coming race would be a much more moral one than ours, you see; since there would be no morals, no one could break them and be wicked.[116]

One is suddenly reminded of Edmund White's observation in *States of Desire* that "Decadence . . . can be read as thwarted manifestations of gay anger,"[117] an insightful contention that pushes much further Hilliard's view that Anglo-Catholicism was in no small measure an aspect of gay rebellion, a source for my own reading here of Cram's churches as in part Trojan horses. Even Parrish admits that the Decadence of Cram and his fellows as discernable in *The Mahogany Tree* "stood for more than a revolt. . . . These iconoclasts had an affirmative creed."[118] And, perhaps just because it was fed importantly by such deep-seated anger of rebellion, that was never lost.

If this is hard to see now, it is because the decadent revolt against mass culture and bourgeois values and industrialism is so often understood today as "anti-modernist." But that by itself this word is quite misleading can be grasped readily in the case of the Visionists, who were a very radical and creative group, and not to be defined merely by so negative a term. What Parrish calls their "affirmative creed" — to husband the past creatively through all their manifold works (including such extensive undertakings, for example, as the whole last phase of the American Gothic Revival and a renaissance in bookmaking still influential today) from a dark age to a better age *of their making* — was targeted clearly and named explicitly: *The XXth Century.*

And was that not a daring enough title proposed for Cram's first aborted journal of the arts in 1887? It does not sound very antimodernist or seem very backward-looking, not even in 1897; it was, in fact, about as progressive a banner as one could raise on the eve of the twentieth century. And that it was recognizable as such to its adherents is clear — despite the migration of the word "modern" since — in the assertion, for example, of the onetime Harvard Bohemian composer Daniel Gregory Mason, who wrote of the 1890s: "In those days the decadence we knew [in 1936, when he was writing] as ultra-modernism was only beginning."[119] Of Cram and his friends one may thus say what Richard Ellmann does of their master and mentor, Wilde, as also of Yeats and Joyce: they really were "not decadents but counter-decadents"; for did they not deliberately go "through decadence to come out on the other side"?[120] And was not the other side modernism?

Consider the example Ellmann gives, Yeats's poem "Leda and the Swan," and the painting by Michelangelo out of which the poem grew. "The incongruities," he observes, "are glossed over by Michelangelo, in Yeats they are heightened. . . . What Yeats does is to let both views of the subject coalesce, to see them with double sight, and this is why [Yeats's] poem is modern as Michelangelo's painting is not."[121] This, too, is why Cram's churches (Freudian as well as Christian landmarks, as it were) are modern and Pugin's, say, are not.

How modern is apparent if one compares Cram's thesis in *The Decadent* with T. S. Eliot's a generation later: "belief gave to Eliot," Russell Kirk has written, "the hope that time might be redeemed."[122] As Eliot himself declared:

The World is trying the experiment of attempting to form a civilized but non-Christian mentality. The experiment will fail; but we must be very patient in awaiting its collapse; meanwhile redeeming the time: so that the Faith may be preserved alive through the dark ages before us; to renew and rebuild civilization, to save the World from suicide.[123]

Cram, who, of course, is *The Decadent* (protagonist as well as author), anticipated the same coming dark age as Eliot, and his response was Eliot's own a half century before Eliot. Although their modernism did not carry the day, as it turned out, Eliot was right in believing that "in a world of fugitives / The person taking the opposite direction / Will appear to run away."[124] But the appearance is misleading. Nor even does the conviction seem to have failed; Thayer Lincoln could still assert in the letter to Cram in the thirties that "what remains with me is the vision itself, and the firm belief that we would now be living in a better world had we been able to make the vision a reality."[125]

What vision was that? The vision of modernism. That is the way I would put it. George Steiner, amazed at how Madame Blavatsky's Theosophy and the Golden Dawn's Rosicrucianism could have instigated Yeats's best work, observed of that poet's correspondence with Maude Gonne that "the key word" in their exchange was "vision" and left it at that.[126] Perhaps wisely. The silence, finally, is deafening. Lincoln also recalled to Cram that it was in the Hall of Isis that Bliss Carman wrote words not unknown even now: "Have little care that life is brief, / Nor less that art is long; / Success is in the silences, / Though fame be in the song."[127] As we have understood Michel Foucault to say before here, there are many kinds of silences.

414

11

KNIGHTS ERRANT

Mark you the floore? that square & speckled stone,
  Which looks so firm and strong,
    Is *Patience*:

And th'other black and grave, wherewith each one
  Is checker'd all along,
    Humilitie:

The gentle rising, which on either hand
  Leads to the Quire above,
    Is *Confidence*:

But the sweet cement, which in one sure band
  Ties the whole frame, is *Love*
    And *Charitie*.

  Hither sometimes Sinne steals, and stains
  The marbles neat and curious veins:
But all is cleansed when the marble weeps.
  Sometimes Death, puffing at the doore,
  Blows all the dust about the floore:
But while he thinks to spoil the room he sweeps.
  Blest be the *Architect*, whose art
  Could build so strong in a weak heart.

— George Herbert, "The Church-floore"

  Our journey has advanced —
  Our feet were almost come
  To that odd Fork in Being's road —

— Emily Dickinson

107. The chancel of All Saints', Ashmont as it appears today: one of the most distinguished congregations of Gothic Revival art in the world.

MORE THAN once during this peregrination of Ralph Adams Cram through the 1890s, we might usefully have paused and inquired what would have been made of this or that of Cram's activities by Cram's chief patrons of this decade, Colonel Peabody and his lady.

What, one wonders, did they make of *The Decadent*? We know from Copeland that it aroused comment.[1] It was the much-talked-of work of their architect, in a place — ruling-class Boston — that was then a very small world in which both the Peabodys were players. The colonel himself was active in many affairs, a member not only of the august Somerset Club but also of the more Bohemian St. Botolph; and Mary Peabody, for all that she was devout, was no naive *femme dévotée*; she was a formidable, strong-minded grande dame, whose name, if it did not appear in *Town Topics* as often (or in as outrageous connections) as Isabella Stewart Gardner's, nonetheless was not unknown even to that society gossip sheet.[2] Speaking of Gardner, that other Anglo-Catholic great lady, what can the Peabodys have thought of *her*?

Or, indeed, for they and all their circle read the *Boston Evening Transcript*, what did they make of Cram's insistent and passionate advocacy through the years of Wagner and the Pre-Raphaelites? Perhaps, most of all, one wonders, what did the colonel and his wife make of that characteristic Pre-Raphaelite figure, the Blessed Damozel? It was, of course, Dante Gabriel Rossetti's wife, Elizabeth Siddal, who died of a drug overdose and whose appearance in Rossetti's paintings Camille Paglia, with some malice but little exaggeration, has described as that of

> a woman of somnambulistic languor . . . rebel[ling] against Victorian convention, her unpinned hair and unstructured medieval gown flowing with lyrical freedom . . . her swollen lips . . . a universal motif of Decadent art, thanks to Burne-Jones and Beardsley.[3]

Yet Nietzsche is right; nature does not jump, neither for Cram *nor* the Peabodys,[4] and it is the biographer's task to "dovetail what can only be seeming incongruities."

As we have seen before, however, the New England mind, even at its most devout, is no simple thing. Remember the explanation Nathan Hale gives as to why Freud and Jung found such significant admirers in Boston, where Hale thought the Unitarian and Transcendentalist tradition nurtured an interest in psychic research in a culture noted as well for its tradition of dissent.[5] Decadence and Freudianism, we have discovered, found their first welcome in America not in New York but in Boston.

The Peabodys — heirs at the highest intellectual level of Unitarian and Transcendentalist thought (Mary Peabody's father was the foremost Unitarian divine in New England), prime exemplars, in their conversion, of the New England proclivity toward dissent and both very active in hospital work (the colonel was in the 1890s the president of Boston's Children's Hospital, his wife president of its convalescent home)[6] — likely were alert to much that Hale refers to. (The colonel and his wife, for instance, moved in social and medical circles where William James and James Putnam were well known.) So, indeed, since they superintended the hospital, did the Sisters of St. Margaret. The nuns, like the Peabodys, led the reverse of a cloistered life; and the chances are that they and the Peabodys did know something of Cram's wild ride through the nineties, as he turned back and forth between such apparently contradictory pursuits as working on the manuscript of *The Decadent* and on the designs for All Saints', Ashmont. Certainly there was one clear intersection of these seeming contradictions and cross-purposes: when Cram in 1896–97 convinced Mary Peabody to commission Sir Edward Burne-Jones to paint All Saints's altarpiece, the projected focus of the high altar chancel.[7]

"THE BLESSED DAMOZEL LEANED OUT . . ."

It must have been a significant choice for Cram, who though he had, perhaps, in his earliest *Transcript* criticism, given Rossetti pride of place, by 1891 had distinctly ceded that position to Burne-Jones. In *Architectural Review* that year, comparing Pre-Raphaelitism with both the Oxford Movement itself and the overall Gothic Revival as the chief "manifestations of the birth of a new life in a land that since the destruction of the Stuart dynasty had been sinking lower and lower in the scale of civilization [note the Jacobite allusion]," Cram named four figures as dominant: in religion, Cardinal Newman; in architecture, John Sedding; in ethics (meaning social ethics, that is, socialism), William Morris; and in painting, Burne-Jones.[8]

A distinguished company. And it is not hard to see Cram's purposes in enrolling that latter master at All Saints'. Burne-Jones had done for Boston only a few stained-glass windows, chiefly two in Trinity Church, Copley Square — a splendid interior, to be sure, but not by Cram's standards of Catholic and liturgical art.[9] And throughout the 1890s Goodhue and Cram naturally dreamed, as All Saints' developed, of making it what Trinity, for all its splendor, was not and never could be, the New World equivalent of churches like Bodley's Church of the Holy Angels, Hoar Cross, or Sedding's Holy Trinity, Sloane Street, where artists such as Burne-Jones and Christopher Whall and William Morris had created glorious aesthete interiors.[10] Peter Anson remarks of Henry Vaughan's master that some of

> the interiors of the churches designed by Bodley . . . express the rhythm of Rossetti's sonnets. . . . When one looks up at [Bodley's] earlier rood-screens, altars, pulpits or the glass . . . one is moved to repeat: "The blessed damozel leaned out / From the gold bar of Heaven; / Her eyes were deeper than the depth / Of waters stilled at even; / She had three lilies in her hand . . . "[11]

Equally, of course, did any Bostonian (surely including the Peabodys) who bought any book (not just *The Decadent*) published by Copeland and Day, who lovingly took Oscar Wilde's lilies as the central motif of the several colophons designed for them by Goodhue; to whom both Cram and Mary Peabody now turned, of course, in the matter of All Saints' chancel's embellishment when Colonel Peabody's death in 1896 brought his widow to share Cram's dream, seeing in a splendid chancel a unique memorial to her husband (*107*).

The project began with the design and erection in 1896–1898 of a dramatic two-story Caen stone reredos (*108*) surmounting Ashmont's high altar, certainly of the school of Newman in its High Church splendor and Seddingesque in its art and craft. Cram's other two heroes were here, too: not only was there provision for Burne-Jones's panels but also there was more than a little of William Morris's social gospel in the fact that, though stylistically the Ashmont reredos is derivative of the great medieval altar screen at Winchester Cathedral, it has also a more modern aspect with a Christian Socialist aura. This comes from the Latino sculptor Domingo Mora. A now little-known Spanish artist who modeled the reredos's figure work for John Evans,[12] Mora, best known today in Boston for his work in Copley Square on the facade of the Boston Public Library and the west porch of Trinity Church, had spent considerable time in Uruguay in the 1870s. Much moved by the sufferings there in those years of fierce civil strife and class warfare, he is credited with having first depicted in his sculpture the oppressed *gaucho* or *campesino*, whose image is evident, too, in the midst of Cram and Goodhue's splendid Gothic reredos at All Saints', where the face of Mora's *Christus Rex*, by no means incongruous but very naturalistic, non-Gothic, and decidedly modern, is a type of the "suffering servant" motif first revealed in Mora's *Victima* in Montevideo.[13]

The reredos is also, as successor of the Advent Lady Chapel sanctuary, the first example of Cram's principles of liturgical art on so large a scale; in fact, the first so large a sculptural commission of Cram and Goodhue at all. Not only did

108. The carved stone reredos of All Saints' rises to great splendor of detail from the boldest and most severe foundation and altar.

they incorporate into the stone screen a dominating inset painted altarpiece, three panels in oils (the very panels intended for Burne-Jones, just above the altar itself), but they conceived of the panels and also the stone figure sculpture as only the chief of many aspects of a great three-dimensional multimedia work of art. An integral part of it (so much so that the exact placement is indicated by lines carved into the stonework) is a suite of jeweled altar cross (*109*) and eight candlesticks; made by Irving and Casson and cast by Thomas McGann with

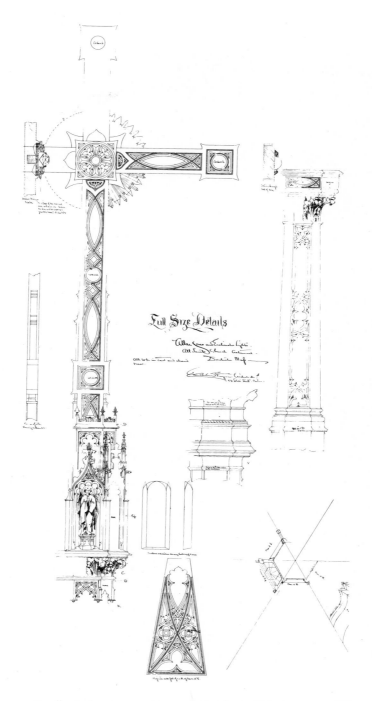

109. Goodhue's elevations, sections, and plans for the high altar cross of All
Saints'. The junior partner's exquisite working drawings often rivaled the
object depicted in artistry.

figures modeled by Kirchmayer, the whole in chiseled brass and gold plate, the suite was unexampled in America at this time. Goodhue also designed the first of several splendid textiles for the altar (the work, in some cases, of the St. Margaret's School of Embroidery).[14] It is a considerable triumph of liturgical art, the All Saints' reredos.

Still, one can imagine what Burne-Jones would have brought to it, how he would have rooted its design even more in the art of its own day, making it as much Pre-Raphaelite, even modern, for example, as medieval in character. Of course, bearing in mind our earlier discussion of the Pre-Raphaelite/Wagner "revelation," such an altarpiece by Burne-Jones at Ashmont would have been modern most characteristically in the way, in H. J. Janson's words, it "radiate[d] an aura of repressed eroticism."[15]

The extent to which the erotic (any more than the socialist) aspects of this work would have registered on churchgoers is arguable. There is a sense in which we all see what we want to see and don't see what we'd rather not. Mora's identification with the oppressed masses, perhaps inappropriate in a memorial to a famous Boston banker and yet another example of irony in Cram's work, may not have registered on Mary Peabody, or if it did, it may not have offended her. We do not know. But if what may or may not have registered with church-goers is in doubt, Mora's artistic intent, and Cram's in commissioning and approving his work, is not. And it is as suave visually as it is provoking (if praiseworthy) religiously; the gaucho *is* robed in sufficient majesty.

Similarly, for an altarpiece Rossetti or Burne-Jones could be expected to calm down somewhat. Philippe Jullian, comparing Rossetti's and Burne-Jones's work to Swinburne's, observes that "painters can never go as far as writers, and Elizabeth Siddal's most sorrowful expressions only vaguely evoked the torments described in [Swinburne's] *Dolores*" — "O daughter of Death and Priapus, / Our Lady of Pain." But if that figure was not very likely to have been proposed for the Ashmont altarpiece, note that the example Janson gives for his observation about repressed eroticism (repressed but nonetheless so evident as to "radiate") is an *Annunciation* by Rossetti. Moreover, Burne-Jones's languid athletes, whether Sir Galahads and Saint Georges, no less than his virgins and maidens, have Elizabeth Siddal's face: "obsessed insomniacs watching over the decline of culture," Camille Paglia has called them.[16] What knights' vigil was projected at Ashmont? Something surely more suitable, at least, than one of Beardsley's provocations — his *Ascension of Saint Rose of Lima*, for example, with its se-ductive Virgin and obscene gesture. But however restrained a work by Burne-Jones is imagined at Ashmont, it is hardly possible to avoid thinking of Octave Mirabeau's characterization of the distinctive Burne-Jones face it was proposed to blazon above the high altar of All Saints': "The rings under the eyes," Mirabeau insisted, ". . . are unique in the whole history of art; it is impossible to tell whether they are the result of masturbation, lesbianism, normal love-making, or tuberculosis."[17]

The ironies and incongruities of this reredos so far noted — socialist art juxtaposed with gold plate and family jewels — would have been underlined wondrously and pointedly by Burne-Jones's radiating Pre-Raphaelite eroticism. Here would have been in some of Cram's earliest important art a stunning example of the general Visionist propensity to produce work needing in the modernist way always to be seen with double sight, as we discussed in the last chapter with reference to "Leda and the Swan." Whereas Michelangelo depicts "the suave perfection of the union of human and divine," Richard Ellmann notes that "under the pressure of Christian doctrine there is no irony recognized in this union"; in Yeats's poem, on the other hand, "the bird, filled with divine power and knowledge, is still the brute blood of the air." Thus indeed does Yeats let both views "coalesce, to see them with double sight" and thus produce a poem as "modern as Michelangelo's painting is not."[18] That double sight coalesces here, too, in Ashmont's reredos because of Mora, but perhaps too subtly. Burne-Jones in his altarpiece would have forced the idea forward more dramatically and heightened an effect now, alas, muted. Perhaps, for Mary Peabody's sake, it was as well that Burne-Jones died. But Louise Guiney, no less genteel as devout, admired — never mind Burne-Jones — Beardsley himself.

"THESE BROKEN BROTHERS"

It is important to note that all this work was undertaken at Ashmont in the wake of the effect in Boston of the tremendous international scandal of Oscar Wilde's trial, to which we have referred here more than once and the full force of which must now be acknowledged.

When Wilde was arrested in 1895, he was carrying a yellow book. No matter that it was not *The Yellow Book*. It might just as well have been. Indeed, in Boston it might just have well have been Wilde's *Salomé* or Cram's *Decadent*. Estelle Jussim records that there was no violence in Boston at Wilde's American publishers, as there was at his London publishers (such things did happen in Boston; a crowd once smashed the Old Corner Bookstore's windows to protest the display of a book by abolitionist Lydia Maria Child), but Wilde's disciples did break for cover, including much of Boston's Bohemia, for whom the Wilde trial was clearly the beginning of the end. "The cry for Beardsley's skin went up at once." And in 1898 he obliged, as it were, dying in the year the Ashmont reredos was erected. He was only twenty-six. His death prostrated Fred Day and very nearly Guiney, too. Riding gallantly (and characteristically heedless of

423

herself) to the defense of the fallen and to savage the Philistines, Guiney demanded of all things of the Roman Catholic Archdiocese of Boston a Requiem Mass for Beardsley. It was held, but it caused such an "uproar" (the word is Jussim's) that Guiney became "seriously frightened." Bohemia in Boston, always fragile, was suddenly very vulnerable.[19]

In fact, it was dying and by 1900 was as dead as Beardsley or Burne-Jones or the proposed All Saints' altarpiece. In 1898 Day made the decision to end Copeland and Day; that October, as it was closing down, Guiney wrote to Day: "I don't think you love Partner as you once did, my fickle child."[20] In 1900 Ralph Adams Cram also made an important decision; he married Elizabeth Carrington Read. His best man was Bertram Goodhue, who, two years later, after his Persian idyll with James Gillespie, married Lydia Bryant. Then in 1903 came the great triumph of the winning by Cram and Goodhue of the West Point competition. And the personal break between the partners, marked inevitably by their marriages, became professional as well with the split of the firm between Cram in the Boston office and Goodhue in the newly opened New York office. Knights errant no more; the nineties were over.

Of all these events, the key one was Cram's marriage, of which much more will be said in Volume Two. The pressures arguing for it, which have been touched on already, persisted in the case of gay people into our own era. As late as the 1940s, Leonard Bernstein's decision to announce his forthcoming marriage, for example, reflected (according to his biographer, Humphrey Burton) the fact that Bernstein's rumored homosexuality was an issue in the matter of whether he would succeed his mentor, Serge Koussevitzky, as conductor of the Boston Symphony Orchestra. Perhaps the only other thing that needs to be said in this volume is that Cram's marriage (like Bernstein's) was on the whole, given the era and its attitudes, a success.[21]

Furthermore, no biography of any of Cram's cohort (except, perhaps, Berenson) would require a second volume, for few of his friends endured to any point. Some — Day, Carman, Guiney, and Copeland — lingered on into sad (or discreet) anticlimaxes: Copeland in Boston (where he became an increasingly outlandish roué and drank himself to death; "no space to grow wings in," lamented Guiney);[22] Carman in repressed provincial obscurity; Guiney herself, exhausted, her muse soon fled, in the English countryside. Day, his leadership role surrendered to Alfred Stieglitz, retired to his Norwood bed (literally) as a Proustian recluse for nearly two decades, living somewhat the tale of Aurelian Blake of Cram's book. Philip Savage, an exceptional talent, as it seemed, to many (his "noble, pure, exacting taste" aroused one critic to exclaim on "the skeptical vigor of his mind and the pagan amplitude of his senses and emotions"),[23] died young, as did not a few of his peers, Dennis Bunker, for instance, within just a few months of his marriage. (Guiney had always worried about Savage — much as Sullivan had about Bunker — once writing Cram: "Pray for Philip Savage, will you? And say never a word of the wherefore, which you will guess instantly. 'Ne obliviscaris vocis qua erentium.' ")[24] Arthur Knapp and Richard Hovey and Herbert Small all were cut down in their thirties; Jack Abbott, George Hallowell, and Henry Randall also died prematurely. The loss of Herbert Small particularly troubled Guiney; "surely," she wrote, "he threw away great gifts."[25]

Listen, moreover, to the way, in *New England: Indian Summer*, Van Wyck Brooks deals with these and other early deaths in Boston's Bohemia, and note the way (in footnotes that I have incorporated into the text through the asterisks) he annexes not only Santayana but Henry Adams to the discussion of the plight of men who were, in some sense, Brooks's peers and friends:

> George Cabot Lodge was extinguished in the battle. He died, like Trumbull Stickney and Philip Henry Savage, in his early thirties, feeling he had lived in a void.* (*". . . the suffocating sense of talking and singing in a vacuum that allowed no echo to return, grew more and more oppressive with each effort to overcome it" — Henry Adams, *The Life of George Cabot Lodge*). . . . Both [Lodge and Stickney] felt that they were Greeks born out of time. . . . The poet Savage was also elegiac. All were alone against the world. . . . * (*"An important element in the tragedy of Oliver [of *The Last Puritan*] . . . is drawn from the fate of a whole string of Harvard poets in the 1880's and 1890's — Sanborn, Philip Savage, Hugh McCulloch, Trumbull Stickney and Cabot Lodge . . . all those friends of mine, Stickney especially, of whom I was very fond, were visibly killed by the lack of air to breathe. . . ." — Letter of Santayana to William Lyons Phelps — Phelps, *Autobiography with Letters*).[26]

Truly, if Brooks did find a pattern in fin-de-siècle Boston, it was one particularly relevant to aesthetes and one not unknown either in London and Paris, where greater figures also died very young. Indeed, the pattern for aesthetes tended toward self-destruction; on which sad fact Ralph Adams Cram mused most eloquently in his old age: "Many of the names have gone into oblivion, sometimes through the frustration of early death or that consequent on too deep an imbibing of the too heady wine of contemporary life."[27] Whispered Guiney to Day in 1901: "May all these broken brothers of ours find peace."[28]

And of Cram himself one may say what Larzer Ziff said of the poet Edwin Arlington Robinson, another Harvard-Boston Bohemian of this era, who, though he, like Cram, had made a name for himself in the 1880s and 1890s, remained always somehow only "promising." If Cram had not yet found his niche or quite won through, if he was listened to but not really heard, that may have been just as well: too often in the nineties he who was heard was destroyed.[29] Cram survived.

The First American Avant-Garde

In retrospect, it is now possible to say that Boston's fin-de-siècle Bohemia will also survive, historically. The generations that had the keenest reasons to obscure it are themselves now long gone. And as always happens, a subsequent generation is now reaching back to reclaim what has been lost track of — nervously, in this case, of course, for somewhere in a corner of Boston's mind the memory of all this and what it might mean has lingered.

Granted, Fred Bullard's music is no longer much heard, nor (except, perhaps, at Dartmouth) Richard Hovey's poetry, nor (south of the Canadian border) Bliss Carman's, either. Nor are prices rising in any spectacular way for the stained glass of Henry Eldridge Goodhue, the way they have for the work of Louis Tiffany, for instance. But museum exhibitions of the work of both Dennis Bunker and George Hallowell have lately been announced and a catalogue of Thomas Meteyard's work published; Connick's glass is now the subject of museum lectures. And it is not for nothing that Louise Guiney has been called, in the wake of Vatican II, the first modern nun. Slowly these names are resurfacing in cultural histories.[30] And a few of Boston's Bohemians have, in fact, survived all along well enough, if only among the cognoscenti. Daniel Berkeley Updike is still regarded as having been one of America's foremost makers of books. Fred Holland Day's legacy as the " 'pater patratus' of American photography, [who] had a large share in creating a new art medium," is increasingly secure, as is the fact that he and Copeland "brought the aesthetic nineties to America"; hardly a small thing.[31] Berenson remains even in death the world's foremost authority on Italian Renaissance art; Bruce Rogers the master of perhaps "the most brilliant typographic achievement of the twentieth century in America"; and Goodhue and Cram themselves among the leading American architects of the twentieth century. Nor are figures such as George Santayana and Ethel Reed and Will Bradley and Isabella Stewart Gardner in danger of obscurity. Susan Thompson has written of Bradley, for instance, that "he did more than anyone to create the beginnings of American twentieth-century style."[32] It may be objected, of course, that by no means were all these figures' achievements attained during their Boston years. But for all of them their Boston years were key. Even Berenson, who lived the rest of his life abroad, so "developed his consciousness of art in Boston," in Shaun O'Connell's happy phrase, that he "carried the city around, a shrine in his head, for the rest of his life."[33]

Already, in fact, though more often still in doctoral dissertations than in bestsellers, scholars like Lawrence Dawler point to the work of what I have called here the Pinckney Street circle (though that name is, of course, an invention of mine); it "displayed a vitality," writes Dawler, "a sense of experiment and excitement, that calls into question the autumnal images that have come to characterize New England at the turn of the twentieth century."[34] He means, of course, Van Wyck Brooks's images, too long dominant—though this is not entirely to discredit Brooks's thesis. Granted, what he saw as absolute decline I see as Boston's benefiting from a changing American landscape of pluralism and diversity on many levels. But it is true that both Hovey and Carman were as often to be found in New York or Europe as in Boston (neither stayed anyplace long, true vagabonds, indeed, true moderns). And many moved away. Berenson departed early, Santayana later. Gelett Burgess was peripheral to Boston's Bohemia and central to San Francisco's because of choice; so, too, *The Chap-Book* was not the last Boston breakthrough to be taken away from Boston upon graduation or whatever. (One thinks of that important modernist magazine, *Horn & Hound*, started at Harvard in the 1930s by Varian Fry and Lincoln Kirstein—who admired Ralph Adams Cram's Gothic world as well as the European modernism of the 1930s, by the way—which migrated not to Chicago, as did the *Chap-Book*, but to New York.) Finally, it must be admitted that Bertram Goodhue was eager to return to New York from Boston when the opportunity presented itself in the early 1900s.

But the traffic went both ways. Will Bradley journeyed to Boston from Chicago, just as *The Chap-Book* went the other way. And Goodhue was able to depart for New York in 1903 only because of success achieved in Boston, having decided as a young man eager to make his fortune in 1891 to leave New York and come *to* Boston. Of course, greener grass was endlessly contemplated at Boston's expense. Hovey once wrote furiously of "priggish, pompous, stilted, affected, ridiculous Boston." But when his biographer goes on to explain, in the manner of Van Wyck Brooks, that Hovey (who in 1894 was about to flee to Europe again) was reacting to Boston's being "a huge museum. Certainly it was no place for new ventures," it is too easy a conclusion.[35] What else was Copeland and Day? And where else in the United States was the equal of it in that very year of 1894, when Hovey's friends published in Boston his and Carman's *Songs from Vagabondia*, not only Hovey's newest but as it turns out his and Carman's most celebrated work? Hovey and Carman, too, achieved their fortune in Boston. And a hundred years later, though the enduring power of any of these achievements will be judged variously—Cram and Goodhue are now rising in significance, Hovey and Carman, for example, descending—the work of all these Pinckney Street Bohemians, and their fellows in the other circles we have referred to here, adds up to quite a sum. So much so that the subtitle of Steven Watson's study of pre-World War I modernism, *Strange Bedfellows*, which really ignores Boston before Amy Lowell, might better be applied to the Pinckney Street circle of the 1890, for this circle could well be called "the first American avant-garde."[36]

Ralph Adams Cram as its leader is, of course, rather a startling role in which to cast him and not the one for which he has been remembered best. Yet his earliest solo work, from the first country and seaside houses (of which almost all memory has disappeared) to All Saints', Ashmont (the overall design of which was Cram's alone), constitutes, as we saw in Chapter 3, a superb body of work that is distinctly protomodern, to use the term Margaret Henderson Floyd uses so pointedly of progressive work of the period she focuses on in *Architecture after Richardson*, the first really thoughtful study of this long misunderstood period between the death of Richardson and the First World War.

Cram was equally a modernist, as he understood the term then, in other realms. In the same decade *Knight Errant* was advertised as a herald of the most advanced thought of its time, a contemporary of Cram could describe him as one of a small group of "literary lefties." And if it seems surprising, for example, that along the cutting edge of the aesthetic-decadent experience in America in the 1890s the first book of the press that introduced America to such things was by Cram, it is because, in the first place, we have forgotten how progressive Boston can often be. Discreetly, of course. But in more than one generation, though its luminaries usually flee to Europe or, in later years, to New York (returning in the summer, perhaps, such is the pull of New England), the first and perhaps most critical chapter of many a "movement" has been written in Boston—especially in college years in Cambridge—and often paid for, too: whether it be the Peabodys' launching of H. H. Richardson in the 1880s and of Cram and Goodhue in the 1890s or Mrs. James Storrow's launching of Walter Gropius in the 1930s.[37] That the Peabodys, for instance, stuck with Cram through the Wilde scandal is by no means a unique example of the New England tradition of dissent and independent judgment.

Recall, too, that what was true generally of the Visionists was supremely true of Cram individually. In the first chapter we laid out a progression of Pre-Raphaelites becoming aesthetes becoming decadents, whom we have now brought here to the verge of being modernists. Daniel Gregory Mason's contemporaneous memory is now becoming scholarly opinion. For example, Karl Beckson writes of "the early twentieth-century re-christening of aestheticism and Decadence *as 'Modernism'* [emphasis added]."[38] One needs only to re-collect Cram's youthful diary complaints about copybook Gothic to realize that we are only too apt, like Van Wyck Brooks before us, to mistake the way "traditionalists"—for Cram *was* such—use words like "original" and "new." T. S. Eliot's thought, in his "Tradition and the Individual Talent," is a case in point. Robert Crunden's summary is masterly:

Critics too often examined new art in terms of what it seemed to have that was new, instead of asking how the new work participated in the traditions of the past. Tradition, [Eliot] insists, is something that cannot be inherited and that must be obtained by great labor. Artists must perceive not only the pastness of their past for the presentness of it. . . . They had to develop their consciousness of the past, keep it steadily in mind when they created. . . . Genuinely mature artists combine the elements of the past in a new way; they do not suddenly create something original.[39]

Cram would have agreed. In 1899, for example, when he compared good modern Gothic to Wagner's *Tristan* and bad modern Gothic to Verdi's *La Traviata*,[40] Cram saw no incongruity in comparing his own (to us at the end of the twentieth century) very "traditional" architecture, not with what he would have called bourgeois Verdian melodrama, but with the most radical and avant-garde music, almost the rock music of its time, that of Wagner. Really, one has only to add to Eliot's testimony Nietzsche's: "it is not being the first to see something new that indicates a genuinely original mind, but seeing the old, the familiar, . . . as *if it were* new."[41]

What better analysis is there of All Saints', Ashmont, at once so traditional and so original! And if we do not quite see, as Claude Bragdon did, that in the 1890s Cram's work there is entirely comparable in originality to Louis Sullivan's, all the more reason as we come now to the endgame of Ashmont, as it were — its interior art — to follow this theme through the work of all the artist-collaborators Cram marshaled there, not just for the great reredos but for completion of the chancel as a whole.

THE MIGRATION OF SYMBOLS

Consider Johannes Kirchmayer's marvelous Ashmont carvings and the sanctuary paneling of 1898 in which they are set, the second of the several stages of the enrichment and completion of All Saints' chancel, begun just after the erection of the reredos. Like that reredos design, with its aspects of Christian Socialism and Pre-Raphaelite eroticism, the Kirchmayer carvings, which record the chief events of the Old and New Testaments, arise out of a denser and more complicated background than is at first apparent.

In the first place, these carvings, which focus strongly on Christ's passion (with which nearly a third of the thirty panels are concerned), are as much about the late nineteenth century as the early first century. For they arise out of Kirchmayer's own memories as a participant in his youth in the late nineteenth-century version of the Oberammergau Passion Play, a celebrated and legendary artistic and religious event of the period, which, like the Bayreuth Wagner Festival, caught the imagination of many more fin-de-siècle Bostonians than

Cram (Isabella Gardner went to Germany in no small measure for the Passion Play in 1890; so, too, did Fred Holland Day).[42] And the link between the Oberammergau and Bayreuth experiences is the more intimate and significant here because, when it was completed in the late 1890s and early 1900s, the All Saints' chancel really was the fulfillment of those early prototypes of Cram's concept of organic, liturgical art — the Church of the Advent's Lady Chapel with its conspicuously Jacobite and Anglo-Catholic iconography and Our Saviour's, Middleborough, chancel with its striking liturgical iconography of the complete cast of a Solemn High Mass carved on all the poppy heads. Both sources, the Oberammergau Passion Play and the Bayreuth-Wagnerian pageant of the Solemn High Mass, coalesced in worship at Ashmont for the first time as conceived by Cram in a great monstrance of his and Goodhue's design; comparable to Parliament's opening in Pugin's House of Lords in London, High Mass at Ashmont is always potentially transcendent in a chancel that is among the most distinguished ensembles of Gothic Revival art in the world.

Then, too, the dense design of symbolism, foliate and figural, in which Goodhue set Kirchmayer's carvings also has a richer resonance than is apparent in the way, for example, the rose and thistle of the episcopal throne conventionally refer to England and Scotland, the countries of Anglican apostolic succession. Beckson, whose study of the significance of the color green and the carnation we dwelt upon in connection with *Black Spirits and White* in Chapter 2, links what we know to have been Cram's chief interests, artistic (medieval art) and religious (Anglo-Catholicism), with another continuing interest of All Saints's architect (the occult) when he notes, in the context of the way the Order of the Golden Dawn's ritual arose out of its devotion to the Rosicrucian occult symbol of the mystical rose of love blossoming from the sacrificial cross, that

> the traditional Christian symbols of the rose and the lily (suggestive of love, death and resurrection) had been used, sometimes in a startlingly secular manner, by such mid-century Pre-Raphaelite artists and poets as Dante Rossetti and Swinburne. By the 1890s, these symbols were increasingly associated with the occult in such works as Wilde's "Rosa Mystica" [and] Yeats's "Rosa Alchemica."[43]

With my previous attempt in mind to transfer some of the meanings of poppies in the book design of Ethel Reed to the choir-stall poppy heads of Cram and Goodhue (Reed's instructor at the Cowles Art School), there can be very little doubt that Beckson is correct overall in his contention that in the "pre-psychoanalytic world" of the 1890s not only words but also "symbols [are] concealed as well as revealed."[44] Moreover, it must be reiterated: to study with this sort of "double sight" the Ashmont chancel, any more than a Cram church as a whole, as a kind of Trojan horse is by no means to diminish its architectural or spiritual importance. Call to mind, however, as you consider this sanctuary, not a Palestrina Mass but the long, ecstatic melodic line of Wagner, and the architecture *and* the spirituality will suddenly be very modern indeed. And, as always with Cram, the work of art will stand on its own.

PURITANS AND VICTORIANS

The underlying significance of this crowning achievement of Cram and Good-hue's decade of the nineties, the completion of All Saints' chancel—fully as important as their other masterpieces of the decade, the exteriors of Our Sav-iour's, Middleborough, St. Stephen's, Fall River, and St. Stephen's, Cohasset—was plainly signaled by Cram's *Catholic World* article of 1894, in which he flatly declared: "New England . . . is weary of Puritanism."[45] Certainly Cram was. His hardening anti-Puritanism is evident in the late nineties in all sorts of ways. Indeed, it could almost be said to have been increasingly an obsession of Ralph Adams Cram: a significant obsession.

The word "Puritan" can have, of course, many meanings; two, as I see it, are particularly pertinent to Cram's thought. First, there is the point of Martin Green's analysis of the Merrymount Press's name. It was, Green wrote, an

> allusion to Thomas Morton's hedonist and licentious establishment near Boston, at-tacked and destroyed by seventeenth-century Puritans. Updike was not hedonist or licentious himself, any more than [his friend and executor] Ned Warren was, but [Updike] was an antipuritan aesthete, and the word "Merrymount" is an antipuritan slogan.[46]

In other words, "Puritan" was often used in a more negative than positive meaning; it described, in Cram's case as in Updike's, more what he was against than what he was for. Second, recall Richard Ellmann's point about Oscar Wilde, that in

> Wilde's time the word "homosexual" was not in use, but there was no less need to find warrant for what it signified. Wilde became the first writer in English since Christopher Marlowe to make a case for it in public. One of his ways of doing so is to attack homosexuality's enemies the puritans.[47]

Considered in the context of David Hilliard's analysis, that Anglo-Catholicism lent itself inevitably to homosexual rebellion as an expression of that at least, if not also of gay anger, Cram's anti-Puritanism takes on new meaning here. This is not to say it loses any of its religious meaning. As we discussed in Chapter 7, the tower as a psychological phallic symbol does not cease to be a religiously aspiring symbol. Meanings merge. And what Cram was for on all fronts was evident on each.

He was, for instance, the animating spirit just after the turn of the century behind Boston's now famous Beacon Hill Christmas festivities, which included public caroling (at one time involving the choir of the Church of the Advent) and lighted candles in house windows, a benign enough business, it seems to us today, but sufficiently a provocation then that Louise Guiney called it "the great anti-Puritan light up."[48] Here, in contrast to my earlier point about how progressive Boston can be, is its sometime backwardness; when Ralph Adams Cram first came to Boston in 1881, Christmas was *not* a legal holiday in Massachusetts. And it was not for another four years that the sons of the Puritans so far forgot themselves as to recognize that festival.

One may be sure it was as grudging a recognition as was that for Cram himself. We have seen already how, like Santayana, Cram attracted the disdain of such as President Eliot. We will see in Volume Two that Cram's eventual success came only after he had married a woman who served as a much-needed abrasive edge (as Goodhue never had, of course) to Cram's passionate (even vulgar-seeming to Brahmins) enthusiasms. A woman whom their elder daughter characterized as more interested in "sacred love" than Cram himself, who was distinctly given to "profane love"; a woman, above all, who, despite severe mental illness, was the consummate wife, mother, and hostess, battling always to keep Cram from his Bohemian friends, Bess Cram was the sort of cool, aristocratic Virginian who did, indeed, attract to her husband the widespread ruling-class patronage he needed.[49] Meanwhile, what would become his chief problem is clear enough in Cram's *Catholic World* article of 1894, which abounds in such tactless phrases as "the pestilence of Puritanism." Even art itself is held by Cram to be "materialized and hardened by Puritanism." In consequence, Cram wrote (lest anyone mistake the point), New England was "reaching toward Catholicism."[50]

He meant, of course, *Anglo*-Catholicism, and of the sort Father Hall had taught him, though in a Roman Catholic journal he could hardly say so. In the tradition of Jeremy Taylor, John Keble, Edward Pusey, and John Newman, all of whose attitudes we have noted here in one connection or another, Hall, with his own affinities for both the social gospel and the "particular friendship" (which is to say, socialism and homosexuality), while they ought not to be taken out of context—Hall was a deeply orthodox monk—now signals to us clearly an Anglo-Catholic profile as *anti*-Puritan and relatively liberal as Boston Irish Roman Catholicism was then *pro*-Puritan and archly reactionary. How pro-Puritan is clear in the survival even today of many of Massachusetts's blue laws. For the attitude, spoken of earlier here, of the early church fathers toward sexuality had long since hardened in official Roman Catholic doctrine, which in turn had profound implications for designers like Cram. As Liane Lefaivre has pointed out in her "Eros, Architecture and the *Hypnerotomachia Poliphili*,"

> the dominant official doctrine of the Latin Church, as professed by the patristic theologians, in relation to architecture as in relation to everything else, remains . . . asceticism. The body becomes a symbol for all that is sinful, a metaphor for evil. . . . Any attachment to the things of this world, including building, is condemned as lust. . . . Architecture is condemned as a form of "lust for building" (*libido aedificandi*), of "voluptuousness," of "perverse delectation."[51]

Could President Eliot have put it better? It was so clear, after all, to use the *Hypnerotomachia*'s categories—the contemplative life (*vita contemplativa*), the active life (*vita activa*), and the life of passion (*vita voluptuaria*)[52]—that Cram, above all, chose the third, the passionate, the sensual; "profane love," in Cram's daughter's words; in mine earlier, the vision of Trebizond. Of course, it all rounds the circle, does it not?—explaining why it was *Anglo-* and not Roman Catholicism that spearheaded the late nineteenth-century and early twentieth-century Gothic Revival of Catholic art. But that would hardly have recommended to Boston's Puritans either Cram or his works. Indeed, quite the reverse. For Cram's problem, as we have seen, was that he was, for all his traditionalism, a most conspicuous agent of change in Puritan New England—change that was real in Boston (hence Bohemia) but unwelcome to many (though they might in other realms be quite progressive, as was President Eliot) and therefore all the more strenuously to be resisted. Cram's *Catholic World* article was a volley no Puritan could well mistake.

The historical process, however, was a long one (literary and theatrical censorship did not end in Boston until the post-World War II period), and Puritanism in the 1890s, in the early stages of its death throes in Boston, may then have been *more*, not less, obstreperous than at its height. That Emerson's generation, "though closer to Calvinist Puritanism than [Cram's] was less haunted and hampered by it" has been observed by Martin Green in his *Problem of Boston*, where he noticed insightfully that while Hawthorne might have been "morally baffled by statues in the nude," on the other hand it was quite clear that when "Emerson worried about the ballet's effect on college students, he decided, characteristically, that such problems were for the individual to decide." Emerson and his generation were "not cultural policemen in the sense that . . . even Charles Eliot Norton was"—and, indeed, President Eliot as well—in what Green calls "that sad story of the Macmonnies 'Bacchante,'" a story that still embarrasses Boston a century later.[53]

Today it is hard to comprehend the issue in the first place. *Bacchante* now seems to us charming, as do Cram's Beacon Hill candles and carols. And the

Ashmont chancel a hundred years later scarcely appears to be what would now be called voluptuous. But that would not have been too strong a word for it in the 1890s. No more than Christmas had come unopposed to the Boston of the 1880s had an altar, for example, yet appeared in the 1890s in Trinity Church, Copley Square, and Trinity was by far the most sumptuous non-Roman Catholic church interior in the city.[54] Instead of an altar, Trinity made do with a small wooden table, dwarfed by Phillips Brooks's pulpit. Even the Church of the Advent's high altar reredos, which dated only from 1891, was notably restrained in its statuary.

Ashmont's high altar reredos was, on the other hand, glorious with ranks of gathering saints. Cram was, therefore, distinctly matching the provocation to the locale when he dared much more in his design of the chief glory of the Ashmont chancel: the All Saints' rood screen, a work of 1892–1911, that, although it was not endowed with its Calvary until 1911, was certainly, given the temporary nature of the first rood cross, contemplated from the beginning and perhaps designed in the 1890s. It is a work that proclaims at one and the same time, moreover, not only Cram's virulent anti-Puritanism but his equally strongly held anti-Victorianism—now another surprising aspect for us of Cram, who was so opposed to European modernism in the 1920s and 1930s that it is easily forgotten that in the 1880s and 1890s he was a vigorous proponent of his own modernism and a vociferous opponent of all things Victorian.

It is possible, of course, to dismiss this anti-Victorianism as the usual Oedipal rebellion of one generation against another. But Cram's convictions in this matter went deeper than that. And they have worn well. Consider the magisterial judgment of perhaps the greatest architectural historian of our recent past, the late Sir John Summerson:

> We are accustomed to assess buildings . . . on the assumption that whether they have or have not for us an immediate relevance or emotional appeal they were at least in their time accepted as right. . . . Early and mid-Victorian architecture was, in its own time and in the eyes of its best-informed critics, horribly unsuccessful. . . . Where the Victorians are concerned it would [thus] be very much safer to begin, at least, on the assumption that it was wrong.[55]

Cram's anti-Victorianism (the garden, as it were, in which grew his modernism of the eighties and nineties) was expressed with his usual vehemence. As late as when he was nearing his seventies, a *Transcript* interviewer remarked that Cram had "the same capacity of firing up when moved that I observed in Sarah Bernhardt,"[56] and he must have been a wonder to have heard when in the full fire of his twenties and thirties, when either in person or in print he was always volatile. On one occasion in the 1890s, for instance, an editor (signing himself only "Primus") felt bound to append to a published lecture by Cram a rejoinder that

Cram's lecture "would never make an opponent desire a fair and fruitful discussion. It would simply arouse . . . indignation," wrote the offended editor, who observed archly that "either the time or Mr. Cram is very much out of joint."[57]

Victorian no more than Puritan tastes, however, were likely to elicit anything from Cram other than the harsh criticism of a young man who had argued in print, after all, as early as 1885, at the age of twenty-one, that "there *is* accounting for tastes, distinctly, . . . one man's judgment touching what is beautiful is *not* as good as another's."[58] And Cram's own judgment was that the Victorian period was one in which

> architecture in America fell to a lower level than history had ever before recorded. Even the Dark Ages that followed the Fall of Rome could . . . show no parallel, for even then such building as was done had at least the qualities of modesty and sincerity of purpose. . . . The Centennial Exhibition in Philadelphia in 1876 [showed] that, compared even with contemporary Europe, we were artistic barbarians.[59]

That was the view from 1934; in his autobiography Cram allowed for a certain recovery in the effect in after years of the American Institute of Architects, the MIT and Columbia schools of architecture, and the efficacious influence (for a time) of the Ecole des Beaux-Arts, all this in the wake of Richardson and McKim. His view in the 1890s, however, was necessarily bleaker. In 1896 he went so far in one of his articles to apologize, not for what he said but for the way he said it, calling it, at its end, an "ill-tempered tirade." And so it was; Cram in this case pronounced the church art of the nineties as bedeviled by "a degree of vulgarity that finds no precedent in history," a judgment strikingly similar to that just quoted, of four decades later. In the 1896 article, moreover, he broke the architect's eleventh commandment, citing named examples: the Church of the Advent's rood screen, he announced baldly, was "bad."[60] (Never mind that Cram lived long enough to be asked to tear it down and design a replacement. That he was often in the end judged correct probably just made him the more resented sometimes.)

A comparison of the original Victorian rood screen Cram criticized at the Advent and the one he designed for All Saints', Ashmont, does not at first glance, however, yield quite what one expects.[61] The Ashmont design is in most respects far more richly ornamental, detailed as it is in gold and vivid colors and flesh tones. Evidently anti-Puritan, Ashmont's rood hardly seems anti-Victorian. In fact, another misunderstanding is upon us, for virtually any pre–World War I ornament of any "traditional" sort seems more or less Victorian to us in the post-modernist age a century or more later. Cram's terms were very different. And in the 1894 *Catholic World* article that I have suggested best signals the Ashmont chancel's significance, Cram, inveighing only slightly less

against things Victorian than against things Puritan, made his terms very clear
and in a way by now familiar to us. Apt, as we have seen, to describe church art
and architecture he liked as "manly," Cram in the *Catholic World* let drop the
other shoe, pronouncing the art and decor of the nineties he disparaged, such as
the Advent rood screen, as "effeminate."[62]

There is, first, a sense in which Cram meant by "effeminate" what his celebrated classicist contemporaries, Ogden Codman and Edith Wharton, meant in
their discussion of domestic decor of the period by "ill bred" or "bad taste." And
this view of things (which, as we saw in Cram's early houses, he shared with
Wright and the Arts and Crafts School of thought) was an important aspect of
the anti-Victorianism Cram shared with Wharton and Codman. It is by no
means beside the point to notice that *The Decoration of Houses* (designed and
printed, by the way, by Cram's, Wharton's, and Codman's mutual friend Daniel
Berkeley Updike) was published in the very year of the All Saints' reredos, which,
for all its elaboration, is very tightly ordered and disciplined in form and refined
in taste, quite the opposite of the agitated, high-calorie wedding-cake reredoses
more typical of the nineties. Such Victorian "soda-fountain" reredoses, as Cram
called them, are, indeed, entirely comparable to the "lunatic cells" of the same
period, as Wharton called the typical American parlor she and Codman despised
as much as Cram did the typical church chancel of this decade.[63]

But if the surface of Cram's meaning in his use of "effeminate" links him with
these currents of his era, we have seen that there were roots as well as topsoil to
Cram's meanings, especially in his sexing of art and architecture. This is evident
in a comparison of the original Advent rood screen that Cram so disliked with
the one he himself designed at Ashmont. If the controlling word at the Advent
was "effeminate," at Ashmont, despite its much richer detail, the equally controlling word is "manly." In the Advent design the elaborate metal screen of
many small-scale, fussy details is everything, its tiny crucifix really nothing. At
All Saints' there is only a rood beam (in this as in other ways Cram parted
company with Pugin; Cram, a liturgical modernist, abhorred elaborate rood
screens); whereas at the Advent the screen is everything, at Ashmont it is the
towering and boldly scaled crucifix that is everything. And at Ashmont the
vivid, dominating sculpture of the Christus (distinctly in the full-blooded Latin
manner, probably by Angelo Lualdi)[64] is forceful evidence that "manly" and
"effeminate" are as much erotic as aesthetic standards.

NUDES SACRED AND PROFANE

Two worlds coalesce in Cram's Ashmont Calvary: the immediate significance of
the male nude in the late nineteenth and early twentieth centuries, and the

evolution stretching back behind that period for a thousand and more years of the figure of the crucified in the history of Western church art.

That the subject of the male nude in the late nineteenth century has arisen here repeatedly is inevitable. Whether one thinks of Sargent's watercolor studies for his Boston Library murals or of Theodore Dwight's smuggled-in erotica or the nude youths over the library's main portal or of Ned Warren's and Matthew Prichard's classical figures at the Museum of Fine Arts, or, not really that much further afield, of Whitman's poems or Cram's Whitmanesque story about sand dunes — above all, if one thinks of Fred Holland Day's photography — it was a natural enough interest for the Bohemian circles of Boston, one that reflected the overall mis-en-scène in both Europe and America. As Allen Ellenzweig has described it:

> The male nude [was] . . . most ardently received by a group that had been variously named during the final years of [the] nineteenth century. They were called Uranians, inverts, Decadents, the third sex, aesthetes and sodomites. Indeed, this group's behavior had first been named in print in 1869. . . . "Homosexuality" was the hybrid term adopted.[65]

Moreover, just as in our discussions of the aesthete Boston network generally we found long-overlooked connections between different Bohemian sets not only in Boston but extending as well to England, so in respect of this focus on the nude distinct links between apparently widely separated figures and circles are only now beginning to turn up. For example: no specific link between Theodore Dwight and the Pinckney Street circle was known until Ellenzweig's study disclosed that the mysterious von Pluschow, whose male erotica Dwight smuggled into this country and whose studio in Europe Dwight used for his own erotic photography, was the teacher of the celebrated late nineteenth-century pornographer Baron Wilhelm von Gloeben, the photographer whose work today scholars increasingly couple with Day's own.[66] That Day's work was a formative influence on Minor White and Robert Mapplethorpe is also emphasized by Ellenzweig, thus positioning this aspect of the Visionist circle in a very specific gay historical continuum. (Indeed, Ellenzweig's discussion comes as close to identifying the gay aura of Cram's circle as has any scholarship.)

Day's photography is, I believe, of particular importance to us in connection with the Ashmont Calvary. Ellenzweig writes:

> Day was drawn to Christian themes shortly after the death, in 1898, of his young friend Aubrey Beardsley. . . . As with themes from antiquity, it seems to have been tacitly assumed that the time-honored and sanctified traditions of Christian art would shield any erotic overtones from attack. They would render acceptable what would otherwise seems scandalous. But Day was too candid for his own good. . . . His pictures on Christian themes yielded striking examples of barely mediated

homoeroticism . . . [including crucifixions with various of Day's friends and models, for example] stripped to loincloths and [in] seductive poses reminiscent of Hellenic contrapposto.[67]

How many of these friends were from Pinckney Street seems scarcely worth asking, though in truth it would be hard to say with any precision. Certainly the whole project of what Day called his Sacred Studies made Louise Guiney very nervous.[68] And Cram, so ardently religious, is suddenly suspiciously absent. When exhibited, moreover, they naturally caused a furor; reviews like that in the *British Journal of Photography* castigated Day (*after* the Wilde trial) as "the leader of the Oscar Wilde School,"[69] not always noting as well Day's idealistic as well as erotic motives. As a matter of fact, Day's plein-air sacred scenes particularly, like Kirchmayer's chancel carvings at Ashmont, were inspired in no small measure by the Oberammergau Passion Play.[70] But what mattered much more to many was that Day's work had made the deity an erotic object. So, to be sure, had Thompson in "The Hound of Heaven." But that is a poem — words, not pictures. The Western eye sees all.

The Ashmont Calvary also embodied boldly (*110a*), equally making the deity an erotic object, and its debut caused, as did Day's Sacred Studies, a furor, reflected even thirty years later when the tale was told in the All Saints' parish history of 1945, the author of which wrote of the Calvary as

> a distinct innovation in the United States. . . . On Good Friday the calvary was delivered. . . . The figure on the cross was not a suffering Christ, but a triumphant One. . . . The whole was elaborately carved, painted and gilded. That night the calvary was mounted . . . by Saturday noon it was ready for the crowds that would gather for the Easter services. They looked at it and shook their heads in vigorous disapproval. It presented too great a contrast to the simple cross [without a corpus, which it replaced], and the protests were loud and prolonged. For fifteen months the argument went on, at times growing bitter. As . . . word of the quarrel spread, interested people came to see the calvary, some from long distances. . . . [The] calvary was attracting wide and surprisingly favorable attention [and] . . . in later years there was a real pride in the knowledge that it had served as a model for similar calvaries, [including] . . . in the Cathedral of St. John the Divine, New York City.[71]

Announcement had, indeed, been made at first that the Calvary would be "replaced by another." Later, however, came the apology that Cram was "overwhelmed by other important work." Later still, according to Ashmont's rector, "visitors coming to All Saints' from all parts of the country declared without hesitation their appreciation of this great work of art,"[72] lending some peace to the matter. One begins to wonder (as with the famous anti-Puritan stamp-buying of the 1890s in another Boston suburb to protect Louise Guiney from her attackers) whether Cram — however overwhelmed — did not have some-

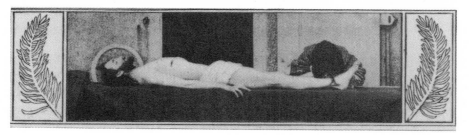

110a, b, c. The "great icon" of the Ashmont Calvary and its rood beam, 1892–1911. *Above*: the Christus shown as restored to its original vividness in the 1930s. *Middle*: one of Day's Sacred Studies, *The Seven Last Words* of 1898, in an architectural enframement (probably designed by Goodhue), the moldings and lettering of which are comparable to Goodhue's on the Ashmont rood beam of 1892. *Below*: *The Entombment* of 1896, another of Day's Sacred Studies, as originally mounted by Day in a similar enframement.

thing to do with all those visitors. Certainly, the Ashmont fracas about Cram's rood, like Guiney's affair in Auburndale and Day's *Sacred Studies* — did not each Bohemian have a characteristic trial by fire, as it were? — discloses, like the nude boys' relief at the Boston Public Library and the subsequent *Bacchante* furor, the bitterness of the Puritan attack of those years.

The Ashmont Christus, furthermore, by its very nature raised special problems. To recall my suggestion that Cram's churches share with Warren's classical sculpture the nature of Trojan horses, it is surely the case that although religion was a more tender nerve to irritate, Cram-type Gothic churches of the most Catholic mien — even despoiling New England town greens — were in their abstract nature a relatively milder provocation compared with Warren's classical male nudes at the museum. But the Ashmont Christus, of course, combined Cram-type church art with the human form quite vividly. As we move from a consideration of one aspect of the rood's context, the male nude in this period, to another aspect, the history of the crucifix in Western art history, we are on the verge here of what can only be called intimate questions. There can be little doubt that by President Eliot's standards the Ashmont Calvary went the *Bacchante* one better. This time the subject was God.

INTIMATE QUESTIONS

It is not widely known that, as Herbert Whone has written, "in iconography there are two crucifixes — Christ suffering and Christ triumphant. . . . Christ's body is always shown fully clothed [and triumphant, from the fifth to the] eleventh century. . . . It was only with the Gothic period that he was portrayed suffering, naked and twisted." Equally significant, before the eleventh century Christ "was fully clothed with eyes open and with two feet nailed separately to the cross [not one on top of the other, helplessly]."[73] (Crowned and vested in high priestly robes, such a Christus, in fact, forms the principal feature of a reredos Cram designed elsewhere for Mary Peabody in this period.)[74]

At Ashmont, however, while the *pose* is clearly that of the triumphant type — the body is neither slumped nor twisted but is straight up, quite unrealistically, against the cross, standing on each foot, side by side, and not bent at the knees, the eyes wide open — the *vesture* is clearly that of the suffering type; which is to say there is nothing beyond the conventional loincloth. The Ashmont Christ is thus a highly unusual combination and one that raises, even more than the conventional crucifix, questions Leo Steinberg has explored brilliantly in his *Sexuality of Christ in Renaissance Art and in Modern Oblivion.* As he put it, the metier of Renaissance artists required that they ask intimate questions that do not well translate into words . . . [such as] even if the body were partly draped, a decision had to be made how much to cover; whether to play the drapery down . . . and whether the loincloth employed, opaque or diaphanous, was to reveal or conceal . . . [for even the doctrine that Christ was ever virgin] was not meant to be taken literally; it was not to be misconstrued as . . . physical disability. . . . Chastity consists not in impotent abstinence, but in potency under check. . . . To relieve [Christ] of [sexual] temptations is to *decarnify the Incarnation itself* [emphasis added]. . . . Modesty, to be sure, recommends covered loins . . . the ensuring conflict provides the tension, the high risk, against which our artists must operate. But if they listened to what the doctrine [of the Incarnation] proclaimed; if even one [artist] disdained to leave its truth merely worded, wanting . . . to see . . . Christ in faultless manhood, . . . conflict . . . was unavoidable.[75]

As Steinberg demonstrates, in painting after painting of the Renaissance, those adoring Christ are deliberately focusing—sometimes quite clearly staring—at his genitals, a focus only too likely to be misunderstood today but intended to document, as it does, the Incarnation. Truly God must be truly Man.[76]

At first glance the conspicuous loincloth on the Ashmont Christus might seem to render this issue moot, but actually the reverse is true. The most overt reference known in Western art to Christ's sexuality—the erection motif—is very strikingly evident in connection with drapery (another instance of mask and signal).[77] And while this motif does not clearly occur at Ashmont, another motif that does is directly relevant to our discussion—a form of what has been called the enhanced loincloth—about which Steinberg asks: "Are there readers who doubt that a cloth can be knotted to allude to the phallus? or who suspect that only a mind misled by modern jargon about symbolic displacement would support such fantasies?" Citing by way of reply sources both literary (Montaigne's *Essays*) and visual (the work of Cosmé Tura), he goes on to describe the enhanced loincloth, an acceptable circumvention in wide usage by the mid-fifteenth century, quite bluntly. It was, he writes, "a potent synecdoche that celebrates the thing covered in the magnificence bestowed on the covering,"[78] an aspect surely very evident at All Saints' in the rood Christus, where the loincloth is so flamboyantly modeled—with a great central upward fold—that its effect is, indeed, to focus attention on the genital area and to lend to the whole figure a kind of heightened, dramatized virility.

How important phallic symbolism is in church art (as an expression no less of religious truth than of psychological), and that it is to be found not just in media controlled closely by artists, such as painting, but in other media (like the art of gesture and ceremonial) controlled solely by the church hierarchy, is clear in H. A. Reinhold's eloquent description in his *Liturgy and Art* of the Easter Vigil rite, an event worthy of Trebizond itself, that has always been the ultimate

Catholic liturgical artistic experience for which Cram designed any church and chancel. On the eve of Easter,

> in the dark of the early night a fire is lit at the gate of the church . . . followed by the blessing of the paschal candle — the ritual representation of the risen Christ; in memory of his sacred wounds five grains of incense are sunk into the body of the candle with the words "Christ, Yesterday and Today, Alpha and Omega, His are the times and the centuries. . . ." Then the large candle is lit from the Easter fire [and carried into the church, where the congregation's candles are lit from it, and set in a great candlestick in the midst of the people, before which is chanted the *Exultat*, an ancient] hymn to the paschal candle as a symbol of Christ.
>
> As the night progresses the church proceeds to bless the baptismal font . . . which is referred to as the womb of the Church. [And then there is] a profoundly mysterious ceremony with all the overtones of phallic symbolism. The paschal candle is three times introduced into the baptismal font while the priest three times sings in ascending scale: "May the power of the Holy Spirit descend upon this brimming font." [The priest then] breathes on the [water in the] font following the form of the Greek letter [psi] for Psyche. . . . And now baptism is conferred. . . . In a triumphant procession the priest moves [to] the altar and celebrates the [first] Easter Resurrection Mass.[79]

Now it may seem that such vivid symbolism is hardly compatible with the chasteness of Christ as proclaimed by the church or, surely, less praiseworthy to a Catholic then or now, with the mind-set of an institution, which, as we have seen, had long regarded sexuality of any kind as problematic. But as John O'Malley, in his *Praise and Blame in Renaissance Rome*, a study of sermons given at the papal court in the mid-sixteenth century, has shown, phallic symbolism — indeed, Christ's own penis — has by no means always been historically a taboo subject, especially on the Feast of the Circumcision. Commenting on how a sermon on the glory of Christ's phallus would likely have been received by a Roman congregation of celibate prelates and monks, Steinberg concludes they would have undoubtedly

> answered that the male member is not disqualified as an emblem of strength for being sexually unemployed. On the contrary. . . . Does such an answer seem sophistical? . . . We hear its echo as late as 1854: "The generative energy . . . when we are continent invigorates and inspires us. Chastity is the flowering of man." The lines were written by our own Henry Thoreau in *Walden*.[80]

All of a sudden we are back in Victorian (and in that sense Puritan) New England, where it perhaps does not need to be said that Cram and his circle were certainly not themselves entirely bored, for all their wider intellectual and romantic ideals, with the male member. In a letter to Cram of this period Gelett Burgess, for example, discoursed eloquently on "the long ambitious strokes of an excited and madly turgescent penis,"[81] a sentence that surely gave memorable form to this interest, which, given Cram's lusty nature, he was likely to have shared exuberantly with Burgess. That notwithstanding, the virtues of heroic male Platonic (and Catholic!) self-mastery were also alive and well in the vicinity of Boston in this era, as we have long since seen. Young men are idealistic, characteristically, as well as lustful; the jump from sermons heard in Renaissance Rome to novels read in Victorian Boston should be a matter of course.

Historically, one could make many a connection. Boston has, famously, more often taken the side of the censors. John Trumbull's *Infant Savior and St. John*, to cite a well-documented example, when exhibited at the Boston Athenaeum in 1828, went unsold by reason of Christ's nudity until the artist repented of his folly and offered a clothed version. By the period of Cram's activity, however, there had been somewhat of a change: two works in Isabella Gardner's collection (Swabian's *Throne of Grace* and Benedetto da Maiano's *Madonna and Child*) established not only, in the case of the latter, divine nudity in the Puritan capital, but in both cases a distinct focus on Christ's phallus. By far the deepest and most significant connection between Renaissance Rome (or ancient Athens, for that matter) and Victorian Boston, however, is the idea that manly virility, far from being compromised by chasteness, is thereby heightened; that such self-mastery constitutes "the flowering of man." Never mind holier or finer—the *flowering*.[82]

Behold the Christ of the Ashmont rood. The fusion of the vesture (which is to say, virtually none) of Christ suffering with the motif of the enhanced loincloth, in the pose of Christ triumphant, yields a beautiful, strong, and triumphantly virile male who—recall the Calvary's surmounting crown; this is Christ—is himself chaste, strong, and uplifting. And, it needs to be said (given the nature of erotic desire), perhaps all the *more* erotic in feeling for that fact. For all the necessary universality and decorum of a such a work in such a place, this Calvary blazons, like a huge "icon" (Cram's very word for the Ashmont rood Calvary), the idealized hero of Boston's youthful Bohemia. So much so that one can hardly help seeing in it the photographic studies of the crucifixion by Fred Holland Day, that ardent admirer of Platonic friendship, whose work was not, I think, far from the mind of the friend whose Calvary this is—a friend, for Cram was himself a Platonic idealist, who in his capacity as art critic is on record as having written of Gertrude Käsebier's and Fred Day's photography in the journal *Photo Era* very pertinent words. Replying to his own query of why photography was becoming in the 1890s and 1900s so much better than painting, Cram pointed out that in his view of things it was because painters increasingly "paint with the intelligence of a camera 'fiend,' while the painter-photographers photograph with the intelligence of old masters."[83]

Another visual connection between the Ashmont rood and Day's photography is the form of the lettering on the rood beam, an elaborately crested and gilded support for the Calvary that instantly reminds one of the architectural enframements (designed, probably, by Goodhue) of a number of Day's Sacred Studies. In fact, late nineteenth- and early twentieth-century pictorialist photography is a source here as well as Renaissance convention or medieval iconography. (Pictorialism, of course, like the Boston School of painting, is often seen as antimodern and *retardataire*, but even in the case of the Boston School that conclusion is increasingly being challenged.)[84] In this connection just how modern the resonances really are in the Ashmont rood is evident in the fact that Day's work, including his enframed Sacred Studies, when exhibited in London in the Royal Photographic Society's exhibition in 1900 "proved as much a cause célèbre in the world of photography," Jussim has written, "as [in painting] the Armory Show of 1913 would be."[85]

This very contemporary image of Christ is not only Cram's and Day's; this is also Father Hall's Christ—and, indeed, Father Hall's Saint John the Beloved Disciple. For this is the Anglo-Catholic Christ preached by the Society of St. John the Evangelist as an alternative to the rigid, Puritanical, Roman Catholicism of England and America a hundred years ago, a teaching that asserted the crucial importance of the Incarnation,[86] the intellectual content of which doctrine Cram himself is on record as having emphasized in the Ashmont Calvary by the symbolism of the two candlesticks that rise from the rood beam on either side of the crucifix. They symbolize, Cram said, Our Lord's dual nature as God enfleshed, God made Man.

The Incarnation was, of course, a doctrine that, as Anglo-Catholics preached it, "revealed the glory of the Church, but . . . also . . . the glory that is in man"; and the consequent belief that the Incarnation is indeed fulfilled in the growing together of every human activity not only "led some Anglo-Catholic priests [such as Father Hall] in the direction of Christian Socialism," but also, in David Hilliard's words, "encouraged a slightly more accommodating attitude toward homosexuality."[87] And one sees this, I believe, in Hall's teaching. However it sounds today, it was very liberal indeed in the 1890s for Hall to have advised in print:

> Whatever your temperament, your natural disposition, remember it needs justice and can be sanctified. . . . You may have qualities that fill you almost with dismay, but you should *remember* that *these very qualities* [emphasis added] are meant to be useful to you, and they will be if disciplined properly and directed in the proper channels.[88]

Recall, too, that the most militant gay activist arguing today for the blessing of "gay marriage"[89] (which Hall would certainly have disparaged) would be hard put to define any same-sex union more positively than did Hall himself of what he would have called the "particular friendship," contrasting, as he always did, Christian marriage and Christian friendship, both of which he would surely have blessed. For Hall did not shrink from teaching not only that marriage and friendship were *comparable* states of Christian life, but that marriage was not necessarily the superior one. Perhaps the more surely because of his own such relationship with Bishop Brent, which survived long absences and great distances over many decades, Hall asserted that friendship was "the most enduring form of love; for it is not broken by death. It outlives the Marriage union as we know it . . .," he concluded; "[Friendship is] a certain foretaste of Heaven."[90]

Shades of Whitmanic friendship, of Edward Carpenter and Francis Thompson, of Hovey's and Carman's comradeship, of Day's heroes and Cram's true knight. And how fitting the words from the Te Deum Cram blazoned beneath the great icon of his Ashmont Calvary: WHEN THOU HADST OVERCOME THE SHARPNESS OF DEATH THOU DIDST OPEN THE KINGDOM OF HEAVEN TO ALL BELIEVERS.

A SOMEWHAT MYSTERIOUS OPTIMISM

Alas, for all this splendor, only one of the famous British masters who had labored on Holy Trinity, Sloane Street, contributed as well to All Saints', Ashmont: Christopher Whall. Yet how fine that the first important example of English Arts and Crafts glass in America should overlook this famous chancel. It was a stroke of luck that Sarah M. Hunnewell, Mrs. Peabody's best friend, should have fallen in with Cram's idea of commissioning this work from Whall just when he was at his crest, after the triumph of his Gloucester Cathedral glass.

This work, too, though in more narrowly artistic circles, caused a frisson. Cram must have been amused when Charles Connick told him (as Connick later related in print) how, when Whall's glass arrived in Boston and was unpacked by the local installers, his unorthodox and seemingly crude panels were greeted with "scornful laughter"; laughter that when the glass was finally put in place turned to "wonder and admiration," so striking was its splendor of line and color. Wrote Connick bluntly: "Whenever a fresh experience of beauty disturbs the drab routine of a commercialized art you may be sure that an ardent spirit is adventuring in the dusty pathways of the stupid."[91]

The Ashmont altarpiece still awaited its master, however, and this time Cram preferred here an untested American youth, his friend George Hallowell. It was a curious choice, and in later years Cram remembered it as such, admitting that his young friend (Hallowell, nearly eleven years Cram's junior, was only twenty-six in 1898 when Burne-Jones died) was

> hardly more than a boy . . . — and had done nothing whatever in the line of religious art; yet with a somewhat mysterious optimism we gave him the altar-piece in All Saints', Ashmont — and he did it! There was something of the North Italian in him, or rather of the Venetian. His feeling for colour, tone and colour-composition, was unique and distinguished; at that time he seemed to combine something (no man can ever achieve more than this "something") of the colour of Giorgione, with hints of the drawing of Dürer, and the result was, to say the least, invigourating.[92]

Hallowell remains something of a puzzle. One thinks somehow of Henry Randall, if only because, to the long panegyric quoted above from his memoirs Cram added the same sort of somewhat overenthusiastic encomium we are all prone to of dear friends whose talents for some reason languish, as it turned out would be the case with both Hallowell and Randall. (Hallowell, insisted Cram in his memoirs, "John Sargent declared to be the painter with the greatest power and promise in America" and "was really one of the great geniuses of the time, as the world would have found out if most untimely death had not brought to an end his achievement.")[93] Cram's judgment of Hallowell was by no means everyone's. Ives Gammell, in his *Boston Painters*, did not even mention Hallowell, though it is only fair to say that Gammell (also, interestingly, invoking Sargent's name) was as effusive as Cram about Hallowell about another painter largely unknown until recently, Dennis Bunker,[94] and in this case one knows what one only suspects about Cram and Hallowell, that the author was fascinated as much by the artist as by the art. But Isabella Gardner (of whom the same was often true) shared Cram's view: visitors to the Gardner Museum will find there three paintings by Hallowell. Today, Hallowell's virile Maine logging scenes and unusual landscapes are increasingly admired.[95]

If Hallowell's work was not then a huge success, it was despite such influential patronage as Gardner's and Cram's. Always a well-respected art critic in Boston, especially as to painters, Cram distinctly puffed Hallowell (of course, in his view deservedly) in a review of the artist's work in *The Red Letter* (yet another avant-garde monthly of the period), where Cram by no means hid the fact that artist and critic had the sort of relationship in which, after perusing for hours innumerable sketches and canvases and notebooks, what was really most important was that "then, after, when the pipe smoke is thick enough, [it was possible to] talk about it all." The talk must have been good. Cram found almost too much to praise in his review, including Hallowell's "almost classical feeling for form," his "strong dramatic impulse" and "remarkable decorative sense [and] singular power . . . over clean, competent line."[96] It is, however, Cram's own categories in this review that are now chiefly of interest, for they highlight very well his artistic values at the end of the nineties.

First, Hallowell's work seemed to Cram admirable for its "manly" quality, an aspect of which is certainly evident in one of the homoerotic images of manly Arcadian struggle that illustrates the review. A second virtue, according to Cram, was that Hallowell's work was "modern"; the "influence of the old men is there," Cram wrote, "but not their dominance." Finally, there was Cram's greatest praise: in an age when "the fashionable art of the day is a Frankenstein — deceptive as to outward appearance, but evil within, as are all things that are man-made and devoid of soul," Hallowell's work was "spiritual."[97]

Manly, modern, spiritual — Cram's values in a phrase — do they not apply as well to the rood Calvary and to the design of All Saints' overall? The prayer is granite, wrote Henry Adams. Of All Saints's exterior what could be more appropriate? And inside, consider the massive chamfered piers without even a hint of a capital. That this is equally true of the chancel is less clear a hundred years later because, in the first place, of the intervening fashion for full frontal textiles that obscure the altar itself, and, in the second place, of the later pedestals to each side that obscure the altar's relationship to the reredos. Actually, as can be seen in the photograph reproduced here (see *108*), taken before the pedestals were added to the composition, the relationship of the lower courses of the reredos and the altar to the ascending courses of the reredos above is very much like that discussed in Chapter 6 between the base and the crown of Cram and Goodhue's church towers. Goodhue's increasing elaboration and delicacy of detail as the reredos rises grows perceptibly out of a base (in the case of the reredos its steps, platform, and lower courses) that is massive and boldly severe after Cram's characteristic manner. Indeed, the same photograph, showing the altar in the days of much briefer quarter frontals, discloses a boldness and severity even greater than Ashmont's exterior: Ralph Adams Cram's first altar is one stark, massive piece of stone, entirely undetailed, weighing four tons. Manly, modern, spiritual!

This is also not a bad accounting in a somewhat different way of the Ashmont altarpiece (*111a, b, c*), for Hallowell's panels are a tour de force of functional (that is to say, decorative, i.e., in a church, liturgical) art that carries off a most difficult charge with considerable panache; using imaginatively, for example, both classical and medieval motifs in a way that reflects no less well than Ashmont's lectern or rood Calvary Cram's theory of Gothic development: that a "modern," not a "Victorian," designer in Gothic, however much he might take

111a, b, c. George Hallowell for Cram and Goodhue, *The Enthronement of the Virgin*, oil on panels, ca. 1903; the altarpiece of All Saints', Ashmont, from a photograph of 1907. Before its installation it was exhibited in London and New York and in Boston at the St. Botolph Club.

medieval work as the primary inspiration, would always have to come to terms with the fact that, for good or ill, for the *neo*-Goth the Renaissance had intervened and would be acknowledged. As Hallowell does here in several ways.

First, and bearing in mind Cram's reference in the case of the Ashmont altarpiece to Giorgione, it is striking that Hallowell's work — very reminiscent (in the manner of the Virgin's enthronement, the placement of Saint George, the architectural and scenic backdrop, and even the pavement of traditional tile patterns) of Giorgione's Castelfranco altarpiece of ca. 1500, his only such work — differs from it significantly in that while Giorgione shows only a medieval architectural backdrop, Hallowell also shows a classical backdrop. Second, compounding Cram and Goodhue's originality in making paintings so dominant an aspect of a huge stone Gothic altar screen, Hallowell introduced through the altarpiece Renaissance perspective into the overall reredos (which, being Gothic, otherwise holds "flatly" to the plane of the wall) and used an

extraordinarily vibrant, jewel-like palette, which could almost be called proto-Art Deco. Here is a very unusual breadth of aesthetic sensibility, ranging from Giorgione to Maxfield Parrish.

The fusion of both classical and medieval sensibilities is evident in the altarpiece not only stylistically but iconographically; just as the medieval legacy is celebrated in the tremendous arches of the cathedral in the background of the Gospel side panel, in the background of the Epistle side panel the classical legacy arises equally conspicuously. The form selected to stand for the latter, moreover, is the *Doric* order. Lest the allusion be missed, recall Serlio's injunction that the most feminine of the orders, the Corinthian, be reserved for works dedicated to virgins, the Ionic for those dedicated to matrons and scholars, and the Doric for works whose dedication was to the great militant male saints such as Peter and Paul and George.[98]

The altarpiece is dedicated to Saint Mary the Virgin (it is entitled *The En-*

thronement of the Virgin)[99] and has more than a little to do with the fact that the donor was Mary Peabody, all of whose benefactions were in a fundamental sense in memory of her lost child, Amelia. But the mis-en-scène depicted goes beyond this to sources more literary, even personal. Consider the two angelic thurifers, one in white vesture, the other in black. Cram, it is known, sent Hallowell on a European sketching tour for the Ashmont job. And it was not many years before Hallowell's tour that Cram wrote *Black Spirits and White*, the title of which these kneeling spirits with their censers seem to illustrate so well. A preference of Cram's own probably also accounts for the presence here of a saint for whom he had a great fondness, Saint Elizabeth of Hungary, to whom (in part because Elizabeth was also his mother's name) Cram would in later years dedicate his own chapel. Often in Cram's work such things occur. In his woodwork in the Lady Chapel of the Church of the Advent cherubim portray the donor's mother, while we have already detected in the altar reredos of Our Saviour's, Middleborough, several faces reminiscent of that reredos's architects and their artist-collaborators.[100]

Furthermore, recalling Cram's observation of the way he thought photography increasingly influenced the art of this period and also our discussion here of how Hallowell's palette at Ashmont reminds one of Maxfield Parrish, I am struck by Richard Guy Wilson's characterization of Parrish's paintings as "photographic, magical realism."[101] For as was the case with the rood, photography may well also inform our study of Hallowell's Ashmont altarpiece. Certainly, my mind's eye, ranging at Ashmont over the thronging medieval knights, bishops, doctors, and mystics of the altarpiece, sees not a little as well of the 1890s Pinckney Street, as disclosed, for instance, in the group photograph of one of Fred Holland Day's dinner parties of 1893 (*112*), where all the assembled Visionists and their friends are in medieval dress—including a "cardinal" in red cassock and ermine (Cram, of course!), as well as a great medieval lady (who else but Louise Guiney?) in the sort of puffed-up velvet medieval dress that, like the coped and mitered "bishop" next to her at Day's table, occurs several times in Hallowell's altarpiece.[102] Like Sargent in an equally serious religious work, *The Frieze of the Prophets* at the Boston Public Library, where we know the prophets are both models and friends of Sargent's, so here in the All Saints' altarpiece Cram and Hallowell may well have celebrated their own contemporaries as well as their historical heroes.

Interestingly, exactly twenty people are shown in the three panels as constituting the Virgin's court at Ashmont, the number, as it happens, Cram mentions in his memoirs as the most ever belonging to the Visionists, some of whom we know were the subject of at least one group portrait, the sketch of 1894 by Goodhue on the cover of *Saint Kavin, A Ballad*. Inspecting Hallowell's altar-

112. A photographic source for the Hallowell altarpiece? The Visionists and their friends are at a medieval costume dinner at Day's house in Norwood, ca. 1893. Day presides, standing at the table's head; to the left (at Day's right hand) is Cram.

piece, in fact, one might construe many a speculative catalogue of resemblances. Hallowell's Saint Barbara, for instance, could be based on a photographic study of that saint by Fred Holland Day, for which it is known Louise Guiney in 1893 was the model.[103] But any such catalogue of historical figures and possible models would waylay us unduly. More likely, Guiney was the model for Our Lady. And who better than the author of *Knight Errant*'s title poem: "And may Our Lady lend to me / Sight of the Dragon soon!" Its slayer, Saint George, stands in the altarpiece to her right hand.

FIDELITIES

What was it the poet laureate (of Anglo-Catholicism no less than England) wrote of Holy Trinity, Sloane Street? "Light six tall tapers to the Flame of Art," Sir John Betjeman began; and he would not have disagreed with me that Ashmont's tapers burn in candlesticks no less worthy than those of Sedding's at Sloane Street; and, too, he would have rejoiced at once in Hallowell's angelic thurifers, their censers sending "incense wreathing to the lily flowers." Indeed, he would have all but chanted his conclusion at Ashmont: "And, with your cool hands white, / Swing the warm censer round my bruised heart. / Drop dove-grey eyes, your penitential showers / On this pale acolyte." Nor would his keen eye have missed two other knights who appear in this altarpiece, both mounted, in the background of the Gospel side panel.

451

If their aspect seems curiously flat and graphic, it is perhaps because that is also true of the cover art of *Knight Errant*, a source for our purposes here both literary and personal, for in retrospect it is surely not harder to name the models of these knights than of the Virgin they ride for; no harder, certainly, than to name the two figures in more ancient dress in the frontispiece of *The Decadent*. In other times and different places, Hallowell's knights might have been not knights but cowboys, or have preferred togas or even that more modern armor, leather jackets. Cram, of course, amidst Hallowell's glowing, vibrant time-warp of saints and Bohemians, preferred knights in medieval armor, perhaps thinking of how in his "Song of Love and Death" of 1875 John Addington Symonds associated the nineteenth-century Romantic concept of chivalry with Whitman's concept of male homosexual love, a connection characteristic enough of the period that it was made, too, by Edward FitzGerald, the translator of *The Rubáiyát of Omar Khayyám*, in his *Euphranor: A Dialogue on Youth* of 1851.[104] Surely this so much more aristocratic gay ideal came even closer than Edward Carpenter's homosexual Christian Socialism to the world of Cram. So much more likely, as we have seen, to have fought for Thebes than for Sparta, Cram would always remain incorruptibly traditionalist, sensualist, Platonist, a new conservative and an old-fashioned liberal, a fin-de-siècle modernist still stubbornly Catholic.

And how fitting that the symbol of so much of this—of the endpoint of Plato's and Dante's ladder of love begun in physical beauty and erotic impulse, as of the true knight's quest for right achievement, self-mastery, and salvation as understood in the Arthurian legend Cram made his own in *Excalibur* (the best thing, he always insisted, that he ever wrote)—how fitting, indeed, that this symbol should be blazoned at the center as the finale of Ashmont's high altar and reredos on one of the last works of art Cram designed for this chancel, in 1910, as Mary Peabody lay dying: the splendid gilt-bronze tabernacle relief by the goldsmith James Wooley that depicts the Holy Grail. That it does so, moreover, as the principal motif of the great symbol of the sacrament of the Eucharist—the Host and Chalice—underlines its historic significance, because this relief is, in fact, the outer door of the tabernacle, the first on any such high altar in any parish church in the Diocese of Massachusetts, a diocese that in those days discouraged as scandalous and papist the reservation and enthronement of the sacrament at the altar's center. Indeed, just two years previously, in connection with the first tabernacle at the Church of Advent in the Lady Chapel, designed by Cram (together with a magnificent jeweled pyx-monstrance [113] to go with it), the bishop of Massachusetts had raised to another bishop the possibility of bringing the then rector of the Advent to trial for that provocation.

Cram, a lover of the Grail opera he had seen at Bayreuth in the 1880s—that

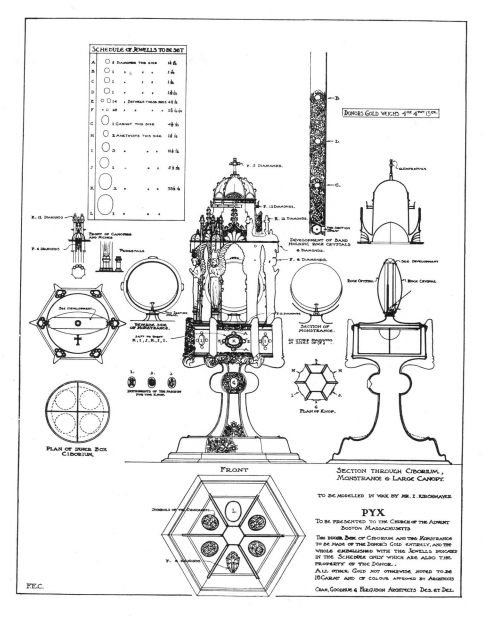

113. Reservation of the Eucharistic bread and wine in a tabernacle and devotions to the sacrament were highly controversial practices among Episcopalians in the early 1900s. This unusual "pyx in a ciborium" design was an ingenious attempt to approximate a discreet Anglican monstrance. *Above*: F. E. Cleveland's plans, elevations, sections, and schedules for the design by Cram for Boston's Church of the Advent. The figures were modeled in wax by Kirchmayer, and the monstrance was made by Arthur Stone.

"shadowy center of a world of male homosexual attractions," as Richard Mohr has called *Parsifal*[105] — understood, of course, in the case of Wagner (as, surely, in the case of Burne-Jones), that there was more to the matter than was evident in conventional church iconography. That other Anglo-Catholic in the next generation, T. S. Eliot, would also understand, and because the Grail has yet another dimension of meaning to us here, Eliot can render us, who have now passed through Pre-Raphaelitism to aestheticism to Decadence in our own quest in this study, one more service by helping us take the final step from Decadence to modernism.

Cram's modernism was not, of course, Eliot's; time moves on. Cram's modernism was, however, in his day modern enough. To speak of his personal life: it is true, for example, that he never learned to drive an automobile. He was born, after all, in 1863, and was approaching fifty before that skill became at all widespread in an era when men like Cram had chauffeurs. Consider, instead, what was newly emerging in Cram's *own* youth: of photography he became, as we have seen, an ardent partisan. Skyscrapers? Cram would confess, when finally given a chance to design one in the 1920s, that he had long yearned for the chance. Of Whitman's poetry and Wagner's music we have spoken much already. Both, admired by Cram, were as artistically and psychologically revolutionary in his youthful era as *The Waste Land* was in Eliot's, when we have William Carlos Williams's words for it, that poem would burst upon the post–World War I era like "an atomic bomb."[106] Listen to how Russell Kirk, the conservative thinker, describes that bomb:

> At the heart of [*The Waste Land*] lies the legend of the Grail. . . . "How may a man be born again and a blasted land made to bloom. . . . [In the Grail legend] questing Knights who entered the Chapel Perilous [there beheld the Grail and] . . . if they found the hardihood to inquire, they would be answered. . . ." So in a civilization reduced to "a heap of broken images" all that is required is "sufficient curiosity," Hugh Kenner comments keenly; "the man who asks what one or another of these fragments means . . . may be the agent of regeneration. The past exists in fragments precisely because nobody cares what is meant; it will unite itself and come alive in the mind of anyone who succeeds in caring . . . in a world where" we know too much, and are convinced of too little.

Eliot, Kirk continues, knew that "the past and the present really are one," that we must all confront "the dead Wizard-Knight, there in the ruinous chapel," and that only if we "face down the horror and dare to ask the questions" is there any hope that we "may be heard and healed."[107]

Ralph Adams Cram, I think, knew it, too. And his life's work, as it turned out, would be to ask what these fragments might mean. Not the least important of them will be evident to the mind's eye in those two knights in the background of the Ashmont altarpiece, who seem to me to invoke Sir John Betjeman's promise that "God guards his aesthetes."[108] And sent to them in the chancel of All Saints' a worthy finale to their fin-de-siècle.

ENTR'ACTE

The decade of the 1890s . . . continues to fascinate . . . a decade of beginnings: of icon-smashing vitality, of modernism. The violent tensions between old and new animated the 1890s, inspiring what may have been the greatest concentrated outpouring of talent since the Renaissance from artists like Hardy, Shaw, Wilde, Whistler, Elgar, Beerbohm, Beardsley, Pinero, Kipling, Conrad and Yeats. . . . From socialism, the New Drama, . . . Uranian love (homosexuality), occultism and decadence to the more particular influences . . . of Whistler, Wagner and Zola. . . . All were anti-Establishment forces seeking to challenge or topple Victorian bourgeois ideals.

> — Margot Peters, review of Karl Beckson's
> *London in the 1890s* (*New York Times Book Review*)

What Karl Beckson has written of the Old World of Wilde and Beardsley and Yeats and Wagner is true as well of their disciples in the New World, Cram and his cohort. For though they were disciples, Boston's Bohemians by no means made history at second hand, as we have seen. After all, Poe and Emerson and Thoreau and (further afield, admittedly) Whitman were important sources for this "concentrated outpouring" in Europe, where in the 1890s and 1900s Europeans, too, learned to admire such things as Day's photography and Cram's churches and Berenson's scholarship. In America, far from merely reflecting intellectual developments abroad, Boston was, from Wilde to Freud, spearheading their thought in the New World and at the dawn of the American century — a century in which no less distinguished a Britisher than Alfred North Whitehead thought Boston would come to be the intellectual capital of the Western world; holding, in fact, the place in modern times of Paris in Cram's beloved Middle Ages. Van Wyck Brooks was wrong; what he called an Indian summer was the dawn of modernism in New England, while the emerging gay subculture of the era Cram led was its herald.

This is admittedly easier to see today in the post-modern era on the eve of the twenty-first century, the late modernism of Andy Warhol and such having so recently, it seems, passed from the scene. But just because we are now virtually at the end of modernism's century, we must make a particular point to try to comprehend the *whole* history of modernism — looking past the late modernism of our own times to not only the high modernism of Picasso and his cohort (cubism in painting or imagism in poetry, for example, or the twelve-tone scale in music) but past high modernism, too, to what was, in fact, early modernism; which is to say, to aestheticism and the Decadence.[1]

Meanwhile, between *Boston Bohemia* and *American Gothic*, as the second volume of this biography will be called, between Cram's youth and his middle age, there is no really satisfactory place at which to take our temporary leave of him, except that it may be that ongoing liturgy, ongoing even today, of the Easter Vigil and the Paschal candle.

It was a liturgy Cram's generation of the eighties and nineties especially appreciated. For example, the author of "The Hound of Heaven" also wrote "From the Night of Forebeing," based on the idea of the light of the Paschal candle shining in the darkness of man's forebeing—in other words, before humanity's creation. And this second poem of Francis Thompson's to arise here, which revolves like the vigil itself around the command "Let there be light," "penetrates," in Brigid Boardman's words, "to the darkest regions of the human spirit. . . . to 'the secret chambers of the brain' and the . . . sources of sensual desire"; to that place where "round and round," Thompson says, "in bacchanal rout reel the swift spheres intemperately,"[2] a place not unlike that of the frantic, ghostly rout of Cram's abiding spirits, both black and white.

It is also a liturgy that depends, not on sentimental gestures of historical reenactment that reveal something but conceal nothing, like the Christmas crèche and the Easter sepulcher, but on *symbol*—the Paschal candle. "Like Jung," Jackson Lears has written, "Cram understood the importance of inherited cultural symbols."[3] Indeed, Cram insisted: "Without those, men cannot live."[4] And the Easter Vigil liturgy of the Paschal candle is suffused with Jung's idea of the symbol's numinous power. John Dourley has written eloquently of this in *The Psyche as Sacrament*:

> The symbol for Jung is a bearer or embodiment of the power of the archetypes of the collective unconscious in their living and changing configurations. . . . The impact of the symbol on consciousness is so great, according to Jung, that it "seizes and possesses the whole personality and is naturally productive of faith." . . . The symbol opens up the depths of oneself and one's surroundings previously closed. The symbol, as it appears in dreams or in other products of the unconscious, makes conscious what was previously unconscious and is directly tailored to the need of the individual's process of becoming aware.[5]

Action precedes belief, or, more learnedly, as someone has said of T. S. Eliot, impersonations become transformations. For Cram the action had begun in Rome with Randall in 1887 at midnight Mass, where Cram may be said to have first "become aware." And of architecture as well as of religion—for "architectural meaning, like erotic knowledge," Alberto Pérez-Gómez has written, "is primarily of the body. . . . Art and architecture speak in the medium of the erotic." For those called to the *vita voluptuaria*, "the life," as Pérez-Gómez put it, "of desire, where fulfillment is never fully present nor fully absent,"[6] the "becoming aware" Jung speaks of is never-ending. Thanks be for Cram, for us, it was his vocation to be the greatest of American church builders. Because, after all, that experience of desire was the deepest and most characteristic experience, I believe, Cram ever knew. It was enough. And to share that experience with the world, *shaping* that world, was ever his greatest exaltation and catharsis; thereby in Jung's sense opening up "the depths of [Cram's] self and [his] surroundings previously closed . . . [to make] conscious what was previously unconscious, [thus] . . . becoming aware."[7] And so the erotic and the aesthetic, action and belief, art and religion, became for Cram, finally, one.

It was a unity upon which Ralph Adams Cram would build a brilliant life.

114. Grotesque of Bertram Goodhue by Lee Lawrie, originally on the West Point Chapel but later ordered removed by the authorities.

CHAPTER NOTES

The following abbreviations and short titles are used in the notes:

PERSONS

RAC	Ralph Adams Cram
FHD	Fred Holland Day
BGG	Bertram Grosvenor Goodhue
LIG	Louise Imogen Guiney

SHORT TITLES AND REPOSITORIES

AABN	*American Architect and Building News*
Beckson	*London in the 1890s* (Hew York: W. W. Norton, 1992)
Brooks, *Indian Summer*	Van Wyck Brooks, *New England: Indian Summer* (New York: E. P. Dutton, 1940)
RAC, *My Life*	Ralph Adams Cram, *My Life in Architecture* (Boston: Little, Brown, 1936)
C&GC/BPL	Cram and Goodhue Collection, Boston Public Library
DAB	*Dictionary of American Biography*
Daniel	Ann Miner Daniel, "The Early Architecture of Ralph Adams Cram, 1889–1902" (Ph.D. dissertation, University of North Carolina, Chapel Hill, 1978)
Ellmann, *Wilde*	Richard Ellmann, *Oscar Wilde* (New York: Random House, 1988)
Finlay	Nancy Finlay, *Artists of the Book in Boston* (Cambridge, MA: Houghton Library, 1985)
Gay, *Education*	Peter Gay, *Education of the Senses*, vol. I, *The Bourgeois Experience: Victoria to Freud* (New York: Oxford University Press, 1984)
Gay, *Tender Passion*	Peter Gay, *The Tender Passion*, vol. II, ibid.
GMA	Gardner Museum Archives
Hilliard	David Hilliard, "UnEnglish and UnManly: Anglo-Catholicism and Homosexuality," *Victorian Studies* 25 (Winter 1982): 181–210.
Jussim	Estelle Jussim, *Slave to Beauty: The Eccentric Life and Controversial Career of F. Holland Day* (Boston: David Godine, 1981)
Lears	T. Jackson Lears, *No Place of Grace* (New York: Pantheon, 1981)
Martin	Robert K. Martin, *The Homosexual Tradition in American Poetry* (Austin, TX, and London: University of Texas Press, 1979)

Nicholas, Notebook	Mary Cram Nicholas, Notebooks, C&GC/BPL
Nicholas, *Notes*	*Notes for Douglass Shand-Tucci*, typewritten pages of Mary Nicholas's responses to lists of persons I put to her as of importance to RAC. All are now in C&GC/BPL.
Paglia	Camille Paglia, *Sexual Personae: Art and Decadence from Nefertiti to Emily Dickinson* (New Haven: Yale University Press, 1990)
Parrish	Stephen Maxfield Parrish, *Currents of the Nineties in Boston and London* (New York and London: Garland Publishing Co., 1987)
Sedgwick, *Epistemology*	Eve Kosofsky Sedgwick, *The Epistemology of the Closet* (Berkeley: University of California Press, 1990)

1 PINCKNEY STREET

1. Quoted in Frances Weston Carruth, *Fictional Rambles in and about Boston* (New York: McClure, Phillips, 1902), 49.

2. The Church of the Advent and St. John's, Bowdoin Street, are easily confused, since both Beacon Hill Anglican parishes grew out of the same history. The Advent, founded in 1844 and staffed after 1872 by the Cowley Fathers, severed all connection with that monastic order after moving to the present church. In 1883 the Cowley Fathers reconstituted what had been the old Church of the Advent as the Mission Church of St. John the Evangelist, which (though no longer associated today with the Cowley Fathers) still exists as an Episcopal parish. RAC, though he became a parishioner at St. John's, often in his youth went to the Advent. Like T. S. Eliot (when in Boston), RAC was in one or another church so often that each parish is associated with him, all the more so as much art by him is to be found at both St. John's and the Advent. But it was St. John's and the Cowley Fathers that claimed RAC's chief loyalty.

For further information on the history of the Cowley Fathers in America, see Chapter 5.

3. Robert Lowell, "91 Revere Street," *Life Studies on For the Union Dead: Robert Lowell* (New York: Farrar, Straus and Giroux, 1971), 15. I am grateful for this source to Paul M. Wright.

4. For the background of William Augustine Cram see RAC, "Fulfillment," *Convictions and Controversies* (Boston: Marshall Jones, 1935), 93–109. RAC conducted extensive genealogical research (mostly through professional genealogists) into his family history, and great piles of this material exist in C&GC/BPL; quite undisturbed, certainly, by this author.

For further background see Mary Cram Nicholas (RAC's older daughter) to DS-T, letter of July 1972, C&GC/BPL. Mrs. Nicholas states that "Emerson and Thoreau [were] both friends of my grandfather, William Augustine Cram; why do you think my father's first name was Ralph?"

5. Interview with Mary Cram Nicholas, 12 December 1975.

6. RAC, *Convictions*, 93.

7. *General Catalogue of Officers and Students of Phillips Exeter Academy from 1783 to 1903* (Exeter, NH, 1903), 64. See also N. F. Carter, *The Native Ministry of New Hampshire* (Concord, NH, 1906), 308.

8. See RAC, *My Life*, 41–47. For a discussion of the work of Rotch and Tilden see

Harry L. Katz, *A Continental Eye: The Art and Architecture of Arthur Rotch* (Boston: Boston Athenaeum, 1985), 1–31. The story RAC told to Laurence Winship is in an undated typescript by Winship, entitled "Cram," now in C&GC/BPL. I am indebted to Rev. Carl Scovell for this source and to Tom Winship for discussing his father's relationship with RAC.

9. RAC to Anne Cram, letter of 28 July 1930.

10. RAC, *The Builder and Woodworker* (Boston, 1882), Plates 17, 33, 51, 52, 53.

11. RAC, *My Life*, 48, 46.

12. Ibid., 46–47.

13. RAC first lived on Dwight Street, where, in 1883, the *Boston Street Directory* locates him as residing at 28; then, in the 1885 and 1886 directories, on Union Park. Thereafter he moved to Beacon Hill. See n. 70, below, and the text at that note.

14. C. A. Ralph [Ralph Adams Cram], "The Danger that Threatens Copley Square," letter to *Boston Evening Transcript*, 3 October 1884, 6. See also RAC, *My Life*, 10. RAC's own designs for Copley Square are discussed in *My Life*, 46.

15. Daniel, 27, 25–26, 85–86 n. 3. See also LIG to RAC, letter of 10 August 1888, C&GC/BPL, in which she writes: "You, who I will affirm, saved Trinity [Copley] Square." This is surely at least one instance, however, where the young RAC was influenced strongly by his employer, for Arthur Rotch had played a leading role (testifying at legislative hearings on behalf of the Boston Art Club, just arrived at Dartmouth and Newbury streets) in getting the commission for the new Boston Public Library away from the rather pedestrian city architect and into the hands of the trustees of the library; this according to Trustee Samuel A. B. Abbott, who in turn was largely responsible for steering the job to Charles Follen McKim. See Walter Muir Whitehill, *The Boston Public Library: A Centennial History* (Cambridge, MA: Harvard University Press, 1956), 140.

16. John Lyman Faxon, "Copley Square's Peril," letter to *Boston Evening Transcript*, 7 October 1884, 6. Cram's reply to the letters responding to his letter of 3 October appeared on 9 October 1884, 6. Faxon was a Boston architect.

17. Nicholas, Notebook II, 6. Cram discourses at some length on Squire Blake in "The Last of the Squires," *Convictions*, 80–92. Blake served in the New Hampshire legislature in 1846. I am grateful to Margaret Perry of the Kensington, New Hampshire, Public Library for her assistance; see her letter to me of 29 August 1992, C&GC/BPL.

18. Ira N. Blake to RAC, letter of 15 October 1885, C&GC/BPL. RAC's grandfather Ira Blake (1799–1869) had two sons, the younger of whom, Ira N. Blake, was the writer of this letter. Ira N. Blake's sister Sarah Elizabeth was RAC's mother. Legal documents having to do with Ira N. Blake's divorce are in the possession of RAC's grandson Ralph Adams Cram II. He and Mrs. Cram kindly sorted out these relationships for me.

19. RAC, *My Life*, 12.

20. Ibid., 7–8.

21. Ellmann, *Wilde*, 183–184.

22. Ibid., 151–152.

23. Mary W. Blanchard, "Near *The Coast of Bohemia*: Boundaries and the Aesthetic Press" (unpublished paper, Rutgers University, Department of History, 1992), 32–33.

24. See Ellmann, *Wilde*, 32–33, 84.

25. Ibid., 156.

26. C. A. Ralph [Ralph Adams Cram], "A Consideration of Rubens II," *Boston*

Evening Transcript, 27 December 1884, 6. RAC's first series of articles, "The Dante Rossettis at the Art Museum," ran on 5, 6, 7, 10, and 12 November 1884.

27. H. W. Janson, *History of Art* (New York: Abrams, 1962), 499.

28. Joseph Horowitz, "Anton Seidl and America's Wagner Cult," in Barry Millington and Stewart Spenser, eds., *Wagner in Performance* (New Haven: Yale University Press, 1992), 173; Eugene Tompkins, *The History of the Boston Theatre, 1854–1901* (Boston: Houghton Mifflin, 1908), 363–364.

29. Horowitz, "Anton Seidl," 179.

30. John Swan, *Music in Boston* (Boston: Boston Public Library, 1977), 46, 93.

31. RAC, *My Life*, 8.

32. Quoted in Sedgwick, *Epistemology*, 171.

33. Carl Schorske, "The Quest for the Grail: Wagner and Morris," in Kurt Wolff and Barrington Moore, eds., *The Critical Spirit*, quoted in Lears, 172. For a discussion of Wagner's overall effect on his era see Gay, *Tender Passion*, 264–266.

34. T. S. Eliot, "The Boston 'Evening Transcript,'" T. S. Eliot, *Collected Poems 1909–1962* (New York: Harcourt, Brace & World, 1970), 20.

35. Nicholas, Notebook II, 9. See also "Miss Nichols" in Nicholas, *Notes*.

36. All these things are in C&GC/BPL.

37. Nicholas, "Miss Nichols," *Notes*.

38. RAC, undated typescript of *My Life in Architecture*, 12, C&GC/BPL.

39. George Santayana, *The Genteel Tradition at Bay*, vol. VII of *The Works of George Santayana*, Triton Edition, 15 vols. (New York: Scribner's, 1936–1940), 129.

40. Mark A. DeWolfe Howe, *A Venture in Remembrance* (Boston: Little, Brown, 1941), 155–157.

41. Sarah Way Sherman, *Sarah Orne Jewett: An American Persephone* (Hanover, NH: University Press of New England, 1989), 74–75.

42. Quoted in Kathryn D. Wheeler-Smith, "Alice Brown: Triumph and Tragedy in Tiverton's Wonderland" (Harvard Extension MLA Thesis, 1991), 9. See also "Alice Brown," *Notable American Women 1607–1950*, Edward T. James et al., eds., 3 vols. (Cambridge, MA: Belknap Press of Harvard University Press, 1971), I, 249–250.

43. E. J. O'Brien, *The Advance of the American Short Story* (New York: Dodd, Mead and Co., 1923), 172.

44. Sherman, *Jewett*, 52–53.

45. For a discussion of Howells's novel see Shaun O'Connell, *Imagining Boston* (Boston: Beacon Press, 1990), 84–88.

46. Helen Howe, *The Gentle Americans* (New York: Harper and Row, 1965), 83.

47. Sherman, *Jewett*, 81.

48. The portrait is now in the Gothic Room of Fenway Court.

49. Louise Hall Tharp, *Mrs. Jack* (Boston: Little, Brown, 1965), 133–134.

50. See "Maud Howe Elliott," *Notable American Women*, I, 575. See also Tharp, *Mrs. Jack*, 127–128.

51. Maud Howe Elliott, *Three Generations* (Boston: Little, Brown, 1923), diary entry for 15 January 1890, 223.

52. Van Wyck Brooks, *An Autobiography* (New York: E. P. Dutton, 1965), 120.

53. Charles Eliot Norton to RAC, letter of 17 January 1892; C&GC/BPL. Although a goodly amount of Norton's correspondence survives in the Houghton Library at Harvard, no letters from RAC are extant there.

54. Leslie J. Workman, " 'My First Real Tutor': John Ruskin and Charles Eliot Norton," *New England Quarterly* 62 (December 1989): 571, 580.

55. Ibid., 574, 580.

56. Ibid., 579. See also 583 and Lears, 243, 247.

57. RAC, *My Life*, 5.

58. Pinckney Street, its houses and residents, are treated authoritatively in Allen Chamberlain, *Beacon Hill: Its Ancient Pastures and Early Mansions* (Boston: Houghton Mifflin, 1925), passim; in Eugenia Kaledin, "Literary Boston," *Victorian Boston Today*, Pauline C. Harrell and Margaret S. Smith, eds. (Boston: The Victorian Society, 1975), 98–99; in Edwin M. Bacon, *Boston: A Guide Book* (Boston: Ginn & Co., 1908), 71; and in George F. Weston, Jr., *Boston Ways* (Boston: Beacon Press, 1957), 70–73. For a more popular but complete secondary source, though dependent on the sources noted above, see A. McVoy McIntyre, *Beacon Hill: A Walking Tour* (Boston: Little, Brown, 1975), 75–92.

59. McIntyre, *Beacon Hill*, 88.

60. For Judge and Mrs. Ruffin see W. E. B. Du Bois, *The Autobiography of W. E. B. Du Bois* (New York: International Publishers, 1968), 137. For Du Bois see O'Connell, *Imagining Boston*, 152. For Barrett Wendell see "Barrett Wendell," *DAB*, X, 649–651, and Paul E. Cohen, "Barrett Wendell and the Harvard Literary Revival," *New England Quarterly* 52 (December 1979): 483–499. For Smith see J. Marcus et al., *Black Heritage Trail* (Boston: Boston 200, 1976).

61. For Townsend and company see Lucius Beebe, "Beacon Hill Bohemia," *Boston and the Boston Legend* (New York: Appleton, 1936), 303. Elliot Paul's association with Harry Crosby is touched on in Geoffrey Wolff, *Black Sun: The Brief Transit and Violent Eclipse of Harry Crosby* (New York: Random House, 1976), 244, 246, 248. I am indebted to Robert and Elizabeth Ives Hunter for this source. For Cheever, see Barbara W. Moore and Gail Weesner, *Beacon Hill* (Boston: Century Hill Press, 1992), 48. For Plath on Sexton and Starbuck, see *The Journals of Sylvia Plath* (New York: Ballantine Books, 1983), 301. I am grateful to Peter Davison for pointing me to this source.

62. Ellmann, *Wilde*, 161. See also Mrs. Thomas Bailey Aldrich, *Crowding Memories* (Boston: Houghton Mifflin, 1920), 247.

Actually, Aldrich had moved from Pinckney Street around the corner to Charles by the time of Wilde's visit.

63. Thomas Beer, *The Mauve Decade* (New York: Knopf, 1941), 150. The rhyme appeared first in the *Tatler* of Chicago, May-September 1896. It is attributed to Richard Hovey in William Linneman, *Richard Hovey* (Boston: G. K. Hall, 1976), 31.

64. McIntyre, *Beacon Hill*, 80; Susan and Michael Southworth, *A.I.A. Guide to Boston* (Chester, CT: Globe Pequot Press, 1987), 184.

65. Martin, 101.

66. Harry Levin, *Matty at Eliot House* (Cambridge, MA: Eliot House, Harvard University, 1982). A bibliography of lengthier treatments is included. Matthiessen's letters to and from his best friend and partner have been published in Louis Hyde, *Rat and the Devil* (Hamden, CT: Archon Books, 1978).

67. W. R. McClure, *Prometheus: A Memoir of Lucien Price* (Boston: privately printed, 1965).

68. Weston, *Boston Ways*, 70.

69. RAC, *My Life*, 4.

70. All Cram's residences are discoverable from the Boston street directories of the years cited in the text at the Boston Public Library. He is first listed as living on Beacon Hill in the 1887 directory.

71. Louis Elson, *The History of American Music* (New York: Macmillan, 1904), 253.

72. Samuel Eliot Morison, *One Boy's Boston* (Boston: Houghton Mifflin, 1962), 44–48.

73. Carruth, *Fictional Rambles*, 47–48.

74. Martin Green, *The Mount Vernon Street Warrens* (New York: Scribner's, 1989), 178.

75. Alice Brown, *Margaret Warrener* (Boston: Houghton Mifflin, 1901), 1–3.

76. The advertisement, the poem, and the correspondence with the tailor are all in C&GC/BPL.

77. Nicholas, Notebook II, 7.

78. Ellen Moers, *The Dandy*, quoted in Beckson, 35.

79. Beckson, 35.

80. RAC, pocket diary, undated, unpaged, C&GC/BPL. On the first page is written "Ralph A. Cram, 85 Devonshire, Rm. 17"—the address of Rotch and Tilden, thus dating the diary 1881–1886.

81. Allan Bloom, *The Closing of the American Mind* (New York: Simon & Schuster, 1987), 134.

82. RAC, *My Life*, 46.

83. Ibid., 8.

84. Ibid., 45.

85. "William Ordway Partridge," *DAB*, XIV, 284–285. See also Albert T. Gardner, *American Sculpture* (New York: Metropolitan Museum of Art, 1965), 77–78.

86. Bernard Berenson, *Sunset and Twilight: From the Diaries of 1947–1958* (New York: Harcourt, Brace and World, 1963), 261, 241.

87. RAC, *My Life*, 15.

88. See Berenson Archive, Harvard University Center for Renaissance Studies, Villa I Tatti. All these letters are noted in Nicky Marino, comp., *The Berenson Archive: An Inventory of Correspondence* (Cambridge, MA: Harvard University Press, 1965). I am indebted to Susan Sinclair for this source.

89. RAC to Bernard Berenson, letter of 26 November 1940, Berenson Archive.

90. Ibid., letter of 10 January 1939, I Tatti.

91. Ibid., letter of 12 May 1941, I Tatti.

92. Ibid., letter of 29 January 1940, I Tatti.

93. Berenson to RAC, letter of 24 June, n.y., I Tatti, C&GC/BPL.

94. RAC, *My Life*, 14.

95. LIG to RAC, letter of 26 May 1887, C&GC/BPL.

96. LIG to FHD, letters of 20 April and 5 May 1891, quoted in Parrish, 43–45.

97. Brooks, *Indian Summer*, 412.

98. Parrish, 17.

99. Brooks, *Indian Summer*, 451.

100. Guiney's father is discussed in the Boston context most pertinently in Brooks, *Indian Summer*, 412. See also "Louise Imogen Guiney," *DAB*, IV, 43–44, and *Notable American Women*, II, 101–102.

101. Alice Brown, *Louise Imogen Guiney* (New York: Macmillan, 1921), 8.

102. See Jussim, 35, and Lears, 126. Henry G. Fairbanks, *Louise Imogen Guiney* (New York: Twayne, 1973), does not raise the issue, but even he speculates about her "normalcy" (61).

103. Fairbanks, *Guiney*, 209, xii.

104. RAC, *My Life*, 16.

105. LIG to RAC, letter of 9 November 1894, C&GC/BPL.

106. LIG to Mrs. Herbert Clarke, 24 July 1896, quoted in Grace Guiney, ed., *Letters of Louise Imogen Guiney*, 2 vols. (New York: Harper, 1926), 116.

107. Alan H. MacDonald, *Richard Hovey: Man and Craftsman* (Durham, NC: Duke University Press, 1957), 184. See also "Richard Hovey," *DAB*, V, 273–274.

108. MacDonald, *Hovey*, 155. See also Linneman, *Hovey*, 305.

109. *Town Topics*, 5 November 1896, quoted in MacDonald, *Hovey*, 192.

110. On Carman's editorship see Ellen B. Ballou, *The Building of the House* (Boston: Houghton Mifflin, 1975), 403, 405.

111. RAC, *My Life*, 89. See also Donald Stevens, *Bliss Carman* (New York: Twayne, 1966).

112. Finlay, 97, 98. See also the *Boston Evening Transcript* obituary, 10 March 1928.

113. Fairbanks, *Guiney*, 181.

114. Gay, *Tender Passion*, 3.

115. Parrish, 2, 55.

116. Jussim, 30, 10.

117. Parrish, 38.

118. Jussim, 36.

119. Ibid., 181, 298 n. 31.

120. Ibid., 10.

121. Jean Gibran and Kahlil Gibran, *Kahlil Gibran* (Boston: New York Graphic Society/Little, Brown, 1975), 54.

122. For crossing class boundaries in the homosexual context, see Allen Ellenzweig, *The Homoerotic Photograph* (New York: Columbia University Press, 1992), 61. See also Beckson, 194.

123. Jussim, 22, 180. For a discussion by Jussim of the nature of Day's affairs see 176–181.

124. Minna A. Smith to FHD, letter of 11 December 1917, quoted in Gibran and Gibran, *Gibran*, 54.

125. LIG to FHD, letter of 10 January 1919, quoted in Jussim, 116. *The Prophet*, although not published until 1923, was in its final form by 1919 and circulated in manuscript. See Gibran and Gibran, *Gibran*; Day is discussed in chapters 3 and 4.

126. Fairbanks, *Guiney*, 56.

127. Jussim, 7. See also note 147 below.

128. Gibran and Gibran, *Gibran*, 41. How seriously Day took his social work is emphasized by Jussim, 117.

129. Jussim, 107. See also Ellenzweig, *Homoerotic Photograph*, 51.

130. Jussim, 118. There was a private viewing at 9 Pinckney on 16 and 17 November 1898, by invitation only. LIG's invitation survives in the Library of Congress; another is at the Norwood Historical Society. The 1898 show was no sudden development. FHD had been experimenting with male nudes for ten years, according to Jussim, 105.

131. Marmaduke Humphrey, "Triumphs in Amateur Photography," *Godey's Magazine,* quoted in Jussim, 119.

132. Jussim, 205.

133. For FHD's professional and personal influence on Minor White and Robert Mapplethorpe see Ellenzweig, *Homoerotic Photograph,* 51, 113.

134. Gay, *Tender Passion,* 258.

135. Clarence Blackall, "Henry Vaughan," *AABN* 112 (11 July 1917): 31.

136. William Morgan, *The Almighty Wall: The Architecture of Henry Vaughan* (New York: Architectural History Foundation, 1983), 138.

137. Ibid.

138. Ibid., 21.

139. Charles Slattery, "American Faces," quoted in Morgan, *Almighty Wall,* 187.

140. Sedgwick, *Epistemology,* 55–56.

141. Martin Green, *The Problem of Boston* (New York: W. W. Norton, 1966), 58.

142. Alan Crawford, *C. R. Ashbee: Architect, Designer, and Romantic Socialist* (New Haven: Yale University Press, 1985), 7–14.

143. Ibid., 10.

144. Nicholas, Notebook II, 6. William Augustine Cram felt that one day science would document and explain particularly thought transference and automatic writing.

145. RAC, *My Life,* 7.

146. Crawford, *Ashbee,* 20.

147. Carpenter's name appears in a list of Day's portraits kindly given me by Verna Curtis, Curator of Photography at the Library of Congress. Also on Curtis's list are the following members of Cram's Pinckney Street circle: John C. Abbott, Herman T. Baldwin, Fred Bullard, Alice Brown, Bliss Carman, RAC, BGG, LIG, Richard Hovey, Ingalls Kimball, Arthur Knapp, Francis Watts Lee, Thomas Meteyard, Ethel Reed, Bruce Rogers, Philip Savage, Herbert Small, Herbert Stone, Stephen Townsend, and D. Dawson-Watson. Another Pinckney Street resident who sat for Day was Leonora Piper. For the Whitman Fellowship International and for review of the American edition of *Ioläus* see Jonathan Katz, *Gay/Lesbian Almanac* (New York: Harper and Row, 1983), 697–698 n. 4. I am indebted to Louis Caldarella for directing me to [Reese, William G. Co.] *Catalogue 134: Literature* (New Haven, nd), entry 990. For Goodspeed's see "A List of Books and Engravings Published by Charles E. Goodspeed, 5A Park Street, Boston, Massachusetts" (np, nd), for a copy of which I am also indebted to Caldarella, who has been kind enough to share with me his knowledge of the historical background of Goodspeed's publishing and of correspondence said to exist between Carpenter and Goodspeed in which Day's name arises. Thirteen books are listed in the Goodspeed catalogue, most printed by Updike, including a volume of poems by Santayana's friend Trumbull Stickney, who is discussed in Chapter 5. For *Ioläus,* see Warren Johansson, "Male Friendship," in Wayne R. Dynes, ed., *Encyclopedia of Homosexuality* (New York: Garland, 1990), 146; and Charles Goodspeed, *Yankee Bookseller* (Boston: Houghton Mifflin, 1937), 157–159.

148. Crawford, *Ashbee,* 20.

149. Emmanuel Cooper, *The Sexual Perspective: Homosexuality and Art in the Last Hundred Years in the West* (London: Routledge and Kegan Paul, 1986), xviii.

150. Ibid., 61–62, 23. For FHD's and LIG's involvement with Anne Whitney see Parrish, 135–137.

151. Cooper, *Sexual Perspective,* xviii.

152. Ibid., 28–31. For a more conservative view of Sargent's sexuality, see Stanley Olson, *John Singer Sargent: His Portrait* (New York: St. Martin's Press, 1986). For an approving essay review, nonetheless pointing out the weaknesses in Olson's failure to speculate, see William A. Coles, "New Perspectives on John Singer Sargent," *New England Quarterly* 61 (March 1988): 122–133, which also discusses the attempt to link Sargent to aestheticism/Decadence by Patricia Hills et al., *John Singer Sargent* (New York: Whitney Museum, 1986).

153. Parrish, 55.

154. Nicholas, Notebook II. See also Jussim, 53.

155. RAC, *My Life*, 8.

156. Ibid., 89.

157. John Boyle O'Reilly, "In Bohemia," *In Bohemia* (Boston: Pilot Publishing Co., 1886).

158. RAC, *My Life*, 89.

159. Ibid., 12, 53–54.

160. RAC evaluates his work for Birge in *My Life*, 53. See Robert Judson Clark, *Arts and Crafts Movement in America* (Princeton: Princeton University Press, 1972), 52 (Fig. 66). I have not been able to locate any of RAC's wallpaper designs. Birge is now part of Sunworthy, and the Birge Archives in the Buffalo Historical Society are in closed storage for the foreseeable future. I am grateful to Richard Cheek for help in locating Birge catalogues of the period.

161. Parrish, 84–86.

162. RAC, *My Life*, 54–55.

163. Green, *Warrens*, 160.

2   BLACK SPIRITS AND WHITE

1. Ernest Samuels, *Bernard Berenson: The Making of a Connoisseur* (Cambridge, MA: Harvard University Press, 1979), 58.

2. Joseph Edgar Chamberlin, *The Boston Transcript* (Boston: Houghton Mifflin, 1930), 213.

3. RAC, *My Life*, 9.

4. Ibid., 38.

5. The quotations are from the undated *Transcript* columns RAC pasted into the scrapbook now in C&GC/BPL.

6. RAC, *My Life*, 58.

7. Nicholas, Notebook II, 7.

8. Ibid., 4–7.

9. Walter Muir Whitehill to William Morgan, blind copy to DS-T, letter of 3 February 1970, C&GC/BPL. William Cram was a distinguished naturalist and author.

10. RAC, *My Life*, 55, 57, 62–63.

11. Ibid., 63. For Randall and his work see "Randall, T. Henry," in Henry F. and Elsie R. Whitney, eds., *Biographical Dictionary of American Architects (Deceased)* (Los Angeles: Hennessy and Ingalls, 1970). 496; see also Mark A. Hewett, *The Architect and the American Country House 1890–1940* (New Haven: Yale University Press, 1990), 140. I am grateful to Claire W. Dewart, Librarian of Trinity Church, Boston, and T. Henry Randall's grandniece, for sending me Randall's entry in the St. John's College *Yearbook*

of 1900 and alerting me to the fact that he had married, the details of which (since the Randalls and the Bradhursts were both prominent families) I was consequently able to trace through the New York business directories and social registers of 1899–1907.

12. RAC, *My Life*, 63.

13. Ibid., 55–56.

14. Ibid., 55, 60–61.

15. Ibid., 84.

16. Michael Cox and R. A. Gilbert, eds., "Select Conspectus of Ghost Stories, 1840–1910," *Victorian Ghost Stories: An Oxford Anthology* (Oxford: Oxford University Press, 1991), 496.

17. See Edward Wagenknecht, *The Fireside Book of Ghost Stories* (Indianapolis: Bobbs-Merrill, 1947). Wagenknecht reprinted "No. 252 Rue de M. le Prince." See also Richard Dalby, ed., *The Mammoth Book of Ghost Stories* (New York: Carroll and Graf, 1990), preface. Dalby chose "In Kropfsberg Keep." Another of RAC's horror stories from *Black Spirits and White*, "The Dead Valley," was reprinted in J. C. and B. H. Wolf, eds., *Ghosts, Castles and Victims: Studies in Gothic Terror* (Greenwich, CT: Fawcett, 1974).

18. RAC, *Black Spirits and White* (Chicago: Stone and Kimball, 1895), dedication page.

19. "Mask and signal" as a textual strategy is cited in Paul G. Schalow's introduction to *The Great Mirror of Male Love* (Stanford: Stanford University Press, 1989), his translation of Ihara Saikaku's *Nanshoku kagami* of 1687. Examples cited by Schalow:

> Shakespeare's sonnets, which obscure the gender of the addressee but give clues to their homoerotic reading; Proust's *A la recherche du temps perdu*, in which the gender of certain characters is switched to avoid stigma while revealing the psychological reality of homoerotic relationships (see [J. E.] Rivers, *Proust and the Art of Love . . .*, 107–152); and Mann's *Der Tod in Venedig*, in which homoerotic feelings appear to serve as a metaphor for aestheticism, physical and spiritual decadence, and death.

See also Leo Strauss, *Persecution and the Art of Writing* (Westport, CT: Greenwood Press, 1976). In the other works I have used here, various terms amounting to the same thing are used; for "concealment and revealment" see Richard Ellmann, "Freud and Literary Biography," *a long the riverrun* (New York: Random House, 1990), 257, 265; for "self-declaration" and "self-concealment" see Martin, 197; for "to communicate and to conceal" see Leslie J. Workman, " 'My First Real Tutor': John Ruskin and Charles Eliot Norton," *New England Quarterly* 62 (December 1989): 579.

20. This discussion is drawn from Beckson, 52–55. See also Wayne R. Dynes, "Flower Symbolism" and "Color Symbolism," in Dynes, ed., *Encyclopedia of Homosexuality* (New York: Garland, 1990), 411–412 and 249–250. He cites examples of green as a gay signifier in the United States as late as the 1950s. For Hichens see *The Chap-Book* 2 (15 November 1894): 37. *The Green Carnation* was published in 1894 in the United States by Mitchell Kennerly of New York.

21. For this series see the unpaged announcement bound in the back of *Black Spirits and White*.

22. RAC, *Black Spirits and White*, 33–52.

23. A. E. Housman, "The Laws of God, the Laws of Men," in Stephen Coote, ed.,

The Penguin Book of Homosexual Verse (Harmondsworth, Middlesex: Penguin, 1983), 239.

24. Sigmund Freud, *The Uncanny*, quoted in D. G. Hartwell, *The Color of Evil* (New York: Doherty Assoc., 1987), 6.

25. Hartwell, *Color of Evil*, 9, 8. See also H. P. Lovecraft, *Supernatural Horror in Literature* (New York: Abramson, 1945), 15.

26. Hartwell, *Color of Evil*, 198, 12, 15.

27. Brigid M. Boardman, *Between Heaven and Charing Cross: The Life of Francis Thompson* (New Haven: Yale University Press, 1988), 372.

28. I am grateful to Boardman for establishing for me that Thompson's poem first appeared simultaneously in England and America, in the latter case under Copeland and Day's imprint.

29. Yet another connection will be established if, as I have reason to hope, Gammell's mural cycle is presented by the Gammell trustees to the Boston Public Library.

30. RAC, *My Life*, 58–59.

31. Francis Thompson, "The Hound of Heaven," *Poems by Francis Thompson* (Portland, ME: Mosher, 1911), 54–60.

32. Holbrook Jackson, *The Eighteen Nineties* (New York: Penguin, 1950 ed.) 172.

33. Though see Boardman, *Thompson*, 372.

34. Daniel, 14.

35. See Robert H. Lord et al., *History of the [Roman Catholic] Archdiocese of Boston* (New York: Sheed and Ward, 1944), 407–415, 760–761.

36. Russell Kirk, *Eliot and His Age* (La Salle, IL: Sherwood, Sugden & Co., 1971), 138–139, 144.

37. Peter Ackroyd, *T.S. Eliot: A Life* (New York: Simon and Schuster, 1984), 159. See also 152 (for kneeling worshippers generally).

38. Brooks, *Indian Summer*, 414.

39. Andrew Mead, "The Rector's Column: Sawdust and Incense," *The Beacon* 6 (Michaelmas 1988): 8.

40. Rose Macaulay, *Letters to a Friend 1950–1952*, Constance Babington-Smith, ed. (New York: Atheneum, 1962), 356.

41. Rose Macaulay, *The Towers of Trebizond* (1956; reprint New York: Carroll and Graf, 1989).

42. Ibid., 72, 70.

43. Ibid., 139–140.

44. John Henry Newman, quoted in Kirk, *Eliot*, 138.

45. C. S. Lewis, "Let's Pretend," *Beyond Personality*, chapter title, quoted and discussed in A. N. Wilson, *C. S. Lewis: A Biography* (New York: W. W. Norton, 1990), 124.

46. Macaulay, *Trebizond*, 161–163.

47. Ibid., 274–275.

48. Robert M. Crunden, Introduction to reprint of George Santayana, "A Brief History of My Opinions," in *The Superfluous Men: Conservative Critics of American Culture 1900–1945* (Austin: University of Texas Press, 1977), 3.

49. RAC, *My Life*, 63.

50. Lears, 205.

51. Sigmund Freud, *Formulations on the Two Principles of Mental Functioning*, quoted in Ellen H. Spitz, *Art and Psyche* (New Haven: Yale University Press, 1985), 13.

52. Barbara Meil Hobson and Paul M. Wright, *Boston, A State of Mind: An Exhibition Record* (Boston: Boston Public Library, 1977), 75.

53. Ibid.

54. Edwin D. Mead, "Boston Memories of Fifty Years," *Fifty Years of Boston* (Boston: Boston Tercentenary Committee, 1932), 36.

55. Ibid. For an architectural outgrowth of socialist activity in Boston see V. Rebecca Zurrier, "Visionary in Boston: The Charlesgate as Housing in a Nationalist Utopia," *Architectura* (Band 22/vol. 22): 120–134.

56. Martin Green, *The Problem of Boston* (New York: W. W. Norton, 1966), 134.

57. RAC, *My Life*, 19–21.

58. According to the *Journal of the Proceedings of the 105th Annual Meeting of the Protestant Episcopal church in the Diocese of Massachusetts* (Boston: Damrell and Upham, 1890), 160, the Church of the Carpenter was at 3 Boylston Place (the Tavern Club was at 14). See also Bernard Markwell, *The Anglican Left* (Brooklyn, NY: Carbon, 1991), 109, called to my notice by Albert M. Tannler.

For Bliss, see "William Dwight Porter Bliss," *DAB*, I, 377–378, and Arthur Mann, *Yankee Reformers in an Urban Age* (Cambridge, MA: Harvard University Press, 1954), passim. In *The Dawn*, Edward Carpenter was praised (April 1895: 9); Francis Watts Lee was an editor (July 1891: 1); William Bayard Hale was a contributor (November 1894: 1); Father Frisby of the Advent was another contributor (February 1894: 9); so was his successor, Father Van Allen (November 1894: 1); as was Father, later Bishop, Charles Brent (December 1894: 9).

59. For Scudder, see "Vida Scudder," *DAB*, Supplement V, 616–617. Scudder's friend Florence Converse was the author of a feminist novel with lesbian overtones, *Diana Victrix*, published by Houghton Mifflin in 1897.

60. Lears, 213.

61. Vida Scudder, *Father Huntington* (New York: Dutton, 1940), 129. See also Scudder, *On Journey* (New York: Dutton, 1937).

62. For RAC's resignation see RAC to William Bliss, letter of 4 May 1891, C&GC/BPL. For Father Hall's encouragement of St. Augustine's Mission see *The Episcopal Diocese of Massachusetts 1784–1983*, Mark A. Duffy, ed. (Boston: The Diocese, 1984), 64. For the ordination of Oscar Mitchell, the black priest, see *The Episcopal Diocese*, 669, and *Journal of the Proceedings of the 109th Annual Meeting of the Convention of the Protestant Episcopal Church in the Diocese of Massachusetts* (Boston: Damrell & Upham, 1895), 117.

63. Lears, 201.

64. Oliver Wendell Holmes, quoted from the *Atlantic* in George L. Richardson, *Arthur C.A. Hall* (Boston: Houghton Mifflin, 1932), 36.

65. RAC is recorded as having been confirmed, in *Names of the Confirmed, Bishop of Massachusetts, Easter Day, 1880-Easter Day 1890* (Boston: Archives of the Episcopal Diocese of Massachusetts), at St. John's, Bowdoin Street, on 3 February 1889.

66. RAC, *My Life*, 67–68. There is, however, some confusion in the matter. In 1889 the governor announced that the first prize of $1,500 had been given to Charles Brigham, the second, $1,200, to John L. Faxon, and the third, $900, to Henry S. McKay. No mention was made of RAC, but his submission is one of three preserved in the State House Archives, and in 1894 it was reproduced in *AABN* 31 (March 1894): 43, thus documenting RAC's assertion in his memoirs that he had won second place. Further-

more, it is possible that some of the features of RAC's design may have influenced the building designed by Brigham. See Ann Beha Associates, *The State House: Historic Structure Report* (Boston: Commonwealth of Massachusetts, 1985), i, 79–80, 83.

67. The first letter in the firm's first letter book is dated 19 April 1889; the first entry in the firm's first account book is dated a month later, 16 May. Both books are extant in C&GC/BPL. One of RAC's watercolor perspectives is dated "A.D. 1888," but this was likely added in later years.

68. C. E. Cotting to Cram and Wentworth, letter of 26 February 1891, C&GC/BPL.

69. RAC, *My Life*, 69.

70. Ibid.

71. Ibid., 69–70. See obituary, Charles Wentworth, *Boston Evening Transcript*, 9 February 1897, where he is described as having been consumptive and an invalid since 1894, since which time he had just traveled. He died in Coronado, California, at the age of thirty-six. He and his wife had no children.

72. Wentworth to RAC, letter dated January 1894, C&GC/BPL.

3 THE PRAYER IS GRANITE

1. RAC, "The Last of the Squires," *Convictions and Controversies* (Boston: Marshall Jones, 1935), 80–82.

2. Ibid., 83, 80.

3. Nicholas, Notebook II, 4.

4. RAC, *My Life*, 26.

5. Ibid., 24, 26.

6. RAC, pocket diary, ca. 1881–1886, unpaged, C&GC/BPL.

7. RAC's work in *The Decorator and Furnisher* ran from November 1885 to November 1887; RAC, *My Life*, 53.

8. Ellmann, *Wilde*, 194.

9. Ibid., 328; see Oscar Wilde, *The Soul of Man under Socialism* (London: Arthur L. Humphreys, 1891, 1895). The words "under Socialism" were omitted in the 1895 edition.

10. See Walter Crane, *An Artist's Reminiscences* (New York: Macmillan, 1907), 371.

11. RAC, "On the Use of Brick in Domestic Architecture, Part I: Workmen's Cottages," *The Brickbuilder* 4 (February 1895): 31–33; "On the Use of Brick in Domestic Architecture, Part II: Workmen's Cottages in Cities," ibid. (May 1895): 99–100.

12. Laurence Winship, "Cram" (unpublished typescript of interview notes in C&GC/BPL), 2; RAC, *My Life*, 70–71.

13. Inquiries of the Buffalo Historical Society have established the fact that the designers of the Birge House were Little and Brown; see Little and Brown, Account Books, vol. A.D., in the library of the Society for the Preservation of New England Antiquities: "George K. Birge, Esq., erection of House and Stable at Buffalo, N.Y., 1898." I am grateful to Laura Congdon for locating this residence. The first entry in Cram and Wentworth's account book is a deposit by Birge. The correspondence runs from September 1889 to May 1891, and payments from Birge continue into 1894. That the house was indeed built is documented by George Gates, "Birge Mansion," *Buffalo Evening News* (4 August 1982), 85.

14. St. John's, Williamstown, first arises in a letter of 9 June 1889 from Wentworth to James Ide, who seems, in another letter, 3 July, from Wentworth, clearly more interested

in his house than in the church schemes Wentworth proposes to bring to Ide's inspection.

15. The Ide House is attributed to White in the National Register forms prepared by the local authorities in Williamstown, Massachusetts Historical Commission files, for knowledge of which I am indebted to Judy McDonnough.

16. RAC, "John D. Sedding," *Architectural Review* 1 (14 December 1891): 9.

17. R. N. Shaw to J. Sedding, letter of 5 February 1882, quoted in Andrew Saint, *Richard Norman Shaw* (New Haven: Yale University Press, 1976), 218.

18. Frank Lloyd Wright, *An Autobiography*, quoted in Brendan Gill, *Many Masks: A Life of Frank Lloyd Wright* (New York: Ballantine, 1987), 115.

19. Sketches for the Parker House at 126 Brattle Street are referred to in a letter of 28 September 1889; work began by 7 June 1890. The house next door, at 128, remodeled by Lois Lilley Howe in 1906, is also by RAC (in 1892), but with Goodhue. See Bainbridge Bunting and Robert H. Nylander, *Report Four: Old Cambridge* (Cambridge, MA: MIT Press, 1973), 123–124.

20. The first payment on the Whittemore House was recorded in September 1889, and payments continued to September 1891. I am much indebted to the Old York Historical Society and to Earl Shuttleworth for introducing me to the present owners, Mr. and Mrs. P. J. Stella, to whom all admirers of RAC's work must be grateful for their devoted care of this important house. See also Scott Carlisle to DS-T, letter of 20 October 1979, C&GC/BPL, and "Moonstone," *York County Coast Star* (17 September 1980), 1. (The Whittemore House was also known as Moonstone.) That the family is that of Charles Wentworth's wife can be established in the Boston *Blue Book*s of 1905, 1906, 1908, which record that Mrs. Charles F. Wentworth and Mrs. Sarah E. Whittemore of 21 Carlton Street, Brookline, had a summer residence at York Harbor, Maine. The Boston Athenaeum has a complete run of these *Blue Book*s.

21. The Swan House in London was erected in 1875–1877 and is illustrated in Roger Dixon and Stefan Muthesius, *Victorian Architecture* (New York: Oxford University Press, 1978), 65.

22. The work by Lutyens, *Les Bois des Moutiers*, in Varengeville, France, is illustrated in Lawrence Weaver, *Houses and Gardens by E. L. Lutyens* (London: Century Life, 1914), xxi. For the relevant Ashbee houses on Cheyne Walk, see Alan Crawford, *C. R. Ashbee: Architect, Designer, and Romantic Socialist* (New Haven: Yale University Press, 1985), 239, 242, 246, 256.

23. Saint, *Shaw*, 230.

24. For Little's work on Beacon Street, as originally designed and built, see G. E. Hooper, *Country House* (Garden City, NY: Doubleday, 1904), 102. For Little's other work of the period, see Walter Knight Sturges, "Arthur Little and the Colonial Revival," *Journal of the Society of Architectural Historians* 32 (May 1973): 158.

25. Richard Guy Wilson, "American Arts and Crafts Architecture," in Wendy Kaplan, *"The Art That Is Life"* (Boston: Museum of Fine Arts, 1987), 102.

26. RAC, "A Country House of Moderate Cost," *Ladies' Home Journal* 18 (January 1901): 15. For a discussion of this house see Daniel, 49–51.

27. RAC, *My Life*, 169.

28. RAC, "The Promise of American House Building," *Low Cost Suburban Houses*, Richardson Wright, ed. (New York: Robert M. McBride Co., 1916), 32; see also 37. I am indebted to Robert Twombly for identifying the Wright house and to Kevin Moloney for introducing me to Professor Twombly.

29. Kevin Nute, *Frank Lloyd Wright and Japan* (New York: Van Nostrand Reinhold, 1993), 11–33 passim. Cram's Japanese architecture is noted but hardly its significance, and his major book, *Impressions of Japanese Architecture and the Allied Arts*, is unfairly and inaccurately described as mostly a compilation of photographs. Nute's study of the influence on Wright of the Boston orientalists is, however, otherwise exemplary and invaluable.

30. Daniel, 42–43. Casa Loma was begun after the Ide House. The first Gale entry is on 17 March 1890; in May the house was still in sketches. Payments continued through September 1894.

31. The published sketch of the Fellner House, "The House of Eugene Fellner, on Aspinwall Hill, Brookline, Massachusetts, Messrs. Cram and Wentworth, architects," appears in *AABA* 39 (11 March 1893): 159, Pl. 898. The earlier, initial version is in the Avery Architectural Library, Columbia University. It has been reproduced in James O'Gorman, *On the Boards* (Philadelphia: University of Pennsylvania Press, 1989), 139. The house first appears in RAC's letter books on 31 March 1891.

32. For Deanery Garden and Orchards, see David Dunster, ed., *Edwin Lutyens* (New York: Rizzoli, 1979), 44–45 and 30–31.

33. The Winslow House, 34 Beacon Street, Chestnut Hill (Newton), appears in RAC's office correspondence first on 12 June 1890, when he wrote to set up a date to show the sketches. The Merriam House, 165 Winthrop Road, Brookline, is first noted in the letter books in May 1891; the Hamlin House, 157 Winthrop, first appears in September 1891. A renter of the Hamlin House in the mid-1890s, John A. Baldwin, so liked the house that in 1898 he commissioned another from RAC, which still stands on the corner of Dean Road and Fisher Avenue in Brookline. A splendid house, it has an elegant entrance porch, which, among other detail, betrays Goodhue's presence, though the house's plan particularly is very reminiscent of the earlier Hamlin House. See Leslie Larkin to DS-T, letter of 9 July 1978, C&GC/BPL (she prepared the National Register submissions for these houses). I am grateful to Marc Cooper, the owner of 165 Winthrop, to Sarah Doherty, the owner of 157 Winthrop, to James Avery of 34 Beacon, and to Kathryn Morison of 233 Fisher for allowing me to inspect all these houses that each has so well preserved.

34. Erwin Panofsky, *Meaning in the Visual Arts* (Garden City, NY: Doubleday, 1955), 232.

35. O'Gorman, *On the Boards*, 138–139.

36. The 1890 Boston Architectural Club exhibition was one of two in which the young firm showed its work that year (the other, at the St. Botolph Club, is discussed in Chapter 6). The catalogue of the 1890 BAC exhibition survives in the Boston Public Library. Five entries are credited to Cram and Wentworth: "(105) Church to be built in Berkshire County, Massachusetts; (257) A Frame of Houses; (258) Design for the Cathedral of St. John the Divine, New York; (292) House at York Harbor, Maine; (370) Study for a Berkshire County church."

37. *Boston Sunday Globe* (25 February 1894), 28. I was first alerted to search for such contemporary documentation—no source at all in the firm's records ever having attributed the Grundmann Studios to RAC—by Beverly Brandt's having made such an attribution in her "Essential Link: Boston Architects and the Society of Arts and Crafts," *Tiller* 2, no. 1 (September-October 1983): 27 n. 4. I am indebted to Paul M. Wright for this source. The artists whose studios were in the Grundmann are noted in several sources

from which I have drawn this information: the *Globe* article cited above; the Boston street directories of the 1890s and 1900s; and Trevor J. Fairbrother et al., *The Bostonians: Painters of an Elegant Age 1870–1930* (Boston: Museum of Fine Arts, 1986).

38. *Boston Sunday Globe* (25 February 1894).

39. LIG to RAC, letter of 20 September 1891, C&GC/BPL. LIG's *Nine Sonnets Written at Oxford* was published by Copeland and Day and designed by Goodhue in 1895.

40. *Boston Herald* (12 September 1891).

41. RAC, *My Life*, 71; C. E. Cotting to Cram and Wentworth, letter of 18 April 1891. The lease (14 April 1890) at 2 Park Square kept RAC there until 1 July 1891 at an annual rent of $350; after which the firm moved to Rooms 1109–1111 on the eleventh floor of the Exchange Building. The lease there (3 March 1891) was for five years at a yearly rent of $1,050. Cotting's letter and the leases are all in C&GC/BPL.

42. RAC, "Frank Ferguson," *Pencil Points* 7 (November 1926): 682. RAC states that Ferguson entered the office "shortly after the establishing of the firm of C&W . . . in 1889," and before the advent of BGG in the fall of 1891. (Ferguson became a partner after Wentworth's death in 1897.)

43. RAC, *My Life*, 49.

44. "Competitive Design, House for Seaside Club, Bridgeport, Conn. Set No. I," ink sketch, C&GC/BPL. That for the Odd Fellows temple, Cincinnati, is also an ink sketch, C&GC/BPL. See also letters of 8 July and 19 August 1890, Cram and Wentworth to Mr. C. W. Manning about the Ohio job, from which the drawing in C&GC/BPL, improperly dated "about 1896," may be correctly dated. The medieval (Romanesque) design is shown in "Competitive Design for the Rockingham County Courthouse, Portsmouth, N.H. . . ." in C&GC/BPL. The classical (Colonial Revival) design is shown in a watercolor labeled "Perspective sketch showing alternative treatment, Rockingham County Courthouse . . ." in the Avery Architectural Library, Columbia University.

45. Cram and Wentworth are not listed in the 1888 *Boston Street Directory*. Their first listing is in the 1889 volume, which means the firm was founded between July 1888 and June 1889.

46. Janet Adams Strong, "The Cathedral Church of Saint John the Divine: Design Competitions in the Shadow of H. H. Richardson, 1889–1891," 3 vols. (Ph.D. dissertation, Brown University, 1990), III, 161–172.

47. Though not published until late 1890 (in *AABN* 30 [19 November]: 138, Pl. 779), this church project, as the firm's first letter book documents, arose first in a letter from the firm to James Ide of 9 June 1889, and sketches had been prepared by 13 July, the date of another letter. RAC's watercolor sketch dated "A.D. 1888" (see Chapter 2, n. 67) is of this church, though the date may have been added some years later when Alexander Hoyle annotated the firm's earliest surviving sketches during the slow period of World War II after RAC's death. St. John's Church does, in fact, somewhat resemble RAC's sketch, especially in the tower, evidence that RAC, even if he lost the job, made some impression with his design. No records survive there at all. See B. W. Dennison to DS-T, letter of 10 November 1976, C&GC/BPL. It seems clear that Ide and/or Gale tried to secure the St. John's job for RAC. A letter of 11 March 189[?] reads in part: "The plans and sketches you refer to were not asked for by anyone having any pretence of authority to act for the church; but as I understand were *voluntarily* sent. Last fall, when the building of a church here seemed to be near, your friends here [identified elsewhere in this letter as Gale and Ide] interested themselves in your favor and with the result that in

November last I received from your Mr. Wentworth a letter (not now at hand) asking in effect that so soon as we would be ready for sketches his firm might be advised . . . and I handed that letter to our rector. . . . I cannot think that Messrs Cram and Wentworth . . . ever had the slightest reason to suppose they had been selected as the architects of St. John's Church." The letter, now in C&GC/BPL, is signed "W. B. Clarke."

48. Daniel, 108–109.

49. The Messiah was published in *AABN* 31 (10 January 1891): 30, Pl. 785. Daniel's analysis of all these early church designs is excellent; my discussion draws heavily on her work.

50. The quotation is from R. Clipston Sturgis to RAC, letter of 5 December 1891; in a letter to RAC of 23 April 1892 Sturgis offered to propose Cram and Wentworth. Both letters are in C&GC/BPL.

51. The Advent high altar credence arises in a letter from the firm to Mr. Cabot of 8 March 1890; a year later it was discussed in letters of 7 and 15 May 1891, with contractors whose unexpectedly high estimate forced RAC to omit the pierced work and reduce the size. That this second RAC design was carried out is clear in a letter from the firm of 14 March 1892 to Messrs. Walsh and Hughes accompanying payment for the credence and raising the question of the further cost of an inscription. All these letters are in C&GC/BPL.

52. This was Cram and Wentworth's third church design, the plans for which had already been made by the firm's letter of 16 June 1890 to L. N. Beard, C&GC/BPL. Again, two sets of plans were prepared.

53. William Morgan, *The Almighty Wall: The Architecture of Henry Vaughan* (New York: Architectural History Foundation, 1983), 154.

54. For biographical essays on Oliver and Mary Peabody, see Douglass Shand-Tucci, *All Saints', Ashmont, Dorchester, Boston: A Centennial History of the Parish* (Boston: The Parish of All Saints, 1975), 28–31, 46–50.

55. For the connection between the Peabodys and John Sturgis (a close friend of Charles Grafton's) I am indebted to Margaret Henderson Floyd. The attribution in Charles S. Damrell's *Half Century of Boston Building* (Boston: Louis P. Hager, 1895) of the Oliver Peabody residence at 25 Commonwealth Avenue to Rotch and Tilden—which would support the view that RAC met the Peabodys through that firm—is incorrect. Damrell meant 125, not 25, and the data he gives for 25 will thus be found in Bainbridge Bunting, *Houses of Boston's Bay: An Architectural History, 1840–1917* (Cambridge, MA: Harvard University Press, 1967), to refer to 125. Contemporary street directories list the owner referred to by both Damrell and Bunting as at 125 Commonwealth.

56. For the early history of Children's Hospital and the Peabodys' association with it see Clement A. Smith, "Devoted Women," in *The Children's Hospital of Boston* (Boston: Little, Brown, 1983), 85–104. For the Society of St. Margaret see Chapter 8.

57. RAC, *Church Building* (Boston: Small, Maynard and Co., 1901), 263–264.

58. John Ruskin, *Seven Lamps of Architecture* (1849).

59. A. W. Pugin, *The True Principles of Pointed or Christian Architecture. . . .*, quoted in Phoebe B. Stanton, *The Gothic Revival and American Church Architecture* (Baltimore: Johns Hopkins Press, 1968), 22.

60. For RAC's first explication of his thesis see his *Description of the Proposed Church of All Saints' in Dorchester . . .* (Boston: Elzevir Press, 1892). Copies exist in the Fogg Museum Library, Harvard University, and in C&GC/BPL.

61. Norton to RAC, letter of 20 February 1892, C&GC/BPL.

62. Montgomery Schuyler, "The Works of Cram, Goodhue and Ferguson," *Architectural Record* 29 (January 1911): 4–112.

63. RAC, *Heart of Europe* (New York: Scribner's, 1915), 131–132.

64. Robert Brown, "All Saints' Church . . .," *Architectural Review* 7 (August 1900): 101–104.

65. RAC, "All Saints' Church, Dorchester," *The Churchman* 79 (15 April 1899): 559.

66. Thomas E. Tallmadge, *The Study of American Architecture* (New York: W. W. Norton, 1936), 260; James F. O'Gorman, "Either in Books or Architecture: Bertram Grosvenor Goodhue in the Nineties," *Harvard Library Bulletin* 35 (Spring 1987): 170.

67. RAC, *Church Building*, 9, 270.

68. RAC, "Notre Dame des Eaux," *Black Spirits and White* (Chicago: Stone and Kimball, 1895), 122–123.

69. Bruce Allsop, *The Study of Architectural History* (London: Studio Vista, 1970), 58.

70. Claude Bragdon, "The Gothic Spirit," *Christian Art* 2 (January 1908): 170.

71. For James see Harold Oxbury, *Great Britons* (New York: Oxford University Press, 1985). James was a graduate of Eton and King's College, Cambridge, a biblical scholar, and medievalist.

72. H. P. Lovecraft, *Supernatural Horror in Literature* (New York: Abramson, 1945), 72.

73. Kathryn Wheeler-Smith, "Alice Brown: Triumph and Tragedy in Tiverton's Wonderland" (Harvard Extension MLA Thesis, 1991), 6, 84.

74. See Mary Cram Nicholas to DS-T, letter of 17 February 1977, C&GC/BPL, which reads in part: "[RAC's] mother, Sarah Elizabeth Blake Cram, the highly intellectual daughter of 'Squire Blake of Kensington,'. . . was a much more practical pragmatic person than her idealist husband; it was hard for her to forgive him for giving up, for conviction, his ministry, pecuniary rewards (such as they were) and the fine reputation he was gaining, to retire with three children and wife to a financially *UN*-affluent life."

75. Wheeler-Smith, "Alice Brown," 42.

76. Frederick Bligh Bond, *Hill of Vision* (Boston: Marshall Jones, 1919).

77. Edith Wharton, *Ethan Frome* (New York: Scribner's, 1911, 1922), Introduction, vi.

78. Henry Adams, *Mont-Saint-Michel and Chartres* (Sentry Edition, Boston: Houghton Mifflin, 1963), 2, 30.

79. Tallmadge, *American Architecture*, 260. Similarly, Henry-Russell Hitchcock notes in his *Architecture, Nineteenth and Twentieth Centuries* (Harmondsworth, Middlesex: Penguin, 1958), 400, that All Saints', Ashmont, is of all RAC's works "the least anachronistic."

80. I refer here to All Saints's overall exterior design; the tower, west porch, and particularly the south porch of 1893–1894 show BGG's influence.

4 THE DESIRE AND PURSUIT OF THE WHOLE

1. Plato, *Symposium*, Seth Bernardete, trans., *The Dialogues of Plato*, Introduction by Erich Segal (London: Bantam, 1986), 254.

2. Evelyn Waugh, *Brideshead Revisited* (Boston: Little, Brown, 1944), 86.

3. Richard Oliver, *Bertram Grosvenor Goodhue* (New York: Architectural History Foundation/MIT Press, 1983), 11–12. BGG's brother Harry began as a student in the Boston Art Students Association and as an apprentice at the Phipps stained-glass firm in 1892, thus surfacing in Boston at about the same time as BGG, just after the death of their father, Charles W. Goodhue, in 1891. BGG is listed in the Cambridge street directories as boarding at 40 Russell Street in 1893, along with his mother, who is listed as the owner. By 1895 mother and son had moved to 7 Buckingham Place, where Harry also is listed. Mrs. Goodhue was still resident there in 1906, a year before her death.

4. See Oliver, *Goodhue*, 1–11.

5. RAC, *My Life*, 76.

6. See *Bertram Grosvenor Goodhue: Architect and Master of Many Arts*, Charles H. Whitaker, ed. (New York: American Institute of Architects Press, 1925), 14. A letter of 18 May 1891 from the firm (the first) to BGG notes an expected meeting, the fact of which is attested to by a further letter of 24 June 1891. From RAC to BGG, this second letter, however, reneges on whatever agreement had been made and suggests that BGG come ahead on an informal basis until the fall, when more permanent arrangements could be considered. One senses a problem not only with jobs in process but also money in hand, and perhaps also a disagreement between RAC and Wentworth, who was cool to BGG in some respects. Although he noted he began as "head draughtsman," presumably it was BGG who provided Montgomery Schuyler (in his "The Works of Cram, Goodhue and Ferguson," *Architectural Record* 29 [January 1911]: 4) with the information there listed, under "Goodhue, Bertram Grosvenor," that in "Nov. 1891 [he] became partner Cram and Wentworth" and that BGG was codesigner of All Saints', Ashmont. But whereas twenty years later BGG might have forgotten the exact month he became a partner, he was scarcely likely ever to have forgotten whether he joined Cram and Wentworth as a draftsman or as a partner (with Wentworth and RAC). And as to being codesigner of All Saints', BGG *was*; for the tower and west and south porches, all erected in 1894, were definitely influenced by him. The only clear documentation contradicts BGG, but hardly very strenuously. It was in January 1892 that he began to sign for the firm under its new name.

In my *Centennial History* of All Saints', Ashmont, I believe I misread the date in BGG's signature on the All Saints' sketches as "89" (i.e., 1889), when it is undoubtedly 1891; the two numeral ones seemed to me previously to be an apostrophe and a smudge. Thus I wrongly identified BGG as a draftsman of RAC's in 1889. See Douglass Shand Tucci, *All Saints', Ashmont, Dorchester, Boston: A Centennial History of the Parish* (Boston: Parish of All Saints', 1975), 19.

7. John Doran to DS-T, letter of 18 November 1975, C&GC/BPL. The text reads in part: there was "no question in my mind that . . . 'All Saints' Church, Dorchester, Mass., Cram, Wentworth and Goodhue . . . ' is by Mr. Cram. However, the foreground and particularly the figures are certainly not by Mr. Cram. Probably they are by Goodhue. Their characteristic techniques are very clear; Cram, for instance, worked over watercolors more than most, while Goodhue's work was more direct."

8. Vestry Minutes, 20 July 1891, All Saints', Ashmont, Archives.

9. See note 6, above. See also *All Saints' Chronicle* 48 (November 1891): 6. In his *Architecture Since 1780* (Cambridge, MA: MIT Press, 1969), Marcus Whiffen, though he correctly identifies All Saints', Ashmont, as "the building whose place in the history of the late [American] Gothic Revival corresponds to that of [McKim, Mead and White's]

Villard Houses in the Second [American] Renaissance Revival," goes on to speculate about the design attribution, suggesting that All Saints's "architects were nominally Cram and Wentworth. However, a talented young draftsman who had joined the office two years before worked on the design, which thus became the first joint work of [RAC and BGG] . . . partners from 1895 until 1913." Though it is interesting that Whiffen is the only scholar to note that the accepted design was by Cram and Wentworth, before construction began BGG's name was added to the credit line invariably used in all contemporary published references after he became a full partner in January 1892.

10. Daniel, 145.

11. RAC, *My Life*, 78–79.

12. Oliver, *Goodhue*, 10.

13. Janet Adams Strong, "The Cathedral Church of Saint John the Divine and New York: Design Competitions in the Shadow of H. H. Richardson, 1889–1891," 3 vols. (Ph.D. dissertation, Brown University, 1990), II, 211–213.

14. James F. O'Gorman, "Either in Books or Architecture: Bertram Grosvenor Goodhue in the Nineties," *Harvard Library Bulletin* 35 (Spring 1987): 170.

15. RAC, *My Life*, 76, 77–78.

16. Charles Maginnis, "Bertram Grosvenor Goodhue," *The Brochure Series* (Boston, 1897), III, 123.

17. RAC, "John D. Sedding," *Architectural Review* 1 (14 December 1891): 9–11.

18. RAC, "The Religious Aspect of Architecture," *Church Notes* 2 (Boston: Church of the Advent, February 1892): 1.

19. Oliver, *Goodhue*, 7.

20. LIG to FHD, letter of 20 November 1891, C&GC/BPL.

21. RAC, *My Life*, 76–77.

22. Ibid., 17.

23. Gelett Burgess, "The Bohemians of Boston," *Enfant Terrible!* 1 (April 1898) [unpaged].

24. The following quotations by Burgess are from his "Where Is Bohemia?" in *The Romance of the Commonplace* (San Francisco: P. Elder and M. Shepard, 1902), 128–132.

25. See Mark Lilly, *Gay Men's Literature in the Twentieth Century* (New York: New York University Press, 1993), 59, 223 n. 3; Byrne R. S. Fone, "This Other Eden: Arcadia and the Homosexual Imagination," *Journal of Homosexuality* (1983), 13–34. For a wider discussion see Wayne R. Dynes, "Arcadia," in Dynes, ed., *Encyclopedia of Homosexuality* (New York: Garland, 1990), 72–73. For Day's summer colony see Patricia G. Berman, "Summer Camp: F. Holland Day and His 'Classical' Models," unpublished ms. kindly lent by the author. For Bliss Carman see his *Pipes of Pan* (written 1894; Toronto: Ryerson Press, 1942), 4, 11.

26. Beckson, 199.

27. Rose Nichols, quoted in Nicholas, Notebook II.

28. For a physical description of RAC, see George Allen, "Cram — The Yankee Medievalist," *Architectural Forum* 55 (July 1931): 79–80. Then sixty-seven, RAC, Allen thought, looked fifty. (This article is in other respects so error-prone as to be by itself unreliable.) For "well-turned limbs" see Nicholas, *Notes*.

29. BGG, *Mexican Memories* (New York: George M. Allen & Co., 1892), 128.

30. RAC, "Partnership," in Whitaker, ed., *Goodhue*, 29.

31. Ibid., 30.

32. RAC, *My Life*, 75.

33. RAC, "Partnership," 30.

34. Michel Foucault, Introduction, *A History of Sexuality* (New York: Pantheon, 1978), I, 27.

35. Beckson, 53–54.

36. John Boswell, *Christianity, Social Tolerance, and Homosexuality: Gay People in Western Europe from the Beginning of the Christian Era to the Fourteenth Century* (Chicago: University of Chicago Press, 1980), 6.

37. Ibid., 192.

38. Brendan Gill, *Many Masks: A Life of Frank Lloyd Wright* (New York: Ballantine, 1987), 99. See also 100–101.

39. Helen Howe, *The Gentle Americans* (New York: Harper and Row, 1965), 140. See also Fred Kaplan, *Henry James* (New York: Morrow, 1991), 515, 538.

40. Kaplan, *James*, 515, 475, 453–454.

41. Gay, *Education*, 132.

42. For Michel Foucault's view, see Sedgwick, *Epistemology*, 83.

43. George Chauncey, Martin Duberman, Martha Vicinus, Introduction, *Hidden from History: Reclaiming the Gay and Lesbian Past*, Martin Duberman, Martha Vicinus, and George Chauncey, Jr., eds. (New York: New American Library, Penguin Books, 1989), 9.

44. John Boswell, "Revolutions, Universals, and Sexual Categories," *Hidden from History*, 35.

45. A. N. Wilson, *C. S. Lewis: A Biography* (New York: W. W. Norton, 1990), xvi.

46. I am indebted to Rev. George Hillman for this quote from his friend Rev. John Moser, ca. 1980.

47. Duberman et al., Introduction, *Hidden from History*, 7.

48. Ellmann, *Wilde*, 471.

49. Sedgwick, *Epistemology*, 49.

50. Gay, *Tender Passion*, 227.

51. Michel Foucault, quoted in David F. Greenberg, *The Construction of Homosexuality* (Chicago: University of Chicago Press, 1988), 487.

52. Don Browning, "Rethinking Homosexuality," *The Christian Century* (11 October 1989): 11. For a good general review of the latest research see Chandler Burr, "Homosexuality and Biology," *The Atlantic* 271 (March 1993): 47–65.

53. Leon Edel, *Henry James: A Life* (New York: Harper and Row, 1985), 497–498.

54. Wentworth to RAC, letter of l May 1895, C&GC/BPL.

55. Karl Miller, *Doubles: Studies in Literary History* (London: Oxford University Press, 1967), 241. See also, for example, Alice Brown's description of Merrymount (Pinckney) Street in Chapter 1. For further discussion of "queer," "nervous," etc., particularly in the works of Oscar Wilde, see Sedgwick, *Epistemology*, 174.

56. Miller, *Doubles*, 241.

57. Elaine Showalter, *Sexual Anarchy: Gender and Culture at the Fin-de-Siècle* (New York: Penguin, 1990), 111–112. For an example in E. P. Warren's life, see Martin Green, *The Mount Vernon Street Warrens* (New York: Scribner's, 1989), 40, where Warren is described as "nervous" as a child.

58. RAC, "No. 252 Rue M. le Prince," *Black Spirits and White* (Chicago: Stone and Kimball, 1895), 3–27.

59. Edward Wagenknecht, Introduction to Part II, *The Fireside Book of Ghost Stories* (Indianapolis: Bobbs-Merrill, 1947), 17–18.

60. Harrison G. Rhodes of Stone and Kimball to RAC, letter of 24 June 1895, C&GC/BPL. Cram's royalty on the book, interestingly, was 10 percent.

61. H. P. Lovecraft, *Supernatural Horror in Literature* (New York: Abramson, 1945), 15.

62. Philip S. Keane, SS, *Sexual Morality: A Catholic Perspective* (New York: Paulist Press, 1977), 12–13.

63. Richard Ellmann, "Freud and Literary Biography," *a long the riverrun* (New York: Random House, 1990), 265–266.

64. Stuart Sutherland, "Evolution Between the Ears," review of Michael Gazzaniga, *Nature's Mind*, in *The New York Times Book Review* (1 March 1993), 16.

65. Robert Hopcke, *Jung, Jungians & Homosexuality* (Boston: Shambhala, 1991), 13.

66. Lears, 208.

67. A. L. Rowse, *Homosexuals in History: Ambivalence in Society, Literature, and the Arts* (New York: Macmillan, 1977), 21–22.

68. Ibid., xi, 13, 114–115, 33, 49.

69. Ibid., 337.

70. Lears, 203.

71. Peter Ackroyd, *T. S. Eliot: A Life* (New York: Simon and Schuster, 1984), 93.

72. RAC, pocket diary, ca. 1881–1886, C&GC/BPL.

73. Greenberg, *Homosexuality*, 203.

74. Ibid., 204, 295.

75. John Addington Symonds, *A Problem in Greek Ethics* (Mew York: Arno, 1975). Symonds's essay was first published privately in 1883. Eight years later he published *A Problem in Modern Ethics*.

76. Boswell, *Christianity*, 27.

77. Humphrey Carpenter, *W. H. Auden: A Biography* (Boston: Houghton Mifflin, 1981), 49.

78. Paul Delany, *The Neo-Pagans: Rupert Brooke and the Ordeal of Youth* (New York: Macmillan, 1987), 43.

79. Boswell, *Christianity*, 42.

80. Martin, 116, 122.

81. Quoted in John McCormick, *George Santayana* (New York: Paragon, 1987), 257.

82. Christine Downing, *Myths and Mysteries of Same-Sex Love* (New York: Continuum, 1991), 129.

83. Ibid., 120.

84. Gay, *Tender Passion*, 47.

85. Downing, *Myths*, 266–269.

86. Maynard Solomon, "Franz Schubert and the Peacocks of Benvenuto Cellini," *Nineteenth-Century Music* 12 (Spring 1989): 202.

87. Jeffrey Richards, "Manly Love and Victorian Society," *Manliness and Morality*, J. A. Mangan and James Walvin, eds. (New York: St. Martin's Press, 1987), 92–122.

88. Stephen Coote, Introduction, *The Penguin Book of Homosexual Verse* (Harmondsworth, Middlesex: Penguin, 1983).

89. Thomas Yingling, *Hart Crane and the Homosexual Text* (Chicago: University of Chicago Press, 1990), 88.

90. C. S. Lewis, *The Allegory of Love* (London: Oxford Unversity Press, 1936), 10.

91. Richards, "Manly Love," 116.

92. Ibid., 108.

93. Edward Rothenstein, "Was Schubert Gay? If He Was, So What?" *New York Times* (4 February 1992).

94. Martin, 112.

95. See Emmanuel Cooper, *The Sexual Perspective: Homosexuality and Art in the Last Hundred Years in the West* (London: Routledge and Kegan Paul, 1986), 39–43.

96. C. S. Lewis, *The Four Loves* (New York: Harcourt Brace Jovanovich, 1960), 91.

97. Ernest Samuels, *Bernard Berenson: The Making of a Connoisseur* (Cambridge, MA: Harvard University Press, 1979), I, 65.

98. Patricia Otoole, *The Five of Hearts: An Intimate Portrait of Henry James and His Friends 1880–1918* (New York: Crown, 1990), 200.

5 THE BELLS OF MY DESIRE

1. See Helen Howe, *The Gentle Americans* (New York: Harper and Row, 1965), 83–84; Mark A. De Wolfe Howe, *Boston: The Place and the People* (New York: Macmillan, 1903), ch. VII, "The Boston Religion," 190–221.

2. E. M. Forster, *Maurice* (New York: W. W. Norton, 1971), 251.

3. William Morgan, *The Almighty Wall: Henry Vaughan* (New York: Architectural History Foundation, 1983), 168 n. 15.

4. Quoted by William Flint, Jr., in MS. history of St. Paul's School Chapel (1933), 3, quoted in Morgan, *Almighty Wall*, 177 n. 4.

5. John Betjeman, *Summoned by Bells* (London: John Murray, 1960), 72.

6. Jonathan Gathorne-Hardy, *The Old School Tie* (New York: Viking, 1977), 166.

7. William Lawrence, "Henry Vaughan," quoted in Morgan, *Almighty Wall*, 178 n. 9.

8. Ann Miner Daniel, "Ralph Adams Cram's Phillips Church, Exeter, New Hampshire," *SECAC Review* (Spring 1980): 217.

9. Gathorne-Hardy, *Old School Tie*, 164–165. See also Beckson, 196.

10. Evelyn Waugh, *A Little Learning* (Boston: Little, Brown, 1964), 160. "Most schoolmasters," wrote Waugh, ". . . are homosexual" (p. 164). See also Lawrence James, *The Golden Warrior* (New York: Paragon House, 1993), 167.

11. Gay, *Tender Passion*, 212; the discussion about Dodd, the student, is on 206–212.

12. John Boswell, *Christianity, Social Tolerance, and Homosexuality: Gay People in Western Europe from the Beginning of the Christian Era to the Fourteenth Century* (Chicago: University of Chicago Press, 1980), 25.

13. Fred Kaplan, *Henry James* (New York: Morrow, 1992), 406. For the relationship of Meteyard and Fullerton, who were classmates at Harvard, see Nicholas Kilmer, *Thomas Buford Meteyard* (New York: Berry-Hill Galleries, 1989), 20, 44.

14. Quoted in Beckson, 202.

15. Ezra Pound, *Pavannes and Divisions* (New York: Knopf, 1918), 46.

16. Ellmann, *Wilde*, 182–183.

17. Xavier Mayne (pseud.; Edward Stevenson), *The Intersexes*, quoted in Jonathan Katz, *Gay/Lesbian Almanac* (New York: Harper and Row, 1983), 329.

18. George Santayana, *The Backgrounds of My Life*, vol. I of *Persons and Places* (New York: Scribner's, 1944–1953), 194.

19. Charles M. Flandrau, *Harvard Episodes* (Boston: Copeland and Day, 1897), 205.

20. George Santayana, *The Middle Span*, vol. II of *Persons and Places*, 29. For the overall Harvard scene (and somewhat the Groton one, too), see also 98–111; and in vol. I, 186–202, 224–237.

21. Flandrau, *Harvard Episodes*, 73, 75, 61.

22. John McCormick, *George Santayana* (New York: Paragon, 1987), 85.

23. Ibid., 103.

24. Van Wyck Brooks, *An Autobiography* (New York: E. P. Dutton, 1965), 102.

25. There is no satisfactory source for Pierre de Chaignon La Rose, one of several instructors (another was Charles Townsend Copeland, the legendary "Copey of Harvard") who taught English A (Rhetoric and English Composition), for which see Holly B. Stevens, *Souvenirs and Prophecies* (New York: Knopf, 1977), 17, 68–70. See also Harvard College Class of 1895 Fiftieth Anniversary Report, 538–540; a pasted-up newspaper obituary (*Boston Globe*, 22 February 1941) under La Rose in the Artists File at the Fine Arts (Research) Department, BPL; Bainbridge Bunting and Margaret Henderson Floyd, *Harvard: An Architectural History* (Cambridge, MA: Harvard University Press, 1985), 43, 290 n. 14; Bainbridge Bunting and Robert H. Nylander, *Report Four: Old Cambridge* (Cambridge, MA: MIT Press, 1973), 156; Stevens, *Souvenirs*, 82–83; Lincoln Kirstein, *Mosaic* (New York: Farrar, Straus, and Giroux, 1994), 86.

As late as 1925 Santayana was still corresponding with La Rose, whose work as a book designer Santayana took very seriously in a letter to La Rose of 19 March of that year, reproduced in Daniel Cory, ed., *The Letters of George Santayana* (New York: Scribner's, 1955), 220–222.

26. Pierre La Rose, "The Signet," *Harvard Graduates Magazine* 10 (June 1902): 513–517. La Rose clearly refers to a remodeling of the entire building by Cram, Goodhue and Ferguson, not merely to the new exterior decor by BGG.

27. See *A Book of Architectural and Decorative Drawings by Bertram Grosvenor Goodhue* (New York: Architectural Book Publishing Co., 1914) for these and many others of BGG's bookplate designs.

28. F. G. Hall et al., *Harvard Celebrities* (Cambridge, MA: Harvard University Press, 1901), 24.

29. Daniel Gregory Mason, "At Harvard in the Nineties," *New England Quarterly* 9 (March 1936): 44, 45, 43, 47, 58, 46. For the reference to theatricals see Stevenson, *Intersexes*, quoted in Katz, *Gay/Lesbian Almanac*, 329.

30. Mason, "At Harvard," 43–44, 48.

31. Brooks, *Autobiography*, 107.

32. Milton Bates, *Wallace Stevens: A Mythology of Self* (Berkeley: University of California Press, 1985), 21. Santayana, in his *Middle Span*, 103, tells the tale a bit differently but substantially confirms it.

33. See Brian Pronger, *The Arena of Masculinity: Sports, Homosexuality and the Meaning of Sex* (New York: St. Martin's, 1990).

34. Emmanuel Cooper, *The Sexual Perspective: Homosexuality and Art in the Last Hundred Years in the West* (London: Routledge & Kegan Paul, 1986), 10.

35. Quoted in Robert Hopcke, *Jung, Jungians & Homosexuality* (Boston: Shambhala, 1991), 27.

36. Forster, *Maurice*, 151.

37. McCormick, *Santayana*, 124.

38. Boswell, *Christianity*, 117. See also Boswell, *Same-Sex Unions in Pre-Modern Europe* (New York: Villard, 1994).

39. Reay Tannahill, *Sex in History* (New York: Scarborough House, 1992), 328.

40. Sedgwick, *Epistemology*, 140.

41. Malcolm Yorke, *Eric Gill* (London: Constable, 1981), 99, 102. The entire chapter, "The excess of amorous nature fertilizes the spiritual field," 99–131, is of interest.

42. Martin S. Bergman, *The Anatomy of Loving* (New York: Fawcett, 1987), 97.

43. Cooper, *Sexual Perspective*, 2.

44. Paul E. Dinter, "Celibacy and Its Discontents," *New York Times* (6 May 1993).

45. Peter Gomes, "Homophobic? Read Your Bible," *New York Times* (17 August 1992).

46. Vern L. Bullough, "Christianity," in Wayne R. Dynes, ed., *Encyclopedia of Homosexuality* (New York: Garland, 1990), 224.

47. George Chauncey, Jr., "Christian Brotherhood or Sexual Perversion?" *Hidden from History: Reclaiming the Gay and Lesbian Past*, Martin Duberman, Martha Vicinus, and George Chauncey, Jr., eds. (New York: New American Library, Penguin Books, 1989), 310–311.

48. Robert Cheney Smith, SSJE, *The Shrine on Bowdoin Street* (Boston: Society of St. John the Evangelist, 1958), 39. For the roles of Shattuck and Burnett at the Advent see John T. Maltzberger, *The Church of the Advent: Early Years* (Boston: Parish of the Advent, 1986), 29–31, 71.

49. See James C. Knox, *Henry Augustus Coit* (New York: Longmans, Green, 1915).

50. John Betjeman, "Holy Trinity, Sloane Street," *Collected Poems* (Boston: Houghton Mifflin, 1971), 59–60.

51. [John F. Bloxam], "The Priest and the Acolyte," *Chameleon* 1, no. 1 (December 1894).

52. Ihara Saikaku, *The Great Mirror of Male Love*, trans. Paul G. Schalow (Stanford: Stanford University Press, 1989), 7; Gay, *Tender Passion*, 236.

53. John Shelton Reed, "'A Female Movement': The Feminization of Nineteenth-Century Anglo-Catholicism," *Anglican and Episcopal History* 57 (June 1988): 200.

54. Ibid., 230.

55. Pusey to Arthur Stanton, in *Arthur Stanton: A Memoir*, quoted in Reed, "Feminization," 236; Bernard Markwell, *The Anglican Left* (Brooklyn, NY: Carbon, 1991), 32–33.

56. Reed, "Feminization," 218.

57. Quoted in Gay, *Tender Passion*, 236.

58. Gay, *Tender Passion*, 238.

59. Hilliard, 181–210.

60. Martin Green, *The Mount Vernon Street Warrens* (New York: Scribner's, 1989), 49.

61. Hilliard, 164.

62. Eve Kosofsky Sedgwick, *Between Men* (New York: Columbia University Press, 1985), 93.

63. See Chapter 8.

64. Catalogue card file of Gardner's library, GMA. See also Adam D. McCoy, *Holy Cross* (Wilton, CT: Morehouse-Barlow, 1987).

65. Robert Speaight, *Eric Gill* (New York: P. J. Kennedy & Sons, 1966), 99–100.

66. Hilliard, 207.

67. Edmund White, *States of Desire: Travels in Gay America* (New York: Penguin, 1980), 62.

68. Basil Cardinal Hume, OSB, *Searching for God* (New York: The Paulist Press, 1977), 49–50.

69. Hilliard, 206–207.

70. Glenn Johnson, "Press On the Kingdom," unpublished ms. ca. 1988, excerpts of which appeared in the Michaelmas 1988 number of *The Beacon* (Boston: Church of the Advent).

71. Winslow A. Erving, Foreword, in Charles Grafton, *A Journey Godward* (London: Mowbray, 1910), 18.

72. A.C.A. Hall, *Catholic, not Protestant, nor Roman Catholic* (New York: James Pott & Co., 1887), 48.

73. Beckson, 203; cf. 49.

74. George Lynde Richardson, *Arthur C.A. Hall* (Boston: Houghton Mifflin, 1932), 24, 32–39, 41; "Arthur C. Hall," *DAB*, IV, 117.

75. A.C.A. Hall, *Self-Discipline* (New York: James Pott & Co., 1896), 25.

76. A.C.A. Hall, *Christ's Temptations and Ours* (New York: Longmans, Green, 1897), 17.

77. Richardson, *Hall*, 5.

78. Ibid., 39, 12.

79. Hall, *Self-Discipline*, 26–27.

80. Ibid., 71.

81. Ibid., 12, 23.

82. A.C.A. Hall, *Christian Friendship* (Boston: Society of St. John the Evangelist, 1886; no. 3 of a series of papers), 88.

83. Boswell, *Christianity*, 215, 218–220.

84. Hall, *Christian Friendship*, 11.

85. Ibid., 14–15.

86. Ibid., 12–13.

87. Hall, *Self-Discipline*, 72–73.

88. A.C.A. Hall, *The Hidden Life of the Heart: Thoughts from the Writings of Father A.C.A. Hall, late of St. John the Evangelist*, ed. A.M.D. (Boston: Joseph George Cupples/Back Bay Bookstore, 1892), 67, 16.

89. Hall, *Christian Friendship*, 4, 7. Hall cites John 13:23.

90. Boswell, *Christianity*, 225. See also 159–160, 187–189.

91. Ibid., 225.

92. Hall cites the Revised Version of 1881–1885.

93. Hall, *Christian Friendship*, 11. Hall himself uses the phrase "Friendship is the union of two souls" (12); he also calls it "a kind of covenant" (8).

94. Alexander Zabriskie, *Bishop Brent* (Philadelphia: Westminster Press, 1948), 28.

95. Richardson, *Hall*, 14; Richardson quotes Hall as saying Brent was one of two men who had "come closest to him in confidence and affection."

96. Zabriskie, *Brent*, 23.

97. "Charles Henry Brent," *DAB*, XI, Supplement I, 115–116; Zabriskie, *Brent*, 41.

98. Zabriskie, *Brent*, 199.

99. Ibid.

100. Leo XIII, *Testem benevolentiae*, quoted in Donna Merwick, *Boston Priests* (Cambridge, MA: Harvard University Press, 1973), 151, 154.

101. Merwick, *Boston Priests*, 162–164.

102. Ibid., 159, 162.

103. Quoted, ibid., 158.

104. Ibid., 165.

105. Jurgen Liias, "Sexually dysfunctional society does not need psychobabble," *Episcopal Times* (Summer 1990), 16.

106. Bergman, *Anatomy of Loving*, 77.

107. Paglia, 524.

108. Ibid., 515, 516, 525.

109. Ibid., 389.

110. RAC, "The White Villa," *Black Spirits and White* (Chicago: Stone and Kimball, 1895), 55–80.

111. See, for example, Ellmann, *Wilde*, 59.

112. John W. Crowley, Editor's Introduction, in Roger Austen, *Genteel Pagan* (Amherst: University of Massachusetts Press, 1991), xxxiii.

113. Martin, 135.

114. Ellmann, *Wilde*, 76.

115. Martin, 114.

6 THE FIGURE IN THE CARPET

1. Justin Kaplan, *Walt Whitman: A Life* (New York: Simon and Schuster, 1980), 248.

2. Ibid., 241, 252, 247.

3. Ibid., 247–249. It was the overt sexuality of "The Children of Adam" section that sparked the dialogue between the two men.

A much larger issue, however, bridges both the "Calamus" poems about "manly love" and "The Children of Adam" poems about "woman love." Each group of poems, both of which appeared for the first time in the 1860 edition of *Leaves of Grass*, was "a daring and original celebration of the drive of sex, not only the creative instinct, but the whole appetite for the context of creation," according to Harold W. Blodgett and Sculley Bradley's *Leaves of Grass, Comprehensive Readers Edition* (New York: New York University Press, 1965), 91. In the same work, moreover, they note of Whitman and Emerson's ongoing dialogue how forthright the former had been, calling his "Letter to Ralph Waldo Emerson" of 1856 "the best statement of [Whitman's] demand for an avowed, empowered, unabashed development of sex" (730–731). The dialogue between the two men on Boston Common could hardly have helped being about *both* groups of poems, however easier it may have been, perhaps, for either of the participants to focus on the "Children of Adam" group.

4. Martin, 34–35.

5. Kaplan, *Walt Whitman*, 249.

6. Gertrude Stein, "Miss Furr and Miss Skeene," *Geography and Plays* (Boston: Four Seas Co., 1922), 17–22; reprinted in *Vanity Fair* (July 1923). See also James R. Mellow,

Charmed Circle: Gertrude Stein and Company (New York: Praeger, 1974), 131, 133–134, and Richard Bridgman, *Gertrude Stein in Pieces* (New York: Oxford University Press, 1970), 94–96, 366. For "gay" see Jonathan Katz, *Gay/Lesbian Almanac* (New York: Harper and Row, 1983), 405, where he notes instances as far back as 1868 of the word's possible use in a homosexual connection.

7. Xavier Mayne (pseud.; Edward Stevenson), *The Intersexes*, quoted in Katz, *Gay/Lesbian Almanac*, 405, 330. George Chauncey, *Gay New York* (New York: Harper Collins, 1994).

8. See Chapter 5, note 93. For Revere Pottery, see that file, BPL Fine Arts Dept.

9. Magnus Hirschfeld, "Homosexuality," quoted in Jonathan Katz, *Gay American History* (rev. ed. New York: Penguin, 1992), 50. This report appears to have first surfaced in Berlin Scientific-Humanitarian Committee, *Monatsberichte* (1907).

10. Antonio A. Giarraputo and William A. Percy, "Boston," in Wayne R. Dynes, ed., *Encyclopedia of Homosexuality* (New York: Garland, 1990), 158. They are also quoting from the *Monatsberichte* of 1907 cited in note 9.

11. Scientific-Humanitarian Committee, *Monthly Reports* 1907, quoted in Katz, *Gay American History*, 382–383.

12. On Bohemian cafés as the ancestors of gay bars see Wayne R. Dynes, "Bohemianism," in Dynes, ed., *Encyclopedia of Homosexuality*, 155. The Pen and Pencil was recalled by Prescott Townsend to a mutual friend of his and this author's. See also Walter Muir Whitehill, *The Neighborhood of the Tavern Club* (Boston: Proceedings of the Bostonian Society, 1971), although it does not explicitly discuss the matter.

13. See Alexander Williams, *A Social History of the Greater Boston Clubs* (Barre, VT: Barre Publishing Co., 1970), 39, and Mark A. De Wolfe Howe, *A Partial (and Not Impartial) Semi-Centennial History of the Tavern Club* (Boston: Tavern Club, 1934), 3, 23.

14. Edward Bacon, *Bacon's Dictionary of Boston* (Boston: Houghton Mifflin, 1886). The fees cited are noted in the entries for the respective clubs: Algonquin, 7; Papyrus, 300; St. Botolph, 354; Somerset, 372–373; Union, 416–417.

15. Elaine Showalter, *Sexual Anarchy: Gender and Culture at the Fin-de-Siècle* (New York: Penguin, 1990), 12–13, 107.

16. Quoted in Katz, *Gay/Lesbian Almanac*, 329.

17. Albert Parry, *Garrets and Pretenders: A History of Bohemianism in America* (reprint New York: Dover, 1960), 138. The original edition was published in 1933.

18. Quoted in Howe, *Tavern Club*, 8–9.

19. Ibid., 24, 23, 14–15.

20. R. H. Ives Gammell, "The Paintings in the Tavern Club," in Edward Weeks, *The Tavern at Seventy-Five* (Boston: Tavern Club, 1959), 144. See also Gammell, *The Boston Painters 1900–1930*, Elizabeth Ives Hunter, ed. (Orleans, MA: Parnassus, 1986), 17–20.

21. See Secretaries' Reports, Archives of the St. Botolph Club, Massachusetts Historical Society. I am grateful to John Brandt for directing me to this source. See also Howe, *Tavern Club*, 43, 84, 115; Thomas Russell Sullivan, *Passages from the Journal of Thomas Russell Sullivan* (Boston: Houghton Mifflin, 1917); Louise Hall Tharp, *Mrs. Jack* (Boston: Little, Brown, 1965), 150, 152, 155 and passim; and Roger Austen, *Genteel Pagan* (Amherst: University of Massachusetts Press, 1991), 128, 130.

22. Austen, *Genteel Pagan*, xxx, 47, 96, 112, 116–117, 125, 126–128, 137, 140, 188 n. 23, 188–189 n. 14. See also Walter Muir Whitehill, *The Boston Public Library: A Centennial History* (Cambridge, MA: Harvard University Press, 1956).

23. Austen, *Genteel Pagan*, 126–127.

24. Larzer Ziff, *The American 1890's: Life and Times of a Lost Generation* (New York: Viking, 1966), 95; Kaplan, *Whitman*, 26.

25. Dwight to Gardner, letter of 18 September 1892, GMA.

26. For Loeffler, see obituaries, *New York Times, Boston Herald*, 21 May 1935; see also Howe, *Tavern Club*, 32; Tharp, *Mrs. Jack*, 114–115; Gammell, *Boston Painters*, 181. For Adamowski, see Tharp, *Mrs. Jack*, 117. For Clayton Johns, see obituary, *Boston Evening Transcript*, 5 March 1932, and Howe, *Tavern Club*, 57. See also Tharp, *Mrs. Jack*, 112; the "contemporary" is quoted without attribution in Tharp, 113.

27. Austen, *Genteel Pagan*, 126; John McCormick, *George Santayana* (New York: Paragon, 1987), 119.

28. Austen, *Genteel Pagan*, 117. See also Henry-Russell Hitchcock, *The Architecture of H. H. Richardson and His Time* (New York, 1936; rev. ed. Cambridge, MA: MIT Press, 1961), 234. I am grateful to Robert Bell Rettig for this citation.

29. John W. Crowley, Editor's Introduction, Austen, *Genteel Pagan*, xxxix.

30. Sullivan, *Journal*, 97–98.

31. Ibid., 109–110.

32. Dwight to Gardner, undated letter, GMA.

33. For Dwight's resignation see Austen, *Genteel Pagan*, 137; and Whitehill, *Boston Public Library*, 129–130.

34. "Saunterings," *Town Topics* 36, no. 12 (12 November 1896): 10. For Gericke's recruiting of Adamowski, see Howe, *Tavern Club*, 37.

35. Austen, *Genteel Pagan*, 127. Sullivan's journal was published in 1917. He married in 1899.

36. Austen, *Genteel Pagan*, 137–138.

37. Bliss Carman, "Paul Verlaine" and "The Bather," in Bliss Carman and Richard Hovey, *More Songs from Vagabondia* (Boston: Small, Maynard, 1896), 59, 33.

38. Carman, "Romany Signs," in Bliss Carman and Richard Hovey, *Last Songs from Vagabondia* (Boston: Small, Maynard, 1901), 56.

39. Russell Sullivan, "Here and Hereafter," quoted in James J. Roche, *Life of John Boyle O'Reilly* (New York: Cassell, 1891), 201–202. For the Papyrus Club, see *Bacon's Dictionary of Boston*, 300; see also Roche, *O'Reilly*, 132–136, 191–192, 196, 221, 234, 241, 243, 361.

40. Roche, *O'Reilly*, 132.

41. Ibid., 200.

42. Mary W. Blanchard, "Near *The Coast of Bohemia*: Boundaries and the Aesthetic Press" (unpublished paper, Rutgers University, Department of History, 1992), Fig. 19 (illustration reproduced from *Puck* magazine, undated), 70.

43. O'Reilly to Stoddard, letter of 21 June 1882, quoted in Roche, *O'Reilly*, 291.

44. Sullivan, *Journal*, 10.

45. Mark A. De Wolfe Howe, *A Venture in Remembrance* (Boston: Little, Brown, 1941), 138.

46. Shaun O'Connell, *Imagining Boston* (Boston: Beacon Press, 1990), 33.

47. Howe, *Tavern Club*, 250; George Santayana, *The Backgrounds of My Life*, vol. I of *Persons and Places* (New York: Scribner's, 1944–1953), 71.

48. Kenyon Cox's original design in oil, dated 1889, has recently been found at the Boston Public Library.

49. Sullivan to Gardner, letter of 21 July 1892, GMA.

50. Whitehill, *Boston Public Library*, 160.

51. Bram Dijkstra, *Idols of Perversity* (New York: Oxford University Press, 1986), 193, 308–309; P. R. Baker, *Stanny* (New York: Collier-Macmillan, 1989), 280.

52. Susan Thompson, "The Blessed Damozel," in Wendy Kaplan, *"The Art That Is Life"* (Boston: Museum of Fine Arts, 1987), 72.

53. Whitehill, *Boston Public Library*, 176–182; see also Howe, *Tavern Club*, 76–77.

54. Whitehill, *Boston Public Library*, 179.

55. Ibid.

56. This will occur in Phase III of the McKim Building restoration begun in 1991.

57. John Boyle O'Reilly to T. R. Sullivan, undated letter ca. 1882, St. Botolph Club Archive, Massachusetts Historical Society. I am grateful to John Brandt for alerting me to this source.

58. Joseph Chamberlain, "American Cities in Fiction — I: Boston," *The Chap-Book* 8 (15 April 1898): 434. Frances Carruth also concludes that the St. Botolph Club is the model of the St. Filipe in *The Pagans*; see her *Fictional Rambles in and about Boston* (New York: McClure, Phillips, 1902), 131.

59. Doris Birmingham, "Boston's St. Botolph Club," *Archives of American Art* (Summer 1992): 26, 31.

60. Ibid., 33.

61. Parrish, 216–217. The Club of Odd Volumes's history makes no mention of Day, though his seal design is reproduced (facing 13), and it is still used in modified form: see Alexander Williams, *Social History of the Club of Odd Volumes* (Boston: Club of Odd Volumes, 1969).

62. *Catalogue* of the 1890 St. Botolph Club Architectural Exhibition (St. Botolph Club Archives, Massachusetts Historical Society). The show took place in October.

63. RAC, "Partnership," in *Bertram Grosvenor Goodhue: Architect and Master of Many Arts*, Charles H. Whitaker, ed. (New York: American Institute of Architects Press, 1925), 29; Howe, *Tavern Club*, 246.

64. BGG, "The Written Work of Ralph Adams Cram," *The Chap-Book* 4 (1 April 1896), 463.

65. Dwight to Gardner, letter of 13 November 1894, GMA; see also Sullivan, *Journal*, 129, 127.

66. James F. O'Gorman, *On the Boards* (Philadelphia: University of Pennsylvania Press, 1989), 137.

67. Martin Green, *The Mount Vernon Street Warrens* (New York: Scribner's, 1989), 55–56, 63.

68. Cynthia Zaitzevsky, *The Architecture of William Ralph Emerson 1837–1917* (Cambridge, MA: Fogg Art Museum, 1969), 21.

69. Walter Muir Whitehill, *Museum of Fine Arts, Boston: A Centennial History*, 2 vols. (Cambridge, MA: Harvard University Press, 1970), I, 143.

70. Green, *Warrens*, 40.

71. Ibid., 40–41, 43.

72. Ibid., 88.

73. Ibid., 41, 59, 58.

74. *Poèmes* (Paris, 1896), 182, cited in Green, *Warrens*, 115.

75. William Sturgis Bigelow to Henry Cabot Lodge, in Akiko Murakata, "Selected

Letters of D. William Sturgis Bigelow" (Ph.D. dissertation, George Washington University, 1971), quoted in Green, *Warrens*, 202.

76. Hilliard, 186.

77. Gay, *Tender Passion*, 202.

78. Green, *Warrens*, 119; Gay, *Tender Passion*, 212.

79. Morris Carter, *Isabella Stewart Gardner and Fenway Court* (Boston: Houghton Mifflin, 1925), 90.

80. Quoted, ibid.

81. Ibid., 91.

82. Tharp, *Mrs. Jack*, 277-278; Nancy Curtis and Richard Nylander, "Introduction," *Beauport* (Boston: David R. Godine, 1990), 7, 11; Herbert Muschamp, "Designing a Framework for Diversity," *New York Times* (19 June 1994); Margaret Henderson Floyd, *Architecture after Richardson* (Chicago: University of Chicago Press, 1994), 85-90, 471 n.63. In the case of Little Harbor, the fundamental source is Woodard Dorr Openo, "The Summer Colony at Little Harbor in Portsmouth, New Hampshire, and Its Relationship to the Colonial Revival Movement," Ph.D. thesis, University of Michigan, Ann Arbor, 1990.

83. RAC, "My Life," unpublished typescript (C&GC/BPL), 12.

84. Catalogue card file of Gardner's personal library, GMA; Gay, *Education*, 365.

85. Dwight to Gardner: the first quotation is from a letter of 18 September 1892, the second from a letter of 15 December 1908; GMA. John La Farge was the well-known artist.

86. I am grateful to Susan Sinclair, the Gardner Museum's archivist, for searching Gardner's guest book and checking the inventory of her personal possessions in situ at her death.

87. Sullivan to Gardner, letter of 31 August 1892, GMA.

88. Ibid., letter of 16 May 1892, GMA.

89. Ibid., letter of 9 March 1889, GMA.

90. Ibid., undated letter, GMA.

91. For the "battle of the casts" see Whitehill, *Museum of Fine Arts*, I, 172-217.

92. Green, *Warrens*, 171; "The *Bacchante* as a Fitting Symbol of the Life within Literature," *Poet Lore* 9 (July-September 1898): 455-457. RAC's views and those of his circle, in various of these matters so key to Boston's Bohemia, are not always discoverable. In the matter of the "battle of the casts" at the Museum of Fine Arts, a passing allusion by RAC in his 1893 lecture at St. John's Chapel of the Episcopal Theological School confirms he took Gardner's and Prichard's side, condemning casts. About the library *Bacchante* I can discover no such allusion, though three of his closest Pinckney Street friends are on record on the subject: Hovey, who in the *Tatler* twitted Boston unmercifully on the subject (Alan H. MacDonald, *Richard Hovey: Man and Craftsman* [Durham, NC: Duke University Press, 1957], 190), and LIG and FHD, who went so far as to exchange letters in which LIG offered to be "a lean and lively Bacchante, in short green cheesecloth and wreath" (Parrish, 299). For an editorial originating in Boston's artistic circles supporting Norton's middle ground see *AABN*, then published in Boston, 17 October 1896 (p. 17), where *Bacchante* is called "a piece of really artistic work . . . [by] an artist of acknowledged ability" but which goes on to assert that "such a subject offered for such a site by an architect who finds Minerva's head the most suitable decoration for the keystone of the [library's] main entrance arch is a curious lapse that verges on

illiteracy." This is the point of view surely of those who later argued for the introduction into the library of Saint Gauden's powerful work *The Puritan*, which according to Margaret Henderson Floyd both W. A. Longfellow and Robert Peabody, two leading Boston architects, favored. It is hard to deny in one sense the force of this argument. See Floyd, *Architecture after Richardson*, 379. Prichard's key role in the design of the Museum of Fine Arts brings to mind the parallel role in the same decade of William Sumner Appleton, another Beacon Hill bachelor of aesthete tastes, who founded the Society for the Preservation of New England Antiquities.

93. Carter to Gardner, undated letter (to "Dea," a nickname he used; see Tharp, *Mrs. Jack*, 307), GMA.

94. Letter of 1908, otherwise undated, quoted in Tharp, 307. Prichard's occupancy is discussed on 257.

95. Morris Carter, *Reminiscences* (Boston: Printed at the Industrial School for Crippled Children, 1964), 43, 33.

96. Ibid., 43.

97. Johns to Gardner, undated letter (marked 1905 in Gardner's hand in pencil), GMA.

98. Fred Kaplan, *Henry James* (New York: Morrow, 1992), 453-454.

99. Carter, *Gardner*, 4.

100. Ibid., 89.

101. For Bourget to Gardner, undated letter, GMA, see Tharp, *Mrs. Jack*, 171 (see also 258); for "Saunterings," *Town Topics*, undated, see 148; and for the remark about the bachelors see 202.

102. Partridge to Gardner, "The Beauty of Thine Eyes," unpublished MS., GMA; Santayana to Gardner, undated letter ca. 1912, GMA.

103. Obituary, *Boston Evening Transcript*, 5 March 1932.

104. Interview with Robert Douglas Hunter, 2 July 1992. I am grateful to Mr. Hunter for sharing with me R. H. Ives Gammell's view of the matter. Gammell, who greatly liked and admired Bunker, strongly suspected suicide.

105. Quoted in Carter, *Gardner*, 60. No source is given.

106. Colin Simpson, *Artful Partners* (New York: Macmillan, 1986), 51.

107. Frank Ashburn, *Peabody of Groton* (Cambridge, MA: Riverside Press, 1967), 155-156.

108. W. A. Gardner to Isabella Gardner, letter of 2 December 1885, GMA.

109. For Copeland see Arthur C. Smith, "To Copeland at Eighty by a Lifelong Pupil," in William Bentinck-Smith, *The Harvard Book* (Cambridge, MA: Harvard University Press, 1960), 93-96; Roger Burlingame, "A Memory of Copey," in Brooks Atkinson, ed., *College In A Yard* (Cambridge, MA: Harvard University Press, 1950), 41-44.

110. For Gardner's influence on Coolidge see Harold Jefferson Coolidge and Robert Howard Lord, *Archibald Cary Coolidge* (Boston: Houghton Mifflin, 1932), 11, 32; for Randolph Hall see Coolidge and Lord, 64-67. The Randolph Hall murals were apparently a private commission of Coolidge's, since an exhaustive search of the relevant Harvard archives of 1897-1914 discloses no reference to them. Even as late as their 1963 restoration, the artist's name, Edward Penfield, was unknown to officials of the Fogg Museum and Adams House, according to correspondence still extant at Adams House made available to me by the present Master, Robert Kiely. Nor is there any note taken of these murals in David Gibson's *Designed to Persuade* (Yonkers, NY: Hudson River Museum,

1984). Through the help of Sinclair Hitchings I found that Theodore Sizer, who Hitchings believes knew Penfield, noted the murals' existence in his *DAB* entry on Penfield.

The existence of Randolph Hall's indoor pool, rumored in an undated historical sketch by Sean Lynn-Jones in the Adams House archives, is documented by *The Official Guide to Harvard*, Stewart Mitchell, ed. (4th ed., Cambridge, MA: Harvard University, 1929), and has been confirmed by me and Robert B. Rettig at an on-site inspection of what are now the University Squash Courts, through the courtesy of Victoria Macy, Assistant to the Master of Adams House, in January 1994. In the sub-basement, amid a dense web of steam pipes, the remains of the pool's elegant tilework are still visible. The Westmorly Tank, though now used as a theater, is still intact.

111. For biographical data on Gardner see Ashburn, *Peabody of Groton*. Gardner himself wrote a charming volume, *Groton Myths and Memories* (Groton, MA: privately printed, 1928).

112. Ashburn, *Peabody of Groton*, 154.

113. Ibid., 156. In a letter to me of 1 November 1991, William Morgan asserts Gardner's house was designed by Vaughan and was called "St. Weobald's Cell."

114. Ibid., 157.

115. William Morgan, *The Almighty Wall: The Architecture of Henry Vaughan* (New York: Architectural History Foundation, 1983), 182 n. 40.

116. William Morgan to DS-T, letter of 1 March 1992, C&GC/BPL.

117. Whitehill, *Museum of Fine Arts*, I, 42.

118. Ibid., 674.

119. Gay, *Tender Passion*, 237; Hilliard, 164, 209.

120. Martin, 183.

121. Nicholas, Notebook II, 12.

122. Hoyle to Caroline N. Clark, letter of 19 December 1956, C&GC/BPL.

123. Eliot to Higginson, letter of 31 March 1896, quoted in Lears, 185.

124. McCormick, *Santayana*, 97.

125. Morison to DS-T, note of 16 December 1975, C&GC/BPL.

126. Brooks, *Indian Summer*, 438.

127. Paglia, 666.

128. Ibid., 629.

129. Hilliard, 206, discusses the sense in which I call Anglo-Catholicism liberal.

130. RAC to William Read, letter of 5 June 1899, C&GC/BPL.

131. Freud to James Jackson Putnam, letter of 16 June 1910, quoted in Nathan G. Hale, ed., *James Jackson Putnam and Psychoanalysis: Letters between Putnam and Sigmund Freud, William James . . .* (Cambridge, MA: Harvard University Press, 1971), 100-101.

132. Nathan G. Hale, *Freud in America*, vol. I of *Freud and the Americans* (New York: Oxford University Press, 1971), 121.

133. Lears, 250.

134. Saul Rosenzweig, *Freud, Jung and Hall the King-Maker* (Seattle: Hogrefe & Huber, 1992), 203, 323 n. 14. Rosenzweig is quoting from Freud's preface to Putnam's collected papers, published in 1921 as the opening volume of the International Psycho-Analytic Library, issued by the International Psychoanalytic Press (London, Vienna, New York).

135. Rosenzweig, *Freud, Jung and Hall*, 13. See also, with respect to Freud, Martin S.

Bergman, *The Anatomy of Loving* (New York: Fawcett, 1987), 160; and with respect to Jung, Gerhard Wehr, *Jung: A Biography* (Boston: Shambhala, 1988), 116, 124.

136. Hale, *Freud*, 21.

137. Ibid., 101.

138. Ibid., 107.

139. See Martin Duberman, *About Time* (New York: Penguin, 1986), 84.

140. Bergman, *Anatomy of Loving*, 157, quoting T. Gould, *Platonic Love* (London: Routledge and Kegan Paul, 1963).

141. Bergman, *Anatomy of Loving*, 179, 219.

142. Gay, *Tender Passion*, 258.

143. Quoted, ibid., 257.

144. Ibid.

145. Quoted in Bergman, *Anatomy of Loving*, 150.

146. For a full discussion see Henry Abelove, "Freud, Male Homosexuality and the Americans," in Henry Abelove et al., eds., *The Lesbian and Gay Studies Reader* (New York: Routledge, 1993), 301–393.

147. For the progressive view today see Richard Isay, *Being Homosexual* (New York: Avon, 1989).

148. Alan Crawford, *C. R. Ashbee* (New Haven: Yale University Press, 1985), 70.

149. Johanna Russ, "To Write 'Like a Woman': Transformations of Identity in the Work of Willa Cather," in *Historical, Literary and Erotic Aspects of Lesbianism*, Monica Kehoe, ed. (New York: Harrington Park Press, 1986), 78–80.

150. Gay, *Education*, 407, 409.

151. Daniel, 54–55.

152. Carroll Smith-Rosenberg, "The Female World of Love and Ritual: Relations between Women in Nineteenth-Century America," quoted in Sarah Way Sherman, *Sarah Orne Jewett: An American Persephone* (Hanover, NH: University Press of New England, 1989), 78.

153. Paglia, 505.

154. LIG to RAC, letter of 8 February 1895, C&GC/BPL.

155. Kaplan, *Whitman*, 24.

156. Robert K. Martin, "Knights-Errant and Gothic Seducers," in *Hidden from History: Reclaiming the Gay and Lesbian Past*, Martin Bauml Duberman, Martha Vicinus, and George Chauncey, Jr., eds. (New York: New American Library, Penguin Books, 1989), 179–180. See also Katz, *Gay American History*, 642 n. 7.

157. Santayana to B. Fuller, letter of 7 February 1914, quoted in McCormick, *Santayana*, 96; Santayana, *The Backgrounds of My Life*, 194.

158. Ziff, *The American 1890's*, 320.

159. "Francis Otto Matthiessen," *DAB*, Supplement IV, 559–561.

160. Quoted in David Bergman, "F. O. Matthiessen: The Critic as Homosexual," *Gaiety Transfigured* (Madison: University of Wisconsin Press, 1991), 92.

161. Russ, "To Write 'Like a Woman,'" 86.

7 Designing Partners, Artful Churches

1. For a discussion of James's young men see Leon Edel, *Henry James: A Life* (New York: Harper, 1985; condensed and revised edition of multivolume biography). For a

franker if not always so full a discussion see Fred Kaplan, *Henry James* (New York: Morrow, 1992).

2. "The Poet Who Kick-Started a Stalled Cézanne," *New York Times* (18 July 1991).

3. See the epigraph to Chapter 4; Walter Hamilton, trans., Introduction to *Plato's Symposium* (London: Penguin, 1951), 12–13, 22, 24, 26.

4. See David Bergman, *Gaiety Transfigured* (Madison: University of Wisconsin Press, 1991), 94.

5. T. L. Steinberg, "Poetry and the Perpendicular Style," *Journal of Aesthetics and Art Criticism* 40 (Fall 1981): 71–79.

6. Martin, 163.

7. RAC, "Partnership" in *Bertram Grosvenor Goodhue: Architect and Master of Many Arts*, Charles H. Whitaker, ed. (New York: American Institute of Architects Press, 1925), 30.

8. Martin Duberman, *About Time* (New York: Penguin, 1991), 66. If the relationship was a physical one, nongays may find of interest the useful guide W. H. Auden proposed as key to understanding such relationships. Though he by no means exhausted the sexual repertory, his views, which I believe have as much to do with archetypes as stereotypes, were that oral sex represents the roles of Son-and/or-Mother; anal sex the roles of Wife-and/or-Husband; and "Plain-sewing" and "Princeton-First Year," or "Princeton Rub" (respectively naval and collegiate slang for mutual masturbation and *coitus contra ventrem*), represent the more brotherly roles.

9. Duberman, *About Time*, 104.

10. See Emmanuel Cooper, *The Sexual Perspective: Homosexuality and Art in the Last Hundred Years in the West* (London: Routledge and Kegan Paul, 1986), 78.

11. Finlay, 8.

12. Jussim, 58. Patricia Berman, "Munch's *Self-Portrait with Cigarette*: Smoking and the Bohemian Persona," *Art Bulletin* 65 (December 1993): 628.

13. Gay, *Education*, 110–111.

14. RAC to BGG, letters from Japan, 1899, C&GC/BPL.

15. Martin S. Bergman, *The Anatomy of Loving* (New York: Fawcett, 1977), 237, 197, 73, 86. The reputed letters were called to my attention by Mary W. Upchurch.

16. David Greenberg, *The Construction of Homosexuality* (Chicago: University of Chicago Press, 1988), 448; John Boswell, *Christianity, Social Tolerance, and Homosexuality: Gay People in Western Europe from the Beginning of the Christian Era to the Fourteenth Century* (Chicago: University of Chicago Press, 1980),44 n. 8.

17. For a full discussion of bisexuality see C. A. Tripp, *The Homosexual Matrix* (New York: Meridian, 1975), 87–90.

18. See A. L. Rowse, *Homosexuals in History: Ambivalence in Society, Literature, and the Arts* (New York: Macmillan, 1977); Thomas Cowan, *Gay Men and Women Who Have Enriched the World* (New Canaan, CT: Mulvey, 1988); and *The Penguin Book of Homosexual Verse* (Harmondsworth, Middlesex: Penguin, 1983). For a more balanced view see Louis Crompton, *Byron and Greek Love* (Berkeley: University of California Press, 1985).

19. Boswell, *Christianity*, 41.

20. Martin Bergman, *Anatomy of Loving*, 247.

21. Ibid., 106. The phrase "the supreme love poetry" is attributed to C. S. Lewis,

quoted by Bergman from John D. Wilson, "The Sonnets," in *The Works of Shakespeare* (Cambridge: Cambridge University Press, 1966), 15.

22. Burgess to RAC, letter of 21 February 1901, C&GC/BPL.

23. BGG to RAC, letter of 15 April 1907, C&GC/BPL.

24. Gay, *Tender Passion*, 340–348.

25. Quoted, ibid., 332. See also 334, 347, 349.

26. Richard Oliver, *Bertram Grosvenor Goodhue* (New York: Architectural History Foundation, 1983), 11, 122.

27. BGG to RAC and Ferguson, letter of 11 February 1910, C&GC/BPL. BGG quotes the phrase without attribution but clearly in reference to RAC.

28. Howard Gardner, *Creating Minds* (New York: HarperCollins, 1993), 279.

29. John Tytell, *Passionate Lives* (Syracuse, NY: Carol Publishing Group, 1991).

30. Gay, *Tender Passion*, 216.

31. Quoted in Gay, *Education*, 287.

32. Carl Capellman, *Pastoral Medicine*, quoted, ibid.

33. Rose Macaulay, *Letters to a Friend 1950–1952*, Constance Babington-Smith, ed. (New York: Atheneum, 1962), 356; Morris Carter, *Isabella Stewart Gardner and Fenway Court* (Boston: Houghton Mifflin, 1925), 4; Thomas Tallmadge, *The Story of Architecture in America* (New York: W. W. Norton, 1927), 263.

34. A. N. Wilson, *C. S. Lewis: A Biography* (New York: W. W. Norton, 1990), 117–118.

35. Philip Hodson, *Who's Who in Wagner's Life and Work* (London: Weidenfeld and Nicholson, 1984), 131–132.

36. Gay, *Tender Passion*, 290.

37. Iris Murdoch, *The Good Apprentice* (New York: Penguin, 1986), 141.

38. Martin Bergman, *Anatomy of Loving*, 258.

39. Quoted in Gay, *Tender Passion*, 290.

40. Ellen H. Spitz, *Art and Psyche* (New Haven: Yale University Press, 1985), 26.

41. Ibid., 29. Spitz quotes both Keble and Abrams from M. H. Abrams, *The Mirror and the Lamp* (New York: Oxford University Press, 1953).

42. Martin Bergman, *Anatomy of Loving*, 250.

43. Cynthia Ozick, "T. S. Eliot at 101," *The New Yorker* (20 November 1989), 128.

44. Abrams, *Mirror and Lamp*, quoted in Spitz, *Art and Psyche*, 29.

45. William Golding, *The Spire* (New York: Harcourt Brace and World, 1964), 184.

46. Richard Taruskin, "Reclaiming Tchaikovsky . . .," *New York Times* (30 June 1991).

47. Tchaikovsky to Mme. von Meck, letter of 21 February 1878, quoted in Gay, *Tender Passion*, 261.

48. Peter Ackroyd, *T.S. Eliot: A Life* (New York: Simon and Schuster, 1984), 38.

49. Hodson, *Wagner*, 132.

50. Sedgwick, *Epistemology*, 168. Wagner, whatever his own tastes, seems to have been surrounded by homosexuality. See Edel, *Henry James: A Life*, 172; Bram Dijkstra, *Idols of Perversity* (New York: Oxford University Press, 1986), 204.

51. Gay, *Tender Passion*, 265.

52. Ibid., 269.

53. Ibid., 264.

54. RAC, *My Life*, 10, 8.

55. Taruskin, "Tchaikovsky," 22.

56. Both scholars are quoted in Edward Rothenstein, "Was Schubert Gay?" *New York Times* (4 February 1992).

57. RAC, "Good and Bad Modern Gothic," *Architectural Review* 6 (August 1899): 118–119.

58. Janet Wolf Bowen, "Architectural Envy: 'A Figure Is Nothing Without a Setting' in Henry James's *The Bostonians*," *New England Quarterly* 65 (March 1992): 5.

59. Paglia, 497.

60. Harold Beaver, "Homosexual Signs: In Memory of Roland Barthes," quoted in Thomas Yingling, *Hart Crane and the Homosexual Text* (Chicago: University of Chicago Press, 1990), 31.

61. Nancy Curtis and Richard Nylander, *Beauport* (Boston: David R. Godine, 1990), 11, 7.

62. John Nicholas Brown to DS-T, letter of 19 November 1983, C&GC/BPL.

63. Hilliard, 205.

64. David Bergman, *Gaiety*, 117.

65. Evelyn Waugh, *A Little Learning* (Boston: Little, Brown, 1964), 160.

66. Eve Kosofsky Sedgwick, *Between Men* (New York: Columbia University Press, 1985), 94.

67. Ibid., 207.

68. See Gay, *Tender Passion*, 251.

69. Louis Sullivan, "Ornament in Architecture," *Engineering Magazine* (20 August 1892; Kindergarten Chat 6, "An Oasis," is about the Marshall Field Warehouse); quoted in Robert Twombly, *Louis Sullivan* (Chicago: University of Chicago Press, 1986), 400.

70. RAC, *My Life*, 32, 33.

71. Twombly, *Sullivan*, 399.

72. Ibid., 401.

73. Ibid., 400.

74. My reference is to the first tower design of 1892. See F. W. Atherton, "Sicut Lilium inter Spinas" (unpublished paper for Professor E. F. Seckler, Harvard College, 1990), 22, 34–37.

75. Daniel, 151–152.

76. Whitney Chadwick and Isabelle de Courtivron, *Significant Others: Creativity and Intimate Partnership* (London: Thames and Hudson, 1993), 204.

77. Brendan Gill, *Many Masks: A Life of Frank Lloyd Wright* (New York: Ballantine, 1987), 79.

78. Nathan G. Hale, *Freud in America*, vol. I of *Freud and the Americans* (New York: Oxford University Press, 1971), 376.

79. *Architecture* 22 (15 July 1910): 97.

80. Cram, Wentworth & Goodhue, "Unsuccessful competitive design for St. Paul's Church, Rochester, New York," *AABN* 53 (12 September 1896): pl. 1081.

81. Montgomery Schuyler, "The Works of Cram, Goodhue and Ferguson," *Architectural Record* 29 (January 1911): 11. For RAC's scheme see "Unsuccessful competitive design for St. Paul's Church," 88, and "Proposed St. Paul's Church, Rochester, N.Y.," *AABN* 53 (12 September 1896): pl. 1081; for BGG's scheme see "Competitive design, St. Paul's Church, Rochester, N.Y.," *Brickbuilder* 5 (August 1896): pls. 39, 40.

82. See Gill, *Many Masks*, 99, 63.

83. Richard Mohr, *Gay Ideas* (Boston: Beacon Press, 1992), 150.

84. C. F. Thwing, "Phillips Brooks, Preacher: Parallelisms and Antitheses to Newman," *Friends of Man* (New York: Macmillan, 1933), 20, 23.

85. RAC, *My Life*, 7.

86. Thwing, "Phillips Brooks," 20. See also James Rigg, *Oxford High Anglicanism and Its Chief Leaders* (London: C. H. Kelly, 1895), 13, 31–32, 109–110, 132, 154, 156; and Geoffrey Faber, *Oxford Apostles* (London: Faber & Faber, 1933), 32–35 and chapter 6 generally.

87. For a discussion of RAC's hero worship of Richardson see Chapter 3.

88. Robert Cheney Smith, SSJE, *The Shrine on Bowdoin Street* (Boston: Society of St. John the Evangelist, 1958), 20.

89. Arthur C. A. Hall, *The Hidden Life of the Heart: Thoughts from the Writings of Father A.C.A. Hall, late of St. John the Evangelist*, ed. A.M.D. (Boston: Joseph George Cupples/Back Bay Bookstore, 1892). A lengthy appendix about the Brooks-Hall controversy is included. Several examples of Hall's "begging letters" to Isabella Gardner are extant, GMA.

90. Frank Ashburn, *Peabody of Groton* (Cambridge, MA: Riverside Press, 1967), 94.

91. Ibid., 66.

92. Edward Wagenknecht, *Ambassadors of Christ* (Oxford: Oxford University Press, 1972), 122, 129, 131. I am not the only person to have recently speculated about Brooks's sexual orientation, the question of which arose in a sermon, "For Integrity," by Rev. Barbara Crafton, an Episcopal priest on the staff of the Seaman's Institute, New York City, in 1992. I discussed this sermon with Crafton through the kind assistance of Rev. Jack Smith, Chaplain of Groton School, and I learned in the first place of it from Groton historian Douglas Brown.

93. Dedicated to "Piety, Character and Hospitality," Phillips Brooks House was opened in 1900 as a home for various of Harvard's religious and charitable organizations.

94. William Bayard Hale, *Phillips Brooks: The Memorial Address January 25, 1893*, in a collection of bound tracts entitled *Episcopiana Massachusetts*, VI, Archives of the Diocese of Massachusetts, unpaged.

95. "William Bayard Hale," *DAB*, IV, 111–113. I am grateful to Dora Murphy, the archivist of the Episcopal Diocese of Massachusetts, for helping me unravel the intricate biography of the former Father Hale.

96. *DAB*, 112. See also "Church of Our Saviour's, Middleborough, Mass.," *The Churchman* (17 December 1898), 897.

97. RAC to Silas McBee, letter of 8 December 1898, C&GC/BPL.

98. One cannot be absolutely certain that it was Holy Spirit to which RAC referred in *My Life* (46); he would have loathed St. Paul's, Andover, just as much (but not more). But a church very like Holy Spirit, illustrated in *Church Building,* is captioned "an example of vicious design." That may be the explanation. RAC knew the Rotches personally and later designed the parish house.

99. George P. Winship, *Daniel Berkeley Updike and the Merrymount Press* (Rochester, NY: Leo Hart, 1947), 7.

100. Berkeley Updike to Ogden Codman, letter of 30 November 1896, letter of 15

October 1902, and attached letter of 14 October 1901 by an unidentified official of St. John's Church, Providence, Rhode Island, to Updike. I am grateful to Laura Congden for alerting me to the second letter and the attachment, which mentions RAC.

101. RAC, *My Life*, 243–244.

102. See *The Education of Henry Adams*, chapter 25. For the context of Adams's images see Brooks, *Indian Summer*, 487–490.

103. Judith Fryer, *Felicitous Space: The Imaginative Structures of Edith Wharton and Willa Cather* (Chapel Hill: University of North Carolina Press, 1986), 97.

104. Charles Maginnis, Introduction, *The Work of Cram and Ferguson . . .* (New York: Pencil Points Press, 1929), fourth page of unpaged front matter.

105. Tallmadge, *Story of Architecture*, 259, 261.

106. RAC, *My Life*, 77–78, 79.

107. I am grateful to D. Gillespie for his reminiscences of the phenomenon of "the man of taste."

108. Daniel, 234.

109. RAC to N. B. Brown, undated letter, at Emmanuel Church, Newport, Rhode Island, quoted in Daniel, 229–230.

110. BGG to N. B. Brown, letter of 7 January 1902, at Emmanuel Church, Newport, quoted in Daniel, 230.

111. RAC, *My Life*, 53–54.

112. Edmund White, *States of Desire: Travels in Gay America* (New York: Penguin, 1980), 255–259.

113. RAC, *My Life*, 105 (discussing the West Point competition designs prepared by him and BGG in Boston. They hired W. W. Bosworth as renderer for the occasion); RAC to Ralph Wentworth Cram, letter of 21 December 1929, C&GC/BPL.

114. John Summerson, *The Classical Language of Architecture* (Cambridge, MA: MIT Press, 1963), 12. The source is Vitruvius, *De architectura*, Books III and IV.

115. RAC, "Good and Bad Modern Gothic," 116. The most explicit treatment of these controversial themes in Cram's circle is to be found in the publication of Gelett Burgess's *A Gage of Youth* (Boston: Small, Maynard and Co., 1902) by Cram's friends Herbert Small and Laurens Maynard. See particularly "Rondel of Perfect Friendship," "Ballad of the Effeminate," and "A Protest of the Illiterate" (16, 42–45), from which last note: " 'Why write about maids and violet shades?' says I / 'Wot's the matter with MEN?' / 'That fad's played out,' he says with a pout, 'and / Beauty's come in again!' / 'Did you ever go out into the show?' I says, 'or feel like a fight?' . . . 'Wot's love and kisses and such-like blisses? Good / God! had ye never a friend?' "

116. Robert Hopcke, *Jung, Jungians & Homosexuality* (Boston: Shambhala, 1991), 83; Edward Rothstein, "Did a Man or a Woman Write That?" *New York Times* (17 July 1994).

117. Martin, 114.

118. David Cohen, "Notes on a Grecian Yearn," *New York Times* (31 March 1993). Plato's argument in the *Symposium* is discussed in Boswell, *Christianity*, 18–20, where Plutarch and other ancient sources are copiously cited. See also Greenberg, *Homosexuality*, 115. Note that Plato thought the most invincible army would be composed of both men and women.

119. Paglia, 26, 22. For the camp side see 557.

120. Sedgwick, *Between Men*, 94.

121. Edward Carpenter, *Selected Writings, Volume One: Sex* (London, GMP, 1984), 234, 274.

122. David Bergman, *Gaiety*, 98.

123. Susan Sontag, "Notes on Camp," *Against Interpretation and Other Essays* (New York: Farrar, Straus and Giroux, 1964), 14.

124. *The Letters of John Keats 1814–1821*, Hyder E. Rollins, ed., 2 vols. (Cambridge, MA: Harvard University Press, 1958), I, 185.

125. Hart Crane, *The Complete Poems and Selected Letters and Prose*, Brom Weber, ed. (New York: Liveright, 1966), 25.

8 White Rose, Purple Rose

1. Thomas Beer, *The Mauve Decade* (New York: Knopf, 1941), 9.

2. Karen Evans Úlehla, ed. and comp., *The Society of Arts and Crafts, Boston, Exhibition Record* (Boston: Boston Public Library, 1981), 189.

3. Harry L. Katz, *A Continental Eye: The Art and Architecture of Arthur Rotch* (Boston: Boston Athenaeum, 1985).

4. *Clark's Boston Blue Book* (Boston: Edward C. Clark, 1983), 432, 444; Edward Weeks, *The Tavern at Seventy-Five* (Boston, Tavern Club, 1959), 183. Rotch was a charter member of the Tavern.

5. RAC, *My Life*, 45.

6. Ibid., 47.

7. Katz, *A Continental Eye*, 24; Margaret Henderson Floyd, *Architectural Education and Boston* (Boston: Boston Architectural Center, 1989), 14–16.

8. Floyd, *Architectural Education*, 14, 40–45.

9. Ibid., 45. This great hall seems to have inspired another and scarcely less grand space at 8 Chestnut Street, ca. 1900. I am indebted to Thomas Townsend for showing it to me.

10. Beverly Brandt, "The Essential Link: Boston Architects and the Society of Arts and Crafts," *Tiller* 2 (September-October 1983): 15.

11. Peter Cormack, "The Charm of Glassiness," a paper delivered at Philadelphia, 27 April—1 May 1994, to be published on an as yet unannounced date in *The Proceedings of the International Seminar on Stained Glass of the 19th and 20th Centuries*. For Vaughan and Kempe, see William Morgan, *The Almighty Wall: The Architecture of Henry Vaughan* (New York: Architectural History Foundation, 1983), 165 n. 18.

12. Brandt, "Essential Link," 8.

13. Ashbee thus advised George Chettlee. See also C. R. Ashbee to F. A. Whiting, letter of 2 April 1910, quoted in Brandt, "Essential Link," 21.

14. Though Wilson's work is illustrated in Montgomery Schuyler, "The Works of Cram, Goodhue and Ferguson," *Architectural Record* 29 (January 1911): 79, it is credited to Wilson only in the caption to Figure CXXXI in RAC, *Church Building* (Boston: Small, Maynard and Co., 1901), 227.

15. Walter S. Sparrow, "Christopher Whall and His Influence," *Royal Institute of British Architects Journal* 90 (July-December 1925): 365–368. See also John E. Tarbox, "Christopher Whall," *Stained Glass* 28 (Autumn 1933): 143; Charles J. Connick, "Christopher Whall," *Bulletin of the Stained Glass Association of America* 19 (Septem-

ber 1925): 5–10; *The Connoisseur* 71 (January-April 1925): 115–116; and "Veronica Whall," *Stained Glass*, 37 (Summer 1942): 51–56.

16. *Victorian Church Art* (London: Victoria and Albert Museum, 1971), N28: 144.

17. Sparrow, "Whall," 365.

18. Emmanuel Cooper, *The Sexual Perspective: Homosexuality and Art in the Last Hundred Years in the West* (London: Routledge & Kegan Paul, 1986), 46; Anthea Callen, *Women Artists of the Arts and Crafts Movement* (New York: Pantheon, 1980), 177; see also 224, 227. In a letter to me of 1 August 1994, Peter Cormack notes that while there is evidence Wilson could have been gay, given his Bohemian reputation, there is no evidence that Whall was. Moreover, Cormack adds that according to Lisa Ticknor, author of *The Spectacle of Women: Imagery of the Suffrage Campaign, 1907–14*, there is "no unequivocal evidence" for Lowndes either. Lowndes, however, shared a house with another woman, usually very good evidence of a lesbian orientation.

19. Sparrow, "Whall," 368.

20. Ibid., 366.

21. RAC, "The Work of Henry Wilson," *Christian Art* 2 (March 1908): 273.

22. Christopher Whall, *Stained Glass Work* (New York: Appleton and Co., 1905), 174.

23. Cormack, "The Charm of Glassiness," 2. The first stained glass at Ashmont, an *Annunciation* of 1893, was given by RAC, BGG, and Wentworth as a thank-offering for their first church. This window, another designed for St. Paul's, Brockton, and a Wentworth memorial window in Our Savior's, Brookline, in which George Hallowell played a part, all came from the studios of Otto Heinigke of Heinigke and Bowen of New York, a firm that before BGG's brother, Harry Goodhue, began to work for them seems to have been RAC's and BGG's choice. A letter from Heinigke in C&GC/BPL, which begins "My dear friend Goodhue" (suggesting that they knew each other in New York), together with Harry Goodhue's work for the firm, indicates that in the 1890s Goodhue was the dominant partner, as one might expect, in matters of stained glass; after Whall, stained glass seems to have become as least as much RAC's province. Eventually this was so much the case that RAC may justly be thought the dominant influence on American stained glass of the first half of the twentieth century. The letter in question (Otto Heinigke to BGG, 13 April 1894) refers as well to Heinigke's "congratulat[ing BGG's] brother on the opportunity he has for [?illegible] from his big brother and sincerely hop[ing] that he may use it with good success." It is likely both Goodhues knew Heinigke from New York days.

24. Charles J. Connick, "Windows of Old France and Modern Notes," *Studio* 78 (December 1923): 44. See also Connick, *Adventures in Light and Colour* (New York: Random House, 1937), 5, 135, 332.

25. *A Tour of All Saints' Church* (Brookline, MA: Parish of All Saints, 1954), 20–21. See also Connick, *Adventures*, 351.

26. Connick to Horace J. Phipps, letter of 20 September 1910, Connick Collection, BPL. Another letter, undated, in C&GC/BPL from RAC to Connick suggests that RAC helped Connick establish his own studio three years later. It reads in part: "I believe I have no further claim on these two life insurance policies which were given me to secure notes I endorsed for you, which notes you assure me have been paid. I am therefore returning these notes to you."

27. For Lawrie, see *Bertram Grosvenor Goodhue: Architect and Master of Many Arts*, Charles H. Whitaker, ed. (New York: American Institute of Architects Press, 1925),

33–36; for John Evans (whose papers are in BPL) and for Irving and Casson, no sources yet exist. Irving and Casson merged eventually with A. H. Davenport Co.; for the latter see Anne Farnam, "A. H. Davenport and Company," *Antiques* 109 (May 1976): 1048–55.

28. William Howe Downes, "General Progress in the Fine Arts," *Fifty Years of Boston* (Boston: Boston Tercentennial Committee, 1930), 335.

29. I. [Johannes] Kirchmayer, "About Woodcarving," *American Magazine of Art* 14 (13 December 1923): 20.

30. RAC, *My Life*, 187.

31. Anne Webb Karnaghan, "Ecclesiastical Carving in America," *International Studio* 85 (September-December 1926): 52–53.

32. Úlehla, *Arts and Crafts*, passim.

33. These, with Arthur Stone and George Germer, were Cram's chief gold- and silversmiths. See RAC, *Church Building*, 222, 224, 324, and *My Life*, 197.

34. [Gardner Museum] *Guide* (Boston: Trustees of the Museum, 1976 ed.), 29; E. P. Denker and B. R. Denker in Wendy Kaplan, *"The Art That Is Life"* (Boston: Museum of Fine Arts, 1987), 390; W. W. Cordingley to RAC, letter of 20 May 1926, GMA.

35. Boston: Merrymount Press, 1900. As much was made, interestingly, of the photography of the book as of the decoration.

36. James O'Gorman, "Either in Books or Architecture: Bertram Grosvenor Goodhue in the Nineties," *Harvard Library Bulletin* 35 (Spring 1987): 174.

37. Susan Otis Thompson, *American Book Design and William Morris* (New York: Bowker, 1977), 44.

38. Finlay, 33–35.

39. RAC, *My Life*, 90. The "Proposal for a Dining Club," dated Boston, April 1896, was signed by Carman, RAC, BGG, Meteyard, and Small and sent to the following: John C. Abbott, Francis H. Bacon, Herman T. Baldwin, M.D., George E. Barton, Prescott Hartford Belknap, J. M. Bowles, Fred F. Bullard, Frank Chaffee, Samuel A. Chevalier, Herbert Copeland, John Cummings, John Cutler, Fred Holland Day, Harry Eldredge Goodhue, George G. Hall, M.D., George Gilman Hall, George H. Hallowell, Walter Blackburn Harte, Oliver B. Henshaw, Oliver Herford, Richard Hovey, Byron S. Hurlbut, T. Edge[r] Kavanagh, John C. D. Kitchen, Arthur T. Knapp, Jonathan Thayer Lincoln, Edgar A. P. Newcomb, Morton G. Nichols, Albert E. Prescott, Thomas Henry Randall, Charles G. D. Roberts, Bruce Rogers, N. S. H. Sanders, Philip Henry Savage, William H. Thomas, D. B. Updike, James E. Whitney, and Allen Hamilton Williams. This may be said to be the pool from which the Bohemians of closer and closer circles to RAC and his cohort were drawn. Note, for instance, the list (Chapter 1, note 147) of those who sat for portraits by Day. The inner circle, of course, was made up of the Visionists.

40. Paul R. Baker, *Stanny: The Gilded Life of Stanford White* (New York: Macmillan, 1989), 273–290.

41. F. S. Bigelow, quoted in Parrish, 51.

42. Finlay, 92. See the forthcoming catalogue of a planned exhibit of Hallowell's work at the Danforth Museum, Lee Lipton, curator. For Heinigke, see note 23.

43. William A. Dwiggins, quoted in George P. Winship, *Daniel Berkeley Updike and the Merrymount Press* (Rochester, NY: Leo Hart, 1947), 128.

44. See Daniel, 174–177.

45. Winship, *Updike*, 20–22.

46. Quoted in Louise Hall Tharp, *Mrs. Jack* (Boston: Little, Brown, 1965), 196–197.

47. Parrish, 56.

48. "Festival of the Boston Art Students Association," *The Bostonian* 1 (January 1895): 354–368. Robert Grant, *The Chippendales* (New York: Scribner, 1909), 26–27.

49. Richard Ellmann, "Henry James among the Aesthetes," *a long the riverrun* (New York: Random House, 1990), 149.

50. "Festival of Boston Art Students," 355, 360, 364.

51. Thomas Russell Sullivan, *Passages from the Journal of Thomas Russell Sullivan* (Boston: Houghton Mifflin, 1917), 226. See also 129.

52. RAC, *My Life*, 84.

53. Parrish, 55.

54. RAC, *My Life*, 84.

55. RAC to FHD, letter of June 1892, quoted in Parrish, 59. Although RAC took his Jacobitism quite seriously, he doubtless agreed with his friend R. Clipston Sturgis that "we admire and applaud Cromwell and love Charles and perhaps feel that we would rather be wrong with Charles than right with Cromwell," an observation made in an article by Sturgis ("The Significance of Christian Art") published by RAC in *Christian Art* 1 (April 1907): 3.

56. [Wallace Goodrich], *The Parish of the Advent in the City of Boston* (Boston: Parish of the Advent, 1944), 195.

57. Morris Carter, *Isabella Stewart Gardner and Fenway Court* (Boston: Houghton Mifflin, 1925), 4.

58. Finlay, 70. The Order of the White Rose is the subject of notes in *The Chap-Book*, for instance, in the issues of 6 (15 February 1897): 275–276; 6 (1 March 1897): 315; 6 (1 April 1897): 388; and 7 (15 February 1898): 274.

59. FHD's collection, including his Jacobite treasures, is discussed in *Verzeichnis von Privat-Bibliotheken*, I, *Vereinigten Staaten, Canada* (Leipzig, 1897), 19. See also Joe W. Kraus, *Messrs. Copeland and Day* (Philadelphia: George F. McManus, 1979), 10.

60. Brooks, *Indian Summer*, 437.

61. Russell Kirk, *Eliot and His Age* (La Salle, IL: Sherwood, Sugden, & Co., 1971), 137, 150, 107.

62. Daniel, 56.

63. *American Architect* 63 (18 March 1899): 88, pl. 1212. A prospectus is in C&GC/BPL. See also Daniel, 56, and Douglass Shand-Tucci, *Built in Boston: City and Suburb 1800–1950* (reprint Amherst: University of Massachusetts Press, 1988), 113.

For probably the first full-fledged low-rise, high-density, upper-middle-class courtyard apartment house in the country, according to "Richmond Court Apartments," an undated, unpaged brochure in C&GC/BPL, RAC and BGG's inspiration was European. Aside from Frank Lloyd Wright's Francis Apartments in Chicago in 1895, endowed with only a rather cramped courtyard, nineteenth-century examples of such courtyard apartment houses are rare in the United States. In his review of Stefanos Polyzoides et al., *Courtyard Housing in Los Angeles* (Berkeley: University of California Press, 1982), which focuses on that city's notable apartments (including Irving Gill's influential work), David Gebhard, writing in *Journal of the Society of Architectural Historians* 42 (May 1983): 189–190, notes that the building type's development came mostly after 1900, which is to place Richmond Court very much at its beginning.

64. RAC, *My Life*, 101.

65. Walter Knight Sturges, "The Long Shadow of Norman Shaw," *Journal of the Society of Architectural Historians* 9: issue 4, 15–20.

66. LIG to RAC, undated letter (ca. 1894), C&GC/BPL. The poem appeared in *The Century* 27 (February 1895): 557.

67. Mrs. Fred Bullard to RAC, undated letter, C&GC/BPL.

68. Marion C. Nichols to RAC, letter of 17 February 1894, C&GC/BPL. Henry Irving did play the role of Charles I, and in Boston in 1883 at the Boston Theatre, so he may well have done so in 1894 (see Eugene Tompkins, *The History of the Boston Theatre* [Boston: Houghton Mifflin, 1908], 309). A search through the Boston newspapers has not been attempted.

69. J. A. Symons, *The Quest for Corvo* (New York: Macmillan, 1934), 66.

70. Ferris Greenslet, *Under the Bridge* (Boston: Houghton Mifflin, 1943), 69–70.

71. Lears, 104, 115.

72. Parrish, 50. See also Kathryn Wheeler-Smith, "Alice Brown: Triumph and Tragedy in Tiverton's Wonderland" (Harvard Extension MLA Thesis, 1991), 12.

73. Elaine Showalter, *Sexual Anarchy: Gender and Culture at the Fin-de-Siècle* (New York: Penguin, 1990), 80–82.

74. A photograph of Bradley in his chair in 1900 is reproduced in Kaplan, *"Art That Is Life,"* 94.

75. RAC's "Saint George of England" appeared in *New England Magazine* 9 (December 1893): 407. For *The Boat of Love*, see *Poet Lore* 42 (1940): 165–177. See also BGG, "The Written Work of Ralph Adams Cram," *The Chap-Book* 4 (1 April 1896): 455–466.

76. Charles Wentworth to Edward Gale, letter of 14 June 1892. For RAC's and BGG's roles in *The Duenna Outwitted*, I am indebted to Stephen Jerome. The undated Xerox from a Brookline [Mass.] newspaper, reporting the event, is now in C&GC/BPL. The history of *The Angelus*, the only play of RAC's to have been performed so far as is known, is not very clear. A letter to RAC of 22 December 1892 from actor-producer Alexander Salvini, then at a hotel in Spokane, Washington, indicates that Salvini liked the play but could not do it at that time. (Salvini was probably the son of Tomasso Salvini, the great nineteenth-century Italian actor so well admired in Boston. See Elliot Norton, *Broadway Down East* [Boston: Boston Public Library, 1978], 39.) According to Franklin H. Sargent, president of the American Academy of the Dramatic Arts, 19 and 23 West Forty-fourth Street, New York, the play was eventually produced. ("Dear Mr. Cram:—The lady who plays in 'The Angelus' is anxious to know about her . . . style, etc., . . . If you could drop her a line and possibly give her a sketch . . .") though when and where the production took place is not known; Sargent's letter does not include a year. In 1897, however, *The Angelus* was still drawing interest. That year the *Boston Evening Record* of 3 August announced a forthcoming production of the play in the fall, of which no further documentation exists except for a letter of 3 December 1897 to RAC from E. S. Willard that refers to Willard's having read *The Angelus* during his American tour of 1897–98. All the letters and the clipping from the *Evening Record* are in C&GC/BPL, but no script of the play survives, and only that for one act of Cram's *John Andover* does.

77. RAC scrapbook, C&GC/BPL. The clipping is from the *Boston Sunday Herald*, 16 January 1895.

78. RAC, *My Life*, 94. There RAC, after noting *Excalibur*, omitted mention of another work of the same period the existence of which he had acknowledged in the typescript but then evidently thought better of including in the final book. The words omitted from the book as printed (in the paragraph on *Excalibur*) read as follows: ". . . for my part I could not resist the dynamic influence of this seething fellowship and I produced a sort of Prisoner of Zenda novel many years later and most injudiciously published under an assumed name and with a title for which I was not responsible."

79. John McCormick, *George Santayana* (New York: Paragon, 1987), 129.

80. See Robert Muccigrosso, "American Gothic: Ralph Adams Cram," *Thought* 47 (New York: Fordham University, March 1972): 105. This is perhaps the only discussion since Cram's death of his dramatic work. See also Chapter 9, n. 65.

81. Sullivan, *Journal*, 133–134.

82. LIG to Philip Savage, *Letters of Louise Imogen Guiney*, Grace Guiney, ed., 2 vols. (New York: Harper's, 1926), I, 246.

83. I will explore all of this at a greater length in my forthcoming *Painting, Sculpture and Craft*, a part of *The Boston Public Library's Sesquicentennial Book* (Boston: The Trustees, 1994).

84. The following quotations are from RAC, "The Influence of the French School on American Architecture," a paper read at the twenty-third annual convention of the American Institute of Architects, Pittsburgh, 14 December 1899; published in *AABN* 66 (25 December 1899): 65–66.

85. RAC to F. F. Tingley, letter of 28 December 1898, C&GC/BPL.

86. Lawrie did a bronze figure for the fountain of Richmond Court, ca. 1899.

87. Van Wyck Brooks, *An Autobiography* (New York: E. P. Dutton, 1965 ed.), 107.

88. Finlay, 47.

89. Brooks, *Autobiography*, 103.

90. Martin Green, *The Mount Vernon Street Warrens* (New York: Scribner's, 1989), 75.

91. Brooks, *Indian Summer,* 447.

92. Brooks, *Autobiography*, 102.

93. RAC, *My Life*, 88.

94. Thayer Lincoln to RAC, letter of 8 January 1935, C&GC/BPL.

95. A short story by Cather appeared in the issue of 21 May 1892.

96. Editorial, *The Mahogany Tree*, no. 16 (9 July 1892), 411.

97. See Jonathan Katz, *Gay/Lesbian Almanac* 704–705.

98. Shirley Everton Johnson, *The Cult of the Purple Rose* (Boston: Gorham Press, 1902), 57–58.

99. "Notes," *The Chap-Book* 5 (15 February 1896): 345.

100. Johnson, *Purple Rose*, 60, 61.

101. Parrish, 86.

102. Nicholas, Notebook II, 6.

9 GAY GOTHIC, DECADENT GOSPEL

1. Parrish, 94.

2. Laurens Maynard, "American Belles-Lettres Typography," *The Printing Art* 8 (September 1906): 17.

3. See RAC, *My Life*, 85–87.

4. The best discussion of Fenollosa and Dow is in Walter Muir Whitehill, *The Museum of Fine Arts, Boston: A Centennial History*, 2 vols. (Cambridge, MA: Harvard University Press, 1970), I, 104–105, 106, 112–115, 119–121, 123–125, 126.

5. LIG to Herbert Clarke, letter of 21 April 1892, *Letters of Louise Imogen Guiney*, Grace Guiney, ed., 2 vols. (New York: Harper's, 1926), I, 31.

6. [RAC], Editorial, *Knight Errant*, 1 (April 1892): 1.

7. LIG to Herbert Clarke, letter of 20 June 1892, *Letters*, I, 38.

8. LIG, "Knight Errant," *Knight Errant* 1 (April 1892): 2.

9. Walter Crane, *An Artist's Reminiscences* (New York: Macmillan, 1907), 371. Crane's own contribution to *Knight Errant*, "Of Aesthetic Pessimism and the New Hope," appeared in the second number, July 1892, 40–43.

10. Finlay, x, 12.

11. Charles Wentworth to RAC, [n.d.] January 1894, C&GC/BPL.

12. Ibid., letter of 22 September 1895, C&GC/BPL.

13. Ibid., letter of 1 May 1895, C&GC/BPL.

14. William A. and Sarah B. Cram to RAC, letter of 23 March 1895, C&GC/BPL.

15. William A. Cram to RAC, letter of 19 June 1895, C&GC/BPL. RAC's parents were not, it should be said, unimpressed, referring in a letter to RAC of 1 January 1895 to "the struggle that you have carried on so bravely for the last two years." That the problem was financial is clear in a letter of 23 January 1895 to T. Guild (of Bates & Guild, publishers of the *Architectural Review*) from RAC (C&GC/BPL), which reads in part: "Our affairs are in as bad a way as yours and I daresay worse. I have *not a cent* in the bank and do not know where to turn for anything."

16. Finlay, 100.

17. Jessica Todd Smith, "Ethel Reed: The Girl in the Poster" (senior thesis, Harvard College, 1991), 104. "Reed [was] a pawn," Smith writes, "in the homosexual/heterosexual debate."

18. Finlay, 100, 102.

19. The following quotations are from Ethel Reed's letters to RAC, ca. 1896–1898 (all undated), C&GC/BPL.

20. Smith, "Ethel Reed," 116.

21. Sarah B. Cram to RAC, letter of 23 March 1895, C&GC/BPL.

22. "Brother Anselm" to "Brother Clement," letter of 21 June 1895, C&GC/BPL.

23. This holograph ms., "The Rule of the American Congregation of the Canons Regular of Saint Norbert," is in C&GC/BPL.

24. "Brother Anselm" to "Brother Clement," letter of 11 March 1895, C&GC/BPL.

25. Ibid., letter of Holy Week, 1895, letter of 6 February 1895, C&GC/BPL.

26. Ibid., letter of 6 February.

27. Ibid., undated letter, C&GC/BPL.

28. Hilliard, 192.

29. Evelyn Waugh, *A Little Learning* (Boston: Little, Brown, 1964), 183.

30. LIG to RAC, letter of 26 June 1891, C&GC/BPL.

31. Ibid., letter of 3 April [year unclear], C&GC/BPL.

32. Episcopal Church Clerical Records, Archives of the Diocese of Massachusetts, establish Garland's identity. Letters from Swanton, VT, signed by Garland, to RAC on the occasion of his engagement also exist in C&GC/BPL.

33. Kenneth S. Rothwell, ed., *A Goodly Heritage: The Episcopal Church in Vermont* (Burlington, VT: Cathedral Church of St. Paul, 1973), 16 (St. Peter's, Bennington); 45 (Holy Trinity, Swanton); 51 (St. James's, Woodstock).

34. "Brother Anselm" to "Brother Clement," letter of 1 April 1895, C&GC/BPL.

35. Ibid.

36. Vaughan designed St. Peter's, Lyndonville, in 1898 and the altar and reredos of St. Peter's, Bennington, in 1909; see William Morgan, *The Almighty Wall: The Architecture of Henry Vaughan* (New York: Architectural History Foundation, 1983), 169 n. 26, 201.

37. George L. Richardson, *Arthur C. A. Hall* (Boston: Houghton Mifflin, 1932), 148. The Bishop's House that Sturgis designed was more of an Oxbridge House-cum-monastery. Wrote Richardson: "One wing was set apart for the library with the chapel above, and the whole central portion of the house was a common room with its great fireplace and massive oak table. The chapel . . . was one of the most exquisite and unique oratories in America. The Bishop had in his mind a small community modelled, perhaps unconsciously, on that group which he had himself joined at Cowley twenty-five years before. . . . The plan also including asking young men who were preparing for holy orders to live at the house. . . . It was the Bishop's delight to work with these young men, guiding them in their studies and in their spiritual life. Regular hours of prayer were kept in the chapel. . . . There were hours of agreeable talk about the fireplace, walks among the woods and cliffs of the point, opportunities . . . among the treasures of the library. Then . . . the bell would sound for service in the chapel—not a perfunctory recitation of the offices [149–150]"; quite the American-Anglican version of Ned Warren's scholarly English community at Lewes.

38. Personal interview with Margaret Henderson Floyd, 23 February 1992. See also Sister Catherine Louise, SSM, *The House of My Pilgrimage* (Boston: St. Margaret's, undated), 69, and a letter of 20 April 1943 to Mary Jenness from an unidentified Cowley father, in SSJE Archives.

39. There is a file labeled "Mower, Martin," on all this in GMA. See also Lincoln Kirstein, *Mosaic* (New York: Farrar, Straus, and Giroux, 1994), 164–169.

40. Sister Catherine Louise, *Pilgrimage*, 29.

41. For Bodley's work in 1856 for the sisters' oratory at East Grinstead see Peter Anson, *Fashions in Church Furnishings* (London: Faith Press, 1960), 166; for his work for the Cowley Fathers, St. John the Evangelist, Oxford, completed in 1898, see Anson, 234; for Vaughan's work for the sisters in Boston see Morgan, *Almighty Wall*, 6–7, 18–19; for Vaughan's work at the Cowley Fathers' Beacon Hill Church of St. John the Evangelist, see Morgan, 165 n. 26.

42. Morgan, *Almighty Wall*, 168 n. 14.

43. Daniel, 250 n. 76.

44. RAC to FHD, undated letter, C&GC/BPL.

45. H. H. Wilcox to RAC, letter of 17 October 1894, C&GC/BPL. The threat to place the matter with lawyers is in a letter of 13 October 1894 from Wilcox to Messrs. Cram and Goodhue, also in C&GC/BPL.

46. See BGG, "The Written Work of Ralph Adams Cram," *The Chap-Book* 4 (1 April 1896): 455–466.

47. RAC, *My Life*, 86.

48. For Copeland and Day see, as an overall review of the firm, Susan Otis Thomp-

son, *American Book Design and William Morris* (New York: Bowker, 1977), 38–54. For a more detailed and comprehensive discussion see Joe W. Kraus, *Messrs. Copeland and Day* (Philadelphia: George F. McManus, 1979), and Parrish, 210–296 ("Copeland and Day, Publishers"). For the key relationship of the firm with the Bodley Head, see James G. Nelson, "Appendix D. The Reception of Bodley Head Books in America," *The Early Nineties* (Cambridge, MA: Harvard University Press, 1971). Nelson gives a complete listing of the Bodley Head's publishing history in the United States, noting that Copeland and Day "got the choice Bodley Head books in America."

49. Jussim, 83. She gives no source for the tale, but it is very much in keeping with Goodhue's often ebullient ways.

50. "Richard Hovey," *DAB*, IX, 273.

51. See Finlay, 84–85.

52. Eve Kosofsky Sedgwick, *Between Men* (New York: Columbia University Press, 1985), 90.

53. H. P. Lovecraft, *Supernatural Horror in Literature* (New York: Abramson, 1945), 1.

54. Robert Taylor, "Aubrey Beardsley: His Age of Anxiety," *Boston Sunday Globe* (26 June 1983); Michael Kimmelman, "Fra Angelico of Satanism Shines at Harvard," *New York Times* (11 June 1989). Thanks in no small measure to Grenville Winthrop, a student of Charles Eliot Norton, Harvard has the greatest Beardsley collection in America.

55. LIG to Louise C. Moulton, letter of 10 September 1894, quoted in Parrish, 95.

56. Elaine Showalter, *Sexual Anarchy: Gender and Culture at the Fin-de-Siècle* (New York: Penguin, 1990), 113, 107.

57. Alice Brown, *Study of Stevenson*, quoted in Showalter, *Sexual Anarchy*, 108.

58. Marion C. Nichols to RAC, letter of 17 February 1894, C&GC/BPL.

59. Gay, *Tender Passion*, 241.

60. Ibid., 221. For a discussion of RAC's *Decadent*, *À Rebours*, and *Dorian Gray* see Jussim, 60. The overall context of inaction in *The Decadent* is very similar to that in *À Rebours*. For contemporary reviewers sensing *Dorian Gray*'s gay overtones see Beckson, 48.

61. Showalter, *Sexual Anarchy*, 171.

62. Martin, 219.

63. Showalter, *Sexual Anarchy*, 15.

64. Martin, 202.

65. Muccigrosso, in his *American Gothic: The Mind and Art of Ralph Adams Cram* (Washington, DC: University Press of America, 1980), argues that the anticapitalist content of *The Decadent* posited the major themes that in the 1920s and 1930s RAC would explore in a series of influential books. RAC's role as a conservative thinker in the post-World War I era is also dealt with in Robert Crunden, *The Superfluous Men: Conservative Critics of American Culture 1900–1945* (Austin: University of Texas Press, 1977).

66. RAC, *The Decadent; or, The Gospel of Inaction* (Boston: Copeland and Day, 1893); the following quotations are from this work, passim. It should be noted that the geisha is clearly sexed by RAC in the text (as opposed to BGG's somewhat epicene treatment in the sketch) and that Aurelian draws "her slim figure toward him, kissing the scarlet mouth." She figures, admittedly, no more prominently than does the black boy in

the red fez, but he is not similarly accosted. Nor anyone else, explicitly, though there is this sentence: "On the floor, before the fire, lay the three men, . . . their dark figures radiating from the queer brazier." For the absurd or satirical subtitle as a mark of "self-deprecating humor, satire and parody" in decadent literature see Beckson, 37.

The Decadent had a very small press run, a first printing of 110 copies. This does not mean it was not influential, however. John Addington Symonds's famous *A Problem of Greek Ethics* was first published, privately, in an edition of only ten copies. Eight years later the second edition consisted of only fifty copies.

67. See Paglia, 506.

68. Sedgwick, *Epistemology*, 172. For the gay resonance of drugs in this context see also Beckson, 34.

69. George Santayana, *The Last Puritan* (New York: Scribner's, 1936), 153–169.

70. Philippe Jullian, *Dreamers of Decadence* (New York: Praeger, 1971), 45; Martin Green, *The Mount Vernon Street Warrens* (New York: Scribner's, 1989), 160.

71. Jussim, 58; Parrish, 77.

72. *Boston Courier* (14 August 1892), quoted in Jussim, 54.

73. LIG to RAC, letter of 16 August 1894, C&GC/BPL. Similarly, Charles Wentworth hated *The Yellow Book*, writing RAC in February 1895, "My aunt sent me the *Yellow Book* for Christmas and I immediately had it changed. I would not own such a piece of putridity" (C&GC/BPL). Another note in regard to *The Decadent* to survive among RAC's papers is from an otherwise anonymous Marshall Oliver of Annapolis, MD. Dated 26 December 1893, it reads in part: "It is interesting and remarkable that a 'farm Yankee' (forgive me; I am one too!) living in a Puritan commonwealth should have conceived of [*The Decadent*]" (C&GC/BPL).

74. FHD to unidentified correspondent, letter of 21 November 1893, quoted in Jussim, 58.

75. Ibid.

76. "A New Publishing Firm — Copeland and Day," *Publishers' Weekly* 44 (2 December 1893): 927.

77. H. Copeland to FHD, letter of 25 June 1894, quoted in Jussim, 87.

That no significant reviews of *The Decadent* have yet come to light is not surprising given Cram's withholding of his name. For a discussion in the same period of a similarly issued work by Henry Adams, *Esther*, that received no attention whatsoever, see Ernest Samuels, *Henry Adams: The Middle Years* (Cambridge, MA: Harvard University Press, 1958), 222–225. Note that only two years later, *Black Spirits and White*, published forthrightly over Cram's name, was not ignored in the same way as *The Decadent*. Although I have discovered only one review for Cram's second book, it was in *The Nation* (27 February 1896, 181–183), a leading journal. Though not much of a rave (the reviewer wrote of *Black Spirits and White* that "its novelty is not dazzling . . . its arrangement is out of proportion to its utility"), Cram was put in good company, his work reviewed alongside that of Sarah Orne Jewett, William Sharp, Louise Guiney, Brander Matthews, Bram Stoker, and Bret Harte, whose *Clarence* was the only book the author of this unsigned review really liked.

78. Goodhue, "The Written Work of Ralph Adams Cram," 466.

79. Ibid., 463, 465–466.

80. Jussim, 59.

10 THE RIDDLE OF THE VISIONISTS

1. F. W. Coburn, "Syriac Suggestions," *Boston Sunday Herald* (22 April 1917).

2. Herbert Copeland to Herbert Stone and Ingalls Kimball, letter of 24 June 1894, quoted in Parrish, 53.

3. Henry D. Blaney, "Rats' Paradise: Province Court," *Old Boston* (Boston: Lee & Shepherd, 1896), 115.

4. RAC, *My Life*, 91.

5. Thayer Lincoln to RAC, letter of 8 January 1935, C&GC/BPL.

6. Herbert Copeland to RAC, undated letter, ca. February 1902, C&GC/BPL.

7. Charles Wentworth to RAC, letter of 1 May 1895, C&GC/BPL.

8. The receipt, dated 9 January 1893, is in C&GC/BPL.

9. T. H. Randall to RAC, letter of 24 January 1895, C&GC/BPL.

10. Wentworth to RAC, letter of 1 May 1895.

11. Finlay, 21; Jessica Todd Smith, "Ethel Reed: The Girl in the Poster" (senior thesis, Harvard College, 1991), 53–54.

12. Margaret Henderson Floyd, *Architecture after Richardson* (Chicago: University of Chicago Press, 1994), 347–350, 374, 376; Ethan Naderman, "Yes: Should We Legalize Drugs? History Answers," *American Heritage* 44 (February-March 1993): 45–47 passim.

13. For RAC's tastes in liquor see RAC to G. Edward Mueller, letter of 8 April 1940. I am grateful to Mr. Ralph Adams Cram II for this source. For BGG's, see Charles Whitaker, "Biography," *Bertram Grosvenor Goodhue: Architect and Master of Many Arts*, Charles H. Whitaker, ed. (New York: American Institute of Architects Press, 1925), 17.

14. [Gelett Burgess], "Some Experiences with Haschisch," *Technology Review*, quoted in Joseph Backus, "Gelett Burgess, a Biography of the Man Who Wrote 'The Purple Cow'" (Ph.D. dissertation, University of California, Berkeley, 1961). I am grateful to Mr. Jan Michowski of the Boston Athenaeum for locating this source.

15. See Chapter 1 and Jussim, 58, 205.

16. Marquess of Queensbury to Lord Alfred Douglas, letter of 1 April 1894, quoted in Ellmann, *Wilde*, 417.

17. Althea Hayter, *Opium and the Romantic Imagination*, quoted in Geoffrey Wolff, *Black Sun: The Brief Transit and Violent Eclipse of Harry Crosby* (New York: Random House, 1976), 164. For this source, I am indebted to Elizabeth Hunter.

18. RAC, *My Life*, 93.

19. The 1924 edition of RAC's *Church Building*, for example, lists on the verso of the half title, under "Books by the Same Author" and "Pamphlets," a total of fourteen works, but neither *The Decadent* nor *Black Spirits and White* is included.

20. Wolff, *Black Sun*, 181. Wolff is quoting Morse Peckham, *The Triumph of Romanticism*.

21. A. J. A. Symons, *The Quest for Corvo* (New York: Macmillan, 1934).

22. RAC, *My Life*, 93.

23. Thayer Lincoln to RAC, letter of 8 January 1935. For the mention of the cat in Cram's autobiography, see *My Life*, 92.

24. Arlo Bates, *The Pagans* (New York: Henry Holt, 1884), 23. See also Finlay, ix. I am indebted to B. Hughes Morris for directing me to this source.

25. Claude Bragdon, *More Lives Than One* (New York: Knopf, 1938), 152.

26. Francis W. Lee to FHD, letter of 7 November 1892, quoted in Jussim, 52.

27. RAC to Bliss Carman, letter of 24 June 1894, quoted in H. P. Grundy, "Bliss Carman and the Pewter Mugs," *Douglas Library Notes* (Queen's University, Antigonish, NS) 17 (1968): 7–14.

28. The nature of the involvement of these women in Boston's Bohemia is unclear. On the general question, which has not been very much studied, see Mary W. Blanchard, "Near *The Coast of Bohemia*: Boundaries and the Aesthetic Press" (unpublished paper, Rutgers University, Department of History, 1992), 22–23. Blanchard (discussing William Dean Howells's *The Coast of Bohemia* of 1893) writes of the room in which so much of the action of that novel takes place that it was

> enclosed and stifling ... an aesthetic hothouse full of "lustrous rugs hung up beside the door ... [and] a great tigerskin with the head on, that sprawled in front of the fireplace." [Here it was that his heroine invited another woman to spend the night, thus] ... hinting at homoerotic forces that were associated with aestheticism and women's participation in a bohemian lifestyle.

The similarity to Cram's great room in *The Decadent* is striking.

29. RAC, *My Life*, 91, 92–93.

30. Albert Parry, *Garrets and Pretenders: A History of Bohemianism in America* (reprint New York: Dover, 1960), 146.

31. Finlay, x, 11.

32. Thayer Lincoln to RAC, letter of 8 January 1935.

33. Bliss Carman, "Vagabondia," *Songs from Vagabondia* (Boston: Copeland and Day, 1894), 4.

34. J. R. Bridge, "Helena Petrovna Blavatsky," *The Arena* (Boston, 12 April 1895): 177–184, places Blavatsky in Boston just prior to the founding of the Theosophical Society. The author calls Boston then "the Mecca of the Spiritualists," though in that venue Madame was not successful at this time. See also Sylvia Cranston, *HPB: The Extraordinary Life and Influence of Helena Blavatsky* (New York: Putnam, 1993), 124, 136–137, 161.

35. Ibid., 388–389.

36. Ibid., 390. See also Bragdon, *More Lives Than One*, 52.

37. The First Spiritualist Temple was erected at a cost of $250,000 in 1885. It is a massive Richardsonian structure.

38. The present Besant Lodge of the Theosophical Society in Boston was founded in 1923, but their records, although sparse, indicate that a predecessor organization existed in the 1890s, and Cranston, in *HPB*, notes that in that era there were twelve American lodges, one of which was surely in Boston, where Madame Blavatsky was well known and had no few disciples.

39. Nicholas, Notebook II, 16; Parrish, 21.

40. Jussim, 46, 269, 285.

41. The English translation given here is by R. J. Schork, professor of classics at the University of Massachusetts Boston, to whom I am much indebted for his help. He points out that in addition to the (presumable) typographical error of *sumnia* (there being no such word in Latin), for which he has suggested *summa* (excellence) or *somnia* (dreams), there is also a mistake in gender: *ordinis* being masculine, the relative pronoun should be *qui*, not *quae*. Considering the historical context of this dedication, I have substituted

"Exarch" for Schork's "leader" (for *Exarcho*); "and brothers" for Schork's "and comrades" (for *fratribusque*); and of the two possibilities presented by Schork, in lieu of *sumnia* I have preferred *somnia* (dreams). I wish to thank the distinguished headmaster of a school celebrated for its classical studies for his learned assistance in this matter.

42. Israel Regardie et al., *The Golden Dawn* (St. Paul, MN: Llewellyn Publications, 1989 ed.). Pasht is illustrated on 655; Isis on 316. See also Beckson, 327.

43. Philippe Jullian, *Dreamers of Decadence* (New York: Praeger, 1971), 94; "Aleister Crowley," *Harper's Encyclopedia of Mystical and Paranormal Experience*, R. E. Guiley, ed. (San Francisco: Harpers, 1991), 129. The *Encyclopedia of Occultism and Parapsychology*, Leslie Shepard, ed. (2d ed., Detroit: Gale Co., 1984), calls Crowley without qualification "the most celebrated occult magician of modern times."

Of several biographies of Crowley, I have relied on the most recent and, it would seem, reasonable: Colin Wilson, *Aleister Crowley* (London: Harper's, 1987). Among a good many appearances in fiction, Crowley was the subject of a novel by Somerset Maugham, *The Magician* (1908). Aside from the summer of 1916, Crowley's closest known association with New England was to have seduced the wife of Amanda Kamaroswami, the Boston Museum of Fine Arts's Curator of Indian Art; see Wilson, *Crowley*, 112. Whether the Golden Dawn still exists in any recognizable form is a subject of some controversy.

44. David S. Reynolds, review of Ann-Janine Morey, *Religion and Sexuality in American Literature*, in *New England Quarterly* 66 (June 1993): 306.

45. John Symonds, "Aleister Crowley," and Kathleen Raine, "The Golden Dawn," in Richard Cavendish, ed., *Man, Myth and Magic* (New York: Marshall Cavendish, 1983), II, 559, and IV, 1131–34. For Charles Williams see Humphrey Carpenter, *The Inklings* (Boston: Houghton Mifflin, 1979), 81–84. For Evelyn Underhill see Christopher G. R. Armstrong, *Evelyn Underhill* (Grand Rapids, MI: Eerdmans, 1975), 36–59. Sax Rohmer was also an initiate of the Golden Dawn.

46. Armstrong, *Underhill*, 37. Rosicrucianism in Boston, unlike Theosophy or Spiritualism or Swedenborgianism, seems never to surface with any definitiveness. Rosicrucian symbols abound in the "Hound of Heaven" mural cycle of R. Ives Gammell (discussed in Chapter 2). Otherwise, the stained-glass artist and Wellesley faculty member Eleanor Ryan is remembered by B. Hughes Morris as having been a Rosicrucian. Do too was Day's protegé Alvin Langdon Coburn.

47. Edward Wagenknecht, ed., *The Fireside Book of Ghost Stories* (Indianapolis: Bobbs-Merrill, 1947), 18; H. P. Lovecraft, *Supernatural Horror in Literature* (New York: Abramson, 1945), 41; see also 38.

48. Armstrong, *Underhill*, 45–47.

49. *Harper's Encyclopedia*, 260.

50. RAC, *My Life*, 92.

51. Finlay, 15, 17–18. Martin Mower did the title page of *Low Tide at Grand Pré*.

52. Henry G. Fairbanks, *Louise Imogen Guiney* (New York: Twayne, 1973), 139, 148.

53. John McCormick, *George Santayana* (New York: Paragon, 1987), 185.

54. Bliss Carman, "The Girl in the Poster," Bliss Carman and Richard Hovey, *Last Songs from Vagabondia* (Boston: Small, Maynard, 1901), 28–31.

55. Parrish, 50.

56. RAC, *My Life*, 95.

57. Louis Elson, *The History of American Music* (New York: Macmillan, 1904), 253.

58. Rupert Hughes, *Contemporary American Composers* (Boston: L. C. Page, 1900), 356–357.

59. Bliss Carman, *Saint Kavin: A Ballad* (Boston: Copeland and Day, 1894), unpaged.

60. Bliss Carman and Richard Hovey, "Concerning Kavin," *More Songs from Vagabondia* (Boston: Small, Maynard, 1896), 21.

61. BGG, "Traumburg," *Architectural Review* 5 (1896): 1–3, 5, 35–37. See also *A Book of Architectural and Decorative Drawings by Bertram Grosvenor Goodhue* (New York: Architectural Book Publishing Co., 1914), and Richard Oliver, *Bertram Grosvenor Goodhue* (New York: Architectural History Foundation, 1983), 31.

62. See Chapter 7.

63. Donald Stevens, *Bliss Carman: Mask and Myth* (New York: Twayne, 1966), 29.

64. Ibid., 26–27, 31.

65. Eve Kosofsky Sedgwick, *Between Men* (New York: Columbia University Press, 1985), 94.

66. Thomas E. Tallmadge, *The Story of Architecture in America* (New York: W. W. Norton, 1927), 259.

67. William Linneman, *Richard Hovey: An American Radical* ((Boston: G. K. Hall, 1976), 34–35.

68. Alan H. MacDonald, *Richard Hovey: Man and Craftsman* (Durham, NC: Duke University Press, 1957), 141.

69. Ibid., 164, 45.

70. Linneman, *Hovey*, 89.

71. Ibid., 24.

72. Wayne R. Dynes, "Aesthetic Movement" in Dynes, ed., *Encyclopedia of Homosexuality* (New York: Garland, 1990), 16–17.

73. RAC, *Church Building*, published by Small, Maynard in 1901 and again in 1914. The 1924 edition was issued by Marshall Jones. The series began in *The Churchman* 80 (16 September 1899): 327–331.

74. Oliver, *Goodhue*, 40.

75. The exterior of the Day chapel is illustrated in Montgomery Schuyler, "The Works of Cram, Goodhue and Ferguson," *Architectural Record* 29 (January 1911): 7; the interior in Jussim, 213. For a photograph of the Scituate studio, see Nicholas Kilmer, *Thomas Buford Meteyard* (New York: Berry-Hill Galleries, 1989), 29, fig. 25. The building still stands, altered, but despite strenuous efforts on my part, the owners allowed me access only to the grounds.

76. "Jonathan [?]" to RAC, letter of 18 January 1895, headed "Fall River"; C&GC/BPL.

77. The office records confirm the assertion of William Carburg and Jack Frost in *Channels of Grace* (Boston: Hawthorne Press, 1954), 12, that RAC designed interior fittings at the Gate of Heaven Church in South Boston, but they record an episcopal throne and altar cards rather than the main altar referred to by Messrs. Carburg and Frost. Another early church commission of which little is known is the chancel of Emmanuel Church, Wakefield, Massachusetts, which the office records indicate was built to RAC's designs in 1892.

78. RAC to LIG, letter of [no day] February 1895, C&GC/BPL.

79. LIG to RAC, letter of 28 March 1895, C&GC/BPL.

80. The following quotations are from RAC, "On the Contemporary Architecture of the Catholic Church," *Catholic World* 58 (February 1894): 644–654.

81. RAC, "John D. Sedding," *Architectural Review* 1 (14 December 1891): 10.

82. "I Feel As If I Had Lost My Home," *Fall River Herald News*, 11 April 1973, quoted in Daniel, 248 n. 5. The story is from one Father Driscoll, reportedly a sometime curate at SS. Peter and Paul.

83. RAC, *My Life*, 105.

84. RAC to Ralph Wentworth Cram, letter of 9 February 1928, C&GC/BPL.

85. For Sedding's keen interest in church art see *Victorian Church Art* (London: Victoria and Albert Museum, 1971), 120–131.

86. Oliver quotes from BGG's correspondence with Lethaby (now in the Goodhue Papers in the Avery Architectural Library at Columbia University) in *Goodhue*, 226, 247 n. 39.

87. LIG to RAC, letter of 14 December 1908, C&GC/BPL.

88. *Victorian Church Art*, 144.

89. "New St. Stephen's Church," *Fall River Daily Herald* (6 December 1897), 1.

90. RAC, *Church Building* (1901 ed.), 79.

91. Alastair Service, *Edwardian Architecture* (New York: Oxford University Press, 1977), 122, 46–47. For a biographical note on Wilson see 212 in that work.

92. William R. Lethaby, *Architecture, Mysticism and Myth* (London, 1891; reprint New York: Braziller, 1975), v–viii. Oliver discusses the significance of these passages to BGG in *Goodhue*, 28–30.

93. Little is known of the order's Scituate cell, as opposed to Norwood. Though Testudo, the Meteyard house burned, the studio (see n. 75 above) survives. See Finlay, 97.

94. RAC, *My Life*, 98–99.

95. RAC, *Impressions of Japanese Architecture and the Allied Arts* (reprint New York: Dover, 1966), 19.

96. RAC, *My Life*, 100.

97. RAC, *Japanese Architecture*, 119–120.

98. RAC, *My Life*, 100–101.

99. Sidney McCall [Mary Fenollosa], *Truth Dexter* (Boston: Little, Brown, 1901), 3. I am indebted to B. Hughes Morris for alerting me to this source.

100. Clay Lancaster, *The Japanese Influence in America* (New York: Walton H. Rawls, 1963), 71.

101. "An Oriental Home," *Boston Sunday Herald* (17 February 1895), 31.

102. Sylvester Morse, *Japanese Homes and Their Surroundings* (New York: Harper and Bros., 1889).

103. Lancaster, *Japanese Influence*, 71. For RAC's discussion see his "Architectural Experiment," *Architectural Record* 8 (July–September 1898): 82–91.

104. "An Oriental Home," 31.

105. I am indebted to Attorney Richard N. LaSalle, whose home the Knapp House now is, for allowing me to inspect this house, and to Mrs. Florence C. Brigham of the Fall River Historical Society for identifying Mr. LaSalle as the owner. Professor Lancaster is wrong to think the house is no longer standing. Though the interior decor has been much altered, even that has largely survived as of the fall of 1992, when I viewed the property. The garden has been obliterated as has the gate house, although some trees remain, and

the tea house interior is hardly recognizable as such. That so much of the original fabric exists, however, is due to Mr. LaSalle's care.

106. "An Oriental Home," 31.

107. Clay Lancaster, "Japanese Buildings in the United States," *Art Bulletin* 35 (September 1953): 217. See also Lancaster, *Japanese Influence*, 75.

108. Quoted, ibid., 71.

109. [Anonymous], "Japanese Architecture and Its Relation to the Coming American Style," *The Craftsman* 10 (May 1906): 192.

110. Lancaster, "Japanese Buildings," 70–75; C. E. Hooper, *Country House* (Garden City, NY: Doubleday, 1904, 1913).

111. William H. Jordy, *American Buildings and Their Architects: Progressive and Academic Ideas at the Turn of the Century* (Garden City, NY: Doubleday, 1976), 227.

112. RAC, *Japanese Architecture*, 19.

113. Bliss Carman, "Phi Beta Kappa Poem: Harvard, 1914," *April Airs* (Boston: Small, Maynard, 1916), 39–42.

114. Jussim, 50.

115. Evelyn Underhill, *The Essentials of Mysticism* (reprint New York: Dutton, 1960), 126–127.

116. Quoted in Parrish, 76–77.

117. Edmund White, *States of Desire: Travels in Gay America* (New York: Penguin, 1980), 256.

118. Parrish, 75.

119. Daniel Gregory Mason, "At Harvard in the Nineties," *New England Quarterly* 9 (March 1936): 66.

120. Ellmann, *a long the riverrun* (New York: Random House, 1990), 17.

121. Ibid., 19.

122. Russell Kirk, *Eliot and His Age* (La Salle, IL: Sherwood, Sugden & Co., 1971), 155.

123. Quoted, ibid.

124. T. S. Eliot, *The Family Reunion* (paperback ed., New York: Harcourt Brace Jovanovich, 1966), 110.

125. Lincoln to RAC, letter of 8 January 1935.

126. George Steiner, "A Terrible Beauty," review of *The Gonne-Yeats Letters, 1893–1938, The New Yorker* (8 February 1983), 110.

127. Bliss Carman, *Songs from Vagabondia*, front endpapers.

11 KNIGHTS ERRANT

1. Herbert Copeland to FHD, letter of 25 June 1894, quoted in Jussim, 89.

2. See "Saunterings," *Town Topics* 29 (30 March 1893), 7.

3. Paglia, 491.

4. Quoted in Ronald Hayman, *A Critical Life: Nietzsche* (New York: Penguin, 1980), viii.

5. Nathan G. Hale, *Freud in America*, vol. I of *Freud and the Americans* (New York: Oxford University Press, 1971), 121.

6. Lendon Snedeker, *One Hundred Years at Children's Hospital* (Boston: Children's Hospital, 1969), 96, 100.

7. RAC, "All Saints' Church, Dorchester," *The Churchman* 79 (April 1899): 563.

8. RAC, "John D. Sedding," *Architectural Review* 1 (14 December 1891): 10.

9. Trinity Church, though a cultural revelation for New England in the largest sense, in its splendor of color of murals and glass, was deeply flawed from the aesthete Anglo-Catholic view, a fact easily misunderstood—by Alan H. MacDonald, for example, in his *Richard Hovey: Man and Craftsman* (Durham, NC: Duke University Press, 1957).

10. Holy Trinity is described in great detail in Peter Anson, *Fashions in Church Furnishings* (London: Faith Press, 1960), 248–251.

11. Ibid., 229.

12. For Mora see Ernest Laroche, "Domingo Mora," *Algunos: Pintores y Escultorres* (Montevideo, 1939), 151–156; *American Art Annual* (1913): 79; "Mora, Domingo," *Thieme-Becker/Kunstler Lexikon* (Leipzig, 1931), XXV, 113; Lorado Taft, *History of American Sculpture* (New York: Macmillan, 1903), 469; and John Wright, *Some Notable Altars* (New York: Macmillan, 1908), 312. For John Evans see Douglass Shand-Tucci, "John Evans Corp.," unpublished paper, C&GC/BPL. The Evans Collection in the Boston Public Library was given by Frederick Davis at the same time as were the Cram and Connick collections.

13. See Silvio Geranio, *Revista de la Sociedad Amigos de la Auquelologia* (Montevideo, 1924), III, 247–268. The sculpture is in the Museum of Fine Arts in Montevideo.

14. Robert Brown, "All Saints' Church . . .," *Architectural Review* 7 (August 1900), describes the artwork most reliably. RAC discusses it in "All Saints' Church," *The Churchman* 79 (15 April 1899): 563. Illustrations of the chancel as RAC developed and enhanced it are found in RAC, *Church Building* (Boston: Small, Maynard, 1901), 42, 90, 101, 105, 106, 107, 153, 167. The first designs for woodwork and altar brasses, very different from those BGG finally designed, were published in *Architectural Review* 11, (3 July 1903), plates 30–31.

15. H. J. Janson, *History of World Art* (New York: Abrams, 1969), 499.

16. Philippe Jullian, *Dreamers of Decadence* (New York: Praeger, 1971), 108; Paglia, 496.

17. Paglia, 508–509, 496.

18. Richard Ellmann, *a long the riverrun* (New York: Random House, 1990), 19.

19. Jussim, 90, 91; Shaun O'Connell, *Imagining Boston* (Boston: Beacon Press, 1990), 55. For the American reaction to Wilde's downfall see Jonathan Katz, *Gay/Lesbian Almanac* (New York: Harper and Row, 1983), 695 n. 25; much more needs to be done on this subject. The requiem for Beardsley was probably held, according to reliable sources in the Archdiocese of Boston who prefer to remain anonymous, at the convent of the Mesdames of the Sacred Heart on Massachusetts Avenue in Boston's South End.

20. LIG to FHD, letter of 30 October 1898, quoted in Parrish, 294.

21. Ellison F. Marvin to Mary Cram Nicholas, letter of 2 June 1977, C&GC/BPL; Humphrey Burton, *Leonard Bernstein* (New York: Doubleday, 1994), 156, 158, 160.

22. LIG to FHD, letter of 23 March 1919, quoted in Parrish, 332.

23. "Philip Savage," *DAB*, XVI, 390–391.

24. LIG to RAC, letter of 12 May 1892, C&GC/BPL.

25. LIG to FHD, letter of 3 January 1904, quoted in Parrish, 297.

26. Brooks, *Indian Summer*, 446–447.

27. RAC, *My Life*, 13.

28. LIG to FHD, letter of 15 February 1901, quoted in Parrish, 332.

29. Larzer Ziff, *The American 1890's: Life and Times of a Lost Generation* (New York: Viking, 1966), 333.

30. Most, for example, arise in Jackson Lears's influential *No Place of Grace.* The fact that such a Bohemia had existed in Boston, memory of which was too quickly fading, did surface once in a while. For example, *Athenaeum Notes* 44 (November 1948): 1, lamented that Alice Brown had not "produced an autobiography, [because had she] a dim, surviving knowledge of a lively little Boston Bohemia of the eighteen-nineties might have been enlarged." Instead, Brown took care to burn LIG's letters!

31. A. L. R. Carter, "The Two Great Exhibitions," quoted in Parrish, 331; Parrish, 240.

32. Susan Otis Thompson, *American Book Design and William Morris* (New York: Bowker, 1977), 66 (for Rogers), 126 (for Bradley).

33. O'Connell, *Imagining Boston,* 55.

34. Lawrence Dawler, Foreword, Finlay, v.

35. MacDonald, *Hovey,* 132.

36. Steven Watson, *Strange Bedfellows: The First American Avant-Garde* (New York: Abbeville, 1991).

37. Reginald Isaacs, *Gropius: An Illustrated Biography of the Creator of the Bauhaus* (Boston: Bulfinch Press/Little, Brown, 1991), 232.

38. Beckson, 45.

39. Robert Crunden, Introduction to Part IV, "Humanism and the Originality of the Artist," *The Superfluous Men: Conservative Critics of American Culture 1900–1945* (Austin: University of Texas Press, 1977), 131. For the essay by T. S. Eliot, "Tradition and the Individual Talent," see Frank Kermode, ed., *Selected Prose of T. S. Eliot* (New York: Harcourt Brace Jovanovich/Farrar, Straus and Giroux, 1975), 37–44.

40. RAC, "Good and Bad Modern Gothic," *Architectural Review* 6 (August 1899): 115–119.

41. Quoted in Hayman, *Nietzsche,* 209.

42. For Gardner's interest in the Oberammergau Passion Play see Morris Carter, *Isabella Stewart Gardner and Fenway Court* (Boston: Houghton Mifflin, 1925), 118–119; her interest in the Bayreuth Wagner Festival is well known. For FHD's interest in the play see Jussim, 41–42, where the author notes that "as a mass-media event of the 1890 season, its only competition was the Wagner festival at Bayreuth." For the Passion Play's influence on FHD's crucifixion series see Jussim, 122, 125.

43. Beckson, 325.

44. Ibid., 52.

45. RAC, "On the Contemporary Architecture of the Catholic Church," *Catholic World* 58 (February 1894), 648.

46. Martin Green, *The Mount Vernon Street Warrens* (New York: Scribner's, 1989), 178.

47. Ellmann, *a long the riverrun,* 9.

48. LIG to RAC, undated note, C&GC/BPL.

49. Nicholas, Notebook II, 26, 21, 22–23.

50. RAC, "Contemporary Architecture of the Catholic Church," 646, 650, 651, 653.

51. Liane Lefaivre, "Eros, Architecture and the *Hypnerotomachia Poliphili,*" *Design Book Review* 18 (Spring 1990): 20.

52. Ibid., 18. See also Alberto Pérez-Gómez, *Polyphilo . . . An Erotic Epiphany of Architecture* (Cambridge, MA: MIT Press, 1992), xvii.

53. Martin Green, *The Problem of Boston* (New York: W. W. Norton, 1966), 110.

54. "The Church in Massachusetts," *The Church Militant* (April 1902): 11. The story reads in part: "Trinity Church is to have a robed choir in the chancel [and] a new organ. . . . The building will be closed during the summer while the necessary changes [presumably choir stalls in the chancel] are being made to accommodate the choir. It is to be hoped that the proposed changes include an altar." Though "Trinity is the nearest we have to a cathedral," the diocesan paper goes on to opine that it is a measure of how low a diocese Massachusetts then was that Trinity is described as being "perhaps in the country" the only church "that has no altar."

55. John Summerson, *Victorian Architecture in England* (New York: W. W. Norton, 1970), 1-2.

56. Redfern Mason, "Music and Architecture Must Harmonize," *The Caecilia* (October 1937): 381 (reprinted from *Boston Evening Transcript*, 21 August 1937).

57. Untitled comment appended to RAC, "On the Religious Aspect of Architecture," *Architectural Record* 1 (January-March 1893): 356-357.

58. RAC, "The Decoration of City Houses: Introduction — The Vestibule," *The Decorator and Furnisher* 7 (November 1885): 38.

59. RAC, *My Life*, 29-31.

60. RAC, "Interior Decoration of Churches," *Architectural Review* 4 (1896): 53, 52, 50.

61. The original Advent rood is illustrated in Mark Wuonola, *Church of the Advent, Boston* (Boston: for the Parish, 1975), 6.

62. RAC, "Contemporary Architecture of the Catholic Church," 653.

63. Ibid., 646; Richard Guy Wilson, "Edith and Ogden: Writing, Decoration and Architecture," Pauline C. Metcalf, ed., *Ogden Codman and the Decoration of Houses* (Boston: David Godine, 1988), 156.

64. It is known that Irving and Casson executed the Ashmont rood, but which of their carvers actually did it is problematic. Certainly Angelo Lualdi is identified with the work in at least one nearly contemporary source, *All Saints' Chronicle* 26 (April 1924): 8, where he is credited with having done only the painting when the rood was installed — surely a mistake, as it is most unlikely the name of Irving and Casson's sculptor would have been omitted in favor of just the decorator. An undated letter does exist in C&GC/ BPL from RAC to All Saints's then rector, Simon Blunt, asking if Kirchmayer was specially sought to do the work, but another letter, of 21 November 1910, from Frank Cleveland of the Cram office to Blunt (after Kirchmayer had left Irving and Casson to become a partner in the William Ross Company) reports that Irving and Casson "claim now to have a sculptor of the highest ability" and strongly advises using this person, presumably Lualdi, who succeeded Kirchmayer at about this time as Irving and Casson's chief modeler. Still, Kirchmayer's rood at St. Mary the Virgin in New York is admittedly somewhat similar: an exceptionally virile Christ is proudly erect on two feet, head straight up and eyes open, forcefully dominant. Alas, the matter cannot be laid to rest at this time.

65. Allen Ellenzweig, *The Homoerotic Photograph* (New York: Columbia University Press, 1992), 15.

66. Ibid., 47-50.

67. Ibid., 51.

68. LIG to FHD, letter of [n.d.] September 1898, quoted in Jussim, 126.

69. Ellenzweig, *Homoerotic Photograph*, 51.

70. Jussim, 41–42.

71. [Alice P. Floyd], *The History of the Parish of All Saints'* (Boston: Parish of All Saints', 1945).

72. *All Saints' Chronicle* 23 (June 1911): 8; 24 (December 1911): 6; 36 (April 1924): 8.

73. Herbert Whone, *Church, Monastery and Cathedral* (Short Hills, NJ: Ridley Enslow, 1977), 58. See also 52–54.

74. This work is illustrated in Montgomery Schuyler, "The Works of Cram, Goodhue and Ferguson," *Architectural Record* 29 (January 1911): 7.

75. Leo Steinberg, *The Sexuality of Christ in Renaissance Art and in Modern Oblivion* (New York: Pantheon, 1983), 16–17.

76. Ibid. For the best précis of Steinberg's thesis see Kenneth Woodward, review of *The Sexuality of Christ, Newsweek* (23 April 1984), Religion page. For RAC's views on the superiority of the triumphant Christ see his editorial in *Christian Art* 2 (February 1908): 256. For his remarks on the question of manliness see *Christian Art* 1 (May 1907): 81. And for the other issues raised by the vivid Ashmont rood see *Christian Art* 1 (June 1907), where RAC wrote: "One must be influenced also by the work of the vast immigration [to the United States] from Southern Europe; all that is best in its art must be assimilated rather than being thrown aside as un-American. That it is possible to thus design in the spirit of the Anglo-Saxon using the more fervid fancies of the Latin . . . is fortunately evinced by facts." Indeed, the Ashmont rood.

77. Steinberg, *Sexuality of Christ*, 137.

78. Ibid., 188, 91.

79. H. A. Reinhold, *Liturgy and Art* (New York: Harper & Row, 1966), 92–94.

80. Steinberg, *Sexuality of Christ*, 187. His source here is John O'Malley, *Praise and Blame in Renaissance Rome*.

81. Gelett Burgess to RAC, letter of 5 April 1901, C&GC/BPL.

82. Steinberg, *Sexuality of Christ*, 177, 36, 107.

83. RAC, "Mrs. Käsebier's Work," *Photo Era* 4 (May 1900): 136. I am grateful to Dr. Barbara L. Michaels for this source. She believes RAC may also have written "Boston Camera Club Exhibit" in the *Boston Evening Transcript* (10 November 1896). See Barbara L. Michaels to DS-T, letter of 25 July 1980, C&GC/BPL.

84. For an exploration of this thesis see Erica E. Hirshler, "Lilian Westcott Hale" (Ph.D. dissertation, Boston University, 1992).

85. See Jussim, 111, 128. Note that while the Ashmont rood Calvary group dates from 1910–1911, the rood beam (with its lettering but without its gilded cresting) dates from before 1897 and probably from 1892.

86. Hilliard, 207.

87. Ibid.

88. Arthur C.A. Hall, *The Hidden Life of the Heart: Thoughts from the Writings of Father A.C.A. Hall, late of St. John the Evangelist*, ed. A.M.D. (Boston: Joseph George Cupples/Back Bay Bookstore, 1892), 66.

89. See John Boswell, *Rediscovering Gay History* (London: Gay Christian Movement, 1985), 18–21.

90. Arthur C.A. Hall, *Christian Friendship* (New York: James Pott & Co., 1886), 17. Students of this period surprised at Hall's teaching (see also Chapter 5) that the bond of friendship endures in the next world, whereas that of marriage does not, should not only recall the teaching of Christ in the New Testament (that in Heaven there is no giving or receiving in marriage; Matthew 22:30) but note as well that Hall's teaching is clearly intended to refer explicitly to same-sex relationships and primarily to male-male relationships. Hall notes that ("in the [ancient] world Friendship had to take the place which marriage and family life fill with us. . . . The wife was certainly not the partner of her husband"[6]). It is also built clearly on the "peculiar intimacy" of Jesus and John (5) and on John's Gospel as, indeed, the "Gospel of Friendship" (4). And the examples in modern life Hall cites are almost entirely of masculine friendships; at one point he even goes so far as to use the phrase "the Friendships of *men*." Hall takes as his text for this lecture 2 John 1:2 — the epistle of that apostle to, as Hall put it, "a private Christian lady, an elderly widow apparently . . . with whom St. John was on terms of more than ordinary intimacy [3]"; a relationship perhaps akin to that Hall himself (and so many other Boston bachelors) had with Isabella Stewart Gardner or even LIG. Hall does not neglect to point out that the friendship bond as well as the marriage bond may exist between husband and wife, and the first of these bonds can endure into the next world even as the second cannot.

91. Charles J. Connick, "Christopher Whall," *Bulletin of the Stained Glass Association* 19 (September 1925): 10.

92. RAC, *My Life*, 195.

93. Ibid., 17, 195.

94. R. H. Ives Gammell, *The Boston Painters 1900–1930*, Elizabeth Ives Hunter, ed. (Orleans, MA: Parnassus, 1986), 16, 17–20.

95. Finlay, 92. I am indebted to Lee Lipton of the Danforth Museum.

96. RAC, "George Hallowell," *The Red Letter* 2 (April 1897): 69. Philip Savage, Ethel Reed, Copeland and Day, Cram and Goodhue and Hallowell all arise frequently in the pages of this little magazine.

97. Ibid.

98. See John Summerson, *The Classical Languages of Architecture* (Cambridge, MA: MIT Press, 1965), 12–13. See also Whone, *Church, Monastery and Cathedral*, 91–92, 63–64. For a discussion of Giorgione's Castelfranco altarpiece see Peter Humphrey, *The Altarpiece in Renaissance Venice* (New Haven: Yale University Press, 1993), 236.

99. The title *The Enthronement of the Virgin* is given in "Hallowell and His Work," *Boston Herald* (1 February 1903), an article marking the exhibition of the altarpiece at the St. Botolph Club in Boston. In RAC's *Christian Art* it was variously called "The Adoration of the Virgin by Saints" and also "The Epiphany," its Low Church title, perhaps. For a contemporary comparison of Hallowell's altarpiece with Sargent's Boston Public Library murals see Will Hutchins, "True and False Standards in Modern Religious Painting," *Christian Art* 3 (July 1908): 161. For another, later, comparison by the present author see Douglass Shand-Tucci, "Ralph Adams Cram and Mrs. Gardner: The Movement Toward a Liturgical Art," *Fenway Court* (1975): 27–34. The altarpiece was also much admired when its watercolor studies were exhibited in London in 1905; see *Studio* 35 (1905): 143–145.

100. Wuonola, *Church of the Advent*, 18.

101. Richard Guy Wilson, "Edith and Ogden," 160.

102. The photograph was taken ca. 1893 in the dining room of the Day house in Norwood. See Jussim, 269.

103. Parrish, 298. Two versions of Saint Barbara as portrayed by LIG are illustrated in Jussim, 125.

104. These associations of Symonds's "Song of Love and Death" and FitzGerald's *Euphranor* are discussed in Beckson, 199–200.

105. Richard Mohr, *Gay Ideas* (Boston: Beacon Press, 1992), 213.

106. William Carlos Williams, *Autobiography*, quoted in Russell Kirk, *Eliot and His Age* (La Salle, IL: Sherwood, Sugden & Co., 1971), 80.

107. Kirk, *Eliot*, 80–81. The quotation from Hugh Kenner is from his *Invisible Poet: T. S. Eliot.*

108. John Betjeman, *Summoned by Bells* (London: John Murray, 1960), 113.

ENTR'ACTE

1. For Karl Beckson's thought see his *London in the 1890s*, 60, 67–70, 185, 255, 266, 287–289, 319, 379. For Wayne Dynes's thought see his "Modernism" in Dynes, ed., *Encyclopedia of Homosexuality* (New York: Garland, 1990), 824–826.

2. Brigid Boardman, *Between Heaven and Charing Cross: The Life of Francis Thompson* (New Haven: Yale University Press, 1988), 217.

3. Lears, 208.

4. Quoted, ibid.

5. John Dourley, *The Psyche as Sacrament* (Toronto: Inner City Books, 1981), 32–33.

6. Alberto Pérez-Gómez, *Polyphilo . . . An Erotic Epiphany of Architecture* (Cambridge, MA: MIT Press, 1992), xvi, xxvi, xviii.

7. Dourley, *Psyche as Sacrament*, 32–33.

THE WORK OF RALPH ADAMS CRAM
1882–1900

PUBLICATIONS AND PUBLISHERS

AABN	*American Architect and Building News*
ARc	*Architectural Record*
ARv	*Architectural Review*
Atlan	*Atlantic Monthly*
B&G	Bates and Guild, Publishers
B&W	*The Builder and Woodworker*
BET	*Boston Evening Transcript*
Brick	*The Brickbuilder*
C&D	Copeland and Day, Publishers
Cen	*The Century Magazine*
Ch-Bk	*Chap-Book*
ChM	*The Church Militant*
Chu	*The Churchman*
CI	*Courrier Innocent*
CN	*Church Notes*, Church of the Advent
CW	*Catholic World*
D&F	*The Decorator and Furnisher*
EP	Elzevir Press
Gor	Gorham Press
H&G	*House and Garden*
Ind	*The Independent*
KEr	*Knight Errant*
MLA	*My Life in Architecture* (RAC)
Moods	*Moods: A Journal Intime*
MTr	*The Mahogany Tree*
NEM	*New England Magazine*
PhE	*Photo Era*
PL	*Poet Lore*
RL	*The Red Letter*
S&K	Stone and Kimball, Publishers
SMC	Small, Maynard and Co., Publishers
TRS	*The Royal Standard*

PERSONS, REPOSITORIES, OTHER ABBREVIATIONS

AB	Firm's Account Books
BGG	Bertram Grosvenor Goodhue

C&GC/BPL	Cram and Goodhue Collection, Boston Public Library
C&W	Cram and Wentworth
CGF	Cram, Goodhue and Ferguson
CWG	Cram, Wentworth and Goodhue
DR	Drawings (often undated) at C&GC/BPL
LB	Firm's Letter Books
PA	Parish Archives (of parish cited)
RAC	Ralph Adams Cram
	(Some of RAC's early work was published under the pseudonym "C. A. Ralph")
*	Indicates "built but since destroyed"
**	Indicates "built and extant"
	A project never built has no symbol.
?	Following an entry indicates the year of the work is not known, but in the author's judgment , it is the year under which the entry appears.

This checklist covers the years 1881–1900. The few post-1900 works mentioned in this volume will appear in the 1900–1942 checklist in Volume Two.

Literary work appears here under the year in which it was written. Usually the assumption is that its writing coincided with its first publication, the date of which is given, but where this is manifestly not the case because the publication date is a number of years later, that date is given in parentheses after the entry. So, too, are the dates of republication.

Architectural work after 1889 (the year Cram founded his firm) is assigned to the year in which a job first appears in the firm's account or letter books (AB or LB, respectively, given in parentheses after the entry); in a small number of cases, because the firm's 1890s records are incomplete, to the year in which a job was first published in an architectural journal, the abbreviation for which in that case (almost invariably in this volume *AABN*) follows the entry. When DR appears following an entry, there is no source other than undated drawings in the C&GC/BPL. BPL alone after an unpublished work refers to a manuscript in the C&GC/BPL. Most of the correspondence and certainly all the account entries are dated; where relevant as documentation these dates are given in the endnotes.

So much of Cram's work, particularly his architectural work, was collaborative, either nominally (as in Cram and Wentworth) or substantially (as in Cram, Wentworth and Goodhue, or as in his musical collaboration with Fred Bullard) that a "credit," as I have called it, has been provided for all work in this checklist, whether to Cram alone (denoted as RAC) or to whatever partnership (CWG, for example, for Cram, Wentworth and Goodhue).

Note that dates given in the text of the volume will often vary by a year or two from those in the checklist, depending upon what aspect of initiative impulse, design development, or construction the discussion in the text focuses on.

To complete the picture of the partners' lives, BGG's independent book designs are also recorded here at the end of each year in a separate note, even if the work was not in association with RAC or any other of the Pinckney Street group. No note is taken of BGG's architectural renderings, however, as few such by RAC after 1892 have been found; nearly all such graphic work was BGG's. Thus the heading Designs/Drawings (Architecture) after 1892 becomes Designs (Architecture).

1882

Designs/Drawings (Architecture)

RAC   "Designs for a Country Cottage," etc., Plates 17, 33, 51, 52, 53 (B&W).

1883

Designs/Drawings (Architecture)

RAC   Project for Copley Square (DR). [?]

1884

Art Criticism and/or Architectural Writings

RAC   "The Danger That Threatens Copley Square" (BET, 3 October).
RAC   "The Copley Square Disgrace" (BET, 9 October).
RAC   "The Dante Rossettis at the Art Museum" (BET as follows: I, "Pre-Raphaelitism," 5 November; II, "Pre-Raphaelitism," 6 November; III, "The Painter," 7 November; IV, "The Pictures," 10 November; V, "The Pictures," 12 November).
RAC   "A Consideration of Rubens" (BET, 24, 27 December).

1885

Art Criticism and/or Architectural Writings

RAC   "Turner and Teniers" (BET, 3 February).
RAC   "Art Notes" (BET throughout year).

Articles/Designs/Drawings (Interior Design)

RAC   "The Decoration of City Houses: Introduction—The Vestibule" (D&F 7 [November]: 38–40).
RAC   "The Decoration of City Houses: Second Part—The Entrance Hall" (D&F 7 [December]: 90–91).

1886

Designs/Drawings (Architecture)

RAC   Suffolk County Courthouse competition project award (MLA).
RAC   Interior and exterior perspectives for Rotch and Tilden of the Church of

the Holy Spirit, Mattapan, MA (PA). Each is reproduced in Harry L. Katz, *A Continental Eye: The Art and Architecture of Arthur Rotch* (Boston: Boston Athenaeum, 1985), 18, 19. Although 36 jobs are credited to Rotch and Tilden between 1881 and 1886 by Katz, drawings by RAC are documented by Katz only in the case of Holy Spirit.

ART CRITICISM AND/OR ARCHITECTURAL WRITINGS

RAC   "Art Notes Abroad" (*BET*, 6 April–3 November).
RAC   "In an English Cathedral Town" (*BET*, 24 December).

ARTICLES/DESIGNS/DRAWINGS (INTERIOR DESIGN)

RAC   "The Decoration of Houses . . . The Dining Room" (*D&F* 7 [February]: 150–151).
RAC   "Studies for the Interior Decoration of City Houses: The Reception Room" (*D&F* 7 [April]: 20–21).
RAC   "Interior Decoration of City Houses—A Smoking Room" (*D&F* 8 [June]: 78–79).
RAC   "Studies for the Interior Decoration of City Houses: The Stairway" (*D&F* 8 [July]: 110–111).
RAC   "Studies for the Interior Decoration of City Houses: The Hall" (*D&F* 8 [September]: 176–177).
RAC   "Studies for the Interior Decoration of City Houses: The Drawing Room" (*D&F* 9 [November]: 48–49).

1887

ART CRITICISM AND/OR ARCHITECTURAL WRITINGS

RAC   "Art Notes" (*BET*; begins to appear in January).

ARTICLES/DESIGNS/DRAWINGS (FURNITURE)

RAC   "A Cabinet" (*D&F* 9 [January]: 128–129).
RAC   "A Lady's Writing Desk" (*D&F* 9 [January]: 126).
RAC   "An Upright Piano and Stool" (*D&F* 9 [February]: 166).
RAC   "A Pier Glass . . ." (*D&F* 10 [May]: 39).
RAC   "A Grand Piano-Forte" (*D&F* 10 [July]: 110–111).
RAC   "A Student's Desk . . . Studies in Furniture Design" (*D&F* 11 [November]: 54).

ARTICLES/DESIGNS/DRAWINGS (INTERIOR DESIGN)

RAC   "Iron in Architecture" (*D&F* 9 [March]: 198–199).
RAC   "The Library" (*D&F* 10 [April]: 6–7).

RAC "A Music Room" (*D&F* 10 [June]: 75–77).

RAC "A Modern English Hall" (*D&F* 11 [October]: 19).

1888

DESIGNS/DRAWINGS (ARCHITECTURE)

RAC Project for the Massachusetts State House Extension (*AABN* 40 [March 31, 1894]).

DESIGNS/DRAWINGS (WALLPAPER)

RAC George K. Birge Co., Buffalo, NY (LB). None found.

1889

DESIGNS/DRAWINGS (ARCHITECTURE)

C&W *Hammond tenements remodeling, Allston or Somerville, MA (AB).

C&W **Ide House, Williamstown, MA (LB).

C&W Birge House(s), Buffalo, NY (AB; it is not clear if one, two, or three houses are indicated).

C&W **Parker House, 124 Brattle St., Cambridge, MA (LB).

C&W St. John's Church, Williamstown, MA (LB).

C&W Cathedral of St. John the Divine, New York City, competition; 2 schemes (*AABN*).

C&W **Whittemore House (The Ledges; Moonstone), York Harbor, ME (LB).

C&W Seaside Club, Bridgeport, CT (LB).

C&W Rockingham County Courthouse, Portsmouth, NH (LB).

DESIGNS/DRAWINGS (WALLPAPER)

RAC George K. Birge Co., Buffalo, NY (AB). None found.

1890

DESIGNS/DRAWINGS (ARCHITECTURE)

C&W Church of the Messiah, Boston (LB).

C&W St. Thomas's Church, Dover, NH (LB).

C&W Odd Fellows Temple, Cincinnati, OH (LB).

C&W *Gale House (Casa Loma), Williamstown, MA (LB).

C&W **Winslow House, Newton, MA (LB).

C&W *Fellner House, Brookline, MA (LB).

1891

EDITORIAL WORK

RAC   Named first editor (with C. Howard Walker) of *Architectural Review*.

ART CRITICISM AND/OR ARCHITECTURAL WRITINGS

RAC   "John D. Sedding" (*ARv* 1 [14 December]: 9–11).

DESIGNS/DRAWINGS (ARCHITECTURE)

C&W   **Merriam House, Brookline, MA (LB).
C&W   **Hamlin House, Brookline, MA (LB).
C&W   *The Gables, Babcock Street, Brookline, MA (AB).
C&W   *Grundmann Studios (including Copley and Allston Halls), Boston, MA.
C&W   Stuart Terrace, Beacon Street, Brookline, MA (AB).
C&W   Clubhouse, Lonsdale, RI (DR).
C&W   Calumet Clubhouse, Winchester, MA (AB).
C&W   First Baptist Church, Bridgeport, CT (DR).
C&W   **Credence, Church of the Advent, Boston (LB).
C&W   **All Saints', Ashmont, Boston (LB).

1892

POETRY

RAC   "Two Sonnets for Pictures of Our Lady" (*KEr* 1 [July]: 44–45).

DRAMA AND COSTUME DESIGN

RAC   *The Angelus* (C&GC/BPL)

EDITORIAL WORK

RAC   *Knight Errant*; four numbers, April 1892–January 1893.

ART CRITICISM, MUSIC CRITICISM, AND/OR ARCHITECTURAL WRITINGS

RAC   *A Description of the Proposed Church of All Saints' in Dorchester* (EP).
RAC   "The Religious Aspect of Architecture" (*CN* 2 [February]: 1–2).
RAC   "Concerning the Restoration of Idealism . . ." and "Essay on Bernardino Luini" (*KEr* 1 [April]: 10–15 and 26–27).
RAC   "An Ave Maria of Arcadelt" (*KEr* 1 [October]: 72).

RAC   Miscellaneous articles (unsigned), *MTr.*

RAC   "Mr. Lang's Private Performance of 'Parsifal' " (*MTr* 1 [17 May]: 300–301).

DESIGNS/DRAWINGS (ARCHITECTURE)

CWG   **128 Brattle St., Cambridge, MA (LB).

CWG   **St. Paul's Church, Brockton, MA (LB).

CWG   St. John the Evangelist's Church, St. Paul, MN (LB).

CWG   **Emmanuel Church chancel, Wakefield, MA, alterations (DR).

CWG   St. Matthew's Cathedral, Dallas, TX (LB). (This cathedral was designed originally in 1891 by BGG.)

CWG   Perry House, Medford, MA (AB).

CWG   Pomfret Clubhouse, [CT?] (DR).

In 1892 BGG illustrated RAC's *Description of the Proposed Church of All Saints'* and as coeditor designed all the numbers of *Knight Errant.*

1893

DRAMA

RAC   *Excalibur* (part I of projected trilogy; published by Gor, [1909]. [?]

POETRY

RAC   "Dante in Exile" (*NEM* 8 [June]: 525).

RAC   "Saint George of England" (*NEM* 9 [December]: 407).

NOVEL

RAC   *The Decadent* (C&D).

ART CRITICISM AND/OR ARCHITECTURAL WRITINGS

RAC   "On the Religious Aspect of Architecture" (*ARc* 1 [January–March]: 351–356).

DESIGNS (ARCHITECTURE)

CWG   **Christ Church, Hyde Park, MA (DR).

CWG   **Church of the New Jerusalem (now Church of the Open Word), Newton, MA (AB).

CWG   Dodge House, Simsbury, CT (AB).

In 1893 BGG designed RAC's *Decadent,* also doing the frontispiece and the initials, and a Book of Common Prayer for Updike.

1894

LYRICS

RAC   *The Boat of Love* (published in *PL* 42 [1940]: 165–177).

ART CRITICISM AND/OR ARCHITECTURAL WRITINGS

RAC   "On the Contemporary Architecture of the Catholic Church" (*CW* 58 [February]: 644–654).

RAC   "On the Use of Brick in Ecclesiastical Architecture" (*Brick* 3 [October]: 195–196).

DESIGNS (ARCHITECTURE)

CWG   **Knapp House, Fall River, MA (DR).

CWG   **All Saints' Church, Brookline, MA (LB; 1899 volume).

CWG   **St. Paul's Church, Malden, MA (AB).

CWG   **St. Andrew's Church, Detroit, MI (AB).

CWG   **Church of the Advent, Lady Chapel Sanctuary interior, Boston (DR).

CWG   First Congregational Church, Plymouth, MA (*AABN*).

CWG   Unitarian Church, Somerville, MA (*AABN*).

In 1894 BGG designed Bliss Carman's *Saint Kavin: A Ballad* and Dante Gabriel Rossetti's *House of Life* for Copeland and Day.

1895

POETRY

RAC   "Dawn" (*Moods* 2 [first part]: unpaged).

RAC   "Nottingham Hunt" (*Cen* 27 [February]: 557).

RAC   "Leo XIII" (*CW* 60 [March]: 505).

SHORT STORIES

RAC   "Notre Dame des Eaux," *Ch-Bk* (1 August 1895).

RAC   *Black Spirits and White* (S&K).

ART CRITICISM AND/OR ARCHITECTURAL WRITINGS

RAC   "On the Use of Brick in Domestic Architecture" (*Brick* as follows: I, "Workmens' Cottages," 4 [February]: 31–33; II, "Workmen's Cottages in Cities," 4 [May]: 99–100; III, [untitled; series title only], 4 [November]: 251–252).

RAC   "The Bells of Christ Church" (*NEM* 11 [January]: 640–647).

Designs (Architecture)

CWG   Chickamauga Memorial Arch, TN? (LB).

CWG   *SS. Peter and Paul's Church, Fall River, MA (AB).

CWG   Church, Holyoke, MA (AB).

CWG   **Phillips Church, Exeter, NH (PA).

CWG   **Newton Corner Methodist Episcopal Church, Newton, MA (AB).

CWG   Merrill House, Little Boars Head, NH (DR).

CWG   Grace Church, Lawrence, MA, alterations (AB).

CWG   **St. John's Church high altar and reredos, Gloucester, MA (DR).

In 1895 BGG illustrated (with his architectural renderings of the church) D. D. Addison's *All Saints' Church, Brookline: A Description*, and did four projects for Copeland and Day: the title page, initials, and page borders of *Esther: A Young Man's Tragedy*, by Wilfrid Scawen Blunt; the cover of *Lovers' Saint Ruth* and the title page of *Nine Sonnets Written at Oxford*, both by Louise Guiney; and the cover of *Apples of Istakhar*, by William Lindsey.

1896

Short Stories

RAC   "How Jamie Rode for the King" (*Ind* 48 [April] 596–600).

Art Criticism and/or Architectural Writings

RAC   "The Case Against the Ecole des Beaux Arts" (*AABN* 54 [26 December]: 107).

RAC   "Interior Decoration of Churches" (*ARv* 4: 50–53).

RAC   "Mrs. Käsebier's Work at the Boston Photo Club" (*BET*, undated clipping).

Designs (Architecture)

CWG   Lonsdale (or Lansdale) parish house, state unknown (AB).

CWG   Public Library, Taunton, MA (likely competition; DR).

CWG   **Public Library, Fall River, MA (AB).

CWG   Church of Our Saviour, Brookline, MA, alterations (AB).

CWG   Christ Church, Waltham, MA (AB).

CWG   New York City Hall (competition entry; *AABN*).

CWG   St. Paul's Church, Rochester, NY (*AABN*).

In 1896 BGG designed the typeface (Merrymount), initials, and page borders for *The Altar Book*, published by Updike's Merrymount Press, and the page borders and initials for Elizabeth Barrett Browning's *Sonnets from the Portuguese* for Copeland and Day.

1897

POETRY

RAC   "Awake Men of France from Your Dreaming" (*CI* [Winter/Spring]: unpaged)

DRAMA

RAC   *John Andover* (BPL).[?].

ART CRITICISM AND/OR ARCHITECTURAL WRITINGS

RAC   "George Hallowell" (*RL* 2 [April]: 69–74).
RAC   "Painting, Sculpture and Architecture" (*Atlan* 77 [April]: 554–68).

DESIGNS (ARCHITECTURE)

CGF   **Our Saviour's, Middleborough, MA (AB).
CGF   Church at Edgartown, MA? (AB).
CGF   **St. Stephen's, Fall River, MA? (AB).
     In 1897 BGG designed the cover of Charles Flandrau's *Harvard Episodes* and the
page borders and initials of *Shakespeare's Sonnets*, both for Copeland and Day.

1898

ARCHITECTURE/PHOTOGRAPHY

RAC   *English Country Churches* (100 plates; B&G). According to the title
page, RAC "selected" the plates; the photographer is not identified.

ART CRITICISM AND/OR ARCHITECTURAL WRITINGS

RAC   "The Early Architecture of Japan" and "The Late Architecture of Japan"
(*ARv* 5: 54–56 and 77–82).
RAC   "An Architectural Experiment" (*ARc* 8 [July–September]: 82–91).
RAC   "The English Country House Type" (*H&G* 4 [November]: 198–203).

DESIGNS (ARCHITECTURE)

CGF   Imperial Japanese Parliament Buildings, Toyko (DR).
CGF   **Sayles Public Library, Pawtucket, RI (LB).
CGF   **Baldwin House, near Dean Road, Chestnut Hill, Brookline, MA (LB).
CGF   Logan House, Bala-Cynwyd, PA (LB).
CGF   *St. Stephen's Mission, Westborough, MA, alterations (*ChM*).

CGF   St. Augustine's Church, location unknown (AB).
CGF   Hammond Houses block, Johnson Avenue, Charlestown, MA (AB).

In 1898 BGG designed the spine decor of *The Quest of Merlin* and *The Marriage of Guenevere*, both by Hovey, the covers of *Along the Trail*, also by Hovey, and *Northland Lyrics*, by William Carman Roberts et al., all for Small, Maynard and Co.; also the cover of *Ships and Havens*, by Henry Van Dyke, for Crowell, a New York publisher.

1899

POLITICAL WRITING

RAC   "Letter of the Prior" and "King Charles the Martyr" (*TRS* 1: 13–18 and 26).

ART CRITICISM AND/OR ARCHITECTURAL WRITING

RAC   "All Saints' Church, Dorchester" (*Chu* 79 [15 April]: 559–564).
RAC   "Church Building" series (*Chu*).
RAC   "The Influence of the French School on American Architecture" (*AABN* 66 [25 December]: 65–66).
RAC   "Good and Bad Modern Gothic" (*ARv* 6 [August]: 115–119).

DESIGNS (ARCHITECTURE)

CGF   Church at Newport Mews, RI (AB).
CGF   Dorchester Heights Monument, South Boston, MA (LB).
CGF   First Parish Church, Cambridge, MA (LB).
CGF   **St. Stephen's, Cohasset, MA (LB).
CGF   Huff House, Greensburg, PA (LB).
CGF   Christ Church, Swansea, MA? (LB).
CGF   Church, Newport News, VA (LB).
CGF   **Richmond Court, Brookline, MA (*AABN*).
CGF   Carnegie Library, Atlanta, GA (LB).
CGF   **26 Elmwood Avenue, Cambridge, MA (LB).

In 1899 BGG designed the cover, title page, and decorations of *Child Verse*, by John B. Tabb, for SMC, and the cover of Bishop Charles Brent's *With God in the World*. He also illustrated Cram's "Church Building" series.

1900

ART CRITICISM (INCLUDING PHOTOGRAPHY) AND/OR ARCHITECTURAL WRITINGS

RAC   "The Cherries of Veno" (*Atlan* 85 [April]: 479–82).
RAC   "Mrs. Käsebier's Work" (*PhE* 4 [May]: 131–136).
RAC   "Japanese Domestic Interiors" (*ARv* 7: 9–15).

DESIGNS (ARCHITECTURE)

CGF	Concord Church, location unknown (AB).
CGF	**Emmanuel Church, Newport, RI (LB).
CGF	**Wheaton Seminary (now Wheaton College), Norton, MA (AB; plan).
CGF	**St. Luke's Convalescent Home Chapel (now a subsidiary part of a modern church complex, St. John's and St. James's, Roxbury, MA, a merger at St. Luke's of two parishes, including the St. James's for which RAC designed the baptistry in 1902, now destroyed; DR).
CGF	Church, Milford (state unknown; DR).
CGF	**11 Kennedy Road, Cambridge, MA (AB).
CGF	St. Patrick's Cathedral, New York City, NY; a competition entry (AB).
CGF	Cathedral of Our Merciful Saviour, Faribault, MN (AB).
CGF	Washington Church, location unknown (AB).

In 1900 BGG designed the page borders and initials of *The Trophies* by José María de Heredia, and the cover, title page, and decorations of *The House of a Hundred Lights*, by Frederic Ridgely Torrence, both for Small, Maynard and Co.

ILLUSTRATION SOURCES

Adams House, Harvard University: 65c, d

Advent, Parish of the, 1844–1944: 22, 45

All Saints', Ashmont, Rector of: 46a (reproduction by Richard Cheek)

All Saints' Chronicle: 110a

American Architect and Building News: 17, 35, 44 (reproduction by Ann Miner Daniel), 49, 51a, b, 71a, 82a, b

Appeal for the New Christ Church, An, Hyde Park, Massachusetts: 70a (reproduction by Ann Miner Daniel)

Architectural Record: 76a, 100

Avery Architectural Library, Columbia University: 34, 39

Bostonian, The: 81

Builder and Woodworker, The: 3

C&GC/BPL. *See* Shand-Tucci, Douglass

Cram, Ralph Adams
   Christian Art: 67, 102, 111a, b, c
   Church Building: 52, 70b, 103, 108
   Decadent, The: 54
   My Life in Architecture: 16, 18, 19, 23, 24, 46b, 48b, 104

Cram, Ralph Adams, II: 2

Cram and Ferguson, Works of: 73, 101, 113

Decorator and Furnisher, The: 25a, b (reproduction courtesy Boston Public Library, Fine Arts Department), 55

Eliot, H. W., Jr., et al., *Harvard Celebrities*: 8

Fairbanks, Henry G., *Louise Imogen Guiney*: 11

Goodhue, Bertram Grosvenor: Architect and Master of Many Arts, ed. Charles H. Whitaker: 71b, 114

Goodhue, Bertram Grosvenor, *Book Decorations* (New York: Grolier, 1931): 99

Goodhue, Bertram Grosvenor: A Book of Architectural and Decorative Drawings by: 66

Gardner Museum Archives: 61, 64a, 74

Holy Spirit, Parish of the, Mattapan, Massachusetts: 4

Hunter, Robert Douglas: Frontispiece II

Kilmer, Nicholas: 86

Lancaster, Clay, *The Japanese Influence in America*: 105a, b

Library of Congress: 7, 13, 14, 110b

Norwood, Massachusetts, Historical Society: 12, 15, 68a (reproduction by Ann Miner Daniel), 94, 112

Oliver, Richard, *Bertram Grosvenor Goodhue*: 50

President and Fellows of Harvard College, Harvard Center for Renaissance Studies, Florence, Berenson Archives: 10, 58

Private collections: Frontispiece I, 5 (reproduction by Ann Miner Daniel), 20, 21, 59 (reproduction by Paul M. Wright), 60, 65a, b, 68b, 69, 84 (photograph by Richard Cheek), 85, 89, 90, 91a, b, 96, 97, 98, 106, 107 (photograph by Jonathan Goell)

Regardie, Israel, *The Golden Dawn*: 95

Shand-Tucci, Douglass: 6, 9, 28, 32, 33a, b, 40, 41 (reproduction by Ann Miner Daniel), 42, 43, 47, 48a, 53a, b, 56, 57, 62, 72, 75, 76b, 77, 78, 79, 80, 83, 87, 88, 109, 110c. All of these prints have been transferred to C&GC/BPL.
   Photographs by: 26, 27, 29, 30, 31, 36, 37, 38, 92

Society for the Preservation of New England Antiquities: 1, 64b, 93

Whitehill, Walter Muir, *The Boston Public Library: A Centennial History*: 63 (engraving by Rudolph Ruzicka, courtesy the Trustees and Director of the Boston Public Library)

INDEX

Cram's work, literary and architectural, appears here under his own name (no account being taken of pseudonyms) or, following individual listings, under the name of the appropriate firm: Cram, Goodhue, and Ferguson; Cram, Wentworth, and Goodhue; Cram and Ferguson; or Cram and Wentworth. Similarly the work of other authors, architects, or artists appears under the individuals' names. Numbers in italics refer to illustrations. A chronological listing of Cram's work can be found in the Checklist.

Burne-Jones, Edward: Whistler's advice to throw him up, 16; influences Mrs. Gardner's costume, 313; scenery by, in *King Arthur*, 325; in *The Decadent*, 364; in *Mahogany Tree*, 412; admired by RAC, 418; and Ashmont altarpiece, 418, 422; masturbation, normal lovemaking, lesbianism, tuberculosis, 422; repressed eroticism, 422, 423; uses Siddal's face, 422

Burnett, Joseph, 179

Burnham, Wilbur, xx

Burton, Humphrey: *Leonard Bernstein*, 254, 424

Burton, Richard: *Arabian Nights*, 323

Butterfield, Herbert, 120

Byron, George Gordon, 259

Byzantium, 17, 30, 72–4

Caesar, Julius, 259

Cambridge University, 51, 52, 121, 384

Camp, x, 270–2

Campbell, Michael: *Lord Dismiss Us*, 167

Capen House, Joseph, Topsfield, Mass., 91

Caravaggio: "The Martyrdom of St. Matthew," 177

Carlyle, Thomas, 32, 52

Carman, Bliss: member Pinckney Street circle, 28, 54; LIG introduces to H. Clarke, 38; assistant editor of *The Atlantic*, 39, 322; involved in *XXth Century*, 55; vagabondia movement and, 139; "The Pipes of Pan," 140; effeminacy of, 171; "The Bather," 212; knew Stoddard, 212; meets T. Dwight, 212; "Verlaine," 212; at lunch club, 322; views of magazine writing of period, 323; involved in *Courrier Innocent*, 331; in *Cult of Purple Rose*, 333; editor of *Chap Book*, 339; read abroad, 356; a Visionist, 380, 389; "Ballad of St. Kavin," 381; Low tide at *Grand Pre*, 386; collaboration with Hovey, 390; widely published, 409; 1914 Harvard Phi Beta Kappa poem, 410–4; portrait by Meteyard, 411; "Have little care . . . ," 414; achieves success with Copeland and Day, 427; in New York, 427; portrait by FHD, 468 n. 147

Carnation, green, as signifier of homosexuality, 61–5, 142, 335

Carnation Series, 65

Carnival Ball, 219, 313–5

Caroline era, 273, 321

Carpenter, Edward, 52–3; *Ioläus* published in Boston, 52, 468 n. 147; ideal of comradeship and Whitman, 139–40; E. Warren compared to, 220; as example of virile mode, 273; masculine and feminine sides compared in work of, 293; and Gorham Press, 334; and Christian Socialism, 366, 452; in *Craftsman*, 409; and Ashmont rood, 445

Carruth, Frances: *Fictional Ramblers in and Around Boston*, 27, 138

Carter, Morris, 222, 225, 228, 229, 230, 264

Carving machine, 306

Casa Loma (Gale House), 96–7, *98, 99*

Casson, Robert, 305. *See also* Irving and Casson

Casts, Battle of. *See under* Museum of Fine Arts, Boston

Cat, Sacred. *See* Pasht

Cather, Willa, 247, 249, 333

Catholic bashing. *See* Roman Catholicism

Catholic University, Washington, D.C., 194, 211

Catholic World, 396, 431, 432, 433, 436

Cavalieri, Tommasso, 152, 173

Century, The, 321, 323

Cézanne, Paul, 254

Chaeronea: Battle of, 167; Order of, 167

Chaffee, Frank, 502 n. 39

Chamberlain, Joseph E., 217; *Boston Evening Transcript*, 59

Chandler, Ira, 382

Channing, William Ellery, 71

Chap-Book, The: on St. Botolph Club, 217; authors appearing in, 339; published by Stone and Kimball, 341; *Black Spirits and White* extracted in, 368; on RAC's writings, 369; moves to Chicago, 427

Charlemagne, 143

Charles I of England: martyrdom, 145; and Anglicanism, 183; in RAC's family history, 317; at Richmond Palace, 319; Stuart context, 321; Van Wyck Brooks on cult of, 330; in glass at Bowdoin Street, 349; in *The Decadent*, 364; Order of the White Rose, 373; as character in play, 504 n. 68

Charles Street, Boston, 19, 24, 25, 210, 226, 244, 313

Chauncy, George, Jr., 178; *Gay New York*, 204–5

Cheever, John, 26

Chelsea, London, 24, 246, 301

62729245567

INDEX

Mannerism, 102–4, 269
Mapplethorpe, Robert, 45, 437; *Chest*, 280
Marcus Aurelius, 365
Marcuse, Herbert: *Eros and Civilization*, 337, 359
Marijuana, 376
Markwell, Bernard: *The Anglican Left*, 77, 181
Marliave's Restaurant, Boston, 54–5, 172, 228
Marlowe, Christopher, 431
Marriage, heterosexual, 190
Marriage, homosexual. *See under* Same-sex unions: Marriage "of the soul"; Particular friendship,
Martin, Robert K., 86, 155, 159, 198, 204, 255, 292
Mary of Scotland, 317
Marxism, 24, 76, 77. *See also* Christian Socialism; Socialism
Masculine/feminine continuum (in men), 56–7, 274–84, 288–93, 323–4; virile gay type and gender appropriate behavior, 144, 166–7, 172–3, 192, 234–5, 249, 272–3, 389, 499 n. 115; effete gay type and gender inappropriate behavior, 152, 167, 171, 221, 232, 235; manliness earned by moral effort, not instinctive, 153; knightly tradition, 158; Plato on manliness, 167; warrior aspect, 167; Doric style, 291
Mask and signal, as literary technique, 23, 63–6, 142, 224–5, 270, 325, 365, 470 n. 19
Mass, Solemn High, 285, 308. *See also* Art, liturgical
Massachusetts Eye and Ear Infirmary, Boston, xv
Massachusetts Institute of Technology, School of Architecture, 6, 62, 377, 435
Massachusetts State House Extension, 78–9, 79
Masturbation, 159, 423, 495 n. 8
Mathers, S. McGregor, 383
Matise, Henri, 226
Matsuki, Bunkio, 408
Matthiessen, F. O., 26, 248, 249, 254
Maupin, Armisted: *Tales of the City*, "Babycakes," 125, 140
Maurice (*Maurice*), 139, 173
Maurier, Frederick Dennison, 52, 77, 192
Maynard, Brother, 353
Maynard, Laurens, 322, 341
Mayne, Xavier: *The Intersexes*, 204, 205, 207
McCahill, Father, 396

McCall, Sidney [Mary Fenolossa]: *Truth Dexter*, 405
McClary, Susan, 269
McClure's Magazine, 323
McCormack, George: *George Santayana*, 174
McCulloch, Hugh, 425
McGann, Malcolm (*The Decadent*), 363, 364
McGann, Thomas, 420
McIntyre, A. McVoy: *Beacon Hill*, 24
McKim, Charles F., 216, 288, 330, 435
McKim, Mead and White, 62, 110, 209; Boston Public Library (McKim Building), 21, 53, 56, 237, 326–7, 419, 437, 440, 463 n. 15; Library seal controversy, 214–6, 215; and *Bacchante* controversy, 216, 217, 227–8, 240, 435, 440, 491–2 n. 92; influence of, on RAC's library designs, 329–30; and Arthur Rotch, 463 n. 15
Mead, Andrew, 72
Mead, Edwin, 76
Medieval Academy of America, xii
Medus, Jacques and Sarah, 211
Mellon family, 114
Melville, Herman, 25, 203; *Moby Dick*, 24; *Billy Budd*, 146
Memorial Hall, Harvard University, 387
Mencken, H. L., xvi
Mercer, Henry, 308
Merrymount Press, Boston, 28, 311, 341, 356, 431
Merrymount Street (*Margaret Warrener*), 28
Merwick, Diane: *Boston Priests*, 193–4
Metalious, Grace: *Peyton Place*, 48, 121
Meteyard, Thomas Bufford, 38–9; in Pinckney Street circle, 28, 54; and Carman, 39; Scituate colony, 139, 331; knew M. Fullerton, 168; at lunch club, 322; portrait of RAC, 344; a Visionist, 380; designed *Songs from Vagabondia*, 386; in 1914 Harvard Phi Beta Kappa poem, 410; portrait, 411
Methodism, 258
Metropolitan Museum, New York, 33
Mexico, 353, 397. *See also* Baroque style
Michelangelo, 26, 173, 176, 252, 423; *Pieta*, 72, 233; Laurentian Library, 102; *Last Judgement*, 176; Doni Tondo, 177; *Leda and the Swan*, 413
Middle Ages, 73, 85, 120, 158, 177, 265, 291, 411
Middlebrook, Diane Wood, xviii
Middlesex School, Concord, Mass., 163
Millay, Edna St. Vincent, 37

557